Beyond Primitivism

"This volume confronts a most pressing issue in the study of religion. It should be received with acclaim and serve as a landmark text in the field."

Terry Rey, Ph.D., Associate Professor of African and Caribbean Religions, Florida International University

"Includes contributors of world renown and influence...an excellent text for classroom teaching and a valuable contribution to academic scholarship on modernity and social change."

Kamari M. Clarke, Yale University

What role do indigenous religions play in today's world?

Beyond Primitivism is a complete appraisal of indigenous religions as practiced across America, Africa, Asia, and the Pacific today. At a time when local traditions across the world are colliding with global culture, it explores the future of indigenous faiths as they encounter modernity and globalization. Against those who claim that indigenous religions are irrelevant in modern societies and are fast becoming extinct, *Beyond Primitivism* argues for them as dynamic, progressive forces of continuing vitality and influence. Its essays on Haitian Vodou, Korean shamanism, the Sri Lankan "Wild Man," and other themes reveal the relevance of native religions to millions of believers worldwide, challenging the perception that they are vanishing from the face of the globe and demanding a much greater recognition of their importance.

Jacob K. Olupona is Professor of Comparative Religion at the University of California, Davis. He is the author of *Kingship, Religion and Rituals in a Nigerian Community* (Almqvist & Wiksell International, 1991), and *African Traditional Religions in Contemporary Society* (Paragon House, 1991). He is also the editor of *African Spirituality* (Herder & Herder, 2001), and co-editor of *Religious Plurality in Africa* (Mouton de Gruyter, 1993).

Beyond Primitivism

Indigenous religious traditions and modernity

Edited by Jacob K. Olupona

Routledge
Taylor & Francis Group

NEW YORK AND LONDON

First published 2004
by Routledge
270 Madison Ave, New York NY 10016

Simultaneously published in the UK
by Routledge
2 Park Square, Milton Park, Abingdon, Oxon, OX14 4RN

Routledge is an imprint of the Taylor & Francis Group

Transferred to Digital Printing 2006

© 2004 Jacob K. Olupona, selection and editorial material;
individual chapters, the contributors

Typeset in Galliard by Taylor & Francis Books Ltd

British Library Cataloguing in Publication Data
A catalogue record for this book is available from the British Library

Library of Congress Cataloging in Publication Data
A catalog record for this book has been requested

ISBN 0–415–27319–6 (hbk)
ISBN 0–415–27320–X (pbk)

Printed and bound by CPI Antony Rowe, Eastbourne

With gratitude to my teachers at Boston University (1977–1983): Merlin Swartz, Dennis Tedlock, Alan Olson, Herbert Mason, Daniel McCall, and Peter Berger

Contents

Illustrations

Figures

Boxes

Tables

Contributors

Michio Araki was, until his retirement, Professor at the Institute of Philosophy, Tsukuba University, Japan. He is the co-author of *Kindaika to shukyo bumu, Kokugakuin Daigaku Nihon Bunka Kenkyujo hen* (Dohosha, 1990).

Karen McCarthy Brown is Professor of Anthropology of Religion at the Caspersen School of Graduate Studies and the Theological School of Drew University. She is the author of *Mama Lola: A Vodou Priestess in Brooklyn* (University of California Press, 2001) and *Tracing the Spirit: Ethnographic Essays on Haitian Art: From the Collection of the Davenport Museum of Art* (Davenport Museum of Art and University of Washington Press, 1995).

David Carrasco is Professor of History of Religions, Harvard University. He is editor-in-chief of *The Oxford Encyclopedia of Mesoamerican Cultures: The Civilizations of Mexico and Central America* (Oxford University Press, 2001), and the author of, among many other works, *Quetzalcoatl and the Irony of Empire: Myths and Prophecies in the Aztec Traditions* (University of Colorado Press, 2001) and *City of Sacrifice: The Aztec Empire and the Role of Violence in Civilization* (Beacon, 1999).

David Chidester is Professor of Comparative Religion, University of Cape Town, South Africa, and the author of *Christianity: A Global History* (Allen Lane, 2000) and *Savage Systems: Colonialism and Comparative Religion in Southern Africa* (University of Virginia Press, 1996).

Steven J. Friesen is Associate Professor and Chair of Religious Studies at the University of Missouri, Columbia. He is the author of *Imperial Cults and the Apocalypse of John: Reading Revelation in the Ruins* (Oxford University Press, 2001) and *Twice Neokoros: Ephesus, Asia, and the Cult of the Flavian Imperial Family* (E.J. Brill, 1993). He is also the editor of *Ancestors in Post-contact Religion: Roots, Ruptures, and Modernity's Memory* (Harvard University Press for the Center for the Study of World Religions, Harvard Divinity School, 2001).

Armin W. Geertz is Professor, Department of the Study of Religion, University of Aarhus, Denmark, and the author of *The Invention of Prophecy: Continuity and Meaning in Hopi Indian Religion* (University of California Press, 1994). He is also co-editor of *Perspectives on Method and Theory in the Study of Religion: Adjunct Proceedings of the XVIIth Congress of the International Association, Mexico City, 1995* (International Association for the History of Religions Congress).

Naomi Janowitz is Program Director and Professor of Religious Studies at the University of California, Davis. She is the author of *Icons of Power: Ritual Practices in Late Antiquity* (Penn State University Press, 2002).

Chris Jocks is a member of the faculty, Native American Studies, Dartmouth College.

Flora Edouwaye S. Kaplan is Professor of Anthropology and Museum Studies at New York University. She is the editor of *Queens, Queen Mothers, Priestesses, and Power: Case Studies in African Gender* (New York Academy of Sciences, 1997) and *Images of Power: Art of the Royal Court of Benin: Exhibition Dates at New York University, the Grey Art Gallery, January 23–February 21, 1981* (New York University, 1981). She is the author of *A Mexican Folk Pottery Tradition: Cognition and Style in Material Culture in the Valley of Puebla* (Southern Illinois University Press, 1994).

Laurel Kendall is curator of Asian Ethnographic Collections, American Museum of Natural History, and Adjunct Professor at Columbia University, where she received her Ph.D. with distinction in anthropology in 1979. She is the author of *Shamans, Housewives, and Other Restless Spirits* (University of Hawaii Press, 1987), *The Life and Hard Times of a Korean Shaman* (University of Hawaii Press, 1988), *Getting Married in Korea* (University of California Press, 1996), and numerous articles on the subjects of Korean popular religion, gender, and modernity. She has also edited several volumes on these subjects.

Whalen W. Lai is Professor of East Asian Languages and Cultures and Religious Studies, University of California, Davis. He is the co-author (with Michael von Brück) of *Buddhismus und Christentum (Christianity and Buddhism: A Multicultural History of their Dialogue)* (Orbis Books, 2001), and author of three essays, including "Sinitic Mandalas: the Wu-wei-t'u of Ts'ao-shan," in *Early Ch'an in China and Tibet* (Asian Humanities Press, 1983), a book that he co-edited. He is also the author of the entries on China in *Encyclopaedia of Asian Philosophy*, edited by Oliver Leaman (Routledge, 2001), and of over seventy-five articles in various academic journals.

Bruce Lincoln is the Caroline E. Haskell Professor of the History of Religions at the University of Chicago Divinity School. He is the author of *Theorizing Myth: Narrative, Ideology, and Scholarship* (University of Chicago Press, 1999).

Charles H. Long is Professor Emeritus, and author of *Significations: Signs, Symbols, and Images in the Interpretation of Religion* (Fortress Press, 1991). From 1991 to 1996 he was Director of the Research Center for Black Studies and Professor of History of Religions at the University of California, Santa Barbara.

Alfredo López Austin is Chief Investigator, Institute of Anthropological Research, and Professor of Mesoamerican History and Culture, National Autonomous University of México (UNAM). He is the author of *The Rabbit on the Face of the Moon: Mythology in the Mesoamerican Tradition* (University of Utah Press, 1996) and co-author of *Pasado Indígena (Mexico's Indigenous Past)* (University of Oklahoma Press, 2001).

Helen McCarthy is a contributor to *Archeological Synthesis and Research Design: Yosemite National Park, California* (Yosemite National Park, National Park Service, US Department of the Interior, 1999) and co-author of *Ethnography and Prehistory of the North Coast Range, California* (University of California Press, 1985).

Mary N. MacDonald is Professor at the Department of Religious Studies, Le Moyne College, Syracuse, New York. She is the author of *Mararoko: A Study in Melanesian Religion* (Peter Lang, 1991) and the compiler of *Melanesia: An Annotated Bibliography for Church Workers* (Goroka, Papua New Guinea, 1988).

John C. Mohawk is Professor at the State University of New York, Buffalo. He is the author of *Utopian Legacies: A History of Conquest and Oppression in the Western World* (Clear Light Publications, 1999), *A Basic Call to Consciousness: The Hau de no sau nee (Six Nations) Address to the Western World, Geneva, Switzerland, Autumn 1977* (published by *Akewesasne Notes*, the official newspaper of the Mohawk Nation), and co-author of *Exiled in the Land of the Free: Democracy, Indian Nations, and the U.S. Constitution* (Clear Light Publications, 1992).

Gananath Obeyesekere is Professor Emeritus, Anthropology Department, Princeton University. He is the author of *The Work of Culture: Symbolic Transformation in Psychoanalysis and Anthropology* (University of Chicago Press, 1990), *The Apotheosis of James Cook: European Mythmaking in the Pacific* (Princeton University Press, 1997), and co-author (with Richard Gombrich) of *Buddhism Transformed: Religious Changes in Sri Lanka* (Princeton University Press, 1988).

Jacob K. Olupona is Professor of Comparative Religion at the University of California, Davis. He is the author of *Kingship, Religion and Rituals in a Nigerian Community: A Phenomenological Study of Ondo Yoruba Festivals* (Almqvist & Wiksell International, 1991) and *African Traditional Religions in Contemporary Society* (Paragon House, 1991). He is also the editor of *African Spirituality* (Herder & Herder, 2001) and co-editor of *Religious Plurality in Africa* (Mouton de Gruyter, 1993).

Håkan Rydving is Professor in the History of Religions, Department of Theology, Uppsala University, Sweden, and author of *The End of Drum-Time: Religious Change Among the Lule Saami, 1670s–1740s* (Coronet Books, 1995).

Katarina V. Sjöberg is the author of *The Return of the Ainu: Cultural Mobilization and the Practice of Ethnicity in Japan* (Harwood Academic Publishers, 1993).

Garry W. Trompf, Sydney Branch Director of the Centre for Millennial Studies, is Professor in the History of Ideas, University of Sydney, Department of Studies in Religion; previously, he was Professor of History at the University of Papua New Guinea. He is the author of *Early Christian Historiography: Narratives of Retributive Justice* (Continuum, 2000) and *Payback: The Logic of Retribution in Melanesian Religions* (Cambridge University Press, 1994). He is also the editor of *Cargo Cults and Millenarian Movements: Transoceanic Comparisons of New Religious Movements* (Mouton de Gruyter, 1990).

Aram A. Yengoyan is Professor, Department of Anthropology, University of California, Davis. He is co-editor of *Philippine Society and the Individual: Selected Essays of Frank Lynch, 1949–1976* (Center for South and Southeast Asian Studies, University of Michigan, 1984) and *The Imagination of Reality: Essays in Southeast Asian Coherence Systems* (Ablex, 1990).

Preface

|

This volume represents the contributions of scholars who participated in a conference we called to respond to a perceptible lack in Western institutions in the study of "indigenous" religions. This lack is especially indicated in the history of religion programs offered at many US universities. Western religious scholarship, generally the world over, has privileged "world" religions by an absolute linguistic separation into two classes of religious studies: "indigenous" religions and "world" religions. This arbitrary and capricious bifurcation of religious scholarship fails to acknowledge the universality of religious systems of belief across the globe. It fails to acknowledge the very sacred spiritual traditions of Africa, the Americas, Asia, and wherever indigenous people inhabit the earth. With the advent of global secular ideologies, based on technological innovation, many indigenous traditions will continue to confront their own decline. The privileging of "world" religions is largely informed by a particular academic orientation of scholars, whose traditions developed out of the "axial age" civilization paradigm.

While the "world" religious traditions of Buddhism, Judaism, Hinduism, Islam, and Christianity are amply studied and represented in the academy, the study of "indigenous" religions is speciously cut off from religious studies. Routinely, indigenous religions are restricted to anthropology or folklore. To correct this anomaly, to sensitize the larger academic community to the significance of native religious traditions in the world today, and to provide a rationale for their study, my colleagues in the American Academy of Religion formed a study group to raise awareness of this incongruity in lectures and sessions at the annual meeting of the American Academy of Religion. The central purpose of this study group is to create a forum in which to discuss theoretical and substantive issues, to investigate and understand indigenous and native traditions, and to augment the few available resources of the academy for examining indigenous religions.

Our study group began to attract a critical mass of internationally known scholars, whose primary interests epitomize the diversity of world religions. Because of the restraints of space, only the contributions of a very few scholars of indigenous religions are mentioned here in this volume. There are many thousands of indigenous religions in every continent across the globe that remain unrepresented. Showing significant empathy for the study of indigenous religion in American universities, a variety of scholarly opinions is represented in the study group by leading scholars: Tu Weiming of Harvard University; Jill Raitt of the University of Missouri, Columbia; the venerable Huston Smith, Professor Emeritus of the University of California, Berkeley; and Ewert Cousins of Fordham University, New York. Subsequently, many other scholars of indigenous traditions have joined in the discussion: Inés Talamantez, Mary McDonald, Charles Long, David Carrasco, Philip Arnold, and Diane Bell.

In 1993, Steven Friesen, of the University of Missouri, Columbia, Diane Bell, and I coordinated the initial planning conversations in extremely productive sessions during the annual meetings of the American Academy of Religion. Under the academic study of religion, Tu Weiming, then Director of the Institute of Culture and Communication at the East–West Center, Honolulu, Hawaii, advanced the profile of indigenous religious traditions. Weiming organized a series of conferences on world spirituality, featuring indigenous religious traditions. Subsequently, Steven Friesen edited a volume on ancestral spirituality published by the Center for the Study of World Religions. Undeniably, these efforts, and the efforts of others, encouraged recognition of indigenous religious traditions in the academy.

In March 1996, during the height of these conversations, I organized an international conference, "Beyond 'Primitivism': Indigenous Religious Traditions and Modernity," at the University of California, Davis. Some of the best and brightest indigenous religions scholars attended from thirteen countries around the world. Up and coming scholars also participated, responding to papers presented. Several younger scholars – Simeon Ilesanmi, Teresia Hinga, Julian Kunnie, and Inés Hernández-Ávila – have assumed positions of authority and leadership in their respective fields and programs. This international conference brought together a truly interactive group, examining and reinterpreting deep religious epistemology, from diverse traditions: Native American, African, Mesoamerican, Japanese, and Australian Aboriginal.

The conference and ensuing book, *Beyond Primitivism: Indigenous Religious Traditions and Modernity*, concluded that some academic perspectives on indigenous religious traditions are misguided. They are categorized in Robert Redfield's phrase as "Little Tradition." On the contrary, indigenous religious traditions are entirely relevant to the modernity project. Indigenous traditions and cultures continue to play important roles in forming and refashioning world cultures, beliefs, and identities of the modern nation-state. More scholars now recognize that ethnic or indigenous African, Cuban, Brazilian, Latin, Caribbean, Native, and African-American cultures maintain widespread influences on the "popular" cultures of present-day societies. These influences are forming the debates on globalization in contemporary society, environmental and ecological crises, world capitalism, and reproductive health. Contemporary issues are anchored in indigenous religious beliefs and cultures, acting as agencies of local indigenous knowledge.

At the October 2001 inaugural meeting of the new editorial board, established to revise Mircea Eliade's *Encyclopedia of Religion*, Professor Wendy Donigen of the University of Chicago remarked that more than half of the nine committee members present were scholars of indigenous religious traditions. These developments indicate general progress in the discipline. Significantly, conversations among ourselves and outsiders developed meaningful dialogue between two groups of scholars: (1) historians of religion – concerned with world religions in Asia, Europe, and the Mediterranean – and (2) scholars of indigenous religion – concerned with innovative scholarship in the theory and practice of indigenous religious tradition.

Despite these gains, there remains today a significant and arbitrary bias in Western religious scholarship that ignores "indigenous" religions in their own right. Current academic scholarship fails to make comparisons between the different indigenous religious traditions, especially beyond the boundaries of the so-called "great" religious traditions of Western hegemony and culture. We look in vain for judicious scholarly works comparing and contrasting, say, the sacred traditions of Asia, the Americas, and Africa. Where is the scholarship that compares, for example, Yoruba Òrìsà with Shinto and Mayan practices, or Australian Aboriginal beliefs with Baganda?

The University of California, Davis, conference, "Beyond 'Primitivism': Indigenous Religious Traditions and Modernity," was successful in terms of attendance, intensity of interaction, participation of scholars, and public awareness. The significant contributions of my colleagues and students made this conference and ensuing volume possible. I would like to acknowledge and gratefully thank these scholars for their most important roles: Bobbie Bolden, Emily Albu, Naomi Janowitz, Georges Van den Abbeele, Ron Saufley, John Stewart, Inés Hernández-Ávila, and George Chantez. Our staff contributed considerably to the conference, especially Aklil Bekele in African-American and African Studies. I thank my current research assistants, especially Mark Davis and Marilu Carter, as well as the program's MSO, Connie Zeiller.

Several foundations contributed generously to this conference. We thankfully acknowledge the funding provided by the Wenner-Gren Anthropological Foundations; the Spalding Foundation, England; the Niwano Foundation, Japan; the Davis Humanities Institute, College of Letters and Science; the University of California Humanities Institute, Irvine, California; and the Office of the President of the University of California, Oakland.

Introduction

Jacob K. Olupona

This book represents the collaborative work of international scholars who spoke at the 28–31 March 1996 conference, "Beyond 'Primitivism': Indigenous Religious Traditions and Modernity," held at the University of California, Davis. The African-American and African Studies Program, the Religious Studies Program, and the Davis Humanities Institute hosted the conference. Forty distinguished scholars attended from fourteen countries in Africa, Asia, the Americas, and Europe. They examined issues ranging from the relationship between indigenous religious traditions and modernity to the status of indigenous religions in particular fields of academic study. The Davis conference sought to extend a discussion to all areas in which indigenous religions maintain a strong presence, in an effort to enhance our understanding of indigenous traditions around the world and to make a compelling case to integrate indigenous religions into teaching and religious studies.

Scholars attending the conference explored the question of modernity and indigenous religious traditions through various theoretical and case-study approaches. Their diverse views indicate a lack of consensus, and this lack defines modernity. This lack prevails because there is no single modernity but, rather, there are numerous "modernities." Secularization, globalization, and the expansion of "dominant" world religions affect indigenous peoples throughout the world. In every case, indigenous peoples have developed their responses to the challenges of multi-faceted modernity.

Discourse on modernity reflects the presence of multiple "modernities" in multiple case studies. This pattern is also reflected in the theoretical realm, in which scholars debate the very definitions under scrutiny. Scholars scrutinize even the study of modernity itself, as some scholars now refer to a widespread condition known as postmodernity. To examine these approaches, we must first establish a working definition of modernity. Scholar Anthony Giddens, in *The Consequences of Modernity*, is one who has wrestled with the definition, describing modernity as the trend or modes of social life or organization that emerged in Europe from the seventeenth century onwards, subsequently attaining worldwide influence.[1] Modernity is associated with the secularization of Protestant Christianity, humanism, and the prominence of scientific thought in Western culture.

Additionally, modernity is associated with the phenomena of colonialism and neocolonialism. As Western nations began to explore and colonize the world, they severely affected the lives of indigenous peoples at all levels – socio-economic, political, cultural, and religious. Around the globe, entire cultures were affected in numerous ways, ranging from the occupation of indigenous lands, the destruction of ancient empires, and economic hegemony, to the sacrilege of a golf course constructed over sacred burial mounds or the discarded debris of the Second World War, interpreted by Pacific Islanders as signs of the Gods in "cargo cults."

Tradition and modernity

The term modernity contains ambiguity that makes a precise definition difficult. Often it refers to the effects of the growing imposition of Western Christianity, secularism, and technology throughout the world. To analyze the term, we should look at the work of such theorists as Peter Berger, Anthony Giddens, Robin Horton, and Zwi Werblowsky, who examine the question of whether science and secular humanism's claims of superiority are valid in the face of indigenous and traditional practices. Likewise, the question of modernity leads to further speculation regarding the nature of tradition itself. How static is tradition in the face of the challenges of modernity? The very notions of time, progress, and the relative value of technology and culture are all legitimate themes for analysis.

From a sociological perspective, Berger attempts to create an analysis of modernity through a five-category model.[2] In essence, Berger claims that modernity can be seen as comprising five categories: abstraction, futurity, individualization, liberation, and secularization. In the case of abstraction, Berger argues for the theoretical links between Marx's conception of capitalism as a source of alienation and reification, Durkheim's reflections on organic solidarity, and Weber's discontent with rationalization. For Berger, the abstraction of modernity is rooted in the underlying institutional processes on which modernity rests. These include the capitalist market, the bureaucratized state, the technological economy, the large city with its heterogeneous agglomeration of people, and the media of mass communication.

Berger's second category of modernity is futurity. Berger says futurity occurs when there is a profound change in the temporal structure of human experience, in which the future becomes a primary orientation for both imagination and activity. Of all distortions of modernity, it is time that has had the greatest effect. Berger advocates that this temporal transformation takes place on three levels. On the level of everyday life, clocks and watches become dominant. On the level of personal biography, the individual's life is perceived and actively planned as a career. On the level of the entire society, national governments begin to map out projects in terms of a plan. At each level, this new temporality conflicts with the way in which Western culture traditionally conceptualizes time.

Berger's third category of modernity is individualization. Modernization has entailed a progressive separation of the individual from all collective entities, and as a result has brought about a contraposition between individual and society. This trend towards anomie comes from the simultaneous institutional trend towards abstraction and the resulting alienation of people who interact with these institutions.

His fourth category is liberation. An essential element of modernization is that large areas of human life, previously considered to be dominated by fate, are now viewed as occasions for individual choice. Berger proclaims this trend as a fundamental rebellion against the divinely instituted human condition. In other words, tradition is no longer binding, and the status quo can be changed. The loss of belief in fate has weakened tradition to the extent that individuals must choose between alternative beliefs, whether they wish it or not. Ironically, liberation reduces an individual's options by challenging fate, the social order, and the certainty of life.

Finally, the fifth category of modernity is secularization. Berger claims that modernization has brought a massive threat to the plausibility of religious belief and experience. Secularization has meant a weakening of the plausibility of religious perceptions of reality among large numbers of people. Berger maintains that any critique of modernity must address these five categories.

Similar to Berger, Anthony Giddens puts forward the idea of discontinuities of modernity.[3] Giddens builds on the ideas of Marx and Durkheim to develop an economic and sociological interpretation of modernity. He explains that modernity creates discontinuities such as the pace of change, scope of change, the intrinsic nature of modern institutions (such as urbanization increased by population growth), and such themes as security versus danger and trust versus risk. Giddens asserts that modernity changes our fundamental notions of trust. The core component of modernity includes the growth of the paradigms of capitalism. As capitalism sought expansion through new markets, so modernity expanded throughout the world. This is evident in the growing trend towards capitalist globalization.

The theme of capitalist integration is fundamental to Giddens, as he recognizes two bodies of literature emerging, which explore the effects of "development" and the indigenous world. The first body of literature, the international relations view, examines nation-states as actors. Giddens views this perception as problematic, since it only examines one dimension. By contrast, the second body of literature can be referred to as world systems theory. Developed by Immanuel Wallerstein, Antonio Gramsci, and Franz Fanon, this theory examines modernity in the light of neocolonialism and dependency theory. Using a basic force model similar to the "realpolitik" of Hans J. Morganthau, world systems theory sees interstate relations in the context of core, semi-periphery, and periphery relations.[4]

Robin Horton takes a slightly different approach in defining modernity by challenging the notion that there is a fundamental difference between modernity and indigenous beliefs.[5] Horton maintains that there is a basic continuity of structure and intentions between traditional religions and modern scientific thought. In essence, the solution of the traditionalists to the challenge of modernity has not been a complete rejection of scientific humanism. Rather, Horton argues that "traditionalists" have demonstrated their own cognitive efficiency through the creation of adaptive mechanisms and institutions. Because these adapted or "hybrid" mechanisms and institutions serve communal needs and functions, Horton questions whether they can be deemed inferior to scientific theorizing.

The flexibility, awareness, and coexistence of alternatives are part of the African response to modern Western mechanistic materialism, although Western culture may not sufficiently acknowledge these indigenous responses to modernity. Horton's theory maintains that social anthropologists and African practitioners have occasionally maintained a fallacy of timelessness for pragmatic reasons. African practitioners benefit from the belief that their adaptive traditions are static because they are motivated to maintain their status of legitimacy. If an adapted tradition is believed to have been part of an endless succession of beliefs, it obtains a level of legitimacy. Conversely, the social anthropologists' research may be based upon observations made within a very small window of time, shorter than the observers' generation. As social scientists, they may lack the resources or willingness to acknowledge change over time in the "traditional" society.

Horton asserts that this change can take numerous forms, depending upon what is needed. A simple taboo, for example, may represent a mechanism of adaptive innovation. In other words, it may just be a way of storing an unknown until a culture's traditions can readjust to a new development. These processes of change and innovation become evident in the patterns of selection and transformation that occur when religious devotees convert to monotheistic Islam and Christianity. Horton believes that the structure and content of the existing cosmology and the nature of events challenging this cosmology ease the process of conversion.

Thus [selection] accounts for the way in which the messages of the world religions are accepted in some circumstances and rejected in others. Again, it accounts for the high degree of selection and remolding, which so often brings despair to the hearts of the proselytes of these religions. At the same time, this approach reveals "conversion" as a further actualization of the traditional cosmologies' vast potential for creative elaboration in response to the challenge of new experience.[6]

Even the process of conversion is not absolute. Indigenous cultures are not entirely discarded for secularized Christianity or Islam. Many basic underlying beliefs of indigenous traditions are retained in the adoption of monotheistic beliefs.[7]

Conversely, Zwi Werblowsky challenges the conventional dichotomy between modernity and tradition, advocating that modernity *is* a tradition and a culture itself.[8] Werblowsky traces the tradition of enlightened criticism to successive skeptics – from the early deists to Hume, Voltaire, Kant, Hegel, and Feuerbach, as well as Marx, Weber, Durkheim, and Freud. The skeptics represent a culture and tradition in themselves. Werblowsky asserts that the issue is not so much a conflict between culture and modernity as it is the rivalry between a tradition of modernity and alternative beliefs. One's worldview or *Weltanschauung* determines one's interpretation of modernity. In *Religion, Modernity and Postmodernity*, Paul Heelas defines the difference between modernity and postmodernity as the difference between differentiation and de-differentiations.[9] These two dimensions recognize contradictory axes on which modernity and postmodernity are analyzed.

In terms of differentiation, modernity emphasizes contrasts. Westernization created a perceived division of labor between work and home as well as the construction of "tribal" or national identities. According to Heelas, these divisions occur as modernity is predisposed to create taxonomies. Classifications help explain how things work by distinguishing between essence and finding relevant mechanisms of operation.

By contrast, de-differentiation involves ideas of unification, such as Kantian ideas of unconditional and categorical imperatives. De-differentiation is characterized by a fluidity of denomination as ideas are merged together. This tendency is no more apparent than in the deregulation of the religious realm. Building on the ideas of James Beckford, Heelas asserts that this tendency reflects a "willingness to combine symbols from (previously) disparate codes or frameworks of meaning." A popular example is "zennis," combining Zen and tennis.

The diversity of these views reflects the existence of multiple "modernities." In China, India, the Caribbean, Africa, the Americas, and in every other region of the world of indigenous peoples we can see multiple "modernities" as cultures adapt, synthesize, and resist modernity. To conceptualize the diverse reactions to modernity, we look to recent scholarship for guidance. For example, in examining questions of culture and tradition, Kwame Gyekeye points out that in understanding the nexus between tradition and modernity, we should first understand that culture and tradition are not interchangeable.[10] What is relevant to any culture today does not routinely become tradition. Tradition must not only be passed on from one generation to another, it must also be accepted. Gyekeye refers to the philosopher H.B. Acton's definition of tradition: "belief or practice transmitted from one generation to another and accepted as authoritative or deferred to, without argument."[11] Gyekeye defines tradition as "any cultural product that was created or pursued by past generations and that, having been accepted and preserved, in whole or in part, by successive generations, has been maintained to the present."[12]

Gyekeye sees tradition as a selective process. A society not only absorbs the traditions of its current culture but also selects aspects from unfamiliar cultures. This selective process leads to some degree of flexibility, as a society can discard old norms as it changes or imports new cultural values. This leads us to question the extent of modernity's effect on tradition. The culture that imports Western science and technology changes existing patterns of tradition. In opposition to traditional communities, imported concepts such as Western humanism promote the exercise of individual capabilities and the cult of reason. By exchanging large families and extended family obligations for higher standards of living, individualistic practices often conflict with indigenous traditions. Likewise, modernity is associated with causality and empirical observation. However, African and other cultures, for example, view causality as a function of spiritual and mystical power. Consequently, modernity constitutes a significant threat to existing traditions. As many indigenous cultures across the globe strive to modernize their societies, they must weigh the costs associated with modernity. Urbanism, mass exodus from rural areas, and population increases, as well as the ensuing increased demands for employment, housing, and education, are introducing new cultural norms that may compete with or replace existing traditional values.

Other scholars raise questions of authenticity and modernity. Not all scholars of religious studies agree on the extent of modernity's influence on indigenous religions. Considering the Middle East, for example, Robert Lee states that in discussing traditional values and modernity, we must consider the concept of authenticity.[13] Building on the ideas of Muhammad Iqbal, Lee notes that the fundamental idea of authenticity is to value the self, that is to say, "to be who you are without desiring to be someone else." Lee views this identity of the self as a fundamental desire for maintaining tradition and the status quo, as opposed to a desire for embracing an identity superimposed by modernity. This desire explains the general rejection of a European concept of progress among Islamic intelligentsia. Lee argues that Europeans lament the erosion of identity, not from any commitment to quaint traditions or disregard for the dangers of nationalist fervor, but from a conviction that the comprehension of reality can only begin with an existential understanding of the self. Ironically, excessive focus of the individual on the self diminishes the development of social solidarity in society, which is fundamental to the well-being of society.

Lee developed his concepts of community by borrowing from the ideas of Sayyid Qutb. Qutb advocates the idea of a Muslim brotherhood, in which the values of human dignity constitute the true values of modernity. Qutb believes that since faith in God is the most important value, this faith has a greater utility than the challenge of Western individualism. Only by being part of a greater Islamic brotherhood can one achieve this condition.

By contrast, other scholars maintain that indigenous peoples largely welcome modernity. Ian Mabbett, in *Modern China: The Mirage of Modernity*, explores the condition of China since its twentieth-century integration into the modern world. However, Mabbett maintains that although China has become a modern Communist state, it has not completely abandoned its traditional past. China, like Japan, pursued a path of modernization; however, pursuit of modernity has not brought the individualization so typically corrosive to traditional communal, collectivist thought. More importantly, Mabbett argues that China's bureaucratization and embrace of Communism do not represent a clean break with its traditional past.[14] Although there are differences between orthodox

Confucianism and Communism, modernizing trends may accommodate traditional Confucian values, such as the maintenance of a bureaucracy of commoners, not aristocrats, who are ideally recruited by their abilities and devotion to an established orthodoxy of the state. Like Communism, Confucianism advocates a code of social morality that depreciates all otherworldly religious beliefs and practices that deny the legitimacy of any alternative claims on the citizen's intellectual loyalty. Like Confucianism, Communism seeks to contain any religious movement that inhibits communal organization not expressly licensed by the state. Lisa Rofel, in *Other Modernities: Gendered Yearnings in China after Socialism*, makes a similar argument by examining the lives of three generations of workers in Chinese silk factories.[15] Rofel is concerned with the efforts of Chinese workers to maintain their strong family and traditional life in light of the needs of industrialization. This process is a fundamental struggle but one recognized as necessary for many Chinese workers for China to become a great power.

China's situation is not unique. Many Asian powers embrace Westernization. In *Changing Values in Asia: Their Impact on Governance and Development*, Han Sung-Joo examines modernity in the context of the industrializing states of Asia.[16] These states recognize the economic and political incentives in adopting pro-Western economies, but at the same time they are wrestling with preserving their own indigenous identities.

Finally, there has been discourse on modernity as a course of change and conflict within society itself. Looking at Indian society, Achin Vanaik writes that within the last twenty-five years, the dynamics of modernity in India reflect pressures within Indian society towards fundamentalism and communalism.[17] These events stem from the introduction of capitalist industrialization, the rise of science, the Age of Enlightenment, and the emergence and consolidation of Indian civil society. These trends triggered a pattern of secularization characterized by a decline in the importance of religion, an increase in the relative separation or replacement of religious institutions or compartmentalized secular institutions, and the growing importance of rational thought and activity.

Responding to the pressures of modernity, Hindu nationalism is fundamentally linked with what Vanaik terms communalism. Vanaik argues that communalism or religious fundamentalism, as a response to modernity, is an expression of a particular state of mind or distinctive personality type. Vanaik sees fundamentalism as a response of self-hating behaviors to a secular, desacralized world. Vanaik argues that although fundamentalism or communalism represents a rejection of modernity, fundamentalism is not as traditional as it might seem. Many fundamentalist or communal institutional challenges to modernity are in fact traditional institutions adapted or modernized to meet the new demands of the contemporary society. For India, modernity is the most formidable challenge yet to religion. Religious systems are responding by carrying out internal reforms in beliefs and practices to reassert their contemporary relevance. Indians have also responded by adopting modern means to pursue traditional goals and values. This is no more evident than in the rise of the Bharatiya Janata Party (BJP).

Similarly, scholars often attempt to examine the effect of modernity on communities within the modern state. How does a minority culture maintain distinctiveness in a homogeneous society? Many scholars of religious studies, for example, attempt to define Jewish identity. Bryan Cheyette and Laura Marcus, in *Modernity, Culture and "the Jew"*, organized a symposium of scholars addressing modernity and Judaism.[18] Cheyette and Marcus observed the work of cultural theorists who had examined the relationship between Judaism and modernity. Theorists quoted in *Modernity, Culture and "the Jew"* attempt to locate

Judaism as it relates to Western culture. However, they also attempt to explore the ways in which Jews have historically been excluded from mainstream societies in order for ascendant ethnic and sexual identities to be formed and maintained. In essence, the argument follows that anti-Semitism is a defining feature that has kept Jewish identity distinct from other ethnicities and identities. Although practitioners of Judaism are almost fully integrated into Western technologies and cultures, ironically the alienation of racism has maintained Jewish traditions and culture in the context of modernity. Specifically, this trend is evident in the effects of the state of Israel on Jewish identity. Cheyette and Marcus argue that there is virtue in ambivalence, which has characterized Jewish history and culture. They situate Jewish history in the context of current debates about gender, sexual, and ethnic identity.

Similarly, Laurence Silberstein maintains that analysis of Jewish fundamentalism is theoretically challenging given the preponderance of studies on Christian and Islamic fundamentalism.[19] Fundamentalism allows a means to control the mechanisms of cultural production. Silberstein maintains that the study of Jewish fundamentalism serves as an important vehicle for scholars to analyze the essential ideological conflicts within the Jewish world, particularly within the state of Israel. Whatever other characteristics they have in common, those Jews whom the dominant society labels as "fundamentalists" engage in and are fully committed to a struggle to generate, disseminate, and transmit a particular view of Judaism, Jewish history, and Jewish identity. Accordingly, Jewish fundamentalists are engaged in a struggle over the power to delimit discourse and establish the appropriate meaning and usage of key terms drawn from traditional Judaism. Jewish fundamentalists and their opponents seek to hegemonize conflicting conceptions of history, identity, society, culture, and tradition.

Silberstein argues that Israel represents a most conspicuous, concentrated site of confrontation between Judaism and modernity. Within that society, the ideological and cultural struggles indicate great conflict over meaning, identity, and power within the Jewish world as a whole. Specifically, Zionist interpretations of Judaism, Jewish identity, and Jewish history provide the basic myths, symbols, and rituals through which a significant proportion of Jews form and express their self-understanding as Jews, setting the terms and the limits of contemporary Jewish discourse.

Modernity and methodology

Rooted in the theoretical and substantive issues of modernity, this volume's twenty-two chapters examine modernity using contextual case studies of peoples of the Americas, Europe, Asia, Africa, and the Pacific Islands. Although the contributors take varied approaches to the issues of modernity, many scholars share a consensus regarding change and adaptability. This consensus is based on the ability of indigenous peoples to maintain cultural identities through the creation of new beliefs and institutions that allow them to adapt to new challenges.

Examining theoretical bases, religious studies scholars Janowitz, Geertz, Chidester, Long and Rydving provide us with several approaches with which to analyze modernity. In "Do Jews make good Protestants? The cross-cultural study of ritual," Naomi Janowitz examines whether or not Protestant paradigms have corrupted and biased Western views in examining other religions. Relying on S.J. Tambiah's theory, Janowitz develops a critique of Eurocentric, Protestant-derived theories of ritual. Janowitz asserts that under Protestant paradigms, ritual has become the object of critical examination only when perceived (by Western evaluators) as exotic, bizarre, or absurd.

This perception allows the question of demarcation to be advanced. How does one distinguish between magic, religion, and science? The question has plagued the study of indigenous religions. For many theorists, including Tambiah, Janowitz asserts that a relativist position has been adopted in response to this criticism: in essence, the norms of one culture are non-transferable when studying or judging another culture.

Janowitz argues that even theorists such as Robin Horton do not subscribe to a true relativist position. Horton maintains that although traditional African thought contains unique characteristics, its basic structure is similar to the logic of Western scientific rationalism. Janowitz uses Tambiah's arguments to assert that Horton represents another Westernized, Eurocentric form that devalues African thought as "childlike" or "primitive." Classifying African thought as "proto"-logical or rational by Western standards indicates a motive to subvert that thought as inferior to scientific humanism.

Janowitz suggests that the Protestant view sees magic in the context of the old biblical Hebrew opposition to Canaanite rivalry. Magic may be interpreted as evil and primitive, and seen as outside the context of rational discourse. However, Janowitz regards the Protestant notion of magic as substantially divergent from biblical versions. Whereas Protestants consider magic misguided and useless, the Old Testament acknowledges the concept of magic as the use of forbidden powers. Biblical denouncements represent pragmatic attempts to curtail a reliance on the gods of other peoples. Janowitz provides examples, such as the Hittite ritual of "*ambassi*," to demonstrate that the ritual of goat sacrifice, for example, differs only slightly from Hebrew traditions. It is not necessarily the ritual or the magic itself that is evil, according to biblical decree, but rather the *rival faiths* themselves that challenge the "true" Jewish doctrine.

Janowitz encourages us to pay attention to Protestant paradigms by adapting relativist positions. Both magic and ritual represent flexible variants of Christian religion, whether their origins are Jewish or Christian-in-transition-to-Protestantism.

Additional methodological insight is evident in Armin Geertz's chapter, "Can we move beyond primitivism? On recovering the indigenes of indigenous religions in the academic study of religion." Geertz provides a methodological and theoretical argument to explore a discrepancy between

> the indisputably central and inclusive role played by indigenous cultures in the development of theory in the social and cultural sciences on the one hand, and, on the other, the systematic exclusion, marginalization, and invisibility of living indigenous peoples in those same sciences.

Geertz suggests that this discrepancy is explained through the history and evolution of "primitivism" in European and American thought. Geertz argues that these criticisms begin with the early notions of the primitivism outlook. Cultural primitivism is fundamentally important. Ethnocentric scholars romanticized the benefits of the "simple life" as a stereotype. These views contrast with what Geertz calls evolutionism. The integration of Darwinism served to change the romantic outlook of cultural primitivism. From both schools emerged modern primitivism and the first serious efforts of modern scholarship to address the issues of modernity. These views have led, in turn, to what Geertz refers to as a new primitivism. A "theology of nostalgia" has emerged in modern scholarship as relativist arguments ask us to re-evaluate our earlier views. For example, many scholars view tourism as a form of cultural imperialism. Finally, Geertz ends his taxonomy with a discussion of radical humanism. Under this paradigm, practitioners maintain that in order to prosper in a rational society, technological processes and communications must override other priorities.

Geertz believes that importing deconstruction-inherited traditions from Western ideology requires the important counterbalancing task of constructing more ethical and accurate models and paradigms. As a practical solution, he proposes a "cleansing of the Age of Enlightenment," a critical rationality, and a reassertion of certain aspects of the Age of Enlightenment project. Geertz's Enlightenment thesis provoked a predictable discussion that continued throughout the conference. Reacting to criticism of the Enlightenment thesis, especially the accusation that "it got us into this predicament," or that the Enlightenment never afforded humanism for the colonized, Geertz observed that it is erroneous to assume a causal relationship between the Age of Enlightenment and colonial subjects.

David Chidester's chapter, "'Classify and conquer': Friedrich Max Müller, indigenous religious traditions, and imperial comparative religion," examines Max Müller as one of the founders of comparative analysis. Chidester's analysis portrays Max Müller's interest in comparative religion as an imperial, pro-British enterprise. Max Müller acknowledges that knowledge and power play a significant role in the emergence of comparative religion, helping to correct faulty paradigms perpetuating the fabrication that indigenous African peoples have no "true" religion. The experiences of Southern Africa, as well as India, prompted Max Müller to be the first intellectual to attempt to combine early notions of social science and anthropology as a means of "liberal imperialism." Chidester demonstrates how Max Müller, together with Wilhelm Beck and Henry Callaway, developed language as a unit of analysis to distinguish patterns of comparison.

Charles Long examines language as a product of imperialist thinking. In "A postcolonial meaning of religion: some reflections from the indigenous world," Long confronts the linguistic ambiguity that underlies Western discussion of indigenous traditions, especially the power structure inherent in language. Long analyzes the term "indigenous," which means, in its conventional sense, "home," recalling the colonial power structure and colonial projects that were established away from the colonizers' homes. Long observes that history, as we understand it today, reflects little truth about the relationships and encounters between indigenous peoples and colonialists. Borrowing Michel Foucault's phrase, Long suggests the need for an "archeology of knowledge" to analyze key terms in religious studies, such as primitivism, native, spirit, and religion. Long observes that modern world systems have created the notion of "primitive." From a psychology of language, the label of "primitivism" serves as an ideological justification for Western hegemony. Long reminds us to be mindful of cultural, ideological, and linguistic parameters, which often convey our very speech at cross-purposes.

In another case study, "Saami responses to Christianity: resistance and change," Håkan Rydving has looked at the Saami people of the Eurasian Arctic and Sub-Arctic, documenting incursions of "modernity." Doubly threatened, the Saami have encountered modernity in the forms of Soviet Marxism and Scandinavian Christianity. The Soviet Union persecuted the Saami until the post-Soviet era. Moreover, the Scandinavian Protestant missionary campaigns from the late 1600s onwards represent the most severe and long-standing threat to ancient Saami traditions.

Rydving investigates the centuries-long confrontation between Scandinavians and the Saami, gathering evidence indicated by the lack of respect for or interest in indigenous peoples and their cultures. Scandinavian religious texts are a sign of the lack of scholarly interest in the Saami. Although accentuating Saami drums and drumming, little emphasis was placed on the spiritual significance of the drumming or on Saami belief systems and culture. The first efforts to suppress Saami religious beliefs began when the Scandinavians confiscated their drums. The drums were seized during "drum hunts" dating as far back as the 1600s. The Saami continued to resist, and even those who converted to Christianity resisted total conversion, for they continued to drum in divination and shamanistic rituals.

Protestant missionaries went to extreme measures to suppress Saami religious practices. Rydving notes that throughout the 1700s, missionaries continued to burn Saami shrines and altars. However, the missionaries failed to subdue Saami beliefs entirely because of gender-based linguistic differences. Rydving tells us that ceremonies differed for females and males. While males were fluent in the language of the invaders, females usually spoke only Saami, making it much more difficult for outside authorities to suppress or identify religious practices among Saami women. Consequently, Saami traditions and beliefs survived centuries of Protestant missionary conversion campaigns. Saami religious beliefs continue to survive today.

The Americas

Many scholars have investigated the religions of the Americas. Moreover, scholars such as Mohawk, López Austin, Carrasco, McCarthy Brown, and McCarthy have developed case studies by examining characteristics of Mesoamerican Catholicism as a proscriptive analogy between European immigrants and indigenous peoples in the Americas. In exploring the origins of the European colonization of North America, John Mohawk develops a historical narrative, "Tribal religious traditions are constantly devalued in Western discourse on religion." Mohawk interprets the history of the colonial West, influenced by a European perception of indigenous religious traditions and peoples. The European meta-narrative of perfectibility and human agency failed to include indigenous knowledge, religion, and peoples. The Western version of its own history fails to incorporate later alternative views of reality. John Mohawk sees the current resurgence in indigenous spirituality as a form of resistance against colonialism and the forces that dominate native religion and cultures.

Mohawk argues that the imposition of European beliefs dates back to the beginnings of Western culture. In essence, Greek philosophy encouraged Europeans to believe that the forces of fate were within their own hands. Combined with social Darwinism, superior military technology, and the eventual resources of the Industrial Revolution, these attitudes led to the expansion of Western discourse through a series of imperialistic Crusades. Mohawk asserts that the first Crusade of the conquest occurred with the attack upon the Gaunche people of the Canary Islands. This attack served as a template for conquests throughout the New World.

Robert Held has critically assessed the European Inquisition, based on artifacts and illustrated documents from an international exhibition which opened to the public in Florence, Italy, in 1983, and closed in Barcelona, Spain, in 1986. Held describes the Inquisition's spread to the Americas: "By 1500 the Inquisition had been exte[n]ded to the New World, particularly to Peru and Mexico, where it destroyed entire civilisations – genocide by torture, although the good friars used to baptise babies and children before throwing them to starving dogs or cremating them alive."[20] Georges Van Den Abbeele agrees with Robert Held's disquieting conclusions: the Europeans imported to the New World the methods and technology of torture developed during the Inquisition.[21] However, early scholars at the time defended European conquests and Spanish *conquistadores*. Using Aristotelian principles, John Locke, in his Second Treatise of Government, defended Spain's treatment of the peoples of the Americas, as did the influential Juan Gines de Sepulveda. European intellectuals justified torture as "the civilizing of lesser peoples" who "failed" to use the resources of the New World and thus needed to be brought to the Christian faith.

Alfredo López Austin's chapter, "Guidelines for the study of Mesoamerican religious traditions," provides an account of how two separate religious traditions in Mesoamerica have combined since the Spanish era. Beginning with a narrative of the pre-Spanish Mesoamerican religion, López Austin describes the synthesis between these indigenous beliefs and Catholicism. Discussing the colonial era, López Austin argues that the disappearance of former Mesoamerican institutions and temples elevated a series of new cults, as Mesoamericans were encouraged to adopt Catholicism. Although nominally Christian, these cults retained their Mesoamerican elements. In many cases, a refined polytheism emerged with characteristics of Christian dualism (God and the Devil) and the Trinity, concepts familiar to polytheistic Mesoamerican cultures. Likewise, the existence of Catholic saints also allowed for the integration of Mesoamerican deities into new cultural fusions. López Austin maintains that Mesoamerican cultures accepted a fusion of two faiths; Christ was revered as a supernatural deity of the sun and the Virgin Mary as Earth Mother Goddess. Although some Mesoamerican spiritual elements disappeared, indigenous peoples maintained significant religious traditions in colonial and postcolonial eras.

In "Jaguar Christians in the contact zone: concealed narratives in the histories of religions in the Americas," David Carrasco makes a similar point by reinterpreting a widespread myth about the European conquest of the Americas. Carrasco says: "The emphasis on conquest inevitably favors the Spanish epistemology as triumphant, and the Spanish Christian program as the effective willing servant of the European desire to erase and obliterate the indigenous world." This view of total European success is imprecise. There was no complete or total conquest of indigenous beliefs as much as there was a fusion of beliefs. Although Latin American peoples of African and Native American descent accepted many external Christian forms, they also practiced their faiths in unobtrusive or understated forms.

Turning to the indigenous peoples of North America, Chris Jocks accounts for the contemporary Mohawk people's enduring resistance to invasions of their homelands in "Modernity, resistance, and the Iroquois Longhouse people." Jocks argues that the history of the Mohawks and modernity is a history of struggle. He begins with an example of long-standing confrontation between the Mohawks and the Canadian army. The Mohawks are attempting to prevent construction of a golf course on sacred burial grounds. This recent confrontation is symbolic of the entire history of the Mohawk struggle to maintain their economy, autonomy, and cultural identity. The Mohawks exhibit strength and resistance, from the Longhouse as an institution to a student walkout to establish a Mohawk-controlled Kahnawaike Survival School.

Jocks examines Iroquois resistance. Their educational system, for example, resists the homogenizing efforts of modernity. Jocks also calls for a re-examination of the way scholars think about religion, because, for example, European-American religious perspectives fail to take into account other forms of religious thought. Jocks questions whether non-Western religious practice and thought can be properly understood by Westerners. Religion to the Iroquois represents not merely a system of symbols, amenable to description in linguistic terms; rather, it represents a system of relationships among individuals and the long-standing memory of the collective over many generations.

Affirming John Mohawk's thesis, Jocks observes that European-American narratives situate Native Americans in the most inopportune and unexpected times, outside the central core narratives. European-Americans perceive Native Americans as "primitive, savages," unstable, weak, "uncivilized," and unable to sustain themselves. During the nineteenth century, across the entire continents of the Americas, European soldiers and immigrants carried out policies of genocide, forced removal, and warfare against Native Americans.

Romanticized as "settlers or pioneers," European migrants even practiced biological warfare by distributing infected blankets from smallpox hospitals to Native Americans. Popular film of the "wild" West justified war, occupation, and the violent "taming" of the American Frontier, because Native Americans were being "civilized." John Mohawk emphasizes that the romanticized myths of conquest and violence were unrepresentative of the conqueror. The few acknowledged instances of violence were seen as deviations from the true "gentle" character of European-American "civilization." Jocks argues that European conquest and genocide in the Americas must be accurately portrayed to understand the insidious nature of colonialism and the inability of indigenous cultures to sustain themselves. Jocks suggests that these tendencies are a normal side effect of modernity. Modernity is designed to maximize efficiency by encouraging homogenization. Modernity's internal drive subverts indigenous cultures such as the Mohawk Nation. Faced with modernity, the Mohawks must learn how to heal internal divisions. It is an ongoing struggle.

Bruce Lincoln skillfully calls our attention to the methodological and moral fallacy of dealing with "world religions" in a-historic fashion in the chapter, "'He, not they, best protected the village': religious and other conflicts in twentieth-century Guatemala." Lincoln encourages us to be mindful of economic investment and military deployment, and other "extra-doctrinal" interests that may facilitate the expansion of "world religions" often in situations of vastly unequal power. "At any given moment and in any given locale," the balance of power between indigenous and "world" religions is reflected in the details of religious discourse. Lincoln illustrates his analysis by drawing on Guatemalan religious narratives in which the struggle for power finds expression in blended Mayan and Chimalteco Genesis-Crucifixion narratives. Jesús transforms the "Jews" into rich and powerful spirit guardians who defend the mountains. The dominant Europeanized ladino elite, depicted as soul-stealing devils, is identified with those most antithetical to the Indian community. Lincoln brings us up to date, recounting severe economic exploitation (1937), political reform (1946), and military repression (1983): events involving the United Fruit Company, the CIA, and with US backing, military death squads in the "most savage campaign of repression against intellectuals, opposition politicians, organized labor, and above all, the nation's peasant and Indian population." He concludes by advocating a dialectic religious model that expresses transformation of both indigenous Mayans and exogenous Spaniards.

In "Vodou in the 'Tenth Department': New York's Haitian community," Karen McCarthy Brown looks at the Haitian diaspora in the context of New York City, observing the efforts of communities to maintain their Vodou faith. Haiti is composed of nine "Departments," prompting Haitians to refer to New York as the "Tenth Department." Haitians in the United States must contend with blatant US racist stereotypes in opposition to their indigenous beliefs. For the practitioner and devotee, Vodou, or "serving the spirits," permeates all areas of daily life. Yet Western culture has wildly sensationalized, vilified, and reviled Vodou as "evil." Westerners have never considered Vodou to be a religion, and thus Haitians must practice in understated forms, sometimes adopting the names of Catholic saints for their deities.

McCarthy Brown maintains that New York City Haitians, caught between both worlds, adopt different ways of speaking. McCarthy Brown speaks of everyday Haitian life through Mama Lola, the central character in her classic study of Vodou religion. Mama Lola uses a pattern of speaking that simultaneously maintains Catholic, American, and Vodou traditions. McCarthy Brown notes the example of the "home-grown" taping of news, flown in from Haiti, copied, and distributed to viewers daily. McCarthy Brown underscores the significance of West African indigenous elements combined with Western traditions, producing a *bricolage* of religious practices also known as "creolization." African-derived spirituality in the Americas, such as African-Cuban *Santería* and African-Brazilian *Candomblé* practices, has influenced contemporary US innovative culture. McCarthy Brown explains that Vodou is not characterized by a theology or a belief system because no continuous official history exists to establish authenticity. Instead, "streams of changing continuity" characterize African-influenced practices. Haitian families and groups participate in and act out Haitian religious practices, but not necessarily as belief systems.

Helen McCarthy argues for the right of Native American peoples to control their native heritage, symbols, and tribal identity through access to their sacred mountains in California. McCarthy argues for these rights in her chapter entitled "Assaulting California's sacred mountains: shamans vs. New Age merchants of Nirvana." She begins a dialog on the significance of these sacred mountains as conduits of spiritual power. Many indigenous Californian peoples have produced their own myths of creation. The free expression of creation myths requires that native Californians and their shamans have access to these sacred places to interact with the spirits. In this context, reclaiming "public space" as spiritual space affects the study of religion, demanding an examination of the effects of tourism, recreational hikers, climbers, geologists, or anthropologists who invade sacred sites. McCarthy makes the case that any successful interaction of shamans with their sacred places requires access to these sites, solitude, and seclusion to conduct sacred religious ceremonies.

McCarthy contends that the sacred mountainous regions of California often represent vortices of power, for example Mount Lassen and Mount Shasta. Even New Age practitioners, says McCarthy, recognize the spiritual power of Mount Shasta. However, such practitioners may unintentionally pollute or defile sacred spiritual spaces by hiking in the mountains and by bathing, invading the perimeters, or throwing crystals in sacred springs. Public agencies that have jurisdiction over California wildlands may allow Native Americans to conduct sacred ceremonies and rituals, but the multi-use policy of federal, state, and local agencies represents an inconsistency that favors other users and allows them to violate the sanctity of these places. McCarthy calls upon these agencies to change their policies to respect the practices of indigenous peoples by restricting access to significant sacred mountains of California.

Participants in the "Beyond 'Primitivism'" conference sparked lively and spirited debate among themselves. One such debate asked if indigenous people themselves incorporate New Age rituals and symbols into their traditions. Often indigenous people allow New Age devotees or gambling enterprises on their land to gain economic benefits. Indigenous traditions then become an economic commodity, especially based on a touristic economy. One is reminded here of similar commercializations of indigenous traditions, such as African traditions in Europe and the Americas, Mexican dances in the United States, and sacred mountains in Zimbabwe. Concluding the session, participants questioned how a religious community might sustain itself, given the economic intrusion of commodification. Native Americans and many other indigenous peoples across the globe may be unable to protect their sacred symbols and land from the economic incursions of modernity. However, rural sociologists and community developers are struggling to help indigenous communities gain skills to withstand or to compete with the invasions of modernity, invasions that begin with missionaries, loggers, miners, surveyors, geologists, anthropologists, and developers.

Africa and Asia

Flora Edouwaye Kaplan examines the nature of indigenous contact with world religions, as well as indigenous peoples' responses to often violent and abrupt encounters over systems of belief. In "Understanding sacrifice and sanctity in Benin indigenous religion, Nigeria: a case study," Kaplan explores the resistance of traditional cultures that continue to form the basis of ethnic and national identity in the modern state. Kaplan asks why some religious communities resist change while others fail to resist change. Using the religion of Benin as a case study, Kaplan examines myth, symbol, institutional religion, and reaction to change. Focusing on the figure of the Oba of the Nigerian Edo-speaking peoples, Kaplan argues that the culture of Benin survived because of inherent flexibility. Belief that their king was the son of a high god was readily adaptable to Western notions of Jesus as the "Son" of their God. Accordingly, the people of Benin maintained significant traditional religious beliefs while accepting overlays of Christian form.

Looking at case studies scattered across widespread regions of Asia, scholars offer diverse treatments of modernity to examine its encroachment on the indigenous peoples of Asia today. Scholars such as Lai, Araki, Sjöberg, Kendall, Yengoyan, and Obeyesekere offer case studies of resistance to modernity. These case studies range from a discussion of non-institutional religious practices in Japan to Earth Mother sects seen in late nineteenth-century China. Whalen Lai begins with "The *Earth Mother Scripture*: unmasking the neo-archaic." Lai analyzes an ancient Chinese text, the Earth Mother Sutra, as an example of the revival of primal religion under Chinese imperial rule. Lai argues that no clear indication emerged of China responding to the predicament of modernity, as with the resurgence of Korean and Japanese shamanistic cults in the same period. Rather, in China, spirit writing was revived as a professed medium for new revelatory texts. Lai's chapter raises an interesting issue about the relationship between indigenous religions and written texts, and the use of written texts as sources for the study of indigenous traditions.

According to Lai, the revival of the *Earth Mother Scripture* is analogous to earlier Earth Mother movements, such as prehistoric China's cult of Hou T'u and T'u Ti. In great detail, Lai describes these earlier movements, contrasting them with the 1880 revival. For the modern movement, the *Earth Mother Scripture* constitutes a written word, teaching the ethics of obligation and kindness to all humans. Lai notes that "the Earth Mother cult returns the sectarian cult of the Eternal Mother to an earlier and simpler form of piety."

Michio Araki describes the Western influences that fostered the decline of traditional religious Buddhist sects and Shinto shrines in favor of new religious movements (NRMs). In "Popular religions and modernity in Japan," Araki examines the broad implications of this process, applying a "Western approach" to Japanese traditions while calling for a closer examination of the concepts applied to the study of Japanese popular religion and native traditions. Araki's study provides an opportunity for scholars to ask about NRMs in Japan, especially the one led by the controversial, semi-divine, and charismatic leader, Asahore. Araki notes that the government does not support NRMs because they work against homogenous Japanese identity and the nation. Whereas in the post-war period the Japanese government tolerated NRMs, recently NRMs have become a political issue because scandalous NRMs have attempted to manipulate the Japanese. The suppression of heterodoxical religious movements is related to the suppression of the religious life of native people. The difference, though, is that the suppression of native traditions, such as those of the Ainu, is related to earlier histories of colonization and competition for land and resources.

As evidence for his thesis, Araki emphasizes four eras in which religious movements were linked to modernization and modernity. The first era occurred at the beginning of the Meiji period. A group of popular religions known as the Kurozumi-Kyo and Konko-Kyo emerged, promising to deliver a personal religious experience nurtured in the traditions of folk religion. A second era is represented by the development of NRMs, including the Omoto-Kyo and Hito-no-michi religions, in the intensity and development of the modern imperial state and capitalist industrialization at the beginning of the nine-teenth century. A third era emerged before and after the Second World War. Sects such as the Tensho-Kotai-jingu-Kyo and Seicho-no-ie emerged, struggling with traditional values in the modern imperial state and a post-war democratic state. A fourth era occurred with the rise of groups such as the Agon-shu in the 1970s. This movement attempted to control the post-industrial or postmodern society, increased urbanization, and rapid economic development and prosperity.

Araki suggests that much of the impetus for these movements signifies a desire for the Japanese to emulate, overcome, and distinguish themselves from Western values. These new sects reflect efforts to integrate or maintain folk traditions and non-institutionalized values, as a means of addressing the challenges of modernity. Although the Japanese may accept the values of technology as "civilization," they reject the Christian religion itself. The Japanese selectively combine folk values with certain aspects of Western civilization deemed essential to the progress of Japanese society.

In "Rethinking indigenous religious traditions: the case of the Ainu," Katarina Sjöberg studies the Ainu of Japan. She looks at the Hokkaido Ainu traditions that are perceived to be disappearing under efforts to integrate them into mainstream Japanese culture. Sjöberg argues that despite widespread notions of their decline, some religious traditions of the Ainu remain viable and resilient. Sjöberg examines these traditions in the context of transformative processes, religion, and culture in modern Japan. Sjöberg argues that indigenous religious traditions do not vanish; rather, they are integrated into mainstream society.

Sjöberg offers evidence for this argument in an Ainu account of human origin. Contrary to the popular understanding that regards the Japanese as homogenous, early Ainu culture created a religious and cultural identity distinct from that of mainstream Japan. Increased tourism and academic interest in the Ainu encouraged a revival of Ainu indigenous beliefs. This revival encouraged the elite to promote the Ainu religion, rituals, and religious practices. Sjöberg suggests ironically that interactions between Ainu and Western cultures actually strengthened the Ainu culture in Japan.

Laurel Kendall explores religion as a construct or category applicable to Korean shamanic practices. In "Korean shamans and the definition of 'religion': a view from the grass roots," Kendall observes Auntie Chun, an aspiring Korean shaman, examining relevant anthropo-logical theories and historical studies. Kendall uses religion as applied to the Korean shaman facing the dilemma of modernity. Kendall's work resonates with the continuity paradigm suggested by Karen McCarthy Brown and Bruce Lincoln. Although shamanism fails to conform to classic Western notions of religion, shamanism represents a stream of continuity with the Korean past. Korean shamans, such as Auntie Chun, are caught between the demands of Buddhism and Christianity, challenged by the forces of modernity in Korean nationalists and Japanese colonizers.

Kendall suggests that moderns view the perceived need to extirpate superstition as "progress." The Japanese repressed shamanism in Korea, while many Koreans themselves viewed shamanism as superstition, as contrary to the logic and ideology of modernization. In the name of development, for example, South Korea's President Park Chung-Hee initiated the repression of shamanism with his campaigns for anti-superstition. Although opposed by Protestant Christians and class divisions in Korean society, shamanism survived as an understated practice. However, these trends are now reversed. In the post-1970s era, cultural nationalists moved shamanism in Korean intellectual discourse from the realm of superstition to that of religion and culture. Once viewed as backward and detrimental to Korean development, many now embrace shamanism as an intricate component of Korean nationalism and identity.

Kendall observes that shamanism is viewed as the domain of the female, based on divisions such as "outside" and "inside." "Inside" is perceived as a female sphere of influence regarding "private" issues, and "outside" as the "male and public realm." After increased economic interest and governmental requirements, shamanism became fashionable, developing a professional appearance supported by schools and study groups. Although often portrayed as disreputable, occasionally one may see well-spoken shamans appearing on television, representing themselves as national treasures. How do these trends relate to the emergence and popularity of Christian Pentecostal movements and the success of Christianity in modern Korea? Some Korean Christians believe that shamanic practices are accepted because "Satan" has a vested interest in shamanism. On the other hand, there is a striking similarity between the two religions insofar as Pentecostalism, like Korean Shamanism, sees prayer as an instrument to success.

Versed in the Mandaya traditions of the Philippines, Aram Yengoyan analyzes the dual influences of Islam and Christianity in "Mandaya myth, memory, and the heroic religious tradition: between Islam and Christianity." Yengoyan finds that the Mandaya coexist with Christianity and Islam, selectively incorporating other traditions. Yengoyan reviews the Mandaya religious system and oratory forms used in myth and history, observing that the impact of Islam and Christianity on the Mandaya is best understood on two levels: socioeconomic and religious. The interaction is not unique, showing that religious systems are often influenced by local contexts as well as world religions.

In developing this analysis, Yengoyan examines the Mandaya pantheon extensively, describing beliefs and traditions, as well as traditional oration and myth. Despite fierce attacks from the Moro people, the Spanish, and the American military, the Mandaya have been able to preserve much of their culture in the face of conquest and modernity.

Gananath Obeyesekere examines the adaptability and resilience of the Väddas or Veddas, the indigenous forest peoples of Sri Lanka, in the context of the hegemony of Sinhala Buddhism. In "The Väddas: representations of the Wild Man in Sri Lanka," Obeyesekere maintains that the conversion of the Väddas to Sinhala occurred under unique endogenous social processes.

Obeyesekere argues that scholars must first recognize that the Väddas are victims of the defamation and vilification of out-group writers, historians, and anthropologists. Many early scholars failed to understand, and thus denied, the existence of religion, laws, and civil society in Vädda culture. Maligned as "wild men," the Väddas were demeaned or romanticized as "uncivilized." Obeyesekere attempts to counter these claims by examining Vädda myth and belief systems, which represent intricate, sophisticated ritual, malleable to their social functions.

Although Vedda religious beliefs are similar to those of Sinhala, they represent no pure form of Buddhism. While both groups revere similar deities and practice similar rituals, the Väddas reject Buddhist beliefs in rebirth and karma. These beliefs represent a synthesis of traditions, since Vedda society significantly values hunting. Only with increasing dependence on rice cultivation have the Väddas converted to Buddhist beliefs in reincarnation and respect for life.

The Pacific Islands

Recent scholars have strengthened the research on modernity and the religions of indigenous cultures. Scholars such as Trompf, MacDonald, and Friesen have concentrated upon the island peoples of New Guinea and Hawaii, making available diverse views on the impact of tourism, cargo, and Christianity. Garry Trompf's "On wondering about wonder: Melanesians and the cargo" examines those influential Western theorists who formulated notions of "primitivism" and "wonder" in the context of Melanesian cargo cults. After reviewing theorists such as Max Müller, ironically Trompf asserts that Melanesian "wonder" directed at Western cultural products parallels Western wonder directed at indigenous Melanesian cultural products. Trompf observes that exotic, mysterious items, of course, entail experimentation, usually by imitation and imagined possession, stimulated by belief in "magical manipulations" of "like objects" and mimicry. Magic constitutes a conduit for power, allowing the believer to adapt to and recognize the existence of the Western world. Trompf maintains that Melanesian interaction with Westerners and their artifacts created a sense of wonder for both Melanesians and Westerners.

Mary MacDonald examines the relationships between Melanesian beliefs and modernity. In "Thinking and teaching with the indigenous traditions of Melanesia," MacDonald provides a personal account of her experiences in Melanesia. Beginning with a narrative of the cultures, languages, and demographics of the island, MacDonald provides an optimistic view of Christian influences and modernity. Describing cargo cults such as the Kema or the bachelor cults of the Huli, MacDonald refers to the notion of sacred geography. That these indigenous groups interact with Christianity is of fundamental importance. MacDonald notes that Christianity offers the opportunity to forge a common identity. As these tribes integrate further with Western culture, they increasingly accept Christianity, becoming ever more unified under a common religion.

MacDonald argues further that 90 per cent of Melanesians identify themselves as Christian, while at the same time they continue to affirm the traditions of their ancestors. Most Melanesians use both indigenous and Christian ritual and mythology when confronting their daily concerns about health, wealth, and fertility. In negotiating regional and national concerns, Melanesians tend to appeal to global Christian "norms," which they see as extensions of indigenous wisdom. Jesus, for example, represents the ideal brother, concerned not only for his own clan, but also for all people.

In "The Hawaiian lei on a voyage through modernities: a study in post-contact religion," Steven Friesen examines the impact of modernity on the Hawaiian Islands. Some scholars, including Friesen, question the meaning and usefulness of the terms "indige-nous" and "modernity." Colonial archives do not contain information about a monolithic modernity; instead, they reveal many "modernities" at any given time and place, moderni-ties that are negotiated or imposed at specific historical moments. Friesen traces the changing views of the floral lei, as it moved through the modernities of early twentieth-century Hawaii. Friesen cites the single incident of the creation of Lei Day as a case study to examine modernity's challenge to the Hawaiian people. The Hawaiian floral lei is an object of cultural significance to the indigenous Hawaiians. By 1920, only 20 per cent of Hawaii's population consisted of indigenous Hawaiians. In the face of a diminished popu-lation, the "Caucasian-in-paradise" paradigm romanticized the islands and its indigenous peoples. The lei was appropriated to advertise the islands to mainland tourists.

Imposed as a type of European "May Day," Lei Day represented a kind of Eurocentric spin on the original religious lei ritual of the Hawaiian people. Consequently, Lei Day failed to eliminate conflict in daily life in the territorial era. It restricted the options, and allowed for the coexistence of a limited range of minority options. Friesen suggests that the significance of the lei was substantially different in the pre-colonial as compared to the postcolonial era. In the Kingdom of Hawaii, the lei was a religious object. It was a symbol of the physical poetics of community life. In the Territory of Hawaii, although the lei remained a religious object, it became a commodified native craft in an occupied colonial setting. Friesen believes that in this case, modernity preserved the symbolic value of the lei, but also destroyed its earlier sanctity.

The scholars in this volume attest to the claim that there is not just "one" modernity. Their case studies demonstrate that there are many "modernities." Across the globe, hundreds of indigenous cultures have developed their particular responses to modernity, based upon the dynamic characteristics and histories of the indigenous peoples. Common to the scholarship collected here is a notion of adaptability and resilience. Indigenous peoples have found ways to resist external influences and/or to fuse their own beliefs with those of the world religions introduced into local regions. The fusion of many Asian, Caribbean, Latin American, and African variants of Christianity and Islam provides evidence of the flexibility and pragmatism of indigenous peoples worldwide.

Notes

1   Anthony Giddens, *The Consequences of Modernity*, Stanford: Stanford University Press, 1990, 1.
2   Peter Berger, *Facing up to Modernity*, New York: Basic Books, 1977, 71–8.
3   Giddens, *Consequences*, 1.
4   Anthony Giddens, "The consequences of modernity," in Patrick Williams and Laura Chrisman (eds) *Colonial Discourse and Post-colonial Theory: A Reader*, New York: Columbia University Press, 1994.
5   Robin Horton, *Patterns of Thought in Africa and the West: Essays on Magic, Religion and Science*, Cambridge: Cambridge University Press, 1993.
6   *Ibid.*, 316.
7   *Ibid.*, 317.
8   Zwi Werblowsky, *Beyond Tradition and Modernity*, London: Athlone Press, 1976.
9   Paul Heelas (ed.), *Religion, Modernity and Postmodernity*, Oxford: Blackwell, 1998.
10   Kwame Gyekeye, *Tradition and Modernity: Philosophical Reflections on the African Experience*, Oxford: Oxford University Press, 1997.
11   H.B. Acton, "Tradition and some other forms of order," *Proceedings of the Aristotelian Society*, n.s., vol. 53 (1952–53): 2.

12 *Ibid.*, 221.
13 Robert D. Lee, *Overcoming Tradition and Modernity: The Search for Islamic Authenticity*, Boulder: Westview Press, 1997.
14 Ian Mabbett, *Modern China: The Mirage of Modernity*, London: Croom Helm, 1985.
15 Lisa Rofel, *Other Modernities: Gendered Yearnings in China after Socialism*, Berkeley: University of California Press, 1999.
16 Han Sung-Joo, *Changing Values in Asia: Their Impact on Governance and Development*, Japan: Japan Center for International Exchange, 1999.
17 Achin Vanaik, *The Furies of Indian Communalism: Religion, Modernity, and Secularization*, London: Verso, 1997.
18 Bryan Cheyette and Laura Marcus (eds), *Modernity, Culture and "the Jew,"* Oxford: Blackwell, 1998.
19 Laurence Silberstein, *Jewish Fundamentalism in Comparative Perspective: Religion, Ideology, and the Crisis of Modernity*, New York: New York University Press, 1993.
20 Robert Held, *Inquisition: A Bilingual Guide to the Exhibition of Torture Instruments from the Middle Ages to the Industrial Era*, Florence, Italy: Qua D'Arno, 1985, 15.
21 Georges Van Den Abbeele, lecture, University of California, Davis, 1997.

References

Ahmed, Akbar, *Postmodernism and Islam: Predicament and Promise*, London: Routledge, 1992.

Balogun, Odun, *Tradition and Modernity in the African Short Story*, New York: Greenwood Press, 1991.

Clifford, James, *Routes: Travel and Transition in the Late Twentieth Century*, Cambridge, MA: Harvard University Press, 1997.

Dallmayr, Fred and G.N. Defy (eds), *Between Tradition and Modernity*, Walnut Creek: Altamira Press, 1998.

Geras, Norman and Robert Wokler (eds), *The Enlightenment and Modernity*, New York: St. Martin's Press Inc., 2000.

McGuire, Meredith B., *Religion: The Social Context*, 4th edn, Belmont, CA: International Publishing Company, 1997.

Miller, Daniel, *Modernity – an Ethnographic Approach: Dualism and Mass Consumption in Trinidad*, Oxford: Berg, 1994.

Mudimbe, V.Y., *The Surreptitious Speech: Présence Africaine and the Politics of Otherness 1947–1987*, Chicago and London: University of Chicago Press, 1992.

Stillman, Norman A., *Sephardic Religious Responses to Modernity*, New York: Harwood Academic Publishers, 1995.

Von Der Mehden, Fred, *Religion and Modernization in Southeast Asia*, Syracuse: Syracuse University Press, 1986.

Williams, Patrick and Laura Chrisman (eds), *Colonial Discourse and Post-colonial Theory: A Reader*, New York: Columbia University Press, 1994.

Part I

Modernity and methodology

Chapter 1

Do Jews make good Protestants?

The cross-cultural study of ritual[1]

Naomi Janowitz

Usually, a ritual becomes the object of investigation only when it is perceived to be exotic, bizarre, nonsensical, or absurd. That is to say, when it is *someone else's ritual*. The "someone else" has classically been an indigenous person; the investigators, in the main, Protestants. The distorting lens of Protestant-based theories of ritual is addressed in S.J. Tambiah's book, *Magic, Science, Religion and the Scope of Rationality*. He presents a thorough critique of scholars such as Edmund Tylor and James George Frazer, demonstrating the straitjacket that their theories constructed for analyzing indigenous rituals.

Despite decades of such critiques, the legacy of these scholars continues to shape debates about ritual. Tambiah's elegant critique of much prior scholarship and his own influential observations about ritual demands careful consideration. In the first section of this chapter, I will address some of the theoretical problems Tambiah raises for us about comparing "Western" and "indigenous" rituals; in the second part, I will examine a test case, Israelite and Ancient Near Eastern scapegoat rituals, chosen because it intersects with material Tambiah discusses. We will see both the tenacity of and the distortions brought by Protestant-based theories of ritual, problems that are at the core of improving our study of indigenous religions. I will offer some suggestions about alternative terminology that can be used in the study of rituals.

Relativism and the problem of efficacy

Tambiah's short book addresses what is often called the demarcation question, that is to say, how to distinguish between magic, religion, and science. In an attempt to avoid using Western notions of science to judge traditional/indigenous rituals, he delineates a variant of the now-common "relativist" position. According to relativist theories, the norms from one society for definitions of rationality should not be used to study, and judge, another culture. He posits that

> it is when we transport the universal rationality of scientific causality and the alleged rationality of surrounding moral, economic and political sciences with the claims to objective rules of judgment...and try to use them as yardsticks for measuring, understanding and evaluating other cultures and civilization that we run into the vexed problems of relativity, commensurability, and translation of culture.

(1990: 132)

These vexed problems are epitomized for Tambiah in Robin Horton's controversial continuity thesis. This thesis, which compares African traditional thought with Western science, has two parts: (1) the structure of traditional African thought is similar to the structure of Western scientific theories; and (2) nevertheless, African thought is dissimilar to Western science in other ways.[2] By making this comparison, Horton appears to many scholars to present indigenous peoples as attempting to indulge, rather poorly, in scientific thinking when they employ traditional modes of thought. For Tambiah, this is just another version of earlier claims that traditional thought is childlike or primitive.

Both halves of Horton's thesis had come under serious attack before Tambiah's critique.[3] Some of the criticisms of Horton are based on his notion of science, which appeared to some to suffer from its positivistic stance.[4] A simple reference to Thomas Kuhn is thought to be sufficient to destroy the basis for Horton's position, and thus his equation of African and Western thought.[5] This criticism does not, however, demolish Horton's enterprise, but simply sends his supporters in search of a more up-to-date philosophy of science.[6]

Another tack taken in refutation of Horton's comparison is to argue that traditional thought is distinct from scientific thought and does not overlap in any way. Any attempt to compare them is a "category mistake." Scientific thought relies on notions of cause and effect while religious thought does not. According to this view, ritual is a purely symbolic activity whose practitioners do not expect a particular outcome from their ritual activities.[7] Instead, they are participating in a symbolic expression of cultural concepts. Beattie, for example, argues that "myth dramatizes the universe, science analyzes it" (1966: 65). Ritual is not an attempt to assert human influence but a meditation on the limitations of being human.[8]

The motivation behind this type of theory is laudable since it frees the "natives" from believing in what appear to be ridiculously simple or misguided notions of cause and effect. Indeed, as Penner notes, "one of the strengths of the symbolic approach is its criticism of ethnocentric explanations of religious beliefs and practices" (1989: 71). However, a symbolic approach to ritual is fraught with problems, two of which will be discussed here briefly.[9]

First, at a theoretical level, a symbolic approach does not tell us what the rituals are symbolic of, nor how to decode the symbols. Clifford Geertz, for example, places symbols at the heart of his definition of religion but does not tell us how symbols work (Asad 1993). The notion of symbol is used by Geertz "sometimes as an aspect of reality, sometimes of its representation" (*ibid.*: 30).[10]

Second, symbolic explanations negate the statements by participants who believe that their rituals are supposed to have specific effects. The implicit accusation that participants are wrong in their understanding of rituals is not itself grounds for rejecting symbolic theories, but negating their direct statements about rituals is an odd way to develop more indigenous-friendly interpretations. The theorist may be rescuing the indigenous people from accusations of misguided action, but he is also telling them that they do not understand their actions.

In sum, symbolic theories may look less pejorative on the surface, but they fail to offer a theoretical basis for the analysis of symbols. Symbolic theories cannot account for the perceived efficacy of rituals and they eviscerate ritual of any real purpose.[11]

Returning to Tambiah, he tries to vitiate Horton's comparisons by emphasizing the "expressive-performative" or "participatory" aspects of ritual. "Participation" appears to be an alternative ordering or reality to causality (Tambiah 1990: 108). This stance brings Tambiah very close to the symbolic theorists, leaving him vulnerable to all the criticisms of their position.

In addition, Tambiah's own two concluding examples undermine his argument. His first example concerns Sri Lanka and South India, where smallpox epidemics were attributed to the anger of a mother goddess. Control of the disease was attempted through annual religious festivals. Tambiah notes that with the introduction of modern vaccines, the festivals died out (*ibid.*: 133). The Western germ theory replaced the indigenous explanation on the basis of its better record of cure and prevention. The smallpox-averting rituals had a major participatory component, but this component was not enough to save them when the goal-directed dimensions were no longer important.

Tambiah's second example compares Indian (ayurveda) and Western healing systems for mental illness:

> [T]hey may both agree that certain behavioral and somatic systems – such as withdrawal from social relations, a depressed emotional state, lack of appetite, and so on – are indices of mental ill-health...But if each system in its context is no more rational and efficacious than the other, then we are faced with the conundrum whether it is possible to delineate a single transcultural context-independent profile of mental states like hysteria or depression.
>
> (*ibid.*: 134ff.)

The Western philosopher of science is apt to be delighted, not dismayed, that ayurveda is as efficacious as Western modes of dealing with mental health. The various branches of psychiatry, psychoanalysis, and psychotherapy are not strong cases for definitions of science because of their comparatively weak empirical success.[12] This example calls for a reconsideration of the demarcation question in relation to the *Western material itself* (is psychotherapy a science?) and not in relation to an East–West comparison. The question must be: if "Western" science is able to come up with a more effective therapy for mental illness, would that replace traditional Indian methods? If so, we will only be able to explain this situation by using concepts of efficacy, which Tambiah rejects.

In both cases we see that, despite his notion of category mistake, Tambiah does allow for a valid trans-cultural judgment (*ibid.*: 132ff.). This trans-cultural judgment looks suspiciously similar to Horton's attempts. Apparently, Tambiah has no way to explain to us which rituals will be replaced with the introduction of modern science, and which will not, unless he turns to the very notions of efficacy that he rejects. Tambiah realizes that "elements of participation are not lacking in scientific discourses" (*ibid.*: 109). Hence, it is not clear why having located some participatory component in a ritual immunizes it against comparative judgment predicated on the efficacy of the causal component.

Unsurprisingly, the case in which Tambiah's distinction between scientific "causality" and ritual "participation" appears to be valid is Protestant-based theories of ritual. These theories are locatable in a specific cultural and historical context. As Horton himself pointed out, once non-theistic paradigms in science achieved unprecedented success in explanation, prediction, and control of the natural world, Christian theologians redefined religion, restricting it to spheres where it was safe from scientific refutation. From then on, assertions about natural science based on Scripture and assertions about deities (especially their non-existence) based on "science" could both be labeled category mistakes. Secularization is a cultural process which influences not only the concepts of science but also those of religion. Looking over the specific historical debates which have led to a Western differentiation of religion from science, it seems impossible to claim that "traditional thought" possessed this identical differentiation.

Similar ambiguities plague Tambiah's characterization of "scientific" versus "persuasive" analogies. In his influential article "The form and meaning of magical acts," Tambiah argues that these two types of analogy are distinct, and that "persuasive" analogies should not be judged by the same standards as "scientific" analogies (1985).[13] In one analogy the Mujiwu compare a tree which has many roots and a woman who wants to have many children. Tambiah explains that

> [t]here is no intrinsic reason why the tree should be similar to a mother and the roots to children, but the analogy which says that roots are to the tree as children are to the mother makes relational sense that can be used to "transfer" effect.
>
> (*ibid.*: 76)

Here Tambiah begs the question: what is "relational sense" and how exactly is it employed to transfer effects? The premise of an analogy is some similarity weaker than identity between two objects; a particular aspect of one is imputed to resemble, for some reason, a corresponding aspect of the other. The more the similarity compels the second correspondence, the more persuasive it is. If by "relational sense" Tambiah is referring to culturally dependent criteria of the probative force of a similarity, then this is a statement about analogies in general.

One of the examples Tambiah gives is the treatment of scabies with chicken excrement. Not only do the two look the same, as has often been pointed out, but Tambiah also argues that part of the negative analogy is the relationship of excrement as a waste product (unwanted) to the scabby skin on the child as an unwanted adherence to the body. Thus a "persuasive analogy" appears to have both a positive and a negative component, pointing out how something is *not* like something else as much as how it is similar.

However, Tambiah does not show us how to tell when natives think that the negative part of a possible analogy would turn it into an unpersuasive analogy, that is to say, one where the evident dissimilarity leads to rejection of the putative conclusion. This is not surprising, because natives are aware of the positive analogies, as Tambiah notes, but appear never to point out the negative ones. It is not difficult to construct negative analogies out of positive ones because the two items are never identical. Until the relationship of the negative analogy to the positive analogy is clarified, an observer can construct his own negative analogy based on speculation about the natives' methods of reasoning without being able to prove or disprove them.

Finally, Tambiah's work is widely cited for his use of speech act theory, as outlined by J.L. Austin. Scholars eager for a means of characterizing the compulsive nature or perceived efficacy of ritual turned with enthusiasm to Austin's *How to do Things with Words*. Austin attempts to capture and describe the sense people have that verbal formulas have effects and accomplish ends. In particular, he created the term "performativity" to capture the sense of "doing" of some types of speech.[14] However, it should be noted in passing that Austin's model is not a sufficient theoretical model for finding "performativity" in any language or ritual system. His categories stem from English verbs, and no argument has ever been made that the functions of these forms are easily transferable to other languages.[15] A more useful theory of "performativity" would have to explain at a theoretical level how certain linguistic forms are related to their context of use (have a perceived efficacy).

To compound the problem of simply adopting Austin's notion of "performativity," Tambiah creates by analogy a category "performative act." This step is crucial for him, yet no argument is made that other types of action are best understood by analogy to language. Exchanging blood, Tambiah's example of a "performative act with no speech," is indeed an action – that would be hard to dispute. To call an action "doing something" is a tautology. That a ritual is an action which is constituted as mere acting, done for no reason other than for just the acting of the action, makes ritual meaningless once again.

Tambiah rejects strong relativism, noting that this position is untenable. This is a common position. Penner, for example, writes: "How could we validate the position that meanings...are culturally determined, since that position itself must arise out of a particular 'form of life' or '*lebenswelt*?' To answer these questions, relativists must somehow rise above the position they are taking" (1989: 75). Tambiah has challenged us to carve out a tenable weak relativism, an issue I will return to in the conclusion.

The tenacity of Protestant theories of ritual

At the beginning of his study, Tambiah examines early modern Protestant definitions of magic and religion, definitions which would later influence scholars such as Tylor and Frazer. Searching for the origins of these early modern definitions leads Tambiah in turn to biblical theories of magic: "Protestant theologians of the late sixteenth century seem to be resurrecting or repeating the dichotomy already constructed in early Israel" (1990: 19). The ultimate source of Protestant theories of magic, then, is the distinction between true religion and false magic found throughout the Hebrew Bible.

What interests me is that I believe that Tambiah's schema is correct, but *in reverse*. Early Israelites were not good Protestants, but Protestant terminology shapes many interpretations of Israelite religion. In his discussion of the biblical material, Tambiah relies heavily on the work of Yehezkiel Kaufmann (1960).[16] Kaufmann's depiction of Israelite theology presents a monotheistic, above-nature deity sharply distinct from other Ancient Near Eastern deities. The Israelite god is the only heavenly power, unchallenged even by powerful demons. Since the biblical god created the world *ex nihilo*, nothing exists outside of his realm of power. Nature itself is established by divine decree, and therefore subjected to his will.

While there are differences between biblical beliefs and the belief systems of other Ancient Near Eastern cultures, Kaufmann's dichotomy is too sharply drawn.[17] What is most striking with regard to our concerns is that the particular strategy Kaufmann used for differentiating the Israelites from their neighbors was to present the former as "Protestantly" as possible. The Ancient Near Eastern rituals are based on magic, and only the Israelites have a moral and interior dimension to their practices.

Since Kaufmann chose to present Israelite religion as "Protestantly" as possible, it is no surprise when in turn Tambiah finds Protestant concepts in Kaufmann's presentation of biblical beliefs about magic:

> In its quintessential form – and this is the early Judaic legacy that has colored subsequent Western thought – magic is ritual action that is held to be automatically effective, and ritual action that dabbles with forces and objects that are outside the scope, or independent of the gods.
>
> (Tambiah 1990: 7)

Tambiah does note one major difference between biblical and Protestant ideas: the Bible sees magical practices as effective, while Protestants consider them to be misguided and useless. It is at this juncture that magic becomes simply fraud, and it sets the modern definition apart from most prior uses.

The gap between biblical and Protestant definitions of magic is wider than he posits. It is hard to find a good description of the use of the Hebrew terms that translate into English as "magic" and "witch." They do not appear to refer to something outside the realm of the gods in the Bible. Instead, many of the terms refer to various divinatory practices. The biblical denunciations have an almost "practical" tone to them (Levine 1974: 89). Practices are prohibited which rely on other people's gods or which are outside of the control of the biblical authorities. The concept of "magic" as the use of forbidden powers is more important than the notion of working automatically.

Tambiah, following Kaufmann, appears to accept at face value the Israelite denunciations of pagan religion as "magic." Tambiah also states: "In actual fact magic declined before the technological revolution, and was rejected before the discovery of new remedies to fill the gap" (1990: 22). We do not know *what* it is that declined according to this statement. Again, it is Protestantism that leads the way theoretically in Tambiah's demarcation. Following Keith Thomas, Tambiah states that while the medieval church had "blurred" the line between magic and religion, it was reasserted by the Protestant Reformation. Many medieval practices look magical to Protestants; that does not mean that the medieval church blurred a distinction.

Decades after Kaufmann, we can see the continuing, almost unavoidable, use of a Protestant lens to compare rituals in the study of Israelite religion. A good example of this is the analysis of the scapegoat ritual from Leviticus 16, often compared with similar Hittite and Babylonian rituals. Discussed in only a few brief sentences (Leviticus 16:6–10, 20–2, 26), this Atonement Day ritual involved selecting two goats, over which Aaron cast lots, designating one for the Israelite deity and one for Azazel (see Table 1.1, Example 5). The priest then placed his hands on the goat for Azazel, recited Israel's sins, and sent the goat out into the wilderness. The person who sent the goat away was considered ritually unclean and could not return to the camp until he had ritually bathed (Leviticus 16:26).

The meaning of this ritual has been the source of controversy. The ancient Aramaic translators of the Bible interpreted "Azazel" as a place name, referring to some part of the wilderness. Based in part on comparisons with parallel Hittite and Babylonians rituals, some scholars argue that Azazel was originally the name of a demon. These rituals purge society of some form of impurity, disease, or evil by displacing it onto an animal which is then sent off to a supernatural being who lives in the wilderness.

One such parallel rite is the Hittite "Ritual of Uhhamuwa" for ending a plague, discussed along with several other scapegoat rites by David Wright (1987: 55–7). In this ritual, colored threads are placed on a ram, which is then driven away while a prayer is said asking the god to act peacefully with the land (see Table 1.1, Example 1). According to Wright's analysis, a plague is transferred to an animal using the colored threads (transfer of evil/disposal), the animal is decorated so as to appease the angry deity (appeasement), but the animal is not killed (no sacrifice).

The Hittite rite, Wright argues, includes both transfer/disposal of evil and appeasement of the deity, while the biblical scapegoat ritual is only a rite of disposal. The biblical goat is not decorated before it is sent out, so its function is not appeasement (*ibid.*: 54).[18] "Azazel" has no real identity any more in Israelite religion. The goat is a neutral "sin-holder" which simply carries the sins away (*ibid.*: 49).

The text of the Uhhamuwa ritual, however, does not explicitly tell us that the meaning of the placing of the colored threads on the animal is the transfer of the plague. For this point, Wright has to refer to another text that does make this point explicit. In the Hittite "Ritual of Pulisa," threads symbolize the evil affecting a king (*ibid*.: 48; see Table 1.1, Example 3). Thus we find that some versions of the scapegoat ritual are elided or tele-scoped versions of other rituals. We have to weigh, then, the question of whether the elided part of the ritual has the same meaning as made explicit in the fuller rite. Do we want to supply the missing meaning even when that missing meaning is the *absence* of some portion (no decoration = no appeasement)?[19]

Most significantly for us, Wright has chosen to see the telescoped rite as having the same meaning for the two Hittite examples (attaching threads means attaching evil even when not stated). For the biblical rites, however, telescoping means improving the rite by jettisoning "magical" aspects.

> Incantations like the one in the Huwarlu ritual would be theologically unthinkable in the Priestly material, since they attribute the effectiveness of the rite to the cathartic instruments rather than to God. The sins are not removed because the scapegoat has the power by itself to receive them and bear them away. They are removed because of the divine power and supervision accompanying the performance of the ceremony.
>
> (*ibid*.: 60)

Table 1.1 Wright's analysis of scapegoat rituals

Name of ritual	Action	Wright's analysis
1 Hittite Ritual of Uhhamuwa	Coloured threads	Transfer/disposal of evil, appeasement
	Incantation	Relies on cathartic instruments, not deity
	Goat driven away, not killed	No sacrifice
2 Akitu Babylonian atonement rite	Priest purifies sanctuary with water	Automatic, no human intention
	Slaughterer wipes walls of sanctuary with body of ram, says incantation, then throws carcass in river	
3 Hittite Ritual of Pulisa	Threads symbolize evils affecting a king	Transfer/disposal of evil, appeasement
	Prisoner used as substitute for the king	
4 Hittite Ritual of Ambazzi	Transfer and disposal only	No substitution, no appeasement
5 Biblical Day of Purgation (Leviticus 16)	Two goats, cast lots, one for Azazel, one sin offering, bull sacrifice, goat blood sprinkled	No colored threads, no appeasement, no substitution, only disposal, no killing so no sacrifice
	High priest confesses sin	Azazel is simply a placeholder

Source: Wright (1987).

In his recent study, Israel Knohl argues cogently that the Priestly source does not avoid incantations as a way of avoiding "magic" but instead avoids any and every form of spoken request (1995: 148). In addition, numerous rituals parallel the biblical scapegoat ritual, each in slightly different ways; the contours of the Israelite rite look different depending on which comparison is chosen. Some Ancient Near Eastern sacrificial rituals also have transfer but no appeasement.[20] The Hittite "Ritual of Ambazzi," for example, is "conceptually similar to the biblical scapegoat rite because it lacks the idea of substitution and appeasement of an evil-causing deity by means of the dispatched animal. It is merely a rite of transfer and disposal as is the biblical rite" (Wright 1987: 57). Thus the "non-magical" form of transfer-only ritual exists in other cultures as well and is not evidence of the inferiority of non-Israelite practices.

It is not clear that in any of the scapegoat rituals the scapegoat effects the transformation "by itself" and that divine power is not part of the equation. By reading divine presence into the Israelite rite and a cathartic instrument into the use of incantations, the superiority of the Israelite ritual is emphasized using a Protestant model.

Wright argues that the scapegoat is not a sacrifice since the goat is not harmed. However, the goat is not harmed in parallel Ancient Near Eastern rituals either.[21] The concern is for getting the sins away from the community; this does not prove that the goat was or was not considered a sacrifice in any of these cultures. We cannot be absolutely certain what Azazel was meant to do with the goat, but the rite does not appear to be for the goat's benefit. Why would any deity or demon take a load of sins if not for the fact that they were packaged in goat meat?

Striking a similar note, Jacob Milgrom points to the inferiority of the Babylonian atonement rite, in which the body of a ram is used to wipe off the walls of the sanctuary and the carcass is then thrown into a river (Milgrom 1991). This ritual has an automatic sense about it, according to Milgrom, and, as with such rites, no role for human intention. Such comparisons, he argues, point to the unique theology of the Priestly source of Leviticus 16. Israelite religion completely rejected the pagan notions of the demonic and of impurity as real forces. According to Milgrom, the basic premise of pagan religion is that deities are themselves dependent on a "metadivine" level and that humans can tap into this realm to acquire magical power to coerce gods (*ibid.*: 42). Israelite priests rejected magic, and now sin was the result of human action and not automatic forces. Israelites have "free will" and the Atonement Day/Day of Purgation scapegoat ritual proves this.

> The ethical impulse attains its zenith in the great Day of Purgation, Yom Kippur. What originally was only a rite to purge the sanctuary has been expanded to include a rite of purge the people...The scape goat, which initially eliminated the sanctuary's impurities, now became the vehicle of purging their source – the human heart.
>
> (*ibid.*: 51)

Purifying the heart, ethics, rejection of magic – the Israelites have been made to look as Protestant as possible. Evil is now "under control" and people are not prey to the cosmic forces and demons who attacked the practitioners of Ancient Near Eastern religion. We end up with the ironic stance that in order to distinguish the Israelites from their neighbors, the Ancient Near Eastern practitioners are depicted as the "Jews" of the ancient world. They lack the notion of free will, indulge in magical practices, and depend on external rites instead of spiritualized practices.

The Ancient Near Eastern practitioners did not consider their practices to be magic. The use of this word alone should make us suspicious of the analysis. It is impossible to tell from the outside which practitioners have ethical intentions in their hearts and which do not. The Priestly cult represents a subset of the much wider set of cultic activities, but none of them are unique to the Israelites. Gary Anderson puts it bluntly: "The distinctiveness of the Israelite cult is nothing other than the limitation of cultic activity to one particular patron deity" (1987: 3).

We are still left with our central dilemma: how can we compare all these types of ritual action? Comparing them is made even more complicated by the fact that we do not know how to describe the individual elements of each ritual and how these elements "stand for" other things (threads for evil) and thus function as particular types of signs (elements that "stand for" other elements). We turn here to the terminology for signs developed by Charles Peirce, following the growing number of scholars who have employed his mode of analysis successfully in anthropology, psychoanalysis, and literary studies.[22] According to Peirce, a sign does not simply "stand for" an object in the familiar way in which, for example, a name stands for an object. Instead, for a sign to have meaning, it must include a triadic relationship between the object itself, a sign which represents that object, and an interpretant, that is to say, the "translation, explanation, meaning or conceptualization of the sign-object relation in a subsequent sign representing the same object" (Parmentier 1994: 5). Each sign "stands for" its object in different ways depending on the particular relationship between the three dimensions of the sign (object, sign, and interpretant). The specific terms Peirce uses for the three distinct ways of "standing for" are icon, index, and symbol.[23]

Peirce defines the first type of sign, an icon, as "a sign which would possess the character which renders it significant, even though the object had no existence; such as a lead pencil streak in representing a geometrical line" (1940: 104). If we think about the example of the line, its form is important, indeed crucial, to its function. Alter the form, then the meaning is altered.

Icons are not arbitrary in the way that we generally think of words as collections of sounds arbitrarily chosen to represent objects. All icons have formal resemblances to the entities they represent. Maps are iconic; if they were totally arbitrary then they would not be much help in finding one's way. International signs try to be as iconic as possible so that people from a variety of cultures can understand them. Hence the iconic representations of men and women on bathroom doors.[24]

These icons are especially important since they establish divine presences in rituals. Any ritual in which a deity is thought to be present will have some form of iconic representation of the deity, that is to say, a representation which stands for the deity in a non-arbitrary manner. A deity is not simply referred to in a ritual, but is physically present in some sign with formal links to the deity.

Peirce's second type of sign is an index, which is linked to what it stands for by a "pointing" relationship, such as smoke to fire or a weather vane to wind. This type of sign must be in spatial-temporal contiguity with that which it represents. Someone yelling "come here" can only be understood when "here" is made clear by the context.

Establishing "pointing to" relationships is very important in rituals, since these relationships link up all the components which are part of the ritual setting. The "here" in which a particular ritual takes place is established by the very ritual itself, where the setting is created, whether it is a room in which a deity is thought to live or one of the highest heavens. When a person wears an amulet or sits on a divine throne, divine power is brought into spatial-temporal connection with that person.

The symbol, Peirce's third type of sign, has an arbitrary relationship with that which it represents, lacking both the formal and spatial relations of the other two types of sign. American stop signs are arbitrarily chosen to represent the concept of stopping at a junction. Given this arbitrary relationship, the form of the symbol is not motivated by its sign in any way. These signs are based entirely on social convention and thus vary from culture to culture. Words, for example, are based on social convention.[25] Symbols are likely to have complex and shifting clusters of meaning that are hard to understand in cross-cultural contexts.[26]

Let us return to the scapegoat rituals. Part of the problem of comparing the different rites is that they are mixtures of iconic, indexical, and symbolic modes of representation. In the Babylonian atonement ritual, wiping off the walls of the sanctuary is a literal map of the goal of "wiping away" sin; the form of the action is part of its meaning. The iconic action carries in it its own replacement; wiping away sin can also be "represented" in a more symbolic fashion, where the actions of "wiping" might be represented instead by a wave (or by throwing the cleansing agent on a selected spot). The question can then be asked whether it is necessary to use any actual iconic detergent, or whether the "cleaning" could just be done at another level and represented by just waving without sprinkling anything at all. Each iconic mode of representation can easily be replaced until the entire ritual can be done by anyone in any place entirely "in his heart."

We are reminded here of Tambiah's struggle with analogies. Analogical thought (and action) is often a way of incorporating iconic models into a ritual. Each analogy presents an exact image of some dimension of the sought-after ends of the ritual. The transformational force does not come from the analogy per se. The analogy is activated by socially understood (often divine) forces that are directed to the goals via the mapping of the goals as part of the ritual itself. Each ritual is a specific example of a general type of action, which is socially understood to bring about such-and-such a state.[27]

We have already considered Wright's claim that colored threads are used to transfer sins onto an animal. The action of tying the threads again maps the direct placement of sins onto the goat. It is easy to imagine the tying on of the threads falling away at some future date. Someone will invariably ask, is it necessary to actually tie the threads to the goat since the thread is already a representation of something else? Colored threads "stand for" sins in a symbolic manner. That is to say, they are arbitrarily chosen to represent some form of evil in the rite. This ritual is both iconic (sending the goat out of the community representing the sending out of the evil) and symbolic (the threads representing the evil).

In general, iconic models are likely to be open to scrutiny, with an almost relentless drive to reinterpret signs in the direction of symbols. At the same time, all rituals have iconic aspects that make them effective and encode their goals. This leaves every ritual open to the charge of being "magical"; the sending out of the goat in the biblical rite will be roundly denounced as "magic" by future generations.

Rituals, wherever in the world they are found, produce a series of echoes whereby the ritual is altered by substitution. At each stage, looking backwards makes the prior level look more "magical" and the substituted one more "ethical." These substitutions are complex mixtures of semiotic signs, often with "iconic" symbols being replaced with "symbolic" ones. In modified sacrifices, for example, the "standing for" relationship of the item sacrificed is made more obvious in the discourse about the ritual, and the item may look less and less like the origin model (a god in the form of a man). Again, this looks like a move away from "magic." *However, a ritual must retain at some level an iconic relationship to both the source of power and the goals, or the ritual will not have any efficacy.* This means that given the right context, even the ritual of wiping one's heart clean of sin without doing anything else will still be open to the charge of "magic."

While Jews may *want* to be Protestants, since so many claims about the rise of science are attached to Protestant theology, for most of their history they have been more like the ancient Israelites. Luckily, as noted above, claims about relativity of culture are only claims about habitual modes of thought and action, and not about potential ones. Jews who want to become Protestants have found the path open.

Notes

1 This paper was delivered at the "Beyond Primitivism" conference held at the University of California, Davis, in March 1996. I wish to thank Jacob Olupona for organizing and directing the conference.
2 The theory was first proposed in 1967 and then modified in 1982. In his update, Horton begins the reconstruction of the similarity thesis without Correspondence Rules (see below), theory-neutral distinctions between observational and theoretical statements, and other problematic elements of positivist philosophy. He also abandons Popper's open/closed dichotomy.
3 The volumes edited by Wilson (1970), Horton and Finnegan (1973), Krausz (1989), and Hollis and Lukes (1982) all contain attacks on and rebuttals of Horton's work.
4 Horton, for example, uses the notion of Correspondence Rules. Until the 1960s, Correspondence Rules were used by historians of science as a standard mode of describing the relationship between a theoretical statement and an observation. Correspondence Rules have fallen into disrepute, having as their basis a logico-positivist conception of science. See Suppe (1979:17ff.).
5 While much of Kuhn's philosophy of science has in turn been rejected, his criticisms of Correspondence Rules were important in their demise. See Suppe (1979: 4n).
6 That is to say, the demise of Correspondence Rules only refutes one piece of Horton's evidence, not his theoretical stance. Horton could simply update his history of science, and the debate continues.
7 For this position see, among others, Winch (1964) and J.Z. Smith (1982).
8 According to J.Z. Smith, interpretations of ritual that include theories of efficacy are posited by anthropologists who take at face value the fantastic descriptions of ritual articulated by the natives, descriptions which the natives themselves do not believe (1982).
9 See the criticisms by Penner (1989: 69–72).
10 Asad contrasts Geertz's ill-defined use of symbol with C.S. Peirce's system (Asad 1993: 30 n3). Peircean terminology is discussed below.
11 On this point, see the important comments about symbolic anthropology in Parmentier (1994: 47–69, esp. 69).
12 Many historians of science, such as Popper, relegate them to proto-scientific status.
13 Tambiah does not define a "scientific" analogy, which is also a serious problem. Although sometimes inspirational, analogy is no longer a method of scientific *proof.*
14 Austin outlines three types of speech act: locutionary, illocutionary, and perlocutionary. Those acts which are understood to carry out a deed in the very speaking, the perlocutionary acts, are of particular interest to scholars of ritual.
15 As Silverstein explains,

> [Austin] discovered certain lexical items – segmental, referential, presupposing, deductible, maximally transparent forms – called "performatives," that seemed to be a key to the non-referential functions of one's own language. It is not by chance that these performatives, such as promise, christen, dub, etc., were discovered first by the linguistically naive native

speakers of Oxford; they satisfy all our criteria. But unfortunately, accurate though they may be for certain of our more transparent speech functions in English, they cannot merely be treated as a universal set to be ferreted out by inaccurate translation techniques in the most remote corners of the globe. Indeed, they represent only a tiny fraction of the functioning of our [own] language, though a fraction that is easily susceptible of native awareness.

(1981: 19–20)

16 In his review of Tambiah's book, Dell Hymes writes: "His initial accounts (of the Western legacy) are modestly derived from others, and what is said about Christianity and Judaism misses so much of their complexity that one suspects a lesson as to the inadequacy of all such sketches" (1990: 951).

17 In many biblical texts the Israelite deity is only one of many supernatural forces; at best, pure monotheism is a late development in the biblical texts. See, for example, Psalms 82:1, 6–7, which states: "God takes his stand in the assembly of El, among the gods he pronounces judgment. I have said, 'you are gods, sons of the Highest all of you, But you shall die like a man, fall like a prince.'" As B. Levine states: "We have yet to find in the Hebrew Bible an explicit statement of Yahweh's omnipotence, in the sense that there is no other power of any sort except his. There are, of course, statements to the effect that he is the only real deity...but nowhere do we find the notion clearly expressed that Yahweh's rule is entirely free from opposition or conflict" (1974: 79 n65). Creation is better described as making order out of chaos, with parts of the cosmos pre-existing the creative work of the deity. For such creation imagery, see Isaiah 44:24–8, 45:18, 51:9–11; Proverbs 8:22–31; Psalms 74:12–17, 89:1–14, 104; Jeremiah 5:22; Job 26, 38–9; and Isaiah 51. For an important discussion of creation texts, see Levenson (1994). A clear statement of creation *ex nihilo* does not occur until the second century CE; see Winston (1971: 185–202, 1986: 88–91).

18 Also lacking is the idea of substitution, as found in rituals where, for example, a prisoner is offered to a god as a substitute for a king.

19 In the second biblical creation story, we are not given a reason for the creation of Adam; when the story is read in conjunction with Ancient Near Eastern stories, where the gods create people in order for them to till the gods' garden, we see an elided reason (Adam as gardener). Giving a reason leaves one open to the charge that the reason is not very good. The biblical version is more mysterious, and perhaps more mysterious in the long run equals more profound.

20 The Mesopotamian rituals often lack substitution and appeasement (Wright 1987: 72).

21 See Wright (1987), where he states that "the Hittite literature too does not always show a concern to complete the disposal rite by doing something to prevent the return of a living bearer of impurity" (55). Indeed, the only references to directly killing the goat are found in the Mishnah.

22 See note 10 above.

23 The term symbol is thus preserved for a specific kind of sign. Here, Peirce thought that he was returning to a definition of symbol that was closer to its ancient usage based on the Greek root "to throw together."

24 A particularly rich example of an icon is a personal signature. In the American legal system, it is necessary to establish one's signature. This is usually done by signing a signature guarantee, a paper which states that a certain signature is in fact one's signature. Once the icon is established, it is a legally binding representation of that person. Deities are also represented in rituals by means of culturally specific notions of, as it were, signature guarantees.

25 A possible exception is onomatopoeic words, which are thought to be formally linked to that which they represent.

26 When a meaning is easily located it may be because the symbol is in effect "dead." See Parmentier (1994: 47–69).

27 On this point, see Parmentier (1994).

References

Anderson, Gary (1987) *Sacrifices and Offerings in Ancient Israel: Studies in their Social and Political Importance*, Atlanta: Scholars Press.
Asad, Talal (1993) "The construction of religion as an anthropological category," *Genealogies of Religion*, Baltimore: Johns Hopkins University Press, 27–54.
Beattie, J. (1966), "Ritual and social change," *Man*, n.s., 1(1): 60–74.
Grant, Robert (1952) *Miracle and Natural Law in Graeco-Roman and Early Christian Thought*, Amsterdam: North-Holland.
Hollis, Martin and Steven Lukes (eds) (1982) *Rationality and Relativism*, Oxford: Basil Blackwell.
Horton, Robin (1967) "African traditional thought and Western science," *Africa* 38: 50–71, 155–87.
—— (1976) "Professor Winch on safari," *European Journal of Sociology* 17: 157–80.
—— (1982) "Tradition and modernity revisited," in Hollis and Lukes, 201–60.
Horton, Robin and Ruth Finnegan (eds) (1973) *Modes of Thought*, London: Faber & Faber.
Hymes, D. (1990) "Review of S.J. Tambiah's *Magic, Science, Religion and the Scope of Rationality*," *Times Literary Supplement* 4562: 951.
Kaufmann, Y. (1960) *The Religion of Israel*, Chicago: University of Chicago Press.
Kearins, J.M. (1981) "Visual spatial memory in Australian Aboriginal children of desert regions," *Cognitive Psychology* 13: 434–60.
—— (1986) "Visual spatial memory in Aboriginal and white Australian children," *Australian Journal of Psychology* 38(3): 203–14.
Knohl, Israel (1995) *The Sanctuary of Silence: The Priestly Torah and the Holiness School*, Minneapolis: Fortress Press.
Krausz, Michael (ed.) (1989) *Relativism: Interpretation and Confrontation*, Notre Dame: University of Notre Dame Press.
Levenson, Jon (1994) *Creation and the Persistence of Evil*, Princeton: Princeton University Press.
Levine, B. (1974) *In the Presence of the Lord*, Leiden: Brill.
Lucy, John (1992a) *Grammatical Categories and Cognition*, Cambridge: Cambridge University Press.
—— (1992b) *Language Diversity and Thought: A Reformulation of the Linguistic Relativity Hypothesis*, Cambridge: Cambridge University Press.
Milgrom, Jacob (1991) *Leviticus 1–16: A New Translation*, New York: Doubleday.
Parmentier, Richard (1994) *Signs in Society: Studies in Semiotic Anthropology*, Bloomington: Indiana University Press.
Peirce, C. (1940) *The Philosophical Writings of Charles Peirce*, New York: Dover.
Penner, Hans H. (1989) *Impasse and Resolution*, Toronto Studies in Religion 8, New York: Peter Lang.
Rumsey, A. (1990) "Wording, meaning, and linguistic ideology," *American Anthropologist* 92: 346–61.
Sahlins, Marshall (1976) "Colors and cultures," *Semiotica* 16: 1–22.
Silverstein, M. (1981) "Metaforces of power in traditional oratory," unpublished lecture.
Smith, Jonathan Z. (1982) "The bare facts of ritual," *Imagining Religion: From Babylon to Jonestown*, Chicago: University of Chicago Press.
Smith, Morton (1952) "The common theology of the Ancient Near East," *Journal of Biblical Literature* 71: 135–47.
Suppe, Frederick (ed.) (1979) *The Structure of Scientific Theories*, 2nd edn, Urbana: University of Illinois Press.
Tambiah, S.J. (1985) "The form and meaning of magical acts," *Culture, Thought and Social Action: An Anthropological Perspective*, Cambridge, MA: Harvard University Press, 60–86.
—— (1990) *Magic, Science, Religion and the Scope of Rationality*, Cambridge: Cambridge University Press.

Wertsch, James (1991) *Voices of the Mind: A Sociocultural Approach to Mediated Action*, Cambridge, MA: Harvard University Press.

Wilson, Brian R. (ed.) (1970) *Rationality*, Oxford: Basil Blackwell.

Winch, Peter (1964) "Understanding a primitive society," *American Philosophical Quarterly* 1(4): 307–24.

Winston, David (1971) "The Book of Wisdom's theory of cosmogony," *History of Religions* 11(1): 185–202.

—— (1986) "Creation ex nihilo revisited: a reply to Jonathan Goldstein," *Journal of Jewish Studies* 37(1): 88–91.

Wright, David (1987) *The Disposal of Impurity: Elimination Rites in the Bible and in Hittite and Mesopotamian Literature*, Atlanta: Scholars Press.

Chapter 2

Can we move beyond primitivism?

On recovering the indigenes of indigenous religions in the academic study of religion

Armin W. Geertz

This chapter will explore the strange discrepancy between the indisputably central and inclusive role played by indigenous cultures in the development of theory in the social and cultural sciences on the one hand, and, on the other, the systematic exclusion, marginalization, and invisibility of living indigenous peoples in those same sciences. I suggest that a possible route to explaining this discrepancy is through the history of primitivism and evolutionism in European and American thought. It is important at the outset to emphasize that "primitivism" is a concept that has both positive (that is to say, romantic) as well as negative connotations. Even though the notion has often been used in a positive sense, it still draws on illusory ideas about indigenous peoples, and therefore I strongly advocate its demise. The problem, however, is that the phenomenon of primitivism is so firmly rooted in human culture (not just, by the way, in European and American cultures) that I fear any attempt to eradicate it would simply be quixotic. But I think it is our job as scholars to point out the inconsistencies and irrationalities of our cultures, indigenous as well as Western.

The route to be followed in tracing the history of primitivism is difficult because so many strands of thought arise from what can be called the "anonymous ideology" of primitivism. Basically, the route of classical primitivism is from antiquity through Medieval Scholastics, the Renaissance, the Enlightenment, and the Romantic period. Surprisingly, primitivist notions (in the romantic sense) continued even more strongly during the heyday of evolutionism in the nineteenth century. One of the many reasons for this was because the full and true impact of Darwinism did not hit Western science until the 1930s! Thus, the absurd notions about "primitive societies" promoted by evolutionists were in fact expressions of a vulgar evolutionism that were more tied in with Victorian ideology than with anything that Darwin had to say. Another reason for the continuance of primitivist notions during the early nineteenth century, in America at least, was that Americans were deeply involved in constructing the "American myth" of innocence and restoration. These constructive efforts became attached to social Darwinism during the latter half of the nineteenth century. Primitivism in modernist guise thrived undaunted at the turn of the twentieth century mainly as a literary and artistic movement with firm roots in the primitivism of Romanticism. The new primitivism since the 1960s is a revival found in all sorts of academic and popular movements and philosophies that continue virtually unabated. Some of these have played central roles in the development of religious studies in the United States, the most prominent being theologians of various persuasions (including feminist theologians), Eliadeans, the postmodernists, and some orientalism critics.

Primitivism

Primitivism is a philosophical position that has characterized Europeans throughout their history. From antiquity through to the Middle Ages, the Enlightenment, and the Romantic period, to the beginning of the twentieth century and even up until today, primitivism has played various roles in philosophy, history, the sciences, literature, and art history. I will try to sketch out some of these phases with the help of those who have analyzed this phenomenon in an effort to get at the heart of European and American attitudes towards indigenous peoples. Without undue effort, I think it can be established that these attitudes have very little to do with real, live indigenous peoples, even though these attitudes have definitely affected indigenous peoples in a most concrete sense.

During the 1930s, philosophers Arthur Lovejoy and George Boas from Johns Hopkins University, together with Gilbert Chinard and Ronald S. Crane, initiated an ambitious project called "A documentary history of primitivism and related ideas." Out of this project a series was published entitled *Contributions to the History of Primitivism*, which resulted in several volumes as early as the mid-1930s.[1] The series was designed to record the history of primitivism or, essentially, the history "of civilized man's misgivings about his performances, about his prospects – and about himself."[2]

Primitivism was not a novelty of the seventeenth or eighteenth centuries. The primitivism of that period clearly had its counterparts in classical antiquity, whereas the primitivism of the twentieth century had its roots in Romanticism and was also a reaction to nineteenth-century evolutionary theory. Thus, in order to understand the primitivism of today, we will need to look more closely at the nineteenth century.

Lovejoy and Boas's book *Primitivism and Related Ideas in Antiquity* (1935) was slated to be the first of a four-volume series. This first volume documented primitivistic ideas in classical literature. The second was to be a documentation of such ideas in medieval literature, but having realized that it was too ambitious, the authors decided to restrict themselves to the Patristic period. The Second World War, however, stopped the project, but Boas took it up again in a collection of essays entitled *Essays on Primitivism and Related Ideas in the Middle Ages* (1948). Unfortunately, the original documentary project was abandoned.

Primitivism covers two distinct tendencies in historical and philosophical thinking that, according to Lovejoy and Boas, seem to have separate historical origins, namely *chronological primitivism* and *cultural primitivism*. Even though they are both associated with one another, they are answers to different questions (see Figure 2.1). According to Lovejoy and Boas:

> Chronological primitivism is one of the many answers which may be and have been given to the question: What is the temporal distribution of good, or value, in the history of mankind, or, more generally, in the entire history of the world? It is, in short, a kind of philosophy of history, a theory, or a customary assumption, as to the time – past or present or future – at which the most excellent condition of human life, or the best state of the world in general, must be supposed to occur.[3]

Cultural primitivism, on the other hand, is "the discontent of the civilized with civilization." It is, according to Lovejoy and Boas, "the belief of men living in a relatively highly evolved and complex cultural condition that a life far simpler and less sophisticated in some or in all respects is a more desirable life."[4] A cardinal idea among cultural primitivists is that the simpler life has in fact been lived somewhere at some time (and thus has affinities with chronological primitivism). But the main characteristic of cultural primitivism is that the ideal mode of life is thought to be led by contemporary so-called primitive or savage peoples, especially peoples in far-off exotic places. Thus, a basic motivating factor in cultural primitivism is the *attraction of the exotic*.

Chronological primitivism can be classified into two main types of theories: (1) those in which the time process as a whole or the history of the human race is *finite*; and (2) those in which the time process or the history of the human race is *infinite*.

Finitist theories conceive of history as being a succession of events having a beginning at some time in the past. There are two types of finitist theories: (1) the bilateral type that conceives of the historical process as having both a beginning and an end; and (2) the

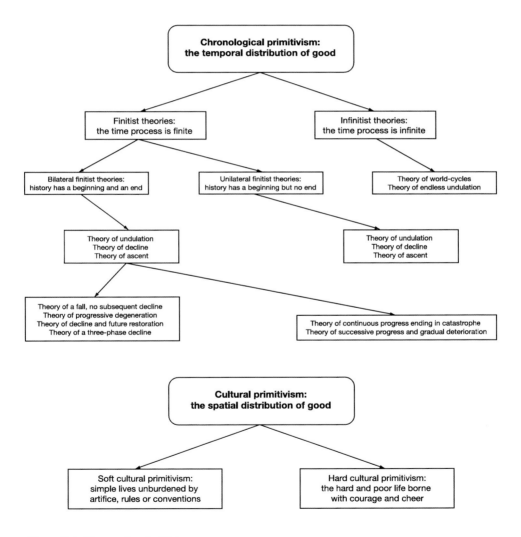

Figure 2.1 Types of primitivism

Source: Lovejoy and Boas (1935: 1–11).

unilateral type that conceives of the historical process as having a beginning, but no end in the future. The first type of theory, bilateral, is the most usual in Christian thought. Of the known bilateral finitist theories, there are three, namely the theory of undulation, the theory of decline, and the theory of ascent.[5]

The *theory of undulation* sees history as a series of periods like waves or undulations or successions of empires that rise, decline, and fall, in which there is no difference in the amount of good that exists in these periods. The *theory of decline* sees the highest degree of excellence in humanity's life at the beginning of history. This theory is the general assumption of chronological primitivism and assumes four varieties depending on the view held as to the course of history: the theory of a fall without subsequent decline; the theory of progressive degeneration; the theory of decline and future restoration; and the three-phase theory of decline. The *theory of ascent*, being antithetic to chronological primitivism, sees excellence not at the beginning but at the end of history. There are two main forms: the theory of continuous progress, wherein there is a gradual increase or diffusion of goodness, happiness, or enlightenment until all is brought to an end through catastrophe; and the theory of successive progress and decline, wherein the beginning was the poorest, but the best having come more or less progressively into history is succeeded by gradual deterioration. Lovejoy and Boas note that "a good deal that has been called primitivism, both in ancient and modern thought, has…in fact…[been a] variety of the theory of progress and decline."[6]

The unilateral finitist theories are characterized by the same types as those of the bilateral theories, except that the former omit the assumption of a future.

Infinitist theories, the second major type of chronological primitivism, are found to include two types: the theory of world-cycles, and the theory of endless undulation. The *theory of world-cycles* conceives of an "endless reiteration of essentially the same states of the world as a whole, in precisely the same order."[7] The *theory of endless undulation* is the "supposition that the assumed infinite succession of events is neither repetitious in any fixed order, nor yet characterized by any definite tendency towards either the augmentation or decrease of value."[8] Lovejoy and Boas point out that the idea of progress has affinities with chronological primitivism, but chronological primitivism is antithetical to the belief in a general *law* of progress during which value accumulates. Chronological primitivism looks to the past, and if the future plays a role, it is only as an anticipated recovery of what has been lost. But it should be noted that the authors point out that often it is difficult to distinguish various forms of primitivism with precision.

Cultural primitivism can be divided into two types, namely soft and hard cultural primitivism. *Soft cultural primitivism* is the idea that primitive people have simpler lives, unburdened by apparatus, rules, regulations, and conventionalities. The primitive individual is relatively exempt from pressure from the social group and more able to allow impulses, emotions, and self-expression their full outlet. Furthermore, the primitive male is conceived by cultural primitivists as being a person of infinite leisure:

> Thus cultural primitivism, whether as a mere escape for the imagination or as a practical ideal, has often owed its appeal to men's recalcitrance to some or most of the inhibitions imposed by current moral codes, or to the alluring dream, or the hope, of a life with little or no toil or strain of body or mind.[9]

Hard cultural primitivism, on the other hand, is often the instrument of preachers of the ethics of renunciation, austerity, self-discipline, and poverty. It is the idea that the life of primitive man is harder, materially poorer, and contains fewer enjoyments, but that the savage is content with little, inured to hardship, and bears the conditions of life with courage and cheer.[10] These two contrasting types of cultural primitivism have been evident throughout primitivism's history.

Nature and the natural

One of the most persistent notions in the history of European ideas and especially in the history of primitivism is the use of the term "nature" as a norm for what is good. Lovejoy and Boas point out that this understanding of nature is as equivocal as it is widespread, and that knowledge of its range of meanings "is an indispensable prerequisite for any discriminating reading of a large part of classical, medieval and modern literature and philosophy."[11] An important point is that not all the normative uses of the term "nature" support primitivist thought. Some have in fact had the opposite tendency. Lovejoy and Boas argue that there are nine major senses of the term that are important to the history of primitivism (see also Box 2.1):

a   nature as intrinsic or objective character[12]
b   as moral, judicial or customary validity[13]
c   as universal validity[14]
d   as the general cosmic order[15]
e   as the healthy state of living beings[16]
f   as the original state of living beings[17]
g   as that which exists apart from man and human contrivance[18]
h   as the intuitive or spontaneous in humans[19]
i   as the natural state of social life.[20]

Thus there are at least seven varieties of *states of nature*:

1   the temporal state of nature (original condition), which when considered to be the ideal state is essential to chronological primitivism, whereas the following are essential to cultural primitivism, cf. (b) and (d) above
2   the technological state of nature (free from artifact), cf. (g)
3   the economic state of nature (communism)
4   the marital state of nature (polygamy)
5   the dietetic state of nature (vegetarianism)
6   the juristic state of nature (anarchism), cf. (i)
7   the ethical state of nature (humanity in unity with itself), cf. (b) and (h).[21]

A more extreme form of cultural primitivism that has clear affinities with contemporary ecology movements can be called *theriophily*, or *animalitarianism*.[22] This idea assumes that the life of animals in general is superior to that of mankind. They are more normal, natural, or more fortunate than humans. In fact the interesting thing about theriophily is not its conception of animals but its conception of humans. This persuasion considers humans to be by nature "unnatural" animals! This persuasion nurtured a fundamental self-disparagement, and it became manifested in the analyses of human behavior by thinkers such as Hobbes, La Rochefoucauld, La Bruyère, Mandeville, and Swift during the

Box 2.1
The meanings of "nature" in the history of primitivism

a   That which anything is "by nature" as its intrinsic or objective character, in contrast with subjective appearances or with human beliefs about it – an antithesis applied first to the objects of the external world.

b   "Nature" in contrast with "law," "custom" or "convention," as the objectively valid in the realm of morals, existing positive law or custom being assumed to deviate from this objective standard partially or completely.

c   That which is true or valid "by nature" as what is universally known to or accepted by mankind, in contrast with beliefs or standards peculiar to particular nations, periods or individuals – an interpretation of the criterion of objective validity implied by (b).

d   "Nature" as the general cosmic order, optimistically conceived as good, or as divinely ordained, in contrast with supposed deviations from this order arising from human error or depravity – "Nature" in this sense tending from an early period to be more or less vaguely personified.

e   The "natural" state of a living being as its healthy condition, in contrast with conditions of disease or impairment of functions – a sense already common in the Hippocratic writings.

f   The "natural" state of any being as its congenital or original condition; hence, in the case of mankind, or of a given people, its primeval state, in contrast with subsequent historic alterations or accretions.

g   "Nature" as that which exists apart from man and without human effort or contrivance, in contrast with "art," i.e., with all that is artificial or man-made.

h   "Nature" as that *in* man which is not due to taking thought or to deliberate choice: hence, those modes of human desire, emotion, or behavior which are instinctive or spontaneous, in contrast with those which are due to the laboring intellect, to premeditation, to self-consciousness, or to instruction.

i   The "natural" state of human social life as that in which the only government is that of the family or the patriarchal clan, in contrast with that in which there exist formal and "artificial" political institutions and laws.

States of nature

1   *The temporal state of nature* – cf. (b) and (d) above: the original condition of things, and especially the state of man as nature first made him, whatever this condition may be supposed to have been. When this alone is conceived as the ideal state, chronological primitivism may be found apart from explicit cultural primitivism. The remaining six senses designate modes or aspects of the ideal of the latter.

2   *The technological state of nature* – cf. (g): the condition of human life in which it is most free from the intrusion of "art," i.e., in which none, or at most only the simplest and most rudimentary, of the practical arts are known. With this is often and naturally

associated a more or less extreme sort of practical anti-intellectualism – the view that intellectual pursuits are in themselves a sort of abnormality and that the progress of knowledge has not made man happier or better, but rather the reverse.

3 *The economic state of nature*: human society without private property, and in particular, without property in land – in other words, economic communism. With this, in consequence partly, perhaps, of Plato's influence, was closely associated, especially in the minds of ancient primitivistic writers, another sort of communism, viz.:

4 *The marital state of nature*: community of wives and children; in its extreme form, sexual promiscuity, including incest.

5 *The dietetic state of nature*: vegetarianism, an early and rather frequent feature of ancient chronological primitivism, not usually on hygienic grounds but as an expression of the feeling that bloodshed in all its forms is sinful, that man in an ideal state should, or at all events once did, live at peace with the animals as well as with his own kind. It was therefore commonly associated with the denunciation of animal sacrifices. With the cultural primitivism which eulogized savage peoples it could, naturally, not easily be combined.

6 *The juristic state of nature* – cf. (i): society without organized political government, or without any except the "natural" government of the family or clan – in other words, anarchism, in the proper sense of the term.

7 *The ethical state of nature* – cf. (b) and (h): the control of human life by so-called "natural" – which does not, in this connection, always imply egoistic or purely sensuous – impulses, without deliberate and selfconscious moral effort, the constraint of rules, or the sense of sin: man in unity with himself, with no "civil war in the cave."

(Lovejoy and Boas 1935: 12–15)

late seventeenth and eighteenth centuries. Theriophily is closely allied to anti-intellectualism, and it is interesting to note that Descartes' famous tenet, that animals lack reason and souls and act mechanically, was formulated in an attack on Montaigne's disciple, the prominent theriophilist of the seventeenth century, Charron.[23]

When studying primitivist thought, it is important to determine what concept of nature the writer has in mind. Lovejoy and Boas claim that the most frequent types in antiquity are the technological and the economic states of nature, where private ownership, mining, metallurgy, and even fire-making were considered to be as much to the detriment as to the benefit of humankind. Thus the disparagement over the present was made more effective with primitivists' ideas about the past or about exotic peoples. Primitivism has in fact been an essential tool of most reformers up until recent times:

Equalitarians, communists, philosophical anarchists, pacifists, insurgents against existing moral codes, including those of sexual relations, vegetarians, to whom may be added deists, the propagandists of "natural religion," who also had their ancient counterparts – all these have sought and, as they believed, found a sanction for their preachments and their programs in the supposed example of primeval man or of living savages.[24]

For these reformers, both in antiquity and the Enlightenment, the assumption of "the essential simplicity of the social problem," or the return to "Nature's simple plan," has been their fundamental premise. But this premise bears with it a contradiction, since the primitivist notion of the "nature" of humankind is misanthropic. Consequently, chronological primitivists have spent a great deal of energy developing theories and explanations of why humankind fell from its elevated "natural" state. Christian thought plays a prominent role among these.

American primitivism

Before moving on to evolutionary theories, which appeared during the nineteenth century as an interim in the otherwise highly related – if not continuous – conceptions of primitivism, it is important to describe the nineteenth-century American myth, called the "American Adam" by R.W.B. Lewis[25] and the "illusion of innocence" by Richard T. Hughes and C. Leonard Allen.[26] The construction of this myth demonstrated that the United States during the late eighteenth and early nineteenth centuries was a nation driven by primitivism, and this drive helps to explain the prevalence of primitivism in the contemporary United States.

According to R.W.B. Lewis, almost every intellectual spokesman, whether novelist, poet, essayist, critic, historian, or preacher, seems to have been actively involved in constructing a new society:

> the American myth saw life and history as just beginning. It described the world as starting up again under fresh initiative, in a divinely granted second chance for the human race, after the first chance had been so disastrously fumbled in the darkening Old World. It introduced a new kind of hero, the heroic embodiment of a new set of ideal human attributes…The new habits to be engendered on the new American scene were suggested by the image of a radically new personality, the hero of the new adventure: an individual emancipated from history, happily bereft of ancestry, untouched and undefiled by the usual inheritances of family and race; an individual standing alone, self-reliant and self-propelling, ready to confront whatever awaited him with the aid of his own unique and inherent resources. It was not surprising, in a Bible-reading generation, that the new hero…was most easily identified with Adam before the Fall. Adam was the first, the archetypal, man. His moral position was prior to experience, and in his very newness he was fundamentally innocent. The world and history lay all before him. And he was the type of creator, the poet par excellence, creating language itself by naming the elements of the scene about him.[27]

Lewis advises that there is no monothetic "American experience" – he argues well for at least three strands, that is to say, the party of hope, the party of memory, and the party of irony[28] – but it is important to note that the agreements, disagreements, and arguments centered around the theme of the new Adam.

What are the illusions involved? Those of freedom from the past, of restoring it, and of innocence. The illusion of freedom from the past is peculiar to Americans. Lewis notes that since Emerson, America has persistently been a "one-generation culture," with the unfortunate effect being not incoherence "but the sheer dullness of unconscious repetition":

We regularly return, decade after decade and with the same pain and amazement, to all the old conflicts, programs, and discoveries. We consume our powers in hoisting ourselves back to the plane of understanding reached a century ago and at intervals since.[29]

The illusion of restoration, of returning to the primal perfection, is not peculiar to American culture, but the American version of that common human idea saw the conceived *contemporary perfection* as a return to primal perfection and thus was an attitude of considerable potency in American thought.[30] Richard T. Hughes and C. Leonard Allen focus their study on this particular aspect of American primitivism, which they term the myth of restoration, of restoring the first times. The myth, according to Hughes and Allen, was "a beacon summoning Americans to perfection." This illusion led naturally to the third illusion, that of innocence:

> The illusion thereby fostered in the minds of these Americans is that they are an inno-cent and fundamentally natural people who, in effect, have stepped outside of history, thereby escaping the powerful influences of history, culture, and tradition. These Americans therefore have often confused the historic particularities of their limited experience with universal norms that should be embraced, they have thought, by all people in all cultures and all times…From time to time, therefore, throughout American history, both in the specific religious traditions and in the nation at large, a persistent and tenacious paradox has emerged: the spectacle of a people, convinced of its own pure beginnings, compelling others to be free.[31]

The realization of the illusory nature of this idea of innocence, when confronted by histor-ical realities, led Americans to what Lewis calls "the chilling skepticism" of the mid-twentieth century and, in the aftermath, paradoxically produced a willful return to innocence.[32] That topic will be taken up in the section on the new primitivism.

Between the American Revolution and the Civil War, the United States abounded in millennialisms of various kinds based on the fundamental attempt to recover the primor-dial past that had been lost in degenerate history.[33] On the sliding scale from right-wing denominations to left-wing sects, everyone was seeking, in the words of Sidney Mead, to embrace "the idea of building anew in the American wilderness on the true and ancient foundations."[34] American institutions such as democracy and free enterprise were and still are considered to be natural and to reflect the way the Creator intended things to be.[35] The urge to restorationism, on American soil at least, is correctly identified by Hughes and Allen as equivalent to primitivism, the urge in other words to restore what seems to be primitive or prior to history.[36]

A great deal of the price for this grand myth of restorationism was paid not only in terms of the history of ideas, but also and more emphatically in terms of war and bondage for indigenous peoples, specifically Native Americans and Afro-Americans. Hughes and Allen formulate it clearly:

> While virtually identifying the new American nation with the primordium, primitivists in this nation consigned both Mexicans and Indians to the finite sphere of human history and proceeded to extinguish not only their liberties but, in many instances, their lives…Even more ironic was the fact that primordial theology, employed by the founders to secure liberty, could be particularized so that those not sharing in the

"primal particularities" were simply excluded from the blessings of freedom...So well rooted was the restoration perspective in the American experience that with the advent of the Civil War, even southern clerics...employed primitivism to deny freedom to blacks and to defend both slavery and the Confederacy.[37]

On the basis of the conceived "mandate of creation" (Genesis 1: 28 – to subdue the earth), Native Americans were removed from their ancestral lands because of their "imperfect possession" of the earth.[38] After the Civil War, flourishing industrial capitalism was further explained in terms of social Darwinism, thus enforcing the American conviction that its civilization had been decreed by "Nature and Nature's God."[39]

Evolutionism

In connection with the evolutionism of the nineteenth century, we come face to face with primitivism in the highly negative sense. It was evolutionary theory, especially social Darwinism, that served as the ideological *raison d'être* of free enterprise capitalism, colonial policy, and scientific racism.

Evolutionism should in principle have been a departure from the many primitivist theories of history. In Eiseley's words, the primitivism of the eighteenth century was in the nineteenth century especially challenged by the emerging sense of time brought on by astronomical and paleontological studies:

> It was time of enormous dimensions...The historic ever-changing, irreversible, on-flowing continuum of events was being linked to galaxies and suns and worlds...Man was adjusting himself, not just to time in unlimited quantities, but rather *to complete historicity, to the emergence of the endlessly new*...Instead of the "natural government" of the eighteenth century, the old principle of plenitude, of God's infinite creativeness, now led directly to a war of nature in which, through time, living creatures are jostled in or out of existence, expand or contract at one another's expense. The infinite creativeness remained as given, but the carefully balanced equilibrium was the illusion of an unhistorical outlook.[40]

Besides the expansion of the timescale, other challenges were brought to bear on the traditional worldview, such as the concept of a changing universe, the elimination of design (teleology and creationism), the elimination of miracles (in evolutionary history), and the inclusion of humanity within nature (as an animal subordinate to evolutionary principles).[41] Even though the major scientific discovery was, in the opinion of Loren Eiseley, Darwin's theory, there was a host of inventions and discoveries that evidently rocked the European world: Baron Cuvier's announcement in 1801 that he had discovered in his paleontological work twenty-three species of animals no longer in existence; the establishment of historical geology at the end of the eighteenth century by James Hutton; the discovery of stratigraphy around the turn of the nineteenth century by William Smith; Gustav Kirchhoff's discovery of the relationship between heated metals and spectrum analysis in 1859; and Mendel's genetic theory published in 1865 but not understood until much later.

Peter J. Bowler has systematically and persuasively refuted the idea that there ever was a Darwinian revolution during the nineteenth century.[42] His analyses show that the leading evolutionists of the nineteenth century were stubborn upholders of progressionist theory and clearly refused to accept among other things Darwin's principle of natural selection. According to Bowler, the Darwinian revolution did not occur until the 1930s when the theory of natural selection was coupled with genetic theory. In the aftermath of that revolution, the so-called "Darwin industry" arose in commemoration of the centenary of the *Origin of Species* in 1959, involving an intense publishing activity of books and articles by and/or about Charles Darwin. A kind of revival arose for the centenary of Darwin's death in 1982. As Bowler notes, the assumption that Darwinism became the dominant force in late nineteenth-century evolutionism arose in part "because it satisfied the values of biologists who were certain that natural selection is the most fruitful explanation of evolution."[43] In other words, there has occurred quite a bit of mythmaking that sees pre-Darwinian evolutionary theories as attempts to grope their way towards Darwinism. This mythmaking literature thus casts a slur on the complexities of nineteenth-century evolutionism.[44]

There were in fact two strong rivals (among many) to Darwinian theory. One was Lamarckism and the other was Chambers' developmentalism. Finally, a proclaimed follower of Darwin, Ernst Haeckel, reconstructed the history of life based on a progressionist vision of evolution. Thus Charles Darwin was not able to check the tide of progressionist theory, and in fact he was used in its service, not all that unwittingly, I might add. Even though he criticized progressionism privately, his *Origin of Species* was interpreted as supporting it. The final sentences in his book could hardly be understood other than metaphysically:

> Thus, from the war of nature, from famine and death, the most exalted object which we are capable of conceiving, namely, the production of the higher animals, directly follows. There is grandeur in this view of life, with its several powers, having been originally breathed into a few forms or into one; and that, whilst this planet has gone cycling on according to the fixed law of gravity, from so simple a beginning endless forms most beautiful and most wonderful have been, and are being, evolved.[45]

Progressionism is a metaphysical doctrine of universal progress that constitutes, in the words of Arthur O. Lovejoy, the temporalizing of the great Chain of Being.[46] The great Chain of Being was derived from Platonic and Neo-Platonic philosophy, but continued until the nineteenth century as one of the most persistent and widely held presuppositions concerning the constitutive pattern of the universe in Western thought:

> the conception of the universe as a "Great Chain of Being," composed of an immense, or...of an infinite, number of links ranging in hierarchical order from the meagerest kind of existents, which barely escape non-existence, through "every possible" grade up to the *ens perfectissimum* – or, in a somewhat more orthodox version, to the highest possible kind of creature, between which and the Absolute Being the disparity was assumed to be infinite – every one of them differing from that immediately above and that immediately below it by the "least possible" degree of difference.[47]

Lovejoy claims that the history of the idea of the Chain of Being is "the history of a failure" because it perceives the world as static and constant, and existence as the expression of a system of eternal truths "inherent in the very logic of being."[48] But this need not concern us here. What is more important for us is that attempts were made during the eighteenth century by Charles Bonnet[49] and Jean-Baptiste Robinet[50] among others to temporalize this rigid and static scheme of things by introducing the idea that the Chain can be conceived of as "the program of nature" being carried out gradually and exceedingly slowly in cosmic history. As Lovejoy writes: "The Demiurgus is not in a hurry; and his goodness is sufficiently exhibited if, soon or late, every Idea finds its manifestation in the sensible order."[51] Thus the static Chain of Being became a unilinear process of ascent to greater perfection.

There were many different attempts to work out the details of this process, but the important names at the beginning of the nineteenth century were Erasmus Darwin[52] and Jean-Baptiste Pierre Antoine de Monet Lamarck.[53] They succeeded in combining evolutionary theory with deism. Their main idea is that development is not random but, rather, consists of phases of progressive advance from lower to higher types following the divine plan laid out once and for all by God at the beginning of time.

Peter J. Bowler has argued that social Darwinism had nothing to do with Darwin's evolutionary theory, but was in fact progressionist ideology that played an important social, political, and cultural role in the Victorian period. The nineteenth century was the century of enormous and rapid social change in both Europe and the United States. The British Industrial Revolution was in full swing, the Indian Empire was being established, great discoveries were being made in every field of the arts and sciences, and especially positivism and the new historiography were breaking onto the scene. The Victorians were fascinated with the past, and the reason for this, according to Bowler, was that it was "the product of an age obsessed with change, desperately hoping that history itself might supply the reassurance that could no longer be derived from ancient beliefs."[54] The Victorians were looking for reassurance in the belief that social evolution was moving in a purposeful direction. Therefore, their interest in history was not simply to develop the new historiography or to collect interesting and arcane facts on human cultures, religions, and history, but rather to invent the past:

> The idea of progress was imposed upon history to create the sense of order that the Victorians craved. In a very real sense they *invented* the past, since all the factual discoveries of antiquaries and archaeologists had to be interpreted within a conceptual scheme that satisfied the cultural demands of the age.

> The idea of progress was of central importance because it offered a compromise between the old creationism and the more extreme manifestations of the new materialism…The concept of evolution supplied an answer to this question by suggesting that all phases of the universe's development, from the creation of life through to the expansion of European civilization around the globe, were aspects of a general progressive scheme designed to create order out of chaos.[55]

Even such a seemingly physical science as the newly professionalized geology was in the Victorian period primarily a *historical* science, in which geologists devoted a great deal of energy to making their discoveries "fit in" with the general scheme of things. Everyone was involved in this grand project of inventing humanity's past, even the founding fathers of the disciplines of the study of religion: Max Müller's comparative science of religion and comparative linguistics;[56] Herbert Spencer's sociology and psychology;[57] Lewis

Henry Morgan's sociology;[58] John Lubbock's psychology;[59] and Edward B. Tylor's anthropology.[60] Even Darwin himself was caught in the struggle between progressionism and his own theory. This is especially evident in his book *The Descent of Man and Selection in Relation to Sex* (1871), when he explicitly draws on Spencer, Lubbock, Tylor, Morgan, and Max Müller in his chapters on intellectual, moral, and cultural evolution.[61]

Tragically, one of the effects of a progressionism that identifies itself as the high point of development is that those individuals or societies that do not meet the standards are ruthlessly pushed aside:

> A ruthless attitude towards failure was characteristic not so much of Darwin's theory of branching evolution, but of the Victorians' wider faith in their own superiority. "Lower" races were stagnant failures, relics of earlier episodes in the history of mankind's ascent, with nothing further to contribute towards the march of progress. Darwin became a convenient symbol of this more ruthless attitude to failure, but his theory was in some respects only an aberrant product of the progressionism that was the true source of "social Darwinism."[62]

Adam Kuper, in his stimulating book *The Invention of Primitive Society*, notes that Victorian conceptions of "primitive society" were highly fictional. Even though some evolutionists were reacting against primitivists, the images they painted of the evolution of social types were just as stereotypical and, unfortunately, even more persistent:

> The persistence of the model is peculiarly problematic since various of its basic assumptions were quite directly contradicted by ethnographic evidence and by the logic of evolutionary theory itself. The difficulties were clearly stated by some of the leading scholars in the field (notably Westermarck, Boas and Malinowski). Notwithstanding, social anthropologists busied themselves for over a hundred years with the manipulation of a fantasy – a fantasy which had been constructed by speculative lawyers in the late nineteenth century. This is a fact which must provoke thought, and not among anthropologists alone.[63]

Many monographs dealing with "primitive society" were produced by lawyers. The main figures were the British specialist in Roman law Henry Maine,[64] the Swiss professor in Roman law Johannes Bachofen,[65] the French scholar N.-D. Fustel de Coulanges,[66] the Scottish lawyer J.M. McLennan,[67] and the American lawyer Lewis Henry Morgan. The anthropologists Edward B. Tylor and James George Frazer specialized in the origin of religion and left the origin of human society to the lawyers. But, as noted above, the kinds of evolutionary theory preferred by the new anthropologists were Lamarckian's progressive-development theory and the conservative religious theory of progressionism. Or else the new evolutionists were maintaining ideological agendas. Henry Maine, for example, wrote his book *Ancient Law* in order to refute the theory of government and law associated with Rousseau, and in particular that of Bentham and the Utilitarians, as it was being applied in Indian affairs.[68]

So we see once again that it was not living indigenous peoples that were at the core of evolutionary theory. On the contrary, until the emergence of fieldwork ethnography, evolutionary theories about so-called primitive society were the handmaidens of colonial, domestic, and ideological concerns. Some may have been fighting good causes, like Henry Maine, but the locus of interest was not indigenous peoples as such.

It is important for us to realize that the study of religion and its origins grew out of this period of exhilaration, ideology, and colonialism. The Romantic period stumbled on new textual material that expanded Western knowledge of non-Western cultures and civilizations beyond all expectations (see Box 2.2). The wave of new information, new sources on foreign religions, and new historical epochs added fuel to the fire of Romanticism and to the whole of the century. It also led to the establishment of the first chairs in the history of religions in Europe, and it gave rise to the paradigm of the century, the grand primitivist notion of Nature Mythologies. The longings of the Romantic for another time or another place, a distant paradise, or a future utopia were primary concerns. Primitivist notions in the study of religion thus flourished, as did the other human and social sciences, side by side with evolutionary ones and survived right up to the beginning of the twentieth century. That they have never left us is a complicated story of continuity and transformation.

Box 2.2
Great cultural discoveries of the nineteenth century

1780–1800	the translation of Bhagavadgita, Shakuntala, the Laws of Manu (1785–94); Bonaparte visits Egypt, during which Bouchard discovers the Rosetta Stone (1798–99)
1800–1820	the translation of the Upanisads (1802); *Description de l'Egypte*, 20 vols (1809–22); archaeological expeditions to Assyrian and Babylonian sites (1811); Bopp's comparative grammar: Sanskrit, Greek, Latin, Persian, and Germanic (1816); Valley of the Kings is discovered (1817); Champollion deciphers the hieroglyphs (1822)
1820–1840	*Corpus Inscriptionum Græcorum* (1828–77); Grimm's *Deutsche Mythologie* (1832)
1840–1860	Stone Age evidence found at Somme (1841); the Vedas are translated in the *Sacred Books of the East* by F. Max Müller (1849–74); translation of the Avesta (1850); the cuneiform is deciphered (the Epic of Gilgamesh), and Layard's work on the libraries of Assurnasipal, Sennacherib, and the temple of Nebo (1851–57)
1860–1880	Lenormant excavates Eleusis (1860); the Caves of Dordogne are found to harbor remains older than the Stone Age (1863); *Corpus Inscriptionum Latinarum* (1863–85); Schliemann's work at Troy, Mycene, Orchomenos, and Tiryns (1870–80); *Corpus Inscriptionum Atticarum* (1873–82); the cave paintings in Altamira (1880)
1880–1900	Tell el-Armarna tablets with correspondence between the Egyptians, Palestinians, and Syrians written in the Babylonian language (1887); Winckler discovers the archives of Boghazkoy, and Hittite is identified as being an Indo-European language (1896); de Morgan finds Susa, the capital of Elam, with tablets dating around 4000 BCE containing among other things the Laws of Hammurabi (1897); Evans finds the labyrinth of Minos in Knosis on Crete (1900)

Conceptions of primitive man

Unfortunately, the evolutionists left behind a formidable jungle of terminology and notions about indigenous peoples that have plagued cultural research up to the present. As opposed to the study of literary cultures, the study of oral cultures was the study of the *antitheses* of Western culture. Much of the theoretical literature on social types is clothed in evolutionary dichotomies: primitive vs. civilized; oral vs. literate; pre-industrial vs. industrial; *Gemeinschaft* vs. *Gesellschaft*; community vs. association; folk vs. urban; rural vs. urban; mechanical solidarity vs. organic solidarity; sacred vs. secular; status society vs. contract society; traditional-value rationality vs. purposive rationality; and so on.

The idea is widespread that even though Western scientists cannot find a satisfactory coverall term for indigenous cultures, most people – scholars as well as the general public – assume that everybody knows what they are talking about anyway. During the 1950s and 1960s, anthropologists Edward Dozier,[69] Lois Mednick,[70] Catherine H. Berndt,[71] Francis Hsu,[72] and others challenged this assumption through a simple analysis of the actual uses of the term "primitive." They argued that its use in a wide variety of publications was ambiguous, inconsistent, and demeaning. From a terminological perspective, it was argued that it names a category of cultures that do not in fact exist, that do not have characteristics that are not shared by all other cultures and peoples, and that therefore is of very little intellectual or analytical advantage.[73] Thus the use of the term can be justified neither empirically nor theoretically.

Hsu has shown that, empirically, the various dichotomies can be reversed or problematized. There are small societies in Europe that are highly urbanized, whereas there are rural societies on an enormous scale in China. The kinship systems of many industrialized Western societies are extremely simple in comparison with the highly complex kinship system of the technologically simple Australian Aborigines. The present or former absence of a written language does not indicate very much in terms of social complexity: there are cultures with highly organized political structures such as the Yoruba and the Dahomey, and societies that have no centralized government such as the Inuit or the Kaska Indians. "Even the criteria of abstract thinking versus concrete thinking," notes Hsu, "are not fool-proof for differentiating the primitive from the civilized. Is the Arunta or Murngin type of social organization less abstract than the Arab or Chinese traders' profit calculations?"[74]

Hsu raises the important question of what exactly is meant by the term "primitive":

> The most troublesome meaning of the term "primitive" is that connected with various shades of inferiority. Sometimes we can unquestionably determine that some single items or usages of a culture are more inferior or less inferior than others in the same culture or in other cultures. In this sense, we can describe hand-pushed carts as more primitive than horsecarts and horsecarts as more primitive than automobiles…But the primitiveness of other single items is by no means so easy to settle. For example, is the custom of sending children to boarding school or to summer camp more or less primitive than that of continuous parental supervision of the children at home? Is a totalitarian system of government more or less primitive than tribal rule or benevolent despotism? Is a religious system based upon monotheism with a history of heresy persecution, witch hunting, and holy crusades more or less primitive than another with a *laissez-faire* attitude toward different creeds and ritual practices? Is the custom of taking care of aged parents at home more primitive than that of leaving them to themselves or in institutions?[75]

A further problem is that despite the empirical evidence, attempts are continually being made to divide humanity into two fundamentally different types: the primitive and the modern. Statistical tests have proven this to be very problematical. The test developed by Rose and Willoughby during the 1950s, based on the Human Relations Area Files, was hampered by the fact that twenty of the cultures had already been scaled for developmental ratings on more or less arbitrary uses of the terms primitive and modern. But the main problem was that of the seventy-two possible categories, only sixteen responded satisfactorily to the scale. Two categories that would be considered central in determining development, namely social stratification and communication, were found to be non-scalable. The data was also very much dependent on the sources of information, which, if varied in a particular region, like Indonesia for example, could easily lead to different results. Furthermore, elements of simplicity in modern cultures could not satisfactorily be measured.[76]

Most researchers, at least in the recent past, have held implicit developmental schemes in mind when using the term "primitive," even though it has been shown that, for example, biological evolution is neither ortholinear nor unilinear. As Ashley Montagu noted in 1962, developmental schemes rely on premises that are not necessarily true, analogous, or related. Four of these are: that what developed later in time is more advanced than earlier developments; that the more advanced evolved from the less advanced; that the more advanced is "better"; and that contemporary primitives are closer to prehistoric than to modern humanity.[77]

The term "primitive" is anathema in anthropology today, but it is still being used in non-Western countries such as India, China, and Japan. And its euphemisms can be found, for example, in African scholarship. It has been argued that all cultures have concepts of the primitive as a necessary ingredient in formulating their own identity.[78] And so it is with the West. The problem is that Western terminology, having become the lingua franca of scientific discourse, is faced with ethical problems when non-Western scholars enter the scientific arena.

Modern primitivism

As Lovejoy and Boas point out, the nineteenth-century myth of progress began to crumble at the turn of the twentieth century. Europeans and Americans were having increased misgivings about the values of their civilization, and public thought was being plagued by doubts and apprehensions, which reached an epitome with the First World War.[79]

Modern primitivism was a reaction to this growing sense of malaise. Its reformulation as cultural critique was basically the work of a handful of artists and poets in Europe. Those responsible for the cult of primitivism were primarily Guillaume Apollinaire, and his friends Pablo Picasso, Francis Picabia, and Marcel Duchamp. Proclaiming "the Negro Enlightenment" and "the New Spirit" during the second decade of the twentieth century, Apollinaire and his generation had discovered truth in the domain of ethnology.[80] The discovery of "Negro and naïve art" was the return to first principles and to fundamentals. It freed early twentieth-century artists from the Western aesthetic and provided a formal vocabulary and new approach to reality. As Samaltanos notes: "The cult of the childlike and the naïve freed art from its 'seriousness.' It encouraged the exploration of the ridiculous, the irrational, the improbable, and the absurd."[81]

More importantly for Apollinaire, art now became a religion and the artist became a healer of the spirit. The cathartic and therapeutic functions of art in ancient and primitive times were now being reinstated by modern man's return to innocence. Returning to the primitive state, the artist became reborn and wise. Paul Klee said in 1902: "I want to be as though new-born, knowing absolutely nothing about Europe, ignoring poets and fashions, to be almost primitive."[82] Modern man, according to Apollinaire, had now become "a superior savage."[83]

These artists were basically amateur ethnologists. They knew little or nothing about indigenous or tribal cultures, and did not much care. Primitivism thus had the same function in art history as it did in the general history of the idea, namely a term denoting the Western conception of the Other – sometimes pejorative, sometimes positive. Until the beginning of the twentieth century, the term "primitive" in art history simply meant anything that departed from the "Greco-Roman line of Western realism that had been reaffirmed and systematized in the Renaissance."[84] What was meant was any artistic style that was simplistic and "sincere," from the Romanesque and Byzantine to the Peruvian and Javanese cultures. Gauguin, for example, called Egyptian, Aztecan, Japanese, Persian, Indian, Javanese, and later Polynesian art styles "primitive."[85] During the first decades of the twentieth century, with the artistic "discovery" of African and Oceanic masks and sculptures, the term "primitive art" increasingly became restricted to tribal objects. Interestingly enough the transformation of "primitive art" from the archaic to the tribal was based on the Cubists' explorations of the abstract forms of tribal art in an aesthetic sense. Thus, even though living indigenous cultures were not the primary concern here, their cultural objects made an important impact on Western art and brought about important changes in Western attitudes to aesthetics and values.

By the end of the Second World War, this phase of art history and of Western primitivism had ended.

The new primitivism: the counter-culture

Gaile McGregor has characterized the mid-century birth of what she calls "neo-primitivism":

> During the 50s, writers like Herbert Marcuse touted technology as the great liberator. During the 60s, as science, "taken over" by the military-industrial establishment, became inextricably implicated in "the ideology of domination and manipulation" (Robinson), this technophilia turned into technophobia. Technophobia in turn stimulated neo-primitivism. Neo-primitivism stimulated a cult of "naturalness" which became expressed as a kind of aggressive political and psycho-sexual experimentation. Less appealing in practice than in theory, this, finally, triggered a reactive neo-puritanism.[86]

There are several strands of thought and activity that I would like to take up as expressions of the new primitivism of the early 1960s. The most obvious is the hippie movement, or the cult of naturalness as McGregor calls it. The second strand consists of the philosophical expressions of the new primitivism as exemplified at the University of Chicago. And the third concerns the artistic and theatrical forms. Generally it could be said that the various movements of the 1960s were attempts to come to terms with the realization of the illusory nature of the American myth and its manifest destiny, attempts that William McLoughlin has grouped under "the Fourth Great Awakening," which, like most awakenings, is concerned with reorientation, meaning, and self-understanding in a therapeutic or cathartic revitalization.[87]

The hippie movement has been compared to the Dadaist and Surrealist movements, which were critical responses to industrialism and the First World War with a re-emphasis on experience and vision. What clearly became the hallmark of the hippie movement was its combination of experience and vision with an anti-rationality and anti-intellectualism.[88] As Nathan Adler argues, the "unresponsive, dehumanized rationality of technological and bureaucratic systems that take people into account only as expendable resources and the stuff of kill ratios" left many people with the feeling of impotency and a world bereft of meaning.[89] Thus the urge to return to the purity of the past, the return to nature and the natural, and the enthusiasm for organic foods and macrobiotics are attempts to extract spiritual purity from material impurity:

> In youth groups and communes, people seek the "real self," in a return to purity, nature, and innocence. As they gather glass, paper, and tin and return these to the cycle of nature, are they paralleling the gnostic desire to gather and return to the divine its alienated fragments?[90]

Adler argues that the hippie movement was an antinomian social movement that replaced traditional values with improvised new roles and the institutionalization of new ways of defining the self.[91] Victor Turner picks up on this aspect of the hippie movement by arguing that it was a clear expression of spontaneous communitas, emphasizing as it did spontaneity, immediacy, existence in the here and now, and its opposition to the structures of laws and customs of the past.[92] In my view, it can also be seen as a willful return to the well-known assumptions of primitivism. The reasons for this willful return to primitivism are relatively easy to understand: the hippie generation is the generation that lived under the evil shadow of thermonuclear annihilation, not, as Theodore Roszak notes, an evil defined by the fact of the bomb but by its *ethos*, the mad gambling with the universal extinction of our species. The primitivism of the hippies was a clear refusal to accept the essential criminality of technocracy.[93] It was in fact a celebration of the conceived ancient values of humanity. Roszak claims that their fascination with magic and ritual, tribal lore, and psychedelic experience were attempts to resuscitate the shamanism of the past, understood to mean the communication of the powers of nature to the human community.[94] The decades following witnessed actual attempts to practice what came to be known as "New Shamanism," promoted by Carlos Castaneda and Michael Harner.[95] New Shamanism today has become a New Age industry in its own right, with missions throughout many parts of the world.

According to William McLoughlin, the counter-culture that developed during the 1960s represents very much a rejection of American values, in five profound ways:

> It has rejected the dualistic view of man and nature, man and God, this world and the next, that is so ingrained in Western thought. It espouses a new sense of time, or timelessness – a preference for measuring life in terms of eternity rather than in terms of the near future or millennial future. It admires the East instead of considering its wisdom backward, quaint, or incomplete. It prefers to think of humanity in terms of "the family of man" instead of in terms of particular ethnic groups, races, classes, or "chosen" people; it tends also to think of man as merely one form of life among all the others, not necessarily superior to them or empowered to have dominion over

them. Finally, it would rather be passive than activist in the current crisis because, by the old-light version of progress (via technical manipulation of man and the environment), any change is bound to be more destructive than constructive.[96]

These standpoints are all clearly related to primitivistic ideas, and in particular to the notions of nature listed in Box 2.1 (see p. 42–3). The old idea of dominion over nature had an appeal to "Calvinistic forefathers facing virgin forests," but the influence of Eastern thought urged the West to

> reconsider its concept of postmillennial progress (the dream of bringing heaven to earth) and consider that the earth may be all man has to live with. In place of linear, step-at-a-time Western engineering and linguistics, the Oriental world view offered "total consciousness" and "intuitive awareness" – seeing the whole universe or, rather, the wholeness of the universe…To lose one's self in a sense of oneness with nature or harmony with the universe is truly to find one's innermost being.[97]

It is difficult to give true justice to the complexities of a counter-cultural age that believed Jesus was the first hippie and that sent 300,000 revivalist pilgrims to a rock festival at Woodstock to sing with Joni Mitchell about transforming the death bombers in Vietnam into butterflies. The point for this chapter, however, should be clear.

The new primitivism: Chicago history of religions

It is my contention that Mircea Eliade's vision of a *new humanism* was a formulation of the *new primitivism* in religious studies in the United States. The urge to help heal humanity of its lost harmony and to regenerate it through the idealizing study of archaic religions is a classical primitivist stance. It was also a theology of nostalgia. It can be said that Eliade's new humanism was exactly its opposite, namely an anti-humanism.[98]

Eliade, like others of his time, was deeply involved in the revolutionary struggle in Rumania during the 1930s and 1940s, which Eliade called a period of the terror of History, and this period of terror greatly influenced Eliade's ideas about history and reality.[99] His aversion to history and historicism was consequently ontological and methodological.[100] Ivan Strenski claims that Eliade's creative hermeneutics was a method to "transvalue" the disaster of his Rumanian past. Strenski summarizes the role that this past had in grounding Eliade's later methodological stance:

1 The radical traditionalism of the Rumanian right becomes for Eliade not a mere political programme; but a sweeping ontological judgement upon the material, secular, modern world, asserting the value of nostalgia for the archaic, cosmic and telluric, understood as fundamental human categories.
2 The profound mythico-religious, Rumanian Orthodox *cum* "Volkish" feelings of the Rumanian right become for Eliade the basis of his dominant religious viewpoint and of the particular *sort* of universal religious vision he embraces – archaic, cosmic and telluric.[101]

These basic assumptions are amply documented in Eliade's work. His despair of the malaise of the modern world is evident in every volume he wrote, and his solution for the world was a return to the archaic and primitive states of ahistorical, religious being. In the introduction to his book *The Sacred and the Profane*, which was first published in 1957, we find the following, typical claim:

> The man of the archaic societies tends to live as much as possible *in* the sacred or in close proximity to consecrated objects. The tendency is perfectly understandable, because, for primitives as for the man of all pre-modern societies, the *sacred* is equivalent to a *power*, and, in the last analysis, to *reality*...Thus it is easy to understand that religious man deeply desires *to be*, to participate in *reality*, to be saturated with power. Our chief concern in the following pages will be to elucidate this subject – to show in what ways religious man attempts to remain as long as possible in a sacred universe, and hence what his total experience of life proves to be in comparison with the experience of the man without religious feeling, of the man who lives, or wishes to live, in a desacralized world.[102]

Eliade's primitivism is clearly in evidence here. Later in the same book he claims: "The man of the traditional societies is admittedly a *homo religiosus*"[103] – in other words, the central theoretical object of all of Eliade's books on religion is epitomized by indigenous and archaic religion. Eliade has been strongly criticized for his ideas about primitives. Anthropologist John A. Saliba criticizes Eliade for holding that contemporary indigenous peoples represent a replica of the past or of a primordial state.[104] Saliba demonstrates in his book that most of Eliade's statements about indigenous peoples are simply wrong, a state of affairs that is well known to the history of primitivism.

In proclaiming his new humanism, Eliade was specifically associating his interests with other primitivist movements, such as Cubism and Surrealism, as well as with the cultural upheaval of the early 1960s. In fact, in his programmatic article, he claims that the new humanism will make it possible for Asians and "so-called primitive peoples" to appear on the "horizon of greater history" and to "reenter history."[105] But what he had in mind was that the historian of religions would be able to approach the religious expressions of a culture "from within" due to his understanding of the existential situations expressed in the religious documents at his disposal.[106] And in the preface to *The Quest*, he claims that his methodology is both a propaedeutic and a spiritual technique brought on by the inner transformation of the researcher having devoted his research to the deciphering and understanding of the messages sent to man by the sacred.[107] Thus, the scholar must return to the ancient existential states, decipher the structures of the sacred, and through a special hermeneutics translate for modern man its pre-reflective language. To be human is to be religious; in other words, the *natural* condition of mankind is that it is religious.

Such statements could be taken to be eminently humanistic, but as many have pointed out, Eliade's approach is from the "top down": he is not interested in historical, living religions, cultures, and people, but in what the sacred has revealed through these cultures to a theoretical object called *homo religiosus*. Furthermore, his approach requires a special hermeneutic that has little in common with other human and cultural sciences.

The new primitivism: New Shamanism

The cultural crises of the 1960s went hand in hand with criticisms raised in the philosophy of science, but in the United States the crises took a turn that was peculiarly American.

Nowhere else in the Western world did so many academics confuse fact with fiction or existential therapy with science so persistently as in the United States. The call to establish new dissenting academies by gestalt therapist Paul Goodman, among others, was met, and many such academies were established and still exist. This trend in the academic world thrived on primitivistic assumptions and especially on the celebration and romantization of the exotic. Even today in religious studies a significant amount of university teaching consists of acting out primitivistic ideas. One example of this is the work of William G. Doty, a respected member of the American Academy of Religion. In his Eliadean-inspired book on myths and rituals, he claims that he does not advocate a return to primitivism, but his book is nonetheless grounded in primitivistic ideas such as the following:

> Our own alienation from our bodies, and from satisfying corporate ritual, may indicate that much is to be learned from other (earlier, more "primitive") societies in which the individual has been more consistently related to the universal, the ectypal to the archetypal, and the natural to the cultural orders.[108]

Doty's university pedagogics consists of a blend of Joseph Campbell's Jungian comparativism and the myths of various cultures in free association with his own and his students' dream worlds.[109] This approach, in my opinion, can only lead to confusion about other cultures and about cultural science in general.

This kind of approach was already evident during the 1960s, when scholars even accepted, for example, Alan Watts, D.T. Suzuki, and Carlos Castaneda as accurate chroniclers of non-Western religions. It is relatively easy to understand why the first two might be taken seriously. After all, Suzuki was himself Japanese and must therefore have known what he was talking about. But he and Watts were both important missionaries of the theosophical reinterpretation of the "true Buddhism," and due to their prolific talents, they literally established a monopoly on the Western "understanding" of Japanese Buddhism.[110] Both of them were publishing as early as the 1930s, but their books met with increasing interest right up to the 1960s, after which they became exceedingly popular. Even today, they are venerated in occult and New Age circles. Alan Watts is best known for his book *The Spirit of Zen*, which, although first written in 1935, was by 1960 in its eighth printing of the third edition.[111] He inspired important beat generation writers such as Gary Snyder, Jack Kerouac, and Allen Ginsberg. And he also inspired Mircea Eliade. Eliade, on the other hand, came to inspire the new drug culture with his book *Shamanism*.[112]

What is more difficult to understand is why Carlos Castaneda was ever taken seriously. A doctoral candidate in anthropology from UCLA wanting to specialize in Yaqui ethnomedicine, Carlos Castaneda enthralled his readers with the magic of psychotropic experiences under the mysterious guidance of his Yaqui teacher, Don Juan Matus. Through each subsequent volume of his work, Castaneda keenly met the existential preoccupations of his American audience, but his tales became more and more outrageous: from the use of *Datura* and peyote, the reader follows Castaneda's growing maturity and his realization that Don Juan's teachings have nothing to do with drugs and everything to do with New Age ideals. Castaneda has had an undeniable cultural impact through nine volumes of powerful narrative, and he became a central figure in the New Age movement.[113] He also became one of the editors of the New Shamanistic magazine, *Shaman's Drum*, and his teachings are promoted in the video *Carlos Castaneda's*

Tensegrity,[114] in which various occult techniques mentioned in his writings are demonstrated. Furthermore, his writings have become the subject of the works of New Age analysts. One example is Victor Sanchez's book *The Teachings of Don Carlos*.[115] Another is the two-volume work by an author who simply calls himself Tomas, *The Promise of Power*, a 776-page concordance of Castaneda's books, and a companion volume entitled *Creative Victory*.[116]

The interesting thing here is the reaction of academic anthropology. Despite the careful documentation of Castaneda's hoax by his critic Richard de Mille and others,[117] the UCLA faculty would not admit to any error, and by 1976, eighteen anthropologists had publicly accepted Castaneda's books as factual accounts.[118] At the American Anthropological Association meeting in 1978, a special session was arranged on "Fraud and publishing ethics," during which the head of Castaneda's doctoral committee, Walter Goldschmidt, presented a statement defending Castaneda by claiming that "Castaneda's work had the virtue of originality and was in the tradition of anomalistic phenomenology, where a person's own experience is appropriate for examination,"[119] and he denied that any error was made by the committee and that it would not entertain questions of validity or authenticity. The Castaneda controversy is symptomatic of a tendency in the American academy.

A second example of such a figure is that of Castaneda's friend, anthropologist Michael J. Harner. Harner was Associate Professor of Anthropology on the Graduate Faculty of the New School for Social Research in New York and chairman of the anthropology program there during the 1970s. He also taught at Columbia University, Yale University, and the University of California, Berkeley, and was co-chairman of the Anthropology Section of the New York Academy of Sciences. He conducted four expeditions to the upper Amazon rain forest beginning in 1956, and has done research on the Jívaro, Achuara, and Conibo-Shipibo Indians, all of whom use hallucinogenic drugs in their shamanism. Harner also began to use these drugs. His first hallucinatory experience, during which he claims to have met the reptilian masters of the universe, drove him to seek more knowledge of shamanism. In 1964 he became an apprentice to Akachu, a shaman among the Untsuri Shuar in Ecuador.[120] From the Wintun and Pomo in California, the Coast Salish in Washington State, and the Lakota in South Dakota, Harner reported in his 1980 practical shamanism handbook, *The Way of the Shaman*, that he had learned to practice shamanism without the use of drugs. He then proclaimed his mission to be as follows: "Now it seems time to help transmit some practical aspects of this ancient human legacy to those who have been cut off from it for centuries,"[121] and with his book, Harner offers "an introductory handbook of shamanic methodology for health and healing."[122]

By 1983, Harner had established an organization called "The Foundation for Shamanic Studies," which, according to the first newsletter, is "dedicated to the preservation, study, and teaching of shamanic knowledge for the welfare of the Planet and its inhabitants."[123] P.C. Johnson has demonstrated that contrary to its claims of "preservation," Harner's foundation is a case study in New Age ritual appropriation: in the first place, what Harner claims to be the shamanistic "core" is in fact innovative in at least three related areas – "universalization (shamanism as culturally non-contingent), individualization (shamanism as malleable to individual needs in the religious marketplace) and the turn to shamanism as a technique of psychotherapy";[124] and secondly, the Foundation established itself "as an authority by the installation of its own language and power to choose what and who to 'preserve' through financial support and archival memory."[125] As Johnson cogently notes:

Its stated intention to preserve traditional forms of shamanism is obscured by its creation of a new, distinct form – a form which, while it claims universal, non-contingent status, clearly relies on its own proper context, namely that of radical modernity and the discourse of mobility and individual agency.[126]

Reactions to New Shamanism on the part of Native Americans is unmistakably clear. New Shamanism is generally viewed not only as being presumptuous, but most often imperialistic and sacrilegious.[127]

But there are Native Americans who actively participate in New Age religiosity. One of the more famous of these is Sun Bear, also known as Vincent LaDuke, who was born on the White Earth Chippewa Reservation in Minnesota. After many years pursuing a personal spiritual search, Sun Bear founded the Bear Tribe in 1966 with three non-Native American women in Reno, Nevada. Combining American occultism with Native American spirituality, Sun Bear initiated the famous Medicine Wheel gatherings in 1974 that became one of the principal ceremonies of the New Age. Sun Bear has had considerable influence on New Age writers such as Lynn V. Andrews and Rolling Thunder, and is a prolific writer of books and articles on self-help shamanism, but there have also been threats of violence against Native Americans who offer workshops at Sun Bear's Medicine Wheels.[128]

It might be argued that these examples of New Shamanism are extreme and unusual, but this is not the case. In fact it is becoming so widespread that even many reputable academic presses are now trying to attract the same kind of audiences.[129] Despite eloquent defenders,[130] the fact remains that this stance does not bring us any closer to the real people we are purportedly studying. Nor does it help us pursue the study of particular religions or even of religion in general. It simply reaffirms the age-old European and American need to romanticize the exotic in order to address our own spiritual, ideological, and religious needs. Thus, there is very little room for living indigenes who do not conform to our stereotypes.

According to Richard de Mille, Barbara G. Myerhoff, who has been very much a part of the trends mentioned in this section, writes in contrast to her friend Castaneda:

Indigenous traditions deserve accurate and respectful preservation, and these records must be distinguished from imaginative works...It is the obligation of the lettered to make written records of the lore of the unlettered simply a record – not a mirror of ourselves or our needs and fantasies.[131]

Postmodern primitivism

The primitivism of the 1980s was so widespread that radically diverse authors and movements could share it as a common fundamental viewpoint. The mention here of two extreme examples will suffice. The first is the tremendously popular restorationist Allan Bloom, whose book *The Closing of the American Mind* attempted to restore the primitivistic American Eden during the Reagan era in which other cultures, ethnic festivals, and the women's movement were to be excluded.[132] The second is that of the Green politics promoted by Charlene Spretnak, whereby archaic religions, the worship of Nature, the celebration of otherness, and ecofeminism provide alternatives to modernity.[133]

Postmodern primitivism in contemporary art and theater has followed similar lines. William Rubin describes the new primitivism in art in the following way:

The kind of twentieth-century primitivism that relates to individual works of tribal art began to wane after World War II. Artists did not entirely stop collecting tribal sculpture or looking to it for ideas. But this object-to-object relationship has been largely displaced, especially in the last fifteen years, by a more tenuous, more elliptical, and, above all, more intellectualized primitivism, which takes its inspiration primarily from *ideas* about the way tribal objects functioned and about the societies from which they came. Prepared to some extent by Surrealist attitudes toward the Primitive, this "Conceptual primitivism" – which includes certain hybrid objects, Earthworks, Environments, Happenings (varieties of "shamanistic" theater) and other activities – draws its inspiration more from texts than works of art, from the writing of Bataille and Leiris, among others, and especially from the structuralism of Lévi-Strauss.[134]

Two examples taken from Kirk Varnedoe's analysis of contemporary primitivism in art may be mentioned, examples that move each in their own directions.[135] The first is the political primitivism of the German artist Joseph Beuys, whose works of art proclaim social renewal, but also draw on symbolism that harks back to German chthonic mythology. Through the use of totemic animals, he attempts to orchestrate the shaman's role as a redemptive force "for a reawakened German national consciousness," which is reminiscent of earlier attempts by German National Socialism to use "a Northern sense of self-in-nature" for their particular purposes.[136]

The second example draws on the widespread feminist primitivism. The idea here is coupled with the nostalgia of collectivism, or primal determinism, where the simpler and suppressed truths of primitive deities promise release from modernity. This kind of art attempts to reduce identity to gender, and culture to biology. In Varnedoe's words, this art draws on an iconography of blood and organs "reacting against an earlier formalism associated with male hegemony" in which "womblike spaces and visceral symbols" replace the "oneiric male sadism of Surrealism."[137] These symbols are incorporated in objects and rituals that are claimed to be linked to tribal and/or prehistoric cults, whereby this art form celebrates "a 'natural' order of tribal life yoked to the imperium of blood and soil."[138]

The visceral and telluric are also central to the so-called "modern primitivists" of the theater. The medium of expression is the bodies of the artists themselves. Through various techniques of mutilation, borrowed from ethnographic monographs on such practices in indigenous societies, the modern primitivists attempt to surpass the cultural veneer and go directly to the sources of emotion. Ultimately this art form, though disclaiming any romanticization of indigenous cultures, nonetheless hopes to find a more ideal society.[139] This utopian ideal is somehow to be accomplished through pain:

> *All* sensual experience functions to free us from "normal" social restraints, to awaken our deadened bodies to life. All such activity points toward a goal: the creation of the "complete" or "integrated" man and woman, and in this we are yet prisoners digging an imaginary tunnel to freedom...It is necessary to uncover the mass of repressed desires lying within the unconscious so that a *New Eroticism* embracing the common identity of pain and pleasure, delirium and reason, and founded on a *full knowledge* of evil and perversion, may arise to inspire radically improved social relations.[140]

One of the more outspoken practitioners of this art is Fakir Musafar, advertised as a Silicon Valley ad executive "who has practiced every known body modification."[141] Born in 1930, Musafar found his role models from the age of 12 in indigenous practices depicted in *National Geographic*. He took the name Fakir Musafa from a nineteenth-century Sufi who lived for eighteen years with daggers and other objects inserted in his body. In 1985, Musafa produced the film *Dances Sacred and Profane*, in which he performs the Sun Dance and a Kavandi Bearing, and has since given lectures, slide shows, ritual demonstrations, and so on. He claims to have visionary and psychic abilities, and these abilities, as well as his drive to modify his body, are the result of prior lives. In the life immediately prior to this one, Musafar claims to have been the wandering spirit of a Lakota warrior. Musafar claims further that his mutilation practices lead to transcendent spiritual events of self-transformation. By separating oneself from the body's pain, one enters an altered state of consciousness. Musafar claims that there are hundreds of different kinds of altered states, and that he has developed systematic techniques to accomplish them. Here Musafar explains what modern primitives are:

> The whole purpose of "modern primitive" practices is to get more and more spontaneous in the expression of *pleasure with insight*...We used the term to describe a non-tribal person who responds to primal urges and does something with the body.[142]

There are seven methods of modifying or working on the body according to Musafar. These are contortion, constriction, deprivation, encumberment, fire, penetration, and suspension. And these practices can bring spiritual benefit, social status or adornment, and/or sexual pleasure.

Like New Age primitivism, postmodern primitivism has also given voice to many artists wishing to re-establish links with their native heritage, and it has furthermore helped Western artists to become sensitized to the ethical, political, and historical issues involving non-Western cultures today. But primitivism conceived of as a flight or liberation from civilization is also, and perhaps even more so, as this chapter has demonstrated, an ever-more suppressive drive deeper into that civilization. As Varnedoe writes:

> At its most banal, self-styled political primitivism has yielded harmless role-playing, conjurings of Atlantean fantasies, and astrological or alchemical mysticism. In other manifestations, however, it has been the arena for iconographies of regression that give more serious pause and that need examining in regard to the politics of primitivism old and new.[143]

Conclusion

Despite the urgent necessity to move beyond primitivism, I do not think that this is something we are capable of accomplishing. It would require more than Western and non-Western scholars are prepared to offer, and it would involve struggling against massive tides of general cultural values and historical contingencies around the globe.

If it were possible to move beyond primitivism, how might this be done? Primitivism in the negative sense is basically outdated, even though one may meet racists in European and American academies now and then. But it is still evident, in sophisticated ways, in much of Western philosophy. Jürgen Habermas, for example, mentioned earlier, who otherwise is a brilliant critic of social oppression in any guise, nonetheless reads into contemporary Western reflection the end result of a development out of traditional, "archaic," "mythical," and "closed" societies (read: "indigenous").[144] This is unfortunate, since much of his thought on communicative action could serve to help cultural science out of its present cul-de-sac.[145]

Moving beyond primitivism today, however, would primarily mean moving beyond primitivism in the positive sense, in other words, in the sense that *promotes the romantic idea of indigenous cultures*, which I have argued here keeps real indigenous peoples out of the picture just as effectively as the scientific racism of the nineteenth century! The way out of this must surely lie in developing approaches that are not intrinsically associated with primitivist notions (in the positive sense) of values lost in some mythical past and/or only found in indigenous or archaic cultures. The answer must also be found outside the realm of religious doctrine, mainly because most religions, including indigenous ones, are implacably primitivistic (about themselves in the positive sense and about others in the negative sense). I suggest that a way to move beyond primitivism is not along the path of intuitive empathy, creative hermeneutics, the misunderstood interplay of mutually absolute discourses, or misanthropic ecological ideologies, but rather through a radical revitalization of the Enlightenment project.

This suggestion, however, does not have the appeal that it should. Many Enlightenment thinkers were indeed racists, and worse.[146] As Terry Eagleton has noted, what is good about postmodernism is that it has helped "reviled and humiliated groups" to "recover something of their history and self-hood":

> This, as I've argued, is the trend's most precious achievement; and one cannot realistically expect that those involved in a painful struggle for recognition will be much enthused right now by transfigured notions of universality, especially when these ideas spring from groups which have traditionally been their enemies…There is indeed a bad kind of universalism; but there is a bad kind of particularism too. If Enlightenment universalism is exclusivist in practice, ethnic particularism can be exclusivist in both practice and theory. Little is to be gained by simply substituting the one for the other, though there is perhaps little to be gained either by arguing the point now.[147]

Eagleton has also argued that much of postmodernism has sprung from or taken root in the United States, and reflects "that country's most intractable political problems":

> It is then perhaps a little ethnocentric of this anti-ethnocentrism, though hardly a gesture unknown to that nation, to project its own political backyard onto the world at large…If postmodernism is a form of culturalism, it is because among other reasons it refuses to recognize that what different ethnic groups have in common socially and economically is finally more important than their cultural differences. More important for what? For the purposes of their political emancipation…It is because of its commitment to minorities that postmodernism questions the notion of a general humanity; but it is difficult to see how some such appeal would not be necessary for defending minorities against racist assault.[148]

For the record, I must emphatically state that being critical of positive primitivism is an expression neither of capitulating to the Right nor of supporting chauvinism, colonialism, racism, authoritarianism, or instrumentalism. It is, on the contrary, a celebration of what characterizes us as humans, namely critical rationality. Following social activist Murray Bookchin, I agree that "until the current antihumanistic tendencies are subjected to serious criticism, we cannot even begin to address the more tangible problems of our time that antihumanism obscures and distorts." [149]

Notes

1 Arthur O. Lovejoy and George Boas, *Primitivism and Related Ideas in Antiquity*, with supplementary essays by W.F. Albright and P.-E. Dumont, Baltimore: Johns Hopkins Press, 1935; Lahontan, *Dialogues curieux entre l'auteur et un sauvage de bon sens qui a voyagé, et Mémoires de l'Amérique septentrionale*, ed. Gilbert Chinard, Baltimore: Johns Hopkins Press, 1931; George Boas, *The Happy Beast in French Thought of the Seventeenth Century*, Baltimore: Johns Hopkins Press, 1933 (reprinted New York: Octagon Books, 1966); Lois Whitney, *Primitivism and the Idea of Progress in English Popular Literature of the Eighteenth Century*, Baltimore: Johns Hopkins Press, 1934; Denis Diderot, *Supplément au voyage de Bougainville*, ed. Gilbert Chinard, Baltimore: Johns Hopkins Press, 1935; and George Boas, *Essays on Primitivism and Related Ideas in the Middle Ages*, Baltimore: Johns Hopkins Press, 1948.
2 Lovejoy and Boas, *Primitivism and Related Ideas in Antiquity*, ix.
3 *Ibid.*, 1.
4 *Ibid.*, 7.
5 *Ibid.*, 2–4.
6 *Ibid.*, 4.
7 *Ibid.*, 4–5.
8 *Ibid.*, 6.
9 *Ibid.*, 9.
10 *Ibid.*, 10.
11 *Ibid.*, 12.
12 Aristotle, *Phys.*, 193a 9; Theophrastus, *De sensibus*, 63, 70.
13 Antiphon, *Ox. Pap.*, XI, 1364; Plato, *Gorgias*, 482e; Euripides, *Bacchae*, 896; Aristotle, *Topica*, 173a 7; Democritus in Diels, *Fragm. Der Vorsokr.*, II, 54, 2ff.
14 Aristotle, *Nic. Eth.*, V, 10; Cicero, *Tusc. Disp.*, I, 30; Justinian I, 2 and 11. This is the principal source of the uniformitarianism or standardizing tendency of the seventeenth and eighteenth centuries. As Lovejoy and Boas write, it is "antithetic to political or moral relativism, and also to the Romantic cultivation of diversity and idiosyncrasy" (*Primitivism and Related Ideas in Antiquity*, 455).
15 Euripides, *Troades*, 886; Euripides, *Fragm. Inc.*, 910; Philolaus (?) in Diels, *Fragm. Der Vorsokratiker*, I, 239; Plato, *Lysis.*, 214b; Cicero, *De re pub.*, III, i, 1; *De fin.*, V, xiii, 38; *De nat. deor.*, I, xx, 53; *Paradoxa*, 14; Philo Jud., *De opificio mundi*, I, 3; Montaigne, *Essais*, I, 30.
16 Hippocrates, *On Airs*, II, 58.
17 Democritus, *Fragm.*, 33 and 183; Plato, *Republic*, 409d, 410b; Pindar, *Ol.*, IX, 100ff., II, 93ff.; Hippocrates, *On Law*, II; Varro, *De re rust.*, II, i, 3; and innumerable later writers.
18 Hippocrates, *On Diet*, I, vi, 486; *On Epidemics*, VI, v, 314; Democritus, *Fragm.*, 33; Plato, *Laws*, 888e–890a; Cicero, *De finibus*, IV, 16.
19 Critias, *Fragm.*, 19; Plato, *Cratyl.*, 400a; *Republic*, 375e, 530c; *Apol.* 22c; Aristotle, *Met.*, 107b 3, 1075a 11; *Politics*, I, 1252a 28; Aristophanes, *Clouds*, 1078; Cicero, *De finibus*, III, v, 17; Rousseau, *Disc. sur. L'inégalité*, Pt. I.
20 Cicero, *Pro Sestio*, 91–2; Hobbes, *Leviathan*, XIII; Rousseau, *État de guerre*, par. 6; Locke, Pufendorf, and other juristic writers.
21 Lovejoy and Boas, *Primitivism and Related Ideas in Antiquity*, 12–15.
22 On theriophily, see George Boas, *The Happy Beast in French Thought of the Seventeenth Century*, Baltimore: Johns Hopkins Press, 1933 (reprinted New York: Octagon Books, 1966). On animalitarianism, see Lovejoy and Boas, *Primitivism and Related Ideas in Antiquity*, 19–22.
23 Boas, *The Happy Beast in French Thought of the Seventeenth Century*, 2.
24 Lovejoy and Boas, *Primitivism and Related Ideas in Antiquity*, 16.
25 R.W.B. Lewis, *The American Adam: Innocence, Tragedy and Tradition in the Nineteenth Century*, Chicago: University of Chicago Press, 1955.

26 Richard T. Hughes and C. Leonard Allen, *Illusions of Innocence: Protestant Primitivism in America, 1630–1875*, Chicago and London: University of Chicago Press, 1988.

27 Lewis, *The American Adam*, 5.

28 *Ibid.*, 7–8.

29 *Ibid.*, 9.

30 *Ibid.*, 9.

31 Hughes and Allen, *Illusions of Innocence*, xiii.

32 Lewis, *The American Adam*, 197.

33 See, for example, Leonard I. Sweet, "Millennialism in America: recent studies," *Theological Studies* 40 (1979): 510–31, and Hillel Schwartz, "The end of the beginning: millenarian studies, 1969–1975," *Religious Studies Review* 2 (1976): 1–15.

34 Sidney E. Mead, *The Lively Experiment: The Shaping of Christianity in America*, New York: Harper & Row, 1963, 108–13, and "The theology of the republic and the orthodox mind," *Journal of the American Academy of Religion* 44 (1976): 105–13. See also Fred Somkin, *Unquiet Eagle: Memory and Desire in the Idea of American Freedom, 1815–1860*, Ithaca: Cornell University Press, 1967.

35 Hughes and Allen, *Illusions of Innocence*, 4. They write, rightly in my opinion, that American foreign policy, "often dominated by redemptive themes, rests ultimately on the conviction that America has restored pure, natural, and primal norms while other nations remain snared in the web of history, tradition, and artificial contrivance" (*ibid.*, 3).

36 *Ibid.*, 4.

37 *Ibid.*, 22–3.

38 See Robert F. Berkhofer, Jr., *The White Man's Indian: Images of the American Indian from Columbus to the Present*, New York: Vintage Books, 1978 (2nd edn 1979) for a detailed analysis of the various ways Native Americans have been understood in the American imagination. He notes that the Indian became an important subject for the newly established national literature under the impetus of the Romantic movement during the turn of the nineteenth century, reaching its height in the 1820s and 1830s but declining in the decade leading up to the Civil War (*ibid.*, 86). Both the noble and the savage Indian were ideal subjects for American high culture. See also Catherine L. Albanese's chapter on this aspect of American thinking ("Republican nature: from the revolution that was lawful to the destiny that was manifest") in her book *Nature Religion in America: From the Algonkian Indians to the New Age*, Chicago and London: University of Chicago Press, 1990, 47–79. For parallel studies on the Native American as a literary, artistic, and/or philosophical motif in American history, see Henry Nash Smith, *Virgin Land: The American West as Symbol and Myth*, New York: Random House, 1950; Roy Harvey Pearce, *Savagism and Civilization: A Study of the Indian and the American Mind*, Baltimore and London: Johns Hopkins Press, 1953 (rev. edn 1965); E. McClung Fleming, "Symbols of the United States: from Indian Queen to Uncle Sam," in Ray B. Browne, Richard H. Crowder, Virgil L. Lokke and William T. Stafford (eds) *Frontiers of American Culture*, Lafayette: Purdue University Press, 1968, 1–24, and "The American image as Indian Princess, 1765–1783," *Winterthur Portfolio* 2 (1968): 65–81; Peter N. Carroll, *Puritanism and the Wilderness: The Intellectual Significance of the New England Frontier, 1629–1700*, New York: Columbia University Press, 1969; Richard Slotkin, *Regeneration through Violence: The Mythology of the American Frontier, 1600–1860*, Middletown: Wesleyan University Press, 1973; Rayna Green, "The Pocahontas perplex: the image of Indian women in American culture," *The Massachusetts Review* 16 (1976): 698–714; Fredi Chiappelli, Michael J.B. Allen and Robert L. Benson (eds) *First Images of America*, 2 vols, Berkeley: University of California Press, 1976; J.M. Powell, *Mirrors of the New World: Images and Image-Makers in the Settlement Process*, Kent: W. Dawson, 1977; Ray Allen Billington, *Land of Savagery, Land of Promise: The European Image of the American Frontier*, New York: W.W. Norton, 1981; Raymond W. Stedman, *Shadows of the Indian: Stereotypes in American Culture*, Norman: University of Oklahoma Press, 1982; and Åsebrit Sundquist, *Pocahontas & Co. The Fictional American Indian Woman in Nineteenth Century Literature: A Study of Method*, Oslo: University of Oslo Press, 1984. Sundquist's book is a statistical analysis of stereotypes in nineteenth-century American fiction.

39 Hughes and Allen, *Illusions of Innocence*, 215. See also Emily S. Rosenberg, *Spreading the American Dream: American Economic and Cultural Expansion, 1890–1945*, New York: Hill & Wang, 1982.

40 Loren Eiseley, *Darwin's Century: Evolution and the Men Who Discovered It*, New York: Doubleday, 1958 (Anchor Books edn 1961), 329–31.

41 Concerning these new views, see Peter J. Bowler, *Theories of Human Evolution: A Century of Debate, 1844–1944*, Baltimore: Johns Hopkins University Press, 1986, 4–8.

42 Bowler, *Theories of Human Evolution*; *The Non-Darwinian Revolution: Reinterpreting a Historical Myth*, Baltimore: Johns Hopkins University Press, 1988; *The Invention of Progress: The Victorians and the Past*, Oxford: Basil Blackwell, 1989.

43 Bowler, *The Non-Darwinian Revolution*, 15.

44 Bowler mentions the above-quoted Loren Eiseley as one of the mythmakers.

45 Charles Darwin, *On the Origin of Species*, facsimile of the 1859 first edition, Cambridge: Harvard University Press, 1964, 490.

46 Arthur O. Lovejoy, *The Great Chain of Being: A Study of the History of an Idea*, Cambridge and London: Harvard University Press, 1936, 242ff. This book is a collection of his William James lectures that were delivered at Harvard University in 1933.

47 Lovejoy, *The Great Chain of Being*, 59.

48 *Ibid.*, 329.

49 Charles Bonnet, *Considérations sur les corps organisés*, Paris, 1762; *Contemplation de la nature*, Paris, 1764; and *Palingénésie philosophique*, Paris, 1769.

50 Jean-Baptiste Robinet, *De la nature*, Paris, 1761–66.

51 Lovejoy, *The Great Chain of Being*, 244.

52 Erasmus Darwin, *The Botanic Garden: a Poem in Two Parts*, 2 vols, London, 1791; *Zoonomia: or the Laws of Organic Life*, 2 vols, London, 1794–96; and *The Temple of Nature*, London, 1803.

53 Jean-Baptiste Pierre Antoine de Monet Lamarck, *Histoire naturelle des animaux sans vertèbres*, 6 vols, Paris, 1815–22; and *Philosophie zoologique: ou exposition des considérations relatives à l'histoire naturelle des animaux*, 2 vols, Paris, 1873.

54 Bowler, *The Invention of Progress*, 3.

55 *Ibid.*, 3 and 5.

56 F. Max Müller, *Lectures on the Science of Language Delivered at the Royal Institution of Great Britain*, 2 vols, London: Longmans, Green, Longman, and Roberts, 1861; *Chips from a German Workshop*, 4 vols, London: Longmans, Green, and Co., 1867; *Introduction to the Science of Religion: Four Lectures Delivered at the Royal Institution, with Two Essays on False Analogies, and the Philosophy of Mythology*, London: Longmans, Green, and Co., 1873; *Lectures on the Origin and Growth of Religion as Illustrated by the Religions of India*, London: Longmans, Green, and Co., 1878; and *Selected Essays on Language, Mythology and Religion*, 2 vols, London: Longmans, Green, and Co., 1881.

57 Herbert Spencer's ambitious ten-volume *A System of Synthetic Philosophy* dealt with biology, psychology, sociology, and ethics. The most important in the present context are *The Principles of Psychology*, 2 vols, London and Edinburgh: Williams & Norgate, 1870, and *The Principles of Sociology*, 3 vols, London and Edinburgh: Williams & Norgate, 1897.

58 Lewis Henry Morgan, *League of the Ho-de-no-sau-nee, or Iroquois*, Rochester: Sage & Bros., 1851; *Systems of Consanguinity and Affinity of the Human Family*, Washington: Smithsonian Institution, 1871; and *Ancient Society: Researches in the Lines of Human Progress from Savagery through Barbarism to Civilization*, New York: Holt, 1877.

59 John Lubbock, *Pre-Historic Times, as Illustrated by Ancient Remains and the Manners and Customs of Modern Savages*, London and Edinburgh: Williams & Norgate, 1865; *The Origin of Civilization and the Primitive Condition of Man: Mental and Social Condition of Savages*, London and Edinburgh: Longmans, Green, and Co., 1870; and *Prehistoric Times as Illustrated by Ancient Remains and the Manners and Customs of Savages*, New York: D. Appleton, 1872.

60 Edward B. Tylor, *Anahuac or Mexico and the Mexicans, Ancient and Modern*, London: Longmans, Green, Longman, and Roberts, 1861; *Researches into the Early History of Mankind and the Development of Civilization*, London: John Murray, 1865; *Primitive Culture: Researches into the Development of Mythology, Philosophy, Religion, Language, Art, and Custom*, 2 vols, London: John Murray, 1871; and *Anthropology: An Introduction to the Study of Man and Civilization*, New York: D. Appleton, 1881.

61 Charles Darwin, *The Descent of Man and Selection in Relation to Sex*, London: John Murray, 1871, Chapters IV, V, and XXI.

62 Bowler, *The Invention of Progress*, 14. Bowler may have been a little too eager to disassociate Darwin from the scientific racism of the Victorian period. He was of course less aggressive than the vulgar social Darwinists, but there is no doubt that the "savage" cultures of his age ranked low on Darwin's own scale of thinking. See, for example, one of the final paragraphs in *The Descent of Man*:

> The main conclusion arrived at in this work, namely that man is descended from some lowly organised form, will, I regret to think, be highly distasteful to many. But there can hardly be a doubt that we are descended from barbarians. The astonishment which I felt on first seeing a party of Fuegians on a wild and broken shore will never be forgotten by me, for the reflection at once rushed into my mind – such were our ancestors. These men were absolutely naked and bedaubed with paint, their long hair was tangled, their mouths frothed with excitement, and their expression was wild, startled, and distrustful. They possessed hardly any arts, and like wild animals lived on what they could catch; they had no government, and were merciless to every one not of their own small tribe. He who has seen a savage in his native land will not feel much shame, if forced to acknowledge that the blood of some more humble creature flows in his veins. For my own part I would as soon be descended from that heroic little monkey, who braved his dreaded enemy in order to save the life of his keeper, or from that old baboon, who descending from the mountains, carried away in triumph his young comrade from a crowd of astonished dogs – as from a savage who delights to torture his enemies, offers up bloody sacrifices, practises infanticide without remorse, treats his wives like slaves, knows no decency, and is haunted by the grossest superstitions.
>
> (1913 reprint of the 2nd edn, 1874, 946)

63 Adam Kuper, *The Invention of Primitive Society. Transformations of an Illusion*, London and New York: Routledge, 1988, 8.
64 Henry Maine, *Ancient Law*, London: John Murray, 1861; *Lectures on the Early History of Institutions*, New York: Holt, 1875; and *Dissertations on Early Law and Custom*, London: John Murray, 1883.
65 Johann Jacob Bachofen, *Das Mutterrecht: Eine Untersuchung über die Gynaikokratie der alten Welt nach ihrer religiösen und rectlichen Natur*, Basel: Schwabe, 1861.
66 N.-D. Fustel de Coulanges, *La Cité Antique: Étude sur le culte, droit, les institutions de la Grèce et de Rome*, Paris: Durand, 1864.
67 J.M. McLennan, *Primitive Marriage: an Inquiry into the Origin of the Form of Capture in Marriage Ceremonies*, Edinburgh: Black, 1865.
68 Kuper, *The Invention of Primitive Society*, 17ff.
69 Edward P. Dozier, "The concepts of 'primitive' and 'native' in anthropology," *Yearbook of Anthropology*, 1955.
70 Lois Mednick, "Memorandum on the use of *primitive*," *Current Anthropology* 1 (1960): 441–5.
71 Catherine H. Berndt, "The concept of primitive," *Sociologus* 10 (1960): 50–69.
72 Francis L.K. Hsu, "Rethinking the concept 'Primitive,'" *Current Anthropology* 5 (1964): 169–78.
73 See Hsu's conclusions after an exhaustive analysis of the use of the term in anthropological literature, *ibid.*, 173–4.
74 *Ibid.*, 174.
75 *Ibid.*, 174.
76 E. Rose and G. Willoughby, "Cultural profiles and emphases," *American Journal of Sociology* 63 (1958): 476–90.
77 Ashley Montagu, "The fallacy of the 'primitive,'" *The Journal of the American Medical Association* 179 (1962): 962–3. See also his *The Concept of the Primitive*, New York: The Free Press, 1968.
78 See, for example, Robert A. Brightman's interesting article on concepts of the primitive among the Missinippi Cree, "Primitivism in Missinippi Cree: historical consciousness," *Man* 25 (1990): 108–28.
79 Lovejoy and Boas, *Primitivism and Related Ideas in Antiquity*, xi.
80 Guillaume Apollinaire, "L'Esprit nouveau et les poètes," letter to André Breton, 24 November 1917, quoted in Katia Samaltanos, *Apollinaire: Catalyst for Primitivism, Picabia, and Duchamp*, Ann Arbor: UMI Research Press, 1981 (2nd edn 1984), 3.

81 *Ibid.*, 108.

82 Quoted in Wassili Kandinsky, *The Art of Spiritual Harmony*, London: Constable, 1914, 6.

83 Quoted in Samaltanos, *Apollinaire*, 107.

84 William Rubin, "Modernist primitivism: an introduction," in William Rubin (ed.) *"Primitivism" in 20th Century Art: Affinity of the Tribal and the Modern*, vol. I, New York: The Museum of Modern Art, 1984, 2.

85 *Ibid.*, 2.

86 Gaile McGregor, *The Noble Savage in the New World Garden: Notes Toward a Syntactic of Place*, Toronto: University of Toronto Press and Bowling Green: Bowling Green State University Popular Press, 1988, 1.

87 As McLoughlin writes: "Through awakenings a nation grows in wisdom, in respect for itself, and into more harmonious relations with other peoples and the physical universe…They are essentially folk movements, the means by which a people or a nation reshapes its identity, transforms its patterns of thought and action, and sustains a healthy relationship with environmental and social change" (William G. McLoughlin, *Revivals, Awakenings, and Reform: An Essay on Religion and Social Change in America, 1607–1977*, Chicago and London: University of Chicago Press, 1978, 2.)

88 Nathan Adler, "Ritual, release, and orientation: maintenance of the self in the antinomian personality," in Irving I. Zaretsky and Mark P. Leone (eds) *Religious Movements in Contemporary America*, Princeton: Princeton University Press, 1974, 285–6.

89 *Ibid.*, 286.

90 *Ibid.*, 286.

91 Other sociologists have promoted the same argument. See, for example, S.N. Eisenstadt, "Generational conflict and intellectual antinomianism," *The Annals of the American Academy of Political and Social Science* 395 (1971): 68–79, and *Tradition, Change, and Modernity*, New York: John Wiley & Sons, 1973, 244–7; and Edward A. Shils, "Dreams of plenitude, nightmares of scarcity," in S.M. Lipset and P.G. Altbach (eds) *Students in Revolt*, Boston: Houghton Mifflin Co., 1969, 1–35.

92 Victor W. Turner, *The Ritual Process: Structure and Anti-Structure*, New York: Aldine and London: Pelican, 1974 (first published 1969), 99–100.

93 Theodore Roszak, *The Making of a Counter Culture: Reflections on the Technocratic Society and Its Youthful Opposition*, Garden City: Doubleday (Anchor Books edn), 1969, 47.

94 *Ibid.*, 265.

95 See my chapter on the hippies and other movements that found their way out to the Hopi Indian Reservation, entitled "*Hippie-Sinom* (Hippie People) and the crisis of meaning," in Armin W. Geertz, *The Invention of Prophecy: Continuity and Meaning in Hopi Indian Religion*, Los Angeles: University of California Press, 1994, 288–319.

96 McLoughlin, *Revivals, Awakenings, and Reform*, 199.

97 *Ibid.*, 201.

98 Mircea Eliade, *The Myth of the Eternal Return or, Cosmos and History*, Princeton: Princeton University Press, 1954 (2nd edn 1971), and *The Quest. History and Meaning in Religion*, Chicago and London: University of Chicago Press, 1969 (2nd edn 1975).

99 Ivan Strenski, *Four Theories of Myth in Twentieth-Century History: Cassirer, Eliade, Lévi-Strauss and Malinowski*, Houndmills and London: Macmillan, 1987, 70–103.

100 A typical statement of his on this subject is the following: "historicism arises as a decomposition product of Christianity; it accords decisive importance to the historical event (which is an idea whose origin is Christian) but to the *historical event as such*, that is, by denying it any possibility of revealing a transhistorical, soteriological intent" (*The Sacred and the Profane: The Nature of Religion*, New York: Harcourt, Brace & World Inc., 1959 (translation of original 1957 German edition), 112).

101 Strenski, *Four Theories of Myth in Twentieth-Century History*, 102. Even Strenski's critic Carl Olson admits to this aspect of Eliade: "Eliade's patriotic fervour is evident in his notion of 'Romanianism', a non-political nationalism that embodied a messianic sense of the divinely-chosen nature of the Rumanian nation with a special mission to fulfill in the world" (*The Theology and Philosophy of Eliade. A Search for the Centre*, Houndmills and London: Macmillan, 1992, 5).

102 Eliade, *The Sacred and the Profane*, 13.

103 *Ibid.*, 15.
104 John A. Saliba, *'Homo Religiosus' in Mircea Eliade: An Anthropological Evaluation*, Leiden: E.J. Brill, 1976, 121.
105 Eliade, *The Quest*, 2. The chapter entitled "A new humanism" is a revised and expanded version of his article from the inaugural issue of *History of Religions* 1 (1961): 1–8, entitled "History of religions and a new humanism."
106 Eliade, *The Quest*, 3.
107 *Ibid.*, iv–v.
108 William G. Doty, *Mythography: The Study of Myths and Rituals*, Tuscaloosa: University of Alabama Press, 1986, 35.
109 Doty, *Mythography*, 38–9.
110 In fact many of the foremost Buddhologists were Theosophists, such as Caroline Rhys Davis (her husband T.W. Rhys Davis claimed not to be, but he was for many years the president of the Buddhist Society which had direct connections with the theosophical Maha Bodhi Society through Dharmapala), A. David-Neel, Christmas Humphreys (the founder of the theosophical Buddhist Lodge which later became the Buddhist Society), and Edward Conze.
111 Alan W. Watts, *The Spirit of Zen: A Way of Life, Work and Art in the Far East*, New York: Grove Press, 1960. Other widely read books by Watts include *Psychotherapy East and West*, New York: Pantheon, 1961; *The Joyous Cosmology: Adventures in the Chemistry of Consciousness*, New York: Vintage Books, 1962; and *This Is It*, New York: Collier Books, 1967. D.T. Suzuki is best known for his collection of essays, *Zen Buddhism*, ed. William Barrett, New York: Doubleday, 1956. Other widely read books were *Manual of Zen Buddhism*, New York: Grove Press, 1960, and the three-volume series, *Essays in Zen Buddhism*, London: Rider & Co., 1949–53 (reprinted 1970).
112 Mircea Eliade, *Shamanism: Archaic Techniques of Ecstasy*, London: Routledge & Kegan Paul, 1964 (originally published as *Le Chamanisme et les techniques archaïques de l'extase*, trans. Willard R. Trask, Paris: Librairie Payot, 1951).
113 Carlos Castaneda, *The Teachings of Don Juan. A Yaqui Way of Knowledge*, Los Angeles: University of California Press, 1968; *A Separate Reality. Further Conversations with Don Juan*, New York: Simon & Schuster, 1971; *Journey to Ixtlan. The Lessons of Don Juan*, New York: Simon & Schuster, 1972; *Tales of Power*, New York: Simon & Schuster, 1974; *The Second Ring of Power*, New York: Simon & Schuster, 1977; *The Eagle's Gift*, New York: Simon & Schuster, 1981; *The Fire from Within*, New York: Simon & Schuster, 1984; *The Power of Silence. Further Lessons of Don Juan*, New York: Simon & Schuster, 1988; and *The Art of Dreaming*, New York: HarperCollins, 1993.
114 *Carlos Castaneda's Tensegrity: Twelve Basic Movements to Gather Energy and Promote Well-Being*, Los Angeles: Elemental Films, 1995.
115 Victor Sanchez, *The Teachings of Don Carlos: Practical Applications of the Works of Carlos Castaneda*, Sante Fe: Bear & Co., 1995.
116 Tomas, *The Promise of Power: Reflections on the Toltec Warriors' Dialogue from the Collected Works of Carlos Castaneda*, Charlottesville: Hampton Roads Publishing, 1995, and *Creative Victory: Reflections on the Process of Power from the Collected Works of Carlos Castaneda*, York Beach: Samual Weiser, 1995.
117 Richard de Mille, *Castaneda's Journey: The Power and the Allegory*, Santa Barbara: Capra Press, 1976, and *The Don Juan Papers: Further Castaneda Controversies*, Belmont: Wadsworth, 1980.
118 *Ibid.* (1990 edn), 120.
119 *Ibid.* (1990 edn), 130.
120 Michael J. Harner, "The sound of rushing water," in Michael J. Harner (ed.) *Hallucinogens and Shamanism*, Oxford: Oxford University Press, 1973 (2nd edn 1979), 16. See also Harner's monograph on the Jívaro, *The Jívaro: People of the Sacred Waterfalls*, New York: Doubleday/Natural History Press, 1972. Concerning his first vision, see his book *The Way of the Shaman*, San Francisco: Harper & Row, 1980, 4–5.
121 *Ibid.*, 19.
122 *Ibid.*, xvii.
123 Newsletter of the Foundation, vol. 4(1) (1991): 2.
124 P.C. Johnson, "Shamanism from Ecuador to Chicago: a case study in New Age ritual appropriation," *Religion. An International Journal* 25 (1995): 163–78, 171.
125 *Ibid.*, 172.

126 *Ibid.*, 173.
127 For commentary on the relationship between the Hopi Indians and New Agers, see Geertz, *The Invention of Prophecy*, 288ff., and "Contemporary problems in the study of Native American religions with special reference to the Hopis," in Lee Irwin (ed.) *Contemporary Issues in the Study of Native American Religion*, Lincoln: University of Nebraska Press, 1996/97, 393–414.
128 J. Gordon Melton, Jerome Clark and Aidan A. Kelly, *New Age Almanac*, New York: Visible Ink Press, 1991, 438–40. See Sun Bear and Wabun Wind, *Black Dawn, Bright Day: Indian Prophecies for the Millennium that Reveal the Fate of the Earth*, New York: Simon & Schuster, 1992. See also the discussion in Albanese, *Nature Religion in America*, 156ff. (concerning threats of violence, see 162).
129 Indiana University Press is a good example of this. In publishing Felicitas D. Goodman's *Where the Spirits Ride the Wind: Trance Journeys and Other Ecstatic Experiences* (1990), it has definitely left the academic field. Stanley Krippner's claim on the back cover of Goodman's book, that she "has opened up a new area of study for the social sciences, as well as utilizing new methods of scientific study of human behavior and experience," reminds us of the Castaneda situation. See my review, "Archaic ontology and white shamanism," *Religion. An International Journal* 23 (1993): 369–72.
130 See, for example, Donald Joralemon, "The selling of the shaman and the problem of informant legitimacy," *Journal of Anthropological Research* 46(2) (1990): 105–18, and Catharine Albanese.
131 De Mille, *The Don Juan Papers* (1990 edn), vi.
132 Allan Bloom, *The Closing of the American Mind: How Higher Education Has Failed Democracy and Impoverished the Souls of Today's Students*, New York: Simon & Schuster, 1987. See an analysis of his mission in Hughes and Allen, *Illusions of Innocence*, 226ff.
133 Charlene Spretnak, *Spiritual Dimensions of Green Politics*, Santa Fe: Bear & Co., 1986. See the discussion in Albanese, *Nature Religion in America*, 171ff. See also Charlene Spretnak (ed.), *The Politics of Women's Spirituality: Essays on the Rise of Spiritual Power within the Feminist Movement*, Garden City: Doubleday (Anchor Books edn), 1982; Jonathan Porritt, *Seeing Green: The Politics of Ecology Explained*, New York: Basil Blackwell, 1985; and Margot Adler, *Drawing Down the Moon: Witches, Druids, Goddess-Worshippers, and Other Pagans in America Today*, rev. edn, Boston: Beacon, 1986.
134 Rubin, *"Primitivism" in 20th Century Art*, vol. I, 10.
135 Kirk Varnedoe, "Contemporary explorations," in Rubin, *"Primitivism" in 20th Century Art*, vol. II, 661–85.
136 *Ibid.*, 680–2. Among other works, Varnedoe mentions Beuys' "I like America and America likes me" from 1974, which consisted of a week-long performance at the René Block Gallery in New York during which Beuys lived in a cage with a live coyote "who was specially chosen as an animal of importance to American Indians but despised by the American white man."
137 *Ibid.*, 680.
138 See Lucy Lippard, "Feminism and prehistory," *Overlay: Contemporary Art and the Art of Prehistory*, New York: Pantheon, 1983, discussed in Varnedoe, "Contemporary explorations," 680.
139 See V. Vale and Andrea Juno's introduction to the special issue of *Re/Search* entitled *Modern Primitives: An Investigation of Contemporary Adornment & Ritual*, San Francisco: V/Search, 1989, 4–5.
140 *Ibid.*, 5.
141 The following information is taken from a condensation of interviews conducted by Vale and Juno with Fakir Musafar during 1982 to 1986, in *ibid.*, 6–24.
142 *Ibid.*, 13.
143 Varnedoe, "Contemporary explorations," 679.
144 Jürgen Habermas, *Theorie des kommunikativen Handelns*, vol. 1, 4th edn, Frankfurt am Main: Suhrkamp Verlag, 1987, 72–113 (English translation: *The Theory of Communicative Action*, vol. 1, Boston: Beacon, 1984, 43–74).
145 See the challenges raised in Amy Gutman (ed.), *Multiculturalism: Examining the Politics of Recognition*, Princeton: Princeton University Press, 1994, which contains papers by Habermas and other leading social theorists such as Charles Taylor.

146 See Emmanuel Chukwudi Eze, *Race and the Enlightenment: A Reader*, Cambridge, MA and Oxford: Blackwell, 1997.

147 Terry Eagleton, *The Illusions of Postmodernism*, Cambridge, MA and Oxford: Blackwell, 1996, 121.

148 *Ibid.*, 122–3.

149 Murray Bookchin, *Re-enchanting Humanity. A Defense of the Human Spirit against Antihumanism, Misanthropy, Mysticism, and Primitivism*, London and New York: Cassell, 1995, 33. Jonathan Z. Smith has expressed similar sympathies: "We cannot judge another culture by reference to ourselves [but] we may judge (both another and ourselves), if our criteria are universal 'rules of reason.' The anthropology of the last century, the study of religions in the academy, has contributed to making more difficult a naive, ethnocentric formulation of the 'rules of reason,' but this does not require that such 'rules' be denied, or suggest that we should slacken in our attempts to formulate them" (*Imagining Religion: From Babylon to Jonestown*, Chicago and London: University of Chicago Press, 1982, 105). See also his recent article "Nothing human is alien to me," *Religion. An International Journal* 26(4) (1996): 297–309.

Chapter 3

"Classify and conquer"

Friedrich Max Müller, indigenous religious traditions, and imperial comparative religion

David Chidester

> Let us take the old saying, *Divide et impera*, and translate it somewhat freely by "Classify and conquer."
>
> Friedrich Max Müller

As many historians have recognized, nineteenth-century science was frequently entangled with the requirements of empire. In a recent study of the geologist Robert Murchison, Robert A. Stafford has argued that the "mediation provided by natural science gave Europeans intellectual as well as actual authority over colonial environments by classifying and ultimately containing their awesome dimensions. This new level of control, linked with the technology representing its practical application, also conferred prestige on the metropolitan power as a civilizing force, helping legitimate imperial rule vis-à-vis subject races, domestic masses, and rival great powers." In its practical effects, imperial science was an important element in Europe's "grid of cultural, political, economic, and military domination" (Stafford 1989: 223). Like the natural sciences, the human sciences could also reinforce imperial authority, particularly through the power of representation. During the nineteenth century, the construction of an "English" or "British" national identity depended heavily upon the "colonization" of others through the process of representing them. As Philip Dodd has noted, "a great deal of the power of the dominant version of Englishness during the last years of the nineteenth century and the early years of the twentieth century lay in its ability to represent both itself to others and those others to themselves" (Dodd 1986: 2; see also Hind 1984; Chrisman 1990; Said 1993). Arguably, these imperial sciences were inherently ambiguous, because they contained not only an implicit sense of global power, but also the pervasive anxiety of powerlessness in the face of perceived degeneration at home and resistance to imperial authority abroad (Pick 1989: 237). Nevertheless, natural and human sciences during the nineteenth century were clearly engaged in the imperial project of maintaining, extending, and reinforcing empire.

In Britain, during the second half of the nineteenth century, comparative religion emerged as an important imperial enterprise, at the nexus of science and representation, that promised to extend the global scope of knowledge and power within the British Empire. This science of comparative religion addressed not only internal debates within a European tradition, but also the intellectual and practical dilemmas posed by increased exposure to "exotic" or "savage" forms of religious life from all over the world, but particularly those beliefs and practices encountered in the colonized regions of "exotic" India and "savage" South Africa. In developing this science of imperial comparative religion, the production of theory – the process of turning raw religious materials into intellectual manufactured goods – involved a complex process of intercultural mediation. In fact, relations between imperial center and colonized periphery resulted in a triple mediation in the formation of theory in imperial comparative religion. This process can be clearly identified in relations between British imperial comparative religion and a colonized periphery such as South Africa.

First, metropolitan theorists applied a comparative method, or what came to be known as "the" comparative method, that allowed them to use the raw religious materials from colonized peripheries to mediate between contemporary "savages" and the "primitive" ancestors of humanity (see Ackerknecht 1969; Bock 1966; Dundes 1986; Eggan 1965; Hammel 1980; Hoenigswald 1963). "Though the belief of African and Melanesian savages is more recent in point of time," as F. Max Müller observed in his foundational 1870 lectures on the science of religion, "it represents an earlier and far more primitive phase in point of growth, and is therefore as instructive to the student of religion as the study of uncultivated dialects has proved to the student of language" (1873: 25). As Edward B. Tylor put it, the "hypothetical primitive condition corresponds in a considerable degree to modern savage tribes, who, in spite of their difference and distance…seem remains of an early state of the human race at large" (1971 [1871]: I, 16). Whatever their differences, metropolitan theorists, such as Max Müller, Tylor, John Lubbock, Herbert Spencer, Andrew Lang, W. Robertson Smith, and James Frazer, deployed a comparative method that inferred characteristics of the "primitive" ancestors of humanity from reports about contemporary "savages" living on the colonized peripheries of empire.

Second, on the periphery, European observers, primarily travelers, missionaries, and colonial agents, mediated between the metropolitan theorists and indigenous peoples. As Max Müller often observed, he relied upon the authority of European scholars on the colonized periphery, experts such as Wilhelm Bleek, Henry Callaway, and Theophilus Hahn in South Africa, who had mastered the local languages, collected the myths, and documented the customs of "savages." By his own account, Max Müller corresponded with these local experts on the periphery and submitted his tentative work to them for correction. He referred to them as the "highest authorities" (1897: I, 33, 183). Other local experts in South Africa, such as the historian George McCall Theal, the author Dudley Kidd, and the missionary ethnographer H.A. Junod, developed similar relationships with metropolitan theorists (see Theal 1919; Kidd 1904; Junod 1927).

However, the informants employed by the local experts were themselves engaged in a third mediation between indigenous tradition and the force of European colonization. Comparative religionists in their own right, many of these African informants can be identified – William Ngidi, Mpengula Mbande, Qing, Spoon, Mboza, Tobane, Mankhelu – but many others remain nameless translators, or converts at remote mission stations, or even prisoners at Cape Town's Breakwater Prison (see Harries 1981; Deacon 1986). Nevertheless, they acted as important intercultural mediators in the formation of theory in comparative religion. As a result of their own ambivalent position, often as recent Christian converts, these informants mediated the contradictions of the colonial context in ways that in turn colonized the production of theory in the science of comparative religion.

This triple mediation mixed and merged in complex ways in the formation of imperial comparative religion. Where indigenous informants recorded religious arguments and tensions, changes and innovations, confusions and contradictions, or often their own Christian critiques of indigenous religion, the local experts on the periphery distilled a system, a distinct, coherent, and functional religious system. When their reports about that local system got to the metropolitan center, however, imperial theorists treated their data as unmediated raw materials for reconstructing the origin and development of religion in a linear progression from primitive to civilized. In most cases, this complex, contradictory mediation became thoroughly and perhaps intentionally obscured in the process of theoretical production. Although clearly dependent upon colonization, the theorists of imperial comparative religion consistently erased any traces of that dependence by developing theories about the prehistoric rather than the historical situation of empire in which they were operating. However, at least one theorist, Friedrich Max Müller, occasionally allowed the traces to show.

England, India, and South Africa

During the last year of his life, Friedrich Max Müller (1823–1900), the eminent Indologist, philologist, mythologist, and founder of the modern science of comparative religion, was preoccupied with the South African War (1899–1902). As England sent imperial troops against the Boer republics of the Transvaal and Orange Free State, Max Müller, weakened by illness, wrote essays on the religions of China, dictated his autobiography, and worried about the imperial situation in South Africa. "To the end he enjoyed being read to," his wife recalled, "and took keen interest in the newspapers, and all that concerned the war in South Africa" (Max Müller 1902: II, 419). Max Müller's interest in this imperial conflict resulted in the last of his publications to appear before his death, a pamphlet, *The Question of Right between England and the Transvaal*, which was printed and widely distributed by the Imperial South African Association. Drawing together in translation a series of essays that had originally appeared between February and April 1900 in the *Deutsche Revue*, this pamphlet was a lively defense of England's imperial sovereignty over South Africa. England's claim, Max Müller argued, was based not on greed for land and gold, but on treaties signed at the time of the Congress of Vienna in 1814 that ensured English suzerainty over all of South Africa. He recalled that England's right over the entire region had been demonstrated by the emancipation of slaves in 1834, the annexation of the Orange River State in 1848, the Sand River Convention of 1852, and the granting of conditional independence to the Transvaal Republic in 1881. That history, Max Müller contended, demonstrated England's legal right. By contrast, Boer claims, which could be based, for example, on the prior Dutch settlement of the Cape, were "prehistoric things which can have no legal value." Based on international law and historical precedent, therefore, Max Müller concluded that England held "supreme authority in South Africa" (1900: 5, 12). As a result, Boer resistance was nothing more than unjustified rebellion against legitimate imperial authority.

How do we account for this interest in South Africa? First, Max Müller indicated that he had a personal, family connection with South Africa by recalling that his cousin, Captain John Elliot, had been killed during the first Anglo-Boer War. The Boers, Max Müller argued, had remembered their martyrs, but "their own misdeeds, as the coldblooded murder of Captain John Elliot, a cousin of mine, have been forgotten, and never revenged" (1900: 6, 28). Second, in Germany, public sentiment about the South African War had been mobilized against England. As a German immigrant at Oxford for nearly half a century, Max Müller was concerned not merely with defending his adopted country, but also with maintaining close relations between England and Germany. Beginning his defense of England's right to South Africa with an appeal for Anglo-Saxon unity, he argued that England and Germany shared common interests because "blood is thicker than ink" (1900: 1). However, German response to Max Müller's intervention in the public debate about the South African War was overwhelmingly negative. As one German correspondent proposed, Max Müller should be hung on the gallows between British Foreign Minister Chamberlain and South African mining magnate Cecil Rhodes, "the thieves on the right-hand and the left!" (Max Müller 1900: 29). According to his biographer, this polemic cast a shadow over Max Müller's entire career, providing "one of the reasons why his name was forgotten in Germany" (Chaudhuri 1974: 254). Third, the immediate pretext of the war, England's defense of the rights of English foreigners, or "uitlanders," in the Transvaal Republic, might have resonated with Max Müller's own position in England as an "uitlander," a foreigner who had adopted a British imperial perspective on the world. From that perspective, England presided over a beneficent global order. If, as Max Müller asserted, Canada, Australia, New Zealand, the West Indies, West Africa, Malta, Gibraltar, Cyprus, and Ceylon were all satisfied with "this desperate yoke of English sovereignty, why not the Boers, who even enjoy greater privileges than they do?" (1900: 23). Significantly, Max Müller omitted India, the land of his greatest professional interest and expertise, from this inventory of contented submission to the political yoke of the British Empire. However, he did draw a pointed analogy by asserting that England "can retire from South Africa as little as from India" (1900: 11). These two imperial possessions, he suggested, were essential for maintaining the global power and authority of the British Empire.

As an academic expert on the language, myth, and religion of India, Max Müller's scholarly work often depended upon the resources and intersected with the interests of the British Empire. While his edition of the *Rig Veda* was made possible by the support of the East India Company, his academic authority was occasionally drawn upon to provide symbolic reinforcement for British rule over India. For example, he translated "God Save the Queen" into Sanskrit in 1882; he advocated the Ilbert Bill in 1884, which upheld the Proclamation of the Empress of India, because it demonstrated that "the Imperial word has been kept sacred"; and he provided a Sanskrit translation in 1890 for the erection of a statue to the Prince Consort in Windsor Park as part of the Women's Jubilee offering to the Queen (1902: II, 124–5, 157, 256–7). In response to the opening of the Colonial and Indian Exhibition in 1886, Max Müller remarked, "It is well that England should sometimes be reminded of her real greatness and her enormous responsibilities" (1902: II, 191).

Like the Colonial and Indian Exhibition, the South African War was also an occasion for reminding England of its imperial power, rights, and responsibilities. Therefore, at the end of his life, Max Müller assumed a dual mission in defending the English abroad and reminding the English at home of their global empire, an imperial order that was fixed on the twin poles of India and South Africa.

As his pamphlet on the South African War revealed, Max Müller had undertaken a fairly thorough reading of journalism, history, travel literature, and novels about South Africa. Anyone who had followed his academic career closely, however, would not have been surprised by this interest in the region. Max Müller had a long history of professional involvement with the study of South African language, myth, and religion. Although he could claim specialized expertise on the subject of India, his broader academic reputation was built on lectures, essays, and books that dealt with general comparative themes in the fields of philology, mythology, and the science of religion. In those fields, Max Müller often invoked South African evidence to draw comparative conclusions. His use of those materials revealed significant facets of what I am calling imperial comparative religion – its global scope, its mode of intellectual production, and the complex process of intercultural mediation that made it possible.

Classifying

The series of four lectures Max Müller delivered at the Royal Institution during February and March 1870 has often been regarded as the founding gesture of the comparative study of religion (see, for example, Sharpe 1986: 35). Defining religion broadly as "the faculty of apprehending the Infinite," Max Müller attempted to place the study of religion on a scientific foundation (1873: 20). A science of religion had to be based on comparison, since, as Max Müller insisted, "all higher knowledge is acquired by comparison, and rests on comparison" (1873: 12). In adopting a global scope for the science of religion, Max Müller argued that comparison had to be guided by classification. "Let us take the old saying, *Divide et impera*," he declared, "and translate it somewhat freely by 'Classify and conquer'" (1873: 122–3). More than merely a rhetorical flourish, this motto signaled Max Müller's imperial project, the promotion of a science of religion that generated global knowledge and power. In developing his imperial science, he dismissed several possible classifications, such as the distinctions between true and false, revealed and natural, national and individual, or polytheistic, dualistic, and monotheistic religions, on the grounds that they were not sufficiently scientific (1873: 122–43). Only a classification based on language, he argued, could provide a firm foundation for a science of religion. Accordingly, he classified the world of religion by reinstating his taxonomy of language – Aryan, Semitic, and Turanian – as the organizing principle of the global empire of religion. In Max Müller's taxonomy, each language family had developed distinctive religions, the Aryan (Hinduism, Buddhism, and Zoroastrianism), the Semitic (Judaism, Christianity, and Islam) and the Turanian (Confucianism and Taoism). "With these eight religions," Max Müller observed, "the library of the Sacred Books of the whole human race is complete" (1873: 106). However, with this global inventory of world religions, the science of religion had only just begun.

> But after we have collected this library of the sacred books of the world, with their indispensable commentaries, are we in possession of the requisite materials for studying the growth and decay of the religious convictions of mankind at large? Far from it. The largest portion of mankind, – ay, and some of the most valiant champions in the religious and intellectual struggles of the world, would be unrepresented in our theological library.
>
> (1873: 116)

Max Müller's concern for including religions without books in the science of religion mirrored his attention to spoken dialects in the science of comparative philology. As he observed in his 1862 lectures on the science of language, "Dialects which have never produced any literature at all, the jargons of savage tribes, the clicks of the Hottentots…are as important, nay for the solution of some of our problems, more important, than the poetry of Homer, or the prose of Cicero." Frequently, he complained that literacy shackled language, as its creativity and regeneration, its "continual combustion," was blocked by "literary interference" (1862: 23, 49). If religions without books were to be included in a science of global comparison, however, they could only be incorporated, ironically, if they were transformed into texts. Their spoken character had to be recorded and transcribed. A truly global science of religion, therefore, had to be engaged in the production of new sacred texts for the non-textual religions of the world.

The mode of intellectual production that generated new sacred texts for non-literate religions emerged as an international enterprise. Raw religious materials, which were contained in the reports of travelers, missionaries, and colonial administrators, were extracted, exported, and transformed into intellectual manufactured goods at metropolitan centers of theory production. As Max Müller acknowledged, missionaries, in particular, had provided useful accounts of religious beliefs and practices among "savages." Like many other metropolitan theorists, however, Max Müller frequently advocated a more thorough and extensive collection of these raw materials from the colonized peripheries of the British Empire. In 1870 Max Müller appealed to the Colonial Office to initiate a centralized plan of ethnographic collection. He repeated that request in 1872, noting that "accurate knowledge of really wild-grown and autochthonic forms of religion would be of the greatest advantage for a comparative study of religions, a branch of inquiry which will become more important with every year" (1902: II, 84). While the Colonial Office refused to dedicate resources for this project, Max Müller repeated his appeal yet again in 1874 and in 1880.

Even without official imperial support, Max Müller could nevertheless conclude that in the empire of religion there was "no lack of materials for the student of the Science of Religion" (1873: 101). But to obtain those materials Max Müller had to rely on reports from the periphery by local scholars, especially by the South African experts, Wilhelm Bleek, Henry Callaway, and Theophilus Hahn. In the process, however, as the colonial situation in which these "experts" worked influenced their research findings, many of the frontier conflicts and contradictions of South Africa were introduced into Max Müller's global science of imperial comparative religion.

When John William Colenso arrived in Natal to assume his responsibilities as Anglican Bishop in 1855, he was accompanied by the philologist Wilhelm Bleek and the priest Henry Callaway (see Guy 1983). Over the next decades, while Colenso scandalized British theology with his critical biblical scholarship, Bleek and Callaway became leading authorities on the indigenous religion of South Africa. Max Müller established and maintained fairly close contact with all three. In 1865 he described clerical attempts to censure or silence Colenso as "a disgrace to the nineteenth century." While in the midst of preparing his lectures on the science of religion in 1870, Max Müller defended Colenso in a letter to Dean Stanley, proposing that Colenso had merely demonstrated that "the Old Testament was not originally written in the language of the nineteenth century, but in old, heavy, poetical phraseology." In 1874, while Colenso was visiting Oxford as his guest, Max Müller again defended the bishop. "The time will come," Max Müller observed, "when they will thank Colenso for having shown that the Old Testament is a genuine old book, full of all the contradictions and impossibilities which we have a right to expect in old books" (1902: I, 307, 372–3, 469).

At the end of his life, as he reflected in his autobiography on the practical religion that he had learned from his mother, Max Müller noted that he "never was frightened or shaken by the critical writings of Strauss or Ewald, of Renan or Colenso" (1901: 294). Clearly, Max Müller's defense of Colenso indicated that he was conversant with one of the major religious controversies of the nineteenth century. Although he disagreed with Colenso's mathematical method, Max Müller nevertheless argued that the bishop had performed a service to the science of religion by demonstrating that the Bible was a poetic rather than a literal or scientific text. While Colenso contributed to his understanding of the religion of the book, the philologist Wilhelm Bleek and the priest Henry Callaway directly influenced Max Müller's theoretical work in the science of religion by providing access to indigenous religions without books.

Max Müller and Wilhelm Bleek

Sharing the same patron, the Prussian diplomat and scholar Baron Christian von Bunsen, Max Müller and Wilhelm Bleek had much in common. Both had been encouraged by Bunsen to study language as the key to ancient history, myth, and religion. Max Müller responded not only by developing principles of classification based on language, but also by proposing a linguistic theory of the origin of religious myth. Under the notorious phrase, the "disease of language," Max Müller argued that myth resulted from a primitive proclivity for transposing words for natural phenomena into supernatural persons. As he proposed in his first series of lectures on the science of language in 1861,

> Mythology, which was the bane of the ancient world, is in truth a disease of language. A myth means a word, but a word which, from being a name or an attribute, has been allowed to assume a more substantial existence. Most of the Greek, the Roman, the Indian, and other heathen gods are nothing but poetical names, which were gradually allowed to assume a divine personality never contemplated by their original inventors.
>
> (1862: 11)

In his second series of lectures on language, Max Müller reiterated this generative theory of myth. "The mischief begins when language forgets itself," he declared, "and makes us mistake the Word for the Thing, the Quality for the Substance, the *Nomen* for the *Numen*" (1864: 580).

In between these two series of lectures, however, Max Müller had received corroboration from South Africa that lent new substance and precision to his theoretical speculations about the linguistic origin of myth. "I received lately," Max Müller noted, "a Comparative Grammar of the South-African Languages, printed at the Cape, written by a most learned and ingenious scholar, Dr. Bleek" (1864: 11–12). In that comparative grammar, Wilhelm Bleek had classified the indigenous languages of South Africa into two major families, the "Hottentot" and the "Bantu." The "Hottentot" language was spoken by Khoikhoi people in the Cape, while the "Bantu" language family comprised Africans who would emerge from the nineteenth century under the designations Xhosa, Zulu, and Sotho-Tswana. Although he argued that the study of these languages promised to answer many questions in the science of language, replacing, he hoped, Oriental with African studies as the leading field in comparative philology, Bleek also stressed the importance of South African languages for the study of religion.

As Bleek found, these two families of language could be distinguished on the grounds that the "Hottentot" language organized nouns by grammatical gender while the "Bantu" languages did not. Accordingly, because they spoke a sex-denoting language that attributed gender to nouns, the "Hottentots" had developed a rich mythology that personified the moon and sun, the night and dawn, as supernatural beings. Therefore, this mythological personification of heavenly phenomena, or what Bleek called the sidereal religion of the "Hottentots," was generated by the grammatical structure of their language. By contrast, the "Bantu" languages, without grammatical gender, had not supported the personification of nouns upon which the development of myth depended. Instead of sidereal religion, the grammatical structure of the "Bantu" languages supported the emergence of an alternative type of religion, the worship of the dead. According to Bleek's theory, therefore, two original forms of religion – sidereal worship and ancestor worship – were derived from the two different grammatical structures which had been preserved in their most "primitive" forms among the indigenous peoples of South Africa.

When he gave his lectures on the science of religion in 1870, Max Müller invoked Bleek's findings as crucial evidence in support of a theory of religion that was based upon language. Indeed, as Max Müller quoted Bleek quoting Max Müller, he indicated the symbiotic relationship between their theoretical projects. As Max Müller explained,

> In order to guess with some hope of success at the original meaning of ancient tradi-tions, it is absolutely necessary that we should be familiar with the genius of the language in which such traditions took their origin. Languages, for example, which do not denote grammatical gender, will be free from many mythological stories which in Sanskrit, Greek, and Latin are inevitable. Dr. Bleek, the indefatigable student of African languages, has frequently dwelt on this fact. In the Preface to his Comparative Grammar of the South-African Languages, published in 1862, he says: "The forms of a language may be said to constitute in some degree the skeleton frame of the human mind whose thoughts they express…How dependent, for example, the highest prod-ucts of the human mind, the religious ideas and conceptions of even highly civilized nations, may be upon this manner of speaking has been shown by Max Müller, in his essay on Comparative Mythology (Oxford Essays, 1856). This will become more evident from our African researches."
>
> (1873: 54–5)

Not only did he confirm the premise that language held the key to religion, Bleek actu-ally advanced the theoretical work of Max Müller by broadening the base of relevant evidence. In South Africa, Bleek's "African researches" suggested a global classification of both language and religion into two general families, the sex-denoting languages, which included the "Hottentots," but also the Semitic and the Aryan, and the prefix-pronominal languages, which included the "Bantu," Negro, and Polynesian. Max Müller invoked Bleek's findings as confirmation of his own theory. He even deployed Bleek's researches in a polemical aside against Edward B. Tylor, who might have had interesting things to say about "savage" religion, "but, not admitting the identity of language and thought, he thinks that the simple anthropomorphic view is the fundamental principle of mythology, and that 'the disease of language' comes in at a later period only" (1873: 56, n1; see also Tylor 1866: 80). According to Max Müller, therefore, Bleek had convincingly demon-strated the linguistic origin of religion. Following Bleek, Max Müller concluded that "the religions of savages, too, will have to submit hereafter to the same treatment which we apply to the sacred traditions of the Semitic and Aryan nations." And, as Bleek had shown, "there is no solid foundation for the study of the religion of savages except the study of their languages" (1873: 56).

However, in certain respects, Bleek's researches actually undermined Max Müller's theoretical project. On the colonial periphery, Bleek found that Max Müller's global classification, his method of dividing and conquering the empire of religion, was inadequate. Instead of identifying three families, the Aryan, Semitic, and Turanian, Bleek found two that had emerged on the colonial frontier in South Africa, the "Hottentot" and the "Bantu." Reinscribing this colonial distinction in his theory of the origin of religion, Bleek found two originals represented by "Hottentot" sidereal worship and "Bantu" ancestor worship. In pushing this distinction further, however, Bleek argued that ancestor worship, practiced by the Xhosa, Zulu, and Sotho-Tswana people of South Africa, had preserved the original form of religion performed by "primitive" human beings before sex-denoting languages had "filled the sky with gods" (Bleek 1869: xv–xvi). Therefore, although language was certainly foundational, the "disease of language" that had generated mythic personifications occurred, according to Bleek, at a later period in human evolution.

In addition to his comparative grammar, Bleek compiled a book on Zulu religion, which, significantly in the light of the demand to produce new sacred texts for indigenous religions without books, arranged oral testimony into chapters and verses as if it represented a Zulu Bible (Bleek 1952 [1857]). Bleek also documented "Hottentot" folklore in his popular compendium *Reynard the Fox in South Africa* (1864), which played a significant role in theoretical debates over the historical diffusion or independent parallel development of myth, religion, and culture. Towards the end of his life, as he served as librarian for the collection of Cape Governor Sir George Grey, Bleek recorded the myths and customs of the "Bushmen," relying upon informants who were imprisoned in the Breakwater Prison at the Cape Town harbor (see Bleek 1873, 1875; Bleek and Lloyd 1911). By the 1870s, as the "Bushmen" appeared as the leading contenders for the title of "*Urmenschen*" in imperial comparative religion, they seemed to be actually disappearing. The "Bushmen," as Bleek lamented, were a "dying out race." As he struggled to preserve their language, myth, and religion, Bleek was also dying, adding urgency to his salvage ethnography. Max Müller indicated that he appreciated Bleek's dilemma:

> Dr. Bleek, the excellent librarian of Sir George Grey's Library at the Cape, who has devoted the whole of his life to the study of savage dialects and whose Comparative Grammar of the South African languages will hold its place by the side of Bopp's, Diez's, and Caldwell's Comparative Grammars, is most anxious that there should be a permanent linguistic and ethnological station established at the Cape...Dr. Bleek has lately been enabled to write down several volumes of traditional literature from the mouths of some Bushman prisoners, and he says, "my powers and my life are drawing to an end, and unless I have some young men to assist me, and carry on my work, much of what I have done will be lost." There is no time to be lost, and I trust, therefore, that my appeal will not be considered importunate by the present Colonial Minister.
>
> (1875: 360–61; 1881: II, 28)

When he republished this essay in 1881, Max Müller noted that Bleek had subsequently died in 1875, but that there was hope that a successor would be appointed. That successor as librarian of the Grey collection, the missionary, linguist, and ethnographer Theophilus Hahn, maintained the close link between Max Müller and South Africa. Hahn's major work on the religion of the "Hottentots," which Max Müller arranged to be published, showed the influence of the linguistic approach to the analysis of sidereal religion (Hahn 1881; see also Max Müller 1882). Therefore, through Theophilus Hahn, Max Müller was able to remain conversant with one side of Bleek's classification of religion.

The other side, which was represented by the "Bantu," or often simply by the Zulu, was developed by the researches of the priest, missionary, medical doctor, and ethnographer Henry Callaway, who emerged as the leading nineteenth-century authority on Zulu religion and, by extension, on all "savage" religion. Although situated on the colonial periphery, Callaway, like Bleek, acted as a mediator in the formation of theory within the science of imperial comparative religion.

Max Müller and Henry Callaway

The Anglican priest Henry Callaway provided the most important link between the imperial theorists of comparative religion and southern Africa. In addition to his work as priest, missionary, and medical doctor, Callaway took an active interest in comparative religion and anthropology (see Callaway 1866–68, 1868–70, 1872, 1874, 1878, 1880a, 1880b). From his mission station at Springvale, near Pietermaritzburg, Callaway engaged in researches on Zulu religion that enabled him to know the Zulu religious system better than the Zulu did, because, as he claimed in 1862, he had "entered far deeper, than the natives themselves could penetrate" (Callaway to Bishop Gray, 8 July 1862, 9.10.c.6, South African Library Manuscripts). As a local expert, Callaway mediated between Zulu indigenous religious tradition in South Africa and theorists in England. He served as local secretary in Natal of the Anthropological Society in London and corresponded with Max Müller and Edward B. Tylor (Benham 1896: 215, 239, 341). However, it was Callaway's major text, *The Religious System of the Amazulu* (1868–70), that marked his real contribution, because this collection of oral testimony, arranged in two columns, with the original Zulu juxtaposed with an English translation, seemed to provide direct access to a "savage" religion from the mouths of the "savages" themselves.

In his 1870 lectures, Max Müller used Callaway's findings to consider "the old controversy whether there are any tribes of human beings entirely devoid of religious sentiment." Although Zulus had been accused of lacking any trace of religion, Callaway, by learning their language and gaining their confidence, had extracted a coherent account of the Zulu religious system. In Max Müller's summary,

> They all believe, first of all, in an ancestor of each particular family and clan, and also in a common ancestor of the whole race of man. That ancestor is generally called the Unkulunkulu, which means the great-great-grandfather. When pressed as to the father of this great-great-grandfather the general answer of the Zulus seems to be that he "branched off from a reed," or that he "came from a bed of reeds."

In Sanskrit, Max Müller observed, the term *parvan*, a knot or joint in a cane, could signify a family, while the term *vamsa*, a reed or bamboo cane, could refer to a human race or lineage. Involving a similar metaphorical extension, the Zulu term for reed, *uhlanga*, could indicate the original source of all life. However, through the "disease of language," the term "was personified, and thus became the mythical ancestor of the human race" (1873: 61).

Drawing on Callaway's evidence, Max Müller could support his linguistic theory of the origin of myth. However, Henry Callaway's account of a Zulu religious system was entangled in the local conditions of a specific colonial frontier on at least three counts. First, Callaway framed his research agenda in terms of what he saw as the needs of the Christian mission. In this regard, he conducted his research on Zulu religion in the context of a theological polemic against Bishop Colenso. On theological grounds, Callaway argued that Colenso's adoption of the God-name *uNkulunkulu* was inappropriate for a frontier mission that had to distinguish itself from a surrounding heathendom. Accordingly, Callaway discovered, against the findings of both Colenso and Bleek, that *uNkulunkulu* was understood by Zulus not as God, but as their original ancestor.

Second, Callaway collected evidence for this conclusion primarily from informants who had sought refuge at his mission station in Springvale. Like the residents of other Christian missions, these informants were social outcasts or refugees from African communities (Etherington 1987: 80; 1978: 68, 95, 102). Furthermore, since they came from different regions that ranged from the remote northern Zulu territory to the eastern Cape, Callaway's informants had undergone different experiences of the expanding colonial frontier. As a result, instead of holding a single, coherent Zulu religious system, Callaway's informants asserted a spectrum of religious positions that can be correlated with varying degrees of colonial contact. At least seven different religious positions can be distilled from the oral testimony Callaway collected. Located in the colonial situation, Zulu religious statements can be correlated with the advance of the mission and administration, whereby, for example, it can be said that relatively intact political groupings to the north regarded *uNkulunkulu* as the ancestor of their particular tribes, political groupings broken or displaced by colonial warfare redefined *uNkulunkulu* as the original ancestor of all human beings, and Zulus in conversation with the mission had learned a new theological discourse in which *uNkulunkulu* could be understood as a supreme being.

Third, positioned at the center of this colonial argument, Callaway's principal informant and assistant, the convert, catechist, and eventually deacon, Mpengula Mbande, actually authored *The Religious System of the Amazulu*. Although Callaway transcribed and edited the volume, providing footnotes and occasional commentary, the majority of the text appeared in the words of Mbande, reflecting, at many points, Mbande's own ambiguous position on the colonial frontier as a recent Christian convert. Mediating between the colonial mission and traditional African society, Mpengula Mbande's ambivalent personal position defined the dominant perspective on Zulu religion that emerged in Henry Callaway's *The Religious System of the Amazulu*. As a Christian, however, Mbande mediated intercultural relations in that colonial situation by advancing his own scathing Christian critique of indigenous Zulu religion, insisting, at one point, that whatever African traditionalists said about religion "has no point; it is altogether blunt" (Callaway 1868–70: 22). Nevertheless, Mbande's account became the standard version of an indigenous Zulu religious system.

In one of his most important contributions to *The Religious System of the Amazulu*, Mpengula Mbande related the "account which black men give white men of their origin." According to this creation myth, black men emerged first from the *uhlanga*, the place of the origin of all nations, coming out, however, with only a few things. They emerged with some cattle, corn, spears, and picks for digging the earth. Arrogantly, with their few possessions, the black men thought that they possessed all things. When the white men emerged, however, they came out with ox-drawn wagons, bearing abundant goods, and able to traverse great distances. By displaying this new, unexpected use for cattle, the whites demonstrated a superior wisdom that had been drawn from the *uhlanga*. In relation to the power and possessions of white men, black men recognized that they were defenseless. As Mbande explained,

We saw that, in fact, we black men came out without a single thing; we came out naked; we left everything behind, because we came out first. But as for the white men, we saw that they scraped out the last bit of wisdom; for there is every thing, which is too much for us, they know; they know all things which we do not know; we saw that we came out in a hurry; but they waited for all things, that they might not leave any behind. So in truth they came out with them. Therefore, we honour them, saying, "It is they who came out possessed of all things from the great Spirit; it is they who came out possessed of all goodness; we came out possessed with the folly of utter ignorance." Now it is as if they were becoming our fathers, for they come to us possessed of all things. Now they tell us all things, which we too might have known had we waited; it is because we did not wait that we are now children in comparison with them.

Therefore, Mpengula Mbande concluded, Europeans had not achieved victory over Africans by their superior force of arms. Rather, their wisdom had conquered. According to Mbande, European colonizers had been "victorious by sitting still." They had not required military force. The wisdom, wealth, and virtue that whites had drawn from the *uhlanga* were sufficient to overpower the black people, who reflected among themselves, as Mbande reported, that "these men who can do such things, it is not proper that we should think of contending with them, as if because their works conquer us, they would conquer us by weapons" (Callaway 1868–70: 79–80).

In this mythic account, therefore, Mpengula Mbande recorded an indigenous religious rationale for submission to the colonial government and its Christian mission. Obviously, this myth was not some primordial Zulu cosmogony. It was a critical reflection on the contemporary Zulu colonial situation. In Mbande's account, this story was the relevant creation myth in the living religious system of the Zulus. In Max Müller's handling of this myth, as we recall, *uhlanga*, the original source of all life, illustrated the "disease of language" through which the term "reed," or "bed of reeds," was "personified, and thus became the mythical ancestor of the human race." However, for Mbande, the primordium was clearly located in the colonial situation. Accordingly, Zulu religion revealed its most dynamic, creative character not in trying to recover a forgotten past, but in the struggle to make sense out of the violent oppositions of the colonial present.

Rather than a single, coherent Zulu religious system, therefore, *The Religious System of the Amazulu* contained an intercultural argument, orchestrated around Mpengula Mbande's Christian critique, that displayed the religious tensions and contradictions of the colonial situation in Natal. Accordingly, this text provided an unstable foundation for theory building in the science of imperial comparative religion. By the 1890s, Max Müller had to confront the instability of that foundation directly. Although still recognized as the greatest authority on Zulu religion, and, by extension, on "savage" religion in general, Henry Callaway was challenged by alternative reports from Natal. Max Müller noted in 1897 that "we now receive from Zululand itself an account of Unkulunkulu from the hand, as it would seem, of a native, very different from that given by Bishop Callaway." This account, published in the periodical *Inkanyiso Yase Natal*, not only contradicted Callaway's version by identifying *uNkulunkulu* as a sky god, but also by claiming that the biblical stories – Adam and Eve, the Flood, the story of Joseph – were all part of indigenous Zulu tradition. "If our Zulu informant can say that Bishop Callaway 'got bogged in a philosophical mess,'" Max Müller lamented, "what would he say of us if attempting to build on such boggy foundations tall structures of mythological philosophy?" Max

Müller's concern pointed to a crisis in imperial comparative religion. "If we can no longer quote Callaway on Zulus, or Hahn on Hottentots," he complained, "whom shall we quote?" (1897: I, 204–5).

This dilemma was inherent in the triple mediation that had created the conditions of possibility for an imperial comparative religion. Max Müller's theoretical mediation between colonized "savages" and the original "primitives" of humanity depended upon quoting Henry Callaway, while Callaway's mediation between the colonized periphery of South Africa and the metropolitan centers of theory production in Europe depended upon quoting Mpengula Mbande. In the colonial context of Natal, however, Mbande was faced with his own problem of mediation, a problem he addressed, among other ways, in the idiom of religious myth. Although he certainly quoted elements of a traditional religious heritage, Mbande reconfigured those traditional resources in response to the colonial present, producing, perhaps not without some measure of irony, the original myth "which black men give white men of their origin." Mbande was celebrated in missionary literature as "an educated, intelligent, Christian native" (SPCK 1875: 29). He was proclaimed as a "Zulu philosopher" (Schneider 1891: 66). However, in the missionary agenda, Mbande's account was valued because it exposed the "degradation" of indigenous African religion. As Thomas B. Jenkinson observed, "the account given by the late Native Deacon Umpengula of the state of the native mind on the subject of their ancestor worship and degraded state is very good" (1882: 28). In London, as interreligious conflicts on the frontier were absorbed into the emerging science of comparative religion, Mpengula Mbande's mythic account became authoritative. However, in the earliest book-length overview of African traditional religion, when Mbande's myth was quoted it was found to be "valuable only as showing the workings of the native mind when brought into contact with the superiority of Europeans" (Rowley 1877: 43). In these blatantly racist terms, therefore, Mbande was incorporated at the center of empire into an imperial comparative religion.

As middlemen in this exchange, Wilhelm Bleek and Henry Callaway simultaneously enabled and undermined Max Müller's science of religion. By providing access to religions without books, they made it possible for Max Müller to fashion a global science of religion that included indigenous religious traditions. At the same time, however, because they incorporated local colonial conflicts and contradictions into their research findings, Bleek and Callaway provided extremely unstable foundations for global theory building. By the end of his career, Max Müller had been forced to recognize this inherent instability in the construction of theory within imperial comparative religion. Perhaps Max Müller's vigorous defense of England's imperial power in his last publication to appear before his death should be read as a compensatory gesture in response to a growing uneasiness about the foundations of imperial knowledge in the global science of comparative religion. With the failure of knowledge, Max Müller had to settle for an assertion of power.

Conquering

The preceding discussion calls for a reassessment of the history of the academic study of religion. Obviously, nineteenth-century comparative religion was fed by many intellectual streams. The philology of Max Müller, the evolutionary anthropology of Tylor, the folk-lore studies of Lang, and the nascent support provided by Frazer for the practice of local ethnography all contributed to the formation of a comparative study of religion. Despite their internal disagreements, these scholars collaborated in the production of an imperial comparative religion, contributing, in different ways, to its global scope, its centralized intellectual production, and the complex relations of intercultural mediation that linked the imperial center with the colonized peripheries of empire.

Central to any reassessment of the history of comparative religion is the question of the relation between knowledge and power. Although they could be regarded, for the most part, as liberal imperialists, the theorists of imperial comparative religion were not obviously in positions of political power in Britain. Max Müller, for example, might have corresponded regularly with Gladstone, but he had no direct influence on imperial policy, even failing to interest the Colonial Office in supporting the collection of ethnographic data. Nevertheless, Max Müller operated at the symbolic nexus of knowledge and power that made the Empire a reality. Present at the opening by Queen Victoria of the Colonial and Indian Exhibition in 1886, Max Müller reflected on the vast global power represented by that imperial ceremony:

> I feel grateful that I went and witnessed what was not a mere festivity, but an historical event. Behind the gorgeous throne and the simple dignified presence of the Queen, one saw a whole Empire stretching out, such as the world has never known, and an accumulation of thought, labour, power, and wealth that could be matched nowhere else. It is well that England should sometimes be reminded of her real greatness and her enormous responsibilities.
>
> (1902: II, 191)

Max Müller's testimony hinted at the location of power in imperial comparative religion. First, comparative religion was a science of symbols that could distinguish between mere ceremonies and real historical events. As we recall, in Max Müller's pamphlet on the South African War, England's sovereignty was based on real historical events; Boer claims were allegedly based on "prehistoric things which can have no legal value" (1900: 5). Imperial ritual, Max Müller suggested, was entirely different from such "prehistoric things." Since the Empire relied heavily upon new imperial symbols, myths, and rituals – those "invented traditions" that signified British power at both the center and periphery of empire – imperial comparative religion could certify their reality in and through the process of disempowering the alternative symbolic forms of the "exotic" or "savage" colonized. While the colonized acted out "mere festivity," the "disease of language," "primordial stupidity," "superstitious survivals," or a "magical mentality," British imperial ceremony enacted a real historical event.

Second, as the Queen's throne displayed the entire Empire, imperial comparative religion also focused and condensed its vast global scope. In nineteenth-century comparative religion, "one saw a whole Empire stretching out, such as the world has never known." For Max Müller, and other imperial theorists, the empire of religion stretched not only from the center to the periphery, but also from the present to the past, even extending to the origin of humanity. These two global extensions, in space and time, were necessarily related, as imperial theorists mediated between the colonized "savages" and the original "primitives" of the human race. However, the time and space of imperial comparative religion also configured global power. "To be able to exercise intellectual power over the problematic mythology of the past," as Steven Connor has observed, "was a promise of being able to exercise the same power over the subject races who were the producers of such mythologies" (1988: 221). Like imperial exhibitions, imperial comparative religion collected, condensed, and displayed the Empire as a sign and signal of its global scope and domination.

Third, as Max Müller testified, imperial power was the power of centralized accumulation, not only the gathering of wealth and the exploitation of labor for the benefit of the metropolitan center, but also the accumulation of thought "that could be matched nowhere else." In the practice of imperial comparative religion, this accumulation of thought, the concentration of ways of thinking about others, was, by unspoken definition, as a matter of implicit principle, incomparable, a kind of knowledge "that could be matched nowhere else." It could compare, without being compared. As we have seen, relations between center and periphery in imperial comparative religion, the complex triple mediation that made it possible, were asymmetrical relations of power. In his list of ethnographic questions about uncivilized or semi-civilized peoples for "men on the spot," James Frazer posed the enquiry, "Do they eat everything?" (1888: 433). William Ngidi, Bishop Colenso's Zulu collaborator, had his own response to that question. As recorded by Max Müller's disciple, G.W. Cox, William Ngidi observed, "I hope that now you know that the Zulus are set at loggerheads by the coming of white men, who want to eat up their land" (Cox 1888: II, 614). Comparing without being compared, eating without being eaten, imperial comparative religion accumulated knowledge from colonized lands.

Fourth, Max Müller celebrated the imperial pageantry because it was "well that England should sometimes be reminded of her real greatness and her enormous responsibilities." At the end of his life, defending England's sovereignty in southern Africa, Max Müller took the opportunity to again remind England of that greatness and responsibility by insisting that England "can retire from South Africa as little as from India" (1900: 11). As Max Müller suggested, these two imperial possessions, the twin poles of his academic work, were essential for maintaining the global power and authority of the British Empire. With power, however, also came responsibility. Max Müller, along with other imperial theorists, assumed that imperial rule was actually beneficial for the people under its domain. While Max Müller was defending the justice of England's cause in the South African War, E. Sidney Hartland drew up a memorandum, "On the imperfection of our knowledge of the black races of the Transvaal and the Orange River Colony," that he presented to the Anthropological Section of the British Association for the Advancement of Science in September 1900. "Our information on the customs, institutions, and beliefs of the native races of those countries is derived chiefly from fragmentary notices by missionaries, which are not to be implicitly trusted," Hartland observed. "An accurate study of the native customs, institutions, and beliefs was an urgent necessity both for missionaries and for purposes of government" (Hartland 1900: 22–3; see also Hartland 1901). In response, A.C. Haddon, who also had a long-standing interest in southern Africa, reminded Hartland that such a scientific study would be good not only for the Christian mission and colonial government, but also for the "natives" of the region. According to Haddon, "It was most important that we should take the present favorable opportunity to study and record the traditional laws and customs of the natives of the Orange River and Transvaal Colonies both for the sake of science and of the natives themselves" (Hartland 1900: 24). In the midst of the South African War, therefore, imperial comparative religion continued to remind the British Empire of both its greatness and its responsibilities.

Still, the question of power remains. If nineteenth-century comparative religion was fashioned at the intersection of academic discourse and imperial force, has the study of religion subsequently undergone a process of intellectual decolonization? Has it become self-critical of its own interests? Has it renounced the imperial privileges such as observation, representation, generalization, colonization, and control that made it possible? Here I think some progress has been made, even if the academic study of religion, in this regard, lags behind postcolonial developments in other disciplines within the human and social sciences. Even in such post-imperial or postcolonial initiatives, however, the problematic of power seems to remain intractable. On the one hand, renunciation appears as an option, as Edward Said, for example, has argued that a post-imperial scholarship "means not trying to rule others, not trying to classify them or put them in hierarchies, above all, not constantly reiterating how 'our' culture or country is number one" (1993: 408). On the other hand, utopian dreams are tempting, visions of a world, as David Spurr has noted, "in which the play of difference could range free of the structures of inequality" (1993: 201). Somewhere between renunciation and utopia, the one potentially paralyzing, the other practically impossible, comparative religion – as opening, as conversation, as interplay of difference, as the contrapuntal comparison of comparisons – might have a place in a post-imperial, postcolonial world.

References

Ackerknecht, Edwin, "On the comparative method in anthropology," in Robert F. Spencer (ed.) *Method and Perspective in Anthropology*, Gloucester, MA: Peter Smith, 1969, 117–25.

Benham, Marian S., *Henry Callaway M.D., D.D., First Bishop of Kaffraria: His Life History and Work: A Memoir*, London: Macmillan, 1896.

Bleek, W.H.I., "Researches into the relations between the Hottentots and Kafirs," *Cape Monthly Magazine* 1 (January–June), 1857, 199–208, 289–96.

——, *A Comparative Grammar of South African Languages. Part One*, London: Trübner, 1862.

——, *Reynard the Fox in South Africa; or Hottentot Fables and Tales*, London: Trübner, 1864.

——, *On the Origin of Language*, ed. Ernst Haeckel, trans. Thomas Davidson, New York: L.W. Schmidt, 1869.

——, "Scientific reasons for the study of the Bushman language," *Cape Monthly Magazine* (n.s.) 7, 1873, 149–53.

——, *A Brief Account of Bushman Folklore and Other Texts*, Cape Town: J.C. Juta, 1875.

——, *Zulu Legends*, ed. J.A. Engelbrecht, Pretoria: Van Schaik, 1952 [1857].

Bleek, W.H.I. and Lucy C. Lloyd, *Specimens of Bushman Folklore*, London: George Allen, 1911.

Bock, Kenneth E., "The comparative method of anthropology," *Comparative Studies in Society and History* 8, 1966, 269–80.

Callaway, Henry, *Nursery Tales, Traditions, and Histories of the Zulus*, 2 vols, Springvale: J.A. Blair and London: Trübner, 1866–68.

——, *The Religious System of the Amazulu*, Springvale: Springvale Mission, 1868–70 (reprinted Cape Town: Struik, 1970).

——, "On divination and analogous phenomena among the natives of Natal," *Proceedings of the Anthropological Institute* 1, 1872, 163–83.

——, *A Fragment on Comparative Religion*, Natal: Callaway, 1874.

——, "South African folk-lore," *Cape Monthly Magazine* 16(94) (February), 1878, 109–10.

——, "On the religious sentiment amongst the tribes of South Africa: lecture delivered at Kokstad," *Cape Monthly Magazine* (n.s.) 2(5), 1880a, 87–102.

——, "A fragment illustrative of religious ideas among the Kafirs," *Folklore* 2(4) (July), 1880b, 56–60.

Chaudhuri, Nirad C., *Scholar Extraordinary: The Life of Professor the Right Honourable Friedrich Max Müller, P.C.*, London: Chatto & Windus, 1974.

Chidester, David, *Savage Systems: Colonialism and Comparative Religion in Southern Africa*, Charlottesville: University Press of Virginia, 1996.

Chrisman, Laura, "The imperial unconscious? Representations of imperial discourse," *Critical Quarterly* 32(3), 1990, 36–58.

Connor, Steven, "Myth and meta-myth in Max Müller and Walter Pater," in J.B. Bullen (ed.) *The Sun is God: Painting, Literature, and Mythology in the Nineteenth Century*, Oxford: Clarendon Press, 1988.

Cox, G.W., *The Life of John William Colenso*, 2 vols, London: Macmillan, 1888.

Deacon, Janette, "'My place is the bitterpits': The home territory of Bleek and Lloyd's /Xam San Informants," *African Studies* 45, 1986, 135–55.

Dodd, Philip, "Englishness and the national culture," in Robert Colls and Philip Dodd (eds) *Englishness: Politics and Culture 1880–1920*, London: Croom Helm, 1986, 1–28.

Dundes, Alan, "The anthropologist and the comparative method in folklore," *Journal of Folklore Research* 23, 1986, 125–46.

Eggan, Fred, "Some reflections on comparative method in anthropology," in Melford E. Spiro (ed.) *Context and Meaning in Cultural Anthropology*, New York: The Free Press, 1965, 357–72.

Etherington, Norman, *Preachers, Peasants, and Politics in Southeast Africa, 1835–1880: African Christian Communities in Natal, Pondoland, and Zululand*, London: Royal Historical Society, 1978.

——, "Missionary doctors and African healers in mid-Victorian South Africa," *South African Historical Journal* 19, 1987, 77–91.

Frazer, J.G., "Questions on the manners, customs, religion, superstition, etc. of uncivilized or semi-civilized peoples," *The Journal of the Anthropological Institute* 18, 1888, 431–9.

Guy, Jeff, *The Heretic: A Study of the Life of John William Colenso*, Johannesburg: Ravan Press, 1983.

Hahn, Theophilus, *Tsuni-//Goam, the Supreme Being of the Khoi-khoi*, London: Trübner, 1881.

Hammel, E.A., "The comparative method in anthropological perspective," *Comparative Studies of Society and History* 22, 1980, 145–55.

Harries, Patrick, "The anthropologist as historian and liberal: H.-A. Junod and the Thonga," *Journal of Southern African Studies* 8(1), 1981, 37–50.

Hartland, E. Sidney, "On the imperfection of our knowledge of the black races of the Transvaal and the Orange River Colony," *Journal of the Royal Anthropological Institute of Great Britain and Ireland* 30 (n.s.) 3, 1900, 22–4.

——, "Some problems of early religion in the light of South African folklore," *Folklore* 12, 1901, 15–40.

Hind, Robert J., "'We have no colonies': similarities within the British imperial experience," *Comparative Studies in Society and History* 26, 1984, 3–35.

Hoenigswald, Henry M., "On the history of the comparative method," *Anthropological Linguistics* 5, 1963, 1–11.

Jenkinson, Thomas B., *Amazulu: The Zulus, their Past, History, Manners, Customs, and Language*, London: W.H. Allen & Co., 1882.

Junod, Henri A., *Life of a South African Tribe*, 2 vols, 2nd edn, London: Macmillan, 1927.

Kidd, Dudley, *The Essential Kafir*, London: Macmillan, 1904.

——, *Savage Childhood*, London: Macmillan, 1906.

Lang, Andrew, "South African religion," in *Magic and Religion*, London: Longmans, Green, and Co., 1901, 224–40.

Max Müller, F., "Comparative mythology," in *Oxford Essays*, London: John W. Parker, 1856.

——, *Lectures on the Science of Language*, 2nd edn, London: Longmans, Green, 1862.

——, *Lectures on the Science of Language: Second Series*, London: Longman, Green, Longman, Roberts, & Green, 1864.

——, *Introduction to the Science of Religion: Four Lectures delivered at the Royal Institution with Two Essays of False Analogies, and the Philosophy of Mythology*, London: Longmans, Green, 1873.

——, *Chips from a German Workshop*, vol. 4, London: Longmans, 1875.

——, *Selected Essays on Language, Mythology, and Religion*, 2 vols, London: Longmans, Green, 1881.

——, "Mythology among the Hottentots," *The Nineteenth Century*, January, 1882, 110–25.

——, *Contributions to the Science of Mythology*, London: Longmans, Green, 1897.

——, *The Question of Right between England and the Transvaal: Letters by the Right Hon. F. Max Müller with Rejoinders by Professor Theodore Mommsen*, London: Imperial South African Association, 1900.

——, *My Autobiography: A Fragment*, London: Longmans, Green, 1901.

——, *The Life and Letters of the Right Honourable Friedrich Max Müller*, ed. Georgina Grenfell Max Müller, 2 vols, London: Longmans, Green, 1902.

Pick, Daniel, *Faces of Degeneration: A European Disorder, c.1848–c.1918*, Cambridge: Cambridge University Press, 1989.

Rowley, Henry, *The Religion of the Africans*, London: W. Wells Gardner, 1877.

Said, Edward W., *Culture and Imperialism*, London: Chatto & Windus, 1993.

Schneider, Wilhelm, *Die Religion der afrikanischen Naturvölker*, Munster: Aschendorff, 1891.

Sharpe, Eric J., *Comparative Religion*, 2nd edn, LaSalle, IL: Open Court, 1986.

SPCK, *May, the Little Bush Girl*, London: Society for Promoting Christian Knowledge, 1875.

Spurr, David, *The Rhetoric of Empire: Colonial Discourse in Journalism, Travel Writing, and Imperial Administration*, Durham: Duke University Press, 1993.

Stafford, Robert A., *Scientist of Empire: Sir Roderick Murchison, Scientific Exploration, and Victorian Imperialism*, Cambridge: Cambridge University Press, 1989.

Theal, George McCall, *Ethnography and Condition of South Africa before A.D. 1505*, London: George Allen & Unwin, 1919.

Tylor, E.B., "The religion of savages," *Fortnightly Review* 6, 1866, 71–86.

——, *Primitive Culture*, London: John Murray, 1971 [1871].

Chapter 4

A postcolonial meaning of religion
Some reflections from the indigenous world

Charles H. Long

Where is the indigenous located?

I begin with two anecdotes: I am told on good authority that when Alexander the Great made his incursions into India in the third century BCE he was met by Buddhist monks who viewed him with an enquiring detachment. Instead of being in awe of his great army, they are reported to have asked him the following questions: "Who are you? Do you have a home? Why aren't you at home?" Perry Miller, in his classic *The Errand Into the Wilderness*, is careful to point out the two interrelated meanings of the notion of "errand." On the one hand, "errand" refers to a particular task that has been assumed or authorized, a task that must be accomplished. On the other hand, "errand" equally refers to the specific task that is to be accomplished.[1] The distinction is subtle, but for Miller, an essential truth about New England Puritanism is defined by this distinction. Is the "errand" the task itself or is it the process of fulfilling the task? Does the "errand" define the specificity of the task that is to be done?

I have begun with these anecdotes because they pose for me the problematic surrounding the term, "indigenous." On the one hand, "indigenous," from the Latin, means literally being born from within, which leads to the notion of being produced or living naturally in a particular region. In other words, "indigenous" refers to what, in a conventional sense, we define as home, whether that home is defined geographically, ethnically, or religiously.

This is a rather straightforward understanding of the notion of indigenous. Things are not, however, quite so simple, for the term is called forth not by those cultures and peoples who are referred to when we use the term. It is, rather, occasioned by those typified by Alexander the Great and their progenies, the conquerors and imperialists – the Romans, and modern Western culture, among others. The term indigenous is called forth within the structure of those who have chosen to understand the source of human value through the processes and practices of "not being at home."

Observe the awkwardness of certain terms used to designate indigenous peoples and cultures: for example, "pre-Columbian," "Native American," "traditional," "pre-colonial." In other words, all indigenous cultures must of necessity admit of the impingement of the "other" roving cultures upon them as a dimension of their identity. Thus, although the notion of the indigenous implies the identity and reality of a people prior to the impingement of the worlds of modernity, in point of fact the "indigenous" has little meaning apart from the colonial and imperial cultures in the modern period. I hope that the movement in linguistic usage from "primitive" to "indigenous" means that we are no longer speaking of an a priori romantic and exotic reality that reveals the "elementary forms of the religious and social life of humankind."

Time, religion, and contact

Sidney Mead, the American religious historian, had the following to say about the movement of European colonists and conquerors across the American landscape. In speaking of this movement, he said: "The quality of their hearts and spirits was formed in that crucible – and in a short time."[2] Mead's statement describes a general cultural ontological-cultural epistemology that is coincidental with a certain practice of the world – a world in movement, a world that understands its space as a place that is "not at home." In a similar fashion, Ian Watt points out with respect to *Robinson Crusoe* that "the hero has a home and family, and leaves them for the classic reason of *homo economicus* – that it is necessary to better his economic condition…Crusoe's 'original sin' is really the dynamic tendency of capitalism itself, whose aim is never merely to maintain the status quo, but to transform it incessantly."[3]

This specific understanding of time in *Robinson Crusoe* follows on from more general meanings of the temporality in Western culture. Henri Baudet's *Paradise on Earth* has the subtitle *Some Thoughts on European Images of Non-European Man.* Baudet spells out two basic and antithetical tendencies that define the ambiguity of the West regarding others and outsiders. One is political; here, the military, socio-economic, and missionary strategies loom large. These modes mark the concrete relationships that the West establishes with others.

The other tendency is that of the imagination; it is the domain of images and symbols formed of the indigenous cultures outside the West. These imaginative configurations are not derived from concrete relationships; they are not the result of observation, experience, or perceptible reality, but rather have their origin in a psychological urge. The intricate mixture of these two tendencies in the origin and formation of the West enables us to understand how, in the search for new lands – lost utopias and paradises – empirical lands and peoples are symbolized and brought within the political and imaginative orbit of the West.

In a related manner, Bernard McGrane, in *Beyond Anthropology,*[4] sets forth the constructions of the "other" that dominated the Renaissance, the Enlightenment, and the nineteenth century. For McGrane, the historical (contingency) of these models makes them conceivable not as counterparts to modern anthropology, still less as actual versions of the real others, but instead as discursive forms that are distinctive to epochs and epistemic order. In the Renaissance, the inhabitants of remote parts of the world are not monsters, as they had been in Pliny's *Natural History* and in the fringes of medieval maps. They are non-Christians and, more particularly, potential Christians of the kind sought by Columbus. In the early eighteenth century, according to McGrane, what became crucial was not religious lack but rather the ignorance of the "other." Anthropology did not exist – there was rather the negativity of a psychology of error and an epistemology of all the forms of untruth.

Johannes Fabian, in another turn around the same theme, devotes his *Time and the Other* to the pernicious methodological blindness of anthropology and ethnology that fails to take account of the fact that the anthropological fieldworker and the culture he/she studies exist within the same time/space continuum. What began as knowledge or an object of knowledge defined by distance now turns into an ideology of time as evolution or progressive history.

Karl Jaspers, in defining the axial age, has rightly rejected the identification of the center of human history with the beginnings of Christianity and its influence in world history. In so doing, he has equally rejected the notion that Christianity is destined to bring about the unity of humankind. Jaspers, however, has not rejected the notion that there is a center in history nor that humanity is destined to be unified. He found the original hint for his notion of the axial age in two previous thinkers, Lasaulx and Viktor von Strauss.

In locating the axial age within a certain historical period covering almost a millennium and expressed in several cultures, Jaspers posits the future unity of humanity upon a certain structural meaning of humanity that emerged in several cultures in different parts of the world during this fortuitous millennium. One summarizing statement regarding the axial age is stated as follows:

> What is now about this age, in all three areas of the world is that man becomes conscious of Being as a whole, of himself and his limitations. He experiences the terror of the world and his powerlessness. Face to face with the void he strives for liberation and redemption. By consciously recognizing his limits he sets himself the highest goals. He experiences absoluteness in the depths of selfhood and in the lucidity of transcendence.[5]

This is a highly metaphysical, if not a theological, statement regarding the nature of humanity and history. One might structure a discussion of it within the framework of metaphysics of history *à la* Hegel, Troeltsch, Toynbee, or Kroeber. It implies that there is a certain necessity in the order of the world that appears at a particular moment in history, and that this order ordains a destiny for the previous and subsequent history of the world. It is clear that such a statement, even if true, could emerge only from one of those cultures of the originative axial period. The statement further implies that cultures and historical periods excluded from the axial age or its subsequent influences must be defined negatively in relationship to the axial age.

He speaks, for example, of the general modification of humanity during this period as "spiritualization," a modification in which the unquestioned grasp on life is loosened, the calm of the polarities becomes the disquiet of Opposites[6] and antinomies; it is the time for the philosophers. It is the time when the specifically human in man appears.

I have problems with the evolutionary moral tone of Jaspers. There is no way to prove, apart from self-serving, the metaphysical, theological, or spiritual-moral evolution of humanity. It can, at best, be regarded as an insightful assertion. One may, however, affirm the meaning of the axial age without such presuppositions. I should like to affirm the fundamental meanings of Jaspers' position and see if it is possible for these concerns to be seen as general characteristics of the human in all times and places. What seems unique to the axial age is the specific historical situation presented at this time.[7]

An alternative position is possible on the basis of a work such as Paul Wheatley's *The Pivot of the Four Quarters*. In this work, Wheatley, as cultural-historical geographer, raises the issue within the framework of the "neolithic revolution" problem. In my opinion, this assumption provides a more solid basis for the axial age; it need not, however, substitute for the issue as put by Jaspers, but it cannot be avoided. One must ask the prior question about the nature of the kinds of societies we are dealing with during the axial age. How many of these kinds of societies are there and what are the demographics of these groups? Are they farmers or are they mercantilists, or both? What is the nature and character of trade, etc.? I am not playing the positivist game here. In Wheatley's work these questions are asked and answered with due regard for spiritual matters. Wheatley undertakes to analyze the religious and cultural meaning of "centeredness" in six cultures where we are able to document urban genesis – the beginnings of that mode of human habitation we call the city or the urban form.

In the first instance, he rejects the position of V. Gordon Childe and his Marxist-inspired theory of the "neolithic revolution," as enunciated in the aptly titled work *Man Makes Himself*. He rather sets forth an alternate theory, one already adumbrated by Thorkild Jacobsen in his Mesopotamian studies. The first urban communities are based upon a ceremonial center. The ceremonial center is the site of the revelation of sacrality; it sets forth the possibility for the effective use of space. One might say that this is the archetypal meaning of space as a human container. The ceremonial center allows for the "domestication" of space. The urban community may occupy the site of the ceremonial center or be founded at some distance from it; in any case, the ceremonial center is the power that generates the creation and sustenance of every other form of the space of the urban environment.

In all six of these centers of urban genesis, in the Ancient Near East, Asia, Africa, and Mesoamerica, similar processes are at work. A particular urban form identified with the ceremonial center becomes the locus of power and thus creates all the areas around it as peripheries, dependent upon the power of the center. The relationship between the center and the periphery fluctuates between the centrifugal and the centripetal dynamics of power. Power moves from the center to the periphery and then back to the center. Power is authenticated to the extent that it participates within the center, and all powers and meanings at the periphery must seek their legitimization through their participation in the center.

It is within this structure that the axial age civilizations appeared. Through the discovery of agriculture, the domestication of animals, and the intensification of the range, quantity, and the materials that formed the exchanges within these societies, new definitions and possibilities for the understanding of human existence were forced upon these cultures. To put it another way, they have increased the range and modes of dependencies necessary for the life of the human community. These dependencies brought about a situation not only for a new and specific form of human dependence upon the human, but also for the dependence of the human community upon that modality of life and experience that revealed the very possibility for the urban genesis itself. Thus, the sacred expressed in forms that undergird and sustain the urban mode with all of its exchanges, demographics, dependencies, and intensities.

At this point I should like to expand on the allusion I made in note 7 above to Eliade's notion of primitive ontology. Since the publication of Jaspers' work in 1949, the very stylization in which we make scholarly conversation about non-citied cultures has changed. We no longer ask the "how natives think" type of questions, nor do we presuppose a kind of non-rational or pre-logical mind. If, indeed, we think about issues of this sort at all, then they are thought of in terms of the structural meaning of human consciousness itself. In the works of Claude Lévi-Strauss, and even more so in works such as Marshall Sahlins' *Stone Age Economics*, we are able to discern a possibility for the meaning of spiritualization related to and emerging within the matrix of the materiality and sociality of the common life. Sahlins' work, inspired by the seminal thesis of Marcel Mauss's *Essai sur le don*, should cause us pause regarding the centrality of the meaning of the axial age and of human spirituality.

The notion of the axial age is an alternative to the crude Marxist "suddenlies" of V. Gordon Childe and for its overgeneralized metaphysical and conjectural history. One might say on a more evenhanded level that the axial age may be characterized as the first crisis of the citied traditions of the world. Insofar as these traditions were the latest and most innovative modes of human community since the beginnings of *Homo sapiens sapiens* on the face of the earth, this was a crisis involving the problematics of the domestication of the environment as well as the domestication of the human consciousness.

If we follow through on this notion, then there is no reason why we should not have included Islam and Mohammed as part of the axial age. Why worry about five hundred years or so if the structural principles are the same, especially since we are dealing with temporal quantities in one thousand-year units anyway? I say that the axial period witnessed the first and most severe crisis of the "citied" tradition. In one sense the structural orders and its center-periphery order worked. They worked and they were repeated. But through this repetition something new and revelatory was emerging within the very modality of the social order. Prior to the city traditions, human discoveries were always discoveries within the realm of the not-human (nature?). These discoveries, which were at the same time sacred revelations, enabled the human community to discover some aspect of their own being, simultaneously with and in a fashion analogous to the discovery of the "otherness" in the forms of nature.

With the establishment of the neolithic and the intensification of the dynamics of the urban form, the arena of the human being and the human community became the field of exploration. In other words, the consciousness as "wild" moves into the "fields" of the human as the non-domesticated realm of investigation. But such enquiry should not be equated with the task and vocation of the "philosopher" as the person of leisure. The task is forced upon various members of these communities because of the complex issues that are attendant on the intensification of the urban form. There is of course the classification of persons and groups in relationship to their labor. There is a distinction between those who are "native-born" and those who are foreign, for example, traders, prisoners-of-war, slaves, etc. The urban form, having made itself a center of an entire territory, can no longer order itself in terms of the intimacies of kinship and face-to-face relations, nor in terms of a "common language" in the cultural or empirical sense. This is the first and most severe situation of the meaning of heterogeneity as a characteristic of the urban form. I should rather see the meaning of the axial in these terms than in the way these things are talked about in Jaspers' metaphysical-theological language. But this is not just a biased preference; it allows me to set forth some notion of the meaning of the "primal" or the "primitive" in relationship to the meaning of the power, structure, and languages of the centers of urban genesis.

In all the centers of urban genesis there are cultural languages that make modulated distinctions between the privileged groups at or near the center and those on the peripheries, and those totally outside the peripheries. In other words, it is always from the centers of urban genesis that those outside these centers are defined and characterized. They must necessarily be regarded in this manner, for the project of the center must always express a universal and all-encompassing ideal; it must have a place for everything and everybody, and if fortune smiles, everything and everybody will be in their respective places.

For the most part, the traditions of all the centers of primary urban genesis have always attempted to define and conquer through military and cultural power all the other areas and arenas made possible through their configurations of power and sacrality. The latest expression of the normativity of this structure occurred in what we now call Western Europe, beginning in the late fifteenth century and extending into the present. This period witnessed the movement of the basic concerns of the human community from the Mediterranean to the world of the Atlantic rim, and from this origin to the entire globe. It is within this movement that the new recognition of the "primal" and the "primitive" must be noted. This last configuration of urban genesis carries some of the characteristics of the older axial age. But, unlike the axial age, it is more dependent ideologically, economically, and militarily upon the cultures at the periphery and even outside the periphery; as a matter of fact, this new axiality must of necessity express a fluidity of borders between centers and peripheries.

The new "primitives" and the "otherness" of the world

One cannot imagine the meaning of the modern "primitive" or "primal" as we have it in present-day usage apart from the modern world system. This system was well on its way by the middle of the seventeenth century, but its origin lies in that series of voyages commencing with the Portuguese explorations of the islands off the west coast of Africa and then of the coast of West Africa itself. This series of voyages reached their peak with Columbus's voyages to the New World; these voyages set the stage for the European conquest of the oceans of the world.

Through these voyages, European explorers and navigators were introduced to an entire new world of humanity. At the same time, the status of the identity of Western European humanity was at stake. It was in the crux of these discoveries of extra-European cultures that these peoples and their customs were epistemologically categorized within the perceptions of "otherness" and exotica. The early conquest and exploitation of the cultures of Mesoamerica by the Spanish were carried out through an ideology of exotica as "otherness" rather than in the terms of the "primitive."

It was only later in the nineteenth century that the notion of the "primitive" appeared as a scientific term of the anthropological sciences. The category appeared in the discourses of the human sciences devoted to the search for origins. Extant cultures of our world were made the analog for the conjectural history of the earliest human cultures. These cultures were looked upon as "survivals," as cultures immobilized in time, having failed to advance at the rhythms of the dynamic progress of the world. These areas of the world were characterized as being on the periphery of the centers of the new world order, which was located in the metropolitan centers of Western Europe and in the United States.

The centers of the new world system were in Europe; the peripheral areas in other parts of the world provided in one way or another "raw materials" that were then refined or traded through the intermediation of the centers of trade and mercantilism. There thus existed a necessary and causal relationship between the centers and the peripheries. The new world system did not, however, create a language that was capable of speaking of this "relationship" outside of purely economic, scientific objective, or sentimental terms. While related intensely within the structures of the new world system, these cultures were recreated in the languages of a distant and faraway past.

It may be that only in a crisis of this new world system will we be afforded the chance to rethink the meaning of those cultures and peoples who have been tragically caught up into the machinations of the nations and peoples who were the makers of the modern world system. It may be in a period (other than now) when the legitimating languages of the new world system (colonialism, imperialism, etc.) have lost their efficacy that we will have a chance to rethink the realities of those persons and cultures designated as "primitives" during the long period when their reception and recognition as humans was designated and compromised by their place in the economic and ideological meaning of the last vestiges of the axial age.

Vision of the vanquished: the human as heterogeneity[8]

The fact that there was this long-term relationship, which produced neither a language of reciprocity nor one expressing the dynamics of contact and relationship from the point of view of the representatives of the normative centers of power, was due to a cultural rather than a personal or individual predilection. It has its origins in the number of orientations and movements in the Western world. One might make a case for a certain kind of Calvinism that stressed an inwardness of piety as a mode of objective subjectivity. Or one might turn to the pervasive effects of the Cartesian Meditations as forming the basis for the meaning of a subjectivity that is capable of denying all "outside" meanings or things in the creation of consciousness. In any case, the modem world system generated a stylistics of the objectivity of consciousness that was able to deal with the ambiguities of the mercantilism of the new world system.

Such a stylization of thought could, on the one hand, move towards a universalism, as later expressed in Enlightenment theories of the human, while at the same time affirm the legitimacy of the mercantile enterprise with all of its exploitation of the cultures and peoples of the "primitive" cultures. I do not think that this is simply and only a matter of personal or cultural deceit; rather, it is part and parcel of the ambiguity of the very notion of "centeredness" or "axiality" when it defines the totality of the relationships between itself and others. In this sense, there probably never has been a true center; rather, in the language of J.Z. Smith, we have had, more often than not, "wobbling pivots."

It is precisely the meaning of the center as a "wobbling pivot" that finds its expression in those "primitive" or "primal" traditions of modernity. Forced willy-nilly into a new meaning of the axiality of the new world system, they have been forced to come to terms with the actuality of the relationship between themselves and the institutions of the new order in the world. By and large, their accounts of the last half of the millennium have not been considered. Nathan Wachtel states the issue clearly:

> For generations of western historians, Europe was both the centre and the standard by which the history of mankind could be measured. According to a simple, linear representation of human development, all societies were thought to pass through identical stages on the path to progress and civilization, with Europe as the most advanced model. In the onward march, non-European societies brought up the rear as examples of less civilized states. Such a view of history provided an ideological justification for Western expansion and world-wide hegemony.[9]

I should like at this point to refer to two modes of the meaning of spirituality that have come from the side of the "primal traditions." One of them, cargoism, represents the attempt on the part of the cultures of Melanesia to come to terms with the facts of contact and colonialism. The members of the cargo cult raise the fundamental issue of the relationship of their culture to the substantive meaning of Western culture, especially as this relationship is mediated through the ideology of Christianity on the one hand, and the commodities of the West on the other. What is most interesting about the cargo cult is the perception on the part of the Melanesians that the commodities of the Western world carry spiritual significance. It is the "spiritual" significance – that which Marcel Mauss refers to in his description of the *hau* or spirit of the gift among the Polynesians – that is adumbrated here. Whereas the Westerners had categorized their gift of spirit in terms of the "gift of the Christian gospel," the Melanesians saw their true gift related to the substantiality of the cargo/commodity.

Maurice Lienhardt, who had spent most of his adult life as a Protestant missionary among the Melanesians, returned to Melanesia for a visit after the end of the Second World War. He was very surprised when one of his old friends, who was a convert to Christianity, responded to his musings on the fact that the one thing the missionaries had brought to Melanesia was the meaning of "spirit." His old friend corrected him spontaneously and in a state of shock. He said: "You did not teach us spirit, you taught us the body!" In other words, it was a new meaning and mode of materiality that had been conveyed to them. The old friend told him that they already knew about the spirit before the coming of the missionaries.

What we might learn from cargoism is a new and profound meaning of the intricate relationship between spirituality and materiality. It is this meaning that has been lost within the cultural and ideological languages of the West. The reverse of this is the case in most cultures that had to undergo the creative conquest and ideological domination of the Western world. But this is not simply a task of putting together "body" and "mind." If taken seriously, it calls for a new way of talking about human constitution itself – a way that must be at least as serious as the Meditations of Descartes or the various commentaries on Calvin's *Institutes*.

The other issue arising from the study of "primal traditions" that I wish to discuss is that of the meaning of the "fetish," or "fetishisms." Since this term was introduced into Western cultural language by Charles de Brosses, it has become a subject of discourse for almost all the disciplines of the human sciences, as well as having its own meaning in popular culture. It was used as a foil for the evolutionary development of humankind by both Kant and Hegel, and, of course, its popular usage is probably due to the currency given to it by Freud and the psychoanalytical movement.

William Pietz has shown us that this term, if mined correctly, reveals a great deal about the interrelationship between the actual situations of the contact and the reciprocities that were being forged in the new world of mercantilism.

The first characteristic to be identified in the notion of the fetish is that of the fetish object's irreducible materiality.[10] The truth of the fetish resides in its status as a material embodiment; its truth is not that of the idol, for the idol's truth lies in its relation of iconic resemblance to some immaterial model or entity. This was the basis for the distinction between the *feitico* and the *idolo* in medieval Portuguese. For Charles de Brosses, who coined the term *fetichisme* in 1757, the fetish was essentially a material and terrestrial entity. Fetishism was thus to be distinguished from cults of celestial bodies (whose truth might be a sort of proto-deist intimation of the rational order of nature rather than the direct worship of natural bodies themselves). Secondly, and as equally important, is the theme of singularity and repetition. The fetish has an ordering power derived from its status as the fixation or inscription of a unique originating event that has brought together previous "heterogeneous" elements into a novel entity. But the heterogeneous components appropriated into an identity by a fetish are not only material elements. They are equally desires and beliefs and narrative structures establishing a practice that is fixed and fixated by the fetish, whose power is precisely the power to repeat its originating act of forging an identity of articulated relations between otherwise heterogeneous things.

There are two other themes related to the problem of the fetish in addition to its materiality, repetitive power, and singular fixation of heterogeneous elements: these are the themes of social value and personal individuality. The problem of the non-universality and connectedness of social value emerged in an intense form at the beginning of the European voyages to sub-Saharan Africa. Thus one of the Cadamostos, who sailed to Senegal under Portuguese charter in the late 1450s, was moved to write of the natives of Gambia: "Gold is much prized among them, in my opinion, more than by us, for they regard it as very precious; nevertheless they traded it very cheaply, taking in exchange articles of little value in our eyes."

Now, it is important to note that the situation from which emerged the accounts that led to the notion of fetishism are defined by the trade, commerce, contact, and intercourse between the communities on the coast of West Africa and the Europeans, mainly Portuguese traders. Pietz, in one section of his articles, defines this geographical situation as one of intense heterogeneity, even of anarchy. The inhabitants of these coastal regions were not simply members of the African communities that were located on the coast. They consisted of all sorts – Christians, Muslims, Africans, even Jews, and every admixture among and between them. We are reminded here of the same kinds of communities of brigands described by Fernand Braudel as inhabiting the north-west coasts of the African Mediterranean.

The problem of the fetish anticipates the meaning of the relationship of value to heterogeneity and the meaning of the constitution of the human consciousness within the structures of heterogeneity. Pietz implies quite strongly that it is through the discourse surrounding the fetish that the possibility of a movement from the Christian theological meaning of materiality to the modem world system meaning of materiality in terms of its situational value within the structure of a fluid market came about. What did not occur, however, was the accompanying meaning of human consciousness in terms of its possible heterogeneity of "doubleness."

> Fetish has always named the incomprehensible mystery of the power of material things to be collective social objects experienced by individuals as truly embodying determinate values of virtues, always as judged from a cross-cultural perspective of relative infinite degradations...Fetish discourse always posits this double consciousness of absorbed credulity. The site of this later disillusioned judgment by its very nature seems to represent a power of the ultimate degradation and by implication, of the radical creation of value. Because of this it seems to hold an illusory attractive power of its own; that of seeming to be the Archimedian point of man at last more open and cured of his obsessions, [Michael Leiris] the impossible home of a man without fetishes.[11]

Throughout this chapter I have argued by implication for a methodological approach that embodies a theory of practice. In so doing, I am attempting to situate the problem of "mind," or second-order reflection. I do not think that there is any such thing as "pure reason"; such a notion has heuristic but not absolute value. If, for example, I chose linguistics as a metaphor for my methodological approach, in the manner of a Claude Lévi-Strauss, it would not be structural linguistics but pidgin and creole linguistics – a linguistic theory that arises out of the history of colonialism and contact. In creole linguistics, we contemplate the absolute fact that humans possess language but that this language is acquired in contingent and heterogeneous situations. As one of the most brilliant creole linguists puts it, "Catastrophe is the rule, uniformitarianism is the law."[12]

Notes

1 Perry Miller, *The Errand Into the Wilderness*, The Academy Library, New York: Harper Torchbooks, 1964, *passim* Ch. 1.
2 Sidney E. Mead, *The Lively Experiment*, New York: Harper & Row, 1963, 11.
3 Quoted in Nicholas Thomas, *Colonialism's Culture*, Princeton: Princeton University Press, 1994, 5.
4 Bernard McGrane, *Beyond Anthropology*, New York: Columbia University Press, 1994, 51.
5 Karl Jaspers, *The Origin and Goal of History*, trans. Michael Bullock, Westport, CT: The Greenwood Press, 1976, 2.
6 *Ibid.*, 3.
7 It would be interesting to compare Jaspers' position with that of Mircea Eliade and his delineation of a "primitive ontology," as well as his presentation of the archaic as a corrective and reformist meaning for contemporary cultures. One must note that Eliade tended to conflate archaic and "traditional societies." Some of his traditional societies would coincide with some of Jaspers' axial age cultures.
8 The phrase "vision of the vanquished" is taken from the title of a book by Nathan Wachtel, *The Vision of the Vanquished: The Spanish Conquest of Peru Through Indian Eyes*, New York: Barnes & Noble, 1977.
9 Wachtel, *op. cit.*, p. 1.
10 I am indebted to William Pietz for the following articles: "The problem of the fetish I," *RES*, 9, (Spring 1985), pp. 5–7; "The problem of the fetish II: the origin of the fetish," *RES*, 13, (Spring 1987), pp. 23–46; and "The problem of the fetish IIIa: Bosman's Guinea and the enlightenment theory of fetishism," *RES*, 16, (Autumn 1988), pp. 105–24.
11 William Pietz, "The problem of the fetish," *RES*, 9, (Spring 1985), p. 15
12 Robert Nicolai, "Is Songay a creole language?," in Glenn G. Gilbert (ed.) *Pidgin and Creole Languages: Essays in Memory of John E. Reinecke*, Honolulu: University of Hawaii Press, 1987.

Chapter 5

Saami responses to Christianity
Resistance and change

Håkan Rydving

The religious situation in the Arctic and Sub-Arctic regions of Eurasia differs a great deal from people to people, between the Saami in the west and the Chukchi in the east. Some of the peoples have been Christian for centuries, while among others the indigenous religions have been alive in all secrecy throughout the decades of the Soviet era. Most of the religious functionaries were executed in the middle of the 1930s when the north – some twenty years after the Russian revolution of 1917 – was integrated into Stalin's empire. Only some aspects of the religions are known today to the peoples themselves. However, several of the indigenous religions of these peoples have been revitalized since the breakdown of the Soviet Union. Thus, bear ceremonials, sacrifices, and "shamanistic" rituals are today performed once again. In the Republic of Yakutia in Siberia, "shamanism" has even been proclaimed the official religion.

Among the Saami, the religious situation is different. The Saami, who today are a people of about 70,000 to 80,000 in number, living in Scandinavia, Finland, and the north-western part of Russia, have been Christians since the eighteenth century, following seven to eight hundred years of missionary propaganda. I am going to focus on the period between the late seventeenth and the first half of the eighteenth century, since that was a time of the most intense religious confrontation and change. I will, however, begin with a few examples of opinions about the Saami in European thought from the seventeenth century to the present.

On a copperplate engraving from the 1680s, the Saamis – or Lapps as they were called at that time – are presented as "the most remarkable people in Europe." Even if the engraving is typical of its time, this characteristic is anything but bound to the end of the seventeenth century. From the oldest written report from the early Middle Ages, the Saamis have been presented and looked upon as exotic and different, both by their Nordic neighbors and by the peoples of Central and Southern Europe. The predominant opinion was that the Saamis were sorcerers. A curious chapter in the still unwritten history of European ideas regarding the Saami was formed by the report of how the Protestant army used Saamis to enchant the soldiers on the Catholic side during the Thirty Years War at the beginning of the century. Although this was a rumor without any ground, it was presented repeatedly during the whole of the century.

Even during the following century, the Saamis were still regarded as sorcerers and as adorers of the devil. In England, Daniel Defoe published an imaginative biography of Duncan Campbell, a soothsayer Defoe, of course, furnished with a Saami mother. And in France, Voltaire linked in with similar lines of thought when the hero of his novel *Candide* gave money to "Lappish sorcerers" in order to secure a fair wind. It was no surprise that the Swedish botanist Carolus Linnaeus gained special popularity when he appeared in his Saami dress and with his Saami drum during his visits to academic institutions in Europe. But Saami sacred drums and sacrificial sites were burned and destroyed during the seventeenth and eighteenth centuries, and their sacred stones were taken away by collectors and placed in private homes and in museums during the nineteenth and twentieth centuries. During the late nineteenth century, the anatomists who wanted Saami skulls and bones for their collections did not hesitate to dig up old graves, assisted by local clergymen.

At the beginning of the new millennium, Saamis are still frequently identified with a distorted picture of their indigenous religious heritage. It happens when participants in incentive journeys encounter Saami culture through a person who is pretending to be a Saami. He or she paints his or her face in order to look dirty (as if that was a Saami characteristic!). He or she sings in a way that resembles a Saami chant, a *vuolle*, and then tells the participants their fortunes. It happens when Saamis in Scandinavian television series are described as persons who use drums in order to solve political questions. And, in the spirit of the New Age movement, courses on "shamanism" are given in Saami-land and pretend, in four or five days, to teach what the *noajdde*, the most important of the Saami ritual specialists, did in the sixteenth century.

There is almost no knowledge about Saami culture and history among the non-Saami majority of the Nordic countries. In the schools, very little – if anything – is taught. And the same is true for the universities. It is symptomatic that one of the latest Scandinavian introductory book on the history of religions, published in Denmark a few years ago, although it includes chapters on African, Native American, and indigenous Australian religions, does not say anything at all about the three non-Scandinavian indigenous religions of the Nordic countries. There is nothing about the indigenous religions of the Finns, the Saami, or the Inuit of Greenland. The further away the peoples who call themselves indigenous are, the more interesting they seem to be.

Following these introductory remarks, I will now return to the most intense period of religious confrontation and change, that of 1670–1750.[1] We are fortunate to have a great number of written sources from this period. Since missionaries and other foreigners wrote most of them, they can only be used as sources with the utmost caution and after extensive source criticism. But the material does include Saami voices and it gives us an uncommon opportunity to analyze a process of religious change at length. My examples have been taken from the Lule Saami.[2]

Drums and sacrificial sites: symbols of Saami resistance

Much of the religious confrontation between the Danish and Swedish authorities[3] and the Saami during the seventeenth and eighteenth centuries was centered on the Saami drums. In spite of the fact that most of the Saami were baptized and married (and were going to be buried) according to Christian ritual, in the middle of the seventeenth century many Saamis still used the traditional drums for various rituals. The role of the drums as symbols of Saami resistance is well attested to in the sources from this period. For many of the Saami, the drums represented their threatened culture, the resistance against the Christian claim to exclusiveness, and a striving to preserve traditional values, that is to say, "the good" that had to be saved. For the Christian authorities, on the other hand, the drums symbolized the explicit nucleus of the elusive Saami "paganism," that is to say, "the evil" that had to be annihilated. During the second half of the 1680s, the hunt for drums was intensified in Sweden. The penalties for possession and use were reinforced, and the Saami were exhorted to hand in the drums to the district courts. Drums were collected and burned or transported to Stockholm for storage. As a means of evading the decree, there is evidence, at least in some places, that newly made drums were handed over to the authorities, while the old, inherited ones were kept.

When drums were confiscated, the Saami were forced to deliver them to a person in authority,[4] but in order to destroy or profane sacrificial sites the missionary had to go to the place himself, something which could involve great hardship for anyone not used to traveling in mountainous country. In spite of this, the Norwegian missionaries especially were eager to search for sacrificial sites and destroy them. For example, one of the missionaries burned forty sacrificial altars during the Lent of 1722, and seventeen altars during the winter of 1726–27.

Among the missionaries, the opinion that punishments would deter people from "idolatry," "superstition," and "sorcery" – to mention but a few of the common designations used for non-Christian (or non-Lutheran) religion – was prevalent. However, this idea was only seldom made as explicit as among some missionaries in northernmost Norway, who were of the opinion that the Word of God had no effect on the Saami, and that therefore, as they state, "a good flogging is the most powerful means of conversion."[5] New ideas, influenced by the individualism of pietism and the rationalism of the philosophy of the Enlightenment, certainly spread to Scandinavia from Central Europe. But these ideas about how "pagans" were to be persuaded to become Christians only changed to a limited extent the methods used by the ecclesiastical and judicial authorities in Denmark–Norway and Sweden–Finland against what was left of the indigenous religion among the Saami. Both countries used punishments (torture, and, in some exceptional cases, capital punishment) as a means to coerce Saamis into abandoning the indigenous religion and into following Christian religious practices instead.

Despite the harsh treatment, a Saami resistance began to form itself. In different parts of Saami-land, and in different ways, *noajddes* and other Saamis tried to revitalize the indigenous religion so that it would better resist the pressure from the missionaries. Saamis who were exposed to propaganda and compulsion were exhorted to stand firm in their beliefs and not desert the customs of their ancestors.

Sacrileges and punishments were the concrete manifestations of the confrontations between the Christian national authorities and the Saami. However, the severe methods of the authorities were successful. The Saami were frightened into going to the churches and into following the regulations that had been drawn up – at least when they were in the proximity of a clergyman or someone else who could report them. As gradually more and more Saamis made common cause with the new religion and its representatives, it became increasingly difficult to keep drums and sacrifices secret from the clergy and the district courts. A consequence of this was that women and children, who were considered to be more inclined to disclose the indigenous religion, were kept away from the religious rituals of the men so that they would not have anything to reveal. A way of escaping church activities was to stay for longer periods – sometimes several years – in the border areas in the mountains where the clergymen never came.

Saami responses to the missionary activities

Only rarely did the situation of the religious encounter make it possible for Saamis to present arguments in defense of the indigenous religion and even more rarely to present their attitudes about the Christian religion – not least because criticizing church and clergy was a delicate task. The few Saami statements that have been preserved are, therefore, expressed with the utmost moderation. They do not reflect Saami powerlessness and anger in the face of demands for religious uniformity, but they still provide an insight – however insufficient – into Saami opinions. A special problem is that Saamis who avoided confrontation are not encountered in this material, except in the few instances when they were detected and reported to the authorities. The sources are silent about them. It is therefore difficult to estimate how representative the preserved statements really are. Nevertheless, it is clear that different Saamis reacted in different ways.

Because of the Saamis' (well-founded) fear of reprisals, the great majority of the statements with unfavorable opinions about the clergy do not come from Saamis themselves, but from non-Saamis. From the accounts of travelers and other casual visitors, it is evident that many of the clergymen who worked among the Saami did not function as the good examples they were supposed to be. The abuse of alcohol was widespread, and many of them were, to use an expression found in one of the sources, "not very edifying."[6]

It is much more difficult to obtain information about how Saamis looked upon the clergymen and the Christian religion. It is easily noted that the few Saami utterances that have been preserved do not apply to the content of the Christian religion, but to the forms of the missionary work. What the Saami who dared express their opinions objected to most of all, when the clergymen listened, were those aspects of the Christian religion that involved restrictions on the traditional way of life, such as the compulsion to attend church and to send their children to school. Another reason for negative attitudes was that the true aims of the missionaries often seemed to be shrouded in mystery. Saamis suspected that the clergy were going to punish them or pick them for service in the armed forces. A special source of irritation was when missionaries forced Saamis to attend religious inquiries and services on short notice and on untimely occasions.

There are not many examples of how Saamis argued when they commented on the religious confrontation. On a few occasions, the clergymen asked Saamis why they performed certain rituals, and the answers they received reflect some of the Saami arguments in support of their religion. In spite of this, they have to be taken with a pinch of salt, since it is possible that the answers also reflect Saami opinions about what was proper to tell a clergyman. At any rate, they are examples of arguments in favor of the indigenous religion. It is difficult to get closer to the reasons for the adherence to the old customs. The question is rather how representative the preserved arguments are. They have been preserved because the persons (most of them clergymen) who wrote the manuscripts that function as our sources for some reason found them interesting and worth mentioning. Nothing is known about other arguments or about what arguments Saamis themselves regarded as the most important ones. The problem of the one-sidedness of the sources is here brought to a head.

The only extensive example of how Saamis argued has been reproduced by the missionary Pehr Högström. Through an encounter with Anders Erson Snadda, an open-minded Saami from the Gájddom community in the northern part of the Lule Saami area, Högström received information about how traditionalists in his congregation reasoned. He writes:

a certain Lapp named Snadda asked me if I would endure, if he said his thoughts frankly according to his conviction held until now. He said that he had heard it said by old people, how happily and in what prosperity the people lived when they freely made use of these sanctuaries, and also how many strange destinies and peculiar events his people had been subjected to, and how a general poverty had increased since so many obstacles had been lain in the way of the use of these customs. He referred to the so-called Nederbyn community, that in former times consisted of a hundred rich and wealthy tax-paying Lapps; but since they began to deviate from the customs of their ancestors, they have become scattered, and nowadays there are in the whole of the community, not more than a few, and most of them are beggars. He told about his father, that he used the drum [*goabdes*], and was well; he himself had now put it aside, but found himself not understanding anything else, but soon having to walk before others' doors [i.e. beg]. He believed that God gives as well, yes as soon, his food to the evil and to witches, as to the pious. He was of the opinion that when the wolf comes, he is not likely to have greater consideration for my reindeer than his. He feared that [his community Gájddom] would soon be waste, if people continued to discard the old customs: which probably they had seen beforehand, who in time had begun to go away and already had fled, etc. To all this, the other Lapps added their words, from which I could notice that they were of the same opinion as he.[7]

Snadda's points of view are interesting for several reasons. His interpretation of the economic decline as having been caused by the fact that the indigenous sacred places had fallen into disuse was a forceful argument in favor of the indigenous religion. So were his arguments against the idea that Christians would not be afflicted by evil, something he possibly had heard in sermons. If the Christian religion did not involve any advantage, why should the Saami abandon the indigenous religion? If Snadda is representative of Saami views, then we can conclude that the reason why Saamis attended church was not that the Christian religion was considered attractive. Rather, it was that "many obstacles had been laid in the way" for the indigenous customs when sacrificial sites had been destroyed and the persons who performed sacrifices or used the traditional drums were put on trial.

Gender and religious change

In the source material for indigenous Saami religion there is an imbalance between how men's and women's religious customs and ideas are described. In spite of the fact that it is nearly only men's rituals that are related, the authors have in most cases written as if all Saamis performed the sacrifices they describe. The sacrificial cult presented in the sources was, however, not an aspect of Saami religion as a whole. Above all, it was an aspect of the Saami men's religion. This one-sidedness of the descriptions is due to the fact that it was not possible for the male missionaries to get acquainted with the religious world of the women. It is more remarkable that recent scholars (male and female alike) have not sufficiently emphasized that this deficiency in the sources makes the picture of indigenous Saami religion defective.

This division of female and male rituals was strict, but there were rituals in which both men and women participated. Sometimes women participated in rituals within the male sphere, for example during the bear ceremonials. Women did not participate when the bear was killed, but they met the men with a *vuolle* (chant) when they came back from the hunt and spat chewed alder bark on the first man who entered the *goahte* (tent). No woman was allowed to come to the special *goahte* where the bear was boiled, but after the ceremonies for the men a ritual was performed with female participants only. The women were supposed to try to hit the bearskin with a bow and arrow while blindfolded. Here, the prohibition on women using hunting equipment was suspended.[8] There were also rituals where men participated in the women's sphere, for example when the father performed sacrifices at the naming ceremonial, or when men at the *Ruohtta* festival at midwinter carried out a certain sacrifice with the purpose of preventing the god *Ruohtta* from hurting the women's genitals.[9]

Men and women participated together in other rituals, too. A woman[10] sometimes[11] performed the ritual *vuolle* in the ritual that was connected with the *noajdde*'s seance. Sometimes both men and women performed it.[12] If the male rituals, above all, concerned economy, wind, and weather, it was the women who carried out the rituals connected with home and family.

The division of female and male gods corresponded, in the main, to the sex of those who worshipped each deity. Men worshipped the gods while women worshipped the goddesses. The most important exception was *Sáráhkká*, who was "the special tutelary spirit of the woman, the home and the family."[13] She was worshipped by both men and women, near the fireplace in the middle of the *goahte*, and was, in some areas, the most important of all the deities.

From what has been said thus far, it is evident that the men's religion and the women's religion both contrasted with and complemented each other. Seen in this light, it is clear that the roles of men and women in the religious sphere changed when the indigenous religion was abandoned. Since the indigenous restrictions on men as regards the religious sphere of the women were in force during sacred times only, while the men's sacred places and objects always (or at least more often) were forbidden for women, the process of religious change was different for the two sexes. The gender roles in daily life were not altered by the religious change. The different duties were distributed in about the same way as before. Within the religious sphere there were, on the other hand, considerable changes, not least because the Christian religion is not, in the same way, divided according to gender.

Through the narrower spatial base of their lives, Saami women had few contacts with Scandinavians. Most of them, therefore, only spoke Saami, while the men, who represented the family outwards, to a much greater extent knew a Scandinavian language. The Church's representatives' first contacts with Saamis had been made with the men, and right up to the 1750s the missionary work was concentrated to such aspects of the indigenous religion that belonged to the men's sphere. During the seventeenth century, it was nearly only the men's religion that the clergymen had heard of. One of the sources may illustrate this point. In the parts of the manuscript where the author deals with religion, phenomena that belonged to the men's sphere are the only ones dealt with: the drums, the thunder god, the most important sacrificial sites, the sun god, and the bear rituals.[14] When in the beginning of the 1690s a bishop writes of the Saami women that they are not "instructed in such devilish tricks that the men do,"[15] the statement exemplifies the fact that the clergy were becoming more conscious of the differences in religion between the genders. Also, it shows that the bishop had drawn the wrong conclusions by implying that women did not keep to the indigenous religion to the same extent as the men did.

The attacks on the indigenous religion were thus directed towards the religion of the men. This was also the case after the Norwegian missions had begun in the second decade of the eighteenth century, and was especially due to the fact that the missionaries above all interrogated the *noajddes* (who were men). What the missionaries did not know anything about, they thought did not exist. Women therefore were regarded as being easier to convert, in spite of the fact that their knowledge of Norwegian was poorer. Gradually, however, the missionaries began to receive information about the women's indigenous religiosity. It is not impossible that the Saami wife of one of the missionaries played an important part as an intermediary.

As long as the missionaries concentrated on the religion of the men in the belief that it was the religion of all the Saami, it must have been easier for the women to pass on their religious knowledge, and one would have expected that female elements would dominate later traditions. Since, however, more recent interest in oral traditions about the indigenous religion has been directed above all towards "shamanism," drums, and sacrificial sites, that is to say aspects of male religion, very little is known about how female religion changed, and whether it was capable of surviving any longer than the male religion. However, it appears plausible to me that this was the case. Otherwise, the best-known example of how the indigenous religion survived in the new religious situation is how *Sáráhkká* was identified with Mary – the only female element in the new religion. The popularity of Mary among the Saami is attested to in the missionary accounts, and it is confirmed by the symbolism of silver ornaments (the use of the monogram of Mary) and by the *vuolles* (chants) to Mary. An odd example is found in a statement in the diary of Olof Rudbeck, a Swedish scientist and linguistic researcher who made a journey to Lapland in 1695. There he tells us that he had heard that "the Lapps formerly on certain occasions have called out to Sara and Mary."[16] "Sara" can hardly have been anyone else than *Sáráhkká*.

The relationship between men and women in daily life did not alter very much because of the religious change, but their religious functions did. In the indigenous religion, the religiosity of men and women differed a great deal, but both sexes could act as functionaries in religious rituals. In the new religion, there was no corresponding clear dichotomy of female and male in every aspect of religion. Rather, the main dividing line ran between the (Saami) lay persons and the (almost exclusively Scandinavian) clergy. The religious roles of both men and women changed, since the many rituals that had been performed in the family by its own members, some by men, others by women, were replaced by rituals with a foreign person – who could only be a man – acting as functionary. Theoretically, the Saami men could – in contrast to the women – become functionaries in the new religion, but very few did. Neither the Saami men nor the women were to perform rituals any longer. Both sexes were thus reduced from religious subjects to objects.

Conclusion

It is necessary to be acquainted with the concrete areas of conflict exemplified in the previous pages in order to grasp the phases of the process of change, but concentrating on these points has one great weakness. It gives a much too simplistic picture of the religious encounter, presenting a picture in black and white, Saami *contra* non-Saami, traditionalist *contra* Christian. The longer the religious confrontation continued, the more obvious it became that the most important opposition was not the one between Saamis and clergymen, but the internal conflicts between different groups of Saamis. Also, the degree of commitment in the religious confrontation varied. Some were active while others were more passive. In order to put the few, separate, and disparate examples in the sources in relation to one another, one might (as a theoretical model) divide possible Saami reactions into five groups in the following way:[17]

1   Traditionalist activists: those who actively supported the indigenous religious heritage and opposed the Christian religion, i.e. agents of the status quo;
2   Passive traditionalists: those who sympathized with the indigenous religious heritage without actively struggling, either for the indigenous religion or against the Christian one;
3   Neutralists: those who lived in both systems without giving priority to either of them, or who ignored the religious dimension;
4   Passivist Christians: those who sympathized with the Christian religion without actively struggling, either for the Christian religion or against the indigenous religion;
5   Christian activists: those who actively supported the Christian religion and opposed the indigenous religious heritage, i.e. agents of change.

Of course, nothing is known about the relative size of each of the five groups. However, with the help of this model, the process of religious change can be suggested as having involved a gradual decrease of groups 1 and 2 and an increase of groups 4 and 5.

Notes

1   The process of religious change among the Saami has been looked upon as an example of how religious forms of modernity have been taken over by indigenous peoples. I do not agree with this characterization. In my opinion, the use of the neo-evolutionary tradition/modernity dichotomy ought to be avoided. I agree with the Comaroffs when they state that these types of binary contrast "reduce complex continuities and contradictions to the aesthetics of nice oppositions." See Jean Comaroff and John Comaroff, *Modernity and its Malcontents: Ritual and Power in Postcolonial Africa*, Chicago: University of Chicago Press, 1993, xii.
2   For a fuller treatment of the themes dealt with in this chapter, see Håkan Rydving, *The End of Drum-Time: Religious Change among the Lule Saami, 1670s–1740s*, Stockholm: Almqvist & Wiksell International, 1995.
3   Norway belonged to Denmark between 1537 and 1814, and Finland was a part of Sweden until 1810.
4   Thomas von Westen, one of the leading missionaries, is reported to have confiscated more than 100 drums during his journeys.
5   Anon., "En kort Underretning," *Kjeldeskriftfondet*, manuscript 232, Kjeldeskriftsavdelningen (Source Department), National Archives of Norway, Oslo, c.1750, 28.
6   P. Högström, *Missions-Förrätningar i Lapmarken*, Stockholm, 1774, 55.
7   *Ibid.*, 34–5.
8   S. Rheen, "En Kortt Relation," *Bidrag till kännedom om de svenska landsmålen ock svenskt folkliv* 17(1), 1897 (1671), 43ff.
9   P. Högström, *Beskrifning öfwer de til Sweriges Krona lydande Lapmarker*, Stockholm, 1747, 189.
10   J. Kildal, "Afguderiets Dempelse," *Nordlands og Troms finner i eldre håndskrifter*, Oslo, 1945 (1730 and later), 140.
11   Or: during certain rituals; or: in certain areas (?). Here, as well as in many other cases, it is impossible to decide if the different statements are due to the deficiencies of the sources or to regional or other differences in the indigenous religion.
12   S. Rheen, "En Kortt Relation," 34.
13   L. Bäckman, "Female – divine and human: a study of the position of the woman in religion and society in northern Eurasia," *The Hunters: Their Culture and Way of Life*, Tromsø: Universitetsforlaget, 1982, 156.

14   S. Rheen, "En Kortt Relation," 29ff.

15   M. Steuchius, "Anmärkningar...till Schefferi Lapponia," *Bidrag till kännedom om de svenska landsmålen ock svenskt folkliv* 17(2), 1899 (early 1690s), 83.

16   O. Rudbeck, "[D]agbok från Lapplandsresan," *Svenska Linnésällskapets årsskrift 1970/1971*, Uppsala, 1973 (1695), 94.

17   The idea for this grouping has been taken from A.A. Lebedev, "Sekul'arizacija naselenija socialisticeskogo goroda," *K obscestvu, svobodnomy ot religii*, Moskva, 1970, 135ff.

Part II

The Americas

Tribal religious traditions are constantly devalued in Western discourse on religion

John C. Mohawk

There have been changes, transformations, and challenges to the prevailing meta-narratives in Western culture. The West claims descent from Mediterranean cultures from the ancient world, as though Western history is more or less continuous and uninterrupted. That is not exactly accurate. The West descends more from two divisions of Christianity, the Greek and the Roman Churches, than from the Greek and Roman cultures.

The West was once a very rural place – a feudal place – for a long time. It is a product of that tradition of Western feudalism, and most of its institutions were formed during that time. To understand its history and why most non-Western and especially indigenous cultures are not centered or even given serious attention, we must review and understand the original narrative arose during the Age of Feudalism and that provided the West with an identity.

The West's meta-narrative was vastly expanded in the eleventh century. At that time it centered on a story of a people who descended from the group that embraced a Christian tradition. This Christian tradition included an interpretation of historical events that urged that the Son of God came to earth and died for our sins – the sins not only of believers but of everyone on earth – and then ascended to heaven. It constituted a very complex and emotionally powerful story that sought to impart meaning to human experiences around suffering, loss, and death. At that time, the followers of this tradition almost universally believed that the Son of God was about to return and that the believers were or should be required to defend the faith. Acting ostensibly on this belief, a succession of popes launched the Crusades, the European foreign wars of conquest of peoples and territory in order to secure the Holy Land in anticipation of the second coming of Christ, but also avowedly for the purpose of seizing the assets of unbelievers. These wars lasted about two centuries.

The Crusades brought a lot more than warfare to the West. The Crusades involved an incident wherein a rural and relatively unsophisticated culture attacked an ancient civilization. When the Crusaders arrived in Asia Minor they encountered things that they had never imagined existed, including spices and porcelain, sugar and textiles, and many things they could not buy at home. One of the most important things that resulted from the Crusades was trade with the East. The road to the Orient began at Constantinople and then continued through passes and mountains all the way into the Gobi desert and China.

Around the year 1300 – the Crusades can be said to have ended circa 1291, following a lot of mostly failed military efforts in the Levant – we find the introduction to Western Europe of chemically propelled weapons – firearms – using gunpowder, which had probably been invented in China. The Christians were particularly well positioned to take advantage of gunpowder because they were master bell makers and the technology of casting bronze bells readily transferred to the production of cannon. The world's best bell makers quickly became the world's foremost cannon manufacturers.

Firearms appeared at the moment in history when cross-Mediterranean trade for products encountered during the Crusades was becoming increasingly important in Western Europe. European trade during this period was centered in southern Italy and the major barrier to such trade was piracy. Seafaring technology had changed little from the days of the Greeks and Phoenicians, and Mediterranean vessels of the period were primarily propelled by oarsmen.

The arrival of cannon raised interesting new possibilities. These trading vessels could protect themselves from pirates, but there was a problem around where to position them. Putting heavy cannons on the upper decks created a balance problem, and they quickly realized they needed to place the guns closer to the water. That strategy displaced the oarsmen, and thus was launched a search for technology that would replace the oarsmen in order to be able to use the cannon and propel the ship at the same time. They already had sails, but they did not have the kind of sailing technology they needed for cross-Mediterranean trade by merchant vessels that carried cannon. In the fourteenth century in the Po Valley of Italy they created a naval military academy that conducted scientific experiments in search of improved sailing techniques. As a result of these sequential events, the trade which arose from the Crusades paved the way for European peoples to invent the technology of sailing that would enable cross-oceanic travel and to launch into what is called the biological expansion of Europe.

The continued expansion of Islam during the fifteenth century was viewed with alarm. A Turkish invasion signaled another round of conquests by an invading people, which upset an established balance of power in the region and which eventually threatened Constantinople and the trade routes to the East. When Constantinople fell, some of the trading possibilities were cut off. Another problem, at least for those so situated, was that the more remote Western nations such as Portugal and Spain found themselves in a position where they were unable in any real sense to benefit from trade centered in the eastern Mediterranean between Italy and the Bosporus and Egypt.

To remedy this situation, Spain and Portugal started out fairly early on trying to find a way to get to China by water. They soon found themselves in the Atlantic, and their explorations produced unexpected discoveries. By 1441, Portuguese vessels were exploring the West African coast and had arrived in Lisbon with the first black African slaves, the sale of which helped pay for the voyage. One of these slaves, a Moor, offered that he could obtain twelve slaves in exchange for himself, and another Portuguese ship was soon on its way to procure more slaves, the first commodity of European exploration of the Atlantic.

A Portuguese explorer by the name of Lancerotte was carried by storm to one of the Canary Islands, which today carries his name. A population of Gaunche people, estimated to be about 80,000 in number, already occupied the Canaries, and the "discovery" of their homeland marked the beginnings of the modern age of European colonization. Colonies did not happen because people needed new farm land. They happened because nation-states needed new revenue streams.

The first victims of the new age of conquest were to be the Gaunche people of the Canary Islands. European invaders landed and began a military operation in 1404. Further explorations led to the discovery and colonization of the Azores and of Madeira.

Madeira was especially important because it was here, on an unoccupied island, that colonization made important strides. Madeira was cleared, irrigation ditches were dug, and in a short time sugar was introduced. Slaves, first from the Canaries and soon from Africa, were brought in to do the hard work. Sugar, a commodity that had become in demand as a result of the Crusades, was successful. Within less than a generation, Madeira was the most successful producer of sugar and profits to the Crown of any place in the world. The desirability of having offshore colonies had been established, and the potential could but stimulate the imagination. Thus before Columbus was born (circa 1451), there already existed in the eastern Atlantic the embryonic institutions that would propel the modern era: a practice of offshore conquests and colonization, plantations, the birth of the factory (sugar refining) system, trade with Europe, and slavery.

That first meta-narrative was about European identity. The Europeans were the people who were carrying on the tradition of Christ and humankind's salvation through his death on the Cross, a marvelous and powerfully attractive narrative that sought meaning in the experiences of suffering and death, loss and misery. There has been plenty of suffering in European history, and people have always been engaged in the search for meaning in their lives. To encounter a European of this era was to encounter a Christian, and to carry on a conversation with one was to invite an immersion into their meta-narrative. It was essential to an understanding of their motivations for entering into the Crusades and the subsequent quest for expansion and colonization, but Christianity was not the only meta-narrative in the Western experience.

In the fifteenth century the Western nations were anticipating the second coming of Christ, but what they in fact experienced was the second coming of Plato. In a sense, Greek philosophers had never completely abandoned this story. Augustine had been influenced by Plato and had incorporated his works into the Christian consciousness in the fifth century. In the middle of the thirteenth century the works of Aristotle filtered into Western Europe and were embraced by Thomas Aquinas, whose *Summa Theologia* was in turn embraced by the Roman Catholic Church as an embodiment of its official philosophy. When Constantinople fell to the Turks and became Istanbul in 1454, the last surviving city of the Roman Empire disappeared. Even before its final collapse, Greek-speaking scholars had found their way to cities in Italy where they taught the Greek language and the philosophical texts of antiquity. Before long, educated Western Europeans were speaking Greek and quoting Plato. This rediscovery of and re-identification with the Greeks of antiquity coincided with the birth of Western imperialism and provided both an inspiration and a framework for its emerging intellectual ideology.

Western Europeans imagined themselves to be the descendants of the great civilizations of the ancient Mediterranean, and this provides an example of how a meta-narrative can work. They already possessed the Old Testament, a story which was significantly different from and certainly only indirectly related to European experience, and had embraced and revered the ancient Hebrew patriarchs as their own. They now embraced the texts of the Greeks as one of the streams of the narrative of European identity. They also proceeded to revere the words of the ancient Greeks as much as those of the ancient Hebrews. The Greeks gave us the words "xenophobia" and "ethnocentrism." Christians had long practiced versions of intolerance, which these words could well represent, but Greek philosophy provided context, ideology, and a kind of legitimacy to such concepts.

Plato tells us that Socrates believed in morality. Socrates' motivation for founding the tradition that would evolve into Western philosophy was his idea that morality was arrived at through clear thinking based on information. Given enough information and an under-standing of disciplined thought, one would arrive at a moral choice. An immoral choice was a result of a lack of information and disciplined thought. Plato, who was much inspired by Socrates, articulates a tenet of Greek thought that lives with us even now. He started with the idea that for every question there is only one correct answer, and that there is a way to find out what that correct answer is. That correct answer will be consis-tent with all the other known correct answers in the world.

This is very interesting and revolutionary because prior to Plato, it had been thought that humans lived in a condition that was determined by forces beyond human control. The Greek philosophers developed a belief that humankind's fate lies in the hands of humans. Plato argues for the supremacy of human agency and provides in his *Republic* a utopian vision for Western culture. He argues that the perfect government would be one composed of philosophers, of educated people – those bright enough and informed enough to have the answers to solve the problems of the day. In the fifteenth century these ideas were embraced with a passion that can be somewhat difficult for contemporary people to imagine.

Greek philosophy enjoyed enormous popularity among the educated classes in Western Europe at a time when technology had enabled them to cross and re-cross the great oceans carrying the world's most sophisticated military technology, and with a self-identity which allowed them to adopt a version of the ethnocentricity that characterized their heroes of antiquity, the Greeks of the Classical Age. Therein lay the definitions that would serve them so well: the idea that Europeans had inherited an intellectual tradition which offered limitless potential for solving the problems of mankind, and the idea, clearly artic-ulated by Aristotle, that privileged classes of philosophers and creators of civilization arose out of nature. Aristotle also provided the idea that there were people who were not so endowed, people who were not Greeks, or at least not middle- and upper-class Greek males, including women and children, whom nature had not endowed with the power of creative thought – a main tenet of Aristotle, found in *Politics*, Books 3 and 4 – and rules by which this utopian project accepted or rejected thought and behavior as a legitimate part of the process that defined all of this.

Christopher Columbus crossed the Atlantic in 1492, discovered the Indians of the islands of the Caribbean, and returned home to gather more ships and people to continue his enterprise. What followed was absolutely astonishing. The Indians of the Caribbean, Columbus noted, were not schooled in the arts of European warfare. The Spanish descended on them with a fury probably hitherto unmatched. The Indians were ordered to find gold. There was little gold in the islands, and those who did not fulfill their quota were subject to punishment. Old woodcuts show Spanish soldiers cutting off people's hands and noses because they had failed to supply gold. The carnage was abso-lutely horrific.

They tortured people on the slightest whim. There are anecdotal accounts, intended to display the general demeanor of the Spanish, or Hispanola, that give context to the Indians' experience. They hung people in groups of thirteen, ostensibly to represent Christ and the twelve disciples. One story tells of a Spanish officer who complained of all the screaming because it was interrupting his sleep. Another story tells of two young boys carrying a pet parrot who encounter two Spanish soldiers on a path. The soldiers behead the boys and steal the parrot. There are stories of soldiers who begin hacking Indian arms and legs, just to test their manly strength and the sharpness of their blades;

stories of Indian women who cannot conceive children because the Spanish will not allow men and women to live together except for a few days a year. And when they give birth, the diet is so poor they cannot produce milk for their offspring. The story of Spanish cruelty on the islands is one that is almost impossible to match. And Spanish torture attests to the depths of depravity of the Christians. Contemporary accounts illustrate how to extend for as long as possible the torture to the victim who lingers in agony. The Indian population of these islands plummeted dramatically under the Spanish boot, and soon African slaves were being imported to replace the Indians. But the cruelty continued, from the slaughter that accompanied the capture of the Africans, to the rape, torture, and deprivations that accompanied travel to the coasts, to the horrors of the transatlantic voyage in disease- and filth-laden ships. Once African slaves arrived on the plantations, they could expect an average of seven years of backbreaking labor until, exhausted and in ill health, they died.

Europeans responded to all this with an elaboration of their own meta-narrative. Machiavelli wrote *The Prince* in 1516. Much of his book is a description of the way in which wealth and power had been acquired in Europe during this period, and an argument that it was the duty of the prince to do whatever was necessary to acquire power because such were the rules of the game. He is viewed by some as a political pragmatist, but he is also a writer who in fact argues that the combination of intelligence and access to information will not produce a moral decision, that indeed a moral decision is immaterial to the pursuit of power. His is the only book published that year which is regularly read today and is included on many lists of the world's greatest books. It has been stated that Cortez acted as though he had read Machiavelli during the conquest of Mexico, but it is more accurate to say that Machiavelli was describing men such as Cortez.

The excesses of the Spanish conquests in the Americas were reported in such detail and with such indignation by men such as Bartolome de las Casas that in 1550, the Spanish Crown called a temporary halt to further conquest. The king ordered the Council of the Indies to convene to consider whether the assault on the Indians was just warfare, morally justified in the laws of the Church and Western philosophy.

The resulting debate took place in Valladolid, Spain. The lawyer for the conquistadors was Gines Juan de Sepulveda, an Aristotelian scholar. The lawyer for the Indians was Bartolome de las Casas. De las Casas argued the obvious humanity of the Indians. He presented proof that the Indians had developed the art of writing, were knowledgeable in astronomy, had schools which paralleled European universities, and that some of them made marvelous converts to Christianity.

De Sepulveda argued that the conquest was just and necessary because the Indians were sub-human. He cited Aristotle's ideas about natural slavery, and garnered every argument that supported the idea of the superiority of every aspect of European culture over every aspect of Indian culture. The Indians, he asserted, were brutes in the shape of human beings, not real human beings at all. Such brutes did not possess souls, any more than a burro possessed a soul. The Spanish, by taking their lands and enslaving their persons, were doing them a favor by placing them in the sphere of a much superior Spanish Catholic culture, which presumably privileged them to toil in the interests of their superior masters. Indeed, every rationalization of racial superiority was called upon to justify the Spanish behavior towards the Indians, and most of it was culled from the great books of antiquity in relatively scholarly fashion. De Sepulveda has been called the father of modern racism, but the record indicates that the racism was present long before the debate at Valladolid. He was, however, one of the earliest to embrace and articulate the racist principles that were part of Europe's meta-narrative of the superiority of its intellectual tradition.

This tradition continues through a long list of writers who express, and are acknowledged as expressing, Western thought. In his work, *Meditationes Sacrae* (1597), *De Haeresibus*, Francis Bacon states that knowledge is power, and offers that the project of science is justified in using the techniques of the inquisition to discover the secrets of nature. His is one of the cornerstone books of the philosophy of science. John Locke offers, in his *Second Treatise on Government*, that because the Indians use land differently than Englishmen, the latter are justified in forcibly taking that land and banishing the Indian from it for ever.

From the earliest moments of Western philosophy, people in positions of privilege wrote rationalizations for their positions, argued the justice of people in subordinate positions, and rationalized social hierarchy; and these ideas, thoughts, and stories contributed to the meta-narrative of Western superiority, which would evolve into the foundations of white supremacy when those who had been subordinated through history could be identified by color. Racism had, for centuries, been defined by membership of groups, but until the European expansion, within the Western discourse, those groups had been arguably white. Racism in Western history began as white-on-white racism. Also, such an institution as slavery had previously tended to place the victim in this position temporarily and was often not hereditary. That also changed in the sixteenth century.

In the nineteenth century, biologists such as Charles Darwin began their efforts to explain the biological diversity of species. Others soon saw in Darwin's explanation the idea that some species were superior (survival of the fittest) to others, and it soon became clear that selective propagation could produce desirable characteristics in certain plants. If it worked with plants, why not humans? Social Darwinism was a logical, if wrong-headed, unintended consequence of the project of science, but it was also consistent with a very ancient tradition of explaining why the winners were entitled to oppress and exploit the losers, which went all the way back to Aristotle and had been enshrined in the Western meta-narrative at least since the fifteenth century.

The idea that human agency could produce desirable characteristics through selective breeding led some, especially in Europe, to imagine a kind of utopian future. If selective breeding could create improved human beings, such intentionally improved humans would possess such qualities of intelligence, creativity, and moral superiority that they would be able to solve all the problems of mankind. This, combined with the generally unchallenged assertions that Aryans were a superior race, led somewhat logically to an assertion that perfect Aryans would represent the perfection of humanity.

The Industrial Revolution, which was centered in Europe, provided Europeans with the weaponry and other tools needed to conquer the rest of the world. They undertook this project with considerable energy and enjoyed almost perfect success. By 1890, an estimated 85 per cent of the globe was under European – or Euro-American, Euro-South American, Euro-Australian, or whatever – control. The intellectual community did not choose to consider this a product of good fortune, or even of military conquest. Rather, they formed an idea of the natural superiority of their own group, which they then dubbed the Aryans. They needed no further proof other than their history of success in subjugating practically the whole world.

Aryan superiority combined with excesses in utopian race theories to produce the idea that not only were the Aryans a superior race, they were also destined through conscious development to create the humans who could best reach humanity's highest potential. Thus, projects such as the Hitler youth were begun. The belief was that Aryans should not need to compete with inferior peoples for the resources of the world that would be needed by future generations of Aryans. The only possible solution to this problem would be the genocide of non-Aryans. Nazi Germany was not an aberration of Western thought. It was fully within its traditions, using all the rationalizations of racial superiority of mainstream Western intellectual thought to reach a conclusion that required on the part of the Aryans the kind of bold action that Machiavelli had outlined as the duty of a prince. The result was wholesale slaughter on a scale not seen since the Spanish conquest. Had the Germans won, *Mein Kampf* would surely have been listed among the world's greatest books.

Even as the Second World War was under way, another chapter of the West's own story – of how it came to be the way it is – was being written. The 1940 World's Fair in Flushing, USA, offered the new theme of a technological utopia about to be born. A number of great American companies were offering a better life through technology. Indeed, their themes were "Better living through chemistry," and they claimed that they had a plan that would eventually solve all of humankind's problems through technology. This utopian ideology, which pretends it is not an ideology at all, and has its roots in Plato and a millennium of European thought which rationalizes the destruction of peoples as a necessary evil on the road to a perfect future, is very much alive with us today. It is amply described as the rationalization of the dispossession of indigenous peoples in John Bodner's book, *Victims of Progress.*

Western philosophy became a meta-narrative that claimed that it was the story of the search for the perfect way of life that would solve all of humankind's problems, just as Christianity had made the same claim for people's spiritual lives. The reason that indigenous cultural values and religious traditions are devalued in the West is that they are not perceived to be part of this quest for a utopian future. They are not part of the discourse of the West, and do not qualify for serious consideration. These are distinct, unrelated narratives, and, as such, are classified somewhat disparagingly as "folk traditions," not philosophy. They are thought to arise from superstitions, such as the kind Socrates ridiculed. They cannot achieve value because they are structurally devalued in the context of a meta-narrative that seeks to rationalize expansion, hierarchy, colonization, and the objectification of nature, patriarchy, and a long list of other characteristics that define and describe Western culture. Since these indigenous traditions do not support, enhance, or otherwise further the projects of Western domination, they are treated as though they are of no value at all.

Chapter 7

Guidelines for the study of Mesoamerican religious traditions[1]

Alfredo López Austin

The Mesoamerican unit

Somewhere in what today constitutes Mexican territory, about 4,500 years ago – around the twenty-fifth century BCE – groups of people who were growers of corn and other domesticated species achieved such dependence on their crops that they gradually became sedentary. In this manner, they abandoned their ancient practices of seasonal migrations that alternated agriculture with hunting and fishing. The life of these initial sedentaries, alongside the transformations that change implies, gave birth to the Mesoamerican tradition. Thus, sedentarism gradually extended throughout vast areas, and with the passing of time Mesoamerica embraced southern Mexico, all of Guatemala, Belize and El Salvador, Western Honduras, the Pacific coast of Nicaragua, and north-western Costa Rica.

Insulated from extra-continental contact, Mesoamerica underwent a long process of evolution. Within four millennia it had developed certain forms of living, ranging from an initial type of egalitarian society that lived in simple agricultural villages, to powerful states with a high degree of political and social organization. Its ethnic composition was heterogeneous. Among the many peoples that belonged to this Mesoamerican cultural complex, some of the more well known are the Olmec, the Teotihuacan, the Mayan, the Zapotec, the Mixtec, the Mexica (or Aztec), and many others.

If we had to ask ourselves about the most notable characteristics of the ancient cultural complex, the Mesoamerican geography would have to be considered. Criss-crossed by many mountain ranges, this ecological diversity was one of the important factors of a process with paradoxical results: on the one hand, it produced a variety of cultural manifestations in Mesoamerican societies; on the other, it gave birth to a cultural unit common to all societies. In effect, the geographical diversity of Mesoamerica, added to the vast linguistic and ethnic differences of its inhabitants and to their distinct local and regional histories, crystallized, through several centuries, in varied cultural expressions. Among those who inhabited such contrasting environments, such as the high valleys of Central Mexico or southern Guatemala, the tropical rainforests, the pleasant valleys of Oaxaca, the northern arid plains and marine coasts, they differed considerably in their utilization of natural resources, in their social and political organizations, and in their artistic expressions. That said, diversity itself resulted in unity. The random orography and the climatic variety encouraged, from a very early time, productive specialization in micro environments, and, from then on, a constant interchange of products was encouraged. The interchange was, if not the only one, one of the principal forces in the interrelation among the agriculturists. The permanent contact produced an early common history that resulted in a strong cultural unity, combined with local differences. In this manner, the nucleus of a shared tradition was constructed.

The cultural unity can be clearly appreciated in the religious concepts of the peoples of Mesoamerica. At the root of the different religious beliefs and practices, the same view of the world is to be found, which served, later on, as an aggregate of codes for communication between the indigenous societies throughout history.

In 1519, Mesoamerica was invaded by a European nation that demolished the ancient civilization, in the process subjugating the indigenous peoples to a colonial situation that produced negative effects which continue to the present day among the direct descendants. The Spaniards landed in the coastal regions of the Gulf of Mexico, and, after an offensive that took advantage of the political discord among the indigenous peoples, conquered the city of Mexico-Tenochtitlan to begin from there the progressive domination of the entire Mesoamerican territory. Colonial dependency lasted for 300 years. In the first quarter of the nineteenth century, Mexico achieved political autonomy, severing its ties with Spain. Independence, however, did not free the indigenous populations from regimes that pretended to integrate them into a so-called national culture. This political milieu aggrieves the social and economic domain that has maintained the communities, for centuries, in cultural dependency and poverty.

The two great periods of Mesoamerican religious tradition

The Spaniards ideologically justified the invasion, conquest, and colonization of the American continent in terms of a so-called divine mission: the expansion and imposition of Christianity. From a European perspective, the Spaniards saw themselves as the carriers of a message of salvation that was intended to keep millions of souls away from the eternal sufferings of hell. Catholicism was imposed on the territories under Spanish control, and initiated a ferocious persecution of whoever resisted accepting the strange faith. Nevertheless, ancient Mesoamerican religion did not disappear completely. The ancient concepts, in unison with those imposed by the Conquistadors, united contradictorily to give birth to numerous indigenous religious beliefs that surfaced during the colonial situation. These are the religions that persist in the present. This enunciated process allows the separation of the history of Mesoamerican religious tradition into two distinct periods.

The first period of the history of Mesoamerican religious tradition

This period corresponds to the forty centuries of the existence of Mesoamerican religion and can be divided into two parts. One, a formative type that dates from 2500 to 1200 BCE, is defined as the epoch of non-hierarchical societies. Archeologically this corresponds to the so-called early pre-classical period of Mesoamerica. During this time, the first villagers established the cosmological bases of a religion strongly influenced by seasonal cycles. In their world-view, the development of the corn plant was one of the principal archetypes. Another, intrinsically tied to the former, was the archetype of the alternating powers of fire and water, derived from the division of the year into two seasons, the dry and rainy seasons. This opposition constituted one of the most important pairings in a firmly dualistic world-view. Regarding the configuration of the cosmos, the agriculturists' prevailing conception was of a division into three great levels that were superimposed onto one another. The first level, the heavens, corresponded to the living areas of the superior gods, who sent life to the surface of the earth. The second level, the world of human beings, was formed by the surface of the earth and four inferior celestial levels through which the Sun, the Moon, Venus, stars, wind, and clouds traveled. The third level, the underworld, was the place of death, from which there emerged periodically the forces of water, the development and greenness of nature. The three levels were united by five cosmic trees; growing out of the principal tree was the center, or navel, of the world and the four remaining trees, on the four directions of the terrestrial surface. The gods and their influences traveled from one level to another through the empty interiors of the five cosmic trees.

The second part of the first period corresponds to an era of much more complex social and political organization. When ranking social systems emerged, the power of the governing elite was founded in the primitive concept of the cosmos. Around 1150 BCE, and for a long period of 750 years (the mid-pre-classic period), an aggregate of sacred symbols was distributed through all of Mesoamerica, associated with the emblems and representations of power. Many of them are found inscribed, carved, or painted onto luxury items or prestigious objects that could have only belonged to the ruling families. This artistic style is very peculiar and has been given the name of Olmec. The reasons for its vast distribution continue to be a mystery. But it is probable that said style was an element of prestige adapted by the elite of varying Mesoamerican nations as part of their ideological support system. It can also be supposed that the code was accepted by the governed since they could find in that symbolism one more expression of their ancient beliefs.

After the dominance of the Olmec phenomenon, unifier of religious symbols, came the period known as late pre-classic. Within this period the diversity among the Mesoamerican cultures was accentuated in the strengthening of regional political centers and their cultural development. Nevertheless, religion and power continued to unite, eventually coming together in a complete and narrow form. Around 200 CE (the beginning of the early classic period), the first cities appeared. By 600 CE, one of the cities, Teotihuacan, achieved its apex thanks to the fact that it had maintained itself as the center of a network of commerce that stretched throughout the Mesoamerican territory. With a splendor that came after Teotihuacan, between 600 and 900 CE, the Mayan civilization reached its peak. This period is known as the late classic and is characterized by great advancements in the development of writing, calendars, astronomy, architecture, and the arts. However, after 650 CE, an unexplained and prolonged collapse of the principal urban centers began. Due to the power vacuum created after the collapse of the most important urban centers, Mesoamerica entered into a long bellicose process in which states struggled for hegemony.

The military regimes had their golden age in the period known as the post-classic. Among the nations engaged in the war for hegemony, one finds the Toltec and the Mexica in Central Mexico, the Mixtec in Oaxaca, the Tarascan in the West, the Mayan in the Yucatan Peninsula, and the Cakchiquel and Quiche in the mountains of southern Guatemala. The constant struggle for power continued until the moment of the Spanish invasion, and was, without a doubt, one of the factors that facilitated the conquest of Mesoamerican territory.

It is clear that during this long period, which ran from 400 BCE to 1521 CE, Mesoamerican religion (in its cultural variants) underwent great transformations. However, one of its most persistent and important characteristics was its function as the sustenance of power. To this was owed the supernatural character of the rulers, who sometimes were identified with divinities; the intellectual development of the priesthood and its control over the most important branches of knowledge; the highest point in the development of calendars, astronomy, writing, and numerical notation; the mixing of popular and state worship; the aggrandizement of state worship; and the increase in human sacrifices, especially during periods of military expansion.

The second period of the history of Mesoamerican religious tradition

This period corresponds to the emergence of indigenous religions during the colonial period. The Spaniards, moved by their need to control conquered territory, and the need to open up areas for the imposition of Christianity, committed themselves to the persecution of native priests, and to the destruction of institutions and the most notable material manifestations of indigenous religions. The history of the conquest holds that some priests were sentenced to death indefensibly by the ferocious dogs of the Europeans. The temples were dismantled; images of gods were destroyed; native rituals were prohibited; and the link between political power and indigenous religion was broken. At the same time, the Christian religious missionaries hurriedly started the process of imposing the Christian faith and transforming indigenous family life, now under the canon of Christian dogma, and began to persecute popular forms of worship, most especially those related to the supernatural protection of the human subject, to domestic activities, and to labor.

The immediate result of the Spanish offensive against the different forms of religious and indigenous belief was the disappearance of state religion along with its wise men, its fatuous celebrations, its art, its architecture, and its close ties with the governing apparatus, ties which were abolished in the Mesoamerican superior strata. Nevertheless, popular religiosity subsisted alongside the domestic sphere, with respect to the caring of the body, daily labor, and village social relations. In short, the traditional nucleus that had started to form with the space and time concepts of the first farmers of the Mesoamerican early pre-classic period subsisted, on top of which there started to be constructed during later times the great religious apparatus tied to political power.

The structure of the Mesoamerican rural religion received the new faith imposed by the Europeans. It was a difficult process, not only because of the effort involved in comprehending a foreign faith, but because of the problems resulting from the adaptation of a form of worship and a dogma very different from the old indigenous religion. Moreover, autonomous worship itself presented enormous problems: worship had lost its normative institutions; it went underground; the priests were labeled as rebels and conspirators, and hence persecuted; and, as a result, indigenous religion in its original forms no longer responded to the social and political reality of colonial times.

Arising from that situation, cults were born. Beliefs and institutions that had been inscribed in the cultural indigenous religious matrix, nourished as much by Mesoamerican as by Christian elements, surged as a colonial product, nominally Christian and subordinated to a foreign ecclesiastical institution. The colonial nature made them acquire the character of new vehicles of social, religious, political, and economic organization, and with high frequency were converted into mediums of resistance against the oppression of the victorious invaders. But, at the same time, these vehicles served as one of the mediums by which the Spaniards influenced the mentality of the native population and kept it under control and surveillance.

One of the most notable peculiarities of these cults, beliefs, and institutions was their heterogeneity. The ancient unity of Mesoamerican religion was derived as much from its common nucleus as from its characteristic as an ideological code in the interrelations of the different Mesoamerican nations. This characteristic was considerably weakened when communications among the various indigenous nations decreased as a consequence of colonial life. Moreover, the qualitative and quantitative variants of Spanish domination over the distinct indigenous communities created the space for a considerable diversity of relations of domination. The different degrees of control exercised over the indigenous population produced an enormous gamut of beliefs, practices, and institutions that constituted, at one end of the spectrum – where the presence of the authority was accentuated – a less orthodox Christianity, and at the other – in regions separated from the direct control of the evangelist – an indigenous world-view little altered by exogenous thought.

That said, it is impossible to talk of "a colonial indigenous religion." It is preferable to refer, in plural terms, to "the colonial indigenous religions," even though all of them have shared, to the present day, a strong agricultural nature, a double Mesoamerican-Christian source, and a cohesive tendency to resist colonial oppression.

As for the double Mesoamerican-Christian source, colonial indigenous religions present characteristics that can be found, although not necessarily in all of them, at least in the greater part of them:

Regarding the Christian tradition on which they inscribe themselves:

1   Colonial indigenous religions are recognized as Christian, independent of the distance that they maintain with the central dogmas of Christianity. This is due to a sincere affiliation of the believers.
2   After the declared and pretended monotheism, there exists a refined polytheism; however, this is easily adaptable to the Christian dualism (God/the Devil), to the trinity dogma, to the worship of the saints, to the worship of the Virgin Mary, and to the many proper patronages of Catholicism. Supernatural and sacred characters of Christianity are re-symbolized, and frequently Christ acquires solar characteristics; the Virgin Mary, the attributes of Mother Earth; and the Devil is seen as the patron of animals, ruler of the forests, and owner of the subterranean resources.
3   Catholic liturgy is adopted, although it is often re-symbolized and re-functionalized.
4   They are found under the tutelage of an external clergy that ties the faithful with the foreign church, ungraspable, incomprehensible, distant, and less comprehending.

Regarding the Mesoamerican tradition:

1   Colonial indigenous religions recognize the authority of tradition, to which they frequently refer using the title *el costumbre*. They endow the principles and knowledge, transmitted over generations, with the characteristics of truths revealed and founded at the beginning of the world.
2   They maintain, as components structuring a world-view of religious thought, a great many of the ancient space and time concepts. To this world-view correspond polytheism,

the attribution of a soul to all living creatures, the belief in the possibility of sharing the soul with other living beings, the idea of the cyclic relation of life and death, etc.

3   They conserve conciliatory rituals, above all the ones related to the agricultural fields and the veneration of mountains and caves. Therapeutics tied to supernatural forces occupied an important place in indigenous practices.

4   The organizing particularities of ritual, conciliation, and, in general terms, the relationship with nature, made necessary the intervention of officials, representatives, and specialists: the delegates of the various religious positions, the doctors, the prayers, the soothsayers, and even the wizards.

The usefulness of comparative studies of the two religious traditions

The historical particularity of the diverse colonial indigenous religions makes difficult their study as a general process in the context of Mexican reality. Nevertheless, to understand them historically in a global context, one should start with the aspects that are common to all of them. Given that all of the religious traditions suffered the conflicting confluence of two traditional streams of thought, it is important to point out first of all the big differences between Mesoamerican religion and Christianity. In effect, all of the colonial indigenous religions, from the beginning, were required to combine two systems of thought into one, congruently, which signified a truly intellectual effort given the enormous inequality that existed between both religions. The study of this process is indispensable, and, consequently, it is necessary to eradicate generalized opinions with little historical support. For example, it is commonly said that the Christian elements of the colonial religions are mere coverings of a persistent Mesoamerican faith. Even though during the early colonial times this was partially true, syncretism and the production of new systems was soon under way in a prolonged transformation that continues to the present day.

The purpose of this presentation is to conclude with a proposal for the study of Mesoamerican religious traditions. This final proposal is the enunciation of the most notable differences that exist between the pre-Hispanic religions and Christianity. My purpose is twofold: first, to set the basis – with reference to the science of history – for some central and common aspects of the particular study of each of the colonial indigenous religions; secondly, to contribute – from the discipline of the science of history – to the defense of the human rights of conscience and worship. There are a considerable number of individuals nowadays who are discriminated against by the hegemonic Mexican society, with attacks or contempt directed against the various aspects of their traditional culture, one of which is, without a doubt, the religious aspect.

Discrimination has had very diverse faces. One of them prevailed during early colonial times – and has not yet completely disappeared at the beginning of the twenty-first century. It places the indigenous population – at least the population which does not follow Christian religion – at the mercy of the forces of the Devil and condemns them, therefore, to eternal perdition. The only way to salvation, of course, is through the acceptance of the guidance of the evangelists. Another of the faces of discrimination categorizes indigenous peoples as ignorant, lacking the capacity to comprehend the fundamental basics of Christianity due to the fact, mainly, of scarce intellectual capacity, and to the long continuance of deformed "superstitions" of the evangelical teachings. A third face, of an evangelical kind, presupposes a historical hierarchy of religions on top of which rests monotheism. Following this mode of reasoning, every polytheistic society is placed in an inferior position with respect to the ranking of civilized societies. From any one of these and other perspectives, colonial indigenous religions have been neglected and subjected to outside intervention throughout the centuries, and the judgments that have been formulated about them have been considered sufficient to justify teachings which contribute to the permanence of a system of exploitation and indignity.

My purpose is to contribute, from a scientific perspective, to the defense of human rights. I do not advocate an aggregate of religions. My interest is directed neither to the preservation nor to the disappearance of creed. I defend the right of conscience and worship, and with it other rights that are restricted or violated due to religious discrimination. I consider that the scientific position, foreign to any creed, removes the polemic to neutral ground, making it more balanced. This is necessary since the debate, throughout the centuries, has been made from the perspective of the dominant faith in society. A scientific study of the history of the different colonial indigenous religions would be able to guarantee an appropriate objectivity with which to examine in depth the comparison that I merely enunciate here.

A comparison between Mesoamerican religion and Christianity

It is very risky to point out the general characteristics of either the Christian or the Mesoamerican religions, since they cannot be considered monolithic creeds or monolith practices. Evidently, religions are transformed with the passage of time, they vary from society to society, and frequently there is no agreement between the daily and popular practical vision of the faithful and the theological perspective. Nevertheless, to make an initial comparison, one might present an abstraction of what was previously put forward, *grosso modo*, that could form the basis of a more precise analysis in the future. However, I consider that in this very general presentation, as well as in the presentations that may be put forward after this one, it is preferable to follow the popular forms of religiosity, which have a greater historical weight in the collision of the two systems of thought. Parting from what has been said above, including the discussion of the major existing differences between both religions, I point out the following:

1   Christianity is proclaimed as a monotheistic religion. Mesoamerican religion, on the other hand, recognized the existence of multiple gods, to whose plurality and heterogeneity is attributed diversity and the mobility of the world, since from the various essences were derived the attributes of living beings; the play of their interventions created time and determined the transformation of the cosmos. Because of this, while Mesoamerican religion had among its clear and explicit principles the contraposition of the divine forces, Christianity was confronted with the enormous problem of the justification of opposites, resolved with the adoption of a duality in the supernatural in which two opposing centers of power in the pairing of God/the Devil are created. This not only occasions serious theological disquisition, but it leaves one of the pair members, the Devil, in an ambiguous position, since in spite of its supernatural character, with powers over creation and a personality of its own, it is not recognized as a god.

2   In accordance with the aforementioned, while for Mesoamerican dualism there was in everything alive a complementary opposition, in Christianity there is necessarily an irreducible opposition between good and evil. The Mesoamerican subject did not conceive of the existence of absolutely good nor absolutely evil gods. All the gods having free will, passions, and inclinations similar to those of human beings, they behaved with a free will such that their resolutions could be harmful or kind for the totality of human beings, for particular sectors of them, or for individuals. In spite of the fact that there were very many pairs of opposites in their cosmos (heaven/earth, life/death, light/darkness, dry/wet, hot/cold, male/female, above/below, etc.), in Mesoamerican thought the cosmic opposition of good/evil is not registered as having existed.

3   For the Mesoamerican subject, the existence of human life was given in an adequate space–time framework, optimum and definitive. The world was conceived as a place full of suffering, in which it was necessary to undertake multiple efforts to survive; but, at the same time, it was a place where the sufferings of human beings were extenuated by the pleasures created by the gods. The world was also a place for the debates and the disputes of the gods, proof of which was the constant transformation of nature. Strife, time, change, and history constituted an indissoluble unity. Following these basics, it was thought that the history of humanity had its beginning in the moment of creation and its ending in a cataclysmic end to human existence. For the Christian subject, on the other hand, the world of human beings is imperfect, full of wickedness; but, consequently, it is transitory, since it is expected that evil will be defeated. After this, the rightful will accomplish the true life, joyful, in absolute virtue. In other words, for the Mesoamerican subject, opposition gave meaning to the world, while for the Christian subject, opposition is an imperfect state that will only be corrected in the process of separating and dividing the opposite essences.

4   Conscious of living in a world of contradictions and opposites, the Mesoamerican subject searched for equilibrium in life. His/her morale had a high practical meaning, since s/he regarded the majority of supernatural consequences, which may be the result of his/her behavior, to have a bearing on life on earth. For the Mesomerican subject, life in the world was the only life truly complete, since the world was the meeting place where all the components of the human being were kept together. In effect, it was thought that the human being was made up of elements of heavy matter and numerous spirits, each one having different functions. Death was imagined as the disintegration of the components of the person. Once the components were separated, one of the spirits journeyed to the beyond, where it could fulfill its cosmic functions or undergo suffering. It needs to be taken into account, however, that said sufferings had more of a purifying character than that of punishment. The purified spirit, cleansed of all acquired memory during the life of the individual, served to give birth to another human being. It was a recyclable process, with which the perpetuation of the species was explained. The same was thought of the remaining living beings: their specific essences were subjected to the cycles of life and death. But, going back to the human being, it was believed that the purifying process lasted for a determinate time, on occasion for four years. Differing from what was said above, the Christian subject understands his/her existence on earth as a brief passage in the context of his/her true existence, conceived as salvation or as eternal punishment.

The concept of atrocious punishments resulting from certain earthly behaviors, an idea present in various religions of salvation/eternal damnation, was inconceivable to the Mesoamerican subjects.

5   Christianity is characterized as a religion with universal pretensions, exclusive and intolerant of other creeds. The Christian subject considers that every human being should belong to the Christian faith; s/he also considers that this is the only true faith. Christianity, therefore, aims at the conversion of the "infidels" and the non-orthodox. In the Mesoamerican religion, on the other hand, it was held that peculiarities in belief and worship were normal within the whole of the different human groups. Each group had, from the time of creation, a tutelage god who shared his essence with his protégés, and their particular beliefs, their peculiar forms of worship, their language, their ethnic group, their profession, and their character were part and parcel of the heritage which said god had left behind to his children. Historical data regarding campaigns to make converts is non-existent in Mesoamerica because religious affiliation was thought of as something innate, belonging to the specific god of each human group. On the other hand, all the patron gods formed part of an immense pantheon recognized by the faithful.

6   The aforementioned difference between Christianity and Mesoamerican religion has determined the forms of their political usage. The universal pretensions of Christianity have justified throughout history the use of force as a vehicle of inclusion. As with other religions that share with Christianity this characteristic, its expansive and militant actions directed towards the absorption of the subjugated have been out of the ordinary. Its conquests have obtained not only the subjugation of the conquered, but also the destruction of their cultures, an action which is justified by the need to eradicate autochthonous creeds. Mesoamerican religion was also utilized as a justification for hegemonic expansion; the campaigns of the nations of the late post-classic period are well documented, among them those of the Mexica and Tarascan who assumed the function of saviors and organizers of the world. These nations took as their role the feeding of the gods with the blood and hearts of captured enemies during combat, and, with this mission, they embarked on the subjugation of their neighbors. Nevertheless, this did not result in the destruction of the cultural institutions of the defeated, and their religious assimilation went no further than the acknowledgment on their part of the superior position of the gods of the victorious in the hierarchy of the Mesoamerican pantheon – and, therefore, the obligation to become politically subjected to said gods and to provide the tribute established after defeat.

7   As a universal religion, Christianity distanced itself from many of the cultures from which it originated, since little by little it had to adapt to the life conditions of the nations within its remit. On the other hand, Mesoamerican religion, in its multiple versions, kept its ties with the diverse cultural mediums that nourished it. The result, for Christianity, was a relative separation of the distinct spheres of social action, including the religious one. Mesoamerican religion, on the other hand, was diluted throughout all spheres of social action.

8   As a result of the relative autonomy of the fields of knowledge within Christianity, is has witnessed not only the separation of but also, on multiple occasions, opposition and conflict between religion and science, between faith and reason. On the other hand, for the Mesoamerican subject, the above separation was an impossi-

bility. All of its systems of intellectual comprehension of the world formed part of a macro system. Nowadays we call this macro system a cosmovision. This constituted the point of reference of all Mesoamerican knowledge; the one that provided all knowledge with a high degree of congruency and with a profound meaning to human life.

Note

1   Translated by Gabriel S. Torres.

Chapter 8

Jaguar Christians in the contact zone

Concealed narratives in the histories of religions in the Americas

David Carrasco

They may someday be considered American classics, but today they are labeled ethnographic texts of dubious value for the history of religions. I am speaking of the fourteen *Books of Chilam Balam* (Books of the Spokesmen of the Jaguar) of the Yucatecan Maya, which contain the history and cosmovisions, transmitted over a thousand years, and reflecting the influences of at least three thoroughly different cultures, the Classic Maya, the Nahuatl cultures from central Mexico who invaded Yucatan, and the European civilizations of Spanish and Republican Mexico. One stunning representative of this corpus is the *Book of Chilam Balam of Tizimin*, which covers the historical and liturgical changes of the Yucatecan ceremonial centers from the seventh to the nineteenth century, with explicit coverage of each twenty-year period from 1441 to 1848. The sections of the *Tizimin* manuscript are dominated by both a sense of cyclical repetitions *and* prophecies of an ancient future! But what catches my attention is another remarkable kind of difference in the text: the radically different ways, in comparison to Spanish accounts, that the Maya viewed the history of their interactions with the Spaniards. Munroe Edmonson, in *The Ancient Future of the Itza: The Book of Chilam Balam of Tizimin* (1982), summarizes this disjunction as follows:

> Perhaps the most startling aspect of the *Book of Tizimin* when it is viewed historically is the autistic disjunction between Mayan and Spanish views of the same broad epoch. There are consistent correspondences on numerous points, but the focus of attention is totally different. The Spaniards chronicled their *entradas*, the sequences of their officials, their laws, discoveries, and conquests. They themselves appear in Itza history, however, as an annoying but shadowy and largely irrelevant presence, alluded to by nicknames. Their tribute was regarded as a temporary burden, destined to be returned at the appropriate time. The thrust of Mayan history is a concern with the Indian lords and priests, with the cosmology that justified their rule, and with the Indian civil war that was perceived as the real dimensions of colonial history.
>
> In effect, this is a secret history…It is astonishing to learn from the Tizimin that the ancient Mayan cities – Mayapan, Uxmal, Chichen Itza, Coba even Merida itself – continued to serve as symbolic reference points for a lively and indigenous religious and political life centuries after their pyramids had fallen into ruins.
>
> (Edmonson 1982: xx)

I am interested in exploring this "different focus of attention" and this sense of a "secret history," especially as they are related to colonial encounters and postcolonial interpretations. And despite the disjunction, there are also a few crucial moments when the focus of attention is shared with the Spaniards. Please reflect with me on a fragment of the text from Chapter 11, which the translator, Edmonson, entitled "Divided rule."

The passage begins by identifying the city of Merida (a colonial city built on top of a Maya site) as the "seat" or central place of a twenty-year period during which Yax Chac was ruler. The text alludes to a civil war between Maya communities resulting in the death of the ruler and a famine, and it goes on to describe a *decision the Maya then made* – the decision to ask the Spaniards to baptize them into the Christian religion. The result was that they became, in my terms, Jaguar Christians.

Following the report of the civil war between the enemy Maya communities and a famine striking the land, the Spokesman of the Jaguar narrates as follows:

> And scattered was the song
> Of his word to the world.
> …Many were the singers
> And no one was not a singer
> Sung to were children
> Sung to were men, Sung to were wives, Sung to were boys, Sung to were girls
> So be it; your younger brothers are coming!
> Your older brothers are arriving
> To change your pants,
> To change your clothes,
> To whiten your dress
> To whiten your pants –
> The foreign judges,
> The bearded men
> Of Heaven Born Merida,
> The seat of the lands.
> And they
> Are the Sun Priests
> Of the living God
> The True God.
> He shall be worshipped
> In one Communion
> On earth Below:
> An additional
> Rule
> And for the fatherless,
> And for the motherless –
> Jaguar was the head
> And urged his people
> To be sprinkled in the changed city.
> So came about
> Its founding,
> And it was the founding of the three-part rule
> In Heaven Born Merida…

> (in *ibid.*: 43–5)

I begin with this complex text of religious change to identify *one* of the interpretive positions scholars of the history of religions in the Americas are surely in, which can be referred to as the "postcolonial world" and is labeled elsewhere by Charles H. Long as the New Arché of Enlightenment/Colonialism. When reading into or, better, reading *from within* the contours, conflicts, terrors, and the dynamic changes of colonial and postcolonial narratives, we are in an interpretive space that Mary Louis Pratt calls the "contact zone." This useful analogy comes from her book, *Imperial Eyes: Travel Writing and Transculturation* (1992). The spatial sense of the analogy "contact zone" attracts others, myself included, who refer to this interpretive position with a number of stimulating spatial analogies. For example:

- "critical landscape" (Ian Chambers);
- "the undone interval" (Trinh T. Minh-ha);
- "street buzz" (Allesandro Triulzi); or
- "thinking at the limit" (Stuart Hall).

I insist that we follow these spatial tropes and consider Pratt's opening description of a contact zone, keeping in mind the Jaguar Christians just referred to. Pratt describes the contact zone as a place of tense cultural interface. The "contact zone" is

> the space of colonial encounters, the space in which peoples geographically and historically separated come into contact with each other and establish ongoing relations, usually involving conditions of coercion, radical inequality, and intractable conflict...often within radically asymmetrical relations of power. By using the term contact, I aim to foreground the interactive, improvisational dimensions of colonial encounters so easily ignored or suppressed by diffusionest accounts of conquest and domination.
>
> (Pratt 1992: 7)

The improvisation of narratives takes place as an expression of "transculturation" when dominated peoples *select and invent* from materials transmitted to them from both the dominant culture and their own indigenous traditions. They work with what they absorb and what they apply. I am impressed with the theme of creative work, of translation and transculturation that takes place in the contact zone.

Reconsider the text of the Jaguar Christians while keeping in mind Pratt's emphasis on the asymmetrical relations of power and the improvisational dimensions of encounters. First, we are told that singers are spreading the word throughout the Maya communities ("scattered was the song/...Many were the singers") that some people have arrived, the Spaniards who are referred to not as strangers but in terms of respect and kinship (as younger and older brothers). They have come to change you, the Spokesman of the Jaguar announces, to change your clothes and the color of your clothes. These new arrivals turn out to be the people in dubious authority – they have more power than the Maya and they reside in the seat of power – these bearded men in "Heaven Born Merida." This city has a celestial prestige, it is born in heaven! At this point we can suspect an improvisation, a "translation" of indigenous ideas into the narrative, for in some pre-Hispanic documents, pyramids, temples, and other ceremonial buildings descend from heaven to earth and give orientation and make an *axis mundi* in the community! The presence of the native voice and improvisation continues in the next passage about the "Sun Priests/Of the living God/The True God." The Sun Priests were Maya leaders in charge of religious organizations, solar gods, calendar cycles, and agriculture and its most precious fruit, corn. Here, the indigenous term refers to the Catholic priests. The phrase "True God," or *Hahal Ku* in Maya, is the indigenous term for the Christian God, but since we have seen one type of theological dexterity, where the Christian priest becomes a Sun Priest, why not suspect another – gods of the contact zone. This is likely when we realize that the *Hahal Ku*, or True God (Christian God), and the *Hunah Ku*, or Sole, Creator God (the Maya god), were merged into one God around this period (see Edmonson 1982: 44). The reference to the Catholic Mass, "He shall be worshipped/In one Communion/On earth Below," presents us with the question of who was being worshipped and how. The final message in the fragment about "An additional/Rule" refers to the internal violence and the impact of Spanish coercion on the natives, for the latter have been left fatherless and motherless, and they have lost their families, their lineage, and perhaps even some access to their ancestors. Then we meet the Jaguar, the highest native official in Maya communities who controlled public offices, land titles, and tribute rights in local communities. "Jaguar was the head," and he tells his people to be "sprinkled" or baptized in the changed city.

In his introduction to the *Book of Chilam Balam of Tizimin*, Edmonson tells us how calculating the Maya were in being converted to Christianity, reflecting again the issue of improvisation. It was not the Spaniards who converted them; rather, it was the Itza who went to the Spaniards when their calendar calculations and prophecies were in line and asked to be sprinkled and to worship the True God. Edmonson describes the Maya initiatives to become Christian in 1695, when their calendar calculations told them that "the time was right...and [they] sent an embassy to Merida to ask the governor to convert them. Obliging with their usual obtuse alacrity, the Spaniards arrived before 8 Ahau began and forced the Indians into armed opposition" (Edmonson 1982: xix).

Returning now to Pratt's theoretical assist, I extend it to argue that historians of religions working in the Americas are dealing with texts produced in the contact zones of both the New Worlds of the Europeans and the New Worlds of the Indians. But they are also dealing, interpreting, writing, and translating from within situations of the contact zones. One writer who boldly affirms that she works from within a contact zone and is not just studying other people's contact zones is Gloria Anzaldua, the Mexican-American author of the celebrated *Borderlands/La Frontera* (1987). Walter Mignolo, in *The Darker Side of the Renaissance: Literacy, Territoriality and Colonization* (1997), identifies Anzaldua as having achieved an interpretive breakthrough, a different way of thinking and writing about religion and language in Latin America. He writes:

> Anzaldua's great theoretical contribution is to create a space-in-between *from where* to think rather than a hybrid space *to talk about*, a hybrid thinking space of Spanish/Latin American and Amerindian legacies as the condition for a possibility for Spanish/Latin American and Amerindian postcolonial theories.
>
> (Mignolo 1997: xiii)

I repeat, the work of the contact zone is one of transculturation, a term first used by Fernando Ortiz in his book *Cuban Counterpoint: Tobacco and Sugar* (1995). As Ortiz and others have noted, when dominated peoples choose and select from materials transmitted to them from the dominant and indigenous cultures, their creative work is always incomplete and open-ended. I am emphasizing this point to encourage historians of religions to give *greater value to the creative possibilities of incomplete, open-ended contact zones and narratives.*

An aside!

As we proceed, there is a subtext to be acknowledged. It is my own now long-term debt and response to certain theoretical contributions of Jonathan Z. Smith around the category of space and place. Beginning with his initial statement of the dialectics of the locative and utopian visions of place in *Map is Not Territory*, to his *To Take Place: Towards a Theory of Ritual*, and more recently in his architecturally arresting essay, "Comparing situations," Smith has provided very useful models and language. Do locative and utopian visions of place get enriched, changed, or significantly altered when confronted with colonial and postcolonial narratives and theories? With the contact zone? With an Anzaldua? With Jaguar Christians? I attempted a mid-course correction of Smith's locative space in my book *To Change Place: Aztec Ceremonial Landscapes* (1998), where I argued for another major category that should be located in the middle, in between the locative and the utopian models and pointing in both directions, which I called *"a metamorphic vision of place."* In the metamorphic vision of place, the processes of change, improvisation, and places *which change through ritual improvisation* suggest something that is neither locative nor utopian. I wrote:

> In a recent series of explorations into the ceremonial patterns of Aztec religion, another conception of spatial order and transformation that is less fixed, more dynamic and momentary has become apparent to me. Sacred space and ceremonial landscapes in Aztec ceremonies expand and retract, meander and transform, link and fold into one another in a "metamorphic vision of place" or, to add to Smith's spectrums of places, the motion and movement of Aztec rituals suggest the title "To Change Place." Deity impersonators, pilgrimages, processions, and mock battles alternate, change, and move beyond static conceptions of sacralized space and social place...It is a vision of place in which change and transformation are the sustained patterns. People change places, the places are transformed by hierophanies, and the humans are momentarily and ultimately changed. It is my suggestion that this metamorphic vision of place reflects a total worldview.
>
> (Carrasco 1998: 33)

I mention this conversation with Jonathan Z. Smith here as a way of thinking theoretically and comparatively about the two concealed narratives that focus this chapter. For we will encounter colonial and postcolonial narratives that conform to and depart from the locative and the utopian – even considering Smith's creative enlargement of the models in his recent book, *Divine Drudgery* (1990). We will encounter in the Cristos de Caña of Mexico a *camouflaged vision of place*. And we will encounter in the myth and ritual of Maximon, a deity of the Atiteco Maya, *not a locative space but, borrowing a strategy from Toni Morrison, a "not-locative" space*, which is not so much utopian as an ambiguous space – one in which Maya and Christian deities have mixed genders, have sexual relations with one another, and replace each other as the flowering tree.

Conquest, the Cristos de Caña, and the camouflaged place

The examples and descriptions above have traditionally and conveniently been handled under the ubiquitous and lazy category of syncretism, a term which the recent *HarperCollins Dictionary of Religion* evaluates as "a term of dubious heritage and limited usefulness often employed to ascribe insincerity, confusion, or other negative qualities to a nascent religious group" (1042). Inga Clendinnen, in her helpful essay, "Ways to the sacred: reconstructing 'religion' in sixteenth century Mexico," goes even further when she writes: "syncretism is not even a teachable proposition because we are not faced with a creative mixing of divergent traditions but with the inexactability of a profoundly different way of conceptualizing the world and man's place within it" (1990: 108). But the best discussion by far of the history and limits of this term appears in the extraordinary book by William B. Taylor, *Magistrates of the Sacred: Priests and Parishioners in Eighteenth Century Mexico* (1996). Taylor, who by the way read with me a number of the classic works of the history of religions, has a section called "Beyond syncretism" in which he also discusses what went on before "syncretism" was the interpretive translation of religious change in Latin American studies. Two models, still influential in anthropological discourse today, are the models of "religious change as conquest" and "religious change as resistance." I will summarize both these models briefly to introduce the next two sections.

Religious change and conquest

The model of difference, religious change, and conquest highlights the crushing experiences of European domination. Consider on the one hand Pablo Neruda's poetic characterization of the long event of conquest and colonialism in his Nobel Prize lecture, "Hacia la Ciudad Esplendida," in which he writes:

> We have inherited this damaged life of peoples dragging behind them the burden of the condemnation of centuries, the most paradisial of peoples, the purest, those who with stones and metals made marvelous towers, jewels of dazzling brilliance – peoples who were suddenly despoiled and silenced in the fearful epochs of colonialism which still linger on.
>
> (1974: 31)

This image of the conquest has been the favorite way of imagining the process of encounter and the forces behind religious change. It puts emphasis on a single, definitive, sustained act of European domination, an act dramatically described by Aldous Huxley during his travels in Guatemala:

> The strength of the Indians is a strength of resistance, of passivity. Matched against these eager, violently active creatures from across the sea, they had no chance – no more chance than a rock against a sledge hammer. True the Indian rock was a very large one, but the Spanish hammer, though small, was wielded with terrific force. Under its quick reiterated blows, the strangely sculptured monolith of American civilization broke into fragments. The bits are still there, indestructible and perhaps some day they may be fused together in a shapely whole; meanwhile they merely testify, in their scattered nullity to the amazing force of the Spanish hammer.
>
> (unpublished manuscript)

In fact there was enormous material destruction in terms of fields, towns, cities, and human beings. When we turn to the statistics of conquest, we learn that the human population in America went from around 80 million people in 1492 to less than 10 million in 1600. In Mesoamerica, there were 25 million people in 1519 but only 1 million native Americans living in the same territory in 1592. This conquest of bodies was supported by a sustained theological, ethical discourse in Spain and New Spain, designed to eliminate the "other," to do away with the native American as body and soul. As the Argentinian novelist Cesar Aira says profoundly, "The Indians clearly seen were a pure absence, but made of the most exclusive quality of presence. Thus, the fear that they provoked" (Fuentes 1992: 8). But the "conquest" model of difference and religious change, which rightly emphasizes the role of violence in the formation of the social world, leaves Native Americans and the miscegenated peoples without a history, a response, a narrative of their own.

One critique of this approach is found in the Cristos de Caña, the hollow, papier mâché-like images of Christ on the Cross, made of plants and produced in Mexico by Indians during the colonial period. They show that the *forms* of the colonial Indians' Christianity were more orthodox than the content! – outwardly looking, as though a real conquest of native ways to the sacred had been, if not hammered, then reworked artistically to appear more European than those made by Europeans. Readers may have seen the Cristo de Caña that was displayed in the 1992 exhibition "Mexico, Splendor of Thirty Centuries," which illustrated the combination of artistry and violence in the life-size figure of the crucified Jesus. These Christs were made from "corn stalks and corn pitch, orchid-bulb glue, carpenter's paste, and a fine clay stucco surface wrapped around a wooden frame – made by Indians indicating that their Christianity [what I earlier called a Jaguar Christianity] appears outwardly well formed to a European eye" (Taylor 1996: 61). But a closer look at an accidental discovery of what was inside reveals that these were objects of the contact zone! Taylor, in his masterful study, writes:

> These light crucifixes from the early colonial period, whose materials connected Christ's passage through birth, death and resurrection to the regeneration of the sacred food plant, maize, sometimes contained writing that would have added to the figures' sacred energy, at least for the maker.
>
> (*ibid.*: 61)

In the case of a Cristo de Caña from Mexicaltzingo, an Indian pueblo in the Valley of Mexico south of the city, more improvisation than conquest was at work. It was Antonio Carrillo y Gariel who, while studying Cristos de Caña, discovered what was inside when one fell from a wall and broke open. An examination was made and it was discovered that

> the chest cavity, abdomen, and upper arms were formed around pages of sixteenth-century community tax records in native style and substantial fragments of Nahuatl texts in Roman script...the Nahuatl texts concerned the life of Christ written on Spanish paper to which was added a stencil (perhaps an embroidery pattern) of Raphael's painting, 'il Pasmo de Sicilia,' depicting Christ's fall on the road to Calvary.
>
> (*ibid.*: 61)

The intention here, Taylor continues, was not "to insert secret idols behind altars" (*ibid.*: 61) or to illustrate how conquered the natives were by Christ, but to conceal a secret history – one which narrated that the image of Christ was associated with the community's forced payments to the authorities (through tax records) and the suffering of Indians (falling on the road to Calvary), as well as "bonded to a powerful new means of communication with the sacred (through the Spanish inscriptions about his life)" (*ibid.*: 62). This ritual improvisation is a good example of the indigenous peoples seeking the spiritual knowledge of the Spaniards while keeping their own religious habits alive, taking control of what the outsiders brought in and making use of it in their own terms. I call this a "camouflaged vision of place" that allows, for some people, a false vision of conquest to remain in focus.

Maximon and ways to the sacred

The second model, besides syncretism, that has been used to interpret the Jaguar Christians and the Cristos de Caña is the model of difference and resistance. It rejects the conquest metaphor – there was no spiritual conquest, regardless of what Robert Ricard says in *The Spiritual Conquest of Mexico* (1982) – but accepts the polarity of two worlds in conflict. The difference is dealt with and imagined primarily in terms of resistance and idols behind altars rather than submission. Here the idea is that the Indians used Christianity as a "front" to their own continuing religious commitments, pretending to convert but remaining the same. Scholars such as Gonzalo Aguirre Beltran, Fernando Benitez, and Jorge Klor de Alva argue that the Indians maintained an idols-behind-altars resistance, only pretending to convert to new beliefs. Miguel Leon Portilla among others argues that "the majority of urban and rural natives...simply borrowed from Christianity whatever elements were necessary to appear Christian...without changing their religious convictions" (Taylor 1996: 52).

One outstanding example that on the surface appears as a "difference and resistance" example but reveals the contact-zone and borderland narratives of a shared ritual, is the cult of Maximon, the "Lord of Looking Good," from Santiago Atitlan, Guatemala. It illustrates what Inga Clendinnen argues so well in her work on sixteenth-century Mexico, namely that the Indians' ability to retain their local religions under colonial rule depended upon their "ways of experiencing the sacred." Taylor summarizes Clendinnen's achievement as follows:

> Focusing on religion as practiced rather than religion as belief, and studying the Indians' "loosely scripted" public performance, she reaches a conclusion...that habits of conceiving the sacred continued while various practices and belief changed...Indians in central Mexico adopted a whole series of Christian practices that were familiar or readily understandable to them, such as attendance at mass, penitence by flagellation, pilgrimage, liturgical theater, sacred dancing, and other forms of worshipful movement, but carried them far beyond what the priest regarded as decorous and reverent conduct. There were mass flagellations that spattered blood on bodies and walls; vigorous dancing and mock combat without obvious liturgical purpose or structure, but with much shouting, clanging, and drinking; noisy, apparently inattentive people at Sunday mass; and others slumped on the church floor, reeking of alcohol.
>
> This "undesired exuberance" was a route to the sacred that repeated and enlarged on the ecstatic piety of pre-Christian times. Harsh colonial sanctions against ritual

warfare, human sacrifice, and the open use of hallucinogenic drugs increased the importance of alcohol as a means to approach the sacred through, as Clendinnen suggests, intense evocations of distinctive moods and experiences – in effect being possessed of the sacred. Community leaders were feted with an abundance of alcoholic drinks – pulque, *mezcal* (distilled maguey juice), or *aguardiente de cana* (cane alcohol) – on many ceremonial occasions; and in the late colonial period, the major feast days came to involve large numbers of people, not only dignitaries, in collective drinking...If the Mexica are representative, the ideas behind such ecstatic practices (which included other kinds of dramatic action and emotion, such as blood sacrifices, and the processions, mystery plays, and other ceremonial performances that early Catholic priests encouraged) centered on transformation and submission to the sacred – of consciously entering new phases, of the living human body as a stage in a vegetal cycle of transformation uniting the human and the sacred.

(ibid.: 60)

The present-day Atiteco Maya peoples of Santiago Atitlan, Guatemala, re-imagine and ritually unearth their own ways of conceiving the sacred during the Holy Week ceremonies that coincide with the chief agricultural and cosmological shift of their calendar, the shift from the dry season to the rainy season. They take the story of Christ's passion, crucifixion, and resurrection and reshape it, in part, in their terms – terms of the regeneration of the earth, plants, and time through sexual insemination by their male gods. In this reshaping, the powers of Jesus are taken into the indigenous narratives and transformed by local categories and myth. Some even suggest that his gender is switched back and forth from male to female and back to male through sexual intercourse with the figure of Maximon, who also switches gender. This is clearly neither locative nor utopian but an *ambiguous vision of the place of gender and gods.*

Maximon is alternately referred to as Venerable Grandfather, Venerable Grandchild, Mr. Knotted, and the Lord of Looking Good, according to the time and place of his rituals. We come to understand something of this plurality of meanings by summarizing the myth of his creation. During their cofradia gatherings, the Atitecos say that Maximon was created when sexual disorder was brought to the family of rain gods who lived in and near Santiago Atitlan. There were both thirteen male and thirteen female rain deities, corresponding to the thirteen levels of the sky. The males moved in an east-to-west direction, while the females moved from north to south and also stayed at home. While the male gods were in the mountains making rain, a mortal man sneaked into town and had sexual intercourse with the thirteen female rain goddesses. When the thirteen male deities discovered this violation they were both troubled and impressed by the sexual prowess of the intruder. They decided to create a being who would guard the females and the moral order, and thus they created Maximon. They searched for a special tree, the Flowering Tree, the *Jaloj K'exoj* (from which to cut and carve Maximon's image), that existed at the center of the world and regenerated everything. (In searching, they found the Red Bean Producing Tree, as red beans were used in divination.) All the rain deities then gathered together and created Maximon by injecting their power into the wooden figure in thirteen locations, the shoulders, elbows, wrists, hips, knees, ankles, and heart – each place invigorated by one of the deities. The result of infusing all this magic into Maximon was that when he came to life, he had all their power and was the most attractive, most powerful being in the world. He looked around and shot off into the community – having sexual intercourse with everyone because he could make himself into the most attractive female or the most attractive male, and families of gods and peoples were thrown into jealous and painful conflicts. Maximon was the Lord of Looking Good, the Lord of Liquor, the Lord of Tobacco – that is to say, the Ultimate Party Animal. In an attempt to gain control of Maximon, the rain gods organized a big fiesta in Santiago and invited the best-looking women and men to lure him back. Maximon showed up "dressed to seduce," and the deities jumped him and twisted his neck and broke it to curb his power. To hide his good looks, they placed a mask on the back of his head, which was now facing forward, and Maximon, they say, is blind to the future and only sees the past.

The themes of unbounded sexual desire, opposition, and confrontation between Maximon and Jesus are reworked during Semana Santa, or Holy Week, which is not a Holy Week conquest or resistance to Holy Week, but a drama where the differences of these gods are activated and worked out. During Semana Santa, Maximon takes on the name of "Lord of the Center of Everything That Is" and represents not only the sexual organ but also the five dangerous days in between the end of the dry season and the initiation of the wet season. He is also dressed and analogized as the Flowering Tree. But there is a competing Flowering Tree who is Jesus on the Cross and who is also referred to by that name. Later in the week, he replaces Maximon at the center of the world, but only after private and public encounters between the two.

The Atiteco say that in order for spring to be born and Easter to be completed, Maximon and Jesus need to have sexual and social contact, and this is realized in two ritual settings, one in private and one in public.

The private meeting

The private encounter takes place when fruit is brought into the town from the lowlands and carefully laid out in a private room. This fruit is understood to represent both female entities and Jesus Christ in his female form. Maximon's image is taken into the room at the appropriate time and left laying amid the fruit. The doors are closed and it is suggested by some that Maximon as the "Center of Everything That Is" inseminates the Jesus fruit and gives life-energy to the earth. Some Atiteco also say that Maximon is attacking Jesus' femininity to drive it out so that Jesus will be fully male when he is crucified (Carlsen, personal communication)!

The public meeting

It is Good Friday and Maximon has been carried on the shoulder of the shaman to a private chapel, hung on a pole, and adorned as the Flowering Tree with fruits, plants, and even live animals. It was from there that he was taken two days before to the private encounter with Jesus. A crowd gathers in the *atrio* of the church and Maximon is brought out amid much admiration and excitement and paraded above the people. According to Robert Carlsen, at a certain moment, the image of Jesus, now as Jesus Sepultado, is also brought out of the chapel and into the people's midst. Maximon's image is rushed into the *atrio* and taken up to confront the image of Jesus. Maximon bows to the four quarters of the world and is then rushed back into his chapel.

The Christian sequence of crucifixion and resurrection follows in the next few days. When Jesus is resurrected, his crucified image, dressed much as Maximon was – with fruits, flowers, live animals – is stuck into a hole called the umbilicus of the world, and lifted up into a vertical position. He is now the Flowering Tree. Maximon's image is either put away or taken apart until the next year.

This stunning series of ritual movements illustrates for me, in part, Clendinnen's claim that the Maya ways to the sacred are both continuous and enlarged during the Holy Week ceremonies. The indigenous way to the sacred is via the flowering of the earth through the ritual insemination by their gods, only now it is the Christian Holy Week that becomes the theater for this insemination in the contact zone.

This ritual improvisation is a good example of indigenous dexterity in that it shows how attractive forms and rites are taken from Christianity but used in local ways far beyond the control of Christian priests. For these reasons I call the Maximon drama a "not-locative" space.

In this chapter I have explored how two concealed narratives of sacred regeneration each tie the life of Jesus to the agricultural cycles of the indigenous peoples of Mesoamerica. My purpose has been to show how these narratives, which center on the hidden meanings of images, one made of a corn stalk Jesus and the other of the red bean tree, draw us into the dynamics of concealment that constitute the improvisations which help the participants survive and sometimes thrive. I call these peoples Jaguar Christians to highlight how they do the creative work of making new combinations while never forgetting the terrible asymmetries that re-created them in the contact zone.

References

Anzaldua, Gloria, *Borderlands/La Frontera*, 2nd edn, San Francisco: Aunt Lute Books, 1987.
Carrasco, David, *To Change Place: Aztec Ceremonial Landscapes*, Boulder: University Press of Colorado, 1998.
Chambers, Iain and Lidia Curti (eds), *The Post Colonial Question: Common Skies, Divided Horizons*, London: Routledge, 1996.
Clendinnen, Inga, "Ways to the sacred: reconstructing 'religion' in sixteenth century Mexico," *History and Anthropology* 5, 1990.
Edmonson, Munroe, *The Ancient Future of the Itza: The Book of Chilam Balam of Tizimin*, Austin: University of Texas, 1982.
Fuentes, Carlos, "Novel of the Americas," in Raymond Williams (ed.) *The Novel in the Americas*, Niwot: University Press of Colorado, 1992.
Long, Charles H., *Significations: Signs, Symbols and Images in the Interpretation of Religion*, St. Bonaventure, NY: The Davies Group, 1999.
Mignolo, Walter, *The Darker Side of the Renaissance: Literacy, Territoriality and Colonization*, Ann Arbor: University of Michigan Press, 1997.
Neruda, Pablo, *Toward the Splendid City: Nobel Lecture*, New York: Farrar, Straus, and Giroux, 1974.
Ortiz, Fernando, *Cuban Counterpoint: Tobacco and Sugar*, trans. Harriet de Onis, Durham, NC: Duke University Press, 1995.
Pratt, Mary Louise, *Imperial Eyes: Travel Writing and Transculturation*, London: Routledge, 1992.
Ricard, Robert, *The Spiritual Conquest of Mexico*, Los Angeles: University of California Press, 1982.
Smith, J.Z., *Divine Drudgery: On the Comparison of Early Christianities and the Religions of Late Antiquity*, Chicago: University of Chicago Press, 1990.
Taylor, William B., *Magistrates of the Sacred: Priests and Parishioners in Eighteenth Century Mexico*, Stanford: Stanford University Press, 1996.

Chapter 9

Modernity, resistance, and the Iroquois Longhouse people[1]

Chris Jocks

At first glance, "indigenous religious traditions" do not appear to be large policy concerns of the United States or Canada. The American military campaign to wipe out the Ghost Dance in the late nineteenth century, as well as twentieth-century bureaucratic programs in both the United States and Canada to outlaw traditional ceremonial works such as the Lakota Sun Dance or the North-west Coast Potlatch, seem to belong to bygone days; today, in many places traditional ceremonies have become tourist attractions. Yet a closer look reveals a different story. Legislative and judicial conflicts involving freedom of religion, particularly protection of and access to sacred sites, are only one indication that these traditions will continue to be a thorn in the side of the modern technocratic state. Even police and military conflicts such as the one at Oka in 1990 have strong roots in traditional attitudes, attitudes in which religious thought plays a key role.

But "indigenous religious traditions" should also be a thorn in the side of the academic study of religion – academics, after all, cannot completely disavow their relationship with the modern technocratic state. I am deeply suspicious of the academic study of indigenous traditions – yes, the very field in which I work. I am deeply suspicious lest we merely make the conquest of native peoples nicer by collecting and enshrining "nice things" about the indigenous ways of life that we are in fact endangering. We must search out the deepest levels of critique, lest all of our work, even our most sincere efforts to "understand the other," in the end go into the maw of consumerism gone mad and come out unrecognizable.

We live and work on ground poisoned by our toxic histories, but there is life beneath and above that ground. My contribution here is one attempt to critique – to clean up – a small piece of this ground. My first step is to relinquish where possible the role of the expert whose insights are always superior to those of her or his "subjects." I am a Mohawk man, but the real authorities in the Longhouse world are the folks who are there, on the territories and in the longhouses, in fair weather and foul, showing up for ceremonial times but also showing up the day before and the day after to clean up and get things ready – the ones practicing the songs and helping their children learn the language and asking each other the important questions. The observations and thoughts I am about to relate may be useful or they may not, but read them as a report of my conversations with the tradition, not as the analysis of a superior authority.

Defending the borders

In the backyard of Charlie Patton, a fire was kept burning for two months in the summer of 1990. Oien'kwa'ón:we, native tobacco, was offered daily in the fire, in prayer. The fire was lit shortly after the battle on 11 July between Mohawk and other First Peoples and the Quebec provincial police at Kanehsatà:ke, "The Sandy Place," also known as Oka. In this fight, one man lost his life. The fire continued to burn later that summer as that same police force, along with federal police and the Canadian army, occupied Kahnawà:ke, about twenty-five miles away. That name means "Place by the Rapids," referring to the nearby Lachine Rapids on the St. Lawrence River. The people of both these communities speak of themselves in their traditional language as Kanien'kehá:ka, "People of the Flint Place." In English they are Mohawk. Thus they belong to one of the five Iroquois peoples, sharing deep streams of history and culture. The more traditional-minded among them say they are Longhouse people, Rotinonhsiónni.[2]

The fire in Charlie Patton's backyard was also burning on 28 August of that same year, 1990, when a caravan of vehicles evacuating women, children, and elders from Kahnawà:ke, which was under military blockade, was stoned by an angry mob of Quebec citizens shouting anti-Indian slogans, leading to the second fatality of the conflict, an elderly Kahnawà:ke man who died of a heart attack. Three weeks later, on 18 September, the fire was still burning when Canadian army troops landed by boat and Huey helicopter on Tekakwitha Island, adjacent to the village of Kahnawà:ke. When the army attempted to cross the one-lane bridge that leads into town, a crowd that included not only young men of the Warrior Society, but also women, children, and elders, met the young soldiers with angry words, fists, and bodies, determined to turn back the invasion of their community. Late in the day the army retreated, unable to push back or disperse the crowd with razor wire and tear gas. Later intelligence revealed that the commanders had not expected concerted resistance; they did not know the people of Kahnawà:ke, just as the provincial police had not known those across the river at Kanehsatà:ke.

These failed attempts by the governments of Quebec and Canada to assert jurisdiction over two small Indian communities began when the owners of a golf course gained permission to bulldoze an old, peaceful patch of pine woods where Mohawk people had gathered for as far back as anyone could remember to relax and play, as well as to bury and remember their dead. According to Quebec law, the Mohawks never had title to the woods; according to traditional practice and understanding, they had never lost or given it up. When the local authorities held firm behind the golf club's expansion and demanded, and got, a military confrontation to end the Mohawk protest, average Canadian citizens' carefully cultivated sense of their own decency was offended, and the battle drew wide media attention. For Mohawks, however, this was only one season, one cluster of attempted invasion and injury: one page, really, from a long history of conflict that continues to the present.

Modernity here is represented in at least three ways. First, it is represented by the rule of an abstract system of law in which written arguments and findings are privileged, while oral tradition is considered merely "hearsay" – a system in which ownership is conferred ultimately by conquest, and subsequently by economic privilege; a system in which the taking of property by favored interests is easily made to appear legal. Second, modernity is represented by the supremacy of profitable use of land over profitless historical and spiritual value. Third, modernity is represented by the remarkable insecurity and uneasiness that led to the Canadian army being called out to subdue by force a handful of Indians who only wanted to be left alone.

The roots of this uneasiness and the roots of Mohawk resistance lie in the same poisoned soil, and the resistance is likewise manifold. It is represented here not only by the

fire and the prayers put into it – sent by means of it – but also by the community's militant, uncompromising defiance of the physical threat of invasion. It was represented,
further, by the manner in which many different segments of the community pulled
together to cooperate during the blockade: patrolling the borders of the territory;
providing and distributing food; locating and broadcasting accurate information; burying
local differences and disputes, at least temporarily. Charlie Patton is not a supporter of the
Warrior Society, and the prayers around the fire in his backyard were for peace and the
traditional "Good Mind," ka'nikonhrí:io; but among those visiting and praying at that fire
were armed Mohawk warriors guarding the perimeters of the territory near Charlie's farm.
Finally, resistance to modernity was represented by the array of Mohawk negotiators and
the positions they took as various parties worked without success to resolve the standoff.
Included on the Mohawk side were representatives of several traditionalist constituencies
as well as modern elective governments. Strong disagreement among these constituencies
complicated the negotiations, but they shared at least one fundamental principle: they
negotiated on behalf of an autonomous people, not a municipality or otherwise subject
community.

Longhouse narratives

In various ways and to various degrees, the Longhouse ceremonies, narratives, and
language allow perhaps a quarter of Kahnawà:ke's five to six thousand residents – maybe
more – to participate in a complex, dynamic, and ancient system of thought and action.
Its oldest strands connect today's Longhouse to the consciousness of forebears who
depended for sustenance only on the nutritional and spiritual resources of the forests and
clearings of north-eastern North America. This consciousness is animated by intensified
experiences through which relationships with the other-than-human entities of the forest
were, and to some extent still are, established and maintained, bringing the power to
know and the power to heal to the human community. The rites of the so-called Medicine
Societies include the cultivation of individual experience that continues to enact this
consciousness.

In subsequent centuries, communities of proto-Iroquoian people bound themselves
more closely together as they built horticulture into their way of life. They greeted,
thanked, and celebrated corn, beans, and squash – the "Three Sisters" – and learned new
forms of reciprocity and respect embedded in the seasons, sky, and soil. These find expression in the Longhouse calendar of ceremonies, a cyclical structure composed of many
important ritual and narrative exchanges. In these "doings" can be found a Longhouse
understanding of the way the world works, and the way human beings were intended to
work with it. These practices and narratives persistently focus human mental and
emotional attention on a surrounding, prior domain full of life, power, and mutual dependence. In that power was always a degree of danger, but skill and attention and
good-mindedness could make human life not only possible in the short term but sustainable; and not only sustainable but rich.

Iroquois clans are the basis of traditional structures of relationship, of mutual support,
of decision-making and dispute-resolution. These structures emphasize consensus, clarity
of thought and communication, and the healing of loss and other emotions that render
hearing impossible. The ritual use of wampum, the rites of Condolence, and the entire
system of government contained in the Kaianeren'kó:wa – the Iroquois "Great Peace,"

sometimes also known as "The Great Law" – are some ways in which these values are implemented. In this evolving system, human social relations were designed to follow the same patterns of reciprocity and autonomy that Longhouse people understood to characterize the rest of Creation. Each individual, both genders, each clan, each community, has its place in Creation, just as each other-than-human species does. Each has a part in the "Original Instructions," as modern Longhouse speakers have phrased it. The general rule is non-interference; but when concerted thought or action is needed, cooperation is solicited by persuasion, never forced. This practice remains the ideal in Longhouse social and political relations.

But human beings often fail in their designs – fall short of their ideals. Cycles of revenge, self-indulgence, and violence ensue. "Good Minds" are weakened, and times of extraordinary renewal become necessary. The early nineteenth-century revival of Longhouse traditionalism under the Seneca visionary, Handsome Lake, was one such time. But the Kaianeren'kó:wa also arose in such a time, perhaps a thousand years ago, according to those charged with keeping its memory. At that time, all the Iroquois peoples were brought together into one longhouse, where they rededicated themselves to traditional social, political, and spiritual relations. The narrative that carries this tradition delineates in detail an ingenious system of confederated decision-making that is still in use today, but a different kind of moment constitutes the heart that this political face expresses. In that moment, the heart and mind and body of a single person are transformed. Atotárho, the last holdout against the Great Peace – deformed, twisted, malevolent – is made to discover his human nature when a complete circle of his relatives-to-be stand around him and offer him skén:nen, karihwí:io, ka'shatsténhsera: peace, the good message, and the power to live as human beings were intended.

The physical longhouse is an edifice with doors; it communicates with the world outside. In the final decade of the last century, Longhouse leaders were continuing to think and speak and act on behalf of Iroquois sovereignty, land claims, and the survival of traditional knowledge. But these local concerns are not the entire story. Since early in the last century, Longhouse activists have worked to develop global indigenous networks and movements, frequently sending delegations to international gatherings and tribunals. Moreover, well before environmental issues became popular, Longhouse people were pursuing an indigenous program of environmental education and activism, both locally and elsewhere. Longhouse resistance has opposed itself, then, to at least four distinct but interrelated manifestations of modernity: large-scale, homogenizing corporate economics and politics; consumerist systems of education and culture; genocide against indigenous people; and environmental irresponsibility.

High steel

High steel construction was my grandfather's way of life. For many years he was a foreman, well known and respected by other Mohawk iron-working men, judging from the stories I still hear about him. He led crews that built bridges and skyscrapers from New York City to San Francisco to Alaska, living for months or years at a time in New York and other cities, and returning home to Kahnawà:ke whenever he could. He was everything a young boy could want to emulate: physically strong, opinionated, but fun-loving too, with an air of bravado and freedom. I cannot remember him ever diminishing himself to gain someone else's approval; he demanded, and invariably got, respect. His confidence and sense of self seemed impregnable. His life was full of adventures and conquests, far-away places, and dangerous work done with skill. At the same time, on any matter involving family or future he sought out and heeded the advice of Margaret, his wife, whom we called Ista, "mother." This, when I was young, was my image of Mohawk men.

My grandfather was a devout Catholic, who I doubt ever set foot in a longhouse. A believer in going to mass early, I can still remember him rousing us kids long before six o'clock on Sunday mornings for that purpose. He was not alone; in those days Kahnawà:ke itself was overwhelmingly Catholic, as it had been for three hundred years since its founding as a Jesuit mission in 1667. Yet the life he led bears striking resemblance to Iroquois tradition. Sociologist Morris Freilich in 1958, and anthropologist David Blanchard in 1983, pointed out the direct descent of the iron-working way of life from that of Mohawk warriors and hunters even before the European invasion: in both cases, men spend long months away from the home village, in the company of other men, led by temporary, self-chosen leaders, pursuing work which defies the inertia of comfort and security, and whose danger demands alertness, mental and emotional conditioning, and, of course, physical strength and agility.[3]

There are other similarities. Since their travels took them to cities across the continent and abroad, where they often lived for months or years at a time, Iroquois ironworkers developed a certain cosmopolitanism just as their wide-ranging forebears had, not only long ago as warriors, but in the interim as voyageurs for the French fur trade, as riverboat pilots, and even as entertainers in turn-of-the-century Indian shows. They were not easily intimidated. Yet beneath the bravado and independence, most of these men maintained strong ties with Kahnawà:ke, usually sending the bulk of their pay back to the homeland, and returning home themselves whenever they could. Thus the proud defiance by which the outside world most often knew them was actually employed in support of and in service to the wives and clan mothers back home.

This dynamic combination of independence and relationship, of autonomy and reciprocity, of innovation and conservatism, is a distinctive characteristic of Iroquois culture and history. Indeed, it is encoded in the most fundamental levels of Longhouse narrative: In the Iroquois Creation Narrative, all human life descends from Sky Woman, and the organization of all life on Earth is accomplished by her twin grandchildren, but none of this would have happened but for a scandalous rupture in the peace and harmony of the World Above, causing her to fall to the formless Earth below – or to be pushed, depending on which version one hears! Later, as Creation is organized by the twins, the same pattern is evident: Tawískaron thwarts and confuses the efficient, mechanical order of Okwirá:se's work. Perpetual summer is interrupted by the grip of winter. While some non-native commentators have set the twins in a kind of irresolvable moral opposition, labeling the one as "Evil" and the other as "Good," in fact we are witnessing the expression of a consciousness informed by close observation of natural processes, in which creativity is found in the margins of systems, or, conversely, in the conjunction or juxtaposition of seemingly dissimilar forces.

This is not to say that high steel construction is in every respect analogous to the traditional – that is to say, pre-invasion – roles of Iroquois men, such as hunting, raiding, trading, or diplomacy. Nor is it to say that Catholicism is merely an innovative outer form that has little or no effect on some kind of radical aboriginal religious sensibility. It is to say, however, that while Iroquois people have found it necessary to make many creative adaptations in three hundred years of living shoulder to shoulder with Euro-American civilization, these innovations should not be judged automatically destructive of tradition. Form and content are not always easily distinguished. Theology aside, when Catholicism was the norm at Kahnawà:ke, it was a uniquely Mohawk Catholicism that helped foster a tightly knit community bound by very traditional practices of reciprocity and respect. And high steel construction has given generations of Iroquois men a means to prove their manhood, develop mental and physical skills, and support their families and relatives righteously.

The heyday of both these institutions at Kahnawà:ke is now passed, yet for most of the last century, they supported Mohawk identity and gave it continuity. In their time, they illustrate that even selective assimilation – assimilation, that is to say, under local community control and subject to the community's traditional values – can be a kind of resistance to modernity. Onondaga artist Arnold Jacobs paints an Iroquois ironworker standing on two girders, high above the canyonlands of downtown Manhattan. An eagle stretches and takes flight beside him, and his face turns to the horizon, where deep in the distance a plume of smoke rises from home, a settlement in wooded hills.[4]

Survival school

In the fall of 1978, Mohawk high school students from Kahnawà:ke walked out of their classes en masse to protest against the invisibility of Mohawk history and culture in the non-Indian public school system they attended in the neighboring town of Châteauguay. Five days later, the Kahnawà:ke Survival School opened, staffed initially by volunteers and operating out of living rooms and meeting rooms around town. It was dedicated not to teaching individual survival skills in a competitive economic environment, but to the survival of the community and its Mohawk culture. Courses in Mohawk history, culture, language, and traditional skills were included along with standard high school subject matter, and these changes were soon implemented in local grammar schools as well, the largest of which now teaches in Mohawk language only for grades 1 through 4, and in Mohawk for half of the time for grades 5 and 6.

Women have played key roles in these educational initiatives – women such as Jeannine Iorihwiióston Beauvais, the first principal of the Survival School. Under her administration, the Survival School implemented a traditional decision-making system, in which students and teachers alike met according to clan and deliberated school policy. The salary structure was also traditional: the entire staff, whether teachers, janitors, cooks, or the principal, chose to be paid at the same rate. Basic ceremonial knowledge is only one part of traditional education in the Kahnawà:ke schools today; through the work of the Mohawk Curriculum Centre – again, staffed mostly by women – Longhouse concepts are also utilized in such areas as cosmology, natural science, social values, physical education, and history. Even mathematics curricula are devised to include Iroquois cultural content. The school system conforms to Canadian guidelines with regard to religious instruction per se, which is available in either Longhouse or Catholic versions according to student preference. However, the import of Kahnawà:ke's broad program of cultural education is that along with a strong sense of identity and history, students will have a basic knowledge of the Longhouse world-view and ceremonial practices; any student who does decide to go to the longhouse will better understand what goes on there.

In this instance, modernity is represented by mainstream public North American educational systems, which are designed to teach mainstream cultural knowledge and values. Most commentators would agree that these systems are presently in a period of transition as global economic pressures bring important mainstream cultural assumptions into question. The response to these pressures is sometimes an attempt to "return to basics," and sometimes an increased emphasis on multicultural education. Unfortunately, multicultural education rarely has gone beyond a sort of "it's a small world" approach, acquainting children with interesting, colorful details abstracted from unfamiliar cultures, such as ethnic dress and foods and words. By contrast, the Kahnawà:ke Mohawk response to this side of modernity is penetrating, holistic, and continually evolving. Its determination to rework and take control of all areas of the curriculum demonstrates a recognition that no aspect of education is "value-neutral."

Religion and resistance

At first glance, Kahnawà:ke might seem an odd setting to examine any aspect of Iroquois religious tradition. Other communities, such as those at Onondaga, Cattaraugus, or Ohswéken, have far more robust and unbroken Longhouse traditions than Kahnawà:ke, with its three hundred-year Catholic history. Kahnawà:ke did not even have a longhouse until 1927, and in none of its three current longhouses does the ceremonial or narrative repertoire begin to approach the richness found in the other communities just mentioned. Therefore, if the only choice in understanding native North American traditionalism's resistance to modernity is between an uncompromising resistance to change on the one hand, and crumbling into modernity's flotsam on the other, then Kahnawà:ke would have to be judged a crumbled community from its inception. The resurgence of traditionalism since the 1920s would then be considered not only a poor imitation, but also an exercise in self-deception.

This kind of interpretation has been the norm in mainstream studies of American Indian religious change, and is built on a linear and quantitative approach to religious "data" that is related to "culture trait" methods in anthropology. An ideal, fully developed, preferably pre-invasion baseline version of the tradition is posited, and from it a list of "elements" is abstracted.[5] Any subsequent version of the tradition can then be subjected to the same snapshot treatment, the two lists compared, and a quantitative judgment made as to the relative strength or erosion of the tradition. Elements incorporated or "borrowed" from formerly alien religious systems automatically count as debits against a tradition's continuity quotient. But what qualifies as an element of a religious system? Scholars of religion are trained to identify their subject phenomenologically, but the kinds of phenomena that qualify as religious are usually limited and structured in a particular way: beliefs – propositions – about the nature, origins, and ultimate disposition of life form the center; ceremonial enactment and narrative texts directly express the beliefs and compose an intermediate circle around the center; while social, ethical, and material implications form the periphery.

These approaches can too easily ignore the dynamic, fluid nature of religious thinking and action, which might be compared to the workings of some parts of the brain, whereby the functions of a damaged region can be assumed by another region formerly dedicated to other processes. It might also be compared to a hologram, in which any piece or fragment has the potential to reproduce the original whole through a properly focused application of energy. The analogy can be pushed further. If, as many have suggested, American Indian religious communities include not only human but also other-than-human members, then the fragments whereby tradition is recovered are not limited to products of human intelligence. In a remark I have heard in different contexts, it is asserted that even the disappearance of a ceremony, when no human being is left alive who is able to perform it, is not final, because the animals themselves, or the other beings to whom the ceremony was directed, will remember its essence and will hold it for future generations.

Can we, then, imagine an alternative scheme in which religion is constituted in the spaces between its discrete moments of performance and textualization – of enactment and reflection? If we can understand religion as a relational gestalt, we may be better prepared to qualitatively interpret religious systems in which the assertion of discrete, propositional meaning is performance reserved mostly for inquisitive tourists and anthropologists; in which change is understood in cyclical, seasonal terms; in which what we do and how we do it are masks that do not displace but perhaps conceal – or figure – out of respect what we think or believe. Religion, conceived in this way, is not a system of symbols, a collection of representations; it is, rather, a system of relationships between and among individuals and collectivities, both human and other-than-human.

Only this kind of analysis can explain the survival and continual resurgence of traditional religious thought and action among American Indian people who usually insist that they have no "religion" – that the term has no relevance in their understanding of what they do. Only this kind of analysis can adequately comprehend the many instances in which traditional forms of religious expression resurface after long periods of apparent oblivion and displacement. Only this kind of analysis can begin to accurately interpret the experience of life in a traditional American Indian community, in which our active relations with one another are the most sacred doings imaginable – the source of our being as a people and, so, as individuals.

Seen in this light, it is entirely appropriate to consider tradition and modernity in a place such as Kahnawà:ke. It was from my Longhouse teachers there that I learned this relational model of religion, and it was there that I witnessed and heard about the everyday enactment of these sacred relationships. It was there that I began to understand how relational structures such as reciprocity, generosity, social provision of material security, and gender respect, often cited as typical Indian "traits," are in fact deeply held, fundamental religious acts. The instances I have discussed here are intended to illustrate this assertion. The prayers in Charlie Patton's backyard were religious acts that cleared a space in the midst of conflict and fear, from which skén:nen, karihwí:io, and ka'shatsténhsera – qualities of the "Good Mind" – could be rekindled. In the same way, the activity of ceremonialists and speakers, singers and dancers, jokesters and cooks, and all who play supporting roles in Longhouse "doings," is religious activity. Mohawk ironworkers such as my grandfather do religious work, in a sense, as they defy comfort and security in order to prove themselves, face danger and power in the world, and, in the process, provide for their families, relatives, and community. The future-oriented labor of teachers, administrators, and all who support the work of Kahnawà:ke schools, too, is fundamentally religious, insofar as it explicitly aims to inform and so provide for the survival of a Mohawk identity that is intrinsically religious.

All of these projects resist modernity, and the many ways modernity is designed to maximize efficiency by homogenization. At Kahnawà:ke, this resistance has never been wholly successful. Today, every Mohawk community struggles not only with external pressure to surrender key tenets of culture and identity, but also with deep internal division. Much damage has been done to the traditional fabric, and so the people are not uniformly proud of all their history. Yet their determination to resist remains as strong as ever. Why?

According to one strand of public opinion, buttressed by a few academicians such as anthropologist James A. Clifton, such assertions of Indian identity are essentially "fictions," self-consciously designed to earn public sympathy and, ultimately, financial support.[6] Against such cynicism, my thesis is that Mohawk resistance at Kahnawà:ke and elsewhere is animated by deeply held convictions about what a good life is – values nurtured in a matrix of religious, political, social, economic, and environmental consciousness-in-action. This resistance cannot be well understood if its religious dimensions are ignored, yet approaching these dimensions instigates a re-examination of conventional views regarding religious change and continuity; and of what constitutes religion itself.

So perhaps sometime soon we will be able to give full credit to accounts such as that recorded by the Lakota writer Luther Standing Bear in 1933: He is remembering his boyhood, a time when he was 5 years old and had just killed his first bird. His father celebrated this passage by giving away a horse, to an old man who would have no means of returning the gift. For Standing Bear, the event was not a mere social signifier or means of economic redistribution. "This," he remarks, "was the beginning of my religious training."

Conclusion

When I was a graduate student in religious studies at the University of California, Santa Barbara, pursuing my studies of American Indian religious life, my professor, Inés Talamantez, would encourage her students by explaining the importance of our work. She would say that American Indian religions deserve the same respect the academic world accords to the so-called "great religions" of the world. I agreed and took courage then, and heartily agree today, but we must also try to ensure that what we academics give to American Indian and other indigenous traditions is really respect. We must continue to ask questions such as whether it is respect or colonialism even to assign the label of religion to people who explicitly deny that it describes what they do. If to classify in some measure is to conquer, then better classifications could well be an even more insidious form of conquest!

On the other hand, if those people who bring their experience out of indigenous contexts into the academic discussion are not present, what happens? The native voices are left out, they become irrelevant, and colonialist interpretations fill the void. So, in my own research and teaching I do not so much explicate American Indian religions as tell stories: I try to reconstitute theory from the experiential ground up, searching down into the roots of indigenous epistemology to recover knowledge as something we do rather than something we possess. I also critique academic sources and categories, and so spend considerable time explaining what American Indian thought and practice is not. None of this resolves the inherent conflict, but sometimes it can at least illuminate that poisoned, conflicted ground.

Notes

1   Read at the conference, "Beyond 'Primitivism': Indigenous Religious Traditions and Modernity," University of California, Davis, 28–31 March 1996.
2   I use the term "traditional" to refer to ideas and practices understood to have strong pre-invasion roots, as well as to people who attempt to ground their daily lives – intellectually, affectively, and otherwise – in these ideas or practices.

3   Morris Freilich, "Cultural persistence among the modern Iroquois," *Anthropos* 53 (1958): 473–83, and "Scientific possibilities in Iroquoian studies: an example of Mohawks past and present," *Anthropologica* 5 (1963): 171–86; Davis Blanchard, "High steel! The Kahnawake Mohawk and the high construction trade," *Journal of Ethnic Studies* 11 (1983): 41–60; Richard Hill, *Skywalkers: A History of Indian Ironworkers*, Brantford, Ont.: Woodland Indian Cultural Center, 1987.

4   Arnold Jacobs, "Reflection: Tribute to our Iron Skywalkers," acrylic, 1983.

5   For an example of this genre in the Iroquois setting, see William N. Fenton, "Long-term trends of change among the Iroquois," in Verne F. Ray (ed.) *Cultural Stability and Cultural Change: Proceedings of the 1957 Annual Spring Meeting of the American Ethnological Society*, Seattle: American Ethnological Society, 1957, 30–5.

6   See James A. Clifton, *The Invented Indian: Cultural Fictions and Government Policies*, New Brunswick, NJ: Transaction Books, 1990.

Chapter 10

"He, not they, best protected the village"

Religious and other conflicts in twentieth-century Guatemala

Bruce Lincoln

Preliminary observations

If by "indigenous religions" we mean to denote religious traditions that have not (yet) been influenced or colonized by the global "isms," then such traditions are notoriously difficult to locate, since most of our evidence is not the autonomous self-expression of an ab-original entity ("a story people tell themselves about themselves," in Clifford Geertz's memorable phrase), but a product of contact between indigenous cultures and encroaching others. Indeed, the very mediations that make these data available to anyone other than indigenes also render them most problematic (travelers' accounts, colonial archives, missionary reports, ethnographies, co-authored autobiographies, and studies by those educated in mission schools or Euro-American universities). As a result, our view of the "indigenous" per se is always refracted, if not obstructed: what we observe most clearly is not "the other," but the situation of encounter between that other and an exogenous intruder. This, however, need occasion no regret, for it provides the stimulus and opportunity to transform our understanding of "indigenous" and "world" religions alike.

Thus, the encounter situation reveals the methodological and moral fallacy of treating "world religions" in a-historic fashion, and forces one to recognize these as emergent phenomena, which expanded their territory, numbers, and power always at the expense of others. Here, one needs to enquire about the extra-doctrinal factors that facilitated their expansion by asking, for example, when and how specific areas and populations were identified as targets of opportunity for missionizing and conversion? Who made these determinations, and in consultation with what other interests (the state, the military, chartered monopolies or venture capital, etc.)? Whence came the personnel and material support for such ventures? How were these resources deployed, and what returns were expected on the investment? Perhaps most important, what kind of subjects did missions seek to constitute, and how did they pursue this project? (Proletarianization is likely to be a key issue.) Furthermore, which portions of prior doctrine, canon, and ethical and ritual practice were emphasized, and which ones reinterpreted or occluded for local consumption?

Conversely, focusing on the encounter situation also helps us avoid theorizing an unrealistically pristine "indigenous" and lets us appreciate that local traditions meet advancing world religions in situations of vastly unequal power, within which they mount certain kinds of resistance, while also making strategic accommodation at points they consider less than vital. At the points of most serious contention, one can observe the crudest shows of force, the most audacious bluffs, the subtlest jockeying for position, and the most complex negotiations. Such points are many and varied, and they shift in locus, nature, and intensity as the engagement continues. Over the course of that engagement, the strategic and tactical sense, cultural and material resources, and determination and endurance of the contending parties are constantly put to the test. At any given moment and in any given locale, the details of religious discourse and practice reflect the extant balance of power between indigenous and exogenous populations, traditions, and values. What is more, they provide the means through which interested parties comment upon, maneuver within, and seek to revise that same balance of power.

Jesús, the "Jews," and Guardians of the mountains

I would like to illustrate these points by treating a few incidents drawn from the history of Guatemala, where, for the last half millennium, Spaniard has struggled against Maya, *ladino* against Indian, the cosmopolitan against the local, the intrusive against the enduring.[1] The first is a story Charles Wagley collected in 1937, as part of his work in Santiago Chimaltenango, a Mam-speaking village of the western highlands.

> Before, the earth was flat, and there were no mountains or *barrancas* (canyons). Father José and Mother María Santissima were the first *naturales* (Indians) to live on the earth. The first man was José and he made the earth, and then came María, his wife. José then made men. At that time their burdens were light because there were no hills or *barrancas* to tire them. The world was *puro plano* (perfectly flat). When Father José first made the earth, neither he nor other men could see what they were doing. Then it was always night and people did not know when to sleep and when to work. Then, so he could see men as they went about, Father José made a great machine, the sun, and then, later, he made the moon so people would have some light as they slept. He made the moon so it would follow the sun and made it strong part of the time and weak other nights. But then the sun and the moon were not regular; they did not appear at the same time every day. Then, Jesús Cristo, the first son of José and María, was born. While María was pregnant the Devil came to José and told him that he was not the father of the child. He said that María had many lovers. José did not believe the Devil and sent him away. On the first day after Jesús Cristo was born, he sat up and talked, and in four days he grew to full size. He told Father José that his name was Jesús Cristo and told him that he would not work on this earth, for he had houses and land above. Jesús told his father, "Do not be troubled, Father, for I am going to make another world and you will be able to help me." Then, day by day, the mountains began to appear on the earth and he (Jesús) began to make valleys and *barrancas* for the rivers. He made the moon weaker [than the sun] so there would be night and day. He set three times a day for people to eat and told people when they should sleep. Now a man watches the sun and eats when it is at regular places [in the sky] and sleeps when the sun is gone. Jesús made roads over these mountains for the Indians to travel. The *naturales* were happy but the people of the Devil, when they saw these mountains appear, were angry and said, "We are not accustomed to these hills. It is the work of that man José and his son. It is better that we kill them."[2]

Wagley described this text as a "combined Chimalteco Genesis-Crucifixion story," and he used it to illustrate the ways orthodox doctrines had been reworked by local traditions and orientations. Although Chimaltecos understood themselves as extremely faithful Catholics, they had little contact with the priest, whose service to their community consisted of a brief visit every year or two. In the interim, religion was in the hands of local officials, some of them attached to the Church (*cantores*, *sacristanes*, *mayordomos*) and some not (diviners and healers, Mam *chimanes*) (Wagley 1949: 50). Within these circumstances, as Wagley observed, the Christian savior comes to be portrayed as a culture hero and trickster, who was born as an Indian, in absolutely human fashion, and whose life was lived on local terrain (*ibid*.: 52). I think, however, one can go further.

Through his creative acts, the Jesús of this story introduces valorized dichotomies at the level of heaven, earth, and society. Thus, he made the sun shine brighter than the moon and brought mountains and valleys to a previously flat earth, an act which also divided humanity into two types.[3] One group of people lives and works happily in the highland terrain, and these are said to be "Indians" or *naturales* (as are Jesús, José, and María). Others find it onerous to trek up and down, and presumably prefer life on the coastal plain or in urban centers.

In the next phase of the plot, the mountain-haters set out to kill Jesús, the maker of mountains. Initially the text calls this murderous band "the people of the Devil," thereby associating them with the malicious spirit who earlier tried to destroy the love of José and María by labeling Jesús a bastard. Later, it shifts nomenclature and calls them "Jews," a term missionaries in New Spain borrowed from the Inquisition for use against adherents of indigenous religion, whom they constituted in this fashion as enemies not just of imperial conquest and colonial domination, but of the Church and Christ himself.[4]

This text, however, reworks the conquerors' favored analogic construct – {Spaniard : Indian :: Christian : Jew} – in daring fashion, first by associating Indians with Christians (rather than with Jews), and second by subtextually identifying "Jews" with that group most antithetical to the Indian community: the Europeanized *ladino* elite who have dominated Guatemalan politics and economy since independence.[5] This is skillfully suggested – without being openly or bluntly asserted – in the story's dénouement.[6] Thus, several episodes describe how Jesús evaded these "Jews" for forty days, deceiving them with one hilarious ruse after another, until finally they caught and crucified him.

> Then the Jews placed Jesús' body at the edge of the pueblo. Late that night a burro came along and breathed over the body of Jesús. The breath of the burro made the marks of the nails disappear at once. That same night Jesús went to heaven and has never returned. When the Jews returned next day for the body, they were angry and frightened to find that it had gone. Then, they were afraid and went to many people and asked where Jesús Cristo had gone. They were told that he had gone to heaven. Then the Jews hid behind trees and in the brush in fear, but a great storm came with thunder and lightning and with each flash a Jew was killed. Now only those who live beneath the ground where Jesús placed them are alive.

(*ibid*.: 52)

Here, Jesús transforms the "Jews" into Guardians of the mountains (Spanish *Guardias de los Cerros*, Mam *taajwa witz*): rich, powerful spirits of the wilderness, who are as remote as they are capricious. Capable of helping Chimaltecos should they wish, they more frequently lure naïve Indians into Faustian bargains, as in the following example:

> Two men, Juan Martín and Pascal Hernandez, both of whom died many years ago, were walking near the summit of *Pichon* [the mountain which towers over Chimaltenango], when they met a strange *ladino*. The *ladino* "had long blond hair, wore a shiny coat and a hat with long feathers on it." The *ladino* warned them to stay away from the summit. Both men were afraid, but one asked if he were the Guardian of *Pichon*. The *ladino* at first said "No," but when one of the Chimaltecos asked if the *ladino* might possibly lend them money, he admitted his identity as the Guardian, and lent them money. The Guardian told them to close their eyes, and when they opened them, they were inside the mountain, inside a huge house. "There was a large coffee plantation inside the mountain. Many animals were inside the house; large ferocious dogs were chained to the walls." The Guardian gave them money – "who knows how much." He asked them to repay it after some days and told them to make *costumbre* to him every four days. After the two men had shut and opened their eyes again, they found themselves back at the same spot where they met the Guardian. But after returning to the village, they did not even once make *costumbre* to the Guardian, nor did they make any effort to repay the money. At the same time they were sleeping with each other's wives; "these good friends cheated each other." After several months, both men and their wives died and "all the people knew why." Now the Guardian is punishing them; "they are working inside *Pichon* for the Guardian to repay the money and as a punishment. They will work there for many years on the plantation of the Guardian."

> (*ibid.*: 56–7)

In relatively open fashion, this passage offers a telling critique of money, debt, wage labor, consumption of luxuries, illicit sexuality, and abandonment of traditional religious practice (*costumbre*). Particularly striking is the resemblance of these Guardians of the mountains – who are repeatedly identified as *ladinos* – to the three labor recruiters who visited Chimaltenango each year and used loans, drink, and other stratagems to entrap Chimaltecos in seasonal labor contracts, committing them to work under truly appalling conditions on the large coffee plantations of the western coast.[7] Mirroring the relation of exploitative *ladinos* to vulnerable Indians, the Guardians of the mountains are also regularly contrasted with the protective and usually benevolent saints (*santos*), who reside in the church at the village center, dress in traditional Chimalteco costume, and receive their prayers in Mam, rather than Spanish.[8]

The text with which we began encodes a set of oppositions between the groups and values listed in Table 10.1. Within the episodes of the narrative, victories alternate between the contrasted groups, but no outcome is ever conclusive. Each escape is followed by capture, and capture by escape. Crucifixion leads to resurrection, and lightning-blast death only occasions metamorphosis into spirits of the mountains. Down to the present, the struggle continues.

Understanding the immediate context in which this text was collected helps refine our interpretation. Although the *ladino* population of Chimaltenango was relatively small (six families in a population of 1,500), *ladinos* controlled disproportionate shares of land and wealth, while also monopolizing top political offices, with the support of the Guatemalan state. Moreover, in 1934, the dictatorship of Jorge Ubico (r. 1931–44) introduced measures devastating to Indian interests.[9] Most sweeping in their import were the notorious "Vagrancy Laws" that obliged men with landholdings below a certain level (and this included 43 per cent of Chimaltecos) to work on *ladino* coffee plantations for a minimum of 100 days each year. Of more immediate local concern was a December 1935 ruling that reduced Chimaltenango from a *municipio* to a subordinate hamlet (*aldea*) of San Pedro Necta, a village whose large *ladino* population Chimaltecos viewed with fear and suspicion. In particular, Chimaltecos worried that their loss of legal status and autonomy would leave them unable to protect their ownership of land and leave them no options other than wage labor. Faced with this crisis, the ranking elders (*principales*) of the village decided to contest the novel arrangements, and they chose a relatively young man, Diego Martín, to represent them, because he spoke fluent Spanish, had some experience of government, and was known as a man "who was not afraid of *ladinos*."[10]

After eight days' journey on foot, Martín and four companions reached the capital, where he met with the Minister of the Interior and negotiated a compromise in which Chimaltenango retained its foremost emblems of municipal status, including the title to its lands,[11] while remaining, for the record, an *aldea* of San Pedro (a status it retained until 1948). Chimaltecos hailed this as a victory, and celebrated their delegates' return with a lavish impromptu *fiesta*. Sixteen months later, Diego Martín became Wagley's most valued informant and recited for him the story of Jesús and the "Jews" (*ibid.*: 8–9 and n6).

Table 10.1 Structural contrasts in a Chimalteco creation account

Contrast	Episode
José and María [= *naturales*] : The Devil :: Faith, love, trust : Gossip, suspicion, trouble- making ::	(1)
Mountains : Valleys :: Sun : Moon :: Day : Night :: Work : Rest ::	(2)
Those who like mountains : Those who like plains :: *Naturales* : "People of the Devil" Contentment, labor : Anger, indolence ::	(3)
Jesús and Christians : The Devil and Jews :: Indians : *Ladinos* :: Ingenious survivors : Persistent persecutors ::	(4)
Santos : Guardians of the mountains :: Village center [= culture] : Outlying wilderness [= nature] :: Healers, protectors : Exploiters, enslavers	(5)

Source: Wagley (1949: 51).

The theft of a soul

Diego Martín gave this account in the wake of a limited and local, but materially and symbolically significant, victory, won in a difficult period. Within the genres of mythic narrative and theological speculation, he offered his reflections, as of that precise moment, on the nature of Indians, *ladinos*, and struggles between the two. Now I would like to move from the western to the eastern highlands, from the 1930s to the following decade, from a village with relatively few *ladinos* to one where they accounted for 35 per cent of the population and owned 70 per cent of the land, from one where a priest went unseen for years at a time to one with monthly clerical visits, and from an instance of mythic discourse to one of ritual practice.

The case I have in mind is the ceremony performed in the Pokomám village of San Luis Jilotepeque in the summer of 1946 that provided the basis for John Gillin's classic discussion of "Magical Fright."[12] At the center of these events was an elderly woman whom Gillin gave the pseudonym "Alicia." One day, while walking along the river outside the village, she and her husband, Fernando, quarreled badly, dredging up a long and bitter history that involved episodes of drunkenness, poverty, illness, infidelity, financial irresponsibility, and physical cruelty.[13] Words were exchanged. Tempers flared. Then Fernando picked up a rock, struck Alicia with it, and afterwards she fell ill. Her symptoms included aches, pains, listlessness, fatigue, diarrhea, loss of appetite, insomnia, depression, and an inability to work or carry out household tasks. Untreated, they were utterly debilitating and posed a serious threat to her life, but help was sought from an accomplished *curandero*, whom Gillin referred to as "Manuel."

In the quarrel that prompted the illness, one can perceive two different, but interrelated, sets of tensions. At one level, Alicia and her husband fought about land, money, and status in the community: resources that were scarce and becoming scarcer as the Indians of San Luis lost ground (literally and figuratively) to their *ladino* rivals. In addition, the couple fought about sex, drink, and domestic violence: issues of love, respect, pleasure, pain, intimacy, dignity, fear, and betrayal, where the lines of cleavage were male and female, rather than Indian–*ladino*. These issues were largely relegated to the background by the *curandero* who treated Alicia and the researchers who reported the case, all of whom focused on the former set of difficulties, each for their own reasons and each in their own idiom.[14]

According to Manuel, the *curandero*, the quarrel caused a condition of "Fright" (*espanto* or *susto*), in which Alicia's soul was dislodged from her body and stolen by spirits.[15] To effect a cure, it was necessary to recover her soul from those who now held it, and towards this end he assembled the couple's friends, neighbors, relations, and one of the village's *principales* for a grueling night-long ceremony, culminating in two expeditions. The first of these led from the patient's home to the church in the central plaza, where the *santos* were asked to give their assistance and to sanction the second, more dangerous journey.

> The curer and the *principal*, together with two male helpers, now went to the place where the precipitating fright of the present *espanto* occurred. They carried with them in a gourd the four eggs just used to draw the *aires* out of the patient, digging sticks, pine splinters for light, two candles, and a collection of gifts to be offered to the evil spirits. These gifts included a cigar, a bunch of handmade cigarettes, an earthen pitcher of *chilate* (a maize gruel used as ceremonial drink among the Pokomám), four

cacao seeds, some sweet biscuits, and a small bottle of drinking alcohol. Davidson [Gillin's field assistant] and I accompanied the party. We walked in single file through the darkness, following a dim path among the bushes upstream along the river. Finally, we came to a spot about ten feet above the river, which the curer announced was the place where Alicia had lost her soul. A pine splinter was lighted. While the two helpers started digging a hole in the ground, the curer and the *principal* turned their backs and faced across the river to the west. All previous prayers had been in Pokomám but now the curer spoke in Spanish and in familiar, man-to-man terms. He addressed five spirits, calling them by name and addressing them as *compadres* (a form of ceremonial kinship). The names of the five were "Avelín Caballero Sombrerón, Señor Don Justo Juez, Doña María Diego, Don Manuel Urrutia, and San Graviel [Gabriel]." After saluting the others, he directed his remarks to Don Avelín. He explained in detail that he had brought them a feast to eat and alcohol to drink. He explained that here Alicia had lost her soul through a *susto*. He dwelt upon her symptoms and said that the eggs would bear him out. He said that he knew that his *compadres* knew where her soul was hidden and that they had it in their power to return it to her. As a favor to him, the curer, would they not help him to secure the lost soul? And so on.[16]

Leaving the security of the village, Manuel and the others ventured by night to a place of fear: the spot where the patient had lost her soul. There, they hoped to find the forces responsible and to secure their cooperation in restoring the balance, energy, self-confidence, and sense of purpose without which she could not survive. Their concern, however, went beyond Alicia's condition to that of the community as a whole, for which she served as synecdoche. The wild terrain they entered was not just a physical space, but also a space of their collective imaginary, within which they explored and addressed their communal troubles, especially their relations with *ladino* neighbors.

In terms reminiscent of Chimalteco descriptions of Guardians of the mountains, the San Luiseños voiced their direst fears and entertained a radical critique, depicting *ladinos* as devils (Pokomám *tiéwu*, Spanish *diablos*) who threatened to steal their very souls.[17] Numerous details establish this identification. First, whereas all other ritual proceedings were conducted in Pokomám, these spirits alone were addressed in Spanish. Second, they bore the names and titles of historic *ladinos* well known in San Luis.[18] Third, they dressed in *ladino* fashion, their leader being particularly known for his large *sombrero* and blond hair. Finally, the gifts they received included cigars and cookies: luxury items favored by *ladinos*, but not *naturales*.[19]

Over the course of the ritual, however, the *curandero* revised this narrative of diabolism and guided it towards a satisfying dénouement, revealing in the process that however alien these spirits might be, negotiation with them was both possible and productive. Towards this end, he put on display a repertoire of techniques for success in dealing with powerful others, a repertoire that included flattery, cajolery, and bribery (that is to say, the use of gifts to call forth reciprocity), as well as extreme politesse (especially the euphemistic coding of demands as requests – *por favor*).

Most importantly, Manuel addressed these spirits as *compadres* (literally "co-fathers," that is to say, the godparents of one's children), thereby constituting them as his ritual kin and invoking an institution of extraordinary importance.[20] *Compadrazgo* is one of the few instruments that serves to integrate the Indians and *ladinos* into a single civic and moral community, and one of the few means through which an Indian can make legitimate demands on a *ladino* that obligate him to respond with benevolence. The relationship, however, is asymmetric, and, as such, fraught with perils and uncertainties.

> The important point is that Indians frequently secure *ladino compadres*, whereas *ladinos* never ask an Indian to serve as *padrino*. Thus a bridge of ceremonial kinship is built across caste lines, although a rather patronizing attitude colors the *ladino* view of the relationship, and the Indian *compadre* and godchild are in a subordinate and semi-dependent status, rather than in a position of equality with the *ladinos* involved. One result is that the term "*compadre*" is not much used between Indians and *ladinos*, because it implies an equality which the *ladinos* will not admit. On the other hand, *ladinos* do recognize obligations toward Indian godchildren. I have found no cases or complaints of *ladinos* failing to "do something" for an Indian godchild in case of emergency.
>
> (Gillin 1951: 61)

To call on a *ladino* as "*compadre*" was thus an operation that could bring desired results, but one that could also backfire, should it be considered an unwarranted presumption. In order to succeed, this maneuver had to be carried out with considerable tact, in a voice that conveyed both respect and confidence, without signaling anything that could be read as audacity or fear. Like Diego Martín, Manuel was known as a man very little intimidated by *ladinos*.[21] Moreover, at the time Gillin watched him bargain with the spirits, the *ladinos* of San Luis had never seemed so approachable.

This was the local result of national events. Roughly two years earlier, Jorge Ubico had been driven from the Guatemalan presidency, ushering in a revolutionary government under Juan José Arévalo that was committed to improving the lives of Indians and peasants on coming to power (on 20 October 1944). In San Luis, this news catalyzed a latent cleavage between the wealthiest *ladinos* and those less well situated, who had been disgruntled in the past and were sympathetic to the incoming Arévalistas. When a Pokomám-speaking leader of the latter faction (one of the two *ladinos* – out of 5,500 – who had such competence) spoke to the Indian population about these events, they rallied enthusiastically to the cause, chased the older leaders from the village, and elected a new government, in which a *ladino* of the revolutionary faction became mayor, and Indians, for the first time, held a majority in the municipal council.

In his account of these events, Gillin lists seven reforms that were rapidly introduced, consistent with trends throughout the nation. All of these were important, and they cover such areas as land ownership, education, participation in politics and commerce, as well as an end to all forms of legal discrimination. Two items, however, are particularly helpful in establishing the context within which Manuel negotiated with soul-stealing *ladino* spirits, whom he addressed as *compadres*:

> (1) It was one of the stated goals of the revolution that the Indians should be incorporated into the national culture. The local *ladino* democrats spoke of this frequently and in public, and made a point of fraternizing with Indians up to a point, arranging favors for them, etc.
>
> (5) Indian curing ceremonies, which had formerly been a favorite target for police when they had nothing else to do, were tolerated without interference.[22]

Healers and "murderers," saints and assassins

From 1944 to 1954, reforms of this sort were pursued with ever greater determination, until a coup organized by the CIA at the urging of the United Fruit Company toppled Arévalo's successor, Jacobo Arbenz Gúzman, and brought an abrupt end to Guatemala's experiment with popular democracy.[23] Since that time, the Guatemalan state and army, with significant (if inconsistent) US backing, have carried out the western hemisphere's most savage campaign of repression against intellectuals, opposition politicians, organized labor, and, above all, the nation's peasant and Indian population. Reliable estimates place the number of those killed by the army and death squads in the hundreds of thousands, not to speak of those imprisoned, tortured, and driven into exile.[24] The absolute height of that campaign came during the military dictatorship of Efraím Rios Montt (1982–83), when "counter-insurgency" policies were unconstrained by democratic institutions, international pressure, or any rule of law.[25] Some religious establishments – particularly the evangelical Protestant groups to which Rios Montt belonged and conservative fractions of the Catholic Church – have aligned themselves with the killers; others, with the victims – Maryknoll missions and proponents of liberation theology being noteworthy in this regard. All, however, have pressed – often with considerable success – for what they view as a purer and more proper Christianity, that is to say, one more consistent with that practiced in Europe and North America, and one less accommodating towards local traditions.[26]

When John Watanabe began field work in Santiago Chimaltenango, more than forty years after Wagley had been there, he found that since the early 1950s, Maryknoll missionaries based in San Pedro Necta had been active in the village. Funded from overseas and independent of the archdiocese of Guatemala, they had earned the respect and gratitude of Chimaltecos with the medical, agricultural, and educational reforms they had introduced, and for their concern for the well-being of the community. At the same time, they had established a cadre of catechists, who took control of the church in Chimaltenango from the traditional authorities and instituted what they considered more "orthodox" patterns of worship. In the course of so doing, they also undertook what a Maryknoll priest termed "holy war" against traditional healers and diviners (*chimanes*), whom they derided as charlatans whose cures were inferior to those of Western medicine and whose *costumbre* was a waste of money. At times, they spoke more stridently still, depicting their adversaries as "murderers" (*choolil*), who covertly collaborated with the demonic Guardians of the mountains – spirits whom, at other times, they dismissed as figments of a superstitious imagination.

As a result of their successes – material and polemic – when Watanabe was present in the mid-1980s, there were no more *chimanes* in Chimaltenango. In addition, *costumbre* for healing was no longer practiced and the Guardians of the mountains figured in tales for children, but not as objects of adult belief (Watanabe 1992: 194–216). Still, traditional understandings remained operative in many contexts, as in the stories Chimaltecos told about the events of 1983. Although Chimaltenango escaped the worst excesses of this period, the dangers were very real, particularly when local residents were forced to serve in civil patrols, where their military commanders pressured them to identify and eliminate all "subversives" in their village.[27]

> One night, a civil patrol on the San Pedro road met an imposing figure on a white horse who told them to turn back. When the Chimalteco [members of the squad] told him that they were under pain of death to carry out their patrol, he led them

back to town himself. When the soldiers tried to shoot him, their rifles misfired, and the horseman rode up the steps of the church and disappeared inside. The next night, the army commander, "a hot-headed man," led the patrol himself, and they again encountered the man on the white horse, this time at the edge of town just above the cemetery. The commander tried to shoot him, but the horse reared and knocked him down the hill into the cemetery, and again the horseman rode into town and entered the church. The horseman returned a final time to confront the army commander, warning that if any Chimaltecos were killed, he would kill the soldiers: he, not they, best protected the village. The next day, according to the story, the army withdrew.

(Watanabe 1992: 214–15)

As Watanabe observes, all understood this horseman to be Santiago, patron saint of Chimaltenango and protector of its Indian population. Ordinarily, the equestrian image of Santiago resides in the church at the village center, from which it emerges on his *fiesta* to dance and celebrate with his people. In this narrative, however, the saint makes a different, more aggressive sally to confront and repel a dangerous outsider, who has cast himself as an alternate protector for the village: the "hot-headed" army commander. Conceivably, this character may be implicitly connected to General Rios Montt, that is to say, the commander's commander, the man ultimately responsible for the campaign of terror, and someone whose evangelical commitments made him particularly hostile to the cult of the *santos*.

Many of the contrasts that structure this account resemble those in the other examples considered above: Indian/*ladino*, saint/devil, threatened harmony/intruding violence, urban center/wild periphery. To these are added some novel, but parallel, pairs: church/cemetery, resident/soldier, possibly also Catholic/Protestant. Above all, the narrative contrasts one form of protection that is true, dependable, rooted in local tradition and in the Church, to another that comes from powerful interests outside (the army and the state), and is, in fact, the opposite of what it claims to be: a threat, and not a protection. Implicit throughout is a contrast of "the indigenous" and "the intrusive," but Santiago's origins ought to caution us against too simplistic an understanding of these categories. For the figure who serves as protector and collective representation of the Chimaltecos was imported by earlier intruders, and serves as patron not only of Chimaltenango but also of Spain.

Conclusions

The three examples given above – a creation account, a healing ceremony, and a vision of a *santo* – are small episodes in a much larger history. The first comes from a period of severe economic exploitation (1937); the second, a time of political reform (1946); the third, at the height of military repression (1983). Notwithstanding their individual differences (and there are many), in each instance those whom we have considered addressed their immediate situation with a narrative or performance in which they represented themselves as "good Christians," while depicting adversaries as their religious and moral antitheses: Christ-killing "Jews" and labor-recruiting "Guardians of the mountains" in the first instance; soul-stealing *ladino* devils in the second; (Protestant?) enemies of the saints in the third.

In all three cases, one could probably determine whether elements traceable to Maya origins preponderate over those derived from the Catholic tradition, or vice versa. Thus, the Pokomám *curandero* might be seen to continue Maya practices beneath a Catholic veneer, while the vision of Santiago could be understood as a piece of "folk Catholicism" with a few Maya vestiges. But such a crude analytic, which characterized much of the pioneering ethnography, yields little of value, for the critical issue is not the classification of given items as "indigenous" or "exogenous," nor establishing the relative balance between them, but understanding the uses to which such items are put, regardless of their ultimate derivation. Models of "syncretism" that blur the distinction of indigene and intruder are also potentially quite misleading, particularly when they create the impression that either people or religions have melded in anything that approximates a stable or peaceful synthesis.[28]

Preferable, I think, is a dialectic model that acknowledges the extent to which both parties have been transformed by their encounter, while also recognizing that even as all else changes, their opposition remains and their struggle continues. As a result of the Spanish imperial adventure, two different groups first confronted one another in the early sixteenth century, and among their defining differences were those of religion. Since then, the sacred practices, discourses, and institutions of Mayans and Spaniards, *ladinos* and *naturales*, have served as battlefields, instruments, and stakes of a struggle, the results of which are anything but conclusive. Indeed, it is hard to imagine how a conclusion could ever be reached, for with every religious utterance or performance, relations between the contending parties – who began their marathon match as "the indigenous" and "the invader" – are ever so subtly revised and their balance of power ever so slightly recalibrated.

Notes

1 A spate of good works on the colonial period has appeared in recent years, including Jones (1989), Clendinnen (1987), and Farriss (1984). For more recent periods in Guatemalan history, see Smith (1990), Handy (1984), and Carmack (1983: 215–53).
2 Wagley (1949: 51). All parenthetical phrases appear in the original (see Table 10.1).
3 For a fuller discussion of this mythological theme, see Lincoln (1989: 38–50).
4 See the discussion in Cervantes (1994), esp. 38–9.
5 For different attempts to theorize *ladino*–Indian relations, see Smith (1995: 723–49; 1990); Casaus Arzu (1992); Rosada Granados (1987); Hawkins (1984); Brintnall (1979: 638–52); Warren (1978); Friedlander (1975); Siverts (1969: 101–16); Colby and Van den Berghe (1969); and Stavenhagen (1968: 31–63).
6 Ambiguity offers subordinate groups many strategic advantages, and the Indians of Mesoamerica have mastered the art of constructing texts that maximize this potential. Cf., for example, their Passion Plays, in which "Roman centurions" torment Christ, clad in helmets that invite anyone so inclined to read them as *Conquistadores*.
7 On the practices employed by these recruiters, see Wagley (1941: 73).
8 Regarding the contrast between *santos* and Guardians of the mountains, see the insightful analysis of Watanabe (1990: 131–50; 1992: 61–80).
9 On the Ubico regime, see Handy (1984: 77–101) and Grieb (1979).
10 Wagley (1949: 8–9; see 51, 86–7, 97 for more on Martín). See also Wagley (1941: 78–80), where we learn he was one of the largest landholders in Chimaltenango, something of a womanizer and iconoclast, as well as a man who consciously learned from *ladinos* how best to exploit hired labor.
11 On the almost mystic importance accorded the village's *titulo*, see *ibid.*, 62.
12 Gillin's article first appeared in *Psychiatry* 11 (1948): 387–400, has been reprinted several times, and is most readily available in his collected essays, *Human Ways* (Pittsburgh: University of Pittsburgh Press, 1969, 197–219). The healing ceremony was also observed by Gillin's field assistant, William Davidson, who made it the subject of his Master's thesis (1948). On San Luis in this period, see further Gillin (1969: 35–59; 1951; 1957: 23–7) and Tumin (1952).

13 The chain of recriminations leads back to the beginning of the couple's relationship, which Alicia described to Davidson (1948: 79–80) as follows:

> Fernando, my husband, is two years younger than I. He is the only man that I have ever had. I was never promised to another, nor did I have an affair previously. As a young man, Fernando had nothing and was much given to drink. He and my brothers were in the army together in Guatemala City. After returning from the service, Fernando came to our house one night. He was drunk and he got my family awake. He got my father out of bed and shared a half-bottle of *aguardiente* with him. They sat down to drink and to talk. Fernando had previously spoken with me when I was walking along the street. He had also spoken to my brother about me, but my brother did not like him since he was poor and a drunkard.
>
> After a while my papa asked Fernando what his intentions were. Fernando said that he wanted to marry one of his daughters, me. By this time the bottle had been emptied, and my father said, "What are we going to do about this without having some more *aguardiente*?" Fernando went out and got two more bottles, one for himself and one for papa. They sat down to drink some more and to talk some more. Before much time had passed, both bottles were empty, and my papa was very drunk. He became very friendly with Fernando, and soon told me that I had to marry this Fernando.

At first, Alicia refused to accept this arrangement. Then,

> One day my father brought a big stone into the house and tied me to it. Then he started to whip me. He gave me three lashes, and then I cried out, "If you wish, I shall marry him. But I must be married in the church." My mother objected to my father, but he struck her and yelled to her, "You are getting very brave, aren't you?" So it was that I was married to Fernando against my will.

More immediately, the spouses' quarrel was occasioned by a long series of misfortunes. Treatment of previous illnesses having been expensive (Alicia had been *espontada* on seven earlier occasions!), they had been forced to sell their land. After years of saving, they were ready to buy land again, but Fernando became drunk, dallied with a "loose woman," fell asleep, and when he awoke, the money was gone. Davidson (*ibid.*: 82) gives a fuller account of these events than Gillin, who summarizes them only briefly (1969: 201).

14 In contrast, see the sensitive and moving treatment of Finkler (1994).

15 Gillin was among the first to write about this condition, which figures prominently in Mesoamerican theories of illness and healing. For later discussions, see Signorini (1989) and Rubel *et al.* (1984), along with the literature cited therein.

16 Gillin (1969: 206). Davidson (1948: 116) quotes the phrases with which Manuel began his address to the chief of the spirits. These contain some striking details:

> Good evening, *compadre Lucifer*. Here [Alicia] lost her soul. She is a good woman. She has harmed no one. Now she suffers much. *Santo Lucifer*, I bring you gifts, a good cigar, good cigarettes, good bread, and a good drink. Please allow her soul to go free.

17 A significant difference is that the Chimalteco spirits are not held responsible for soul-loss. They most closely resemble the Zinacanteco Earth Lord: "a fat and greedy *ladino* who wants meat with his tortillas," and who, if not placated with gifts, will "capture the souls of the inhabitants of the house and put them to work as slaves for many years, until the 'iron hurarches he gives them all wear out'" (Vogt 1993: 15–18, 56–8).

18 The leader of the spirits, Don Avelín Caballero Sombrerón, is known only to Manuel, and, according to his rivals, is simply the healer's invention. His name, however, resembles that of Pedro Amalín, one of the *Conquistadores* who captured San Luis in 1530. Don Manuel Urrutia was an *intendente* of the village in the 1890s, while Señor Don Justo Juez and Doña María Diego seem to have similar connections. Rounding out the set is Saint Gabriel, Manuel's patron *santo* (Gillin 1951: 11, 106, 108).

19 Gillin (1969: 207). Davidson (1948: 115) adds white bread to the list.
20 Gillin (1951: 60–2). The fullest discussion of *compadrazgo* in Mesoamerica is Nutini and Bell (1980), with full citation of earlier literature.
21 Davidson notes that he and Gillin stayed in the home of a wealthy *ladino*, in which all their Indian visitors seemed ill at ease, save only Manuel (Davidson 1948: 53–4). He also quotes the response Manuel gave when he asked him what things he feared, a response which indicates his awareness of the then current political situation: "Here we are not afraid of much. We are afraid of revolutions, but they do not come often. Our greatest fear is of the *pesta* which kills our children" (*ibid.*: 49).
22 Gillin (1957: 23–7, esp. 25). Further information may be obtained in Handy (1994: esp. 131–2).
23 On the revolutionary period, see Handy (1994); Villamar (1993); Gleijesis (1991); and Wasserstrom (1975: 443–78). Regarding the coup – which was largely orchestrated by E. Howard Hunt, of Watergate fame – see Schlesinger and Kinzer (1982); Immerman (1982); and De Soto (1978).
24 See Jonas (1991); Handy (1976: 112–39); Carmack (1988); Simon (1987); and McClintock (1985). The many reports filed by human rights organizations also make for grim reading: see Reports (1981/1983; 1983; 1984; 1988; 1989; 1990; 1991; 1995).
25 See Montenegro (1995), as well as the literature cited in the preceding note.
26 Regarding patterns of religious change over the past twenty years, see Wilson (1995); Samandú (1991: 67–114; 1990); Stoll (1990); Annis (1987); Brintnall (1979); and Sexton (1978: 280–302).
27 Regarding the use of civilian patrols to carry out terror at the local level, see Jay *et al.* (1993).
28 For theoretical reflections on the category of syncretism, see Stewart and Shaw (1994). Recent attempts to make use of it for Mesoamerican data include Marzal (1985), Nutini (1988), and Slade (1992).

References

Articles and books

Annis, Sheldon, *God and Production in a Guatemalan Town*, Austin: University of Texas Press, 1987.
Brintnall, Douglas E., "Race relations in the southeastern highlands of Mesoamerica," *American Ethnologist* 6 (1979): 638–52.
——, *Revolt against the Dead: The Modernization of a Mayan Community in the Highlands of Guatemala*, New York: Gordon & Breach, 1979.
Carmack, Robert, "Spanish–Indian relations in highland Guatemala, 1800–1944," in Murdo MacLeod and Robert Wasserstrom (eds) *Spaniards and Indians in South-eastern Mesoamerica*, Lincoln: University of Nebraska Press, 1983, 215–53.
—— (ed.), *Harvest of Violence: The Maya Indians and the Guatemalan Crisis*, Norman: University of Oklahoma Press, 1988.
Casaus Arzu, Marta Elena, *Guatemala: Linaje y racismo*, San Jose: FLACSO, 1992.
Cervantes, Fernando, *The Devil in the New World: The Impact of Diabolism in New Spain*, New Haven: Yale University Press, 1994.
Clendinnen, Inga, *Ambivalent Conquests: Maya and Spaniard in Yucatan, 1517–1570*, Cambridge: Cambridge University Press, 1987.
Colby, Benjamin and Pierre Van den Berghe, *Ixil Country: A Plural Society in Highland Guatemala*, Berkeley: University of California Press, 1969.
Davidson, William, "A method for studying religious cult and healing ceremonies and its application to a Guatemalan Indian curing ceremony," unpublished MA thesis, Duke University Graduate School of Arts and Sciences, 1948.
De Soto, Jose Aybar, *Dependency and Intervention: The Case of Guatemala in 1954*, Boulder: West-view Press, 1978.
Farriss, Nancy, *Maya Society Under Colonial Rule: The Collective Enterprise of Survival*, Princeton: Princeton University Press, 1984.
Finkler, Kaja, *Women in Pain: Gender and Morbidity in Mexico*, Philadelphia: University of Pennsylvania Press, 1994.

Friedlander, Judith, *Being Indian in Hueyapan*, New York: St. Martin's Press, 1975.

Gillin, John, "Magic fright," *Psychiatry* 11 (1948): 387–400.

——, *The Culture of Security in San Carlos: A Study of a Guatemalan Community of Indians and Ladionos*, New Orleans: Tulane University Middle American Research Institute, 1951.

——, "San Luis Jilotepeque: 1942–55," in Richard Adams (ed.) *Political Changes in Guatemalan Indian Communities*, New Orleans: Tulane University Middle American Research Institute, 1957.

——, *Human Ways*, Pittsburgh: University of Pittsburgh Press, 1969.

Gleijesis, Piero, *Hope: The Guatemalan Revolution and the United States, 1944–1954*, Princeton: Princeton University Press, 1991.

Grieb, Kenneth, *Guatemalan Caudillo: The Regime of Jorrge Ubico, Guatemala, 1931–1944*, Athens: Ohio University Press, 1979.

Handy, Jim, "Insurgency and counter-insurgency in Guatemala," in Jan Flora and Edelberto Torres Rivas (eds) *Sociology of "Developing Societies": Central America*, New York: Monthly Review Press, 1976, 112–39.

——, *Gift of the Devil: A History of Guatemala*, Boston: South End Press, 1984.

——, *Revolution in the Countryside: Rural Conflict and Agrarian Reform in Guatemala, 1944–1954*, Chapel Hill: University of North Carolina Press, 1994.

Hawkins, John, *Inverse Images: The Meaning of Culture, Ethnicity and Family in Postcolonial Guatemala*, Albuquerque: University of New Mexico Press, 1984.

Immerman, Richard, *The CIA in Guatemala: The Foreign Policy of Intervention*, Austin: University of Texas Press, 1982.

Jay, Alice, Kerry Kennedy Cuomo, Helet Merkling and Nan Richardson, *Persecution by Proxy: The Civil Patrols in Guatemala*, New York: Robert F. Kennedy Memorial Center for Human Rights, 1993.

Jonas, Susanne, *The Battle for Guatemala: Rebels, Death Squads, and U.S. Power*, Boulder: Westview Press, 1991.

Jones, Grant, *Maya Resistance to Spanish Rule: Time and History on a Colonial Frontier*, Albuquerque: University of New Mexico Press, 1989.

Lincoln, Bruce, *Discourse and the Construction of Society*, New York: Oxford University Press, 1989.

Marzal, Manuel, *El Sincretismo iberoamericano: Un estudio comparativo sobre los quechuas (Cusco), los mayas (Chiapas), y los africanos (Bahia)*, Lima: Pontificia Universidad Catolica del Peru, 1985.

McClintock, Michael, *The American Connection: State Terror and Popular Resistance in El Salvador and Guatemala*, 2 vols, London: Zed Books, 1985.

Montenegro, G. Asturias, *Los 504 dias de Rios Montt*, Guatemala City: Gamma, 1995.

Nutini, Hugo, *Todos Santos in Rural Tlaxcalas: A Syncretic, Expressive, and Symbolic Analysis of the Cult of the Dead*, Princeton: Princeton University Press, 1988.

Nutini, Hugo and Betty Bell, *Ritual Kingship: The Structure and Historical Development of the Compadrazgo System in Rural Tlaxcala*, Princeton: Princeton University Press, 1980.

Rosada Granados, Hector Roberto, *Indios y Ladinos (Un estudio Antropologico)*, San Carlos, Guatemala: Editorial Universitaria, 1987.

Rubel, Arthur, Carl O'Nell and Rolando Collado-Ardón, *Susto: A Folk Illness*, Berkeley: University of California Press, 1984.

Samandú, Luis, *Guatemala. Retos de la iglesia catolica en una sociedad en crisis*, San Jose: DEI/CSUCA, 1990.

—— (ed.), *Protestantismos y Procesos Sociales en Centroamerica*, San Jose: EDUCA, 1991.

Schlesinger, Stephen and Stephen Kinzer, *Bitter Fruit: The Untold Story of the American Coup in Guatemala*, Garden City, NY: Doubleday, 1982.

Sexton, James, "Protestantism and modernization in two Guatemalan towns," *American Ethnologist* 5 (1978): 280–302.

Signorini, Italo, *Los tres ejes de la vida: almas, corpo, enfermedad entre los Nahuas de la Sierra de Puebla*, Xalapa: Editorial UV, 1989.

Simon, Jean-Marie, *Guatemala: Eternal Spring – Eternal Tyranny*, New York: W.W. Norton, 1987.

Siverts, Henning, "Ethnic stability and boundary dynamics in southern Mexico," in Fredrik Barth (ed.) *Ethnic Groups and Boundaries: The Social Organization of Cultural Difference*, Boston: Little, Brown, 1969, 101–16.

Slade, Doren, *Making the World Safe for Existence: Celebration of the Saints among the Sierra Nahuat*, Ann Arbor: University of Michigan Press, 1992.

Smith, Carol A. (ed.), *Guatemala: Seminario sobre la Realidad Etnica*, Centro de Estudios Integrados de Desarrollo Communal (Mexico City), 1990.

——, "Race–class–gender ideology in Guatemala: modern and anti-modern forms," *Comparative Studies in Society and History* 37 (1995): 723–49.

Stavenhagen, Rudolfo, "Classes, colonialism and acculturation," in Joseph Kahl (ed.) *Comparative Perspectives on Stratification: Mexico, Great Britain, Japan*, Boston: Little, Brown, 1968, 31–63.

Stewart, Charles and Rosalind Shaw (eds), *Syncretism/Anti-Syncretism: The Politics of Religious Synthesis*, New York: Routledge, 1994.

Stoll, David, *Is Latin America Turning Protestant? The Politics of Evangelical Growth*, Berkeley: University of California Press, 1990.

Tumin, Melvin, *Caste in a Peasant Society*, Princeton: Princeton University Press, 1952.

Villamar, Marco Antonio, *Significado de la decada 1944–1954 conocido como la revolucion guatamalteca de octubre*, Guatemala City, 1993.

Vogt, Evon Z., *Tortillas for the Gods: A Symbolic Analysis of Zinacanteco Rituals*, Norman: University of Oklahoma Press, 1993.

Wagley, Charles, *Economics of a Guatemalan Village*, Menasha, WI: American Anthropological Association, 1941.

——, *Social and Religious Life of a Guatemalan Village*, Menasha, WI: American Anthropological Association, 1949.

Warren, Kay, *The Symbolism of Subordination: Indian Identity in a Guatemalan Town*, Austin: University of Texas Press, 1978.

Wasserstrom, Robert, "Revolution in Guatemala: peasants and politics under the Arbenz Government," *Comparative Studies in Society and History* 17 (1975): 443–78.

Watanabe, John, *Maya Saints and Souls in a Changing World*, Austin: University of Texas Press, 1960.

——, "From saints to shibboleths: image, structure, and identity in Maya religious syncretism," *American Ethnologist* 17 (1990): 129–48.

——, *Maya Saints and Souls in a Changing World*, Austin: University of Texas Press, 1992.

Wilson, Richard, *Maya Resurgence in Guatemala: Q'eqchi' Experiences*, Norman: University of Oklahoma Press, 1995.

Reports

Guatemala: A Government Program of Political Murder, London: Amnesty International, 1981/1983.

Report on the Situation of Human Rights in the Republic of Guatemala, Washington: General Secretariat of the Organization of American States, 1983.

Guatemala – Tyranny on Trial: Testimony of the Permanent People's Tribunal, San Francisco: Synthesis Publications, 1984.

Closing the Space: Human Rights in Guatemala, New York: Americas Watch, 1988.

Guatemala: Human Rights Violations under the Civilian Government, New York: Amnesty International, 1989.

Guatemala: A Nation of Prisoners, New York: Americas Watch, 1990.

Guatemala: Getting away with Murder, New York: Americas Watch and Somerville, MA: Physicians for Human Rights, 1991.

Guatemala, London: Catholic Institute for International Relations, 1995.

Chapter 11

Vodou in the "Tenth Department"
New York's Haitian community

Karen McCarthy Brown

The wave of Haitian migration to North America began in the late 1950s, when François Duvalier became President of Haiti, and by 1990 had carried 1 million persons to New York, Miami, Boston, Chicago, and Montreal. There are approximately 8 million Haitians and 500,000 of them live in greater New York, as well as the New York and New Jersey communities that participate in the life of the city. This is the largest Haitian diaspora community in the United States. The majority of Haitians serve the Vodou spirits. "Serving the spirits" is the more common expression among Haitians for what journalists and academics, as well as increasing numbers of Haitians themselves, call Vodou.[1]

Vodou communities in New York are family-like networks connecting Haitians with one another and, at times, with members of other ethnic groups. These fictive kinship structures mimic the system of rights and obligations definitive of extended families in rural Haiti, where 80 per cent of Haitians still live. In New York, as in Haiti, Vodou priests and priestesses are known as "papa" and "manman"; their initiates are called "children of the house." The Vodou temple, often the leader's home, functions as a social welfare center. It is a place to gather news about Haiti, process information about New York's dangers and possibilities, and get moral support, perhaps even a small loan, when in trouble. Vodou families in New York City are key to the survival strategies of Haitians. Their function is related to that of Vodou families in Port-au-Prince, where traditional religious ties tend to compensate urban dwellers for the loss of contact with the land and with the built-in security of the extended family.

As a whole, the immigrant community in New York functions as an outpost of Haiti in North America. There are nine administrative districts, or "departments," in Haiti. Haitians in the United States like to call themselves the Tenth Department, and President Aristide appointed to his cabinet a minister for the Tenth Department. Thus Haitians living and practicing their religion in the United States are not so much immigrants, in the traditional sense of that term, as they are transnationals:[2] people with emotional, social, political, economic, and spiritual involvement in two places, and with the ability to move back and forth between these two places in order to make use of each to compensate for what the other lacks.

While Haitians in New York may suffer the melancholy that comes from being away from home, they do not suffer the trauma of cosmic proportions that their African ancestors did when they realized home was irrevocably lost. What makes the difference is that Haitians in New York City can go back home. Even the sizeable number who are undocumented aliens, and therefore cannot travel at the present time, live with the hope that this will not always be their condition.

The image of immigrants in the US press, particularly of those with dark skin, is that of a group of ambitious people out to capture the wealth and opportunity that come with being "American." The naïve chauvinism behind such a view discounts the problems these people flee from and assumes that virtually everyone in the world would prefer, if given a choice, to be a citizen of the United States of America. The poorer the area from which the immigrants come the more likely the general public is to assume their immigration involved unmixed emotions and straightforward motives. While stopping an anticipated "flood" of refugees from Haiti was one of the most accented reasons for the September 1994 US invasion of Haiti, no newspaper I saw even bothered to notice that for weeks following President Aristide's return, the tide was running in the other direction. The American Airlines flights from New York's John F. Kennedy Airport were routinely full going to Haiti and nearly empty coming back. I personally know a handful of people who returned to Haiti to live in the last few months of 1994 after being in the United States for fifteen or twenty years. At least two had resident alien status.

Transnationalism is a phenomenon of the second half of the twentieth century. In part, it is a condition made possible by affordable air travel, fax machines, and computers, as well as by the decreasing significance of nation-states and the increasingly enmeshed global economy. For Haitians, transnationalism is a particularly apt label, because so many of them living in New York were driven to emigrate from Haiti by economic and social processes that originated far closer to New York City than to Haiti. While it is inaccurate to paint Haiti as simply a victim of outside forces and influences, it is nevertheless true that internal corruption has quite often flowed alongside schemes for Haiti generated by the US State Department, USAID, the World Bank, or the CIA. This meddling in Haiti probably has as much to do with the current suffering in Haiti as does Haiti's failed leadership.

Racism, religion, and the Tenth Department

In significant ways, the experience of Haitians coming to the United States has not been like the experience of European immigrant groups, and there are few reasons to believe that, with time, it will come to parallel the Euro-American experience any more than it does now. Ever since Haitians succeeded in liberating themselves from slavery, Haitians and their religion have been feared and reviled. Moreau de St. Mery, a Caribbean planter writing at the time of the Haitian Revolution (1791–1804), who many believe provides the earliest description of Haitian Vodou practice, painted a portrait of the religion replete with fear, lust, and violence.[3] He also characterized its trance states as out of control and, worse, potentially contagious for outsiders who happened to stumble on such rites. Others, writing somewhat later, made the point more directly: all a civilized person had to do was get too close to Haitian religion, and its out-of-control sexuality and violence could overwhelm the observer.[4] Contagion is a recurrent theme in the larger world's image of Haiti.

In the sixteenth century, the island now called Haiti was said to be the source of syphilis in Europe. (Syphilis was most likely brought to the island by Columbus's men.) In the nineteenth century, Haitians were accused of introducing tuberculosis to the US. Then it was AIDS. In the early 1980s, when it was not yet clear that HIV infection had come into Haiti from the United States rather than the reverse, AIDS was known as the 4-H disease: homosexuals, heroine addicts, hemophiliacs, and Haitians were said to be the prime sources of contagion. I heard many stories during that period of New York Haitians losing jobs, apartments, and friends because someone feared they might have AIDS or might practice Vodou or, on more than one occasion, might be involved in the over-determined combination of the two. For a while, prestigious US medical researchers pursued the absurd theory that HIV entered the human population via routine copulation with animals during Haitian Vodou rituals.

The relentlessly racist stereotypes of Haiti and of Vodou affect the lives of Haitians in New York City almost as much as their often precarious economic circumstances do. There is in the United States a perverse will to misunderstand Haitians and their religion. It is almost as if the United States needs Haiti to carry its projections, to justify our own long history of racism. A strikingly persistent line of reasoning about Haiti can be traced from Moreau de St. Mery through to Laurence Harrison, a former chief of USAID, who made strikingly similar arguments in a summer 1993 edition of *Harper's*, at the height of Haitian suffering during the period of Aristide's exile. Vodou, Harrison argued, has no morality and therefore Haiti has no civilization. That is the country's biggest problem, Harrison argued. Haiti's case is hopeless, he concluded, and, not having caused these problems, the United States should do nothing to intervene. There is historical continuity in this attitude. Even though Haitians had fought in the American Revolution, the United States offered Haiti no military aid during their war for independence and, in the early nineteenth century, when Haiti's own revolution left the newly independent country in economic ruin, there was no economic help from the United States.

A hidden religious identity

From late-night "*zombi*" movies to casual references to "voodoo economics," prejudice against Haitian Vodou is pervasive in the US media. Haitians living in the United States who serve the spirits respond by secreting their religious allegiances behind a fabric of half-truths, outright denials, and defensive maneuvers. Even young Haitian children in the United States know that there are two ways of talking: one within the Vodou family, and one outside of it. For example, the son of Mama Lola, a Vodou priestess in Brooklyn who has functioned for a long time as my teacher and friend, once crowed with delight when I affirmed his intuitive decision that it was not a good idea to discuss Papa Gede (the raunchy Vodou spirit of death) with the Catholic priest who was conducting his First Communion classes.

Virtually all Haitians who serve the Vodou spirits are also Catholics, and when another child in the family had her First Communion, Mama Lola actually staged a two-tier celebration. Upstairs was a very Christian event. There was a huge table loaded with food and, in the midst of it, a family Bible placed next to a cake baked in the shape of an open Bible. To acknowledge the diversity among her guests, Mama Lola arranged for both Catholic and Protestant prayers to be offered before the meal. But only some of the people upstairs were invited down to the basement, where a smaller table allowed the Vodou spirits as well to share in the day's feast.

In New York, the concrete evidence of Vodou practice is kept carefully segregated within the private corners of Haitian homes, often behind closed and locked doors. When I first met Mama Lola in the summer of 1978, her altars were in a tiny room in the back of her townhouse basement, a room that she could close and lock when someone came to read the electric meter. Inside the room, however, her altar for the sweet-tempered Rada spirits was out in the open on a big table. The fiery Petwo spirits had their altar on a similar table placed at a right angle to the first, and the Gede's low-to-the-ground, stair-step altar was in a corner of the same room. By 1982, both the Rada and Petwo altars had disappeared behind closed doors. First, the Petwo altar went into a closet in the small basement room. Some months later, a tall metal cabinet with locking double doors was purchased to house the Rada altar. With this arrangement, Mama Lola could lock up her altars before she locked the altar room itself. In 1984, Mama Lola moved from that house because one of the neighbors had started to complain to everyone who would listen about Lola being "a Vodou Lady." In 1987, she moved once more for a similar reason. Recently, however, things have shifted back towards greater openness. I do not know what all the reasons are for this, but I suspect that one concerns the publication of our book, *Mama Lola: A Vodou Priestess in Brooklyn*,[5] in 1991. In the last few years, Mama Lola has seen many positive responses to her religion and to herself as a professional healer within that tradition. Even the curtains have recently come down from the latest incarnation of her spirit altars, and she has expanded the size of her altar room and taken great care in redecorating it. Yet her altars are still located in a basement room that can be safely locked against those who are too curious or too judgmental. As was mentioned above, virtually all Haitians who serve the spirits are also Catholics, and so upstairs in Mama Lola's home – on the living room walls, on her bedside table – the only things an outsider sees are devotional objects for the Catholic saints.

Mama Lola's children and grandchildren knew from when they were very young that the Vodou spirits who counseled and comforted them in the rituals that took place in their homes were not to be acknowledged in their larger social worlds. The habit of having a public and a private religion, and of admitting to the first only, is deeply engrained in the Haitian community. It fits with a larger sense of secretiveness (which includes routinely using one name for "business purposes" and another for friends) born of a feeling that Haitians are neither respected nor welcome in the US. These habits of hiding speak of the power issues that shape Haitian life and religion in New York City in the early twenty-first century. Any attempt to describe immigrant life or Vodou in North American cities that does not give a central place to prejudice misses a major dimension of the Haitian experience.

New York Vodou

Several of the characteristics of New York Haitian Vodou that have emerged in this discussion actually have their roots in earlier developments in Haiti. This is further evidence that Vodou is best understood as a transnational phenomenon, one shaped by forces that transcend any one particular nation-state or culture.

It is important to note that, by and large, it was not migration to New York that caused Haitians to lose contact with the land. For most of them, that process started one, or even two, generations earlier. Significant rural out-migration began fifty years ago in Haiti, and it has continued up to the present. The forces that cause the population to move from the countryside to the cities are poverty, soil erosion, overpopulation, local political corruption, and zealous foreign investors who have periodically tried to amass large tracts of land for business ventures.

The majority of Haitians in New York come from Haiti's cities. (By contrast, in Miami, the majority are from the countryside.) In many cases, it was the parents or grandparents of these urban people who left the rural areas in search of a better way of life. Port-au-Prince, the launching pad for much of the second diaspora, has seen a steady and rapid growth in ghettos as a result of the influx of the rural population. Most Haitians now living in New York therefore encountered urban life, and inevitably also North American culture, well before they emigrated.

New York City turns up the volume and intensifies these processes, but many Haitians come to the United States already quite urbanized and Americanized. Indeed, exposure to things that for a long time were available only in Haiti's cities – US popular music and television, Bruce Lee movies, blue jeans, and Johnny Walker scotch – is what started many young people dreaming of life in New York. It should not be overlooked, however, that more sober reasons for coming to the United States go hand in hand with such fantasies. Often one emigrant represents the survival strategy of an entire family. A black market tourist visa can cost a great deal in Port-au-Prince, so frequently entire families have to invest, and they expect a return on that investment. (Before the most recent round of political upheaval, starting with the downfall of Jean-Claude Duvalier in 1986, a black market visa cost $2,000; during the same period, the average annual income in Haiti was around $200.)

Finally, New York badgers Haitians with racism, an especially virulent form of which singles out their religion for self-righteous and vitriolic attacks; but even this is not an unknown for Haitian immigrants. Haiti's mulatto elite and the Catholic Church hierarchy have periodically tried to destroy the popular African-based religion called Vodou. During the worst of the so-called anti-superstition campaigns in Haiti, Vodou withdrew discretely behind temple walls. The habit of maintaining a secret religious life intensifies and becomes more elaborate in New York City, but the need for it does not come as a rude shock to most Haitians.

Religious transnationalism

What makes this so-called second diaspora different from the slave diaspora is that, this time around, they chose to come – more or less. And this time they can, and do, go back – sometimes for visits and sometimes to stay. Furthermore, Haitians in New York City remain in touch with friends and families in Haiti; they even participate in Haitian politics.

Some examples will make the significance of this apparent. During the upheaval that followed the 1986 departure of President-for-life Jean-Claude Duvalier, Haitians in New York were kept well informed of what was happening in Haiti by video news cassettes. Tapes covering important developments could be purchased in shops on both Nostrand and Flatbush Avenues in Brooklyn, often within twenty-four hours of the events they depicted. This informal news network was able to provide much more extended and graphic visual news coverage than any of the television networks. The tapes, some made by amateurs, were flown in on the daily American Airlines flight from Port-au-Prince and duplicated in a studio in New York.

The direct participation of immigrants in Haitian politics provides another example of their transnationalism. The so-called Tenth Department raised a large percentage of the money expended on the candidacy of the then priest and liberation theologian, Jean-Bertrand Aristide. During his campaign for office, Aristide came to New York and drew crowds that numbered in the thousands. In December 1990, Aristide became the first president in Haiti's history who could make an honest claim to having been democratically elected. When he was ousted in a coup in September 1991, the Tenth Department became a major financial supporter of his government in exile.[6]

In parallel ways, the spiritual life of the Tenth Department is also enmeshed with that of Haiti. In the second diaspora, Haitian Vodou has become a transnational religion. This label is intended to call attention not only to the parallel Vodou ceremonies being performed according to the same ritual calendar, in both Haiti and New York, but also to the interesting circumstances that make Vodou a key player in the exchange of people, goods, and money between Haiti and the continental US.

The Tenth Department pumps a substantial amount of money into the local Haitian economy, approximately $100 million per year.[7] Unlike other monies circulating in Haiti, a significant amount of this money comes in relatively small amounts and goes directly to poor people. Much of the elaborate Vodou ritualizing in Port-au-Prince would probably not be possible without the money Haitian exiles send to friends and family members back home.

Furthermore, some New York Vodou leaders, who are either US citizens or resident aliens, and therefore free to travel, insist on going to Haiti to perform particularly important ceremonies. Mama Lola is one of them. She will not initiate anyone in New York City because, she says, initiates need to be able to put their bare feet on Haitian soil for the ceremonies to be effective. Some prominent diaspora Vodou leaders will initiate people in New York and take on just about any cure there as well, but part of Mama Lola's authority in the diaspora community stems from her willingness to travel.[8]

Once initiated into a Vodou lineage based in Haiti, a person acquires lifelong connections to a family-like network of temples there. Some US priests and priestesses send money to their "brother" and "sister" priests and priestesses in Port-au-Prince, asking that ceremonies be performed in Haiti for their New York clients. Occasionally, items of clothing are sent through the mail as surrogates for the people who need healing or, perhaps, controlling. This process puts money into the hands of the heads of Vodou families in Port-au-Prince, who in turn spread the money throughout the poorest segments of the urban population.

At times, trips to Haiti are occasioned by Mama Lola's healing practice. When she has reached a dead end in an attempt to help one of her clients, Mama Lola may decide to travel to Haiti for one last effort. She recently had some "work" to do for a client about to go on trial for a serious crime. When a volatile political situation and a US embargo on flights to Haiti prevented her from going there, she flew instead to the Dominican Republic, which shares the island of Hispaniola with Haiti. She then picked her herbs and performed her rituals in a location as close to Haiti as she could get.

The elaborate eight-day cycle of rituals for ancestors and family spirits that Mama Lola performed in Haiti in the summer of 1989 also falls into the category of ceremonies that would not be as effective if performed in New York City. Mama Lola spent several thousand dollars on these rites, the first ancestral ceremonies on such a scale that she had been able to stage since she emigrated in 1963. On an economic level alone, these rites had a significant impact on the downtown neighborhood where her mother's house is located; it was in the backyard of that house that Lola performed her family rituals. The most tangible and immediate benefit of the rituals was that more than one hundred people were fed every day for more than a week.

Vodou also generates a number of small-scale international markets for herbs, religious images, beads, flags, and other Vodou paraphernalia. Travelers to Haiti often bring back hard-to-find herbs, tucked discretely into their luggage. But when informal means of keeping Haitian healers supplied with the tools of their trade are insufficient, there are commercial solutions. In large cities such as New York and Miami, *botanicas*, general supply stores of African-based religion in North America, carry a wide selection of fresh and dried herbs from Haiti. One Miami *botanica* even provides shopping carts for its clients to use as they browse the aisles of refrigerated cases holding herbs and roots from all over the world, including several countries in West Africa, as well as Haiti.

Conclusion

Writing for *The Village Voice*, art critic John Berger once described the experience of immigration using elegantly simple geometry. Home, he said, is the "center of the real" and the place where two lines intersect. The vertical is "a path leading upward to the sky and downward to the underworld," thus keeping the person in simultaneous connection with the gods above and the ancestors *beloe*, while the horizontal is a representation of "the traffic of the world...which assures that all journeys end at home." In Berger's image, immigration is to be understood as synonymous with the loss of home, and the attendant loss of contact with ancestors and gods. Berger added that once one has emigrated and, as a result, has no "fixed points as bearings," the traffic of the world dissolves into meaningless wandering. Berger's sense of home as the center of the real has deep resonance in Vodou; the crossroads image, omnipresent in Vodou, is basically the same as Berger's image of the intersecting lines. Yet, at least in the Haitian case, and, one suspects, in others as well, Berger's analysis of the consequences of immigration could not be more wrong.

The key factor for the people of Haiti's second diaspora is that they did not lose Haiti when they left Haiti. In the early twenty-first century, the continuous movement of people, money, goods, and information between New York City and Haiti traces and re-traces the horizontal line of the crossroads figure, anchoring it solidly in place. Spiritual cargo also flows along this horizontal line and unites Haitians in New York with Haiti itself – and from there with the vertical, that is to say with God in heaven and the spirits and ancestors below in Gine, Africa.

Yet it is necessary to add that life in New York is not always a thoroughly comfortable fit for Haitians and their religion. Haitian Vodou is a religion, like the several African traditions out of which it was born, that is characterized by flexibility and a certain natural, unstrained hospitality towards other religious traditions, other cultures, and other value systems. Nevertheless, it is not hard to perceive that Vodou in New York is stretching and straining to accommodate new, and often alien, attitudes, ideas, and places. However, in the final analysis, Vodou accommodates itself to life in New York, refuels itself through contact with Haiti, and, on the whole, thrives.

When Mama Lola tries to account theologically for the transnational character of her spirits, she says: "The spirit is a wind. Everywhere I go, they going too...to protect me." By casting her spirits as the wind, she makes them moveable, dynamic, and powerful. She also lifts them above the boundaries of state and culture. Intuitively, she knows what comes next for the Vodou spirits: the challenge of placing the Haitian spirits in the religious universe of humankind.

Not only their long experience of Catholicism but also the increase of Protestantism in Haiti and in Haitian immigrant communities have heightened Haitians' awareness of the power and utility of transcendent world-views that claim to account for the whole world and, within it, assign each group to their place. When home was "the center of the real," it was not necessary for Haitians to have a world-view that accounted for everything and everybody. But urban life has changed this. Contemporary cities are by definition made up of many realities. Even a city the size of Port-au-Prince – with a population of approximately 1 million people – contains enough human diversity to put a strain on a unified understanding of the world. A city the size and complexity of New York puts considerably more pressure on the local spiritualities that its immigrants bring. The felt need for a universal religious schema is greatly intensified, one that accounts not only for one's own self and one's own beliefs, but which also places that self in relation to the other and, furthermore, delineates the larger reality that encompasses the two. How the Vodou spirits respond to the pressure for such a theological schema will be determined by how they come to understand and to use power in the modern world, how they relate to their neighbors on a day-to-day basis, and, in general, how they negotiate morally. Haitians in New York already have a generation's worth of experience in dealing with pluralism in the human family – more if the experience of being enslaved is counted in this column. Their characteristic openness and flexibility is mirrored in the New York Vodou altars that have begun to collect the spirits of Cuban Santeria and the implements of healers from West Africa. On the issue of living with cultural and religious pluralism, Haitians have something important to contribute to contemporary life in New York. Yet it cannot be avoided that they have little chance of influencing anyone beyond the members of their own communities if they continue to be bullied into carrying the projections and fears of North Americans.

Notes

1   The word comes from the Fon *vodun*, meaning god or spirit. In Haiti, the word Vodou (the correct spelling according to the official Haitian Creole orthography) originally referred to one style of drumming and ritualizing among many such styles. It was outsiders who first applied the word Voodoo to the entire complex of religious action and belief in Haiti.
2   See, for example, Nina Glick-Schiller and Georges Fouron, "'Everywhere we go, we are in danger': Ti Manno and the emergence of a Haitian transnational identity," *American Ethnologist* 17(2) 1990: 329–47, and, by the same authors, *Georges Woke Up Laughing: Long Distance Nationalism and the Search for Home*, Durham, NC: Duke University Press, 2001.
3   M.L.E. Moreau de St. Mery, *Description Topographique, Physique, Civile, Politique, et Historique de la Partie Française de l'Isle de St Domingue*, Paris: Libraire Larousse, 1958 (originally published in 1797).
4   See Robert Lawless, *Haiti's Bad Press: Origins, Development, and Consequences*, Rochester, VT: Schenkman Books, 1992.
5   Karen McCarthy Brown, *Mama Lola: A Vodou Priestess in Brooklyn*, rev. edn, Berkeley: University of California Press, 2001.
6   President Aristide made the Tenth Department official. During his initial short tenure in office, he appointed Gerart Hean-Juste, Director of the Miami Haitian Refugee Center, 1980–91, as the first director of the Tenth Department.
7   Jean Jean-Pierre, "The diaspora: the Tenth Department," in James Ridgeway (ed.) *The Haiti Files: Decoding the Crisis*, Washington, DC: Essential Books/Azul Editions, 1994.
8   Mama Lola goes to the places where the problems manifest themselves – a plot of land, a car, or a house – in order to treat them directly. In addition to Haiti, her healing work in recent years has taken her to Canada, Jamaica, Belize (on two occasions), and also to Boston and several small towns in the southern part of the United States.

Chapter 12

Assaulting California's sacred mountains

Shamans vs. New Age merchants of Nirvana

Helen McCarthy

The religious systems and practices of the indigenous peoples of California have suffered numerous detrimental consequences of colonization and hegemony of Western civilization since the time of effective contact in 1769. Indigenous religious observance endured the initial onslaught of the zealous missionary fathers, the initial colonists in California who made a concerted, proselytizing effort, aimed directly at converting the native people to Christianity through agricultural labor in the missions and intended to obliterate local, pagan religious expressions. The California peoples who survived proved to be resistant to the numerous attempts to force them to relinquish cultural and religious traditions. Some of the regions of strongest persistence are, not surprisingly, in rural areas, where the people live within their ancestral territories and thus have access to their traditional resources, including both materials and, even more importantly, their sacred landscapes. In many cases, these traditional lands are under the jurisdiction of federal and state land management agencies (for example, the Forest Service, the National Park Service, etc.), who, according to public law, must grant Native Americans access to their religious sites and protect those opportunities for the practice of native religion. These lands, however, are also subject to the demands of competing interests, such as lumber companies, ski resort development projects, hydroelectric-generation construction, and "New Age" religions – the whole gamut of modern society.

While on the surface this seems to be a conflict over the use of the lands themselves, ultimately it is over the right of control of native heritage, symbols and tribal identity. Tribal shamans, as traditional guardians of tribal religious expression, are in the forefront of the fight against these modern assaults on their sacred landscapes. There are many struggles today in California between the agents of modernity and the indigenous people over the control of native heritage. But those which pertain specifically to sacred mountains are of particular interest, for it is within this sphere that confrontations with New Agers occur as these contemporary seekers of religious experiences attempt to appropriate native symbols and actuate them for their own redefined purposes. Data here is drawn from my own research regarding four sacred mountains: Mt. Pinos (Ventura/Kern Counties); Chews Ridge (Monterey County); Chanchelulla Peak (Trinity County); and Mt. Shasta (Siskiyou County). The most public controversy has been over Mt. Shasta, which has received national attention in the US Congress having been named in a bill proposing to significantly limit the protection of sacred sites (H.R. 563, introduced by Congressman Herger in 1995). First I will review the cultural context of pre-contact California and the religious essentialisms that have persisted into the contemporary period. I will then discuss the inherent contradictions between California tribal religious practice and modern society which led to the perilous confrontations that are currently manifested across the state and, indeed, the nation.

Pre-contact California religious essentialisms

In the late pre-contact period, California was inhabited by a large, dense population of peoples – circa 350,000 – who supported themselves on a gathering, hunting, and fishing economy. Although they did not practice agriculture, they lived in permanent villages of up to 1,000–1,500 residents, where they stored tons of food supplies, particularly acorns, but also including many varieties of seeds and nuts, as well as dried fish and meat (Cook 1976; Kroeber 1925). These supplies not only sustained the people through winter months, a period of minimal harvest potential, but also existed as a surplus of values that could be realized as prestige/profit through competitive ceremonial feasting and as material profit through the extensive trade network that linked groups north/south and east/west across and beyond California (McCarthy 1993). Shell beads manufactured by coastal tribes served as the standard currency throughout this network.

The political and ceremonial structures in each tribe were expressed through a complex organization that embraced both socio-political and religious powers. The tribe was guided by a chief, who usually inherited his position. He directed the activities in the main town and surrounding satellite villages; in large towns, there might be up to three chiefs representing different divisions. The chief did not have authority but rather great influence, based in part on his primary role as ritual leader, which gave him the power to make the decisions regarding the performance of the cycle of necessary ceremonies. Essentially, these rituals, such as the first-fruits observances, expressed the tribe's thanks to the spiritual world for the continuing well-being of the people. Other ceremonies, particularly the Annual Mourning Ceremonies held for the recently deceased, were large inter-group events that required significant financial backing from the chief's constituents in order to host hundreds or even thousands of guests. Thus the chief had a critical responsibility for maintaining the tribe's relationship within both the social and the cosmological orders, and a number of these ceremonies continue to be practiced today.

In addition to community ceremonials, religion is expressed in other equally important ways, both by ordinary individuals and by spiritual specialists or shamans. The daily world and the spiritual world exist together as a seamless whole, wherein spirits are both immanent and immediate throughout the entire environment – the landscape is everywhere imbued with spiritual power. Many of the most important locations are marked and explained by myths that tell of the dawn of the world, when the world was created, and of "The Time When Animals Were People," before humans as we know them were created. Mythological reality is stitched down to the daily places where women gather, children play, and men hunt, thus generating a sacred landscape within which the people live on intimate terms with the spirits. This integral and inherent relationship between the local geography, the supernatural world, and the human residents is an essentialism of California Indian religion.

While spirits exist ubiquitously across this landscape, their presence is more prevalent and potent in particular places, and these are the locations where individuals go to seek communication with the supernatural world. These spiritually charged places are often at springs, waterfalls, rock formations, caves, or locations high in the mountains with an unimpeded viewshed.[1] The quest for a tutelary spirit is usually assumed by males at puberty, but is also pursued in some groups by women. The goal is to establish a lifelong relationship with a spiritual guide who will extend supernatural power to the individual in various daily as well as potentially extraordinary circumstances. During this initial meeting, the spirit teaches the supplicant a special song that is to be used for future communication between the two. An individual renews this relationship periodically throughout life.

One destined to become a shaman or doctor develops a similar but far more intense relationship with the spiritual world, and might eventually have several spirit guides. In some cases, young, nascent shamans receive spirit dreams long before they actively seek a special relationship. The potent alliance between the shaman and the supernatural is often an inherited affinity, but also requires lengthy training and testing with the spirit guide(s) as well as with accomplished, older shamans in the tribe. This training demands repeated visits to sacred locations specially marked for shamans, most of which are restricted to use only by shamans because of the potency of the spiritual presence there; these are dangerous places for an average individual and thus assiduously avoided by most tribal members. In this endeavor, the trainee requires isolation, privacy, and quietude, and in some cases a particular view or vista that encompasses other power places identified by the tribal cosmology. For some tribes, the ultimate spiritual power lives within a prominent mountain in the local landscape. The shaman who is able to form an alliance with this spirit has extraordinary healing powers and the ability to protect the tribal community from external or supernatural agents of harm. Initially, it is necessary for the shaman to go to the mountain to develop this relationship and to make subsequent visits there, but once the link is firmly established, the shaman can summon the spirit from distant locations. Thus, this essential bond with the spirits of the land bestows the power to the shaman through dreams and visions.

Conflict and competition with contemporary society

From this brief discussion, it is clear that continuing access to these sacred locales is essential for the spiritual well-being of individuals, for the practice of shamanism, and for tribal identity and persistence as articulated through the religious symbolism imbued in the landscape. Tribal members and groups require not only physical access to these locations; they also need the privacy, isolation, and quietude that are inherent in this aspect of their religious practice. It is also obvious that this need for access to specified locations, which have been used for many generations, and which are basically uncontaminated by contemporary activities, creates a situation of extreme vulnerability for those who strive to maintain their religious heritage. When these sacred locations are violated or desecrated by various modern activities and forms of development, the spiritual connections may be permanently lost to the tribe, with no comparable substitute available.

As is well known, indigenous people across this continent were everywhere displaced and removed from their ancestral lands by the Euro-American colonists. This process was vigorously pursued in California as well, with the result that California Indian peoples today have only the most minimal remnants of their former territories under tribal jurisdiction as trust lands. While many areas, of course, have long since been swallowed up by cities and modern development, there nevertheless remain many acres of land under state and federal jurisdiction – the National Forests, National Parks, State Parks, and BLM[2] lands – that are relatively undeveloped. Traditional tribal homes are frequently adjacent to these state and federal lands that encompass their ancestral territories, and it is primarily within these lands that practitioners of traditional religion have had access to some of their most important sacred sites. In fact, the historic loss of so many ancestral lands and concomitantly sacred sites greatly enhances the value of those that remain accessible today.

With a burgeoning population in California, public lands are experiencing increasing pressures from both existing and new activities that often target remote and pristine areas as their foci. For example, the US military recently proposed construction of a high-powered interstellar telescope on the summit of Chews Ridge (Monterey County). This construction would have installed a noisy generator and blocked off the entire top of the ridge with chain-link fence and razor wire, thus preventing access to about 100 acres including the most critical location for Esselen prayer. While the tribe was asked to verify the religious basis of their claim to this property, the real challenge they faced was to establish tribal authenticity after being declared "extinct" early in the twentieth century by anthropologists who conducted research in the area.

In another case, the Chumash are currently opposing new parking lots on Mt. Pinos (Ventura/Kern Counties) designed to accommodate more visitors to the area, which is the mythological center of their world and an extraordinarily sacred mountain; ironically, in pre-contact times, Chumash peoples did not venture onto its slopes except to make a religious offering because the location is so sacred and dangerous. They are now being asked to reveal religious secrets in order to verify religious connections to the site. They are also being asked to confirm current ceremonial use of the location, yet appropriate traditional practice prescribes avoidance. Thus they are required to meet the expectations that the dominant Western society has of religion, expectations which do not correspond well to indigenous Native American religious practices.

The most publicly visible example of this conflict in California, and perhaps nationally, pertains to Mt. Shasta in northern California. Mt. Shasta, located at the head of the Sacramento Valley, is a spectacular volcanic cone that stands alone, rising above 14,000 feet in elevation, the treeless upper slopes above 8,000 feet shimmering under the snow and glaciers. It can be seen and easily distinguished for hundreds of miles as it seems to hover above the surrounding landscape, and is sacred to many of the tribes in the area, including Shasta, Karuk, Wintu, Achomawi and other Pit River tribes, and Modoc. Several of these tribes share a creation myth that tells of the creator making Mt. Shasta from the snow and ice in the clouds where he resided, so that he could step down to earth. He sat on Mt. Shasta and created the creatures of the earth, and later used the mountain as his home – the smoke from his fire could be seen coming out of the top. Some relate that the Legendary People who lived during the Time When Animals Were People went up onto Mt. Shasta when their obligations towards establishing the earth had been discharged and became some of the rock formations that we see today on the upper slopes. They will re-emerge when this current cycle of existence has completed its course.

The treeless upper portions of the mountain where these cosmological events occurred are supernaturally very potent and therefore dangerous. They are the eminent locations for contact with the spiritual powers, and shamans from several tribes acknowledge regular use of the area. In particular, there are some springs that provide especially efficacious spiritual conduits for the shamans. While a number of native spiritual people use this area, they do so only after careful preparation, which includes fasting and prayer that notifies the spirits of their impending visit, and they conduct themselves with the utmost respect. The spiritual leaders feel strongly that this area must not be altered by modern development, since it will disrupt and perhaps entirely end these supernatural communications.

The sacred qualities of the upper slopes, however, are rather immediately threatened by two kinds of activities. The first is the proposed development of a ski resort, including lifts into the sacred cosmological areas and a full range of support developments such as restaurants, condominiums, and so on. There has been a protracted conflict over this proposal between the developers, the Forest Service, and the local tribes. The tribes recently won the last round. In the heavy snows of the 1994–95 winter, an enormous, highly destructive avalanche ripped through the center of the proposed development area. One of the shamans publicly takes credit for it, warning that the spirits are demonstrating their ultimate power to destroy any development that violates their home. While not necessarily conceding the cause of the avalanche to supernatural forces in league with the shaman, the Forest Service is taking the avalanche problem into serious consideration regarding its potential for loss of life and property in a densely populated ski resort.

Perhaps the most insidious and pernicious threat to the traditional use of Mt. Shasta is posed by the New Age religious activities on the mountain. "New Age" practitioners seek new religious ritual and insight through non-Christian/non-Western religious conventions directed towards a cosmic unity of being and power flow. Towards this end, they usurp ritual practices, expressions, and symbols from many other peoples and pile them, layer upon layer, into their own cosmologies and ceremonial observances. In that many of them appear to seek communion and unification with the powers of the earth, they appropriate Native American symbols (among others) which they interpret as generative of harmony and balance with nature. They also seek transcendent locations where they can make contact with the forces of the universe, and many believe that Mt. Shasta emanates a power vortex that establishes it as one of seven such locations worldwide. Consequently, many New Age practitioners come to Mt. Shasta to enter this power grid. There are numerous small shops in Mt. Shasta City that offer all sorts of paraphernalia – from Mayan calendars and Tibetan prayer wheels, to crystals and aroma packets – to amplify one's efforts to develop the desired cosmic connections. The summer of 1989 was hailed by New Agers as a period of "cosmic convergence" because of a rare alignment of the planets, and thousands of believers flocked to Mt. Shasta to join in this convocation of the cosmos.

Actual New Age practices are many and diverse, but nearly all of them that make use of Native American sacred spaces are repugnant to the Native Americans themselves, as these behaviors are disrespectful and desecrating to the sacred places. The first issue is simply that too many people come to these locations, which, for the Native Americans, are places of isolation, solitude, and quiet, and where one fasts. The New Agers are noisy, trample the environment, urinate and defecate near the water, eat, drink alcohol, and leave trash. Some, in their efforts to become one with the cosmos, dance nude and bathe in the sacred springs, both of which are particularly violating acts. One fervent woman appears in a heavily feathered outfit, which she describes as her "guise as Egret Woman," to greet the dawn. Imagine the response to such acts committed in the cathedral of Notre Dame in Paris.

Other problems include the rock designs that many people construct on the virtually vegetation-free slopes above the tree line. Most often they design a medicine wheel, a large circle including various other symbols. According to the local tribal spiritual people, these symbols are appropriated from distant places (from Native American Plains cultures, for example) by individuals who do not understand them. It is tantamount to a religious territorial marker that is out of place, thus expropriating the location from its indigenous context. This misuse and misplacement of inappropriate symbols sets up a kind of spiritual static that complicates communication with resident spirits.

More seriously, many New Age practitioners believe that crystals are effective conduits for cosmic power and are aware that crystals were used by some California Indian shamans. Consequently, they take them as an offering to the mountain, and throw them in the sacred springs, sometimes in such numbers that the natural flow of the water is obstructed. However, they do not understand the basis of Native American use of crystals and power. As one Achomawi spiritual person explains, you cannot just go downtown and buy a crystal and think that you are going to achieve instantly spiritual union or power. It takes years of training to become a spiritual person, and possession of a store-bought crystal does not automatically grant you a relationship with spiritual power. Another side of the issue for Native Americans is that power is raw, that is to say, it can be used for positive or negative purposes, so if it is not controlled and directed by a knowledgeable, trained person, then the power may do a great deal of harm – something that New Agers never seem to consider. Throwing these potentially highly charged objects into the sacred springs is thus extremely contaminating and may cause the resident spirit to withdraw.

Recently, there was a direct confrontation between a New Age group and one of the local shamans. The shaman went with members of her tribe to the location, which is regarded by all other tribes as her special place. Upon arrival, she found New Agers engaged in activities there. They stridently refused to leave and threatened the shaman, who is an elderly woman. She decided to use spiritual help to remove them from her sacred area and, asking her supporters to back her up, went into a trance to summon her powers. She returned from her trance just in time to see them leaving, in a subdued manner.

The Native Americans understand that others recognize the spirituality of Mt. Shasta, but insist that there are appropriate ways to approach the sanctity of the mountain, as did the Buddhist monks a few years ago. In pre-contact times, if an individual (or group) was called to the mountain, the protocol required that he/she should contact the local spiritual person, who would introduce the visitor to the mountain spirit with the appropriate prayers and songs, in the appropriate language. The visitor was instructed on the proper behavior, and went in a respectful manner. This is, in fact, similar to the way in which travelers visit churches and holy lands in most other places. No Christian church or Moslem mosque would be asked to endure the kinds of violations that the sacred locations on Mt. Shasta suffer from New Age activities.

The relationship between the essential nature of Native American religion and modern society is inherently contradictory, thus creating persistent primary conflicts. The articulated religious symbolism is imbued in a landscape that the Native Americans no longer control. Public agencies that do control the land must by law grant Native Americans physical access to their sacred places, but, because of their policy of allowing the multiple use of these lands, they are unwilling to restrict access to any one group. Thus New Agers, the ultimate product of modernity, appropriate Native American symbols and sacred places, jeopardizing traditional religious practice and disarticulating the symbolic connections in the sacred landscapes, thereby challenging not only tribal heritage but even identity.

Notes

1   "Viewshed" is a technical term used in cultural resource management. It signifies more than a view; it is all the places, some of them sacred, within that view.
2   Bureau of Land Management, a federal agency that owns and manages an enormous acreage in the west.

References

Cook, Sherburne F., *The Population of the California Indians 1769–1970*, Berkeley: University of California Press, 1976.
Kroeber, Alfred L., *Handbook of California Indians*, Bureau of American Ethnology Bulletin 78, Washington, DC, 1925.
McCarthy, Helen, "A political economy of western mono acorn production," unpublished Ph.D. thesis, University of California, Davis, 1993.

Part III

Africa and Asia

Chapter 13

Understanding sacrifice and sanctity in Benin indigenous religion, Nigeria

A case study

Flora Edouwaye S. Kaplan

Benin religion presents an interesting case study for the questions raised at the "Beyond 'Primitivism': Indigenous Religious Traditions and Modernity" conference.[1] The conference enquired about the nature of non-Western contact with world religions, apart from major Eastern religions – and the consequences of often abrupt and violent encounters with the West – and the responses and the effect both parties, or more, have on each other in a complex interaction between indigenous religious traditions and modernity. Benin offers several reasons for presentation as a case study. It suggests some answers as to why some traditions continue to form the basis of ethnic and even national identity in a modern nation-state, and why some religions resist change and others do not. Benin illuminates how some structures of indigenous tradition such as myths, symbols, and institutions both respond to contact with foreign traditions and shed light on their reaction to major world religions such as Christianity, Islam, and others.

Introduction

Notions of sacred kingship in Benin were reported from first contacts with the Portuguese in the late fifteenth century. These notions both resemble and violate Western ideas of similar phenomena and challenge us to accept and extend our understanding of these potent ideas in non-Western religions. This case study considers the consequences of West Africa's often abrupt and violent encounters with the West – the responses and the effects both parties (or more) have on each other – and the complex interaction between indigenous religious traditions and twentieth-century modernity. Benin offers an example of resistance in the face of violent colonial encounters. It shows how the contradiction between modernity and indigenous religion is sometimes resolved by the capacity of ancient traditions such as sacred kingship to take on new roles and meanings. At the same time, key indigenous institutions, myths, and symbols provide the basis for both the Benin's resistance and their eventual, selective acceptance of world religions.

At the end of the nineteenth century, Europeans decried Benin religion as "barbaric," especially for its ritual practice of human sacrifice. British accounts of Benin City at the time of their 1897 military expedition against the Benin kingdom painted a gory picture of bloody brutality. They christened the capital city, Benin, "City of Blood" (Bacon 1897). The "Punitive Expedition"'s surgeon, Felix Roth, MRCS, LRCP, vividly described in his diary the remains of human sacrifice the British found along the way and in the kingdom's capital in 1897 (see also Figures 13.1 and 13.2):

Benin City, February 19th – We are now settled down in the above place. It is a misnomer to call it a city; it is a charnel house. All about the houses and street are dead natives, some crucified and sacrificed on trees, others on stage erections, some on the ground, some in pits, and amongst the latter we found several half-dead ones. I suppose there is not another place on the face of the globe so near civilisation where such butcheries are carried on with impunity...In front of the king's compound is an immense wall, fully twenty feet high...This wall must be a few hundred yards long, and at each end are two big ju-ju trees...[and on a framework] live human beings are tied, to die of thirst or heat, and ultimately to be dried up by the sun and eaten by the carrion birds...There were two bodies on the first tree and one on the other. At the base of them the whole ground was strewn with human bones and decomposing bodies, with their heads off...the flesh was off their hands and feet, and the heads had been cut off and removed...All along the road, too, more decapitated bodies were found, blown out by the heat of the sun; the sight was sickening.

(quoted in the appendices to H.L. Roth 1968: ix–xi)

And what then of the Oba himself? Richard Burton, writing in 1862, affirmed that "The Obba (king) of Benin is fetish – hence his power." He noted that the Benin believed he was "a deity himself." In 1801, Beauvais, and later Adams in 1823, reported that "the King could live without food or drink, subject to death, but destined to reappear on earth at the time of a definite period" (*ibid*.: 62–71). The belief in reincarnation was an integral

Figure 13.1 Altars with skulls and the blood of human sacrifices, Queens' compound of the harem, after British military assault, Benin City, 1897

Source: Photograph by R.K. Granville, 1897, courtesy of Liverpool Libraries, Liverpool Record Office, UK.

part of the indigenous religion when I began fieldwork in Benin in the 1980s. It is still widely believed that the Oba does not eat, drink, or sleep, and that he never dies, but is reborn. He is the source of life and the focus of all religious worship. Captain Adams' 1823 description of the King of Benin obtained up to the turn of the last century (except for the consequences). He was:

> fetiche, and the principal object of adoration in his dominions. He occupies a higher post here than the Pope does in Catholic Europe; for he is not only God's viceregent upon earth, but a god himself, whose subjects both obey and adore him as such, although I believe their adoration to arise rather from fear than love; as cases of heresy, if proved, are followed by prompt decapitation.
>
> *(ibid.: 62)*

The British believed that colonial rule would replace human sacrifice and cruelty with Christian religious worship and virtue. They contemptuously ascribed the sanctity of the Oba of Benin, the awe and fear felt by his subjects, and his status as a demi-god to "juju," or magic, not religion. Nonetheless, the British understood his power in two very important respects: it was the major obstacle to seizing control of commerce and to imposing colonial rule. The Oba's "juju" could disrupt the area's coastal commerce and inland trade on the creeks and rivers at his will. A provocative incident – the rash attempt of a British party, led by Acting Consul General Captain James R. Phillips, to pay an uninvited visit to the Oba during a period of religious observance in the capital city – led to their ambush and

Figure 13.2 Covered pit into which sacrificed captives or slaves were thrown. Photograph taken after British military assault near the Oba's Palace, Benin City, 1897

Source: Photograph courtesy of Liverpool Libraries, Liverpool Record Office, UK.

"massacre." It precipitated a long-sought, major military assault on Benin City, thereafter called the "Punitive Expedition" in the West. The results were the executions of several loyal chiefs, and exile of Oba Ovonramwen (1888–1914) from Benin to Old Calabar.[2]

The notion of sanctity refers to a state of godliness – the state of being holy or sacred. As a sacred king, the Oba of Benin was and is set apart for service and worship as a living deity. Sacrifice, by definition, is the act of offering something precious to attain something else. The core concepts of sanctity, sacrifice, and community in Benin are inseparable from the king's person. Their centrality in indigenous religion assured the continuity of the institution of sacred kingship and Benin resistance throughout the colonial period. And, at the same time, the ideas of sanctity and sacrifice associated with a king and community facilitated acceptance of comparable notions in Christian religion, first introduced in the sixteenth century, and again later in the nineteenth century. Thus, an understanding of sacrifice and sanctity in Benin indigenous religion extends our understanding of changes wrought by conquest and colonialism, and of why Christianity played a major role in the late nineteenth and twentieth centuries.

After the British conquest, instead of human beings, large animals – cows, goats, and rams, for example – were sacrificed. These animals and other traditional offerings of cockerels, crocodiles, snails, and fish continue to be offered to specific deities to this day. Sacrifice is integral to religious worship in Benin. Human blood had been the quintessential life force. For the Benin who valued life to the utmost, it was the most precious and efficacious gift that could be made to the gods and king. Blood remains a moral imperative needed to cleanse and renew the Oba's sources of individual and collective power in Benin. The king's person, his head and parts of his body, are anointed with blood on special occasions, and on others with medicines, chalk, and other substances. Blood especially is needed to sustain his power and the power of his coral bead regalia. Blood spilled on Palace altars propitiates the royal ancestors who, like the living Oba, stand for the state. Blood sacrifice assures the continuity essential for social communion, cohesion, and life itself. For a warrior people such as the Benin, the connection between life and blood was obvious. Human sacrifice also rid the body politic of those who threatened the peace and fabric of society. Troublesome war captives, slaves, and habitual criminals were used, periodically emptying the prisons.

Self-sacrifice, like voluntary suicide, is a rarity among the Benin. One remembered instance is preserved in oral tradition, and cited as the ultimate act of love and devotion to the king. Queen Iden, it is said, was the only wife of Oba Ewuakpe who stayed with him when all the other wives, the chiefs, and his people had fled and abandoned him in the Palace. The king had ordered excessive human sacrifices and decreed prolonged sexual abstention throughout the land, in mourning his mother's death. Queen Iden offered herself as a sacrifice to bring the people back to serve the Oba. After her death, Oba Ewuakpe is said to have ruled the kingdom peacefully until about 1712. Her act shamed the others and restored order to the kingdom. For this, Queen Iden, who was childless, has her grave forever respected and remembered in Benin.

Western contact and the Second Dynasty

Long before the coming of the Europeans in the late fifteenth century, Benin was a centralized state and forest empire, with political and spiritual power vested in the Oba, a sacred king. While some trade and contact across the Sahara may have reached Benin earlier, and visitors are reputed to have come in the thirteenth and fourteenth centuries, these early contacts are not well documented in Western literature. The first recorded Western contacts were with Portuguese explorers and traders, followed by English seamen and Dutch, French, English, and other commercial interests. The Benin kingdom maintained its economic, social, religious, and political independence over the ensuing five centuries by restricting direct inland access to foreigners, and by regulating trade.

Early Portuguese visitors had contacts with remembered "warrior obas," beginning with Oba Ewuare, "the Great" (circa 1440–73). This Oba is reputed to have been a "mystic, physician, traveler, and warrior to many parts of present-day Nigeria, Dahomey (the modern Republic of Benin), Ghana, Guinea, and the Congo" (Egharevba 1968: 13). He is said to have conquered "201" towns and villages (meaning many or countless places), some as far away as Igboland to the west of the Niger River. Ewuare is credited with having built many roads in Benin City, including Akpakpava and Utantan, main roads still known and in use today. He is said to have extended the Benin city walls and earthworks, and to have put down rebellions at Owo and Akure. Ewuare brought out many leaders, warriors, and heroes, some of whom were later deified as spirits in the towns and villages where they performed their deeds. They include the Okhuahe of Ikhuen, Ovato N'Igieduma, Emuen of Uhi, N'Ekodin, Ezuku N'Ogan, Ogan N'Ekhua, Ake and Ezalugha N'Ilobi in Isi, Oza of Benin City, Ebomisi N'Ugo, Oravan N' Irhirhi, Ireghezi N'Ekae, and many others (*ibid.*: 13–15; Eweka 1989b: 20). All these personages, remembered events, and accomplishments are attributed to Oba Ewuare's reign, and are part of Benin's rich oral tradition about famous kings.

In 1486, the Portuguese explorer Jão Affonso d'Aveiro negotiated a formal trade agreement with Oba Ozolua, "the Conqueror" (circa 1481–1504). Ozolua also expanded the Benin kingdom by winning many battles. He conquered the Yoruba towns of Owo and Ijebu-Ode and their environs, and fathered many local rulers (for example, the Alani of Idoani, the Olokpe of Okpe in the Akoko-Edo area, the Owa of Owo, the Oguan of Ora, the Awujale of Ijebu-Ode, and others) (Egharevba 1968: 22–3; Eweka 1989b: 22). Oba Ozolua, who was a forward-looking ruler, sent his first son when he was Edaiken, the Crown Prince, to live in Portugal for a time. There, Oba Esigie, as he was known later, learned to read and write the Portuguese language; and he is said to have brought a Portuguese wife with him when he returned to Benin. Later, as Oba, Esigie exchanged ambassadors with the King of Portugal. He is also counted among Benin's great warrior Obas.

Esigie's reign was another period of expansion of the Benin kingdom. The Portuguese aided him in warfare, and their presence is well represented in Benin court art associated with Esigie and his mother, Queen Mother Idia. While some scholars question the value of their military aid beyond lending prestige and intimidating the Oba's adversaries, others point out that guns were effective against northern cavalry. Certainly, Benin bronze plaques record victories against foreign warriors mounted on horses (Law 1976: 126; Gemery and Hogedoren 1978: 247–49, 250; and see Read and Dalton 1899: Plate XIX). Benin castings of equestrian figures celebrate their defeat of northerners, among them the powerful Atah of Idah.

Christianity was first introduced in Esigie's reign (circa 1504–50). He permitted Portuguese Fathers to preach Roman Catholicism, and to establish the churches known today as Aruosa, "the Oba's church." There are three such churches in Benin City: Aruosa

N'Idumwuerie, Aruosa N'Akpakpava, and Aruosa N'Ogbelaka. Nearly two centuries after their establishment, however, near the end of the seventeenth century, the Portuguese Fathers returned to Europe, leaving native priests in their place. It was a period of much political instability and many lapses of faith. From 1661 to 1700, a series of rival brother princes vied with each other, and ruled in brief succession.

Afterwards, in the reign of Oba Akengbuda (circa 1750–1804), a Frenchman, Captain J.F. Landolphe, visited Benin in 1778, and again in 1787. His friend, the botanist Palisot de Beauvais, also visited Benin, in 1801. Several Englishmen came after them in the reign of Oba Osemwede (circa 1816–48): Lieutenant John King, R.N., who came between 1815 and 1821; James Fawckner, in 1825; and Moffat and Smith, in 1838. Captain Richard Burton came to Benin in the time of Oba Adolo (circa 1848–88), as did a number of other visitors, traders, and missionaries. Cyril Punch made several trips to Benin City early in Oba Ovonramwen's reign (1888–1914).

Captain Gallwey was the last British visitor to Benin City before the ill-fated visit of Acting Consul General Captain James R. Phillips, and the "Punitive Expedition" that followed in 1897 (H.L. Roth 1968: 2–3). British superior firepower, artillery, and guns eventually prevailed after the expedition reached Benin City. The Benin warriors fought fiercely for several days, inflicting severe casualties with native weapons and antiquated guns. In his diary, Dr. Roth recorded the aftermath of Acting Consul General Captain Phillips' ill-advised march:

> One of the saddest sights, as we entered the big palaver house, was to notice the effects of the massacred white men. Amongst them we noticed Phillip's helmet in its case, a doctor's bag complete (which belonged to poor Elliot) while, scattered here and there, were the clothes, hats, boots, cameras, and other things so useful to men on the march. Of course we found no arms or ammunition, the natives having most probably used them against us.
>
> (*ibid*.: xii)

Oba Ovonramwen's hereditary governance was soon replaced by a group of Benin chiefs chosen by the British. One of them, Chief Obaseki, became prominent. He was a very able, ambitious, and clever man, who maintained his power for twenty years. In serving the British, Obaseki served himself well, acquiring great wealth. But he was never accepted as a legitimate ruler in place of the Oba. Then, in 1920, he died suddenly, and the British found it expedient to bring back to the throne the Oba's rightful heir, the Edaiken, the Crown Prince, who was crowned Oba Eweka II.

It was left to Oba Eweka II (1914–33) to slowly rebuild the Palace that had been burned and sacked in 1897. The period of Oba Ovonramwen's exile (1897–1914) is known in Western histories as "the interregnum." From the Benin point of view, however, there was no "interregnum." There was always an Oba, albeit one who resided in the east temporarily.[3] The succession in the Second Dynasty was unbroken.

Of course, up to 1914 there was no resident Oba to publicly perform the indigenous festivals of Benin religion. In his absence, the royal guilds that had served the Oba and the ancestors were without their patron. Later, Oba Eweka II established craft schools in the Palace grounds to restore knowledge and practice of Benin arts forcibly abandoned under early colonial rule. "Art" in Benin was both religious and historical. It was certainly not "art for art's sake," but art for life's sake, and quite literally so. The objects that formerly adorned the many ancestral altars inside the Palace included numerous carved ivory tusks, wood rattle staffs, bells, altarpieces, sculptures, etc. They memorialized the royal succession, the events and victories associated with the reigns of past Obas, represented by cast bronze heads of Benin's sacred kings (see Figure 13.3). A few of the Obas are represented publicly today, in a series of contemporary cast composite clay plaques set into the Palace walls (see Figure 13.4). It is the work of a well-known Benin sculptor and artist, Igbinovia Idah, assisted by Peter Osasebor Omodamwen, from the 1950s. Only some of the famous past kings and queens of Benin are shown, together with those of the post-conquest succession: Oba Ovonramwen, Oba Eweka II, and Oba Akenzua II (1933–78).

Figure 13.3 Royal Ancestral Altar, with remains of animal blood sacrifice, "House of the Fathers," *Ugha Erha Oba*, Oba's Palace, Benin City

Source: Photograph by Flora E.S. Kaplan, 1989.

It is notable that the Benin Obas generally enjoyed long reigns, excluding a few scattered exceptions in periods of turmoil. The shortest remembered reigns are connected to specific and unusual events: Oba Ezoti died in 1473 as the result of an accident and after a brief reign lasting only fourteen days. Ogbebo, a usurper, ruled for eight months in 1816 before setting fire to the Palace and killing himself. Other brief reigns noted by Egharevba occurred in the late seventeenth and early nineteenth centuries. Egharevba's king lists record thirty-seven remembered Obas before the thirty-eighth, and present, reigning Oba Erediauwa (1979–).[4] Many famous Obas are also remembered for their cultural and

Figure 13.4 Cast composite clay plaque on Palace wall, Benin City, showing Oba Ozolua (circa 1481–1504). A famous warrior, Oba Ozolua is typically shown triumphant in battle with his cutlass raised and holding a slain enemy. The severed heads signify his great success in battle. Plaque by Igbinovia Idah, assisted by Peter Osasebor Omodamwen, 1950s

Source: Photograph by Flora E.S. Kaplan, 2001.

artistic innovations, their military prowess nothwithstanding. For example, Oba Ewuare (circa 1440–73), a famous warrior Oba, reigned for thirty-three years. He was Prince (*Okhoro*) Ogun before he came to the throne, and is credited with introducing the royal coral beads and the ceremonial red flannel cloth, or *ododo* (Eweka 1989b: 21). Thirty-four Obas of the Second Dynasty, from the thirteenth to the end of the twentieth century, collectively reigned for a total of 645 years, yielding an average of some nineteen years each. If the three twentieth-century Obas are added, making a total of 37 kings having reigned for 735 years, the average is nearer twenty years each. Surely this is an enviable track record compared with that of the kings of Europe and England.

Lest the long reigns seem overstated, the average of the last four Obas of Benin of the late nineteenth century is thirty-two and a half years. Oba Adolo is known to have ruled for forty years (circa 1848–88), and the shorter reign of the exiled Oba Ovonramwen (1888–1914) lasted twenty-six years. Eweka II (1914–33) was on the throne for nineteen years, and Oba Akenzua II reigned for forty-five years (1933–78). The two shorter reigns of the last four Obas (nineteen and twenty-six years respectively) are well within the spans of some earlier Obas (Egharevba 1968; Eweka 1989b; Chief Edogen of Use, personal communication, 1984). Egharevba's dates, in some instances, are supported by informa-tion contained in the reports of European visitors. Archaeological surveys and test pits dug in the 1950s and 1960s in and around Benin City also lend support to Egharevba's early dates (Connah 1975; Darling 1984a, 1984b). Belatedly, historiographies of Egharevba's publications have begun in the past decade (Eisenhofer 1995; Usuanlele and Falola 1994; Ogbomo, forthcoming). When much needed archaeology is again begun in and around Benin and the region, existing chronologies will be refined, and a more complex picture will emerge of Benin and its neighbors.[5]

Pre-dynastic beginnings, sacred kings, and myth

The old people Egharevba interviewed in the late 1920s and 1930s were adults at the time of the British conquest in 1897. They spoke of the *Ogisos*, or "sky kings," who ruled Benin before the present Second Dynasty. The first *Ogiso*, Igodo, became a "king" by virtue of his wisdom and was described as being from heaven, "*Oyevbegie No Riso*" (Oba Erediauwa 1984). Thirty-one *Ogisos* are named, of whom a few were women. According to oral tradition, it took several centuries to centralize the power of the *Ogiso* and to estab-lish succession by primogeniture. It is unclear just how long that took, but in that time Benin expanded its territory by trade and war (Eweka 1989b: 12–15).

When the last *Ogiso*, Owodo, died without an heir, a delegation was sent from Benin to look for his banished son, long thought to have been killed. The Yorubas now say that they were asked to send a Yoruba prince to Benin; the Benin say that the banished son of Owodo was a Benin, Prince Ekaladerhan. He had wandered in the forest until reaching Uhe, where he became its ruler and the first Oduduwa. (Uhe is now identified as the modern Yoruba city of Ile-Ife.) The Benin claim that Oduduwa is a corruption of their words "*Imaghido duwa*," or "*Imado duwa*," which mean, "I have not missed the path to prosperity." They say that the name reflects Prince Ekaladerhan's change in status from an exile to a king at Ife. Oduduwa's son, Oranmiyan, sent to Benin, fathered the boy who became Oba Eweka I, founder of the Second Dynasty. At this time, the title of *Oba* (king) came into use in Benin. The Yoruba claim that "Oba" is their word for a sacred king. The Benin deny the claim, saying that the title derives from the Edo word "oba," meaning "it is hard or difficult." "Oba" is said also to be a shortened form of the name *Obagodo* (*oba* – king – and *godo* – high) (*ibid.*: 18).

Before the *Ogisos* and before the Second Dynasty, there was creation, when sacred kingship and sanctity originated. The Benin believe that Osanobua, the High God, created the world. They have no migration myth of coming from somewhere else. For them, Benin City is the cradle of the world, "*Edo Ore Isi Agbon.*" It is the place they came to from the spirit world, and where they have ever been. According to Benin's creation myth, Osanobua offered his four sons, who would be kings on earth, their choice of gifts to take with them. One chose wealth, one wisdom, and one magical powers, but the youngest son, who became the king of the Benin, chose a snail shell, which was the only thing left and contained only sand. When the four kings arrived on earth, they found it covered with water. The Benin king then turned his snail shell upside down, and out poured sand that became dry land, the only land on earth. The other kings had to ask him for land to settle on. And that is why the Oba of Benin is the owner of all the land (up to the European country, "*Oba Yan Oto Se Evbo Ebo*"), and why the snail shell still figures prominently in Benin coronation rituals (Oba Erediauwa, personal communication, 1984). This myth establishes the Oba as the owner of all the land at the beginning of the world, and as the favored son of the High God, a sacred king, who takes precedence over his brothers.

Tradition, change, and modernity

The Benin are known to other ethnic groups in Nigeria for holding their traditions very close, including their feared use of "medicines" and oaths. Unlike in some ethnic groups where chiefs can invent and award titles, only the Oba has that power. The proliferation of titles common among the newly rich seeking instant recognition and status in Nigeria is absent in Benin, where such recognition must be earned over time. The Oba rewards humble as well as wealthy men with titles based on performance and merit.

As a sacred king, the Oba of Benin is a full-time traditional ruler. Some contemporary traditional rulers are free to don Nigerian national dress or Western-style suits when attending to their business interests, and to travel abroad to London or Houston, Texas, or wherever they like. The Oba remains in Benin to perform many unseen rituals inside the Palace, and others in public, in a continuous cycle throughout the year. His presence and actions are crucial for the continuity and well-being of his people. The clothing the Oba chooses to wear each day is traditional (with some innovations); it is a statement of occasion, intent, mood, and power. The crowns, the beads, the ornaments, and the symbols of power held in the hand are chosen with care according to occasion and ritual need. All have meaning and evoke memory. Privileges of dress accorded to the chiefs are also statements of more than rank; they are statements of the Oba's level of confidence in them, and signals the regard in which the wearer is held. No privilege in Benin is without its history, and each carries responsibility for proper behavior and demeanor.

"You cannot buy a title in Benin" is an oft-repeated statement among other ethnic groups in Nigeria. A title, like all else in Benin, must be earned. Titles conferred by the Oba are for the lifetime of an individual and cannot be taken away, even by the king himself. Should someone later prove disloyal or disgrace himself, he may be declared "an enemy of the Oba," and banished from court. But the title he was given is his unto death.

Change and modernity

The re-introduction of Christianity accompanied British colonial rule. Promising young Benin boys attended missionary schools and became literate in English. They eventually became the teachers, clerks, and clerics prepared to fill the many new and powerful positions in colonial Benin. Many who became part of Nigeria's educated elite were able to move the country forward before and after independence in 1960. Under colonial administration, a new national educational system was created and a colonial court system based on English common law was instituted. Customary courts to deal with local issues of native law and custom were also established in Benin by the British. Their impact was felt especially in matters of custom involving marriage disputes and inheritance. In turn, British common law was itself modified by existing "native law and custom" and underwent considerable changes (Kaplan 1997: 255–6, 288–9, 291, 293). When Oba Eweka II was restored to the throne in 1914, people again started coming to the Palace to plead their cases. They customarily consulted first with family elders at meetings, and then with local traditional chiefs and important people on matters of family and land disputes as they had before. While the means of conflict resolution and governance abruptly changed in the colonial period, the Oba was seen as the court of last resort when agreement could not be reached between contending parties.

In modern, early twenty-first-century Nigeria, marred by rampant corruption at all levels, it is notable that in a period from before his coronation up to the present, no scandal or taint of corruption has been attached to the current Oba of Benin. A major

Figure 13.5 Group of senior town chiefs, *Eghaevbo n'ore*, at "*Igue*." They advance together to "salute" Oba Erediauwa in the compound of the "House of the Fathers," *Ugha Erha Oba*

Source: Photograph by Flora E.S. Kaplan, 1984.

change has been the transformation of land into a commodity that can now be bought and sold. But the Oba's opinions are still valued for their knowledge of tradition, fairness, and impartiality. The present king, Oba Erediauwa, is especially well versed in these matters, having been carefully trained by senior chiefs, and having read law at King's College, Cambridge, in England. His decisions have yet to be overruled by the courts. On occasion, even the state and federal governments have found it useful to seek the Oba's assistance to acquire land they needed in Edo State.

World religions and change

Contemporary Benin was and is besieged by a wide array of proselytizing world religions (virtually all Christian denominations and many Evangelical groups, Muslims, and others). They impart, along with their religious beliefs, overt and covert economic, political, and social ideas and agendas. Church attendance is popular in Benin, especially among women, as is participation in various Christian Pentecostal and Evangelical churches. The women (and men), especially in Protestant denominations, frequently dress in white or will wear the same cloth on Sundays and special occasions. They lend each other support emotionally and financially. Among the major Christian denominations in Benin City are Roman Catholicism, first introduced by the Portuguese in the early sixteenth century; the Anglican faith, brought by the English in the nineteenth and early twentieth centuries; and the popular Baptist churches from the United States of America. Nowadays, there are many other American groups; for example, Jehovah's Witnesses, the Mormons, Oral Roberts, as well as many more small and not-so-small foreign and local groups, such as the late televangelist, Idahosa, who had many followers. Muslims constitute an increasing number of religionists, but not so much among the Benin as among the increasingly multi-ethnic mix in Benin City. Other locally minted and individually inspired Christian groups have dramatically increased in number over the last decade.

What makes the Benin interesting for this study is their evident cultural conservatism in contrast to their acceptance of outside religious forms, and of imposed as well as adopted social, economic, and political change. For nearly five hundred years, a succession of Obas allowed the practice of Roman Catholicism. Since the end of the seventeenth century, the Aruosa churches have been maintained by indigenous priests, led by the *Ohen-Osa*. Oba Erediauwa attends an Arousa church on special occasions and during the celebration of the New Year (see Figures 13.6 and 13.7). He has also gone to the Mosque in Benin City on occasion, and the Mullah maintains active and cordial relations with His Highness.

While many Benin people in the capital city today attend one or another church, most also maintain some form of ancestor worship in their homes. They also attend and/or take part in the ritual life of the Palace. Men of importance in their communities seek to enter one or the other chiefly orders of Palace or town chiefs, accept titles, and move up the chiefly hierarchy. Their wives, extended family, and followers accompany them to the Palace in celebration and provide them with all necessary support. Thus, the Benin neither eschew modernity nor abandon tradition. Both are inextricably bound to the Palace today and are embodied in the sacred person of the Oba, who constitutes a living symbol of Benin ethnic identity. I note here that Islam, in forbidding participation in the indigenous religious system as represented by the Oba and the Palace, has not made significant inroads among the Benin.

The Oba is still viewed with awe, fear, respect, and love. It is widely believed that his pronouncements have the power of prophecy and that they will come to pass. His names, contained in his title, Omo N'Oba N'Edo Uku Akpolokpolo, reveal his centrality to indigenous religion and his oneness with the world: he is "the child" (meaning the beginning of all life), "the father" of all his people (the giver and taker of life), and the "old man" (the most senior and venerated among them). In Benin religious belief, the Oba is the counterpart of the deities in the spirit world. On land, he is the "Lord of the Dry Land"; his counterpart, Olokun, the "Lord of the Waters," is a son of the Benin High God, Osanobua. The Oba is also referred to as the "Leopard of the Home" (the supreme

Figure 13.6 Female chorus singing and playing women's traditional calabashes, *ukuse*, for New Year's Sunday service at the Roman Catholic Aruosa church ("the Oba's church"), Akpakpava Road, Benin City

Source: Photograph by Flora E.S. Kaplan, 1995.

creature of the civilized world), in contrast to the "Leopard of the Bush" (king of the untamed or natural world). His sanctity and centrality to Benin religion set him apart in this world and are his destiny by birth.

Conclusions

Indigenous religious concepts such as sanctity, sacrifice, and community have endured over time and are inseparable from the person of the Oba. One of the questions considered here was: why do some groups continue to have a strong sense of their ethnic identity and indigenous religion? The Benin case suggests an answer lies in the extent to which the Benin social and "political" life is connected to the Palace and replicated at all

Figure 13.7 Oba Erediauwa attending the Aruosa church at New Year, with attendants and some of his chiefs. His senior *Omuada* (right) carries the *Ada*, his ceremonial sword of state

Source: Photograph by Flora E.S. Kaplan, 1991.

levels of society. "Political" is defined here to mean not solely a system of offices and office holders, but more broadly to include those who make decisions affecting others in the use and distribution of resources perceived as scarce. From the Oba's family writ large to the house of the Oba's ancestors, *Ugha Erha Oba*, to the family house of every patrilineal extended family in Benin, and from the humblest homes to the most exalted – commonly held ideas and values that govern everyday life and ritual behavior are shared and deeply felt, forging strong emotional links binding Benin people to the Oba and the Palace.

As a living symbol of Benin ethnicity and its greatness, the Oba is the pivotal figure among Edo-speaking people everywhere in Nigeria and abroad. Benin Palace and town chiefs are drawn from many walks of life, from traditional to modern occupations, positions, professions, corporations, and institutions. Collectively there are among them teachers, businessmen/women, lawyers, doctors, administrators, farmers, loggers, craftsmen, traders, etc. They live in cities, small and large towns, and in villages. Some are highly educated and some are illiterate. They hold their positions, whether as town chiefs outside the Palace or as chiefs inside the Palace, by virtue of the respect and "popularity" (recognition) that they engender in their respective communities. Their achievements are not measured simply in money and wealth, but in their ability to serve both the Oba and the people. The dictum, "You cannot buy a title in Benin," is well known and admired among other ethnic groups in Nigeria. Few titles are hereditary, and those given are only awarded to others after the owner has passed. The finite granting of titles keeps Benin society open and flexible. It allows new ties to be created while preserving old ones. In theory and in practice, then, every man has the chance to be connected to the Palace, to be recognized, and to make his "name." If he performs well and gains popularity, he also has a chance of achieving lasting fame – the most desired social goal. The traditional value of personal achievement is accessible *and* integral to, as well as characteristic of, Benin culture and personality.

Other factors that contribute to a deep sense of ethnic identity in modern Benin include the embedding of cultural history in oral tradition and in the physical features of the landscape. Trees are planted to mark boundaries, events, and to serve as mnemonic devices. For example, a tree planted near the Oba's Palace marked the place where a famed heroine in history, Emotan, had her market stall in the fifteenth century. It was there for centuries. In the colonial period, the Benin say, a Lebanese trader cut it down for obstructing the view from the second storey of his house. A near riot ensued. Oba Akenzua II then commissioned a statue of Emotan to replace the tree – a modern innovation that marks the spot to this day. There are many such local and collective ethnic memories present in Benin oral tradition and in nature, especially in certain trees, rocks, and rivers in Benin. Some are made visible and tangible in modern representations, such as the statue at the Emotan shrine, and the one of Aruanran at Udo; the oral traditions carved on wooden doors; and others now represented by popular commercial carvings, such as "Adesuwa," "The Greedy Hunter," etc.

Other questions addressed in this case study of Benin indigenous religion and modernity asked: why do some religions survive abrupt and violent change, and how do people react to the introduction of new world religions? Secrecy has been an important factor in the survival of Benin religion. Those with knowledge of Benin religious ritual and tradition at the Palace swore oaths of secrecy on pain of death. Colonial authorities were unable to forbid what they themselves were ignorant of – what the Benin knew, believed, and carried in their heads.

While human sacrifices were forbidden with the advent of colonialism, large animals replaced them. Lesser traditional offerings such as cockerels, crocodiles, snails, fish, and chalks continued to be made. Blood remained essential and was used to purify, propitiate, and renew the power and godliness of the Oba. Christian notions of sacrifice and sanctity were associated with Christ, the Son of God, who came to earth and would come again some day. Similar ideas of rebirth and reincarnation, sacrifice, and sanctity were traditionally associated with the Oba, a son of Osanobua, the High God and a sacred king. It did not require a great leap of the imagination for the Benin to then extend their worship to Christ, the king. Now, as in the past, most Benin people accommodate both religious spheres. They equate Christianity with modernity, and indigenous religion with their cultural identity, tradition, and the Oba. The last of these equates with "themselves" as a people and an ethnic group in a pluralist nation-state. The two exist side by side, with the individual determining the degree of identification. Each religion is regarded as a separate arena of action. Conflict arises when representatives of a world religion insist Benin followers reject dual loyalties.

Figure 13.8   Visit of Lord Plymouth, Earl of Plymouth (center), to the Oba of Benin (right) at the Oba's Palace, February 1936. With Lord Plymouth (left) are Governor Hunt, the Resident A.S. Hughes of Benin Province, and several district officers of the Western Province. Also shown are distinguished chiefs and Benin persons, including Reverend Ohuoba, Chief Legemah, and Chief Obahiagbon, as well as (left) the first Benin reverend of the Anglican Church and the postmaster (in English suit), among the first educated people in Benin. Some of the traditional chiefs (right) include Chief Okoro-Otun, the *Iyase* of Benin, Chief Osagie, and Chief Edo (Esamo), among many others.

Source: Photograph by S.O. Alonge, from the collection of Flora E.S. Kaplan.

Foreign world religions, especially proselytizing ones, are powerful outside forces for change in Benin indigenous religion and culture. A senior Benin chief I knew was a late convert to Roman Catholicism. On his deathbed he was faced with the choice of renouncing all but one of his four wives in order to receive the last rites of the Church. On another occasion, an invited Muslim government official refused to enter the compound of a well-known Ogun priest to observe (not participate in) the annual festival being celebrated. Nonetheless, some nationally elected and appointed officials (vice-presidents and ministers) of the Federal Republic of Nigeria (some of whom are Muslims, others Christians) do attend annual public festivals and ceremonies at the Palace as honored guests of the Oba of Benin.

Oba Erediauwa (1979–) actively continues to revive public ceremonies that were either rarely performed or abandoned entirely in the colonial era and period of early independence. Still, for many Benin who accept Christianity, and, to a lesser extent, for those among a smaller group who converted to Islam, the Oba himself, his attendance at important public functions, and the public performance of traditional rituals and masquerades at the Palace are visible manifestations of modern Benin ethnic identity. The cloak of secrecy that still surrounds the Palace and native religion both declares and protects their cultural identity. But it makes the indigenous religion an unlikely candidate for adoption beyond Benin in a modern nation-state.

A final question raised in this case study asked: how do some structures of indigenous traditions such as myths, symbols, and institutions respond to contact with foreign traditions and to world religions? Considering modernity, change, and continuity, it appears, paradoxically, that indigenous religion enabled the Benin to both resist *and* change because it was flexible; at the same time, it was a centralized and highly ranked society. Flexibility was rooted in widespread access to status, achievement, and rewards through the Palace. Men of proven character and ability throughout the kingdom were made chiefs. Young boys who were sent from villages and towns to the city to serve the Oba later returned to their villages with knowledge and ties to the Palace. They also returned with links to others like themselves in Benin City and elsewhere in the region. Some of these young men later became chiefs, as their fathers before them often had been.

So, too, might a young woman "noticed" by a chief or by the Oba himself be taken to the Palace or "given" to the Oba by her parents. She may become an Oba's wife, a queen, able to bring good fortune to her family and community. All who served the Oba also learned to keep secrets. They acquired knowledge to be kept from others, a practice that served the Benin well in the colonial era. The ties and memory of service to the Oba created by contact and marriage are maintained and remembered for generations in the villages and towns, *and* at the Palace. These memories became a part of local oral tradition, creating a sense of cultural continuity and cohesion among the Benin in Nigeria, and wherever they reside today.

It has been suggested here why some structures of indigenous tradition such as myths, symbols, and institutions continue to survive while others do not; and how they reacted to foreign world religions. From the first contacts with the West at the end of the fifteenth century, the Benin readily accepted new technology and change that benefited them. They changed in order not to change beyond what they valued and wanted to achieve, and they kept their sense of who they were as a people. Much later, after 1897, during the early British colonial period, the Benin resisted and dissembled, outwitting, tricking, and serving the new functionaries as their old value system had taught them to do. They used their heads and hands to survive and prosper, in new as well as old ways. They kept their counsel, they were patient, and they guarded their secrets. The Benin also accepted many forms of Christianity, and some accepted Islam. However, to this day, most have not abandoned their ancestors, the Oba, or the Palace. They have, thus far, managed to straddle the divide between world religions and indigenous religious tradition.

Notes

1 An earlier version of this chapter was presented as a paper at the international conference "Beyond 'Primitivism': Indigenous Religious Traditions and Modernity," 28–31 March 1996, University of California, Davis, organized by Jacob K. Olupona. It was part of the session entitled "Indigenous Religious Traditions and Modernity: Cross-Cultural Perspectives (Africa and North America)."

2 The results of the "trial" held by the British were predictable after the Oba had returned to Benin City from six months in the countryside escaping his pursuers. Following the trial, the Oba himself was spirited out of Benin City under cover of darkness and sent into exile in the east. Chief Ologboshere was found to be the instigator of the Benin "massacre" of the Phillips party, not Oba Ovonramwen, and he was later captured and executed on 28 June 1899. The British had taken possession of Benin City on 17 February 1897, ushering in a period of colonial rule that ended when Nigeria declared independence in 1960. Old photographs taken in 1897 show members of the British expedition sitting jauntily amid the ruins of the burned-out Oba's Palace. They are surrounded by thousands of art works in ivory, bronze, and wood taken from the Palace's ancestral altars, storerooms, and private quarters. These art works constituted Benin's historic documents, sacred objects, Palace furnishings, and items of the Oba's regalia. They were later sold in England to museums and collectors in Europe and elsewhere. The funds were then used to offset the military expenses incurred.

3 The Oba passed away in his house at Old Calabar. His body was not immediately brought back to Benin, but, at some time unknown, it was later buried where it belonged, at the Palace in Benin City.

4 Egharevba is the first Western-styled, indigenous, and self-taught historian of Benin. His best-known published work in several English editions is the classic *A Short History of Benin* (1968 [1934]).

5 The tropical forest kingdom of Benin, founded in medieval times and centered in south-western Nigeria, was once a great empire. At times it stretched westward beyond Lagos and eastward beyond the Niger River. Lagos is known to the Benin as "Eko," the site of their ancient war camp. Increasing British colonial control in southern Nigeria from the mid-nineteenth century onwards reduced the size of the territory and the number of other ethnic groups paying tribute to the Benin. The kingdom's independence ended at the close of the nineteenth century with the British conquest. Benin City remains the spiritual and cultural center of the Edo-speaking peoples. Traditionally these peoples include the Ishan, Itsekiri, Urhobo, Etsako, and Isoko, as well as the Edos proper (Bradbury 1957). The Oba's Palace, rebuilt in the 1920s by Oba Eweka II (1917–33), is now considerably smaller, although it still occupies several acres in the heart of the city. The Palace site presently dates to the thirteenth century, but may well date to the eleventh century, or possibly even earlier (Connah 1987: 248–9).

References

Adams, Capt. J., *Remarks on the Country Extending from Cape Palmas to the River Congo*, London, 1823.

Bacon, Reginald Hugh, *Benin, The City of Blood*, London: Edward Arnold, 1897.

Ben-Amos, Paula, *The Art of Benin*, rev. edn, London: British Museum Press, 1995.

Bradbury, R.E., *The Benin Kingdom and the Edo-speaking Peoples of South-Western Nigeria*, with a section on the Itsekiri by P.C. Lloyd, Ethnographic Survey of Africa, Western Africa, Part XIII, London: International African Institute, 1957.

——, *Benin Studies*, London: Oxford University Press, 1973.

Chief Edogen, personal interview, Use Palace, Nigeria, January 1984.

Connah, Graham, *The Archaeology of Benin: Excavations and Other Researches in and Around Benin City, Nigeria*, Oxford: Clarendon Press, 1975.

——, *African Civilizations: Precolonial Cities and States in Tropical Africa: An Archaeological Perspective*, Cambridge: Cambridge University Press, 1987.

Darling, P.J., *Archaeology and History in Southern Nigeria: The Ancient Linear Earthworks of Benin and Ishan. Part I: Fieldwork and Background Information*, Cambridge Monographs in African Archeology 11, Oxford: BAR International Series, 215(i), 1984a.

——, *Archaeology and History in Southern Nigeria: The Ancient Linear Earthworks of Benin and Ishan. Part II: Ceramics and Other Specialist Studies*, Cambridge Monographs in African Archeology 11, Oxford: BAR International Series, 215(ii), 1984b.

Egharevba, Jacob U., *A Short History of Benin*, 4th edn, Ibadan: Ibadan University Press, 1968 (first published 1934).

Eisenhofer, Stefan, "The origins of Benin kingship in the works of Jacob Egharevba," *History in Africa* 22, 1995, 141–63.

Eweka, Prince Ena Basimi, "The Benin monarchy," Archives, Benin Traditional Council, Eweka Court, Oba's Palace, Benin City, 1989a.

—— *A History of Benin*, Ibadan: Ethiope Publishers Ltd., 1989b.

——, "Some aspects of Benin history," Archives, Benin Traditional Council, Eweka Court, Oba's Palace, Benin City, 1990.

——, "The Benin culture," lecture given to the University of Toronto, part of the Celebration of African Heritage by African/Canadian[s], 6 November, 1991.

——, *Evolution of Benin Chieftaincy Titles*, Benin City: University of Benin Press, 1992.

Gemery, H.A. and J.S. Hogedoren, "Technological change, slavery, and the slave trade," in Clive Dewey and A.G. Hopkins (eds) *The Imperial Impact: Studies in the Economic History of Africa and India*, London: Athlone Press, for the Institute of Commonwealth Studies, 1978, 243–58.

Kaplan, Flora E.S., "Runaway wives, native law and custom in Benin, and early colonial courts, Nigeria," in Flora E.S. Kaplan (ed.) *Queens, Queen Mothers, Priestesses, and Power: Case Studies in African Gender, Annals of The New York Academy of Sciences*, vol. 810, 1997, 245–313.

Law, Robin, "Horses, firearms, and political power in pre-colonial West Africa," *Past and Present* 72, 1976, 112–32.

Oba Erediauwa, Oba of Benin, "The evolution of traditional rulership in Nigeria," paper presented at the University of Ibadan, Institute of African Studies, 11 September 1984.

Ogbomo, Onaiwu (ed.), *Jacob Egharevba: Historiographical Perspectives on the Benin/Edo Historian*, forthcoming.

Read, C.H. and O.M. Dalton, *Antiquities from the City of Benin and Other Parts of West Africa in the British Museum*, London: British Museum, 1899 (reprinted New York: Hacker Art Books, 1973).

Roth, H.L., *Great Benin: Its Custom, Art and Horrors*, Halifax, England: A. King and Sons, 1903 (reprinted New York: Barnes & Noble Inc., 1968).

Usuanlele, U. and Toyin Falola, "The scholarship of Jacob Egharevba of Benin," *History in Africa* 22, 1994, 301–18.

Chapter 14

The *Earth Mother Scripture*

Unmasking the neo-archaic

Whalen W. Lai

On the ninth day of the first lunar month in the ninth year of the reign of Ch'ing Emperor Kuang-hsu (1883) at the Earth Mother temple at Shensi, the *Authentic Scripture of the Earth Mother* was revealed during a "flying phoenix" (spirit writing) session. Some time later, the *Wondrous Scripture of the Earth Mother* was received.[1] Then, just this last year (1995), from the twentieth night of the eighth lunar moon (14 October) in Taichung in Central Taiwan, *The True Scripture of the Earth Mother Universally Delivering All* was revealed. As decreed by the Jade Emperor, the Vacuously Empty Earth Mother (and) Great Compassionate Worthy moved the brush that wrote it down. At the time of writing the present chapter, it was still being composed at the Wu-miao Ming-cheng Hall that Philip Clart has been studying since 1994.[2]

In *The Flying Phoenix: Aspects of Chinese Sectarianism in Taiwan*,[3] a study of these *pai-luan* or plantchette societies in present-day Taiwan, Overmyer classifies the *Earth Mother Scripture* under "Liturgical Texts: Sectarian" and as one of the "Spirit-Writing Books from Modern Taiwan." Though it originated in the mainland, it is now found all over Taiwan, due largely to the Compassion Society founded in 1950 that distributes this text free along with a primer on the basics of Buddhism. A long poem in seven-character lines, it does not always conform to the standard format of the spirit-written genre. Overmyer's summary assessment goes as follows:

> The book appears to be an expression of an earth mother cult; its chief concerns are to stress the creative power of the Earth Mother and her ability to bring blessings to those who appeal to her and recite her scripture.
>
> (*The Flying Phoenix*: 73)

The scripture may stand by itself or be paired to a number of other shorter works.[4] Though the Earth Mother goes back to the Great Mother of archaic times, she wears also the guise of the sixteenth-century sectarian cult figure known as the Eternal Mother.[5] The Eternal Mother inherited but also superseded the early Taoist cult of the Queen Mother of the West.[6] She continued but also overshadowed the Buddha Amitabha of the Western Pure Land. By Late T'ang, the paradises of the Queen Mother and of Amitabha had merged in popular perception. By the Sung, going to the "land of ultimate bliss" was synonymous with going to the "peach garden" or the "jasper pool." Under the Yuan (Mongol rule), Pure Land piety fused with the millenarian expectation of the coming of Maitreya. That precipitated the White Lotus rebellion that brought in the Ming dynasty. By Late Ming, the figure of the Eternal Mother appeared and called for a return of her children to her.[7] Because the White Lotus was proscribed by the state, one way to hide the identity of the Eternal Mother was to hide her behind other persona, such as the Earth Mother. Her sectarian movement was based on revealed texts called "precious scrolls." China's modern period – usually dated by the Taiping Rebellion (1853) – witnessed a vogue of spirit writing and a notable rise in "flying phoenix" revelations in the more prosperous coastal areas. If the earliest sectarian text of this type known to Overmyer is the *Yu-lu chin-p'an* (Golden Basin of the Jade Bow), dated to 1880,[8] then the *Earth Mother Scripture* dated its revelation to just three years later. Though both the time and the place of its composition are suspect,[9] the text assumes an imperial order that historically came to an end with the modern Republic of 1912.[10]

A genealogy of the Earth Mother

Although in China Heaven is proverbially father and earth proverbially mother, the generic Ti Mo (Earth Mother) is rarely employed as a name. The most recent (1991) catalogue of China's folk deities (*Chung-kuo min-chien chu-shen*, henceforth CS)[11] does not list it. But then the same applies to the Magna Mater. The Great Goddess was once typically localized. She was known through the form of the *genii locale*. Today, she is better known as T'u-ti Fu-jen, Po, or Liang-liang (lady, wire, matron, maiden). T'u-ti means simply "earth and ground." It is the overarching Heaven that tends to be all-embracing, rising as it did often with city states and their alliance to some sky god that transcended blood kin and local loyalties.

The classic earth deity in China was Hou T'u. Nowadays, this is usually read as Lord of the Earth, but it once could well have been Queen of the Earth, that is to say, a "she" before being recast into a "he." One early record, the *Tso-chuan*, recalls her genealogy as follows: "Kung Kung gave birth to the Horned Dragon who is Hou T'u." Demythologized, it means "From the primeval waters rose the first land."[12] The *Li Chi* placed Hou T'u in the center with or as an aid to the Yellow Emperor (*CS*: 218–19). From Hou T'u (earth) came the Five Cereals. For that gift of grain, Hou T'u's birthday was set on the eighteenth day of the third lunar month[13] (*CS*: 224–5). Earth being linked to the netherworld, Hou T'u also held the office of Lord to the "Dark City" (i.e. Hades).

Patriarchal bias favored seeing Hou T'u as male. A defender of that orthodoxy (cited in *CS*: 224) goes so far as to insist that when the *Book of History* speaks of Wang T'ien and Hou T'u, it does not mean "King Heaven and Queen Earth." Both are male and the two prefixes only paint Heaven as august and Earth as thick. The source also criticized a Yang-chou custom of enshrining a Hou T'u Fu-jen (mistress) image: "That is just ridiculous. If Hou T'u is female, then Hou Ku'ei and Hou Ch'i would also have to be female" (*CS*: 224). That could well have been the case originally.[14] But it appears that during the Han, Hou T'u was indeed worshipped as queen to Heaven as king. Only after the Sui might the Horned Dragon (deemed somehow male) replace her on the altar. But that male identity could well be an elite choice. The common people, then and after, often enshrined a Hou T'u Liang-liang (matron or maiden) instead. During the Sung, a shrine dedicated to this earth deity – it could simply be a marker and not a figure – was often set up next to the grave (*CS*: 225).

Economically, the Earth cult was tied to farming. Peasants honored this giver of grains at the *she* shrine, which at one time could just be a mound decked with greenery, in spring and fall. Each locality had its own *she*. And the typical offerings at harvest would be the first-fruits. The imperial sacrifice to Earth paired it with the sacrifice to Heaven. Ideally then, her share of a full, animal sacrifice was buried – while that for Heaven was burned and sent heavenward, and that to the River would be thrown into the water. Of course, only the Son of Heaven could worship Heaven (which was done at the temple of Heaven); others could not. Owning all domain, the emperor also sacrificed to Earth; this was done at a separate, Earth shrine. The feudal lords honored the *she* of their region and sacrificed to the mountains and rivers in their domains. This subdivision of duty went down the line of the ranks of the nobles. When aristocracy disappeared under the First Emperor, officials of the centralized bureaucracy assumed the duty to worship the *she* at their respective levels. This in effect divided the earth and made natural communities fit the design of that administrative system. Thus a commentary on the *Chou Li* (*CS*: 241) now defines *she* as the community made up of twenty-five households. The number is artificial. Later *she* households were numbered at ten or five. Neighbors grouped together to form a unit to help and to keep watch over one another. The Legalist intended that the unit be held responsible as an incorporated whole for the crime of any one single member. A commentary on the *Filial Classic* (*CS*: 241) remarks: "The *she* refers to the *lording* of the earth; the earth being extensive, it cannot be worshipped *all at once*. So it is customary to fief an area, set up a *she*, and then worship (the earth) in gratitude" (emphasis added). In one sense, the *Earth Mother Scripture* sought to reverse that imperial hierarchy. It would have all men worship her *all at once*.

The archaic Earth cult was affected by two other developments: the cult of the dead and the promise of universal salvation. Euhemerization saw to the deification of men.[15] This affected T'u-ti more. As a groundskeeper, he was not necessarily tied to agriculture. He ruled over non-farm land and he served anyone who happened to be in his area. The first recorded case of a displaced dead person becoming a T'u-ti god occurred in late Han. Chiang Tzu-wen, a man of ill repute, was waylaid by robbers and killed at the foot of Mount Chung. His unquiet soul appeared in early Wu (one of the Three Kingdoms) saying: "I will be the T'u-ti god of this area and grant boon to the people. Instruct them to build me a shrine. Otherwise there would be calamity" (*Shou-shen-chi*: *CS* 242). It is not uncommon for the unquiet dead called *li* to become gods in this way.[16] Their apotheoses result from a rite of pacification that transforms their discontent into benevolence, basically transforming a vengeful spirit into a grateful dead. Benefactors in this life, of course, could also be appointed benevolent T'u-ti at death. The early fifth-century poet Shen Yueh, at the Liang court in the Chinese-ruled South, regularly went home once a year to mourn his father at his grave. The emperor and the prince went out of the city (their seat of power) to welcome Shen Yueh's return. Not wanting to inconvenience his royal highnesses, Shen Yueh had his father's shrine moved to the capital. This, however, left the original chancery at the grave site unused and the monk cantors there unemployed. So Shen Yueh turned this private "merit cloister" over to the Sangha. The monks of the Pu-ch'ing temple thanked Shen Yueh and honored him as their T'u-ti god (*CS*: 246). Down the centuries, quite a number of notable benefactors also ended up becoming gods in this way. Officials on earth in this life, they continued being officials in the next.[17] Lowest of the official bureaucrats, T'u-ti usually came across as very human, an easily approachable home body. More adaptable than Hou T'u to answering all kinds of human prayers, T'u-ti images and shrines proliferated in the medieval period. By the Sung, he was protecting individual houses, courtyards, doorways, orchids, hills, forests, temples, crossroads, street corners, and, as noted already, grave sites – any space that required consecration and a groundskeeper. He too wore many hats, came in various costumes, had wives and kids, and, for doing his job well or badly, regularly got promoted or demoted. He could be reassigned to a different locale – as Hou T'u and the *she* god could not. Many colorful and even comical stories were told of him. Good publicity meant some T'u-ti gods ended up in well-endowed shrines, while others lacking that finesse languished in small, neglected ones. One such lesser figure posted this couplet at his gate: "Though this stone hut has no light, still the moon would be my lamp bright. All alone in this desolate field, still the wind may sweep my shrine clean" (*CS*: 250).

However, if T'u-ti outnumbered Hou T'u, the city god would in turn outrank him. A god of walls and moats in the classical period, he rose to defending the "walled cities" in the age of disunity following the barbaric invasion of 316 CE. With the rebirth of cities under the T'ang, he grew in prominence still. In the spiritual realm, he was the magistrate as T'u-ti was the runner. With urban commerce outpacing village farms, his temples became much better endowed. And unlike T'u-ti, who could multiply easily even in one ward, one city could have only one magistrate and one city god. With the cult of loyalty growing in the Five Dynasties, city gods were often recruited from the pool of loyal officials. So defenders of cities from bandits and enemies graduated into being city gods in greater numbers during the Sung. They also took on a new and necessary task: the care of the displaced and unclaimed dead. All the dead reported to him, a magistrate of the local hell, before any further assignments. The city god received official recognition under the founding emperor of the Ming. Ming T'ai-tsu recruited both the city god and T'u-ti into his administrative system, paring off the terrestrial, the celestial, and the subterranean bureaucracies for good. Officials taking up their posts had to report to their city gods first; it was their duty to sacrifice at the city temples. The responsibility cut both ways. City gods were to help uphold law and order. Failure to do so meant that they could face chastisement by the Son of Heaven, the human link to the celestial realm above. This system lasted through the Manchu dynasty until 1911.

Three millennia separate the prehistoric cult of Hou T'u and the *Earth Mother Scripture* of 1883. Hou T'u was restored to her original gender.[18] Earth, her domain, long cut up to fit some administrative rationality, was reunited in her one body. Her prime standing, long challenged by T'u-ti and the city god, was restored to her. As one guise of the sectarian Eternal Mother, all mankind were reclaimed as her children; they should serve her above all others. What was "indigenous" – localized and particularistic – was drawn upward and made celestial and universalistic.[19] And even as the Ming rule was well known for being despotic – absolute power was wielded unchecked by the monarch – this Eternal Mother was all-powerful but also all-forgiving. And in the modern period, what was primitive and archaic, this Earth Mother of old, remade herself into the Earth Mother of new.

Content analysis

The Earth Mother wrote the *Earth Mother Scripture*. Thus, the *Authentic Scripture* states: "Earth Mother waves her brush and the herb of immortality (the means of salvation) is made manifest."[20] But if she did, she wrote in a fairly elegant hand. The text recites old myths and has access to a knowledge of astrology; it is not the work of the unlettered. And even if its vernacular verses are not always well polished, it presumes a degree of mastery of form worthy of an educated literatus. The ideological pretext is the sectarian cult of the Eternal Mother. She lurks behind the persona of the Earth Mother. Sectarians would recognize such coded references to "mother and children" – that is to say, the goddess and her devotees – "meeting again some day." Hers is a good cover. The untrained eye and the unsuspecting authorities would find little cause to proscribe this worship of the earth that the Classics had well sanctioned.[21] The Compassion Society disseminates this text today probably because it is short, simple, and uncontroversial. A front for the Eternal Mother, the text could well be used by anyone for everyday devotion, with he or she not necessarily knowing the whole sectarian history.

Unlike other sectarian scriptures, the *Earth Mother Scripture* does not include in its preamble any notation on how and through which person of what lineage the revelation came. No heavenly drama precedes its disclosure; no sacred lineage is told at the end. The text contains a psalm, which is used in the ritual offering of incense, and an evocation of her presence, to be used when taking refuge or professing faith. Both of these are fairly short; the work does not include even a standard set of precepts. They are followed by the *Earth Mother Authentic Scripture* and the *Earth Mother Wondrous Scripture*. The latter is clearly a later addition, because at one point the former refers to itself as "this True Scripture has 182 lines, each and every one of which is true." The *Authentic Scripture*, exactly 182 lines long, at that point did not yet know of the existence of the *Wondrous Scripture*.

As with other texts of the Eternal Mother, the *Earth Mother Scripture* has a "Gnostic" agenda. That is to say, it reveals the magnificence of this unknown godhead who, until now, has been neglected, ignored, hidden, or misrepresented. Once the truth of her reality and the accident of her obscurity is explained, there is issued this call to her long-lost children to come home to her. The premise is that the children are adrift in the lower world, so seduced by the physical and material pleasures[22] as to have forgotten their truer and higher destiny. That prior world of light will be restored in the dark hours of the end time. At this point, eschatology rejoins cosmogony.

This Edenic tale of being lost and then found, this motif of alienation and return, is standard also to Western Gnostic literature.[23] Historically, Gnosticism was the prevalent tradition on the Silk Road. This wisdom tradition informed early Mahayana Buddhism. Parables of alienation and return are found in a number of its scriptures, starting with the *Lotus Sutra*. Medieval Taoism took over some of these motifs. And the birth of the White Lotus sectarianism in Yuan just happened to have a second Gnostic infusion of Manichean dualism. Tamer and less otherworldly by comparison, the *Earth Mother Scripture* nonetheless inherited the Gnostic dualism from the later Eternal Mother cult. That cult had an eight-character mantra: "Venerable Mother of the Unborn/Home Village of the Truly Empty." This wisdom couplet captures the secret of the faith: a recognition of a hitherto unknown high goddess, and a hope of being transported back to this original home of hers. The *Earth Mother Scripture* proclaims that same secret. The Earth Mother calls her children, who have been seduced by things of this world and by the lower gods, immortals, and Buddhas, to return to her. The text encourages the recipient to regularly chant the scripture – "seven times in the heart on the holy days," or "daily, always, the whole morning through." My copy has a woodblock print illustrating her youthful Holiness, but it is in no way iconographically distinct.[24] The line that might serve as her mantra is her full title: "The None-Higher, Vacuously Empty Earth Mother (in her) Mysterious Transformations (being able to) Nurture Life and Protect Destiny." This is repeated at the very end of the first text with the closing praise, "Compassionate Worthy, Great Compassionate Worthy" – the only time where it breaks away from the seven characters per line format. The *Wondrous Scripture* then adds the only sure sign of a liturgical instruction and a final poem in five-character lines:

Twenty-four prostrated bows
Intending the merits here acquire
Be generously spread to all
With sincerity revere the Earth Mother
May bountiful grace forever fall.

Such inducement to "chant and copy" as well as "teach and transmit" is standard to all such scriptures. The practice began in China with the early Mahayana sutras from India; it persisted into the native "good books" – popular moral tracts of the Ming period – calling people to "print and distribute this text free." The *Earth Mother Scripture* has that self-promotion built into the revelation. The *Wondrous Scripture* sums up the central teaching of the *Authentic Scripture*, and it mentions "print and disseminate" in the opening lines:

The vacuously empty Earth Mother rules the human lot
Being most honored since the day when chaos gave birth to form
To give birth to Heaven and Earth was my fundamental intent
One Buddhist monk, one Taoist adept, and one layman[25]
From the Earth Mother is transmitted this Earth Mother Scripture
Man and woman should print and distribute it free[26] to ensure peace and prosperity
If you want the world to be prosperous and peaceful
Then everybody everywhere must recite this Earth Mother Scripture
Before the Earth Mother left behind this Earth Mother Scripture
No single family has truly worshipped this goddess of the earth
The legend of the Earth Mother begins with this work
Those who chant this authentic scripture will surely be saved
Everyone that does not so honor the Earth Mother
Will languish after death forever in the halls of hell.

In presenting itself as a new revelation of something old and primeval, the *Earth Mother Scripture* runs into the following paradox, common to many Gnostic gospels: how is it that what was so foundational and obvious became lost and forgotten?

For the welfare of her children, the Earth Mother labored to no end
Yet the sons and daughters never give her thought
Every need the world has she has anticipated
Everything required she has duly supplied
But whereas the seventy-two gods all have their followings
Only I, the Earth Mother, has no congregation to call my own
In every corner of the universe are found the many shrines
Wherein those congregated could hustle and bustle
Only I, this Old Maid,[27] has no building in my name to claim
Somehow as luck goes, mine have fallen through the cracks.

This is probably the weakest of reasons given for the fall into ignorance: simple bad luck. Since then, however, the Earth Mother had worked hard for mankind's welfare, but the *Authentic Scripture* laments:

Ultimately (everything there is or happens) is my doing
But does the world know how much sacrifice I made?

Toil and hardship the Earth Mother bears
Good food and good meals the sons and daughters enjoy.

But are her children grateful? No. Earlier in the same text, it is said:

This Old Maid labors for the sons and *even more so*[28] for the daughters
But sons and daughters forget their debts owed her
What you eat and you wear I have caused to come into being
All things that change and flourish I have nursed and given growth
The money you use for buying and selling – all that I have provided for
Yet who ever remembers me enough to give me thanks?

The blame for her neglect is ultimately placed on mankind.[29] In a more somber mood, the text prophesies that this alienation of mother and child would not be reversed until the end of time:

Since my birth I have suffered million times and more
Never thinking that as the Earth Mother I would somehow be forgott'n
None of my sons and daughters I nursed or carried about
Ever sat by the Yangtze River tearfully my lot to mourn
If Mother and children are ever to meet again
That may not happen until the cosmos in renewal ends

Since the text claims that the Earth Mother was unknown to the world prior to this recent revelation, one would have expected the Earth Mother Temple, where such a message appeared, to have been the first of its kind. Yet since she is also the Eternal Mother in disguise, and there were temples dedicated openly or secretly to her before, that would explain why there is a passing reference to rebuilding existent temples dedicated to her (the Eternal Mother). Such temples might have suffered state persecution and could have been neglected in the interim. From the *Authentic Scripture* (with emphasis added):

Give thanks to and repay the debt owed the vacuously empty Mother
Quickly to *refurbish her temples* and incense to burn
Carve anew images of the Mother so people can come and pray
To make up for the filial piety long due her.

Presumably the images would be patterned after those of the Eternal Mother.

The text sets a new date (different from that of Hou T'u) for the Earth Mother's birthday:

The Earth Mother is born on the eighteenth of the tenth month
At which time every household should recite this Scripture
Lamps, incense, fruit offering should all be laid out
A meeting called, the scripture chanted, and a notice posted.

Besides this lavish celebration on her birthday, a new monthly liturgical calendar is established to observe the holy days or the tabooed fifths of the month (the fifth, fifteenth, and twenty-fifth).[30] The special days were mentioned in the Incense Psalm; the *Wondrous Scripture* fleshes the process out further:

Man and woman, young or old, they all need to remember
Sincerely the Earth Mother Scripture to chant
Quickly, quickly to preach and likewise to transmit
In no time the blessing of a good harvest will come
Always gold and silver candle in offering light
In reverence on the three fifths of each month
(It is not that any other day is not fit for worship
It is just 36 days of observances a year be kept)
All that is required are just six lamps and five incense sticks
Paper gold, paper silver and a cup of plain tea
Let man and woman set up such platforms on those days
Post the announcements so the public can be invited
Seven times from the heart the sacred writ to chant
So that peace on earth may everywhere descend

As a shadow for the Eternal Mother, the Earth Mother is more than just the chthonic, fertility goddess of old. She is a high deity, the mother of all the gods, the immortals, and the Buddhas. All their temples, shrines, monasteries, or nun cloisters are encompassed by her cosmic body. Forgetting her overarching grace and competing among themselves for vain glory, the three teachings forsake what is their common ground. The *Authentic Scripture* states:

Immortals, Buddhas, Sage and Worthies forgot her good will
They boast, their communities compete in some vain show of talent
Ruler, minister, literatus and military forgot her good will
Forgetting how her great compassion is meant for all
Scholar, farmer, artisans and merchants forget her good will
Instead of paying the debt due her, they slight and abuse her.

However, since in truth the Earth Mother is the beginning and the end, the all-in-all, the same text sings her praise and elevates her high above the others. It goes so far as to contradict the orthodox standard that always places Heaven above Earth:

The people of the world knows Heaven as Great
But the Earth Mother dares to even better Heaven
Heaven may claim possession of the one sweet dew
But Earth is where the Five Grains grow
And even if the rain from above is a heavenly boon
More precious still is the Earth's bone and marrow
The (rain) dragon in the thousand lakes is a part of me
The cloud and the wind are of the Earth Mother born.

Elsewhere, the same scripture has Heaven and Earth paired off as a couple: "He as deaf (Heaven) and I as dumb (Earth) are joined in marriage as a pair."[31] All the assurance of the mother's love notwithstanding, there is at the back somewhere this warning of the apocalyptic end:

The Earth Mother never closes her eyes day or night
For fear that if she does, calamity would strike

Had she even looked aside for a split second
The (subterranean) Leviathan would toss and level everything
At that time, there would be no heaven and no earth
Everything in the world would dissolve into a void
The various Buddhas taking flight will flee the world
The bodhisattvas would run as far as the limitless can take them
Ruler, subject, and mankind will all be destroyed
Gods of heaven and worthies on earth will be by fire consumed
Neither east nor west or south and north would there be
As everything is reduced to so much ash and dust.[32]

Of course, for the elect, the promised end is not of destruction but of joy everlasting: the *Authentic Scripture* ends with a scene of lotus flowers in bloom (i.e. enlightenment) and a transformation of the Central Kingdom (China) into a Buddha Realm. In that cosmic Net of Indra, everyone becomes a point of light that is part and parcel of that infinite network of myriad lights reflecting myriad lights. The *Wondrous Scripture* gives a still more graphic description:

As the Earth Mother so profoundly reveals this predestined Dharma
East, west, south, and north turned into the Lotus Womb
Man and woman in their golden (deathless) bodies appear
As great immortals of the highest heaven they will not be reborn again
Cultivation and enlightenment replete, they to the great assembly go
To receive fame and glory at the Peach Garden [of the Queen Mother of the West]
Never again to come down eastward to this mundane realm,[33]
Just forever to attend the birthday banquet of the Earth Mother.

The *Earth Mother Scripture*, though partial towards the cult of the Eternal Mother, does not fall neatly into the two major divisions of that sectarian movement. It stresses chanting, but unlike the sutra-chanting sectarians, it does not explicitly encourage engaging in vegetarianism.[34] It does not make an issue of following the five lay precepts either. It is also unlike the literature of the meditative sectarians. It does not teach breathing techniques or martial arts or healing cures.[35] It shows no loyalty to and lists no specific master–disciple transmission.[36] No prophet or messenger of the Earth Mother is named. And whereas most "spirit writings" of the recent period now regularly opt for a "realized eschatology" (i.e. the last age is already here, the direct communication with the gods being the new dispensation that eliminates the need for the wait), the *Earth Mother Scripture* keeps up that end-time drama and an eschatological crisis.[37] Though promising material boons to the faithful chanters, it is not so grossly materialistic as some recent plantchette teachings that forsake the utopian future. In fact, except for a general line in the *Authentic Scripture* about "Great loyalty and great filial piety (ensuring) great rewards; great kindness and great compassion (bringing about) a long life," the text is not concerned with teaching morality. We may assume that at the practical level, it endorses fairly traditional values. There is no hint of leaving home, of repudiating the family, or of taking arms against the state. At the same time, it does maintain at the theoretical level the total equality of the sexes in a utopia, one family under the Earth Mother with none of the hierarchic norms operative in this world.

If the *Earth Mother Scripture* is one of the earliest spirit writings, it would seem to have avoided that genre's decline into shoring up traditional morality while promising this-worldly rewards. It keeps up the early sectarians' hope for a Gnostic deliverance by combining the quietist piety of the devotional sutra-chanters without actually withdrawing from the world. It works at a popular appeal to all and sundry without the secrecy associated with the lineage transmission of some "inner techniques."

The meaning of the neo-archaic

Modernity has created the category of the "primitive." At one point, its claim to progress even pronounced the imminent demise of anything primitive. But in the midst of the economic miracle that is Taiwan, a cult of the Earth Mother has survived. It still flourishes.[38] The *Earth Mother Scripture* seems to have found its own niche in the present.

The cult spreads, it seems, primarily by print. Clart cites two examples. An Earth Mother temple was set up in P'u-li by a Liang family that has recited the scripture since 1914. When the goddess saved the family from an earthquake in 1917, it built the Pao-hu kung T'ien-t'i t'ang in her honor. The Earth Mother temple in Hua-t'an was founded by another devotee who chanced upon a copy of the scripture in 1946.[39] After the Compassion Society decided to disseminate it in 1950, the text reached a still larger readership. The Earth Mother's latest revelation at the Wu-miao Ming-cheng t'ang came with the boom in communicating with the spiritual realm. Like "neo-paganism" in a post-Christian West, this "neo-archaism" found a new hearing in modern Taiwan. The utilitarian interpretation would tie the plantchette cult to a social sector's need for a means of maximizing their chances of making it in the world.[40] I, however, have chosen to present the *Earth Mother Scripture* as affording men access to a higher *gnosis*, a *sophia* or *sapientia*, and membership of a cosmic family of this Great Mother that rises above the lower knowledge, the *techne* or *scientia*, of the mundane and more fragmented world. Like nineteenth-century Spiritualism in Europe,[41] this wisdom is so independent of the truths of the lower realm that it may accommodate, co-opt, sublate, set aside, or negate the latter, depending on the circumstances. Gnosticism is, of course, a blanket term brandished by the early Church Fathers against "heretics" of many colors. What we know of the Gnostic tradition now is that there were many cultural variations with different goals. It was the mainstream faith on the Silk Road; and to the extent that China inherited it through Mahayana Buddhism, it colored this cult of the Chinese Demeter.

Modernity has often misrepresented what it sees as primitive. Charles Long discusses this issue in Chapter 4 of the present volume with reference to the case of the "cargo cult." Usually presented as the wishful thinking of primitivism, the cult expected these big cargo ships to come loaded with all kinds of modern appliances. The goods were earmarked for the natives even as the white traders came to an evil end. As Long points out, it was as much a "civilized" critique by the indigenous people of the Europeans, who were the real "barbarians." The latter could not stay happy at home; rather, as restless souls, they chose to go running around. They did not know the civilized way of exchanging gifts for sealing friendship. When these Western barbarians took and took and took, did not share, and just hoarded their possessions, they behaved abominably in the eyes of the natives. They violated the basic rule of civility, and so upset the cosmic balance of what is good and decent that it was just a matter of time before the generous natives would be rewarded and these selfish invaders punished. And if the white traders remembered their own tradition, they should know that these "primitives" truly "loved their neighbors," while it was the white man who, too proud to join in that "pot-luck" banquet, were duly left out, "gnashing their teeth" in indignant resentment. These Christian traders – capitalists and imperialists who in time exploited and subjugated – had forgotten how their own faith went back to the exodus of an enslaved people who followed their God, who once had promised them a land of milk and honey, and later celebrated an eschatological feast where the last would be the first and the first be last.[42] In other words, the cargo cult is more than an indigenous people's "primitive" way of responding to the European Other. The cult draws both parties into a larger global conversation, one which is as much an occasion for the European ego to understand better its own pseudo-modern prejudices and its own self-alienation.

As Jordan Paper has shown, in *The Spirits are Drunk: Comparative Approaches to Chinese Religion*,[43] Eurocentric misrepresentation of Chinese religion runs deep. God being eternal and self-evident to the Jesuits, Matteo Ricci once thought he had found Ur-monotheism in the ancient Chinese worship of a Lord on High, so he overlooked the coterminal cult of the Mother Earth. Later, the Protestants, keen on doctrine and less keen about rituals, overlooked how *li* (ceremonies) might be the heart of Chinese religion. Used to seeing the Eucharist as a sacrificial meal, Western theories of ritual focusing on sacrifice were not equipped to understand the Chinese custom of eating and drinking with gods, ghosts, and ancestors. Used to dealing with singular dogmas, the missionaries reported China as having "three religions," thereby implicating a Chinese tendency towards syncretism – when syncretism may exist only in the eyes of the outside beholder. Ultimately, a religion of prophets and priests might find it hard to make sense of shamans and media.[44] The irony is that the Christian missions had little idea how the gospel they planted could be fused with the spirit medium who came up with new revelations that turned the God-Worshipping Society into the Taiping Rebellion (1850–65), the event now used to mark China's entry into her modern era.

The T'ai-p'ing was China's "cargo cult." It expected a Christian Kingdom of the Great Peace to come that would put the "Western devils" in their place. The Boxer Uprising (1900), wherein bare-fisted fighters thought that they were immune to Western bullets, qualifies as China's "ghost dance." Both movements globalized the conflict. England and America helped put down the T'ai-p'ing. Eight foreign nations squashed the Boxers. However, both uprisings can be seen as activistic extensions of the Eternal Mother sectarianism.[45] Both felt the need to exorcise the barbaric ghosts and demons that were then infesting China. But then ghosts and demons, according to Chinese religious rhetoric, were simply outsiders who created havoc, who would not behave in a ritually proper fashion, and whose unpredictable malice required dispelling.[46] Thus Hung Hsiu-ch'uan, who founded the God-Worshipping Society, felt himself commissioned by God to go after the demons. The demons had lost a battle to Jesus in Heaven but had somehow managed to escape to Earth. Hung first started destroying idols as the missionaries had taught him to; but then he identified the demons with the Manchus, the "internal aliens" ruling the Han race; and still later he equated them with the Europeans, the real "foreign devils." The Boxers came "to aid of the Manchus"; their aim was to kill these Western goblins and "eradicate the foreigners." That malaise in the realm of the spirits was just a reflection of the very real uncertainties in the uncivilized behavior of men in the world below.[47]

The *Earth Mother Scripture* is one civilized response to the barbarianism of modernity, even if it happens to be blissfully unaware of the major modern events. It condenses the sectarian teaching to a very simple form – with minimal theogony and ecclesiology. It avoids national politics and places its gnosis above the fall into history. That it persists even as the T'ai-p'ing and the Boxers came and went may be indicative of the continual success of the Great Mother in reinventing herself down the centuries. She is as much above the world as she is deep in the earth. Depending on her manifest form, she can be nature personified, a granter of fertile boons, a cult figure, a sectarian figurehead, a patient mystic, a miracle worker, a harbinger of a lost paradise now regained; or, when circumstances provoke, she might turn millenarian, activistic, and outright anti-establishment. With a long history of mutation behind her, this protean Earth Mother in her latest neo-archaic form proves herself to be resilient. She stands well on her truth and holds up a viable ideal still.

Notes

1   For ease of reference, I will refer to the set as the *Earth Mother Scripture* because my copy of the second text ends with "Thus ends the True Scripture of the None Higher, Vacuously Empty, Earth Mother (who is) Mysteriously Transforming, Life Protecting (and) Destiny Nurturing." I shall refer to the two texts individually as the *Authentic Scripture* and the *Wondrous Scripture* respectively.

2   Clart (as of 1995) is writing his doctoral dissertation on this hall at the University of British Columbia. The hall is dedicated to Kuan Kung, "God of War," who has meanwhile been elevated from duke to becoming the Jade Emperor himself. Since 1994, the Earth Mother has been added to the "already abundantly staffed pantheon" in this temple. The revealed writings are reprinted by installment in the Luan-yu Magazine. Clart was kind to send me (on 26 July 1996) the first three from issues no. 583, 585, and 591.

3   David Jordon and Daniel Overmyer, Princeton: Princeton University Press, 1986.

4   Jordon's copy has only the *Earth Mother Scripture*; Overmyer's has in addition a scripture in honor of Kuan-yin, the Five Grains Scripture, the Eyesight Scripture, the True Scripture of the Sun, and the same of the Moon. My copy does not have the Sun and the Moon Scripture but instead the Wondrous Sand Scripture, the Diamond Incantation, and the Psalm for Taking Refuge. The Preface to Overmyer's ties the Earth Mother to the creatress (female creator) Nu Wa: "After creative chaos was first divided, Empress (Nu) Kua put human relationship into proper order"; mine has no such preface.

5   See Daniel Overmyer, *Folk Buddhist Religion: Dissenting Sects in Late Traditional China*, Cambridge, MA: Harvard University Press, 1976.

6   See Suzanne Cahill, *Transcendence and Divine Passion*, Stanford: Stanford University Press, 1993.

7   The Buddhist "unborn" is a synonym for "empty," but a Taoist reading would take it to mean easily the "eternal" (Mother).

8   See Daniel Overmyer, "Values in sectarian literature: Ming and Ch'ing Pao-chuan," in David Johnson *et al.*, *Popular Literature in Late Imperial China*, Berkeley: University of California Press, 1983, 221.

9   The place is the Earth Mother temple at Ch'eng-ku *yuan* (district), Han-chung *fu* (prefecture) in Shensi province. It is not registered in the local gazette, but it could be a small, sectarian temple.

10   The text does not mention any reigning emperor (except in the date). It prays for "a prosperous state and a peaceful people," and takes for granted the traditional four classes and the old administrative structure. But then there is no mention of the Taiping Rebellion or any political event, which is not uncommon in this genre. The latest revelation (9 December 1995) mentions the "five human relationships," but the running commentary substitutes a sister–sister dyad for the king–minister relationship. The advice it gives addresses problems of modern city living. Instead of promising a good harvest, it instructs people on how not to chase after money.

11   Compiled by Lu Tsung-li and Luan Pao-ch'un and first published in 1986, it has been reissued in two volumes (Taipei: Hsueh-sheng, 1991). It excerpts literary references to gods and goddesses from the early classics to the late dynastic encyclopedias.

12   Kung Kung is the sound of rushing water, or a flood. The dragon is an Ur-being. Horns go with the creature of land, as scales and wings would water and air. Hou T'u is pictured here as a dragon of land rising out of the primeval deep.

13 My copy has the Five Grains Scripture. It has the birthday of the Earth Mother in the fall instead of in the spring.

14 Hou K'uei founded the Hsia dynasty; Hou Ch'i (millet) initiated farming. Millet is the prime of the Five Grains.

15 Reversed Euhemerism attributed to Early China should be distinguished from attested-to Euhemerism in the imperial era. Men could become gods only following the divinization of the First Emperor. Euhemerus, who reported of said practice on an Indian island, was himself a produce of that age of Alexander the Great.

16 P. Steven Sangren explains this logic best in *History and Magical Power in a Chinese Community*, Stanford: Stanford University Press, 1987.

17 This post-Han era with the barbaric invasion was when both T'u-ti and Hou T'u took on more the functions of being officials of the netherworld. Even a 10-year-old murder victim could become a T'u-ti.

18 The elite might prefer to see Hou T'u as male, but the populace might not. Even in early China, the *she* in the Yangtze and Wei River areas worshipped a *she-mu* (earth mother), whereas further north they worshipped a *she-kung* (earth master) (CS: 252). And during the last dynasty, the South kept up a stronger tradition of worshipping a Fu-jen (mistress) at even the T'u-ti shrine.

19 The credit of her becoming "cosmic and salvific" has to go to that "celestialization" process of the medieval era noted earlier. But that medieval, otherworldy movement was "brought down to earth" when a pneumatic Amitabha was overshadowed by this earthly, physical creatress that is the Eternal Mother in Late Ming.

20 Because the text is less than seven "leaves," or double pages, long, such that any Chinese reader can scan through it in no time, I will skip citing it by page number. There is no standardized edition anyway.

21 Zealous officials might not be deterred or fooled by the camouflage. The Eternal Mother had hid herself behind even the worship of the sun.

22 This motif of the fall into lusting after sex, wealth, luxury, and vain glories is told, for example, in one of the earliest Eternal Mother texts, the Lung-hua (Dragon Flower) Ching.

23 Such as in the Song of the Pearl. With the recent studies on the Gnostic tradition, the line between the orthodox and the heretical is getting harder to draw. On the Silk Road, Gnosticism is orthodox.

24 She looks like many of the popular Liang-liang goddesses such as Ma-tsu, the Queen of Heaven, the most popular of them all in Taiwan and along the south-east coastal provinces. See James L. Watson, "Standardizing the gods: the promotion of T'ien Hou ('Empress of Heaven') along the South China coast (960–1960)," in David Johnson, Evelyn S. Rawski and Andrew Nathan (eds) *Popular Culture in Late Imperial China*, Berkeley: University of California Press, 1985. It is not clear if the picture is integral to the original scripture; it was most likely added later for illustrative purposes. The couplet set into the picture, "By imperial decree of the ninth (the highest) Heaven/Earth Mother and Original Ruler," is not a title used in or implicated by the text itself. By being so appointed, it actually demotes her status to being below the August Jade Emperor. The couplet also does not serve as a Gnostic formula such as the one attending the Eternal Mother.

25 The Buddhist and the Taoist traditions have a special class of religious virtuosos (the clerical elite); the Confucian tradition has no such renunciates (it is all lay). The Eternal Mother sent the Buddha, Lao-tzu, and Confucius to save their respective followers. Thus the line here is in effect saying: the Earth Mother gave birth to the three teachings of China.

26 This is the first sure indication that "printing" is seen as the standard way of disseminating this teaching.

27 Literally, "old woman" for mother, as the English "old man" is for father. But I do not want to paint her as being that old, so "old maid" sounds better.

28 Emphasis added. This "even more so" emphasis was pointed out to me by Cheng Yu-yin (unpublished Ph.D. thesis, University of California, Davis).

29 Unlike some Gnostic texts that depict a dramatic fall or a circuitous deception and seduction of the spirit, the text here alleges only a simple forgetfulness.

30 The numerical value of earth is five. I seriously doubt that these days were ever adhered to; the sectarian sutra-chanting societies met at most two times a month – not three. The new revelations being currently received in Taichung from the Mother do not fall on those holy days.

31 Philip Clart, in his 26 July 1996 communication, informs me that he had tracked this pair, the Deaf Celestial and the Mute Terrestrial, to two of the four acolytes attending the God of Learning, Wen-chang. In the myths of the Eternal Mother, sometimes a heavenly lord precedes her, sometimes after her, sometimes paired with her, or, as Fu Hsi and Nu Wa, generated from out of her.

32 The reference to the eyes is to the myth of the Torch Dragon; if he closes his eyes, the world will be swallowed up by darkness. The Leviathan is a giant fish holding up the land in its slumber.

33 China is, to wit, "East of Eden"; this fall from the Eternal Home to this mundane world is told in the Lung-hua Ching.

34 Admittedly there is no discouragement either; the Earth Mother produces all crops and herbs but notably not any "fish or meat" for man's dining table.

35 Of course, chanting the work is supposed to bring boons, including good health and longevity.

36 On the characteristics of these two groups of sectarian texts, see Susan Naquin, "The transmission of White Lotus sectarianism in late Imperial China," in Johnson, Rawski and Nathan (eds) *Popular Culture in Late Imperial China.*

37 The latest revelation from December 1995 has so far kept that out.

38 See Philip Clart, "Sects, cults, and popular religion: aspects of religious change in post-war Taiwan," *B.C.* [British Columbia] *Asian Review* 9 (Winter 1995/96): 120–63. In the 1950s and early 1960s, when Taiwan was experiencing economic hardship, the Christian churches, both ~holic and Protestant, saw significant growth. Being modern, then, somehow goes with being ⸳ – and Christian. With the economic miracle taking off, Taiwan regained her cultural ⸳nd the rate of conversion to Christianity was stalled and finally stagnated. "National ⸳ fashionable; the sectarian I-kuan Tao, once banned, regained respectability college-educated; and the plantchette societies bloomed. Modern education ⸳sbelief; but the educated are not totally immune to such spirit writings. ⸳rsonal communication (26 July 1996). ⸳rdon and Overmyer, *The Flying Phoenix*, finds the "flying phoenix" clientele to be ⸳king success but lacking the proper credential or necessary means, such as a good ⸳. He sees the cult as a calculated blend of belief and disbelief: the members are open to ⸳sibility of spiritual intervention but pragmatic enough to be wary of any unreasonable ⸳d on the part of the cult leaders seeking personal gain. These are not fanatic "true ⸳vers" but shoppers of religious "kirsch." As a voluntary society of near equals, it allows more ⸳edom than the organizations of the official religions. It is also its own support group against any skepticism within and without.

41 Swedenborg etc. is briefly noted by Jordon and Overmyer, *ibid.*. Like much of nineteenth-century European Spiritualism and the still current Theosophical Society, they are all tied to this Gnostic undercurrent in European thought.

42 Liberation theology has taken better cognizance of this moral critique.

43 Albany, NY: SUNY Press, 1995.

44 Paper postulated a difference in early China between a northern, nomadic tradition of the shaman and a southern, rice-cultivating tradition of the medium. Ideal-typically, the shaman flies up in conscious flights and reports of his journeys thereafter, while the gods descend into the medium who, while possessed, is supposed to be unaware of what transpired.

45 This promise of immunity is present among the meditative-and-martial wings of the White Lotus sectarians.

46 Following the established custom that "gods are officials; ghosts are ancestors; ghosts are outsiders." But only in the nineteenth century were the aggressive European demonized as " devils."

47 As to the cult of the "flying phoenix," that tells of a new dynamic in the mutual support between the living and the dead. In traditional village and town cultures, social norms are enforced by the power of the ancestors. The presence of the significant dead, as defined by a nexus of relationships, spans generations. The will of the deceased has to be consulted while their well-being (their whereabouts) is a matter of concern. For authority, Americans can point to a piece of paper and say, "The Constitution states such and such"; but in Chinese villages, the headman can still evoke spirits and say "Grandfather states so and so."

Chapter 15

Popular religions and modernity in Japan

Michio Araki

As is often pointed out, one of the most important religious and social phenomena in modern Japan has been the gradual decline of the established religions of Buddhist sects and Shrine Shinto and the dramatic rise and development of many new religious movements having a strong influence on the cultural and religious life of Japanese people (Araki 1990, 1992). Japanese new religions, however, have been very little appreciated, partly because of the enlightenment policy of the modern imperial regime in Japan and its overall influence on Japanese culture and society, and partly because of modern Western concepts and images of religion that were introduced into modern Japanese universities, which in themselves were modeled after Western universities.

These new religions have thus often been ignored or dismissed as something less than religion, in spite of the fact that these new religions have been created and supported by the common people, have sustained the common people through existential life crises in an ever-changing culture and society, and are the creative transformations in the modern context of folk religious traditions with a long and important history. It is Japanese folk religion that both indigenized Buddhism, initially a foreign religion, and subtly influenced and gradually transformed Christianity in Japan. Folk religion is the very tradition that constitutes the underlying substratum of Japanese religion, running from archaic, prehistoric religion in Japan to the present. It is the organic vessel into which important, yet fragmented, elements of various historic religions have been received and transformed. Being closely linked with folk religion, Japanese new religions are thus of crucial importance for understanding all aspects of Japanese religion.

Understanding the full significance of Japanese new religions requires, however, a greater appreciation of the intentions they embody. New religions in modern times manifest their creativity under the identity of new "popular" religions. They are popular in that they emerged spontaneously from the lives of common people. Though born of folk religious traditions, the new religions manifest more coherent worlds of meaning than folk religion and aim, more or less clearly, at creating an egalitarian world and community. They thus aim to sustain and enhance the lives of common people who are alienated from the structure of the surrounding society, a structure in which the elite (including the state) and the folk, the rulers and the ruled, and the "haves" and the "have-nots" are divided in opposition. New religions envision and try to embody a world of relations beyond the divisions and hierarchical structure of society (Araki 1990). They are religions of the people in the sense that they are created by the people, sustained by the people, and are for the people. Even when they become entangled with the elite and state religion and seem not to be popular religions in actuality, they are still religions of the people in terms of their ideals. Both folk religions and new religions have embodied alternative visions of human experience and potentiality containing both explicit and implicit critiques of aspects of modern civilization.

Both folk religious traditions and the new religions are thus part of a tension and structure running throughout Japanese religious history that may be briefly characterized in terms of the opposition of center and periphery. While both folk traditions and new religions have met with suppression in the modern period, it is important to note here that folk religious traditions have met with opposition, control, and even suppression from the center throughout recorded history.

The new religions reveal a religious structure of "new creation," that is to say, they attempt to create a new world of meaning in which people can live with human dignity and integrity. They attempt to create this new world out of the existential confusion and chaos that arise from rapid changes in culture and society and which are seen as a sort of "primordial chaos" preceding the creation of a new world. This creativity is the mark of those religious movements that Professor Charles Long has referred to as "new archaism." In terms of the theme of the present volume, I would suggest that the study of "indigenous religion and modernity" might be approached through a comparative study of new archaism as linked to the problem of colonialism and religion in the last five hundred years of cultural contact that formed the contemporary world.

The new archaism of Japanese new religions might differ in some degree, however, from the new archaism of new religions of Third World countries due to some peculiarities and ironies of the Japanese situation. Unlike most Third World countries, Japan has never, save for a brief period of occupation, been directly dominated by colonial rule. As is well known, however, the effort to emulate and become equal with the West did lead to Japan becoming a colonial power in parts of East Asia and Southeast Asia. Many still have painful memories of Japanese militarism and colonialism. Japanese society too has suffered from the trauma of having imposed colonial and military rule on parts of East Asia and Southeast Asia. And many of the new religions of Japan have suffered oppression at the hands of the Japanese government that imposed colonial rule on parts of Asia. While Japanese society has thus not experienced the same sort of hard liminality that Third World countries have passed through, it has passed through phases of incredible change, trauma, and transformation.

Let me return, however, to the historical problems of the Westernization and modernization of Japan and their relation to popular new religions. During the past one hundred and fifty years, Japanese society has undergone many phases of radical cultural and social change, involving all aspects of life. Included here are such great transformations as the decline of the feudal Tokugawa regime; the establishment of the modern, imperial Meiji state; the rapid introduction and absorption of policies of modernization and Westernization in the fields of government, law, education, technology, and culture; the development of capitalism and colonialist, militaristic involvement in Asia; the Japanese–Russian War; the further development of industrialization and capitalism as well as further economic and military involvement in Asia; the Second World War, which ended in Japan's defeat; the US occupation and post-war modernization and democratization; and phenomenal economic growth. These rapid changes in society brought forth serious existential crises that have included new types of human alienation and identity crises along with the disintegration of traditional communities and values.

The rise of the new religions in Japan is thus inseparable from contact with the West, from the age of imperialism, and from the spread and absorption of Western ideals, rationalism, technology, and economic models. The rise of the new religions in Japan is inextricably linked with the decision of the Japanese elite to emulate, overcome, and yet distinguish themselves from Western modes of being. It is important to recall here, however, that the very history of Japanese society, culture, and religion might very well be described as a history of cultural contact. It is important to note this point because Japan, despite all the evidence to the contrary, is still often presented as being a homogenous culture with little or any diversity. Indeed, this notion of a homogenous culture owes much to both contact with the West and the Meiji effort to create a modern state to rival Western powers by forming a new center – by creating, under the rubric of "restoration," an imperial system with modern myths of the homogeneity of the Japanese people and culture. This effort led at times to the radical control and even suppression of new religions. While established religions tended to capitulate to government projects, there were signs of resistance among many of the new religions. The degree to which Meiji and subsequent regimes have emulated, mirrored, and reacted to the West also makes it difficult to clearly separate the indigenous and the Western.

While the established religions (traditional Buddhist sects and Shrine Shinto) and their leaders were busily trying to adjust to these ongoing changes and remained aloof from the life and religious needs of common people, new religious movements emerged spontaneously from the lower strata of society. But as soon as these new religions were more or less established within the structure of society, another group of new religions would emerge from even lower strata of society or from the fringes of established new religions. This has been the general historical pattern of the emergence of new religions, repeated until the very recent explosion of new religions – now called new new religions – in "postmodern" Japanese society from the 1970s onwards (*ibid.*: 31–42).

The patterns of development of new religions in Japan suggest many of their characteristics and their cultural and historical implications. The historical development of new religions in modern times can be divided into the following four phases or groups based on the historical period of their emergence and development:

1   The first group or generation of modern new religions includes Kurozumi-kyo (The Teaching of Kurozumi, Kurozumi being the family name of the founder), Konko-kyo (The Teaching of the Light of Kon, Kon being the divine name of the all-embracing Kami, Konjin; Konko also refers to the name of the founder), and Tenri-kyo (The Teaching of Heavenly Reason). These new religions formed the prototypes of popular new religions in Japan and thus reveal the nature and characteristics of popular religions most clearly. They emerged in feudal, agricultural communities located close to urban centers, communities that had been disintegrating due to the radical changes which marked people's lives from the latter part of the Tokugawa period through to the beginning of the Meiji period (approximately 1840–88). Each of these new religions emerged spontaneously through the personal religious experience of their founders, which was grounded and nurtured in the traditions of folk religion, that is to say, the non-institutional, syncretic substratum of Japanese culture and religion.

2   The second group of new religions emerged in the critical period formed by the development of the modern imperial state and capitalistic industrialization, the Japanese–Russian War, the imperialistic invasion of China, and the economic depression

and crisis that led to the outbreak of the Manchurian Incident (approximately 1895–1930). The most representative religions of this period are Omoto-kyo (The Teaching of the Great Origin), Hon-michi (The True Way), and Hito-no-michi (The Way of the Human, later changed to PL Kyodan, The Religious Body of Perfect Liberty). They emerged more or less from the fringes of the first group of new religions, on the peripheries of urban centers, based on the religious experiences of their founders.

3   The third group of religion emerged in the critical situations before and after the Second World War (approximately 1930–70). This period witnessed the traumas of war, the dissolution of the modern imperial state, the questioning of almost all of the traditional values of pre-war institutions, and the effort to build a democratic state with a new constitution and economy. The most representative new religions of this age include Tensho-kotai-jingu-kyo (The Teaching of the Imperial Sun Goddess Amaterasu), Seicho-no-ie (The House of Growth), Sekai-kyusei-kyo (The Teaching of World Messianity), Soka-gakkai (The Value Creating Society), Reiyu-kai (The Association of the Friends of the Spirits), and the Rissho-kosei-kai (The Society for the Establishment of Righteousness and Friendly Relations). Some are Lotus Sutra or Nichiren-related Buddhist lay movements, some were founded by shamanesses, and others are offshoots of the earlier new religions. This period was the second stage of a far-reaching modernization and Westernization of Japanese culture and society. Faced with rapid and radical changes in all aspects of life and society, all of these regions centered on traditional values and elements of folk religion, such as respect for ancestral souls and the continuity of the family. Some of these new religions later engaged in aggressive proselytizing throughout the world. Unlike some of the earlier new religions, this group has almost never experienced serious persecution by the government.

4   The new religions of the fourth group began emerging in the 1970s and were formed in situations of post-industrial or post-modern society, increased urbanization, and rapid economic development and prosperity. While there was in this period a sense that the goals of modernization, rationalization, and Westernization for the sake of the survival of the community had been achieved in the form of economic and technological development, there was also a feeling of fatigue. Although many small new religious groups were created in this period, the most representative among them are Agon-shu (The Agama Sect), Sekai-mahikari-bunmei-kyo (The Teaching of True Light and Civilization of the World), Kofuku-no-kagaku (The Science of Happiness), and also Aum Shinri-kyo (The Teaching of Aum the Supreme Truth), which has recently become known throughout the world because of its attack on the Tokyo subway system.

Although many of them have links with syncretic folk traditions in Japan, these new religions are very much influenced by the mystical vocabularies of foreign traditions of both Eastern and Western origin. They do not place as much emphasis on what earlier groups regarded as central – the fulfillment of the daily needs of people afflicted with sickness, poverty, hunger, and social strife. They do not address their messages to the basic conditions of human existence. The majority of the members of these groups seem to look for answers to their religious needs, but the religious needs of the members of these "new" new religions seem to be clearly different from those of the older new religions.

The teachings of these new religions do not emphasize what was crucial for the earlier new religions – strong ethical values and the creation of new, egalitarian communities.

We can observe among these contemporary movements, however, a strong revival of the mystical belief in spirits and souls, the popularity of shamanic spirit possession, and the importance of charismatic saints and leaders. We see here archaic religious motifs in abundance, not only among these new religious groups, but also in the popular culture of the younger generation, as expressed in literature, comics, television programs, and movies. Especially among the younger generation, many seem to be seeking mystical experience, desiring to be spiritually elevated by mystical means, as if they had completely forgotten about the religio-ethical problems and human concerns in the surrounding community and world. Their tendencies might be indicative of their dissatisfaction with the highly rationalized, secularized space and time of human existence in urban societies today. While they seem materially blessed with an abundance of goods, they do not seem to be blessed with a sense of the real and significant. This in itself seems to me the mark of a serious crisis (Shimazono 1992: 23–62).

Before moving on to a discussion of the cultural and historical meanings of the new religions in modern Japan, it would be best to touch briefly on the characteristics of these new religions. While it is important to focus here on the common characteristics of these popular religious movements, it also needs to be noted that they encompass a variety of types of religiosity and forms of socio-cultural organization. There are, for example, purist, individualistic, reformist, and anti-ritualistic groups among these religious movements. On the other hand, there are also groups that are heavily ritualistic, collectivistic, and magico-religious. Some movements emphasize the interiority of faith, and others an aggressive form of proselytizing directed towards the outside world. Some emphasize a clear break with the social and cultural values of the outside world, while others do not. These new religious movements, in short, manifest a variety of religious modes of being in the world.

They do, however, share the following characteristics:

1 These religions are, as was observed earlier, intimately related to the problems of modernity and modernization in one way or another.
2 These religions emerged from the tradition of Japanese folk religion, which contains not only a wealth of archaic religious motifs and expressions – such as shamanistic possession, belief in spirits and souls, various forms of divination and oracles, magico-religious prayer, various taboos and prohibitions, belief in the protective power of amulets, etc. – but also fragments and elements of the historic, established religions of Buddhism and Shinto. The folk religious traditions also feature many elements derived from Japanese Taoism, often called "popular On-myo-do" (The Way of Yin-Yang), which trickled down from elite and state religions into folk traditions through a variety of syncretic historical and cultural processes. Furthermore, these elements of Buddhism, Shinto, and Taoism that were incorporated into folk traditions include Buddhist deities such as Kannon, Amida, and Maitreya; the deities of official Japanese mythology; deities such as Ne-no-hoshi (Polar Star) and Konjin; notions such as Satori (Nirvana) and Innen (karma); belief in the magical power of the Lotus and Prajna-Paramita Sutras; the notion of Dori (reason or law); the Yin-Yang calendars; Taoist divination and geomancy; and various Buddhist, Shinto, and Taoist practices and rituals. Thus, while it oversimplifies the matter somewhat, the new religions might be seen as various efforts to reintegrate the various traditions of folk religion in

various modern contexts. New religions are based on a religious valorization of the universe and a reassessment of the condition of the modern, historical world from the perspective of folk religious traditions.

3 As we can observe clearly from the life histories and sacred biographies of the originating leaders (the founder, foundress, or often "Kaicho" (Chairperson) or "Socho" (President) in contemporary formulations), the majority of the originating leaders were not trained in the elite religious or cultural traditions; rather, they were common people of the lower strata of Japanese society who themselves suffered the pains of people at the margins of society.

4 These religions emerged "spontaneously," that is to say, without any intervention from the state or elite traditions, were based on the religious experience of the founder or foundress, and were supported by the people.

5 These religions express the importance of charismatic individuals who are believed to intervene between the sacred and the profane to save people and are often called "Iki-gami" (Living Kami) or "Iki-botoke" (Living Buddha).

6 All of these religions are more or less millenarian or messianic, preaching an eschatological doctrine of "Yonaoshi" (World-Healing or World-Mending), and existing in tension or opposition to the present structure of society.

7 All of them try to respond to the daily religious needs of common people in one way or another, although this tendency is rather weak in the new religions.

8 In the initial stages of their development, the archaic technique of spirit possession often plays an important role, whether as a means of delivering oracles and teachings or making more fundamental divine revelations.

9 The teachings are "simple" and "direct," easy for common people to understand. They are also dynamic, in the sense that they can be related to the needs of believers who – being engaged in a daily schedule of work – do not have the leisure time to contemplate an articulated and sophisticated theology and philosophy.

10 The religious experience of a founder or foundress, who usually makes claims for the originality and uniqueness of their religion, its teaching, its practical expression, and its mission, often initiates them. These new religions also intend, as stated earlier, to go beyond the gap between the elite and the folk. This last tendency is particularly present in those groups with explicit egalitarian ideals. Some groups have managed to embody these ideals to a fair degree in their theoretical, practical, and communal forms of expression until or even after they become incorporated into the official structure of the state. This was especially the case in the pre-war period of the new religions, but not so much so in recent movements. Recent movements often establish a rigid hierarchical organization in the initial stages of their development.

11 As long as they keep their egalitarian ideals and spirit of communitas alive (as, for example, when the founder is still active), these religions tend to exist in a dialectical tension with both the outside world and the values and structure of mainstream Japanese society, and are able to maintain their creativity. This can be seen in the cases of Konko-kyo, Tenri-kyo, Hon-michi, Sekai-kyusei-kyo, and Rissho-kosei-kai. But when the oppressive power of the outside world is too strong, this dialectic can become simply destructive, as can be seen in the cases of Omoto-kyo and Renmon-kyo. And when the group is more or less established and loses the existential qualities of liminality, the ideals and creativity of the group become merely ideological and abstract.

12 Following the traditions of folk religion, almost all of the new religions revalorize and reaffirm nature and the cosmos as beautiful and salutary in a variety of forms under a variety of names, such as The Parent-Kami, The Great Life of the Universe, The Kami of Heaven and Earth, or The Sun, Moon, and Earth. The cosmologies of these groups manifest the religiosity of cosmic religion, a religion in which human beings are embraced in a cosmos or universe that is the source of life and power, the saving reality. These religions are open to the cosmos in this sense. But they are also related to history. Their religious expression reveals a mythicization and cosmicization of daily life and history that interprets historical events in terms of myth. Their religious culture is, to use Louis Dumont's term, a "holistic" culture in which everything is interrelated (Burridge 1979; Dumont 1986).

These new religions, however, have been frequently treated as being less than religions, or as being illegitimate religions. The feudal Tokugawa regime, for example, banned any new forms of religion or faith outside of the official, established religions. All the new religious movements under this regime had to borrow the name or support of official religions or go underground in order to conduct their activities. The founded religions of Tenri-kyo and Konko-kyo had to disguise themselves in the lower fringes of official religious organizations in order to cope with repeated suppression.

Under the modern regime of Meiji, which was based upon the contradictory goals of establishing a Western-style nation and restoring a semi-divine state, various aspects of magico-religious folk religion – including the "Yin-Yang" calendar, calendrical divination, folk religious taboos, and new faiths – were banned as "Inshin-jakyo" (the worship of malicious gods and evil religion). The founded religions of Tenri-kyo and Konko-kyo faced repeated suppression under the modern government policy towards religion. With the death of their founders, both groups succumbed to the authority of the government and were made official as parts of "Kyoha Shinto" (Sect Shinto), a political invention of the government used to control new religions and a term which carried the implied connotation of "less than Shinto." The second group of new religions – Omoto-kyo, Hito-no-michi, and Hon-michi – was not officially recognized by the imperial regime. They were treated as "Evil Religions," "Malicious Superstitions," or "quasi-religions," and repeatedly banned. They all had to wait for the establishment of religious freedom under the post-war constitution in order to be recognized as legitimate religions.

Protected by the constitutional separation of church and state and the right of freedom of faith in post-war Japan, the third and fourth groups have not faced such serious suppression. Yet under the pressures of modernization and rationalization, these new religions have often been treated as dubious, as reactionary, and as having negative influences on modernization.

One of the most far-reaching influences of the enlightenment policy of the Meiji regime was the disappearance of religion from the public domain; religions became private matters within the structure of the secular, modern state, although the sacred, inviolable emperor ruled over it. Politicians did not confess their faith, and schools and universities did not teach religion as a basic subject matter for human beings (Yamaori 1995). Japanese intellectuals and leaders attempted to learn earnestly from modern Western sciences and philosophy. Many young scholars and students were continuously dispatched to Western nations to study Western science and technology. As Kanzo Uchimura states, the Japanese accepted Christian civilization but not Christianity itself. Soon, they found themselves in an atmosphere in which they could not be persuasive unless they were skillful at manipulating modern Western scientific concepts and categories. Even Buddhist scholars (figures such as Manshi Kiyosawa, Taiken Kimura, and Kitaro Nishida) had to use Western concepts and categories of philosophy and science to articulate their doctrines and ideas. This is the reason why various sciences, including folklore and the study of religion, have had to follow modern Western models so devoutly until today. Despite this tendency, it should also be noted that these traditions of scholarship also developed some profound and articulate critiques of the West, as can be seen in the work of Okakura, Nishida, Nishitani, and Yanagita.

The predilection to follow Western models can also be seen in the study of religion in Japanese colleges and universities. Bunyu Nanjo, who was very much inspired by German idealism, occupied the first chair for the study of religion at Tokyo University. Scholars who introduced Western theories of religion in various styles succeeded him. They absorbed Western methods and applied them to Japanese phenomena, but neither critically nor cross-culturally. And those scholars who attended the World Parliament of Religion in Chicago in 1893 returned to Japan with an ideology of "progress" and evolutionism and then helped to develop the study of religion in Japan, as well as the Japanese Association of the Study of Religion, which is one of the oldest and largest national organizations for the study of religion in the world. Nevertheless, the Japanese study of religion was directly based on Western models of the science of religion until quite recently.

Indeed, the Japanese study of religion represents the modernism of modern Japan and a form of Japanese Orientalism; it employs Western categories and perspectives, for the most part uncritically, to explain Japanese traditions. This can be seen clearly in the work of Hideo Kishimoto, a Harvard-trained, positivist scholar of religion. Kishimoto conceives of the study of religions in terms of a structural-functionalist model common in Western social-scientific approaches to the study of religion. For Kishimoto, religion is to be grasped as a function of culture in the daily life of people and to be studied "scientifically." His understanding of religion thus clearly reflects the conventional image and concept of religion that was prevalent in society and intellectual circles in post-war Japan as it was striving to rebuild the nation through Westernization and economic development. Kishimoto's orientation is clear in his operational definition of religion: "among general cultural phenomena, religion is a phenomenon centered around those activities believed by people to bestow ultimate meaning on human life and to be concerned with the ultimate solution of human problems." Such phenomena were separated from general cultural phenomena and studied as religion (Kishimoto 1961).

Although he claims scientific objectivity in his study of religion, he is employing the analytic methods of Western social sciences without any serious qualification. His interpretation thus becomes much like those produced by conventional models and categories based on modern, Western Enlightenment notions of religion. Religion is consequently clearly separated for study from other categories of life. An example of the problems that arise here can be seen in Kishimoto's use of the conventional category of belief as the key religious act that defines religious phenomena. The notion of belief is clearly linked with the religious quality of interiority and thus does not serve as a reliable approach to those religions in which interiority and exteriority are not separated. Kishimoto also relies heavily on Paul Tillich's concept of "ultimate concern" as a means of separating religion from other functions of culture and as an analytical tool for interpreting all religious phenomena. By adopting the Western notion of "ultimate concern," Kishimoto thus treats all religious activity not meeting the criteria of "ultimate concern" as less than religious, thus leading to unbalanced and biased value judgments in his own typology of religions. Kishimoto also adopts without critical reflection the then current Western typological categories such as natural religion, animism, monotheism, polytheism, world religion, etc. Kishimoto thus distorts religious phenomena not only by separating religion from other aspects of culture and life, but also by limiting the sphere of religious phenomena to daily life and "belief." His own typological distinctions and those borrowed from the West both distort and render "invisible" many religious phenomena and traditions not preoccupied with "ultimate concern." With Kishimoto, religion becomes a rather well-controlled department of culture based on ordinariness, which is in tune with the preoccupation with modernization and rationalization prevalent at that time in post-war Japanese culture and society.

A similar tendency can be seen in Ichiro Hori's interpretation of the new religions as "residues" of old shamanistic, superstitious primitive religions and thus as anti-modern, reactionary, and harmful to modernization and rationalization. In spite of all the negative aspects he sees in these religions, Hori admits that they are supported by many commoners, but does so in a way that seems to scorn these "common people" (Hori 1968). Even today, many Japanese scholars still use various concepts such as animism, monotheism, fetishism, and ancestor worship without much critique, even though these concepts have largely been discredited in the West.[1] While the time for such a simple faith in modernism and its categories is gone in the West, the application of such Western concepts to the new religions or to the whole of Japanese religious tradition still prevails in Japan.

Both in and out of the academy, the mainstream of modern Japanese culture has thus supported modernization and Westernization, so much so that scholars and intellectuals in modern times concentrated on absorbing every new development of Western science. In the study of religion, Hori is perhaps the most telling example; he employed many Western methods and concepts, which often contradicted one another, without modification. In the process of assimilating such methods, the spirit of Western modernism was also absorbed into Japanese culture and academic institutions. This is how the study of Japanese religions has in practice come to employ the somewhat outdated concepts of Western science to Japanese phenomena. The distortions inherent in such practices and the gaps between Western methods and Japanese phenomena were things some Japanese scholars reflected on with certain misgivings. But often, they were simply employing Western methods without serious critique, as if they were the tools of secular salvation.[2]

The problem of cultural contact in modern Japan raises enormously important questions for the understanding of new religions in Japan, Japanese folk religion, the whole of Japanese religious tradition, and religion in general. We can at least state at this point that this problem requires us to pursue a double or even triple critique of past approaches to the study of religion. This is not to say that we historians of religion should give up Western approaches to the study of religion altogether; it is to say, however, that we must perform double or triple critiques of Western approaches and categories as developed in modern studies of religion, Japanese or otherwise, in order to build up a more authentic study of religion. Reference might be made here to a method of cross-cultural, critical study developed by Joseph M. Kitagawa. In particular, one might examine Kitagawa's double, perhaps triple, critique of Hegelian approaches and "Hegel's ghosts" in his analysis of early Japanese ritual prayers.[3]

Our understanding of religions is, needless to say, always conditioned by our own experience and situation; and all of us, whatever our geographical and cultural point of origin, are implicated and embedded in the seemingly endless instances of cultural contact and exchange that have marked the formation of the modern world. And cultural contact did not begin, of course, with the rise of the West. A critical orientation requires critically unpacking both sides of these processes and layers of contact. When we study Japanese religions, we must at the same time study and understand what happened through the development of the imperialism and colonialism of the West, through the formation of the modern West, which brought forth the present world, including modern Japan. It is also through these developments that all the concepts and categories of religion were created. We must also examine, however, how these concepts and categories were received, reconstituted, and deployed. It was Japanese Confucian rationalism that accepted Western rationalism and secularism without difficulty. And, as suggested earlier, the Japanese did not accept the Christian religion; they accepted Christian civilization. In order to understand ourselves and the rest of the world, we must go beyond our particular horizon or situation, by examining how that horizon or situation has been constructed. For myself, I locate the best examples of such a critical orientation in the work of Joseph M. Kitagawa and Charles H. Long, two historians of religion.

Notes

1   As for the concept of animism, Keiji Yuwata, an anthropologist of religion, is the most eloquent manipulator of the term. He uses the notion of animism uncritically to argue for the uniqueness of Japanese religion. Fetishism is widely used in disciplines such as psychology, philosophy, and economics in Japan but not so much in studies of religion. The notion of ancestor worship is much employed by folklorists such as Choshu Takeda.
2   There have been Japanese scholars, such as Kitaro Nishida and Keiji Nishitani, who have come to grips with the crisis of this modernist academic culture in Japan.
3   See Kitagawa (1991). For further examples of double and triple critiques, see Long (1989).

References

Araki, Michio, "Minzoku Shukyo toshite no Shinshukyo [New religions as folk religion]," in Nobutaka Inoue (ed.) *Kindaika to Rhukyo Bumu* [Modernization and the Religious Boom in Japan], Kyoto-shi: Dohosha, 1990, 19–67.
——, "Modern Japanese New Religions As Cultural and Historical Problem," *Chinese Journal of World Religions*, 1992, pp. 32–35.
Burridge, Kennelm, *Someone, No One: An Essay on Individuality*, Princeton: Princeton University Press, 1979.
Dumont, Louis, *Essays on Individualism: Modern Ideology in Anthropological Perspectives*, Chicago: University of Chicago Press, 1986.
Hori, Ichiro, *Folk Religion in Japan*, Chicago: University of Chicago Press, 1968.
Kishimoto, Hideo, *Shukyogaku* [The Study of Religion], Tokyo: Taimedo, 1961.
Kitagawa, Joseph M., "Preface," *Norito*, trans. Donald L. Philippi, Princeton: Princeton University Press, 1991.
Long, Charles H., *Significations: Signs, Symbols, and Images in the Interpretation of Religion*, New York: Free Press, 1989.
Shimazono, Susumu, *Shin-shinshukyo buumu* [New New Religions and the Religious Boom], Iwanami Booklet No. 237, Tokyo: Iwanami shoten, 1992, 23–62.
Yamaori, Tetsuo, "Aum Jiken to Nihon Shukyo no Shuen [The Aum incident and the end of Japanese religion]," *Shokun*, June 1995.

Chapter 16

Rethinking indigenous religious traditions

The case of the Ainu

Katarina V. Sjöberg

Introduction

This article discusses the religious tradition of the Hokkaido[1] Ainu, Japan's indigenous people. It focuses especially on transformation processes, including aspects regarding development and modernization. Research into the situation of the Ainu has been done with the focus on strategies of assimilating the Ainu. The standard position in Japan, when talking and writing about its culture, is that it is homogenous, despite the fact that there are actually a number of different ethnic groups in Japan. Disregarding the fact that Japan has recently recognized the Ainu as a religious and cultural minority, most literature dealing with the general issues concerning the Ainu way of life maintains the idea that the Ainu, as a group of people, has ceased to exist, implying that their religious tradition has disappeared.[2]

My argument in this article builds on the finding that the religious tradition of the Ainu is alive and well; the Ainu have never forgotten their religious beliefs and values. By this statement, I do not mean that I take an ahistoric static view. Rather, the perspective I have chosen implies an exploring of the religious beliefs and the practicing of them as a social process with various phases: some phases consist of periods when they are relatively stable; during other phases, they are elaborated and enriched; while during still others, they are subjected to retrogressions. The design of the different phases depends, of course, on the surrounding context, that is to say, the conditions the Ainu face during different time periods.

The material used in this chapter comes from my fieldwork among the Hokkaido Ainu, conducted during the years 1985–8, a follow-up study conducted in the year 1995, and archival, historical and more contemporary sources that have provided me with updates concerning the situation since my visits. The main methods used lie within the field of qualitative research techniques, including participant observation, interviews, and the collection of life histories.

Approach

Focusing on the heterogeneity that the Ainu face when interacting with the larger society, and the strategies they employ in coming to terms with new and alien values, allows for an understanding of the multiplex interplay between the Ainu and the dominant ethnic group in Japan, the Wajin.[4] As there are several actors in the arena, there are also several strategies in dialog and encounter with one another. Ainu contact with values and norms belonging to the dominant ethnic group in Japan has taken place over a long time span, and during intervals the Ainu have maneuvered in various ways and on different levels, from the grassroots up. By placing emphasis on a multifaceted reality and by incorporating the Ainu as active players, we are given a means to understand the religious tradition of the Ainu as a product/construction work, subject to the possibility of transformation. This is an enterprise embracing periods of active struggle for practicing religious rights and rules, as well as periods of a more passive behavior, and even periods when the Ainu were eager to forget their own religious beliefs in favor of the beliefs of the dominant ethnic group.[5] One main advantage of this approach is that it departs from a view of the Ainu as passive objects and their tradition as something belonging to the past.

The inherent dynamic of the values behind the religious tradition of the Ainu is exemplified by the fact that their religious ideologies continue to exist not only in memory but also in practice, as shown by the fact that the Ainu at the present time still celebrate different religious ceremonies. These ceremonies include:

1   *Iyomante*,[6] the bear ceremony, a distribution ceremony that includes the killing of a bear;
2   the *Shakushain* ceremony, celebrating the Ainu hero in the battle of *Shaushain* in 1669 and held in honor of Ainu ancestors; and
3   the *Marimo* ceremony, dedicated to a powerful lake god whom the Ainu used to fear because they believed that it fed on humans.

Such ceremonies were at one time considered by the authorities in Japan to be crude, uncivilized, or invented, and, among other things, when Hokkaido territory was annexed to Japan proper, that is to say Honshu, in 1868, the *Iyomante* ceremony was forbidden. Restrictions against this ceremony were not lifted until the late 1970s. Nevertheless, the Ainu never stopped practicing this religious ceremony. Regarding the *Marimo* ceremony, whereas originally it was performed on an individual basis, today it is transformed into a collective ceremony, resulting in the majority of people in Japan viewing this ceremony as an "invention," a view shared by some of the Ainu who, to use an Ainu metaphor, turn their back to this ceremony. Finally, the *Shakushain* ceremony is a ceremony increasing in popularity among the Ainu, resulting in the building of a *Shakushain* statue, a stone monument placed in the Shizunai area where he was born. However, the craftsman is not of Ainu origin, a fact that has caused some tension among the Ainu, who argue that this statue should be removed and replaced by one built by their own people (see Batchelor 1971; Cornell 1964; Sjöberg 1993).

Assuming that the values behind their ceremonies and the performances of them remain intact, aiming at some original understanding of both their "indigenous" status and the religious beliefs behind them, by trying to reconstruct the way they were undertaken during the dim days of the past, or by studying them during periods when they were restricted by prohibitions, is, in my opinion, not realistic. This is a statement equally valid for today's practices, occurring as they do in connection with the flourishing tourist industry. Without any doubt, the religious tradition of the Ainu has undergone transformations of various kinds, making it more suitable to the actual situation of the Ainu during different time periods. At the present time, we have a situation where Ainu religious activities are the focus of many Ainu who take an active part in the "revitalization" of them. This is an enterprise involving a field within which the Ainu debate the relationship of their religious tradition in relation to others' interpretation of it. Moreover, it also involves the building of specific Ainu knowledge centers. A main ambition of these centers is to provide information about variations in Ainu cultural and religious activities and practices. The act of initiating the revitalization of these cultural and religious activities shows that, in practice, there exists a synthesis between tradition and change, which is quite contrary to the assumption, often held by modernization theorists, that tradition and change stand in an antagonistic relationship (Sjöberg 1993).

Trying to explore the inherent meanings of concepts such as "indigenous" and "traditional" is indeed both a challenging and an intriguing task. It involves problems regarding how a contemporary native might interpret his/her "indigenous and traditional" self and also the material written about these issues: for example, whether indigenous peoples recognize themselves and their customs in the texts produced about them. In addition, there is another aspect involved, namely one of a more "selective nature": for example, what kind of – and how – indigenous ideologies and beliefs can be incorporated into the reality these peoples confront today, that is to say, what they choose to emphasize, and what they choose to neglect, their own presentations of these beliefs and ideologies.

No doubt it is true to say that there are many different ways of interpreting and understanding indigenous religious traditions. Many factors are involved, some of which relate to the beholder, including his/her background and, of course, his/her aims and goals. Considering the fact that, in one way or another, all types of interpretation, such as time-specific theoretical approaches and the views of antagonists as well as supporters, are modified to fit specific issues, there are bound to be certain ambiguities.

I hold the view that religious traditions do not disappear, they transform. The various transformation processes that occur are, of course, people's own work. People use various different strategies when adapting to new situations, and the Ainu are certainly no exception.

Negotiating the actual indigenous nature of the religious tradition of the Ainu

The material taken up here aims primarily to give a view of the debates and discussions occurring among scholars of different schools of various disciplines dealing with questions connected with the origins of the Ainu, focusing especially on the Ainu's relation and non-relation to the dominant ethnic group in Japan. Discussing and trying to grasp ideas behind such controversy is, in my view, highly relevant when exploring the religious tradition of the Ainu. This approach highlights issues concerning whose religious tradition actually is under investigation as well as the actual indigenous nature of the religious tradition of the Ainu.

The problems connected with the origins of the Ainu are considerable, and even though research into this issue has been a central part of the studies of the Ainu in general, their origins remain unknown.[7] The problem of Ainu identity can be studied in several different ways, and one approach, largely employed by early scholars, is to solve the problem from the standpoint of the relationship of the Ainu to the aboriginal population of Japan. According to the reports of some of these scholars, the original inhabitants of Japan were not the Ainu but an ancient group known in Ainu legend as the Koropok-un-guru, and it is believed that this population expanded to its greatest number about 3000 BCE.[8] A rival view claims that the close resemblance between Japan's neolithic population and the Ainu must be seen as evidence that the Ainu were the aboriginal settlers of Japan. These views were challenged by a third theory, putting forth an argument that builds on the idea that the aborigines of Japan were the population from which both recent Ainu and the historic Japanese population were derived. According to this view, the Ainu were the result of a mixture of the aboriginal Japanese population, of unknown origin, and the people who later migrated to the islands from the north-eastern parts of Siberia. This view was also challenged, this time by a theory building on the idea that the ancestors of the Ainu came to Hokkaido from the north, whereas the ancestors of the historic Japanese population came from the south of China to the Japanese island of Kyushu and then moved north to Honshu (Levin 1958: 261ff.; Kodama 1970: 263; Peng and Geiser 1977; Ohnuki-Tierney 1981: 204ff.). None of these theories has won over the others (Munro 1911, 1962; Kodama 1970).

According to anthropologist Kodama (1970), researchers dealing with the identity of the Ainu represent five different theories. These are the Mongoloid theory, the Caucasoid theory, the Oceanic Race theory, the Palaeo-Asiatic Tribe theory, and the Rasseninsel theory. The Mongoloid, Caucasoid, and Oceanic Race theories are based on conformities in material culture, customs, weapons, ornaments, utensils, and similarities in ritual and ceremonial performances, as well as on correlations in word arrangements. Since the above correlations and similarities are linked to different theories, one cannot claim superiority over the others. Researchers who support the Rasseninsel and Palaeo-Asiatic Tribe theories are of the opinion that the Ainu do not belong to any race now living. This is based on the fact that there is not yet convincing evidence as regards the craniological, somatological, and cultural material gathered in the studies of the Ainu and the *Jomon* age people, the people who lived in Japan in prehistoric times.[9]

Anthropologist Ohnuki-Tierney (1981) has made a further contribution to the study of the origins of the Ainu. She puts stress on the fact that "the Ainu culture is not monolithic but rich in intracultural variations representing Hokkaido Ainu, Sakhalin Ainu and Kurile Ainu, geographical locations not merely representing a mechanical division of the Ainu but, reflecting clearly distinguishable lifestyles" (21). This is both relevant and interesting since, by placing the focus on a comparison between neighboring Ainu groups rather than on a comparison between the Ainu and neighboring groups of different cultural traditions, Ainu as a "blanket term," to use Ohnuki-Tierney's own terminology, easily reduces the actual practicing of the various lifestyles of the Ainu over time to questions of adaptability to time-specific theoretical approaches of "the grand theory" type.

Apart from the fact that one gets an impression that previous researchers have been more concerned with falsifying each other's theories than with solving the problems of the origins of the Ainu, one also senses a notable emphasis on the differences between the Ainu and the majority ethnic group in Japan. This focus on the Ainu's differences to/non-relation with the dominant ethnic group in Japan is maintained throughout the historical texts produced in Japan.

According to Japan's historical records, the people who did not adopt mainland[10] rule soon became a minority, and their fate was either assimilation or escape. The fact that those who did adopt such rule – the Wajin – succeeded in oppressing those who did not – the Ainu – either by assimilation or by forcing them across the Tsugaru Strait to settle down in Hokkaido, may have influenced Japanese scholars of Wajin descent to present a dark and negative picture of the Ainu. In the historical texts, the Ainu are clearly distinguishable from people of Wajin descent. Attempts to differentiate the Ainu from the people belonging to the dominant ethnic group include various attempts to label them. Of these, the most notable one builds on phrenology, as shown in some of the early works in which the success of the dominant ethnic group is seen as related to "racial" superiority.[11]

Turning to historian Takakura (1960: 8), the reader is informed that the Ainu were in ancient times referred to as, among other names,[12] *Koshi* or *Yumasa*. The former name refers to the location of their territories, whereas the latter is a concept standing for the great fighting qualities of its bearers. However, according to Japan's ancient records, the territories of the Koshi were situated in a region called Izumo in the southern part of Honshu. Since the location of the Koshi people's territory in mythical times was in the southern part of Honshu, and not in the northern part where the Koshi region lay in historic times, we may assume that its location differs according to the kind of time we are dealing with – mythical or historical. This possibility Takakura labels "an interesting corruption." Suffice it to say in this context that studies dealing with questions concerning Ainu residence/territorial rights more or less coincide with the annexation of Hokkaido to Japan proper, contributing to an emphasis, by some scholars, on Ainu relations with the dominant ethnic group in Japan. Yet in most debates and discussions concerning this question, the emphasis is on non-relations. This may be due to the fact that if evidence was found that the Ainu and people of Wajin descent are identical, the Ainu, together with people of Wajin descent, must be recognized as the rightful owners of the land to which the latter claim the exclusive rights (Levin 1958; Kodama 1970; Peng and Geiser 1977).

It is interesting to note that the present Ainu[13] oppose the use of the name *Yumasa*. The present Ainu maintain the idea that they have always been a peace-loving people, resolving conflicts by using models of the consensus type; that is to say, they prefer to solve their conflicts with verbal means. Moreover, the Ainu also oppose the view that they were forced either to escape from Honshu or to assimilate. They prefer a "choice model," arguing that some of their people chose to stay and adapt to the mainland conditions, while others chose to abandon their territories in Honshu. The reason for leaving the Ainu relates to the fact that the conditions in Honshu grew continually worse. This, they argue, was due to such things as the escalation of feuds between feudal lords, *Daimyo*, making living in Honshu miserable for many, including commoners of those now referred to as people of Wajin descent – and among this latter category there were "a surprising number" who adopted an Ainu lifestyle (Takakura 1960).

Initially, intermarriage between the Ainu and people of Wajin descent was frequent, and the two groups of people shared and used the natural resources in Hokkaido in much the same way. Apart from hunting and fishing, their activities also included agriculture, horticulture, and trade with the people from Sakhalin and the island of Kurile, as well as from the mainland. The items that the Ainu traded with the mainland included fish, edible seaweed in large quantities, hawks, and a number of rarities such as bear liver, seal skin, and eagle feathers. These items came to serve as tributes to the imperial court. In return, the Ainu were offered things such as rice, sugar, sake, lacquer ornaments, and cotton cloth (Refsing 1980). Among the Ainu, lacquer ornaments and sake were perceived as highly prestigious goods. These items were, however, not entirely new to the Ainu; rather, they represented "improvements" on the Ainu manufactured counterparts, largely because the mainland lacquer ornaments were more shiny and their sake stronger. These things were essential to the Ainu when performing their religious ceremonies. In their opinion, the more shiny the lacquer ornaments and the stronger the sake, the more honorable the celebrations devoted to their ancestors and gods, which in turn attributed more prestige and higher rank to the leaders of the ceremonies in which such goods were included.[14]

However, the trading activities between the Ainu and people from the mainland developed into a situation not unlike the one in which the native peoples of North America found themselves (see Fagan 1984). It came to involve competition between not only the various *Daimyo* on the mainland but also between Ainu leaders, the *Ekashi*. People from the mainland who saw the power of the *Ekashi* as a threat soon began to barter with anyone to keep prices down and appointed trading partners of their own, giving them power over the distribution of the traded items. Yet their qualifications as powerful tradesmen did not correspond to Ainu demands, but rather to those of the mainland. Nevertheless, initially, the traded goods enriched the cultural and ceremonial life of both the Ainu and their trading partners.[15]

During the early days, there seems to have been little to hinder the Honshu people wishing to settle in Hokkaido. Yet, before long, immigration on a large scale resulted in conflicts between the immigrants and the natives. At the beginning, the former were defeated and driven out of the territories they occupied. Later, however, they turned to the mainland for support, which they received. The support was not sufficient, however, and, as a result, the conflicts went on for a considerable amount of time, until the middle of the sixteenth century, a time at which the authorities on the mainland changed their policy to one of reconciliation. With the reconciliation policy, the prelude to the annexation of Hokkaido to Japan proper began, comprising a period of more than four hundred years, from the sixteenth to the nineteenth century. Speaking in general terms, this period was as rich in positive consequences for people of Wajin descent as it was in negative consequences for the Ainu (and those of the former who had come to Hokkaido and adopted an Ainu lifestyle). For the latter, the period was to bring about a depletion of resources, a general reduction in the power of the *Ekashi*, a weakening of social and political bonds, and the introduction of diseases to which they had no immunity. In short, it meant a decline in terms of population and religious, cultural, and social values. During the period as a whole, the position of the people coming from the mainland, and maintaining a mainland lifestyle, was strengthened, whereas that of the Ainu was continually weakened (see Takakura 1960; Sjöberg 1993).

On the mainland, this period has been depicted as a time of unification, during which those hierarchical and ascriptive values already prevalent in the original mainland society became permanent and static.[16] Meanwhile, in Hokkaido, it was a time of disunity. Continuing depletion of resources caused by the construction of fishing industries, gold prospecting, and intensified hunting activities increased both rivalries between the *Ekashi* and rebellion against intruders from the mainland. As a result, the Ainu became more economically involved with the mainland system, and eventually they came under the control of the military administration in Honshu. This was a system encouraging attempts to transform the Ainu into a peasant community and that stood in direct contrast to the policy preceding it, the early Matsumae Han period (1514–1798), which favored a segregation policy. This rule in Hokkaido was followed by a period of colonization, a period that runs parallel to the Meiji era. With it came Japan's entry to the world market and the start of rapid modernization. Meiji officials were sent to Hokkaido to survey and map the island. During this period, the island was renamed; in previous times, the island had been referred to as Ezo, which was an Ainu name.[17] Apparently, the authorities in Japan thought an Ainu name inappropriate, especially since the island was now to be incorporated into the Japanese nation-state to be.

The takeover, or annexation, of Hokkaido by Japan, an enterprise that extended over a considerable period of time, left the Ainu in a situation of extreme poverty. The cause of this condition was interpreted differently. To the emperor (Utari Kyokai 1987: 7), the cause was the mainland exploitation and the innocence of the Ainu, whereas according to the interpretation of some Ainu, it had to do with "bad relations to their own gods." In their eyes, the gods had deserted them, and some Ainu relate this to the fact that their people had not fulfilled their obligations towards their gods and ancestors. Since, as it turned out, their own disgrace and the favorable situation of the people from the mainland extended over a long period, some of their people thought that the gods of the latter must be more powerful than those who they themselves worshipped. Hence some Ainu devoted much time and effort to being assimilated, whereas some tried to incorporate their own beliefs and values with the mainstream; still others were determined to keep their own values and ideologies "intact."

Against this background, which highlights the controversy that surrounds the nature of the origins of the Ainu and also the intermingling of the Ainu with people of Wajin or other descent, the actual indigenous status of the religious tradition of the Ainu is indeed difficult to establish, let alone who constructs and transforms it. Suffice it to say in this context that the religious tradition underwent changes, of both a regressive and an enriching nature.

The Ainu way of negotiating their religious tradition in the present time

When accounting for the way the Ainu cultural and religious activities are constructed, my argument builds on the idea that this can best be understood if we consider that the potentials of their beliefs and values have been underestimated for centuries, and that to the majority people in Japan, the "Ainu" concept is something unknown. During my stay in Hokkaido in 1988, there were people who thought that "Ainu" was some kind of food, or even a computer (Sjöberg 1993).

Bearing in mind that the recognition of the Ainu as a cultural and religious minority is a fairly recent phenomenon, it is necessary to consider and take into account that their practicing and presentation of their religious values and beliefs intimately relate to issues concerning attempts to rid themselves of the stigma regarding their status as neolithic remnants and the idea that their religious tradition is but an "uncivilized" variation of the one belonging to people of Wajin descent. Hence, today, one main ingredient in the practicing and presentation of their religious tradition concerns factors connected with the judgment of the majority ethnic group. In short, the Ainu are, in a way, trying to establish a recognition of the status of their entire cultural tradition as equal to the one belonging to people of Wajin descent.

According to the anthropological literature, "traditional" Ainu refers to the general category of hunters and gatherers who lived in egalitarian societies with an extensive division of labor both within and between communities (Takakura 1960; Munro 1962; Kodama 1970; Watanabe 1972). In my work (Sjöberg 1993), I discuss the possibility that the "traditional" Ainu were at one time a hierarchical society with a mixed economy and that their status as hunter/gatherers may well be a product of the long and painful integration of Hokkaido into the Meiji state.[18] My argument builds on:

1   material related to the interplay that occurred between the Ainu and people of Wajin and other descent who settled in Hokkaido in the early days;

2   accounts concerning the success of the Ainu in defeating people of Wajin descent
    when the number of the latter increased, causing competition with respect to territo-
    rial rights and how to use them; and
3   material related to the trading relations between the Ainu and the people from the
    mainland.

However, turning to the studies of the "traditional" Ainu lifestyle, one senses a tendency,
among researchers dealing with descriptions/interpretations of the religious tradition of
the Ainu, to focus on elements of a regressive nature, making these permanent. In these
works there is a concentration on presentations of their religious beliefs and values in ahistoric static terms,[19] some of which pigeonhole the whole life of the Ainu according to
subject headings such as "Ainu descent group," "The supernatural world of the Ainu,"
and the like, making no sense at all to the Ainu of today.

During my fieldwork among the Ainu, issues of incompatibility between their own
interpretations of themselves and the picture emerging from the texts produced about
them were a recurring topic of debate. Many Ainu are unwilling to accept "scientific"
interpretations of their religious tradition and take an active part in the critical analysis of
foreign as well as Wajin writings about them.

Against this background, it is necessary to place our point of departure in an area of
research allowing us to explore a field within which the Ainu continually debate the relationship of their religious tradition with reference to others' interpretation of it. During
my stay among the Ainu in 1986, I asked a prominent Ainu leader, who is well read in the
literature written about his people, to explain the essence of Ainu religious belief, and he
expressed himself in the following words:

> When you enter a *Chise* [an Ainu-style house], you find sacred things, placed where
> you expect them to be placed. Everything is familiar to you, because of the informa-
> tion you have received through books or other sources. Now you think you know
> their story. This makes you think you understand them and the context they are in.
> This, in turn, makes you very pleased. You found and understood what was
> expected. True, you understand more than people with no interest in those things,
> but you understand very little compared with us. Why is that, you ask. I will tell
> you. You are involved with theory, but you are not emotionally involved or tied to
> these things and you have no experience of how they work in practice. Therefore
> you see them as objects. As objects they have nothing living in them and they are
> what you call dead matter. To us they are both dead and alive. Let me explain. They
> live lives of their own. They live because they are in their proper surrounding. Only
> in this surrounding can they live. When new or other objects take the place of the
> former, they are placed in harmony with the former. The objects and their order are
> one and the same thing to us. There is nothing if they do not come together.
> Therefore they are both dead and alive at the same time. Alive because they have
> something to tell us who understand to interpret it properly and dead to those who
> do not understand what is delivered. The message they hide from you, we can see
> clearly. Therefore the message they tell you is very different from the message they
> tell us.

(Sjöberg 1993: 56)

From the above, it becomes clear that the Ainu position is that an emotional engagement is an absolute necessity for a proper understanding of their religious tradition. In
other words, their position is that in order to be able to grasp the values and beliefs
behind their religious tradition, one has to be born Ainu, or raised among the Ainu since
childhood. This gives the Ainu the role of purveyors of the "true" view. By virtue of being
Ainu, they are the true experts.

Having stated in the introduction to this article that the religious tradition of the Ainu
is alive and well, questions of how the Ainu themselves interpret their religious tradition
will be the focus of my further discussion concerning recent Ainu practices. Naturally, not
the entire population of Ainu descent takes an interest in their religious inheritance, and
my focus is, of course, not on people belonging to this category. My focus is on those
Ainu who place a strong emphasis on themselves as a distinct cultural and religious group.
Speaking in general terms, we may among the Ainu today discern at least two major identification strategies. One is used by those Ainu who place a strong emphasis on their
cultural and religious heritage, while the other is used by those who de-emphasize their
Ainu origins, preferring instead to point out similarities between themselves and people of
Wajin descent. This latter group makes use of their national identity, Japanese, or
Nihonjin, in a national context, whereas in a regional and local context they identify themselves as Japanese of Ainu descent. These people employ what we might term "double
identities," used in a hierarchical sense, to be found among Ainu who seek their living in
the rural sector, or in other sectors connected with the various industries in the big cities.
The Ainu belonging to the former group identify themselves as Ainu in a national context,
whereas in a regional and local context they use the Ainu term "*un-guru*," a concept
expressing a sense of belonging, to distinguish themselves as Ainu people from different
settlements – for example, *Nibutani un-guru*, *Shiraoi un-guru*, that is to say, people
belonging to such-and-such a settlement, or *kotan*. Ainu belonging to this group can be
said to use their identity for "clarification" purposes, implying a strictly horizontal use of
the identity concept. Ainu who maneuver in this way are occupationally engaged in
various Ainu activities and are to be found both in the countryside and in the big cities
(Sjöberg 1993: 45ff.).

Hence, in order to realize their aims in a society dominated by the majority ethnic
group, the Ainu exploit their specificity in various ways in the integration situation. On
the one hand, they make use of a strategy emphasizing the basic elements in their own
definition of their cultural and religious tradition, recognizing themselves as Ainu in all
contexts and situations. On the other hand, their strategy is characterized by a situation
where the authorities in Japan as well as the Ainu themselves recognize their national
identity, but where the majority people stress non-Wajin elements, or else pretend to be
unaware of their existence – that is to say, people who think of the Ainu concept as some
kind of food etc.

Although many of the Ainu activities related to their material culture, customs, and
religion include purely commercial aspects and have a low profile outside the tourist
seasons, the Ainu engaged in them claim that their commitment is social, cultural, and
religious. In their view, Ainu tourist villages, such as Shiraoi, Akan, and Nibutani in the
Iburi, Kushiro, and Hidaka regions respectively, represent centers or market places where
not only material needs are fulfilled but also, and mainly, social, cultural, and religious
ones. These centers are therefore looked upon, at least in the eyes of the Ainu and in their
present guise, as based on shared feelings of mutual understanding and friendship. In

short, they emanate from a conscious sense of belonging, consolidated by membership in a common tradition, and they function as a kind of public sphere for the Ainu. These tourist centers have become places where Ainu, by putting themselves and their activities on show, can express their group or collective identity, emphasizing the distinctive content of their cultural and religious heritage for the tourists and the larger public, who are invited not only to buy Ainu-made products, but also to see how they are made, and even to experiment in making them themselves. They can also learn about Ainu mythology, ritual, and history, taste Ainu food, and live in Ainu homes. Moreover, the Ainu make great efforts to inform the tourists of important Ainu happenings, gatherings, and meetings, including the organization of field trips of different types involving, for example, camping arrangements where the public can take part in Ainu gatherings, and field trips where the public is invited to areas that used to be powerful Ainu settlements. During these events, the participants are told about former Ainu place names, the ways in which they have been corrupted, and how this has led to the loss of essential knowledge about characteristics of the places. Ainu place names give information not only about the general topography but also about other characteristics, such as the place where benevolent gods live, the river with an abundance of trout, the place where people may hunt but not settle down, and so forth. With the hope of replacing the standard picture of the "traditional" Ainu way of life with a picture of diversity, the participants are also informed about local and regional variants of Ainu language, customs, and religious beliefs. This way of seeking recognition should, in my opinion, not be confused with folklore. Folklore is more concerned with making permanent those aspects of the specific cultural nature of certain values that belong in the past, whereas the activities of the Ainu are concerned with debating, discussing, and exploring the inherent dynamic of the values behind their religious tradition, making them fit the present context. The need to make their existence clear, to put a "face" on their values and beliefs, something akin to presenting a "Mr. Ainu," has become a main ingredient of this enterprise. This is an undertaking primarily linked to the understanding of the course of history preferred by the dominant ethnic group. A common feature of this is an attempt to present the Yamato people, the ancestors of the majority ethnic group, as the conquerors and heroes, and all other peoples as having been either assimilated or driven away (*ibid.*).

To adopt a position from which present Ainu activities are seen as folklore, that is to say, a mere display of their values and beliefs for tourists, is, in my view, a serious misinterpretation by those who fail to see the relationship between these beliefs and their practice. When it comes to the commercialization of their beliefs and traditions, this is something we cannot dismiss. Yet it should not overshadow the time people devote to educate themselves in Ainu matters. This involvement, as well as the skills acquired, must be ascribed its rightful value and viewed as a means to stimulate or activate religiously based practices and activities rather than as ways to support a living or to satisfy purely material needs. However, for people of Wajin descent, the commercial aspect of this display has come to overshadow the ideological content. Accordingly, substance has been de-emphasized, while the display for tourists and the larger public has become dominant. According to this view, museums, exhibition halls, and the like will remain the only possible forum for the survival of the religious traditions of the Ainu, resulting in a "neat" picture of an unproblematic fusion of assimilation and the maintenance of "traditional" values and ideologies.

In my opinion, the way the present Ainu practice their religious beliefs and ceremonies is not merely a question of the actual ceremonial performances and displays; rather, and to

234 Katarina V. Sjöberg

a much higher degree, it is a question of the act of building knowledge both of the proper way of performing these ceremonies and of the various preparation activities. Included here is the building of knowledge of the places and materials essential to the practice of these ceremonies. The initiative to building a knowledge of the religious tradition of the Ainu is largely the work of Mr. Shigeru Kayano, who is of Ainu origin. His interest in his own Ainu inheritance and his concern for and his work with the values and beliefs behind the religious beliefs of the Ainu have inspired many Ainu to follow his example. Today we find Ainu all over Hokkaido who are creating a manifold picture of the "traditional" religious ideologies of the Ainu. At the present time, Kayano is not only commonly accepted as a virtual authority on the religious beliefs of the Ainu; he is also the embodiment of the entire Ainu indigenous cultural tradition. This is an image created as much by his interest in and work with Ainu matters as by his frequent appearances on television and radio where he acts as an official representative of the Ainu people (*ibid.*).

This development can be seen and interpreted as an attempt to enter modernity, as defined by people belonging to the dominant ethnic group in particular, since in order to achieve recognition as a distinct cultural and religious group, the Ainu advertise their ceremonial activities to attract tourist attention and newspaper coverage. By this view, the Ainu are, in a way, creating themselves, experiencing their religious tradition as a part that has been lost, that is to say, something external to themselves, that they strive to regain (Friedman 1994). However, this is a somewhat simplistic interpretation, reducing the religious and cultural substance and content of Ainu activities and practices to a means of exploiting a commercial niche, missing a deeper or more nuanced exploration of the way the present Ainu build an understanding of their own religious and cultural beliefs. Moreover, this interpretation reveals more about the ideology of the state in Japan and its influence on research than about the beliefs and practices behind the religious tradition of the Ainu.

In accounting for the Ainu religious tradition and the changes that have occurred, research has, to a large extent, adopted the state ideology that ranks rather than analyzes, resulting in a view of the Ainu way of life as backward and static, and in conclusions which emphasize that such lifestyle factors are the ultimate cause of their present status as a group of individuals depending on social welfare for their survival. The authorities, in their understanding of the modeling of the religious and cultural activities of the Ainu, have made use of the low percentage (approximately 20 per cent)[20] of Ainu registering as Ainu, together with the high percentage (approximately 80 per cent)[21] of Ainu engaged in the rural sector, to support a view that confirms the success of the policy of assimilation. With this view, issues concerning the inherent dynamic of the religious beliefs and values of the Ainu are neglected – issues that are evident, however, when exploring the religious tradition of the Ainu as a process containing various different phases. There is reason to believe, however, that the former view has been constructed to suit national purposes, a context in which the Ainu belong to a nation that has grounded itself firmly in a territorial and social space inherited from the ancestors of the dominant ethnic group. It is a reality in which people of Ainu and Wajin descent jointly occupy the same national territory, on "equal" terms. Yet this does not correspond to the reality in which the Ainu live and operate; the fact that the Ainu "share" this same space with descendants from the majority ethnic group has not resulted in them being treated as equals. Discrimination against Ainu, manifested in the reluctance of the dominant ethnic group to marry and employ people of Ainu descent, is a common feature. If, officially, the Ainu are as any national citizen, then they are still lower in rank, and their "outcast" position functions as effectively as any ethnic stigmatization. For such reasons, the interests of the Ainu and national interests must be understood in terms of a contradiction. For the Ainu, the stress on cultural and religious factors is an indispensable means of unequivocally defining their own position in the context of the larger society. Witness, for example, the productions and displays for tourists in the public arena, where the production, teaching, learning, discussion, and debating of their cultural and religious heritage have become central processes in the Ainu way of relating to and building an understanding of their own position in the larger society.

Looking back one hundred years ago to when the land of the Ainu was annexed to Japan, the situation was different. At that time, Japan acted as if it was her right to forbid the Ainu to practice their religious tradition, to speak their own language, and to lead a lifestyle according to their beliefs; furthermore, at that time, many Ainu welcomed this development. The image that we, as well as the Ainu, have of their religious tradition, is, of course, the result of their specific history, the interpretation of which, to a considerable extent, is dependent on who the author is and how she/he interprets the reality of history. There is thus no natural continuum in the process of building an image of the Ainu religious tradition in the general sense, but rather a wide spectrum of possible constructs, due not only to the above but also to the fact that people learn from experience and reconsider their views.

Revisiting the Ainu: summer 1995

Having been given the opportunity to return to Hokkaido during the summer of 1995 to update my information, the final part of my discussion attempts to give a view of the most recent developments among the Ainu, focusing especially on the Nibutani Ainu. This focus on Nibutani relates to the fact that this village is the most densely populated of the Ainu villages, and is regarded as the core of Ainu cultural and religious activities in Hokkaido.

Negotiating identity

Returning to Nibutani, my fieldwork base, was an enterprise involving mixed feelings and a great many question marks. Upon arrival in Nibutani, my thoughts were occupied with issues concerning my previous contact and work with the Ainu, wondering if they were familiar with my findings and results. If this was the case, had they incorporated my ideas and thoughts into the general discussion dealing with the relationship of their own interpretation of their cultural and religious tradition with the interpretation of such matters by others?

In my previous writings, when discussing and trying to grasp the essence of the Ainu cultural and religious beliefs and their practice, my emphasis has been on "elements based upon shared feelings of mutual understanding emanating from a conscious sense of belonging and consolidated by a joint participation in a common tradition." My concerns this time, when given an opportunity to update my information, were similar. Interviewing Nibutani's Ainu inhabitants for information concerning these matters, my previous observations and writings seemed to live up to this view of their present situation. They confirmed my previous findings; people spoke with enthusiasm about Ainu networking, about associating with and learning from each other, and about their joint participation in various Ainu religious activities, such as the *Marimo* ceremony in Akan, an Ainu tourist village in the Kushiro area, and the *Iyomante* ceremony in Shiraoi, an Ainu tourist village in the Iburi area. When talking about the *Iyomante* ceremony, people gave voice to their uncertainties concerning opportunities for its continuation. They mentioned problems concerning the length of time and the effort involved in its preparation. The bear cub has to be kept in human custody until it reaches fertility, and thus looked after and fed by members of the "host family." They also mentioned the dangers involved in catching the bear cub and in killing the mature bear, or sending it away to its ancestors. Special emphasis was placed on problems concerning the proper ritual way of killing the animal, with its head placed between wooden logs, a method causing much pain and therefore not allowed by the authorities in Japan. Today's practice of this ceremony adheres to a pattern where the hosting of the bear alternates between the various Ainu tourist villages. The *Iyomante* ceremony performance in Nibutani dates back six years, but people seem to agree on one thing: that there will be no further *Iyomante* ceremonies held in Nibutani.

A powerful leader

Kayano had become a member of the Japanese parliament, the first Ainu ever, a position giving him a means not only to push Ainu matters and concerns more strongly, but also to put Nibutani Ainu in the limelight. Some critical voices emphasize the isolation of the Nibutani Ainu from the rest of the Ainu population in Japan. This may be traced to Kayano himself, who aims at directing the cause of development among the Nibutani Ainu with a firm grip and at preventing Ainu people coming from other Ainu areas to have their say in Ainu matters. As an example of this, people refer to a particular ceremony, initiated by an Ainu woman and gathering people from all over the world. According to the critics: "in Kayano's eyes, this is not an Ainu ceremony but something sprung from the mind of a confused Ainu female." The ceremony referred to is called the *Ichi Man Nen Sai* ceremony. It is a joint Ainu Wajin ceremony, stretching over a period of five days and dating back five years. When I asked Nibutani's Ainu population for some information on this ceremony, they were reluctant to speak. "It is difficult. We do not attend. Nobody does [in Nibutani, that is]. It is more like a hippie gathering. People are dirty. Don't ask me what they are celebrating. I could never figure it out. If you want to attend it is up to you. We cannot stop you."

The Ichi Man Nen Sai ceremony

The *Ichi Man Nen Sai* ceremony was being held during my stay so I decided to attend. It was a camping arrangement held in the bush, one hour's drive from Nibutani. The event gathered some three hundred people from all over the world. Very few Ainu attended, the majority of those present being people of Wajin descent, some of whom had a Rastafarian-like hairstyle and many of whom were dressed in Ainu-style garments and equipped with various Ainu utensils, swords, earrings, necklaces, bags, etc. When asked why they were dressed in Ainu-style garments, they answered: "The Ainu are the original inhabitants of the Japanese islands. They are our ancestors." When asked why they were attending, they answered: "We have come here to pay our respect to Nature. To show our appreciation we sing and dance." Singing and dancing were indeed dominant features of this festival. Some of the songs and dances were of Ainu origin, some had their origins in the cultural traditions of other groups of people, and some were mixtures of various different cultural traditions. Some of the songs were new compositions, such as the one featuring the Ainu ancestor *Shakushain*, which located his origin in Nibutani instead of in Shizunai, where it is located by most historians.

The dam-building project

It was obvious that development had not come to a standstill in Nibutani. The controversial dam-building project on the Saru river was nearly finished. How to stop or prevent this project was a constant topic of debate during my previous encounter with the Nibutani Ainu. At that time, the construction of a dam in this area was seen as a severe crime against nature. Not only would acres of Ainu land be flooded; it would also prevent the salmon from spawning – and the Ainu only catch the salmon after spawning. Salmon is considered Ainu staple food, and in the Ainu language it is called *Shiepe*, where *shi* stands for real, *e* for eating, and *pe* for things – real eating things. In the discussions with the authorities, it was understood that those people whose land would be covered with water would receive compensation in the form of a cash payment. But everybody seemed to agree: money cannot compensate for such damages. Today, however, the dam is nearly finished and in the end only two persons rejected the monetary compensation.[22] Initially, this knowledge made me wonder if the improvement in material living standards among the Ainu, such as the appearance of new cars and newly built houses, should be tied to the dam construction project rather than to a flourishing tourist industry (the two boarding houses in Nibutani were full). However, an interview with the owner of the boarding house (*minshoku*) at which I was staying,[23] and at which I have stayed during my previous visits, gave me a more nuanced picture. After the Ainu had received the money as compensation for the damages caused by the dam's construction, various financial institutes approached them offering loans to improve their situation further; many Ainu were attracted by these offers and many of the new cars and the newly built houses have been financed with such loans. Hence, the dam-building project has come to function as a means of giving these Ainu a favorable credit rating. Some Ainu have used this situation to improve their material living standards, buy cars, build homes, modernize the equipment in the tourist shops or the facilities for tourists at the *minshokus*, and so forth.

The Nibutani Ainu Cultural Museum

There was the two-year-old Nibutani Ainu Culture Museum, built with funding from the prefectural government and located on a hill overlooking the Saru river, with a cluster of Ainu-style houses, *Chise*, to one side, houses built of oak and linden pillars and with thatched roofs. The demand to establish an Ainu museum in Nibutani was also a topic much discussed during my previous visits. At that time, it was wishful thinking, due to both the costs involved and the fact that Nibutani already had one exhibition area, the *Shiryokan*, for the display of Ainu material culture. However, the items exhibited in the *Shiryokan* did not undergo scientific evaluation, and it did not acquire the status of a museum. Hence the necessity to build a proper museum.[24] A guide to the exhibition areas and general information on the museum are presented in the form of a leaflet, placed on the counter and handed to the paying visitors. The museum is divided into three exhibition areas, or sections, comprising:

1   an area exhibiting "traditional daily materials with the following major categories: child care, leisure, wood carving, clothing, meals and housing";

2   an area introducing "spiritual culture by presenting recorded prayers, beliefs, legends and stories. Specially selected *Yukara*, epics, *Kamuiyukara*, myths, and *Uepekere*, old tales, can be heard only in this museum"; and finally

3   an area introducing "materials related to farming, hunting, transportation and funerals."

To a person like myself, familiar with the people and the surrounding area, the museum gives an air of intimacy. The Ainu people appearing on the various video cassettes, documenting such things as the traditional Ainu wedding ceremony, how to build an Ainu-style house, children's games, the *Iyomante* ceremony, etc., are my friends and associates; I know their faces and voices, their pleasures and sorrows. The children playing by the Saru river are grown up now, and, knowing what became of them, watching the video cassettes gives me a feeling of peeping into the future. When I push the button on the tape recorder to listen to the *Yukara*, *Kamuiyukara*, and *Uuepekere*, I hear voices belonging to people I knew but who are now dead; and when listening to lectures in the Ainu language, *Itak*, I hear Kayano's voice, reminding me of both the Ainu language classes I participated in during my previous visits and a meeting with him after having listened to the tape. Furthermore, some of the exhibited items made by local craft men/women I have watched being manufactured. To me, this museum is a living museum, where the items on display function as a focal point for bringing to life the Ainu activities and practices of the past, even allowing glimpses into the future. But what about the Nibutani Ainu, what do they say to this presentation of their religion and culture? Well, for one thing, I heard some Nibutani Ainu complaining about the Ainu smell being absent. They told me: "It does not smell Ainu," meaning that they did not feel at home in the new museum, giving them a feeling of alienation. They continued:

> The style and form of the museum building is not an Ainu-style, it's not even Japanese. It is inspired by Western architects. In some big city this museum would be all right but not here in Nibutani, such a small village. We prefer the *Shiryokan*. It is more Ainu-style.

However, on the whole, the Nibutani Ainu were quite content with the presentation of their religion and material culture, and especially with the idea of placing photos of the local crafts men/women beside their products. When commenting on the video cassettes and other tape recordings, they reflected on using them in ways that reminded me of the way people in general use such equipment to document important happenings in their lives – they all had copies of their own, watching or listening to them occasionally.

The Ship *sanke* ceremony

By and large, my interviews and observations in Nibutani and the activities that were taking place there seemed to adhere to a familiar pattern. When I arrived, tourism was at its peak. My stay in Nibutani coincided with the holiday season in Japan. I saw Ainu people busy in their tourist shops manufacturing Ainu cultural items, giving information on Ainu activities, such as Ainu language classes[25] and lectures on how to manufacture

Ainu-style garments, how to sing Ainu songs, how to dance Ainu dances, etc., and field trips. Above all, people were giving information on the upcoming *Ship sanke* ceremony, which was to take place in Nibutani the following weekend (19–20 August). The *Ship sanke* ceremony is an annual ceremony held for the river god when launching canoes into the Saru river. I had attended this ceremony during my previous visits, at which time it had attracted Ainu people from all over Hokkaido. This time, however, was special; it was to be the very last time that the ceremony would be held in the Saru river. As a result of the dam-building project, the water level in the Saru river was set to rise to such a degree that carrying out the *Ship sanke* ceremony there would become a dangerous enterprise. Hence, this year, the ceremony would, I was told, be the largest ever and gather Ainu people not only from the Hokkaido area but also from Honshu. Various video, film and TV people were expected to turn up to document this important event. As it turned out, the ceremony gathered many people – a lot more than on any previous occasion – but Ainu people from other areas did not turn up. The people assembled were a mixed lot. There were people from the mass media; people representing various indigenous groups from all over the world; scientists and researchers belonging to different schools of various disciplines; tourists from all over Japan; and finally people who traveled around the world with the sole purpose of attending indigenous gatherings and paying indigenous peoples their respect and sympathy. Among this latter group, people coming from Honshu and other Japanese islands were in the majority, and the participants were dressed in Ainu-style clothes, wearing Ainu dresses, *attush*, and Ainu shoes made of bark. On their heads the women wore Ainu head garments and some of the men wore Ainu-style leggings. Their belongings they kept in Ainu-style gathering bags, *Saranip*. I recognized these people as belonging to a group I had met when attending the *Ichi Man Nen Sai* ceremony.

The ceremony began with people assembling in front of the *Shiryokan* to hear the welcoming speech by one of Kayano's sons, acting now as his father's secretary and expected to be his successor. In his speech, which was given in Japanese, Kayano Jr.'s emphasis was on the importance of the ceremony to the Ainu people, and the fact that this was the last time it was to be held on the Saru river. The speech ended with thanks being given to the people who had gathered to participate in the ceremony. Afterwards, people were invited to pay their respects to nature, an act including an Ainu-style invitation to and welcoming of spirits dwelling in nature to take part in the ceremonial performance, and consisting of the drinking of some drops of sake and the sprinkling of some of the liquor on a sacred stone monument. This event was followed by an invitation to participate in a gathering in an Ainu-style house, *Chise*, to watch Ainu leaders, *Ekashi*, performing ritual practices tied to the ceremony. The *Ekashi* were all dressed up in Ainu garments, and when they spoke they used the Ainu language. When listening, I noticed that some of the Ainu words had changed. For example, people were no longer using the term *Saru pet*,[26] but instead were referring to the river as *Shi shi ri muka*. (Recently, in connection with Kayano's plans to write an Ainu–Japanese dictionary, research into Ainu place names has intensified, and many new Ainu concepts, or rather old Ainu concepts, have come to replace those used previously.)

When this part of the ceremony was finished, the people assembled started to dance Ainu-style dances; those who were too old to dance stood back clapping their hands. Apart from the changes in Ainu terminology, in comparison to the ceremonies I had attended previously there were other differences. For example, one important ingredient of the ceremony used to be the building of new canoes, an enterprise involving the selecting and cutting of appropriate trees, the engaging of the most skilled Ainu wood carvers, and also the performing of different rituals tied to the various moments of the working process. This time, no new canoes were built; rather, those used the previous year were used again. Another important ingredient was also missing, the one involving all the participants pulling the canoes from the *Shiryokan* to the launching area on the Saru river, instilling the participants with feelings of responsibility and belonging. This time, big trucks equipped with hydraulic lifts took care of transportation to the Saru river. Furthermore, the whole idea of gathering in the *Chise* was also something new, at least to me. There may have been further changes, but on account of sudden and intense rain, many people refrained from attending the final part of the *Ship sanke* ceremony. The remaining participants numbered but some thirty individuals, consisting of Ainu *Ekashi*, responsible for carrying out the final ritual performance, some scientists, and, of course, the people from the mass media who were documenting the event. Four hours later, the NHK news program broadcast the event on television. When commenting on the developments, people expressed opinions concerning the relationship between the ritual content/substance and the ceremonial performance/display, pointing to the fact that the performance in a way had taken the upper hand, and in their opinion this development was not remarkable as such, considering the immense attraction that this ceremony, or any other Ainu ceremony for that matter, had for the larger public.

The Ainu Nibutani Forum

In 1993, the Ainu Nibutani Forum was held, which gathered indigenous peoples from all over the world to discuss and elaborate on the premises underpinning their present situation, and which resulted in the publication of a report entitled *Gathering in Ainu Moshir, The Land of the Ainu: Messages from Indigenous Peoples in the World* (Nibutani Forum Organizing Committee 1994).[27] This Forum has given Nibutani village a place on the world map. This is what I was told by a man coming from Australia, representing a group of indigenous people from his country. He said: "If you want to meet other indigenous people, or people interested in indigenous matters, you come here to Nibutani." The accuracy of his observation was easily confirmed: during my stay I met people from Siberia, New Zealand, Germany, England, America, Canada, Australia, to name but a few.

The main aims of the Ainu Nibutani Forum were, of course, to share and discuss problems concerning the exploitation of Hokkaido's natural resources, issues concerning the Ainu's status as a religious and cultural group, Ainu educational preferences, steps to be taken in connection with a flourishing tourist industry, and so forth. The initiative that was required to arrange the forum clearly indicates that the Nibutani Ainu wish to perform on an international basis, recognize similarities between their own situation and those of other indigenous groups, and seek a platform for future ideas and practices. Moreover, and most importantly, they reject the idea that issues of identity and belonging are matters of individual choice.

Conclusion

When exploring the indigenous religious tradition of the Ainu, I have chosen to emphasize issues concerning how the Ainu relate to and build an understanding of their position in society as a whole over time, focusing especially on the way the surrounding context has influenced the modeling of their cultural and religious heritage. This can be seen and interpreted as construction/transformation work. This work embodies considerations regarding Ainu negotiations of the actual "authentic" content of their cultural and religious heritage, as well as factors concerning how this is perceived by the majority ethnic group. Taken together, these components constitute a major part of the reasoning behind the Ainu's choice of strategy when defining themselves and their place in the larger society. Needless to say, the content and substance of their own definitions vary over time.

In the case of the Nibutani Ainu, and with reference to the *Ship sanke* ceremony, this has resulted in the development of a preference for hydraulic lifts over humans when transporting "ritual objects," and instead of manufacturing new canoes, the old ones are used again. Regarding the *Iyomante* ceremony, here the contemplation of various obstacles in the performance of this ceremony has resulted in a development whereby the Nibutani Ainu have condemned the survival of the ceremony to the museums, at least for a while. In addition, we have a development whereby joint participation in a common tradition has come to involve not only one's own group, but also indigenous groups from all over the world. This is exemplified by both the Nibutani Ainu Forum held in 1993 and the *Ichi Man Nen Sai* ceremony. Moreover, as the dam-construction project has shown, we can discern a development whereby the exploitation of natural resources works as a means of giving the Ainu a favorable credit rating, thus improving their economic situation and raising their capacity to consume. This has allowed them to invest in new cars and homes as well as in new equipment for manufacturing cultural items for the tourist shops, and to modernize housing facilities for the tourists and the performance of their ceremonies. Needless to say, the improvement in material living standards should not, of course, dwarf the fact that the dam-building project has also had severe negative consequences for the Ainu in this area.

In a way, the developments described above point to the fact that ceremonial performance/display for tourists has taken the upper hand. Yet such developments are not unidirectional. For example, there is an ongoing and lively debate concerning matters of "authentic Ainu origin and content." This is illustrated by the fact that the Ainu have begun to reconsider formerly accepted Ainu concepts, resulting in their plans to work with an Ainu–Japanese dictionary, and also in the expressed opinions that the newly built Ainu museum does not have an Ainu smell. Moreover, it can also be discerned in the Nibutani Ainu's reluctance to participate in the *Ichi Man Nen Sai* ceremony – or in the *Marimo* ceremony. The act of shifting or changing one's emphasis is neither a unidirectional process nor a random construction/transformation. In the case of the *Ichi Man Nen Sai* ceremony, the question of who/what directs/constructs these developments is highlighted. On the one hand, we have the initiator and her strong emphasis on factors binding together indigenous peoples and people who share the same values, resulting in the fact that this ceremony gathers people from all over the world. On the other hand, however, we have Kayano and his strong leadership, resulting in the Nibutani Ainu taking a stand against participation in this ceremony. The Nibutani Ainu appear to have resorted to questioning the ceremony's authentic content, giving the people who participate a "hippie" label. At the present time, we can conclude that the ceremony has, in fact, been going on for five years now and that there are no discernible signs of it ending. Hence, in this context, it functions to join together people of Wajin and Ainu descent, building on elements based on a common attitude to nature. These elements serve to create a feeling of joint participation in a common tradition, a tradition emphasizing "respect for nature"

– the Ainu tradition as they define it. However, for the Nibutani Ainu, the ceremony has come to play a quite different role, functioning to firmly define what is and what is not authentic in the Ainu cultural and religious heritage. In this context, it serves to create a common "authentic" basis of knowledge aiming at directing the practice and performance of the Ainu cultural and religious tradition.

In my view, these two directions are not contradictory; rather, they are complementary. Their different emphases, for example Ainu relation and non-relation, respectively, to the dominant group in Japan, can be seen as a focal point activating internal debates and discussions concerning the relationship of the Ainu religious tradition to others' interpretation of it. This, in turn, functions as a means to establish a continuity with certain aspects of their past. In this sense, it works to open up an opportunity for the Ainu to elaborate, in their practices, literature, and songs, on factors concerning interpretations of the actual authentic content of their cultural and religious heritage.

Notes

1 Also known as Ezo (Yeso).
2 See Kreiner (1993), Fitzhugh and Dubreuil (1999), volumes bringing together research material on the studies of the Ainu religious beliefs, language, history and material culture.
3 From the Magn. Bergvalls Stiftelse and the Scandinavian–Japan Sasakawa Foundation.
4 Wajin is an ethnic concept, whereas the concept of Japanese (*Nihonjin*) is a national concept, and this concept is linked to the ideology of the *Meiji* Restoration established in 1868, when Hokkaido was annexed to Japan. Hence, we have Japanese of Wajin descent and Japanese of Ainu descent, etc. (see, for example, Sjöberg 1993: 3).
5 See, for example, Refsing (1980), who writes: "In a way they [the Ainu] tried to become even more Japanese than the Japanese" (87).
6 According to most reports, the *Iyomante* ceremony is the most precious of all ritual performances practiced by the Ainu. It connects to the hunting activities of the men and it is included in the sacred realm. According to Batchelor, the *Iyomante* ceremony represents "the outward expression of the greatest racial religious act of worship of the Ainu brotherhood" (1932: 37). When the ceremony was "reintroduced," the performance of it took place in August, i.e. during the tourist season in Japan, rather than in February, the proper Ainu time for its performance (see Sjöberg 1993).
7 One theory currently in fashion is that the Ainu, as well as the Ryukyuans, the inhabitants of the Okinawan Islands, represent more or less direct descendants from the Neolithic people of the Jomon culture, the prehistoric culture of Japan (Arutiunov 1999)
8 J. Milne was the first to claim that the Koropok-un-guru was Japan's aboriginal population, and one of the theory's strongest supporters was a Japanese named Tsuboi (see Ohnuki-Tierney 1981: 204ff.). For further information, see Levin (1958: 261); Kodama (1970: 263ff.); and Peng and Geiser (1977: 8).
9 The Paleo-Asiatic Tribe theory concludes: "As the Ainu who lived since ancient times in the Asiatic continent do not belong to any other race of today, they must be called Paleo-Asiatic"; the Rasselinsel theory simply states: "The Ainu do not belong to any of the races in the world of today" (quoted in Kodama 1970: 265).
10 "Although all of Japan is insular, time, history and distance somehow ingrained in the Japanese mind the idea that Hokkaido was an 'island' as against the mainland of Japan [Honshu]" (Takakura 1960: 6).
11 For example, Kajima (1895) writes: "The hardy, tough, intelligent and industrious Japanese...have driven these primitive, kindly, simple-minded, stupid, slothful, dirty people [the Ainu] before them less probably by the sword than simply by superiority of race" (1).
12 Other names used to depict the Ainu are Koshi, Kai, Emishi, Ebizu, Yeso, Ezo, Toi (see Takakura 1960; Kindaichi 1960; Siddle 1995), and possibly also Kumaso, Sobito, and Hayato (see Takakura 1960).

13 Here I am referring to Ainu leaders and intellectuals.

14 Takakura, for example, writes: "However, it was but natural that the more powerful and wealthy of the [Ainu] chiefs...should extend their power...from which there arose chiefs of tremendous power among their people" (1960: 23).

15 It is often suggested that no trade existed between the Ainu and the people from the mainland as the relationship between the two cannot be classified as trade at all, but merely exploitation, since in the end the Ainu were deprived of the right to administer their natural resources and their way of life in accordance with their own beliefs and wishes (see Refsing 1980: 83).

16 A system referred to as the *shi-no-ko-sho*, where *shi* stands for the strata whose duties it were to protect the various fiefs against intrusion and whose position was second in rank to the *Daimyo*, and where *no* stands for the peasant group who served as the foundation of the economy and who looked to their superiors for protection in exchange for taxes rendered. Artisans *ko* and merchants *sho* were almost identical in their status and were bound to the fiefs for protection. Since these groups were not as economically essential as the peasant group for the maintenance of the system, its members were lower in rank (see, for example, Matsumoto 1960).

17 "Kindaichi (1962[*sic*]: 69–71) has argued that the word [Ezo] is, in fact, a corruption of Emishi, which, in turn, is a corruption of an indigenous self-designation" (quoted in Siddle 1995: 75).

18 "Meiji" as a concept stands for "enlightened government," established in 1868 when Hokkaido was annexed to Japan.

19 See, for example, Takakura (1960); Seligman (1962); Cornell (1964); Hilger (1967); Kodama (1970); Batchelor (1971); Watanabe (1972, 1975); Peng and Geiser (1977); Davis (1987); Kreiner (1993).

20 Hokkaido Registration Office, Sapporo, 1988.

21 Hokkaido Registration Office, Sapporo, 1988.

22 This is something that upsets Kayano, one of the two persons who rejected the monetary compensation. However, in my discussions with him, he also showed some empathy with the people who accepted the money: "They are poor people. They need the money."

23 This particular *minshoku* was now equipped with flush toilets, a TV set in each room, and a washing machine.

24 Today, the profile of the *Shiryokan* is somewhat changed; its aim now is to display various cultural items belonging to indigenous groups from all over the world.

25 From the Ainu contribution to the Nibutani Forum held in 1993, the reader gets an idea of the importance the Ainu place on the ability to express oneself in the native tongue. Note the following: "people's words and language are so important. Their native language is so important that a person will feel that he must die early so that the proper words can be spoken for his requiem...When a person is born on earth, who on earth would wish to die early? But my father and his friends wished to die early, because they wanted to have a proper Ainu requiem...That actually demonstrates how important the native language is for the particular group of people. This kind of feeling seems to be very difficult to be shared or understood by other people whose native language was never taken away" (Nibutani Forum Organizing Committee 1994: 23–4).

26 During my previous visits, the proper Ainu name for the river had been the subject of lively discussion and debate. Yet at that time, people seemed to have settled for the term *Saru pet*, where *pet* stands for river in the Ainu language. In Japanese, *pet* has been replaced by the term *betsu*, due to the fact that the Japanese can neither pronounce the word *pet* nor depict it in writing.

27 The various indigenous groups who presented reports were as follows: from the USA, Chippewa, Chemehuevi Abenaki, Tolova, Onondaga, Western Shoshoni; from Canada, Kwagiulth, Nisgaa, Mamalilikala, Namgis, Haida, Heiltsuk, N'akwaxdaw, Sansei, Mohawk, Cree; from the Philippines, Cordelliera; from Sweden, Saami; from Japan, Ainu; from Guatemala, Maya; the Republic of South Africa; and the Republic of Nicaragua.

References

Arutiunov, S.A., "Ainu origin theories" in W.W. Fitzhugh and C.O. Dubreuil (eds) *Ainu Spirit of a Northern People*, Washington DC: National Museum of Natural History Smithsonian Institution and University of Washington Press, 1999

Baba, Y., "Study of minority-majority relations: the Ainu and the Japanese in Hokkaido," *The Japanese Interpreter*, 1980, 60–92.

Batchelor, J., *The Ainu Bear Festival*, Sapporo: Transactions of the Asiatic Society of Japan, 1932.

——, *The Ainu Life and Lore*, New York: Johnson Reprint Corporation, 1971.

Cornell, J., "Ainu assimilation and cultural extinction," *Ethnology* 3, 1964, 287–304.

Davis, G., "Japan's indigenous Indians: the Ainu," *Tokyo Journal*, October 1987, 7–13, 18–19.

Fagan, B., *Clash of Cultures*, New York: E.F. Freeman & Co., 1984.

Fitzhugh, W.W. and Dubreuil, C.O. (eds) *Ainu Spirit of a Northern People*, Washington DC: National Museum of Natural History Smithsonian Institution and University of Washington Press, 1999

Friedman, J., *Cultural Identity and Global Process*, London: Sage, 1994.

Hilger, M., *Together with the Ainu: A Vanishing People*, Oklahoma: University of Oklahoma Press, 1967.

Kajima, S., *The Ainu of Japan: An Album of 22 Splendid Photographs of the the Ainu with Explanations*, Tokyo: Genrokukan Seisaburo, 1895.

Kindaichi, K., *Ainu Go Kenkyo* [The Study of Ainu Languages], Tokyo: Sanseido, 1960.

Kodama, S., *Ainu Historical and Anthropological Studies*, Sapporo: Hokudai University Press, 1970.

Kreiner, J., *European Studies on Ainu Language and Culture*, Muenchen: Iudicium-Verl, 1993.

Levin, M.G., "Ethnic origin of the people of north-eastern Asia," in H.N. Michael (ed.) *Arctic Institute of North America: Anthropology of the North 3*, Toronto: University Press of Toronto, 1958.

Matsumoto, Y.S., "The individuals and the group," *Transactions of the American Philosophical Society* 50, 1960, 1–75.

Milne, J., "Notes on the Koro-pok-guru or Pitdwellers of Yezo and the Kurile Islands," *Transactions of the Asiatic Society of Japan*, X, 1882.

Munro, N., *Prehistoric Japan*, Tokyo: Daiichi Shobo, 1911.

—— (ed.), *Ainu Creed and Cult*, edited with a preface and an additional chapter by B.Z. Seligman, London: Routledge & Kegan Paul, 1962.

Naert, P., *Aiona: En Bok om Ainu – Det Vita Folket I Fjärran Östern*, Stockholm: Natur och Kultur, 1960.

Nibutani Forum Organizing Committee, *Gathering in Ainu Moshir, The Land of the Ainu: Messages from Indigenous Peoples in the World*, Japan: Eikoh Educational and Cultural Institute/Yushisha Co. Ltd., 1994.

Ohnuki-Tierney, E., *Illness and Healing among the Sachalin Ainu: A Symbolic Interpretation*, Cambridge: Cambridge University Press, 1981.

Peng, F.C.C. and P. Geiser, *The Ainu: The Past in the Present*, Hiroshima: Bunka Hyoron Publishing Company, 1977.

Refsing, K., "The Ainu people of Japan," *IWGIA Newsletter* no. 24, 1980, 79–92.

Seligman, B.Z., "Social organization. Postscript," in N. Munro (ed.) *Ainu Creed and Cult*, Cambridge: Cambridge University Press, 1962, 141–58.

Siddle, R., "The Ainu: construction of an image," in John C. Maher and Graynor Macdonald (eds) *Diversity in Japanese Culture and Language*, London: Kegan Paul International, 1995, 73–94.

Sjöberg, K., *The Return of the Ainu*, London: Harwood Academic Publishers, 1993.

Sugiura, K. and H. Befu, "Kinship organization of the Saru Ainu," *Ethnology* 1(3), 1962, 287–301.

Takakura, S., "The Ainu of northern Japan," *Transactions of the American Philosophical Society* 50, 1960, 1–92.

Utari Kyokai, *Statement Submitted to the Fifth Session of the Working Group on Indigenous Population*, Sapporo: Utari Kyokai, 1987.

Watanabe, H., *The Ainu Ecosystem*, Tokyo: Tokyo University Press, 1972.

——, "Subsistence and ecology of northern food gatherers, with special references to the Ainu," in R.B. Lee and I. DeVore (eds) *Man the Hunter*, Chicago: Aldine de Gruyter, 1975, 69–77.

Chapter 17

Korean shamans and the definition of "religion"

A view from the grass roots[1]

Laurel Kendall

there are today and have been in the past relatively few languages into which one can translate the word "religion" – and particularly its plural, "religions" – outside Western civilization. One is tempted, indeed, to ask whether there is a closely equivalent concept in any culture that has not been influenced by the modern West.

(Wilfred Cantwell Smith 1978: 118–19)

Any term used to think broadly about the human condition across cultures will be flimsy and loosely fitting, perhaps even ill-fitting. It helps in our task as interpreters to see the arbitrariness of the categories, for recognition that the arbitrariness lays bare our own prejudgments.

(Lawrence Sullivan 1991: 31)

religion is a necessary thing. It gives strength to the poor and provides a place for them. This is where our shaman practices are weak. We have genuine miracles and inspiration but the educational level of the shamans is low.

("Auntie Chun," 1994)

This chapter injects the voice of a humble Korean woman into our discussion of religion and modernity. Auntie Chun speaks to us from within the Korean shaman world but articulates her singular opinions and experiences. As in Bruce Lincoln's exegesis of ethnographic texts from another part of the world (see Chapter 10 of the present volume), Auntie Chun's micro-narrative opens a window on the history of local encounters between indigenous and world religion. Auntie Chun is a destined shaman, currently employed as a maid-of-all-work in a public shaman shrine. She participates in a religious tradition that is realized in primarily oral traditions, interactions between shaman and client, and crisis-oriented ritual performance, a tradition that, following Karen Brown's apt characterization, may be understood not as a body of text and doctrine, but as a "changing stream of continuity."

Auntie Chun has struggled for years without attaining the full inspiration that would empower her to assume the shaman's role, receive her own clients, give divinations, and convey the authority of the spirits in major rituals. By working in the shrine, she serves the spirits (and observes successful shamans). Prior to this, Auntie Chun traveled other spiritual paths, and she has thought deeply about the things she learned on her journey. Auntie Chun, the destined shaman, is also a student of comparative religion. In this, she poses a challenge to me and my work.

In researching, writing, and lecturing about Korean shamans, I have often found it necessary to explain the ways in which shamanic practices do not conform to Western notions of "religion" but are very much a part of Korean religiosity. Korean shamans do not espouse a distinct doctrine, the "ism" of a purported "shamanism." Mediating between human and spirit, living and dead, they operate within a moral universe defined by essentially Confucian and Buddhist understandings and by historical contingencies that include encounters with Christianity. As technicians of the sacred, they receive their training through loosely structured apprenticeships and perform together in small teams on the basis of shifting alliances (Kendall 1985).

They are not accountable to an overarching ecclesiastical authority, and genuine inspiration and competence can be both ambiguous and subject to contestation (Choi 1987, 1990; Kendall 1996a). Clients seek shamans for instrumental ends as determined by personal crisis and need, and although some clients may enjoy long relationships with a particular shaman and her spirits, they do not generally see themselves as "shamanists" as distinct from "Buddhists" – the use of the term "Buddhist" being an expedient means in Korea of defining oneself as "non-Christian" for the benefit of survey and census.[2]

As an anthropologist working amid the pluralities of philosophy and sacred practice in East Asia, I read with a sense of the great "Aha!" Wilfred Cantwell Smith's (1978) explication of how the term "religion," as organized "church" and explicit "doctrine," was, along with so much of the rest of our intellectual baggage, a product of the Enlightenment, anchored in a specific historical and cultural milieu and with limited descriptive value beyond its reach. But if, as in many other places, the European construct of "religion" is a poor fit with Korean local practices (Smith 1978; Tambiah 1990), this alien notion and its obverse, "superstition," have intruded mightily upon Korean intellectual life and social policies, from "anti-superstition" campaigns to assertions of indigenous monotheism. If a "Buddhist" response to a census-taker's question does not always signify according to Western expectations, this periodic exercise of question and response underscores for the Korean census-taker and respondent that the notion that having a "religion" (or not) is an identifying attribute of self and citizenry. The researcher must ask: At what point do borrowed European constructs cease to be alien? For whom and to what consequence? As we shall see, "religion" is an operable concept for Auntie Chun.

Auntie Chun's story

Anyone who decides to become a Catholic can do so. The Catholics say that even people in Russia can receive baptism. When I was young, I thought that maybe I would become a nun...but you need your parents' permission, and without that, I couldn't do it. I continued to go to the Catholic church, but then I became less avid. You have to observe the sacraments and it's all very complicated. Next, I went to the Protestant church, the Methodists, I went there for a while but that was when I began to dream [probably the visionary dreams that foretell a shaman destiny].

I went into business. I was 90 per cent, a 100 per cent resolved that I wanted to live a quiet life, but it kept falling apart. Tens of times, I was at the point of accomplishing something and then things fell apart and fell apart again. I kept lighting incense and praying...and then, when I would go to see a *kut* [major shaman ritual] at some house, right then, the spirits would come...

I didn't want to have this [to become a shaman], I wanted to be rid of it. I entered a Buddhist temple to suppress it, sitting there beneath the Buddha in his beneficent aura [*kap'i*]...I sat and prayed for two years...I was a cook in a Buddhist temple for two years, but then it was just as before, so I came out of the temple and I've been here [in the shaman shrine] for two months...

In Buddhism the fame and glory [*myŏngye*] of human life are like rice powder, one must perceive the world as no more than a pit filled with rice cake...But the ancestors I have [the spirits who should assist in the shaman profession] are still practicing self-cultivation [*torŭl tangnŭnjosang*] so they haven't yet opened my mouth [to the inspired speech that enables one to perform as a shaman].

Me, I'm still a monk without a tonsure, my prayers don't work. I haven't yet suffered enough, I must suffer some more. I must endure it.

Auntie Chun is a *bricoleur* (Lévi-Strauss 1973: 16–36) who patches together both imagery and understandings that have been gathered, here and there, on her journey. While it is not unusual for shamans to have once been Christians or to have spent time in Buddhist temples, Auntie Chun's patchwork of imagery is unique among the accounts that I have gathered within the Korean shaman world. She describes her prolonged suffering as, simultaneously, a sort of Catholic penance, of which she has not yet done enough, and as a consequence of her familiar spirits' lack of Buddhist "self-cultivation," their failure to lead the lives of good Christians and Buddhists.[3] Here we might seize upon her idiosyncratic synthesis as further confirmation of the arbitrariness of bounded religious entities; Auntie Chun, like many other potential shamans, has crossed and recrossed the boundaries during her personal quest. But despite her own *bricolage*, the boundaries mark "real" entities for Auntie Chun, and she regards them with the eye of a comparativist.

Acknowledging that shamans have a greater capacity for the miraculous than do Christian ministers, she denigrates the shaman's gift as insufficient to her understanding of religion:

The thing we call belief [*sinang*] must be moralistic, universalistic, and virtuous, and shamanic practices [*musok*] have not yet been systematized in that way. This is because of the shamans' [social and intellectual] level; they haven't had much education. But as for miracles, more of these come to the shamans, more than in Buddhism, more than in Christianity...Some people are granted miracles and some are not, but religion is a necessary thing. It gives strength to the poor and provides a place for them. This is where our shaman practices are weak. We have genuine miracles and inspiration but the educational level of the shamans is low. They should be concerned with saving all living things, but they put too much emphasis on the spirits. I mean, it isn't right to give primacy to miracles. Of course there are miracles, there are always miracles, but I feel that the shamans don't yet have the educational level to guide believers on the right and proper path, even while they give them miracles and help. That's because there's nothing systematic to it [shamanic practices]. I firmly believe that if someone should arise from amongst our shaman society within Korea and educate all the shamans in a group, then all sentient beings could be guided. But we don't have any such system yet.

Auntie Chun craves doctrine, orthodoxy, structure, leadership. I find irony. Where the outsider anthropologist deems it inappropriate to reify a "Korean shamanism," Auntie Chun defines shamanic practices as insufficient to her understanding of "religion." Where I find agents of cultural production who mesh the shifting needs and circumstances of their clients to a broad but always reassuringly Korean religiosity, Auntie Chun sees a simple-minded instrumental appeal to the "miraculous" that fails to provide a suffering humanity with an inspirational and morally uplifting doctrine. Where I celebrate strong-minded women, untrammeled by the authority of a religious hierarchy, Auntie Chun sees this lack of organization and leadership as inhibiting the spiritual development of poorly educated shamans and their followers. She longs for a leader, a messiah, who would wed the miraculous powers of the shamans to a theology of salvation.

Where did Auntie Chun come by these ideas? Most probably, her encounters with Buddhist and particularly Christian clergy subjected her to well-articulated arguments intended to highlight the deficiencies of shaman practice, but I have no way of knowing this.[4] Suffice it to recognize that the concept of "religion" (chonggyo), and the value judgments implicit in the term, have taken on a life of their own in Korea, coloring the perceptions of a woman like Auntie Chun. She, in turn, forces me to pause in my own deconstructive housecleaning and listen to ideas that are abroad in the Korean shaman world lest, once again, the messy specificities of a people, a time, and a place be effaced by an over-arching theory.

"Religion" comes to Korea

"Religion" in Korea has a genealogy that is both global and local. Late traditional Korea was a "Confucian" society insofar as its key institutions and values were grounded in notions of morality and propriety derived from Confucian texts. Confucian texts were the core curriculum of the literate elite and the source of critical rites of kinship and passage (such as coming-of-age, marriage, funeral, and ancestor veneration rites), which were seen as both embodying and fostering the virtues attendant upon proper human relationships (Deuchler 1992). Scholars of East Asian thought are often reluctant to characterize "Confucianism" as a "religion" rather than a "philosophy."[5] The Confucian was not a member of a "church" so much as a participant in a pervasive moral order and larger civilization sustained (ideally) by propriety among people and by stable governments administered by virtuous officials.

It was a hegemonic vision, but its realization was never absolute. Although Confucian officials took issue with the practices of Buddhist monks and shamans, and attempted to control and circumscribe them, their own wives made offerings at monasteries and patronized shamans. On appropriate occasions, the Court itself patronized monks and shamans. Confucian officials criticized shamans as potential charlatans who robbed the people, and as women who sang and danced in public,[6] but the fundamental premise behind the practices of women and shamans – the existence of spirits – was not directly assaulted.

"Religion" (chonggyo) and "superstition" (misin; literally, "false belief") came to Korea in the late nineteenth century via Japan, where words had been feverishly coined to express in ideographs new social, political, and philosophical concepts contained in Western books, the new vocabulary of modernity that was assaulting East Asia. As in the post-Reformation English world that Keith Thomas (1971) describes, "superstition" would serve evermore as "religion"'s dark alter ego, the realm of unacceptable practices, of things irrational, invalid, and consequently harmful. But in a religious field where neither "church" nor "doctrine" establishes firm boundaries (save for Korean Christians), the question of what is "superstition," as distinct from acceptable "religious" practice or sentimental "custom," could be vociferously debated. In Korea, the argument persists into the present moment, where things once reviled as embarrassing "superstition" are increasingly revalued as the relics of "national culture" (Choi 1991; Kendall 1998; Kim 1994).

The perceived need to extirpate "superstition" was part and parcel of what modernity – as logic and ideology (Baudrillard 1987) – meant in East Asia. Effacing "superstition" was no less a priority for early Korean nationalists than it was for their Japanese colonizers, who had done the same thing at home (Robinson 1988; Hardacre 1989). In the colonial period (1910–45), shaman practices were discouraged by the strong arm of the colonial police (Ch'oe 1974). Ironically, this history of suppression by the Japanese is invoked today in revivalist public performances of shaman rituals to enhance their luster as national traditions, while aging shamans recall how, in a newly independent Korea, they were routinely harassed by the police. In the 1970s, in the name of "development" (*paltal*), the Park Chung-hee regime initiated "anti-superstition" (*misin t'ap'a*) campaigns that were reminiscent of earlier Japanese colonial efforts (*ibid.*).

Protestant Christianity came to Korea in the 1890s, bearing schools for Western education and hospitals, the institutional accoutrements of enlightenment. Because the missionaries were not of the same nation as the colonizers, the Christian community gave early nationalists a space in which to define themselves against both a failed tradition and the colonial presence that had supplanted it (Clark 1986: Chapter 2). Korea is Protestant Christianity's unique success story in Asia, and Christian concepts of religion have had a great bearing on how many Korean intellectuals view indigenous practice. The awesome absolute of conversion was dramatized in "fetish" burnings, described in missionary accounts as great bonfires of ancestral tablets, spirit placings, and shaman equipment (Gifford 1898: 115; Jones 1902: 51), "destroyed as were the books in Ephesus" (Gifford 1905: 149). A distinct religious identity, forsaking all others, was now a Korean possibility.

Boundaries, however, are negotiable. Written accounts and anecdotes suggest a subtle distinction between the new rationalist converts, whose Christianity absolutely denied the existence of spirits, and practitioners of popular religion, who embraced Christianity as a new, possibly more efficacious way of dealing with them.[7] For more than a century, Korean Christianity and shamanic practice have moved on their orbits as not-quite-parallel worlds, colliding periodically in competitive demonstrations of efficacy (Harvey 1979: 205–34; 1987; Sun n.d.).[8]

Religious identities were at play in the emergence of new social classes in early twentieth-century Korea. For Christian and non-Christian alike, disdain for "superstition" – embodied by shamans – was one means of naturalizing the superiority of a small urban middle class of first-generation professionals and entrepreneurs, disassociated from its rural origins and identified with "science," "progress," and "enlightenment" (Robinson 1988; Eckert 1991: Chapter 2). Similar developments have been noted worldwide where adherence to modernity and progress and contempt for superstition are mustered to justify class domination.[9]

Just as well-born collectors of popular folklore in seventeenth-century England fed a growing sense that the citizens of town and country inhabited different mental worlds (Thomas 1971: 666), the rise of modern folklore studies in early twentieth-century Korea was both a sign and a signification of the distinction between "modern" Korean urbanites and their "traditional" past. As elsewhere, folklore was about the politics of culture (Bauman 1989, cited in Bauman and Sawin 1990: 288), but early Korean folklorists were also fired by the nationalistic longings of a colonized people (Choi 1987; Janelli 1986; Robinson 1988).[10]

The folklorist, historian, and nationalist Ch'oe Namsôn linked contemporary shaman practices to myths of the culture hero Tan'gun, as recorded in ancient texts, and precipitated an intellectual tradition that regards "shamanism" as a unique spiritual force, an ancient monotheism, infusing the Korean people (Janelli 1986; Allen 1990; Walraven 1993).[11] The cultural nationalists moved "shamanism" from the jaws of "superstition" to the embrace of "religion" and "culture" within Korean intellectual discourse. By invoking the pedigree of Tan'gun, ancient shamanism was infused, retrospectively, with nationalist spirituality, a theme that has been taken up again with the revival in the 1970s of an interest in Korean folklore (Janelli 1986; Walraven 1993). The assumption that shamanic practices existed in a purer, truer form in ancient days facilitates their interpretation as "religion" and "culture," but at the cost of regarding their contemporary manifestations as a degraded form, overgrown with the dross of superstition. Auntie Chun is not alone in her judgment that ignorant female practitioners have limited the potential of Korean shamanic practice.[12] As Charles Long reminded us during the "Beyond 'Primitivism'" conference (held on 28–31 March 1996 at the University of California, Davis), when one accepts a vocabulary of domination, when one accepts being defined by its terms, then one accepts a definition of inferiority.

The consequences of historicization

The notion that "shamanism" was the ancient religion of the Korean people is now pervasive; even musicians at a *kut* will discuss the tradition's 5,000-year history. Sophisticated urban shamans, borrowing from the discourse of scholars, describe it as the foundation of Korean culture and art. Historicizing shamanic practices and presenting them as "culture" has had mixed results. At the beginning of the new millennium, public performances can be enjoyed by all Koreans, regardless of religion, so long as the spiritual content of these events is glossed as cultural entertainment.[13] While many shamans feel that the designation of some of their number as Human Cultural Treasures (*Ingan Munhwajae*) has elevated the stature of all who share this formerly despised profession (Kendall 1996a, 1996c), some see this veneration of traditional culture as officialdom's denial of the religious content of their work. One young shaman asked acerbically whether monks and ministers would ever be appointed as Human Cultural Treasures.

In the 1990s, several professional associations claimed to represent the political and cultural interests of shamans, often in direct competition with each other for both members and performance venues.[14] Association leaders, almost invariably men, describe themselves as providing a strong organization with an effective leadership that will champion the interests of the (almost exclusively female) Korean shaman world in the political arena, just as Christian and Buddhist associations – the latter organized in reaction to the formidable Christian presence (Buswell 1992: 143–4) – have effectively defended and advanced their members' interests. Organization is problematic precisely because the shaman world is such a bad fit with common-sense notions of organized "religion."[15] One organization defines the problem as larger than the lack of an ecclesiastical structure, asserting that an effective organization of shamans and their followers will require both monotheism and scriptures. To this end, the group's leaders would have the shamans all worship Tan'gun, the culture hero. The leaders themselves are writing the scriptures. This agenda is no more likely to revolutionize the shaman world than are the dreams of an ambitious young man, a former Christian married to a shaman, who wants to establish a theology school for shamans.

In sum, discourses about shamanic practices as a "religion," measured against other "religions," are being articulated both about and within the Korean shaman world, although usually not by the shamans themselves. Conversations with a great many shamans and shrine-keepers in the summer of 1994 led me to appreciate that they have also come to think of what they do as "religion," but not with Auntie Chun's appetite for comparative theology so much as from political expediency. Ever the potential victims of harassment, they increasingly see their victimization in terms of religious discrimination. If Christians are often the perpetrators of complaints against shamans, then shamans have come to see their own work as somehow equivalent to Christian worship. Shamans complain that Christians can ring church bells at all hours but "noise pollution" laws bring fines and the swift termination of a *kut*. Venerable shrines with long histories fall victim to urban renewal, while the designation of mountain land as "public parks" imposes restrictions on the building of new shrines and on access to mountain pilgrimage sites. Churches and Buddhist temples, the shamans assume, would not be so easily destroyed. Many shamans are aware of the public voice claimed by Christian and Buddhist associations and feel the need for similar advocacy. However, most are cynical with regard to the existing shaman associations, which they see as ineffectual and bothersome.[16]

Conclusion

While "religion" is an awkward concept in Korea, it seems to have stuck. Discourse about "religion" is articulated, here and there, within the Korean shaman world, in part from contact with and even temporary participation in the large and vocal Christian community, and in part from indigenous intellectual traditions that have constructed shamanic practices as a deep-rooted national tradition. At the very least, politics and recent history encourage shamans to define what they do as a "religion" among more powerful and potentially antagonistic "religions."

As with much of the other detritus of Western capitalist societies, we are doomed to re-encounter our discarded scholarly concepts where they have been set at play in new settings around the globe. I am not advocating a wholesale return to old categories grounded in even older certainties. I will never be comfortable writing about a "religion" called "Korean Shamanism" (although I may quietly applaud where shamans appeal discrimination on "religious" grounds). I do recognize that awkward attempts to describe Korean shamanic practices as a "religion" are justifiable responses to decades of persecution under the onus of "superstition." I have learned that it is important to trace the local genealogies of the seemingly familiar and commonsensical in order to appreciate what they become in local consciousness, and when and why (Comaroff 1985).

"Superstition," "culture," "religion" – the words are invested with different stakes for different players as they do battle in the contemporary Korean imagination. If the scholar's task is no longer to sort and categorize, then one faces the more daunting business of witnessing all of the inconsistencies, the shifts, the messiness when worlds collide.

Notes

1 The ethnographic "guts" of this chapter are the product of fieldwork in the Republic of Korea in the summer of 1994, supported by the American Museum of Natural History Belo-Tanenbaum Fund. Seong-ja Kim served as my research assistant with great skill and fortitude. Ann Wright-Parsons assisted in the preparation of this manuscript. Serenity Young gave an early draft a careful and very helpful reading.

2 In the 1970s, I heard both shamans and clients sometimes refer to what they did as "*misin*" (superstition), leaching the word of its prejudicial content for want of any better term (Kendall 1985: 28). By the 1990s, the scholar's term "*musok*" (shamanic practices) had gained wide acceptance within the shaman world.

3 The shamans I have worked with usually described the possessing spirits as having a particular force or power acquired in their past lives, often as shamans or destined shamans, but sometimes in personas identified with warriors or statesmen. Something close to Auntie Chun's characterization appears when the initiate, Chini, speaks for her dead sister who has "received the teaching of the Heavenly King" (Kendall 1996a); she has been working on self-cultivation in the great beyond.

4 Her remarks carry an echo of Christian theologian David Kwang-sun Suh's complaint: "The Shaman concept of Hananism (God) [*sic*] is ahistorical and amoral...There is almost a complete lack of a framework in Shamanism to understand Christology as such...There is no concept of divine incarnation, coming to this world for the salvation of the secular world" (Suh 1983: 49).

5 The Korean designation *kyo* (Chinese *jiao*), applied to Buddhism, Confucianism, Taoism, and even occasionally "shamanism" (*mugyo*), is perhaps best translated as "teaching." "Teaching" admits the possibility of syncretic belief, but has little to say about the practices through which beliefs are realized.

6 See Yi (1976) for the expressed complaints of officials. See Kendall (1985: 30–4) for a discussion of conflicts between officials and shamans as a folkloric motif.

7 Missionaries also noted the frequency with which potential converts came to them to be exorcised of "devils" (Allen 1908: 17; Gale 1898: 246; Gifford 1898: 112–17). Gifford writes of an 82-year-old shaman, "rescued after years of bondage," who accepted Christianity when prayers from the little church in her neighborhood rendered her stiff and mute as she attempted to invoke her spirits (Gifford 1905).

8 Christian exorcists, in competition with shamans, are a persistent theme in the Korean Christian experience and imagination. In his novellas, *Portrait of a Shaman* and *Ulhwa*, Kim Tongni describes the tragic struggle of a shaman mother and Christian son, each grimly determined to exorcise the other of alien spirits.

9 Keith Thomas describes how in England, by the seventeenth century, new intellectual developments had deepened the gulf between the educated urban classes and the "superstitious" lower strata of the rural population (Thomas 1971: 666). A similar split has come to exist in China, where, from the end of the last century, the traditions of the rural population have been "derided as backward and actively suppressed by China's modern political and intellectual elites, whose views on other matters range across the political spectrum from extremes of the Left and the Right" (Cohen 1991: 113). Both Argyrou (1993: 266), writing of Cyprus, and Kapferer (1983: 18, 29), writing of Sri Lanka, describe the middle class's identification with "science" or with more "rational" religious practices as a means of asserting and naturalizing class domination. In urban India, middle-class households adopt new "rationalized" devotional practices that disassociate them from rural "superstition" (Babb 1990). Writing of Nepal, Pigg (1996) notes how those villagers who identify with the "modern" sector, through jobs in teaching or with development projects, shun the "superstitious" practices of village shamans.

10 See also Linke (1990).

11 Ch'oe Namsŏn was not the first to describe Tan'gun as the progenitor of contemporary shamans. Boudewijn Walraven notes that the *Mudang naeryok* (History of the *Mudang*), dated to 1885, had already made this link while disparaging then contemporary shaman practices (Walraven 1993: 10).

12 In another context, I describe the gendered politics of this discussion, of men claiming to inscribe nationalistic meanings on the personalized stories that female shamans perform in their rituals (Kendall 1998).

13 Acceptance of shaman rituals as purely "cultural" events, although widespread, is not absolute. Christian Korean-American communities, whose members are often unaware of the respectability now accorded shaman rituals in Korea, have proven to be very vocal in their opposition when shaman teams are brought to the United States for cultural performances. Within Korea, performances staged on the campuses of Christian universities have also provoked heated debate.

14 By 1994, there were at least four such associations, and another was about to be announced. In the summer of 1994, I interviewed representatives of three of these associations, attended events sponsored by two of them, and asked member and non-member shamans about them.

15 These developments are not, however, the first attempt to organize shamans into a professional association. Boudewijn Walraven notes that at the turn of the last century, a short-lived organization of "Korean-Japanese *mudang*" made an opportunistic attempt to establish a "Church" of shamans, modeled after the role of the Shinto shrine maidens (*miko*) in Japan (Walraven 1993).

16 We even heard allegations that one of these associations used to extort protection money from its constituents in a gangster-like fashion.

References

Allen, Horace W., *Things Korean: A Collection of Sketches*, New York: Fleming H. Revell, 1908.

——, *Anecdotes Missionary and Diplomatic*, New York: Fleming H. Revell, 1990.

Argyrou, Vassos, "Under a spell: the strategic use of magic in Greek Cypriot society," *American Ethnologist* 20(2), 1993, 256–71.

Atkinson, Jane Monnig, "Religions in dialogue: the construction of an Indonesian minority religion," *American Ethnologist* 10(4), 1983, 684–96.

——, "Shamanisms today," *Annual Review of Anthropology* 21, 1992, 307–30.

Babb, Allan, "New media and religious change," *Items* 44(4), 1990, 72–6.

Balzer, Marjorie Mandelstam, "Dilemmas of the spirit: religion and atheism in the Yakut-Sakha Republic," in S. Ramet (ed.) *Religious Policy in the Soviet Union*, Cambridge: Cambridge University Press, 1993, 231–51.

Baudrillard, Jean, "Modernity," *Canadian Journal of Political and Social Theory* 11(3), 1987, 63–73.

Bauman, Richard, "Folklore," in E. Burnouw (ed.) *International Encyclopedia of Communications*, Oxford: Oxford University Press, 1989.

Bauman, Richard and Patricia Sawin, "The politics of participation in folklife festivals," in I. Karp and S. Lavine (eds) *Exhibiting Cultures: The Poetics and Politics of Museum Display*, Washington and London: Smithsonian Institution Press, 1990.

Berger, Peter L., *The Sacred Canopy: Elements of a Sociological Theory of Religion*, Garden City, NY: Doubleday, 1969.

Buswell, Robert E., *The Zen Monastic Experience*, Princeton: Princeton University Press, 1992.

Ch'oe Kil-sông [Kil Seong Choi], "Misin T'ap'ae taehanilgoch'al [A study on the destruction of superstition]," *Han'guk Minsokhak* [Korean Folklore] 7, 1974, 39–54.

Choi, Chungmoo, "The competence of Korean shamans as performers of folklore," unpublished Ph.D. thesis, University of Indiana, 1987.

——, "The artistry and ritual aesthetics of urban Korean shamans," *Journal of Ritual Studies* 3(2), 1990, 235–50.

——, "Nami, Ch'ae, and Oksun: superstar shamans in Korea," in Ruth-Inge Heinze (ed.) *Shamans of the 20th Century*, New York: Irvington Publishers Inc., 1991, 51–61.

Choi, In-Hak, "Non-academic factors in the development of Korean and Japanese folklore scholarship," paper presented to the Annual Meeting of the American Anthropological Association, Chicago, November 1987.

Clark, Donald N., *Christianity in Modern Korea*, Lanham and New York: University Press of America for the Asia Society, 1986.

Cohen, Myron L., "Being Chinese: the peripheralization of traditional identity," "The Living Tree: the Changing Meaning of Being Chinese Today," *Daedalus* 120(2) (special theme issue), 1991, 113–33.

Comaroff, Jean, *Body of Power, Spirit of Resistance: The Culture and History of a South African People*, Chicago: University of Chicago Press, 1985.

Deuchler, Martina, *The Confucian Transformation of Korea: A Study of Society and Ideology*, Cambridge, MA: Council on East Asian Studies, Harvard University, distr. Harvard University Press, 1992.

Eckert, Carter J., *Offspring of Empire: The Koch'ang Kims and the Colonial Origins of Korean Capitalism 1876–1945*, Seattle: University of Washington Press, 1991.

Gale, James S., *Korean Sketches*, New York: Fleming H. Revell, 1898.

Geertz, Clifford, *The Interpretation of Cultures: Selected Essays by Clifford Geertz*, New York: Basic Books, 1973.

Gifford, Daniel L., *Every-day Life in Korea: A Collection of Studies and Stories*, Chicago and New York: Fleming H. Revell, 1898.

——, "Rescued after years of bondage," *The Korea Methodist* 1(11), 1905, 148–9.

Hardacre, Helen, *Shinto and the State 1868–1988*, Princeton: Princeton University Press, 1989.

Harvey, Youngsook Kim, *Six Korean Women: The Socialization of Shamans*, St. Paul: West Publishing Co., 1979.

——, "Possession sickness and women shamans in Korea," in N. Falk and R. Gross (eds) *Unspoken Worlds: Women's Religious Lives in Non-Western Cultures*, New York: Harper & Row, 1980, 41–52.

——, "The Korean shaman and the deaconess: sisters in different guises," in L. Kendall and G. Dix (eds) *Religion and Ritual in Korean Society*, Korea Research Monograph 12, Berkeley: Center for Korean Studies, Institute of East Asian Studies, University of California, 1987, 149–70.

Janelli, Roger L., "The origins of Korean folklore scholarship," *Journal of American Folklore* 99(391), 1986, 24–49.

Jones, George Heber, "The spirit worship of the Koreans," *Transactions of the Korea Branch of the Royal Asiatic Society* 2, 1902, 37–58.

Kapferer, Bruce, *A Celebration of Demons: Exorcism and the Aesthetics of Healing in Sri Lanka*, Bloomington: Indiana University Press, 1983.

Kendall, Laurel, *Shamans, Housewives, and Other Restless Spirits: Women in Korean Ritual Life*, Honolulu: University of Hawaii Press, 1985.

——, "Initiating performance: the story of Chini, an apprentice Korean shaman," in C. Laderman and M. Roseman (eds) *The Performance of Healing*, New York: Routledge, 1996a, 17–58.

——, "Korean Shamans and the spirits of capitalism," *American Anthropologist* 98(3), 1996b, 1–16.

——, *Getting Married in Korea: Of Gender, Morality, and Modernity*, Berkeley: University of California Press, 1996c.

——, "Who speaks for Korean shamans when shamans speak of the nation," in D. Gladney (ed.) *Making Majorities: Constituting the Nation in Japan, Korea, China, Malaysia, Fiji, Turkey and the United States*, Stanford: Stanford University Press, 1998.

Kim, Kwang-ok, "Rituals of resistance: the manipulation of shamanism in contemporary Korea," in C.F. Keyes, L. Kendall and H. Hardacre (eds) *Asian Visions of Authority: Religion and the Modern Nation State in East and Southeast Asia*, Honolulu: University of Hawaii Press, 1994, 195–219.

Kim, Tuk-kwang, *Han'guk chonggyosa* [History of Korean Religion], Seoul: Haemunsa, 1963.

Kim, Yung-Chung (ed. and trans.), *Women of Korea: A History from Ancient Times to 1945*, Seoul: Ewha Woman's University Press, 1977.

Lee, Diana S. and Laurel Kendall, *An Initiation* Kut *for a Korean Shaman*, video, Honolulu: University of Hawaii Press, 1991.

Lee, Hyo-chae [Yi Hyojae], "Protestant missionary work and enlightenment of Korean women," *Korea Journal* 17(11), 1977, 33–50.

Lévi-Strauss, Claude, *The Savage Mind*, Chicago: University of Chicago Press, 1973.

Linke, U., "Folklore, anthropology, and the government of social life," *Comparative Studies of Society and History* 32(1), 1990, 117–48.

Pigg, Stacy Leigh, "The credible and the credulous: the question of 'villagers' beliefs' in Nepal," *Cultural Anthropology* 11(2), 1996, 160–201.

Robinson, Michael E., *Cultural Nationalism in Colonial Korea, 1920–1925*, Seattle: University of Washington Press, 1988.

Smith, Wilfred Cantwell, *The Meaning and End of Religion*, San Francisco: Harper & Row, 1978.

Suh, David Kwang-sun, *Theology, Ideology, and Culture*, Hong Kong: World Student Christian Federation, 1983.

Sullivan, Lawrence, "Dissonant human histories and the vulnerability of understanding," in S. Friesen (ed.) *Local Knowledge, Ancient Wisdom: Challenges in Contemporary Spirituality*, Honolulu: Institute of Culture and Communication, East–West Center, 1991, 26–33.

Sun, Soon-Hwa, "The work and power of Korean shamans and clergywomen," unpublished manuscript, n.d.

Tambiah, Stanley Jeyaraja, *Magic, Science, Religion, and the Scope of Rationality*, Cambridge: Cambridge University Press, 1990.

Thomas, Keith, *Religion and the Decline of Magic*, New York: Scribner, 1971.

Thomas, Nicholas and Caroline Humphrey, "Introduction," in N. Thomas and C. Humphrey (eds.) *Shamanism, History and the State*, Ann Arbor: University of Michigan Press, 1994.

Walraven, Boudewijn, "Our shamanistic past: the Korean government, shamans, and shamanism," *Copenhagen Papers in East and Southeast Asian Studies*, Seminar for Buddhist Studies Monograph 3, 1993, 5–25.

Yi Nung-hwa, *Chosôn musok ko* [Reflections on Korean Shamanism], modern Korean translation of the 1927 edition by Yi Chae-gon, Seoul: Paengnuk, 1976.

Chapter 18

Mandaya myth, memory, and the heroic religious tradition
Between Islam and Christianity

Aram A. Yengoyan

Poised between two prophets (Christian and Muslim), the Mandaya of south-east Mindanao have dealt selectively with matters of religious conversion and cultural hegemony as a means of maintaining a way of life, a portion of which has no counterpart in the world religions that they are encountering. Conversion to Christianity is understood primarily as a means of entering a dominant socio-linguistic group (Cebuano/Bisayan), thus opening new avenues of commercial activity and partial social acceptance. On the other hand, Islam, through its teachers, wandering missionaries, and traders, argues that all features of Mandaya religious action, structure, and thought exist within Islamic religious perspectives, which not only embrace local Mandaya beliefs but are also more powerful. Both world religions operate globally, yet they are limited in terms of the oratory, mnemonics, and genealogical depth that link Mandaya mythical and historical heroes and heroines, and which project the living past onto the present.

The context

Eastern Mindanao is occupied by a number of "tribal" groups who are markedly different from the Islamic populations of southern and central Mindanao, although close similarities with other non-Islamic groups in central and western Mindanao, such as the Bukidnon and the Subanun, do exist. One of the major groups of eastern Mindanao is the Mandaya, who occupy the foothills and mountain areas of eastern Davao province and Surigao del Sur. Interior settlements are generally located up to an elevation of 4,000 feet. In some cases, the Mandaya have moved beyond this elevation, though the effects of swiddening in this ecological zone are highly negative. The push higher into the interior is a result of the extensive nature of Mandaya slash-and-burn cultivation. Although early accounts indicate that the Mandaya were one of the most powerful warring groups in eastern Mindanao, with the decline and disappearance of the *bagani* (warrior) complex during the 1920s, the Mandaya today are scattered throughout their ancestral areas subsisting on rice, corn, and tuber cultivation, and, occasionally, the commercial production of abaca (hemp).

Like many other non-Christian, non-Islamic groups practicing upland rice swidden cultivation, the Mandaya have only recently become involved in a market economy. Abaca production in swiddens that are no longer useful for upland rice is now found scattered throughout the foothills, from the Mati-Tarragona area north to Cateel. Most of these small-scale abaca farms are still maintained by the Mandaya, but in certain localities Cebuano farmers have taken land from the upland Mandaya. The Visayans are also committed to a mixed farm system of rice, corn, and vegetables for household consumption, while abaca is planted as a cash crop.

Initial accounts of the Mandaya come from the Jesuit *cartas* of the 1850s to the 1880s. At this time, the Catholic Church and the Spanish colonial administration were moving southward in eastern Mindanao with the aim of establishing missions and military settlements to curtail the Moro expansion along this coast. With the coming of the Americans after 1900, the missions became municipalities. Today, the towns of Mati, Manay, Caraga, Baganga, Cateel, and Lingig are local coastal settlements. Most of these towns are populated by Mandaya and by Visayans, who had moved into south-east Mindanao by the early 1930s.

Religion and the pantheon of belief

Mandaya religious belief centers on an elaborate hierarchy of spirits (*anito*) and a group of female mediums (*ballyan*) whose general function is the interpretation of the supernatural for everyday life. Besides the various creation legends that have their source in the sky, the Mandaya belief system provides the rationale for human social action as well as dealing with counterfactual events which might or might not occur. Cole (1913: 175–80) notes seven types of spirits for the Mayo Bay district, while Garvan (1931: 190–2) lists various spirits and deities for the Agusan Manobo; however, in both cases, the religious organization among the two tribes is quite similar.

Spirits

Four major spirits exist among the Mandaya, though a number of minor ones are present but are seldom called upon in man's interaction with nature. These spirits are as follows:

Diwata

The *diwata* spirit dwells in the skies and on earth. Although Garvan (1931: 192) appears to attribute a quality of "being" to the *diwata*, the Mandaya *diwata* is divorced from any type of human attribute. The heavenly bound *diwata* is represented on earth by wooden images called *manaog*, which consist of a square pole about four feet tall with notches and elaborate carvings on the upper half. About a foot from the top, a piece of wood is tied horizontally to the vertical pole. This horizontal piece is also carved with notches and drawings, which resemble various animal eyes. Usually each dwelling has a *manaog* placed on the side where the sun is first viewed each morning. *Manaog* images were also reported in the Cateel area by Maxey in 1910, and recently by the writer in upper Caraga, Cateel, and among the Agusan Manobo; however, Cole (1913: 175) noted a complete absence of *manaog* images among the Mayo Bay Mandaya.

Although most *diwata* spirits are considered beneficial or at least helpful, to obtain the assistance of the *diwata* one must offer food and prayers to the *manaog*. Offerings, prayers, and dances are usually the function of a *ballyan*; however, in cases where a *ballyan* is unavailable, one may perform the offerings and prayers for himself or herself, though the possibility of failing to achieve one's needs or desires is greater. Because *diwata* spirits are everywhere at all times, one's behavior is continuously observed; thus, one is unable to escape from the offering of prayers and food to the *diwata* since to neglect such duties is to invite a future disaster.

The *diwata* is not a supreme being; the beliefs and behavior attributed to it tend to reinforce the value system. Sickness, disease, accidents, and other calamities are never related to mechanistic or natural causes; rather, such misfortune is personalized as being due to a lack of prayers, offerings, and obedience to the *diwata*. It is also claimed that since the *diwata* is the cause of misfortune, consequently one must fulfill the ideal behavioral norms to avoid being harmed.

Asuang

These spirits are usually considered malevolent, and are thought to inhabit the tops of tall trees and the bottoms of streams, dark places in which they are unable to be seen; however, they are always associated with the *bud-bud* (*balete*), or banyan, tree. When *asuang* spirits have afflicted one by entering the body, a *ballyan* must be called for curing purposes. Usually a chicken is sacrificed by piercing the animal's throat. Then the *ballyan* dances around the sick man's dwelling, recites her prayers, and squirts blood from the chicken in a manner similar to the way in which one uses a pair of hand bellows to ignite a fire. In other cases, a live chicken is offered to the *asuang*, and, if the patient recovers, the chicken is then released into the wilderness.

Since informants agree that *bud-bud* trees are permanent *asuang* dwellings, areas where such trees are found are completely avoided. If a *balete* tree must be cut for agricultural purposes, a Mandaya will travel to Lucatan, a Moro (Muslim) village on the northern shores of Mayo Bay, to ask a Moro to cut the tree, since the latter are not afraid to do so. An equivalent value of thirty pesos is paid to the Moro for this service. Also, the capping of teeth in gold leaf is a specialty of traveling Moro merchants. Gold teeth among the Mandaya is considered a sign of beauty. The capping of each tooth costs about twenty pesos. After the tree is cut, food – betel nut and occasionally a live chicken – is offered to the *asuang* spirit for three to five nights. Prayers are recited to the *asuang* as an inducement to accept the offerings. Each morning the amount of food left over from the previous night is checked to see whether the offerings have been accepted. If the offerings have been consumed, this indicates that the *asuang* has vacated the region, thus allowing the area to be cleared and cleaned.

Asuang spirits are quite similar to the Agusan Manobo's *bú-sau*, as described by Garvan: "an order of insatiable fiends, who, with some exceptions occupy themselves wantonly in the destruction of human kind" (1931: 191). Cole (1913: 177) lists the *bú-sau* as spirits found among the Mandaya of the northern Davao Gulf, whose function is to look after the welfare of the *bagani* warriors. Garvan does not attribute such a purpose to the Manobo *bú-sau* spirits.

The Mandaya term "*asuang*" is generically similar to the Hiligaynon "*aswang*" and the Bicol "*asuwang*"; however, in the latter two regions, "*aswang*" and "*asuwang*" imply the existence of witches, a phenomenon that is absent among the Mandaya. It should be noted that among the non-Christians of central Panay, western Bisayas, the *aswang* beliefs are quite similar to the *asuang* beliefs of the Mandaya. Lynch (1949: 401–27), citing Castaño, notes that *asuwang* beliefs in Bicol during the late sixteenth century were also limited to spirits, though presently "*asuwang*" implies witches. The attributing of witchcraft to the *asuang* among the lowland Christians may be a result of the replacement of aboriginal beliefs with western European Christianity, folk beliefs, and witchcraft during the era of Spanish missionizing.

Kalaloa Nang Umay

This category (the literal translation of which is winnowing basket of the rice) includes all spirits of the harvest to which offerings are made during the planting and harvesting season. The first fruits of each rice harvest are offered to spirits that dwell in the rice fields. Although tubers and cassava are the basic staples for 80 per cent of the population, there are no spirits or offerings to these products since prestige value in the consumption of root crops is absent. The planting and harvesting ceremonies only apply to rice, which is considered the primary dietary staple. For the ceremonies to occur during each agricultural cycle, the *ballyan* must be consulted as to the performance of the various prayers and dances. Each *ballyan* living within a former *bagani* domain is required to initiate the ceremonies. During both planting and harvesting ceremonies, the *ballyan* sows or harvests the first grains. If the ceremony is held during the planting season, the seeds are thrown into the wind after they have been ritually blessed by the reciting of the necessary prayers and proverbs. With the onset of the harvest season, similar practices are held with the *ballyan* harvesting the first grains and testing the milk content of each pod. If the milk appears in ample quantity, the *ballyan* predicts a good harvest after reciting her prayers. One *ballyan* stated that formerly the first grains harvested were burned and blessed by each *ballyan*. Afterwards, a portion of the burned *umay* (unhusked rice) was given to each man who had a *kaingin* (rice field) to be harvested. Each cultivator would sprinkle the burned, blessed *umay* on the rice fields before harvesting. This would ensure a good harvest.

Daday

Daday (spirits of the dead) appear when a person has recently deceased. Although such spirits are considered harmful, a person may effectively utilize precautionary practices to avoid misfortunes and other calamities. The location where a person became ill, the place at which he passed away, and his habitual dwelling grounds must be avoided for a certain period of time. The family and close relatives of the deceased usually observe a stricter adherence to such precautionary beliefs and behavior than non-kin or distant relatives. Causes of death are usually attributed to supernatural spirits such as the *diwata* or *asuang*. Thus, if a male suddenly dies of unseen causes, or if a falling tree crushes someone to death, the reasons for such a calamity are related to a person having neglected his offerings and prayers to the spirit world. If a child passes away, the causes are listed as the deceased child's parents' neglect of their prayers and offerings to the supernatural, since a child below the "age of reason" is considered unable to harm the spirit world. As stated earlier, mechanistic and natural causes for death are absent in the scheme of cause and effect.

When a male adult has died, the remaining household members call a *ballyan* to initiate the rituals for the dead and the necessary steps to be taken to avoid future calamities. In the death ceremony, a pig is ritually sacrificed by a *ballyan* who pierces the animal below the neck. While the pig is still tied to the altar, each attending relative and visitor sucks and drinks the blood from the wound. The pig is then removed from the altar, quartered and cubed by male attendants, and roasted in bamboo tubes. After each person has drunk the blood and consumed a portion of the pig, the spirits of the dead are said to have entered everyone. While the *ballyan* perform the dances, a few men carve a coffin from the trunk of a *narra* tree. The coffin is taken into the dwelling, and the deceased is placed in a prostrate position along with his bolo and other objects of art. A small *ipil-ipil* branch is set on fire, and the smoke is spread into the coffin by a *ballyan*. This results in the driving away of the *daday* from the deceased. Upon completion, the *ballyan* drops the burning branch from the window to the ground where the participants are located. Everyone watches the direction in which the smoke of the burning branch is moving, since it is believed that this will indicate where the next death is to occur. The coffin is lowered from the dwelling by abaca ropes to the ground, where the relatives carry it to an open grave near the dead man's dwelling. Before departing from the completed ritual, each individual wraps ashes from the fire used for the roasted pig in a banana leaf. Upon reaching the first stream or creek, each person then removes his own apparel and rubs the ashes over his body and washes himself. When approaching the household, everyone again removes their own clothing before entering the dwelling quarters. Later, all clothes are burned to destroy any remnants of the *daday*.

The members of the dead man's household are isolated for three to seven days from neighbors living within the *bagani* domain. At the end of the seventh day, the deceased's dwelling is burned, and the ashes along with his belongings are placed in the open grave and covered. The remaining family members wash themselves with ashes and burn their clothing. The new household head then either erects another dwelling on the opposite side of the *kaingin* or moves to a new area within the *bagani* domain.

The hierarchy of supernatural spirits, beliefs, and omens has been kept intact and reflects little outside influence. Since all happenings, either positive or negative, are personalized and related to spirits, events that bring benefits or harm to all inhabitants are difficult to explain within the realm of beliefs. Within the memory of my oldest consultants, no one could remember any disaster, illness, or plague that had affected all individuals; thus personal happenings and misfortunes are easily explained within the world-view. Yet in 1989, a rat infestation from western Davao and Cotabato affected rice harvests to the degree that the entire year's yield was nothing but straw. Such poor harvests and the resulting hardships have affected those who offer prayers to the *diwata* as well as those who do not, those who are poor as well as those who are well off, and the commoner as well as the *ballyan*. The occurrences are difficult to explain within the existing belief system, since individuals who have behaved in accordance with the prescribed religious dogma have also been negatively affected. Although the present belief system is adhered to, elements of doubt as to the validity of the *diwata* powers are found among those who perpetually neglect their prayers.

Ballyan

The interpretation and transmission of the spirit world to its followers are the primary responsibilities of the *ballyan*, a set of female mediums whose influence is paramount in all matters pertaining to the religious side of life as well as to maintaining the core of tribal customs and beliefs. Although their political influence is nil, their power to interpret the supernatural results of a *bagani* action, which may produce negative effects, is known to all.

Garvan (1931: 200–3) describes the Manobo *bailan* as a priest of either sex whose role is the interpretation of the *diwata*. However, the Mandaya *ballyan* is always a woman, since the duties of a *ballyan* involve behavior fit for a woman only. Furthermore, to describe a Mandaya *ballyan* as a priest is not justified in two respects: first, the role is not one of full-time participation with the supernatural; and secondly, a *ballyan* must support herself by working in her husband's rice fields. The lack of surplus food rules out the existence of any full-time non-economic specialization (with the exception of the *bagani*).

In contrast to the Manobo *ballyan*, who is not designated by distinctive apparel (*ibid*.: 202), the Mandaya *ballyan* is clad in a dark-red, maroon, and black abaca skirt and blouse. The skirt is wrapped around the torso once or twice and extends to the ankles. Blouses, also red with black designs, are long-sleeved. Charms, amulets, dried herbs, and medicinal leaves along with small brass or silver Chinese bells are hung around the neck and wrists with small silver chains.

As mediums, the *ballyan* act as mediators with the spirit world, though each practitioner is considered closer to certain spirits than to others. Thus, a particular *ballyan* is called according to different purposes and needs, since her powers for mediation with a particular spirit are stronger than her colleagues'. At times of planting, harvesting, birth, death, sickness, curing, calamities, etc., *ballyan* are requested to apply their powers for a smooth transformation through these periods of crisis. Dances and seances are held around a wooden altar onto which the sacrifice, either a pig or a chicken, is tied. Each *ballyan* holds a palm branch or palm flower section in both hands and waves them in all directions during the dance. The continuous waving of the palm branches symbolizes the attempt to ward off bad spirits during the ritual. Upon completion of the recitation, prayers, and chants, each woman goes into a trance, at which time they are claimed to be possessed by their personal spirit. The climax is reached when the *ballyan* group has collapsed to the ground and are calling for each spirit to assist them in the wishes of the gathering.

Out of twenty-seven *ballyan* in upper Manay, twenty-two had inherited their position from their mother, their mother's sister, or their father's sister. Though most *ballyan* have inherited their role by learning the practices, dances, and interpretations from a kinsman, one also obtains the *ballyan* status by ascription at birth, or through divine inheritance without previous aspirations or premonitions. Those ascribed at birth as *ballyan* know the rituals and lore enabling them to perform the dances and hold the position at an early age. Others can become *ballyan* at any period in their life cycle if they are struck by *tulanang*, a condition comprising violent physical trances and temporary mental disorders that overcome the individual for a few hours, a day, or a week. Physically, the state resembles an epileptic fit, though the convulsions are usually more violent and erratic. Cognitively, the individual talks and shouts in a disorganized, incoherent manner; however, throughout these vocal outbursts, the other *ballyan* note which spirit is possessing and manifesting itself in the individual. When these periods of convulsion end, the other *ballyan* teach the new *ballyan* the dances and rituals. After learning the rituals, the other *ballyan* consider her as the leading mediator of the spirit that had possessed her.

Thus the *ballyan* hierarchy consists of two groups: (i) natural *ballyan* by ascription; and (ii) *ballyan* by having acquired the status through learning the rituals. Within the first group, those who are *ballyan* at birth are ranked higher than those who gain the power later in life by the *tulanang*. Though each *ballyan*'s forte relates to a certain spirit, those belonging to the first category are considered to have the widest knowledge of and power with all the spirits.

Bagani

Although Garvan (*ibid*.: 203) describes the Manobo *bagani* as a priest of war and blood, whose main role is the sacrifice of captives in war, the Mandaya *bagani* appears not to have religious or supernatural functions and cannot be described as a warrior priest. Captives taken during warfare were sacrificed by the *bagani*; however, such behavior did not involve any supernatural phenomena or interpretation since the sacrifice was made to avenge the death of a cohort or to obtain the powers, courage, and ability of a brave opponent warrior, whose heart was removed and eaten by the *bagani* and his warriors (*maniklad*). Although a *bagani* might be assisted by certain spirits, the primary aim in taking captives was not to fulfill the dictums of his supernatural guides.

The tungud movement

From 1908 to 1910, a great revivalist movement (*tungud*) swept through the Manobo and the Mandaya of the Agusan River valley, from Esperanza to Mati. Although the movement was initially started and spread for religious reasons, it was later used to promote fraud and theft among the groups involved. Since Garvan (*ibid.*: 229–40) provides a detailed account of the religious revival, only the effect of the movement in upper Manay will be discussed. Among the Mayo Bay Mandaya, by the time the movement had reached the coast, the principal and initial tenets of the *tungud* had been replaced by attempts of the coastal Islamic population to arouse the Mandaya against the increasing number of Christians in that area (Cole 1913: 178–80).

The only mention of the *tungud* movement and its accompanying *maybabaya* spirit in upper Manay comes from the single case of Taganaka, who was a resident of upper Bato-Bato. The descendants of Taganaka claim the *diwata* told him that his salvation was only in the heavens, which for the Mandaya are composed of primary forests. The *diwata* told Taganaka to rid himself and his followers of all earthly belongings and journey to the west. Taganaka had his followers burn their homes, kill their pigs, and dispose of their rice. Everyone carried out his orders, but nothing happened, and eventually many died on their journey to the upper Agusan valley. Taganaka's descendants noted that these miracles occurred only in the early American period.

Although the *tungud* had little effect on the upper Manay Mandaya, other Pacific Coast branch groups were influenced to a greater degree. The native population of upper Cateel was involved in the movement probably more than any other group on the east coast, since transportation and access to the Agusan River valley from the headwaters of the Cateel River is not difficult. Most Mandaya who departed from the upper Cateel lost their belongings and were unable to return to their homes.

Oratory in myth and history

Oratory and the overall ability to use and control verbal art is a highly desired quality among the Mandaya. A good speaker not only has a fine sense for turning a phrase, using a metaphor, or stressing repetition, but also possesses the wisdom and experience for animating knowledge and thought in a meaningful way. This combination is rare among individuals. It is difficult (if not impossible) to learn, and it is even more difficult to transmit. Almost all of the warrior leaders (*bagani*) seem to have this ability, but it is clear that one need not be a *bagani* to be a great orator.

Given the changes that have occurred over the past thirty years, it is difficult to assess exactly how the system of oratory formerly worked. From the living memories of older people, however, we do have some idea of how it was structured. First, it appears that the vehicle of expression in oratory ranged from riddles and proverbs to the lengthy recitation of epic poetry (*dawot*), both in its classical and non-classical forms. Oratory also included a variety of oral traditions, such as ritual songs, folk songs, folktales, morality songs, certain kinds of love songs, and some puns. Within this range of genres, no single orator could master the complete inventory of all forms of oration, especially those regarded as classical. A characteristic feature of classical oratory, particularly when it related to obscure accounts, was that very few listeners could provide a precise translation. In many cases, the whole effect was based on sound and lyrical composition. The reaction of the audience was that of a mesmerized body.

A second feature of oratorical structure raises a question about the common "denominators," or themes, that embraced all these different forms of expression, and why some features were part of the oratorical tradition while others were not. In many of the more lengthy accounts, such as the Mandaya *tagadiwatanan* or the *gambong*, which are almost like epics or sagas, the sky is always the major point of reference. In attempting to understand which aspect of the oral tradition falls within oratory, the role of the sky as the source of meaning and action appears to be crucial. For the Mandaya, questions of morality, immorality and amorality, truthfulness and wrongdoing, and evil and goodness – all ethical issues – posited the sky as the initiator of action as well as the source from which the recited story or epic derived. In turn, the sky was also seen as being responsible for the way in which the orator interpreted the account to the audience. The function of oratory and erudition was not only to store and retrieve cultural information, but also to convey values to people who were earthbound. By contrast, puns, riddles, folk stories, and ritual songs took as their source other referents, such as the ground, the forest, a rice field, and occasionally the sea. Relatively few of these accounts could be included as part of the realm of oratory, and their absence in the corpus of oratorical forms indicates that the sky was primary and special in explaining the basic values and cultural codes the Mandaya used to promote and judge action and thought. It appears that stories, poetry, and epics, which had their existence in the sky, were given to humans as a form of revelation that was not to be debated, nor could it be understood in any physical expression. At best, these accounts were accepted as cultural givens. In one sense, oral traditions that use the sky as the only referent of existence are comparable to what in Greek tradition is referred to as "The Word." Most of these oral accounts, either in folk songs or lengthy epics, start with the phrase "*Long naan*" ("It is said").

Mandaya oratory was performed by both men and women; both sexes could achieve a high level of oratory. Men controlled political and military functions, but most of the religious life and ceremonial activities were limited to part-time specialists or practitioners (*ballyan*). Although most religious activities pertained to agricultural and medical matters, many female *ballyan* also had a well-developed sense of oratory. Oratory and high levels of erudition among the *ballyan* occurred frequently during trance-like states commonly linked to ritually charged activities. Yet there were times when women recited and interpreted epics in conjunction with men who were renowned as expert orators. Gatherings in which both sexes participated commonly occurred after the last rice harvest. These gatherings did not appear to be competitive in the sense that one orator would try to out-rival another. In most cases, the quality of one orator as compared with another was not measured by the general ability to recite a legend, but by the emphatic and creative manner in which the moral message was conveyed. This required the use of both informal and colloquial expression and of highly formalized speech.

Oratory is the primary means of stating and conveying what myth and religion are, how they are to be interpreted, and how morality and cultural truths are related to all human situations. Mandaya accounts of *magbabaya* (which is vaguely conceived of as a supreme being), or of *tagamaling* (the fairy spirit who promotes goodness in individuals), require recitation that will allow all members of society to realize what inspires individuals to strive for certain goals. At the same time, the question of wrongdoing is regarded as an enduring form of evil that must be controlled and conquered.

Knowledge promoted via oratory deals primarily with questions of human conduct – actions and thought – on the basis of an understanding of values and morals, in the context of how the individual relates to family, to kinsmen, and to others. Almost all knowledge contained in myths and epics and conveyed through oratory is based on what it means to be a social being and how each individual fits into the social fabric. How the individual and society are constituted is the vital message in Mandaya myth.

Oratory is not the only major expression of the Mandaya concept of humanity; another is mnemonic structure. However, knowledge transmitted through oratory is markedly more generally accessible than knowledge vested in mnemonic structure. In defining these differences, we might conclude that myth is regarded as a revelation, an account accepted at face value and pertaining only to human conduct and thought. Just as myth is something special, oratory is special as well. Even though only a few individuals have oratorical ability, the message of myth is not privatized. It represents a form of collective knowledge that all individuals must comprehend. Even in folktales, where the verbal art of raconteurs makes the message special and unique, it must have meaning for all individuals who consider themselves Mandaya.

If oratory is the expression of myth, where does history fit into the Mandaya cosmology? For the Mandaya, historical statements are events that sometimes have specific referents in the land and the ground, and more often in the forest and in the cultigens the Mandaya have planted. History is the form of events that have transpired. All of these events are recalled or can be recalled through memory.

Memory and history

Mandaya oratorical traditions have their source and existence in myth, which is the primary means for understanding how the individual and society are created and how values are shared. The realm of history deals primarily with what humans have done with their environment, how they have developed through particular cultural events, and how these events relate to one another through genealogy and recent time. Mnemonic devices are probably the most important ways in which time and history converge, while genealogy – either factual or imputed – links individuals and groups to one another.

Nearly all mnemonic devices are related to plants, either cultigens or wild plants, or to localities in which significant cultural events have taken place. Most cultigens, such as rice, other grains, and vegetables, have a growing period of a year or less. Since these crops are planted annually in new swiddens, they are not used as memory devices. Cultigens that last for many years, however, such as fruit trees (durian, mango, banana, *atis*), are used as a primary means of tracking the sequential events attendant to the movement of families from one settlement to another. Each bearing fruit tree still gives the original planter a residual right over the swidden in which it was planted, even many years after the swidden has been abandoned.

Tree growth, especially of those trees that are feared, is another memory device. In this regard, the *bud-bud*, or banyan, is the most important tree, one to which almost all

Mandaya relate certain events. In turn, they avoid contact with it. *Bud-bud* trees are characterized by long branches that extend outwards and by aerial roots that grow from branches towards the ground, take root, and eventually provide additional support. In some cases, the crown of a single banyan tree may cover an area ten to fifteen meters or more in diameter. The dense crown provides a heavy shade so that it is usually very dark underneath these trees. The Mandaya claim that malevolent spirits such as the *asuang* are invariably located in such surroundings. Swiddens are never planted near banyan trees, and Mandaya always avoid walking within shouting distance of them. However, each of these trees signifies a long story of past events that brought harm to someone. Furthermore, the banyan is usually the nesting and resting place for the *limokon*, a white dove that plays an important role in Mandaya concepts of fear and death. Whenever the call of the *limokon* is heard, all activity is stopped and a Mandaya retires to his residence. If the call is unheeded, one is believed to be vulnerable to sickness and death, if not immediately at least relatively soon.

The *bud-bud* tree, the call of the *limokon*, and other frightful signals are not simply warnings for avoidance. They cue the recounting of events in the past and thus the transmitting of history. History – structured by memory – provides cultural continuity. In some cases observed during fieldwork, events that occurred as long as eight or ten generations back were discussed as if they had just happened. Memory is verbally transmitted, but each physical and geographical cue is used to describe events that have occurred and will recur. The concrete cues support and reaffirm the impact of the verbal account.

Memory, as it is conveyed orally and through physical cues, is also important in denoting localities considered dangerous. Not only are parts of the forest regarded with caution, but deep pools of water are also considered places in which danger exists. Deep pools as well as the tracks linking pools are avoided, since evil spirits move along particular trajectories from pool to pool. The means of linkage need not be water; in many cases, spirits will move through the forest, over the land, and even from rice field to rice field. Paths of evil spirits are noted and this information is conveyed through mnemonic means. Directions of spirit movements between pools indicate that spirits travel in a linear direction. Thus, human paths are commonly curved and criss-crossed to avoid contact with such spirits. Throughout the forest and open rice fields, markers indicate the direction in which humans should move. Each locality also has a story about past disasters that befell individuals who did not heed the advice concerning the movement of spirits. Not only is history expressed through spatial and physical referents, but the continuity of action indicates that past events may be used as indicators of what might happen if violations and trespassing provoke malevolent spirits.

Almost all conflicts and raids that resulted in significant warfare are noted in the living memories of individuals, especially among elder males. In discussing the long-past exploits of a leading *bagani*, the elders recall such activities as if they had only recently occurred. However, when one tries to reconstruct the time frame of these attacks, it appears that they took place in the late Spanish period (1880–1900). Although some battles are noted after 1910, the fact of well-established pacification and the gradual demise of the *bagani* by the 1920s and 1930s indicates that the high point of armed conflict ceased more than two or three generations ago.

The exploits of past warfare live on not only in the memories of some individuals; in some cases, mock battles are held to demonstrate how the conflict took place. When elder males travel through clearings, the chants and songs of war are sung and a mock enactment is staged to show who was where, what happened, and who was killed at what spot. Bravery and heroism are noted and stressed as the exploits are repeatedly recalled in a manner meant to evoke all the spirits of the warriors and emphasize their meaning to the living generation. Clearings and localities of war are semi-sacred and future swiddens cannot be located near them. These stories are passed on to children as a means of maintaining a memory of historical events that are not simply locked in time but which also become timeless. Memory is thus used as a means of moving events through time. Since the meaningfulness of these activities is not vested in the fact that they occurred in the past, memory creates a form of history that collapses the immediate past into the present. This feature does not occur with myth, which is related to questions of cosmogony, the origin of things, and how Mandaya humanity is constructed.

Genealogy as a mnemonic device is critical in relating history and culture to and through the present. Most Mandaya genealogies are characterized by their shallowness: they go back two generations, occasionally three, and seldom four. Although kinship terms for cousins extend to fifth cousins, the link between fifth cousins cannot usually be demarcated by tracing genealogical connections. Thus, an individual learns that one is a fifth cousin only by being told. Although the average person lacks any genealogical depth, most genealogical connections spanning three generations relate to how individuals draw kinship ties to a famous *bagani*. Some of these ties, most of which are imputed and fictional, go back six to nine generations and are combined into a conical type of relationship, or what can be called "linking to the axial line." Cultural events relating to large ceremonies, warfare and conflict, pestilence, and population movement are "tacked on" to each axial line. The memories of past events are sequentially linked through conical and axial genealogical connections to founders or particular warriors.

Since the Mandaya are non-literate, the historical dimension of their lives is invoked through memory devices, of which genealogical connections are one of the major means to project past events into the present. The use of geographic, environmental, and sociological idioms in the constitution of memory structures permits us to understand how history is transmitted through a number of cultural vehicles, the content of which is markedly variable.

The tradition of oratory is the major vehicle for expressing how cosmological and ontological forces emerged and what they mean in terms of Mandaya life. However, oratory does not only consist of the transmission of this cultural knowledge. It also involves the ability of the orator to state convincingly and forcefully how these values and philosophical concepts relate to behavior and everyday reality. The moral basis of human action is founded in a close and harmonious connection between the pragmatics of everyday life and the symbolic underpinnings that provide meaning and emotional sustenance to what people are doing.

Between Islam and Christianity

The impact of Islam and Christianity is best understood at two levels. The first is that of the social and economic practices of the Mandaya, those normal quotidian activities that structure how the Mandaya continue to reproduce their daily activities. The second level requires an analysis of the religious and value systems in which local beliefs come into contact with world religions and their respective dogmas, which might or might not have an impact on the realms of world-view and religious structure.

Taking the issue of quotidian culture as a starting point, it is evident that Islam and Christianity have had an essential role in change, but the essentialization of Mandaya value systems and religion has hardly succumbed to changes of the first order. Contact with Islam has come via merchants, occasionally Islamic missionaries and teachers, and also from individual Moros who are hired for certain jobs that the Mandaya fear to do. Moros are called in to fell banyan trees, to cap teeth in gold, and at times they have established commercial links with the Mandaya through the marketing of cash crops such as hemp. But overall the interaction has been sporadic; thus any ongoing daily contact is normally absent.

Yet the Mandaya have internalized the feeling that the Muslims in Mindanao are a strong and fearless people. Through hearing the Moro teachers and missionaries, they have a sense that the Muslims fought and conquered the Spaniards in most parts of Mindanao, and that they were never conquered by the American troops in western and central Mindanao from 1900 to 1913, a time at which the troops led by General John J. Pershing were held to a stalemate that led to the gradual withdrawal of American troops from most parts of Mindanao. The Mandaya know that Pershing gained his fame in the Mexican Revolution and also in the First World War in France, but his sojourns against Muslim Filipinos resulted in heavy American casualties and never gained political hegemony over the Muslims. Thus to the Mandaya, the Muslims are a people who cannot be conquered. This feeling is even more credible given that the Japanese could not subdue the Moro during the Second World War and the Marcos government failed time and again in its conflicts with the Muslims. Consequently, Moros are respected as a people, but Islam as a globalizing religion is distant, foreign, and has little if any connection with the Mandaya religious pantheon.

Mandaya interaction with Christians has been more intense and direct, especially in the coastal communities. The Christians, who are primarily Cebuano speakers, have had a long-term impact on the workings of Mandaya society, but in many ways the lasting influences have been primarily at the level of daily social interactions.

Religious conversion to Christianity is not a recent phenomenon. Contact with the Spanish on the eastern Mindanao coast dates back to the 1840s and 1850s, at which time the Spaniards were trying to establish military posts to counteract the spread of the Moro into the Davao Gulf, Mati, and towns along the eastern coast. Catholic missionaries moved southwards along the east coast, establishing churches and missions at important military and population centers such as Caraga. Garvan summarizes the steps of Christianization in the lower and upper Agusan areas among the Manobo and the Agusan valley branch of the Mandaya. During the period 1877–98, some 5,000 natives of different tribal origins were converted to Christianity. The Christian populations of the Agusan valley are referred to as *conquista*. Jesuits constituted the majority of missionaries during the late Spanish phase and only recently have other Catholic orders and Protestant churches been relatively active.

As the "peasantization" process has continued among the abaca-cultivating Mandaya, certain social changes have occurred. The influx of new elements such as transistor radios, "stateside" clothing, galvanized sheet metal roofs commonly known as the "GI sheet," sewing machines, and so forth, has created further demands of the local population on the outside market and all that this implies. The role and importance of a formal education is recognized not only in learning the basics of reading and writing, but also in an understanding of what the dominant Bisayan ways of life are, how they operate, what they mean, and how they are acquired.

While Mandaya culture – in its organizational aspects – has adapted to the commercial production and marketing of abaca, marked changes have not occurred on the structural level. However, contact with coastal "Bisayans" and other members of dominant Philippine religious groups has brought about changes in self-identification with regard to groups and networks external to the Mandaya. As contact with external populations has increased, the Mandaya have gradually assumed and acquired certain behavioral patterns that only manifest themselves in their dealings with non-Mandaya populations in the widening socio-economic framework.

The major obstacle hindering the Mandaya's interaction with and acceptance by the lowland Bisayan population is the prejudice that lowlanders display towards uplanders. In general, Christians and Muslims regard uplanders or pagan groups as backward, unsophisticated, and superstition-bound people. In most areas, the lowland peoples readily take advantage of upland groups by obtaining lands that are not titled or by reneging on agreements concerning commercial transactions.

In upper Manay and Caraga, those segments of the Mandaya involved in abaca production recognize the necessity of being a "Bisayan," at least when interacting with the coastal populations. Externally, this is easily accomplished by changes in apparel, the cutting of one's hair, and the exclusive use of Bisayan, the lingua franca. However, external changes are only the first step in the uplander's transition to life amid the coastal Bisayan population.

The Mandaya also recognize that all Bisayans are baptized and are Christians. This close association between baptism and being a Bisayan is most important in the interaction of the upland Mandaya with coastal populations. In cases where the Mandaya discussed the meaning and role of baptism, most felt that one became a Bisayan through baptism. The ideal of spiritual rejuvenation, which is commonly connected with baptism, was seldom realized as being crucial, nor was it recognized. The high rate of Mandaya going to a coastal mission or church, being baptized, and returning as "Bisayans" attests to this fact.

Being a Bisayan to the Mandaya, at least in their interactions with the coastal people, connotes that their status is equal to that of the coastal Bisayans. Whereas the foothill Mandaya, who are involved in the production and marketing of abaca and are in close contact with the coastal groups, become baptized as a means of acquiring and assuming the status of a Bisayan, the interior upland rice-cultivating Mandaya are seldom involved in direct interaction with the coastal populations.

The process of "Bisayanization" through baptism is not new; nor does it occur only among the abaca cultivators. Most coastal groups are actually Mandaya, whose conversion dates back to the late Spanish period or the early American era. In such cases, when a person is asked "What are you?," the common reply is "A Bisayan." Upon further enquiry as to what Bisayan island he is from or where his parents or grandparents were from, the findings are that as far as one is able to trace descent, all lineal kin were born in a given locality in eastern Davao or Surigao del Sur. Ultimately, the basis on which a person calls himself a Bisayan is baptism.

Not only does one become a Bisayan by changes in clothing and hair style and through baptism, but also by active participation in a social framework that is part of the "mainstream of Philippine Culture." A Bisayan is one who is fully aware of the national life, one who knows the "ins and outs" of business, politics, and society, and is able to take part in political, social, and religious organizations and activities characteristic of lowland

Philippine culture. For a Mandaya who is gradually coming into the sphere of Philippine economic activity, it is necessary to acquire lowland cultural patterns and attitudes.

Thus, the Christian baptism to a Mandaya signifies a partial change in reference group structure. In dealing with non-Mandaya, a baptized Mandaya calls himself a Bisayan, uses Bisayan as the lingua franca, and selectively manifests activity in lowland Philippine culture. In the foothills, one is a Mandaya, speaks Mandaya, and partakes in all the social and religious aspects of Mandaya social structure.

In summary, Christian baptism is the key to participation in lowland Bisayan culture. The initial step, and usually the only step, in conversion to Christianity is baptism – the spiritual rebirth of one's soul for the ultimate destiny of other supernatural spheres. Practically, to all Christian missionaries working in eastern Mindanao, baptism ideally represents only the first step towards a Christian life. In reality, most missionaries (especially those whose church congregations are low in number) recognize that the odds of following up on all natives who are baptized are very limited. Thus, people are baptized with little or no religious instruction and with the minimum hope that at least a few Mandaya families will reach advanced levels of religious instruction. The dilemma to many a missionary on the remote east coast of Mindanao is: "Shall I or shall I not baptize segments of the aboriginal population although they may never acquire further religious instruction or be seen again?" Whereas many missionaries may assume that the number of baptisms performed is a measure of their success, the crucial issue is to investigate what baptism signifies to those who undergo such an event. The author does not know how widespread the practice is. Though there may be cases where contact between the dominant lowland culture and various non-Christian upland groups is characterized by sporadic interaction, an absence of continuous one-way contact between a dominant and subordinate culture, and few agents for cultural transmission, one may find cases, such as the Mandaya, where the reference group structure and changes allow an individual to partially participate in two networks of social activity with a minimum amount of conflict.

Discussion

As indicated, there are many aspects to what conversion to Islam and Christianity means, as well as to how these processes are to be interpreted. Even in cases where Mandaya are baptized by Christian missionaries, of either Catholic or various Protestant faiths, a return to the traditional homelands only means that they regard themselves as Bisayan or Cebuano when encountering the dominant coastal group. Within the context of Mandaya society, one is a Mandaya through traditional ritual activity relating to the pantheon of spirits, apparel, length of hair, etc. This form of compartmentalization allows individual Mandaya to articulate within Christian and/or Islamic spheres of influence on the level of human interactions that involve economic and social contact and which have minimal or no influence on the sacred qualities of Mandaya religion.

One of the critical features of Mandaya religion is its local, even parochial, quality, which stresses place and region over any other parameter and which embeds religious thought and dogma. An example of this is the importance of oratory. Mandaya realize that Islamic teachers and Christian missionaries do not possess oratorical skills, which are recognized as a gift that certain individuals have while others do not; indeed, even among those with such skills, there are fine gradients of ability. Speech, verbal discourse, and lengthy orations must have a sense of "flowery" style, not only in how the words and phrases are put together, but also in their ability to create inversions through metaphor and irony. Much of this is done in a style that can be understood; that is to say, meaning is generated from words, phrases, and sentences. However, in "classical" expressions of Mandaya, the ideal is that the power of the oration is in its style of delivery and its extreme involution in terms of how phrases sound and not necessarily what they mean. In fact, the ideal is to go beyond meaning in the sense that what is critical lies in not what is said but what is unsaid, in the use of language that is not understood, and in the delivery and the eloquence of the message as poetic, abstract, and opaque.

These qualities of oratory simply are not found in the average individual; furthermore, from their limited contacts with Islamic and Christian missionaries, it is evident that these proselytizers do not possess such gifts. Above all, there is another facet to oratory that is as important as the act of oration itself. The vitality and creativity of oratory is enhanced if the gift of the speech is conveyed in the exact locality in which events embedded in the oratory took place. All verbal accounts of past and present deeds are ideally recited in the exact vicinity or locality in which such events took place. In the case of myths that are linked to the sky, the act of oratory is conveyed under the correct set of constellations that are the source of the myth, epic, saga, etc. Under such conditions, the existence and the invoking of the physical referent virtually creates an enactment of a historical or mythic event through both the orality and the meaning of the action, as well as through how it is visualized. In this context, one well realizes that religious prophets, heroes, and heroines are always coupled to space and place, be it earthly or celestially bound to the parameters that circumscribe the Mandaya religious pantheon. Given these localizing tendencies, it is difficult if not foreign for Mandaya to conceive of religious prophets, events, and processes that are not linked to precise points. Yet, in conversations with Islamic and Christian missionaries, they have heard of the importance of Mecca and Jerusalem to these world religions, they have heard of the biblical holy temple, thus they realize the source or the foundation of these belief systems. The problem concerns how place and locality might be propelled into a worldly religion without the loss of the meaning and impact that these belief systems must express. Mandaya concerns about the transformation from local to global have been partly addressed by Smith (1987), yet the puzzle is far from being resolved.

In summary, cases such as the Mandaya are not unique. Most religious systems are linked and embedded to particular features that seldom extend beyond the social and cultural confines of local contexts. From a comparative perspective, these local contexts must be accepted as essentialisms by which particular societies reproduce themselves. For the Mandaya, oratory combined with celestial referents form the arena that provides the emotional sustenance and intellectual rationalization behind what the belief system means in daily human interaction. For the Pitjantjatjara of central Australia, the domination of myth combined with ground and what is underneath the surface of the earth is essential for comprehending the importance of ritual (see Yengoyan 1989, 1990, 1993). To understand global religious processes and various expressions of modernism and postmodernism, students of religious action and thought might consider starting locally before thinking globally.

Note

The author has done anthropological fieldwork with the Mandaya of south-eastern Mindanao, the Philippines, since 1960. Specific references can be provided to the reader by contacting the author directly.

References

Cole, Fay-Cooper, *The Wild Tribes of the Davao District, Mindanao*, Chicago: Field Museum of Natural History, 1913.

Garvan, John M., *The Manobos of Mindanao*, Memoirs of the National Academy of Sciences, vol. 23, Washington, DC: United States Government Printing Office, 1931.

Lynch, Frank, "*An mga asuwang*: a Bicol belief," *The Philippine Social Sciences and Humanities* 14, 1949, 401–27.

Smith, Jonathan Z., *To Take Place: Toward Theory in Ritual*, Chicago: University of Chicago Press, 1987.

Yengoyan, Aram A., "Language and conceptual dualism: sacred and secular concepts in Australian Aboriginal cosmology and myth," in David Maybury-Lewis and Uri Almagor (eds) *The Attraction of Opposites: Thought and Society in the Dualistic Mode*, Ann Arbor: University of Michigan Press, 1989, 171–90.

——, "Cloths of heaven: Freud, language, and the negation in Pitjantjatjara dreams," in David K. Jordan and Marc J. Swartz (eds) *Personality and the Cultural Construction of Society: Papers in Honor of Melford E. Spiro*, Tuscaloosa: University of Alabama Press, 1990, 201–21.

——, "Religion, morality, and prophetic traditions: conversion among the Pitjantjatjara of central Australia," in Robert W. Hefner (ed.) *Conversion to Christianity: Historical and Anthropological Perspectives on a Great Transformation*, Berkeley: University of California Press, 1993, 233–57.

Chapter 19

The Väddas

Representations of the Wild Man in Sri Lanka[1]

Gananath Obeyesekere

Introduction

For many anthropologists, the Väddas were a "classic" tribe of aboriginal people who lived in the margins of the Sinhala-Buddhist civilization of Sri Lanka. In his 1881 text, Tylor mentions them thus: "In the forests of Ceylon are found the Veddas or 'hunters', shy wild men who build bough huts, and live on game and wild honey" (Tylor 1881: 164). Owing to their racial antiquity and their gentle yet primitive ways, they were the subject of numerous studies by physical anthropologists, studies being continued to this day by teams from Sri Lanka's medical schools. The Väddas came into prominence in social anthropology when the great pioneer of the discipline C.G. Seligmann and his wife Brenda published their book *The Veddas* in 1911 (Seligmann and Seligmann 1911), the same year their distinguished colleague W.H.R. Rivers published his book, *The Todas*, on the people of South India of the same name. The Seligmanns could find only tiny groups of genuine Väddas living in abject misery in the jungles of north-eastern Sri Lanka, an area known as the Bintanne ("plains"). In recent times, their numbers have shrunk further as a result of the Sri Lankan government's development programs. These recent trends and the apathy of the native Sri Lankan Buddhists have led to several Euro-American interventionist movements to save the Väddas and ensure their "cultural survival" and cultural revival. One ethnographer has tried to hold the Sri Lankan government responsible to the United Nations for the violation of the rights of indigenous peoples; another from Berkeley thinks that the Väddas were once noble beings, descendants of the demon king of Sri Lanka, Ravana, immortalized in the great Indian epic, *Ramayana*. While the former is trying to lure back the Väddas to their pristine style of living by hunting with bows and arrows, the latter (more imaginatively) has led groups of Väddas to Kataragama in south-eastern Sri Lanka to the seat of the great god Murugan, or Skanda, in order to resurrect their lost traditions. Also known as the god Kataragama, Murugan is the powerful deity to whom most Sri Lankans pay homage, irrespective of formal religious affiliations. Everyone, including this anthropologist, agrees on one thing: the Väddas are a disappearing tribe that will soon vanish from the world's ethnological museum. The question remains – what happened to the Väddas?

It is easy to show that the Väddas were once a much more ubiquitous presence in Sri Lanka. An invocation sung at a Sinhala ritual called *väddan andagähima*, or "the roll-call of the Väddas," asks them to participate in the *vädi dane*, "the almsgiving of the Väddas." The text asks the god of *Santana* to bring blessings on the audience; *Santana* is the mountain of *hantana* in Kandy, the capital of the last kings of Kandy and of the present

Central Province, and the god is known to the Sinhalas as Hantane Deviyo and to the Väddas as Hantane Maha Vädi Unnäha, "the venerable great Vädda of Hantana." However, contemporary Väddas no longer associate him with the mountain of Hantana; his domain at the beginning of this century is Mavaragala in what is now known as Vädda country, or the Bintanne. The Vädda god of Hantana has retreated from Kandy and his shrunken abode is now in what is considered Vädda territory proper. Yet the text of *väddan andagähima* suggests that Vädda territory was practically coterminous with that of the Sinhalas. In two texts of *väddan andagähima*, one edited by Charles Godakumbure and the other by Mudiyanse Dissanayake, over ninety Vädda villages are mentioned; famous Väddas such as the Dambane and Danigala and Sitala Vanniya Väddas of the Seligmann list are not included, presumably because they were unknown to the composers of these texts. However, Nilgala, which the Seligmanns classify as Vädda territory, is included (Godakumbure 1963: 90–1). No reference is made to Väddas living in Sri Lanka's Sabaragamuva Province either. Some of the Vädda areas, such as Asgiriya, Bogambara, and Hantana, are familiar to those living in and around the modern city of Kandy, while others are well known to many: Batalagala, Gomiriya, Maturata, Hunnasgiriya, Lower Dumbara, Kotmale, Nuvara Eliya, Kehelgamuva, and Uragala. Today, these are all Sinhala (and estate Tamil) areas. These lists are by no means exhaustive, but they are almost always from the area around Kandy, the North Central Province, the Dumbara and Kotmale Valleys, and Uva.

Perhaps one of the most fascinating references to Väddas in areas that are now exclusively Sinhala is a document in which Prince Vijayapala of Matale, south of Kandy, summons several Vädda chiefs from nineteen villages to help him in his fight with his half-brother, King Rajasinha of Kandy (1634–87) (Parker 1909a: 101–2). A large number of Vädda villages mentioned in this text are from the Matale District, now exclusively occupied by Sinhalas. The main duty of these Vädda chiefs was to guard the frontier. Two of them were called "Herat," clearly a Sinhala name, one of them possessed the honorific title "Bandara," reserved for Kandyan nobility, while another was called Kadukara, or "sword bearer," indicating a martial occupation rather than, or in addition to, one of hunting. The Seligmanns would have been thoroughly annoyed with the last of these because they thought the Väddas simply did not have swords!

This particular text suggests that the Väddas were not only living cheek by jowl with Sinhala villages but that they could also be enlisted for military purposes. Knox, the Englishman captured by the Sinhala king and confined to an area outside the kingdom of Kandy in the middle of the seventeenth century, refers to Väddas of the Hurulu Pattu in the North Central Province who fought the Dutch on behalf of the Kandyan king and did a good job of it. The martial virtues of the Väddas were noted as late as 1818, when one of their aristocratic chiefs, Kivulegedera Mohattala, became a major figure in the rebellion that nearly ousted the British, three years after the formal capitulation of the Kandyan kingdom (Peiris 1995: 188–9).

Permeable boundaries: Vädda and Sinhala-Buddhist

The earliest reference to people who live by hunting (those now categorized as "Vädda") comes from the *Mahavamsa*, the great Buddhist chronicle, which describes the Sinhala cultural hero Vijaya who landed in Sri Lanka with his followers on the very day the Buddha died (circa sixth century BCE). He initially married a demoness named Kuveni. Later, Vijaya rejected her and married a Tamil princess from South India, while his followers married the Tamil women who came with her. From this legitimate union sprung the Sinhalas. According to the *Mahavamsa* account, Vijaya's two children from Kuveni fled the area after her death: "Fleeing with speed they went thence to the Sumanakuta. The brother, the elder of the two, when he grew up took his sister, the younger, for his wife, and multiplying with sons and daughters, they dwelt, with the king's leave, there in Malaya (forested mountains). From these sprung the Pulinda" (Geiger 1980: 60). The offspring of Vijaya are not called Väddas in the *Mahavamsa* but Pulindas, another designation for hunting peoples. Moreover, they were in the territory of the god Saman (Sri Pada), which is located in Sabaragamuva, "the province of the hunters," adjacent to today's populous Western and Southern Provinces. After this initial reference, the Buddhist chronicles scarcely mention the Väddas.[2] However, the *Parevi Sandesaya*, written in the mid-fifteenth century, refers to daughters of Väddas in the area below the Sumanakuta Peak, where, according to the *Mahavamsa* myth, the Buddha in his own lifetime placed his footprint (Obeyesekere 1984: 304, 301–6). What is most impressive is that at least one British observer reported in 1805 that "tribes who inhabit the west and southwest quarters of the island between Adam's Peak and the Raygam and Pasdan cories [*korale*s, or districts], are the only Bedahs [Väddas] seen by Europeans, and are much less wild and ferocious than those who live in the forests of Bintan" (Percival 1805: 284). This again is the border between the present Sabaragamuva and Western Provinces, which no one today believes is Vädda territory. Yet the word "Sabaragamuva" means "the country of the *sabara*s" (hunters) and is identical with the etymology of Vädda. It is therefore not surprising to find plenty of references to place names in Sabaragamuva that indicate a previous Vädda presence: *vädi pangu* (Vädda land share), *vädi kumbura* (Vädda rice fields), *vädivatta* (Vädda gardens), and *väddagala* (Vadda mountain), where a Sinhala village is now located. One of the most interesting place names on the border between the Sabaragamuva and Southern Provinces ("Ruhuna" in the old political geography) is known as *habarakada*, "the gateway of the *sabara*s," pointing to an equivalence between Vädda and Sabara. Even now, the tradition that this was where Väddas and Sinhalas met to barter and trade is strong. I also have ritual texts that postdate the fifteenth century, which say that it is a bad omen if you see a Vädda coming from the direction of Ruhuna, the southernmost province of Sri Lanka.

The preceding evidence suggests very strongly that the Väddas were almost everywhere in Sri Lanka particularly before the seventeenth century. By the seventeenth century, it seems that some Väddas were being given Kandyan aristocratic names; they were neighbors of the Sinhalas, but it is not clear from the Vijayapala text that they were rice farmers. However, the Sabaragamuva place names do suggest that some of the Väddas were engaged in rice cultivation, which is nothing unusual because the so-called "village Väddas" are engaged in rice cultivation even today, and their lifeways have been documented by the anthropologist James Brow (1978). If Väddas were all over the nation prior to the seventeenth century and existed in the Sabaragamuva Province up to the nineteenth century in what are Sinhala areas today, then the question is: where have all the Väddas gone? And if the Väddas consisted of those who were wild, those engaged in rice cultivation, and those belonging to a military tradition and who knows what else, and, further, if they were designated by three distinct names all denoting "hunter," then one has to ask the related question: who *were* the Väddas?

Let me start with the first question. There are two possible answers to this, one being that the Väddas are no longer around because they were decimated through diseases introduced by the colonial rulers in the sixteenth century, the other that they were through time exterminated by the Sinhalas or by the European colonialists. Both factors have certainly played a part in the destruction of native peoples all over the world by European invaders and colonizers, but the history of South Asia does not exhibit this pattern. The Väddas were no more or less immune to diseases than the Sinhalas; neither did the British make any attempt to harm the Väddas, who were integrally part of the economy and polity of the nation. The British never settled in Sri Lanka as they did in other places, and while they pillaged Sri Lankan villages in war, there was little violence against native populations during the peace. The deliberate displacement of Väddas from whatever hunting grounds that were left to them in the twentieth century was a product of recent actions by successive native postcolonial governments. Hence the obvious answer: the Vädda villages mentioned earlier are now Sinhala simply because Väddas have been converted into Sinhalas through endogenous social processes.

Now for the second question: who were the Väddas? This is difficult to answer, since the Väddas, unlike the Sinhalas, had no voice in history. Because they were mostly illiterate and non-Buddhist, they are represented by others, initially by the Sinhalas and later and in more detail by the various colonial powers. As James Brow convincingly argues, the term "Vädda" is for the most part a label employed by the Sinhalas for a widespread and important group of people who were different from themselves in some significant ways. It is true that "Vädda," "Pulinda," and "Sabara" meant "hunter," but because we know that there were Väddas who were not hunters, the significance of these labels has to be further examined. Moreover, from our preceding account, Väddas were found in a multiplicity of ecological zones. It is highly improbable that the Väddas who lived in Sabaragamuva were the same Väddas who lived in Uva-Bintanne, in Matale, or in Kandy and its environs. Hence our first conclusion: in all likelihood, "Vädda" was a label given to a variety of different groups by the Sinhalas. Yet, like the label "Sinhala," it was also probably one of several self-referential terms, used by hunting peoples to distinguish themselves from the Sinhala, who were for the most part Buddhist. In one sense, there is no real difference between the two labels "Sinhala" and "Vädda." The large group of people who speak Sinhala are subdivided into various other categories that are also significant to their identity, the most important being caste. Similarly, the Väddas were divided into a multiplicity of groups but, because they did not possess a historical voice, it is difficult to determine what these groups or categories were.

Creation of the Wild Man

The Väddas, as we understand them today, have emerged from studies by Europeans. It is the Europeans who have typologized the Väddas and have represented them to the world outside and to educated Sinhalas. Consider this early description of them from Knox, an astute observer who, in 1681, was writing more extensively about the Sinhalas:

> Of these there be two sorts, Wild and Tame…For as in these Woods there are Wild Beasts, so Wild Men also. The Land of Bintan is all covered with mighty Woods, filled with abundance of Deer. In this Land are many of these wild men: they call themselves Vaddahs, dwelling near no other Inhabitants. They speak the Chingulayes [Sinhala's] Language…They never till the ground for Corn, their Food being only Flesh.
>
> (Knox 1911: 98)

Knox provides a wonderful engraving captioned "A Vadda or Wild Man," which shows a man with his bow and arrow and dagger, smoking a huge pipe, and wearing a thick loin-cloth or *amude*. He then goes on to describe the tame Väddas, who he says owe service obligations to the king, especially tusks, honey and wax, and deer's flesh, which they bring to the *gabadage* or store house. In Knox, the fundamental distinction is between wild and tame, itself a distinction between nature and culture, the wild ones living in a state of nature without the benefits of culture (*ibid.*: 98–9). Hence, says Knox, they are also called *Ramba-Väddas*, or hairy Väddas, who, as children of nature, "never shew themselves" (*ibid.*: 101). He had fleeting glimpses of them when he was running away from the Kandyan kingdom, but he could not possibly have had a close look at them. Consequently, Knox's wonderful drawing of the Vädda must be seen as a product of his fertile imagination and that of his engraver. But why the caption "Wild Man"? I suggest that Knox invented this portrait of the wild man because it was something that his late seventeenth-century public expected to see.

Neither Knox (*ibid.*) nor the later scholarly endeavors can be understood outside the larger context of the European fascination with the wild man. Richard Bernheimer, in his book *Wild Men in the Middle Ages* (1952), has beautifully documented this European obsession. Hayden White and, more recently, Roger Batra have also re-examined this topic.[3] Margaret Hodgen has demonstrated that after the so-called voyages of discovery, the human monsters and wild men of the middle ages were being foisted on the savage, often providing a rationale for the extermination of native peoples. When Columbus traveled into the new world of the Caribbean, he did not find any monstrous beings. Yet he made hesitant references to Amazonians, to a tribe without hair, and to tailed men in a remote part of Cuba (Hodgen 1964: 18–19). These ideas sometimes affected physical perception. Thus in 1560, the Spanish thought they saw giant men in Patagonia, which is the land of patagones, or "big feet" (Wallis 1964: 185). As late as 1765, the English circumnavigator Byron claimed to have seen giants in Patagonia, and it was Wallis and Carteret who, a few years later, disabused the English public regarding Patagonian giants (*ibid.*: 186).

The popular ideas of the wild man also affected science and other forms of literature. For example, the great Linnaeus in his *System of Nature* not only classified the world's fauna and flora but also typologized humans into *Homo sapiens* and *Homo monstrosus* – and among the former were wild men. These notions of savages not being fully human but rather wild men influenced religious reformers like John Wesley. He thought that the American Indians possessed no religion, laws, or conceptions of civil society, and that they murdered their fathers, mothers, and children. Asians and even savage Europeans were not exempt:

> What say you to thousands of Laplanders, Samoiedes and Greenlanders, all of whom live in the high northern latitudes? Are they sheep or oxen? Add to these the myriad of human savages, that are freezing in the snows of Siberia...To compare them with horses or any of our domestic animals would be doing them too much honour.
>
> (Hodgen 1964: 366–7)

Since most of what we know of the Väddas comes from British times, it is necessary to sketch the ideas of wildness that prevailed at the turn of the eighteenth century. The voyages of discovery took an important new turn with the European Enlightenment. Thus

Captain Cook's voyages of discovery that resulted in our knowledge of Polynesian and some Melanesian peoples were sponsored by the Royal Society, the nation's premier scientific organization. As a result, science was conjoined with exploration in the depiction of the lifeways of savages. These voyages were also expeditions for collecting artifacts. Along with masks and baskets, there was a fantastic collecting spree for body parts of savages, perhaps the most significant being the decapitated heads of "cannibals." But this was not all. Hair, bones, and other parts of the savages' anatomies were collected by almost everyone on board for later sale to old curiosity shops in London, and these in turn found their way into museums and anthropology departments. Parallel with this were careful ethnographic descriptions of the lifeways of savages, some of whom, such as the Polynesians, were romanticized while others, such as the Melanesians, were seen as really "wild" or "hard savages," as Bernard Smith calls them (Smith 1985: 34–5). By the late eighteenth and early nineteenth centuries, a new type of wild man had startled the scholarly imagination, namely the Australian Aborigine, living by hunting and gathering in an uncongenial physical environment and in a very low level of technological development. The analogy with the Väddas was so strong that some scholars thought that both belonged to the same human family. It is easy to see how the Väddas and other hunters of South Asia were fitted into the new category of aboriginal. The wild man of the European imagination was fused with the idea of the Aborigine.

The preceding background is necessary in order for us to appreciate the first "scientific studies" of the Väddas, begun in the British period and culminating with the work of the Seligmanns. Prior to this, considerable information on the Väddas had been provided by British civil servants such as Bailey, and most importantly by Parker in *Ancient Ceylon*, and also by Hugh Nevill in such journals as the *Taprobanian* (Parker 1909b). The physical anthropology of the Väddas was studied by Drs. F. and P. Sarasin and by Rudolf Virchow, who in grand style measured their scalps, took body measurements, characterized the shape of their noses and hair, and systematically typologized the Väddas in physical terms.[4] The wild Vädda was given physical identifying features, and it was possible to talk confidently of the Väddoid type in contrast to the Sinhala (without seriously examining whether there were Sinhalas who shared these features). These physical anthropologists and early colonial historians were the first to define the Väddas as aborigines. When the Seligmanns arrived, there was already the notion that the Vädda was a distinct physical type and that the task of the anthropologist was to give that type cultural and sociological specificity.

Even before these scientific studies, the Väddas had become objects of popular and intellectual curiosity. Many Europeans wanted to see the Vädda as a specimen of the wild man, or as a copy of the primitive Australian Aborigine, from the comfort of the government rest (guest) house. As the Seligmanns noted:

> The Veddas have long been regarded as a curiosity in Ceylon and excite almost as much interest as the ruined cities, hence Europeans go to the nearest Rest House on the main road and have the Danigala Veddas brought to them. Naturally the Veddas felt uncomfortable and shy at first, but when they found that they had only to look gruff and grunt replies in order to receive presents they were quite clever enough to keep up the pose. In this they were aided by the always agreeable villagers ever ready to give the white man exactly what he wanted. The white man appeared to be immensely anxious to see a true Vedda, a wild man of the woods, clad only in a scanty

loin cloth, carrying his bow and arrows on which he depended for his subsistence, simple and untrained, indeed, little removed from the very animals he hunted.

(Seligmann and Seligmann 1911: 39)

Naturally, the European curiosity was satisfied by the Nilgala headmen who brought Väddas properly attired as wild men to show them to the Europeans. The Väddas of Dambana were also easily accessible from the government rest house. The Seligmanns called them "show Veddas" because they "have been sent for so often by white visitors that they have learnt certain tricks, which they show directly they see a European" (*ibid*.: 49).

Both the Danigala and Dambana Väddas at that time were no longer exclusively hunters. They had long since taken to swidden cultivation, even keeping cattle, and lived in close contact with neighboring Sinhalas. Some of them had had shotguns since at least the beginning of the twentieth century, while others borrowed guns from the Sinhalas (*ibid*.: 52). But that was not how they represented themselves to outsiders. The Väddas of Dambana and Danigala had taken over the persona of the wild man expected of them by the European. Theirs was a mimesis of savageness: half naked, carrying a bow and arrow and displaying its uses, gruff, morose, distant, and rarely laughing. Some British observers even said that the Väddas did not have a language. The idea that the Väddas did not laugh was widespread; this was simply a phenomenon of their acting the wild-man role, but done so well as to fool Europeans such as Deschamps, who observes that Väddas never laugh nor smile (*ibid*.). Thus the Vädda as a "wild man" was being created for the European by the not-so-wild Väddas. Soon this image was being perpetuated for those middle-class Sinhala who, in their own mimesis of colonialism, had imbibed much of the Vädda mythology created by the Europeans. In the 1950s and 1960s, I witnessed Dambana Väddas line the road to Mahiyangana carrying their bows and arrows and waiting to perform their act of wildness, at which they had become pastmasters. They also demonstrated to the awed Sinhalas the nature of their strange language, which had become known as *vädi basava*, or "Vädda language," helping thereby to further distantiate Vädda from Sinhala.

Although the Seligmanns made acute observations on Vädda ethnography, they too were paradoxically caught in the dilemma of how to represent the "true," "pure," or "genuine" Vädda. The "show Väddas" were phoney Väddas, whereas true Väddas displayed unique physical and cultural characteristics. Throughout their important book, the Seligmanns are concerned with "pure Väddas," some of whom are "purer" than others, "pure" and "purer" being defined in terms of three criteria, namely physical appearance, blood, and cultural integrity. On this basis, the Seligmanns posit a three-fold classification: Väddas, village Väddas, and coast Väddas, and it is the first group who are regarded as true Väddas. The coast Väddas are the least interesting because "they have much Tamil blood in their veins, and though often taller than pure Veddas, some still retain an appearance which suggests their Vedda origin" (*ibid*.: 29). The Seligmanns give short shrift to village Väddas in general and are especially harsh on those, like the Malgode Väddas of Sorabora, who "dropped their old Vedda customs so entirely that the local Sinhalese no longer look upon them as true village Veddas" (*ibid*.: 53). Actually, for the Seligmanns there are no true village Väddas, and they ignore the village Väddas of Anuradhapura carefully documented much later by James Brow. Finally, the Seligmanns are totally dismissive of those Väddas who are "half-bred" and "degenerate," and who "will soon be entirely lost among the Sinhalese" (*ibid*.: 45).

Given their interest in the real Vāddas, one would have thought that the Seligmanns would deal with them at length, but they found that there were not many left. The Danigala Vāddas are physically pure but culturally Sinhala; and the Kovil Vannamai are "badly off and in varying conditions of ill health and malnutrition." The Seligmanns report that "after visiting so many decaying or degenerate communities a refreshing state of affairs was found at Sitala Vanniya." This was the only group that represented both physical and cultural integrity but, unfortunately for the Seligmanns, there were only four families left (*ibid.*: 37–44). It seems that the Seligmanns' construction of Vādda culture and society was based on these four families, supplemented by imaginative reconstructions of "genuine" Vādda culture from the other groups they visited. I follow Brow's pioneering work in thinking that the Vādda culture and social organization described by the Seligmanns are little different from those of their Sinhala neighbors living in the same ecological area, except for their religious and eschatalogical beliefs.

The strength of the Seligmanns' work is in the area of religion. They present elaborate descriptions of the Vādda pantheon, Vādda ceremonial life, and magical practices. But once again they are forced to admit that nearly all of these are shared by the Sinhalas, and indeed in some instances the Sinhalas have an active role in Vādda ritual (*ibid.*: 236). Thus the key ceremonies performed by the Vāddas, such as the *kirikoraha* and the *kolamaduva*, are performed by the Sinhalas in a much more elaborate fashion. Virtually all the deities in the Vādda pantheon are also common to the Sinhalas; and both Sinhala and Vādda believe that their gods are under the suzerainty of the god Skanda, or Kataragama.

One conclusion is irresistible: in their quest for the pure Vādda, the Seligmanns missed what was evidentially clear at the time, namely that there were striking similarities in virtually every aspect of the lives of Vāddas and Sinhalas living in proximity to one another. Therefore, the distinctions between the various peoples subsumed under these two large categories must be sought elsewhere. What, then, are the distinctions? First, in spite of the fuzziness of the physical and cultural boundaries between Vādda and Sinhala, the two labels are used by one group to distinguish themselves from the other and these labels are also mostly self-referential. Secondly, the Seligmanns correctly noted that the Vāddas they studied were not Buddhists and did not believe in *karma* or rebirth, but rather in an ancestor cult of the Nä Yakku (kinfolk deities). The Seligmanns' account is very plausible for two reasons: such cults of deified ancestors are also common to Indian "tribal" groups such as the Soras and similar ancestor cults found the world over. By contrast, the Sinhalas thought of themselves as Buddhist, the idea of rebirth being integral to their faith. This idea was absent in the Vādda cult of the Nä Yakku.

Taming otherness: the collective representations at Mahiyangana

This chapter deals with the Sinhala-Buddhist typologization of the Vāddas, rather than that of the Vāddas themselves whose voices have been muffled by history. Let me begin with the foundation myth. According to the Seligmanns, the Vāddas they studied did not subscribe to this myth, but in my view, the Vāddas begin to do so as they move towards becoming Sinhala. We have already noted that in this myth Vijaya married Kuveni and later banished her and his two children by that marriage; out of this union of brother and sister sprang the Vāddas. The myth implies that the Vāddas are the kin of the Sinhalas, through Vijaya, yet are separate from them, having been banished into the forest and to a life of hunting, a very un-Buddhist profession. The charter myth for the opposition between hunting and Buddhism is known to most Buddhists and is first presented in the *Mahavamsa*, which describes the Buddhist saint (*arahant*) Mahinda flying through the air and landing on the mountain of Mihintale where the king (Devanampiyatissa, 250–210 BCE) was out hunting. Not only was the king converted, but also the place of this archetypally wrong act became a meditation site for the first monks and a center of Buddhist worship and pilgrimage.

These myths have no literal truth value but they do illustrate the manner in which the Väddas were perceived by the dominant group as an alien community in their midst, despite the fact that the two groups were linked by historic and economic ties. This notion of likeness and difference is beautifully expressed in the dramatic ritual known as the *vädi perahära* ("procession of the Väddas"), performed during the annual festival at Mahiyangana. Mahiyangana is in the heart of Vädda country and is also known as the Bintanne ("plains"), the area that Knox says was the haunt of the wild Väddas and also the area studied by the Seligmanns. The *Mahavamsa* mentions Mahiyangana as a place the Buddha himself personally visited and consecrated by his presence. In later times, the collarbone relic of the Buddha was enshrined there. Like the footprint of the Buddha on Sumanakuta Peak in Sabaragamuva, the Buddhist shrine indicated the hegemony of the Buddhists over the hunting population. Today, alongside this Buddhist *stupa* (relic chamber) and temple, there are also shrines for Saman and Skanda, major gods common to both Sinhalas and Väddas. My description of the Vädda procession is based on the rituals I witnessed in the late 1950s and early 1960s.

In one of these rituals, seventy-one Väddas carrying poles representing spears line up near the shrines of the gods Saman and Skanda, led by a "chief" carrying a bow and arrow. After circumambulating the shrine three times in a graceful dance, the Väddas suddenly increase the tempo and, at a signal from the chief, start hooting, yelling, and brandishing their spears, terrifying the assembled Sinhala spectators. They stage several battles in front of the shrine by "assaulting" it, striking their spears on its steps. They then run towards the Buddhist temple and try to enter the premises of the *stupa*, where the Buddha relics are enshrined. Here their path is blocked by two gate keepers (*murakarayo*) who shout, "You can't approach this place. Go back to the royal altar" (*rajavidiya*, the altar of the guardian deity). These mock battles are repeated several times and end with the Väddas placing their "spears" gently against the *stupa* and worshipping it. They then run towards the monks' residence (*pansala*), stage a battle there, and, as at the *stupa*, end up by worshipping the assembled monks. Then, from the monks' residence they head back to the shrine where they again perform a "battle," beating their spears against its stone steps until the spears break into small pieces; finally, they fall prostrate on the ground to worship the gods housed in their shrine (*devale*). After this they run towards the nearby river at "the ferry crossing of the gods" and bathe and purify themselves. Returning to the shrine, calm and self-possessed, they are now permitted to enter the inner sanctum where the priest (*kapurala*) chants an incantation for the gods Saman and Skanda and other major deities, and blesses the Väddas by lustrating them with "sandal water." The ritual ends with the Väddas all shouting "*haro-hara*," which in Sri Lanka is the paean of praise for the god Skanda, the great guardian deity of Sri Lanka and formal overlord of both the Vädda and the Sinhala pantheon.

The differences in the social functions of the rituals performed by the Sinhalas and the Väddas at Mahiyangana are impressive. In the case of the Sinhalas, there are no rituals that separate one group from another: all the assembled Sinhalas form one moral community participating in common worship at Mahiyangana. In the case of the Väddas, the rituals define their status in relation to the dominant religion, in that they are prevented from entering the temple and *stupa*. Though they are made to formally acknowledge the Buddha, they are clearly outside the community of Sinhala-Buddhists. Yet they are not total strangers either: after initially resisting the gods Skanda and Saman, they finally acknowledge the fact that these deities also head their own pantheon. Furthermore, it must be recognized that the guardian deities are not only protectors of the Buddhist religion; they are also protectors of the secular realm. The Väddas are incorporated into the "state" structure, not into the Buddhist "nation" or *sasana* symbolically represented in the *stupa*. Their incorporation into the political order of the Kandyan state is recognized in another part of the *vädi perahära*: the Väddas rub their bodies with honey and then cover themselves with cotton wool. Honey is the substance they used to collect as the king's due, or *rajakariya*. It is likely that some Väddas were also the suppliers of cotton cultivated in forest clearings or small garden plots. We know from Knox that cotton was a crucial local industry, which colonialism destroyed. Supplying cotton must have been an important historical role for some Väddas and this is recognized in the foundation myth itself, which says that when Kuveni first met Vijaya she was spinning cotton.

The level at which the Väddas are incorporated into the larger symbolic order shared by both communities is not that of Buddha worship but rather that of the guardian deities. In the present time, the great guardian god that unites Vädda and Sinhala (and both with Tamils) is Skanda, who is the overlord of the Vädda pantheon (the *Mahavamsa* evidence suggests that in ancient times it was the god Saman). This integration is given further symbolic validation in the mythology of Valli Amma, who was adopted by the Väddas as a child and became Skanda's illegitimate spouse, or second wife. Rituals and practices at Kataragama recognize the Vädda connection in many ways. For example, prior to the present enbourgeoisment of Kataragama, one was permitted to sell venison near the shrine premises, and venison was also offered as part of the *adukku*, or meal, given to the god. Similar techniques of articulating Vädda with Sinhala traditions/culture were practiced in village rituals. Thus, in Sinhala communal thanksgiving rituals after harvest, there is a sequence called the *vädi dane* ("Vädda almsgiving"); it is likely that it too was an attempt to introduce Vädda into the ritual life of the Sinhala village. In some rituals, there are actors who represent Väddas and who are permitted to eat meat substances, not in reality but in mimesis. By contrast, no meat, cooked or otherwise, was ever brought into the ritual arena by Buddhists.

The most interesting incorporation of Vädda into Sinhala village ritual occurs in the ritual cycle known as the *gammaduva* ("village hall"), held in honor of the Buddhist goddess Pattini. The myth goes as follows:

> After the goddess Pattini destroyed the city of Madurai, the Väddas decided to honor her since there was no one like her in the three worlds. The king of the Väddas proclaimed to his people that Pattini was on her way to their "city" after setting Madurai on fire. He ordered his people to clean up the city by removing sticks and stones, so that they might honor this Buddha-to-be. The Väddas then constructed a hall or *maduva* for performing *puja*s in her honor. They hung leopard skins as a canopy, and streamers of betel leaves and branches for decorations. The walls also were of leopard and deer skins. They lit lamps and burned incense in her honor. They had skins for carpets and meals prepared with *uru vi* ("pig rice," an inferior rice).

The Vädda offering, from the point of view of a pure goddess such as Pattini, was outrageously polluting, and hence the god Sakra summoned Dala Kumara, or Gara, the demon who swallows impurities, to earth. The goddess saw him and gave him a warrant to take the offerings for himself. Dala Kumara went to Vädda land, frightened all the Väddas, and gobbled up everything, the food as well as the physical structures. Pattini gave Dala Kumara permission to accept various rituals on her behalf from the Väddas. Then she witnessed the dances, drumming, and other displays of the Väddas in her honor.

What this myth seems to indicate is the following: Väddas are permitted to bring meat offerings to the *gammaduva* rituals for Pattini, but these are accepted by Gara, or Dala Kumara, who consumes impurities. Offerings to Gara are made at an altar or *mässa* outside the ritual arena. In any case, a strong opposition between the meat-eating Väddas and the pure deity of agriculturalists is suggested – a theme I will take up later in this chapter. As I interpret it, the *vädi pujava*, like the previous rituals, is a mechanism for incorporating Vädda into the religious and social structures of adjacent agricultural communities while at the same time recognizing its separateness.

The Nä Yakku cult and its transformations

I have made the case in the preceding discussions that from the Buddhist viewpoint at least, the Väddas are not Buddhist believers in rebirth and *karma*: they are presumed to possess an identity as hunters (even though they were historically agriculturalists, aristocrats, or mercenaries) and in this regard they resemble Sri Lankan castes. Outside of this, both Väddas and their neighboring Sinhalas seem to worship similar deities and practice similar ceremonials. In the Seligmann study, what distinguishes Vädda religion from Sinhala are the Nä Yakku, the spirits of the dead members of one's kin group. Here is the Seligmanns' general account:

As each Vedda community consists of a small number of families who, since cousin marriage prevails, are usually related both by blood and marriage, the *yaku* of the recent dead, called collectively Nae Yakku, are supposed to stand towards the surviving members of the group in the light of friends and relatives, who if well treated will continue to show loving kindness to their survivors, and only if neglected will show disgust and anger by withdrawing their assistance, or becoming even actively hostile. Hence it is generally considered necessary to present an offering to the newly dead within a week or two of their decease; but this is not invariably the case, for a few Veddas said that they would not hold a Nae Yaku ceremony until they specially required the help of the *yaku* or until misfortune threatened or had overtaken them.

(*ibid*.: 127)

In these ceremonies, the priest (*kapurala*) becomes possessed by the spirit of one or several Nä Yakku. The offering generally consists of rice and coconut milk, indicating once again the extent to which these ceremonies have been influenced by the Sinhalas. As in the Sinhala ceremonies, the food, or *adukku*, being offered to the Nä Yakku is eaten by the community as a whole, and in some communities (such as Henebadde) they even anoint the heads of their dogs with the milk offerings because they depended on dogs for hunting. "The strength of the desire for the companionship and communion with the spirits of the kindly dead was very strong, and it was generally felt that shamans, and those frequently possessed by the *yaku*, might have especially good luck on account of their close association with the spirits" (*ibid.*: 130–1). The belief is also strong that the Nä Yakku went as attendants to a major Vädda deity, Kande Yaka ("the deity of the mountain"), a friendly and helpful deity and a patron of hunters (*ibid.*: 132).

How does the dead person become a *yaka* (the singular form of Nä Yakku), or ancestral spirit? The process is simple enough. In the period immediately following a death, the term used is *prana karaya* ("breath being") rather than *yaka*.

> Among the Henebedde Veddas it was thought that the *prana karaya* resorted to Kande Yaka a few days, perhaps three to five, after death, and then obtained permission from him to accept offerings from the living, and thus become numbered among his attendants, the *Nae Yakku*; but beyond the vague idea that the spirit might perhaps exist for a short time at the site where death had occurred, these folk had no knowledge of its state before it reached Kande Yaka.
>
> (*ibid.*: 133)

It is interesting to note that the Bandaraduva Väddas, who have come under Sinhala and Tamil influence, say that the spirit, after staying near the death scene for a few days, leaves it to seek the Kataragama god to obtain his permission to become a *yaka* before "pass[ing] into the train of attendants on Kande Yaka, and so becom[ing] a *Nae Yaku* capable of accepting offerings from the living and in return helping or injuring them" (*ibid.*). These same Väddas believe that, along with the offering to the Nä Yakku, "it was equally important to propitiate the nearest Buddhist priest" (*ibid.*: 234). Unfortunately, the Seligmanns do not tell us what these Väddas meant by "propitiating" the Buddhist monk, but it is probably a formal recognition of suzerainty, as in the *vädi perahära*.

Vädda eschatology is such that Nä Yakku are constantly being produced as people die. First, when death occurs, one must hold a Nä Yakku ceremony to propitiate the dead kinsperson. Secondly, not every dead person can remain in the memory of the living beyond a finite period. Thus, while Nä Yakku are constantly being created, they are also constantly forgotten. The spirits of those who are long dead have a cosmological abode. They congregate in various mountain fastnesses under the aegis of Kande Yaka. However, some prominent ancestors have become more powerful Nä Yakku and continue to exist in memory and in the lives of Väddas. The Seligmanns record a Nä Yakku ceremony in Sitala Vanniya (the abode of "pure" Väddas) in which two important deceased ancestors possessed Kaira and his father-in-law, Handuna. At one time, the spirit of Handuna's own father-in-law, Tuta Gamarala, possessed both of them. Later on, the spirit of Handuna's father, Huda, possessed Kaira. The Seligmanns have a fine description of this ceremony and I refer the reader to their account. Suffice it to say here that the Nä Yakku rituals are of two types, one performed at death and the other when there is a need to propitiate the Nä Yakku, for example during illness or some other misfortune in the family, or, more positively, when specially powerful ancestors are invoked to produce more game. Of the two ancestors invoked in the Sitala Vanniya ritual, the Seligmanns have this to say: "The two *yaku* invoked at this ceremony were remembered by the community as influential men, and had probably been invoked frequently, and thus though still looked upon as attendants of Kande Yaka in a general way, they had probably gained a certain independence" (*ibid.*: 231). This kind of selectivity is also the basis for what is known as the "Bandara cult," the apotheosis of redoubtable dead ancestors popular among the Sinhalas.

Even though the worship of the Nä Yakku forms the striking feature of the ancestor religion of these Väddas, the Sinhalas occupying the same ecological zone as the Väddas also have a Nä Yakku cult, but with some important differences. This indicates once again the blurring of distinctions between Vädda and Sinhala, and at the same time forces us to recognize the differences. Hence I shall now describe the transformation of the Vädda Nä Yakku cult by the Sinhalas living in close proximity to the Väddas of Dambana.[5]

According to my informant Jayasundara's Sinhala conception, the formation of the Nä Yakku begins with desire or attachment or love (*asava, adaraya*). If, let us say, a woman dying by the side of her husband conceives an attachment for him, then she may eventually become a Nä Devi ("kin goddess"). Before the person becomes a Nä Yaka (or a Nä Devi), it is a *prana karaya*, a being possessing *prana*, or breath. The *prana karaya* does not possess any self-consciousness and wanders aimlessly around trees and rocks and such things until it is time for the conventional almsgiving for Buddhist monks three months after death.[6] Let us say that the *prana karaya* takes residence at a huge tree. While being a resident of the tree, it does not know what is happening. It is just born there like a caterpillar. Thus born, this being now tries to obtain a "warrant" from the gods such as Mangara, in charge of cattle, and other deities, including Ira Deviyo (sun god), Sanda Deviyo (moon god), Kataragama Deviyo, Isvara (Siva), Pattini, and others. Having obtained a "warrant," the Nä Yaka then tries to come back to the human world to see its kinfolk. For example, if the dead person had a son and loved the boy, it will go to that house. It makes certain signs to indicate its presence, most commonly by creating noises and frightening the residents, by bringing in serpents and depositing them, and by appearing in dreams. This is to bring to the attention of the household that the dead relative, now a *yaka*, is present.

According to my informant, there are various ways for the Nä Yaka to indicate its presence. It might cause a minor illness in a child, but it could be that no one pays any attention to it. Then it might give another example of its *has kama* ("signs of spiritual power"). A hunter (*vedikkara*) might go out for days and get nothing, but once a Nä Yaka is there to help him, presto (*patas gala*)! – he finds plenty of game. He will have good periods of hunting often by simply shooting at the animal without bothering to take aim; but then nothing happens for a week or two. The person might then become uncomfortable and consult an oracle, or *pena*, who tells him that a Nä Yaka is involved. He then immediately places an *adukku mutti*, or "offering pot," to the Nä Yaka and everything is fine again. When the Nä Yakku provides game in this way, one cannot go hunting with others, only alone. Furthermore, one must be guarded in one's speech and thoughts. If one gets a small animal and says disparagingly, "this is useless," or if one steps over a dead animal (an insult), or when faced with little success one says, "What nonsense! There are no Nä Yakku," then that person will have bad luck. The Nä Yakku can do a lot of good when they want to, and show their power (*has kama*) accordingly.

It seems that the Nä Yakku are capable of doing both good and bad to draw attention to themselves. When the Nä Yakku produce game, this must be recognized by putting aside a special portion (*mas kotasa*) of the animal known as *is malu* or *layil malu*, namely pieces from those parts of the body that cannot be licked by the animal. The blood is washed away, the meat cut into strips and dried. It is forbidden to eat this until the Nä

Yakku have consumed it from the *adukku mutti* placed for them whenever a ritual is performed in their honor. This ritual is central to both the Sinhalas and the Väddas living in the same area. At some point, the Nä Yakku who have come to hover around a human habitation through their great love or craving must be sent away (*elidara karanava*) from the house into the open. This is because the Nä Yakku can do good as well as harm. To put it differently, ambivalence is the characteristic feature of the Nä Yakku. The motivation to hold a ritual is strongest when a Nä Yaka has caused a serious illness or misfortune in the family.

Within the scope of this work, it is not possible to go into a detailed account of the rituals for the Nä Yakku. Consider what happens when a *pena*, or oracle, has identified an illness or misfortune as one caused by the Nä Yakku. The first step is for the priest to make a pledge, or *bara*, to the Nä Yakku by putting aside an *adukku mutti* ("offering pot"), containing rice, *panduru* (dedicated coins), a bangle, and a necklace of beads, and to invoke (*yadinava*) the Nä Yakku. Next, one vows to hold a Nä Yakku ceremony within a fixed period, for example seven days. The *adukku mutti* is then put aside, and if the patient has been afflicted by a recently deceased Nä Yaka, there will be a temporary cure. Following this is the major ceremony held at the specified time to send the Nä Yakku out of the household, but it is held under the aegis of three major gods, Manik Bandara, Kalu Bandara, and Indigolle Deviyo (also known as Gale Yaka, or Gale Bandara). In this example, it is the latter god who is in charge of the Nä Yakku. At the conclusion of the ritual, the *adukku mutti* is placed near the altar of Indigolle Deviyo. The priest dances as Indigolle, as though possessed by that deity. At a certain point he sprays *handun parahada* (sandalwood paste mixed with turmeric) on the family members seated on a mat before Indigolle Deviyo. The priest has a flower in his hand, which he waves before those assembled. At this point, one or more members of the family get possessed, or *vahanava* ("covered"), by the illness causing Nä Yakku, and they become *pissu* ("mad"), that is to say, they start to shake and "dance." This means that the Nä Yakku are in the bodies of those possessed. Once this has occurred, the priest stops his own dance and addresses the Nä Yakku who are now resident in the bodies of those who are *pissu*. He tells them that "you have come from the other world (*paralova*) into this world (*melova*) and born under the control of the *yakka*s and *deva*s (*yaksa damanaya, deva damanaya*) and you have displayed your *has kama* to your relatives and have now come into this household as a Nä Deviyo, but now you have left the house and come for the lovely offering (*ru adukkuva*)." The priest then says that "if you are a recently born Nä Deviyo owing to your love for the living, tell us your name and where you now are and how you have lived." At this point, those possessed identify the intruding Nä Yaka or Nä Yakku (because more than one dead ancestor may be present). The priest then takes the offering (*adukku mutti*) and gives it to the assembled family members. He sprays turmeric water (*kahadiyara*) on each patient and takes him or her aside. When the patient recovers from the possession, he or she is cured. The assembled family then eats the food from the *adukku* while the Nä Yakku go back to their abodes.

What, then, are the differences between the Nä Yakku religion of the Väddas, as described by the Seligmanns, and that of the Sinhalas living in the same ecological zone? It is clear that for both, hunting seems to be a key component of existence, though both practice swidden agriculture. The Sinhala priest gave us accounts of his own hunting exploits without the slightest implication of wrongdoing, even though he is formally a Buddhist. Both groups share the concept of Nä Yakku as well as the major deities who are overlords of the Nä Yakku. There are, though, some interesting linguistic differences. The Väddas tend to use the term *yakku* for all their deities, whereas in general Sinhala usage *yaka*, or *yaksa*, has bad connotations and is opposed to *deviyo/deva* ("god"/"goddess"). But those Sinhalas sharing the same ecological zone as the Väddas use *yaka* or *yakku* (plural) as the latter do; in addition, they use the term Nä Deviyo ("kin gods") synonymously. The Väddas, however, refer to their major gods also as *yakku* – thus Kande Yaka, Indigolle Yaka, and so forth – whereas the Sinhala priest uses the term *deviyo*. As far as the Bandara gods (selectively apotheosed ancestors) are concerned, both the Sinhalas and the Väddas use the same nomenclature, such as Kirti Bandara and Gange Bandara, but sometimes the Sinhalas convert the Vädda deity into a Bandara, for example when Gale Yaka becomes Gale Bandara. However, when the Väddas refer to the overall chief of the pantheon, Skanda, or Kataragama, they refer to him in the Sinhala mode as *deviyo*. There are only a few differences in the rituals, too, except that the Sinhalas have more songs and texts about the deities than do the Väddas, plus their ceremonies seem more elaborate. Thus once again the distinctions between Vädda and Sinhala living in the same zone and having the same occupations become fuzzier and fuzzier.

Yet there *are* some differences that need to be explored. According to the Seligmanns, the Väddas, like many other tribal groups the world over, practice a form of ancestor propitiation, which means that *all* persons at death become Nä Yakku. Thus, at the death of a person there has to be a ritual for the Nä Yakku, though not all groups consistently perform this. The Sinhalas do not share this belief; for them, only *some* become Nä Yakku, and these are the relatives who have had excessive *asava* or *adaraya* for the living. With this notion we are in the realms of Buddhist eschatology, for it is in Buddhism that desire is viewed as bad, as *tanha*, the root of all suffering, or *dukkha*. Thus our Sinhala priest, Jayasundara, says that nowadays only few become Nä Yakku, whereas in "those days" many more did. Other Sinhala priests in former Vädda country who have given up hunting have told us that it is the exceptional relative who becomes a Nä Yaka. Even so, there are many Nä Yakku around.

What happens to the Nä Yakku once they have been sent away at the conclusion of the ritual? Here is Jayasundara's version:

1   Those Nä Yakku who have not sinned too much go to various mountain tops like Mavaragala, Kokkagala, and Sesagala and live there. These places are in the fastnesses or *adaviya* of the god Saman and these *yakku* are under the command of Saman and Kataragama and the immediate command of gods like Indigolle and Kande Deviyo.

2   Those who have committed a lot of *pavu*, or "sin" in the Buddhist sense, are reborn in accordance with their *karma*. If they have done a lot of sin, they will spend time in hell.

3   Those who have done *pin*, or merit, are reborn in a good place (*honda tänaka*), for example in the human world, as soon as the Nä Yakku ritual is completed.

It might seem surprising to hear an inveterate hunter utter these Buddhist sentiments, but then even in the coastal regions there are many Buddhist communities, some fanatically so, comprised of professional fishermen. Our priest is also a Buddhist, and however nominal his Buddhism, it is desire that causes the relative to be born as a deity, and desire is a bad thing in the Buddhist scheme of things. With the *karma* theory, it is impossible for all relatives to be born as Nä Yakku because such things are determined by *karma*. This problem does not arise in the case of those Väddas who believe in neither *karma* nor rebirth; these groups can have an ancestor cult in which all relatives become Nä Yakku. Once people become Buddhist then the Nä Yakku become identified with the *preta*s of Buddhist mythology, a process that I shall now discuss.

I will do this by considering the work of Kiri Banda of the Monaravana shrine near Madagama, Bibile, south of Dambana. One might call him a "reform priest" because he started his career in a manner very similar to that of the previous informant, Jayasundara, but he now practices a cult that is much more permeated with Buddhist ideas. Kiri Banda's earlier practice differed little from Jayasundara's, but he has long since abandoned such practices. He told us that he learned his craft from a Vädda guru. This was nothing unusual, he said, because previous generations (*parampara*), including his father, did it this way. People at that time hunted a lot and practiced mostly swidden agriculture, and hardly any rice cultivation. When he commenced his professional career, Kiri Banda also did "bad things," namely hunting and making offerings of meat to the Nä Yakku. But he came under the influence of his mother who urged him not to sin, and when she died he gave up "bad things" and now he does only *pin daham*, or merit-making. Influenced by his greater piety, he has introduced some changes into his ritual practice. For example, his ritual texts require the giving of meat and fish offerings (*diya-goda mas*) to the Nä Yakku, but the provision of these substances will entail the direct or indirect killing of creatures and he will reap the effects of bad *karma*. Therefore, at the conclusion of the ritual he burns a few of his own bodily hairs for the dead person, or *preta*, because burned substances, or *pulutu*, according to Sinhala custom in general, are desired by demons and *preta*s. *Preta* is a Buddhist term referring to those reborn as inferior spirits owing to their excessive desires or greed. (*Preta* in classical Hinduism also means the spirit of the departed without any bad connotations, like the *prana karaya* of Vädda eschatology.)

Kiri Banda's sketch of Nä Yakku shows that it is still rooted in Vädda ideation. According to him, the Nä Yakku are our close kinfolk; mothers, fathers, brothers and sisters, mother's brothers and father's sisters, and occasionally children, but rarely little ones. In Kiri Banda's experience, most Nä Yakku are old persons who have had desire or greed (*asava*) for their children, property, or for jewelry they have hidden. They are sometimes seen exactly as they were in real life, generally after six o'clock in the evening. They also express their presence with signs, such as bringing snakes into the house. And sometimes they cause illness, and then one has to perform a ritual to get rid of the *preta*. Like the previous priest, Kiri Banda also believes that not all relatives become Nä Yakku. At death, when the *prana* (breath) leaves the body it is like a wind and hovers around the house for a period of seven days.

Kiri Banda gave us a description of present ritual practice that is quite different from Jayasundara's. Before dawn on the seventh day prior to the almsgiving to monks (the standard Buddhist practice), a *prana bat tatuva*, or "tray of rice for the breath being," containing sweets (*kävili*), bananas, rice, vegetables (*malu*), and water, is given to the recently deceased spirit (*prana karaya*) on a chair covered with a cloth. After the incense sticks have been lit, the Buddhist monk utters the standard prayer (*gatha*) that transfers merit to the dead. This is a variation of a well-known practice among Buddhists, better known as *preta tatuva* or *mataka tatuva* (the "preta tray" or "memory tray"). It seems to me that the earlier offering of meat known as the *is tambul* (Kiri Banda's term for

Jayasundara's *is malu* or *yayil malu*), given to the Nä Yakku for the success of the hunt, has been converted into a practice shared by Buddhists at large but with one difference: most Buddhists do not eat the food placed on the tray for the dead person, whereas the people in Kiri Banda's village and the surrounding areas do. This again is a remnant of the idea that the food given to the Nä Yakku – the *is tambul* – should be consumed by members of the household. The Nä Yaka only consumes the essence or smell (*suvanda*). This latter idea is also present in the Buddhist mortuary practice: the tray of food of the sort enjoyed by the dead person is consumed in essence by his wandering breath, or *prana*. This is the last act of consumption; after the almsgiving, the merit is transferred by the monk to the dead person in order to redeem him or her. If Kiri Banda's practice is a transformation of the Vädda practice, is it not possible that the Buddhist practice itself is a transformation of a cult of ancestors of the sort found among the Väddas?

Now, if the deceased was one possessed of good *karma*, he will immediately depart to a good rebirth, by which Kiri Banda meant a human rebirth. Then there are others who cannot achieve an immediate rebirth, but must wait for the next almsgiving three months later. There are yet others for whom this is inadequate, and rebirth for them might take a year or two, or even four or five years. Those who take three months to achieve rebirth are still non-material (*vayu*); they hover around but do not trouble anyone.

In the case of Kiri Banda, there is a real shift in the discourse on Nä Yakku. It is true that the first informant, Jayasundara, also thought that Nä Yakku were what most Sinhala folk call *preta*s, but the word *preta* rarely entered his discourse; it was almost always Nä Yakku and Nä Deviyo ("kin gods or goddesses"). In Kiri Banda's case, these terms are interchangeable. He also referred us to a text that deals with the origin of the Nä Yakku, which is simply based on the *Peta [preta] Vattu*, a late canonical text in Buddhism. He also makes constant references to *preta*s in his ritual songs.

Yet Kiri Banda has to recognize that the Nä Yakku are quite different from the classic descriptions of *preta*s in Buddhist texts and in the imaginations of most Buddhists. So he makes a distinction between the *preta*s of the time of previous Buddhas and other kinds of *preta*s. Those old *preta*s are called *gal preta* ("stone *preta*s") because they are firm and cannot be dislodged. In fact, it is not possible to cure a person afflicted with the *gal preta*. Thus, in spite of the influence of Buddhism on his cult, he also makes a clear distinction between the recently dead and the old *preta*s of the texts. Basically, there are three types of *preta*s or Nä Yakku of the recently dead: those who have done a lot of *pin daham*, or merit, and thus have no problem achieving a human rebirth after the almsgiving cere- mony; those who have had desire or love for the living or for property; and those who seek revenge from the living. Those who cause illnesses by excessive attachment are the easiest to banish with rituals and offerings (*dola pideni*). More difficult are those who have become *preta*s for *vairaya* and *pali* (hatred and revenge): they have to be removed by the power of the Bandara gods and the Kataragama god combined with the power of the priest's own teacher (*guru saktiya*).

Buddhism and the movement towards rice cultivation

I noted earlier that those Sinhalas who live or used to live in the same ecological zone as the Väddas practiced similar rituals because they shared a similar form of life. The Väddas, however, did not subscribe to Buddhism. The movement from Vädda to Sinhala is part of a larger movement whereby those who practiced hunting moved towards rice cultivation.

This is true for the Sinhalas as well as for the Väddas. With rice cultivation, it was possible to become more Buddhist, because one no longer needed hunting for subsistence. Needless to say hunting, like other professions that involved killing, was viewed as a low form of existence. Thus, the answer to the question of where have all the Väddas gone is that they have moved towards agriculture and towards Buddhism. The first and most important shift in this larger movement was one towards swidden cultivation and the raising of cattle. Obviously, swidden cultivation and cattle-raising were able to coexist with hunting, as many Sinhalas and Väddas living in similar zones discovered; but they were also able to coexist with rice cultivation, which then became a three-fold occupation most consonant with being Buddhist.

It is, however, a mistake to think that with rice cultivation and pastoralism there was a suspension of hunting. Prior to the colonial period, the agricultural areas were surrounded by large forests, and people used the resources of these forests for their livelihood in part by hunting. Thus, even in our own times, there are *vedikkaras* (hunters with guns) in Buddhist villages, but this is a devalued occupation because it is a sinful one. The opposition between hunting and agriculture is not just expressed in Buddhist doctrinal and historical texts such as the *Mahavamsa*. It is also expressed in ritual texts such as those pertaining to the goddess Pattini, who is par excellence the deity presiding over the ritual cycle known as the *gammaduva*, practiced in the rice-cum-cattle-raising areas of the Western and Sabaragamuva Provinces. In the *vädi pujava*, which was discussed earlier, she is repelled by the impurity of the Vädda offering of meat and has the demon Gara gobble up these noxious foods.

The vast rice-growing areas in ancient times embraced the great hydraulic civilizations of the dry zones, which in my view were for the most part inhabited by Sinhala Buddhists. The pre-fourteenth-century literature hardly makes any reference to the Väddas, though they must have lived around the periphery of the great agricultural zones. The northern hydraulic zone contained the capital of the Sinhala-Buddhist kings and was known as the *rajarata* (the realm of the kings). That this was not the typical habitat of hunters is recognized in the *Mahavamsa* quotation previously noted: the Pulindas, the offspring of Vijaya and Kuveni, retreated to the Peak in Sabaragamuva, the *adaviya*, or forest domain, of the god Saman and outside the pale of Buddhist civilization. After the abandonment of the old *rajarata* in the thirteenth century, the Väddas perhaps also moved over into that region, such that Knox had fleeting glimpses of them when he was running away. Meanwhile, profound historical changes were taking place in Sri Lanka between the fourteenth and fifteenth centuries with the formation of new kingdoms outside the old hydraulic zones: these were in the Kandyan area in the central highlands, Kotte near Colombo, and the outlying regions that captured the new sea trade with Arabs and then with European powers.

The development of these once forested areas for rice growing paralleled the growing outreach of Buddhism and that of the great guardian gods who were protectors of both Buddhism and the secular realm. The poetry of this period refers not only to the paths that interconnected this vast region but also to the many great Buddhist temples and shrines for the guardian gods. With the introduction into this region of rice cultivation and subsidiary pastoralism (which included cattle as well as buffaloes needed for agriculture), hunting ceased to be the prime and valued form of life. With this powerful movement leading to the growth of rice cultivation, the Väddas were gradually drawn into the dominant economy; *ipso facto* they were also drawn into a hegemonic Buddhism, fostered by intermarriage with the Sinhalas. Thus, when the British arrived on the scene, the so-called wild Väddas were confined for the most part to the *palu rata*, or "desolate lands," the plains of the Vanni, the Bintanne.

One could cite dozens of ritual texts that deal with the movement from hunting to agriculture and sometimes from hunting to pastoralism. These texts also deal with the lives and myths of origin of the gods and goddesses who were associated with this shift. Let me present just *one* of these texts, one that concerns the origin myth of the great god of pastoralism and cattle rearers, the god Mangara, also known as Budusiru. According to one of the Mangara myths, Prince Budusiru was born in the country of Maya in Muladipa ("original land," i.e. India). Astrologers predicted that at 19 years old he would be killed by a wild buffalo in Kadirava (in the southern plains) owing to his bad *karma* from a previous birth, caused because he had sucked the milk from a cow and had deprived the calf of its milk. The king, his father, afraid of his son's prowess, banished him, and he landed in the area between Tangalla and Ambalantota on the south coast of Sri Lanka. He sent a cow herder to capture a wild buffalo while he went with his followers to Kadirava. There he saw a huge golden *nuga* (banyan) tree and rested there. In its hollow was a large beehive, which the bees were entering in three places. Budusiru asked his men to cut the hive, but the god of the tree got angry because it was his tree. The men struck the tree but all their weapons broke, and Budusiru himself dealt a blow with his golden axe and the *nuga* tree opened like a door. In it were various ornaments and most importantly the following: golden lassoes and goads, golden pots and vases, and golden plows and yokes. Mangara and his followers then went to Kadirava with their lassoes and goads and weapons to capture a buffalo, when they eventually saw an extraordinary one in the midst of seven lakes. Mangara tried to noose it with his lasso, but the bull charged at him and killed him and then killed all his followers. Meanwhile, the herder whom he had sent earlier saw the dead king and accosted the deadly animal in the lake and killed it. This herder is the prototype priest of the Mangara cult. He cut up the dead buffalo and used the various body parts for the ritual he performed. Thus:

> The kneecaps were used for hearthstones
> The hide stretched into a canopy
> The intestines were used as curtains
> And the nerves as golden halters...

Now the herder-priest wanted turmeric, presumably to cleanse the ritual arena of pollution, and went to ask the goddess Pattini for some. Pattini was angry because of the pollution of dead animals and humans. She then went to the Naga (snake beings') world, accompanied by Prince Cowherd and Prince Milk, and got *rat hal* (red rice) and turmeric from the Naga king. Now the arena could be cleansed and the milk-boiling ceremony could be performed. When the milk was boiling, Pattini sprayed some on Budusiru and his retinue and they were resurrected. The various parts of the buffalo were also put together and it came alive with a joyous cry. Then Mangara, the glorious god, went and lassoed wild buffalo to capture and tame them.

As I interpret this myth, the followers of Mangara (alias Budusiru) try to take the honey from the *nuga* tree by force. Honey collection is a prime task of the Väddas; it defines their gathering role. But Mangara himself forcibly cuts the *nuga* tree and gets the honey, and in the cavity he gets his own *ayuda* and *abharana*, or ritual weapons and ornaments, and, most importantly, his goads and lassoes and plows. He goes out to kill a wild buffalo; he is the hunter and is killed presumably for this illicit action. The herder then kills the buffalo and cuts it up and uses its body parts for the ritual. Pattini, the deity associated with agriculture, cleanses the pollution and resurrects both Mangara and the buffalo. Consequently, Mangara takes a new course; he becomes someone who ceases to kill buffaloes, capturing and taming them instead – and this, as everyone in the culture knows, is so that they can be used for ploughing and for obtaining milk. Pattini herself provides *rat hal* rice, which presumably will be used for sowing. In other myths, similar processes are depicted: thus Unapane Kiriamma, a goddess worshipped by both Väddas and Sinhalas, has a spouse known as Unapane Vanniya who was responsible for bringing the land in this region under rice cultivation. The implication of such myths is that both Väddas and Sinhalas living in the same region moved from hunting to agriculture, which is the beginning of a process of becoming Buddhist.

Conclusion

In this chapter I have referred to three representations of "Vädda." The first is the early European incorporation of Vädda into the native (European) notion of the wild man. This preoccupation persists to this day in various guises, among both Romantic Europeans and colonized Sinhalas who have appropriated the wild Vädda. Secondly, there are those modern categorizations of "aboriginal," "tribal," and so forth, that we saw in the Seligmanns' hopeless attempt to search for the pure Väddas. Thirdly, there is the Buddhist representation of the Vädda as "hunter," even though there have been Väddas who have defied this simplistic categorization. The Buddhist fiction, however, permits a certain decoding, namely that given the hegemonic nature of that civilization, Väddas were being converted into Buddhists. On the other hand, there are Buddhists living in the same ecological zone nowadays who are culturally allied to Väddas; before modern times, such Buddhists could as easily have become Väddas. I have suggested that one could gloss "hunter" to mean something else as well: that Väddas were non-Buddhist believers in a cult of ancestors known as Nä Yakku. Consequently, I show from the work of the Seligmanns that the idea of the Nä Yakku was fused with the Buddhist notion of *preta* and that Vädda ideation persists in the mortuary rites of Sinhala-Buddhists. Furthermore, I can document other Vädda ritual practices that have become Buddhicized.[7] Hindu beliefs have also been accommodated by Buddhist popular religion in a similar fashion, and have been given Buddhist ethical values. For example, animal sacrifice, so common in Hindu popular religion, has been virtually eliminated in Buddhist popular religion. Thus Kiri Banda, the priest, tells us that although his ritual requires the flesh of animals and fish (*diya goda mas*) to propitiate the Nä Yakku, he substitutes this with burned hair from his own body. There is nothing new here; he is simply borrowing this idea from Buddhist popular religion.

In the Buddhist scheme of things, there are no "indigenous peoples," no "aborigines," no "wild men," no "tribes" of the Western imagination. The origin myth of the Väddas says clearly that they were the offspring of the union of Vijaya with Kuveni, who is defined as a *yakini* (a demoness). From this union sprang the Väddas, who were no more indigenous than the Sinhalas springing from the union of Vijaya and his men with Tamil women. This wonderful recognition of hybridity has not been challenged by Sri Lankans until recent times (as the Tamil side of their ancestry is being forgotten). The Väddas have become Sinhalas and Buddhists over a long historical period; and Buddhists have no doubt become Väddas. The Väddas have also bypassed what many ethnographers thought held good for India: that tribes become low castes as they are integrated into a larger polity. But quite the contrary is true for Sri Lanka. The Väddas, as far as I know, became rice farmers and most of them dropped their Vädda identity and became members of the dominant farmer caste. Moreover, the Väddas have not been seen as an inferior group; they were feared and respected even though they were outside the pale of Buddhist civilization.[8] There is no doubt that that civilization was a hegemonic one. The kings were Buddhist and defenders of the Buddhist faith. But there has been no instance, as far as I know, of "internal colonization" through violence, or of a forcible absorption of Vädda communities into the Buddhist polity (Weber 1976: 490–6). Finally, as far as the theme of the present volume is concerned, neither Vädda religion nor forms of local religion among Buddhist villages (such as shamanism, spirit possession, and the propriation of gods, or *devas*) possess an internal dynamic that impels them towards modernity. That is provided by Theravada Buddhism, which has become a powerful driving force for modernity since the late nineteenth century.

Notes

1   In this chapter, I do not use diacriticals except for certain key words (Vädda, Nä Yakku, Nä Yaka, and Nä Deviyo) and when a word is italicized. Two versions of this paper, written with a different slant, have appeared previously, first as the Ludowyk Lecture 2000 at the University of Peradeniya, Sri Lanka, and a second, with the title "Where have all the Väddas gone?", in Silva (2001). I must also acknowledge the help of my research assistant, Nandana Weerarathne, who helped me track down isolated villages influenced by Vädda culture; and James Brow and Larry Rosen for their comments on an earlier draft of this chapter.

2   For a good historical survey, see K.N.O. Dharmadasa, "Veddas in the history of Sri Lanka," in Dharmadasa and De A. Samarasinghe (1990: 34–47).

3   This literature has been recently reviewed in two important essays by Hayden White (1978a, 1978b). See also Bernheimer (1952) and Campbell (1988). Bernheimer has a neat summary of the wild man on the basis of depictions in art, literature, and sculpture:

> It is a hairy man curiously compounded of human and animal traits, without however sinking to the level of an ape. It exhibits upon its naked anatomy a growth of fur, leaving bare only its face, feet, and hands, at times its knees and elbows, or the breasts of the female of the species. Frequently the creature is shown wielding a heavy club or mace, or the trunk of a tree; and, since its body is usually naked except for a shaggy covering, it may hide its nudity under a strand of twisted foliage worn around the loins.
>
> (1952: 1)

Regarding Roger Batra's (1994) re-examination of this topic, I am not persuaded by his thesis that the European experiences in the Americas led to the erosion of the idea of the "Wild Man."

4   For a good discussion of these issues, see James Brow (1978: 3–39).

5   My informant is a 44-year-old Sinhala priest (*kapurala*), Herat Mudiyanselage Jayasundara of Dambana.

6   The general custom among most Sinhalas is to give alms to monks on behalf of the dead person seven days after the death and again after three months. It seems that this priest has skipped the first round.

7   In my book *The Cult of the Goddess Pattini* (Obeyesekere 1984: 301–4), I show how the well-known Vädda hunting ritual has been converted into different ritual forms among the Sinhalas.

8   For more evidence on this subject, see Dharmadasa and De A. Samarasinghe (1990: 37).

References

Batra, Roger, *Wild Men in the Looking Glass*, Ann Arbor: Michigan University Press, 1994.

Bernheimer, Richard, *Wild Men in the Middle Ages*, Cambridge, MA: Harvard University Press, 1952.

Brow, James, *Vedda Villages of Anuradhapura*, Seattle: University of Washington Press, 1978.

Campbell, Mary, *The Witness and the Other World*, Ithaca and London: Cornell University Press, 1988.

Dharmadasa, K.N.O. and S.W.R de A. Samarasinghe, *The Vanishing Aborigines: Sri Lanka's Veddas in Transition*, New Delhi: Vikas Publishing House, 1990.

Gallagher, R.E. (ed.), *Byron's Journal and His Circumnavigation 1744–66*, Cambridge: Cambridge University Press for the Hakluyt Society, 1964.

Geiger, Wilhelm, *Mahavamsa*, London: Pali Text Society, 1980.

Godakumbure, Charles, *Kohomba Kankariya*, Colombo: Government Press, 1963.

Hodgen, Margeret, *Early Anthropology in the Sixteenth and Seventeenth Centuries*, Philadelphia: University of Philadelphia Press, 1964.

Knox, Robert, *An Historical Relation of the Island of Ceylon*, Glasgow: James Maclehose and Sons, 1911.

Obeyesekere, Gananath, *The Cult of the Goddess Pattini*, Chicago: University of Chicago Press, 1984.

Parker, Henry, *An Account of the Aborigines and of Part of the Early Civilization*, London: Luzac and Co., 1909a.

——, *Ancient Ceylon*, London: Luzac and Co., 1909b.

Peiris, Paul E., *Sinhale and the Patriots*, New Delhi: Navrang, 1995 (first published 1909).

Percival, Robert, *An Account of the Island of Ceylon*, London: C. and R., 1805.

Seligmann, C.G. and Brenda Z. Seligmann, *The Veddas*, Cambridge: Cambridge University Press, 1911.

Silva, Neluka (ed.), *Hybrid Island*, Colombo: Social Scientists Association, 2001.

Smith, Bernard, *European Vision and the North Pacific*, 2nd edn, New Haven and London: Yale University Press, 1985.

Tylor, Edward B., *Anthropology: Introduction to the Study of Man*, London: Macmillan and Co., 1881.

Wallis, Helen, "The Patagonian giants," in R.E. Gallagher (ed.) *Byron's Journal and His Circumnavigation 1744–66*, Cambridge: Cambridge University Press for the Hakluyt Society, 1964.

Weber, Eugen, *Peasants into Frenchmen*, Stanford: Stanford University Press, 1976.

White, Hayden, "The forms of wildness: archaeology of an idea," in *Tropics of Discourse: Essays in Cultural Criticism*, Baltimore: Johns Hopkins University Press, 1978a, 156–82.

——, "The noble savage theme as fetish," in *Tropics of Discourse: Essays in Cultural Criticism*, Baltimore: Johns Hopkins University Press, 1978b, 183–96.

Part IV

The Pacific Islands

Chapter 20

On wondering about wonder
Melanesians and the cargo

Garry W. Trompf

I

When I was a young boy, I used to pore over one particular book that my father had given to my eldest brother. It was an attractive little volume entitled *The Secrets of Other People's Jobs*, and it was littered with photographs and diagrams as to how the many interesting objects in my own observable world – glasses, pots, cans, ships, airplanes – were put together.[1] In the course of my early education I had occasion to join school excursions to witness for myself some of the processes depicted in that book, although it took twenty years for me to see the inside of something like a cotton mill (a hosiery factory), personal penury as a 26-year-old student in Oxford to see a leather-splitting machine (before which I labored for extra cash as a humble t-poler), and the first time I ever saw tins coming off the production line was at 35 when, as a visiting academic, I had taken my family on a long jaunt from San Francisco to Salt Lake City. It was at the last place that I began thinking very much about my students back at the University of Papua New Guinea, where I had taken one of the first two appointments in Religious Studies in Australia (at a time when Papua and New Guinea were still Australian territories). I took photographs madly, mindful much less of this as my own first experience than of young Melanesians who might take more convincing that tins were actually made on assembly lines, and not in some spiritual location. No factories of the kind were in place for them to visit in Port Moresby or Lae, and many of their families were still given to tales of "the Cargo" – of introduced, "European-style" commodities – being manufactured by ancestors or spirit-beings. On reflection, though, there was an immediate lesson to be learned: that I myself had assumed the very worldly existence of things on the basis of photographs (including, in the course of time, television) and not of stricter empirical encounter; and that my reaction to the experience of this already mentally extrapolated world was more of confirmation than of wonder.

Wonder is the focus of this chapter and it is a subject not without some prior attention. It is intriguing to consider how influential Western theorists who constituted modern notions of "primitivity" handled wonder. I take it as of real fascination, indeed, that the alleged founder of capitalism, the Scotsman Adam Smith (1723–90), a man who showed no little interest in new products and artifices, was perhaps the first to devote a third of a treatise – *The History of Astronomy* – to the sentiment of wonder. Wonder, by Smith's definition, is the response to "extraordinary and uncommon objects" (meteors, comets, and eclipses being of obvious singularity among them), and in humanity's earliest state, "every object of nature...considerable enough to attract his attention" will be enough to imbue wonder in the "savage's" mind.[2] To anything quite overawing, such as lightning, he will respond with a reverence that approaches fear, and (like his Neapolitan near-contemporary, Giambattista Vico (1668–1744)), Smith imagined for the "primitive" a heightened anxiety about "the displeasure of...offended deities." Other phenomena "perfectly beautiful and agreeable," on the other hand, were also "the proper objects of reverence and gratitude," still inspiring wonder as proceeding "from some intelligent beings," the sentiment of wonder behind either "consternation" and "complacency" so arising, as philosopher David Hume (1711–76) doubtless influenced Smith to conclude, through early humans not being able to make a connecting, "imaginal" bridge between events, in much the same way as an eighteenth-century Scotsman wondered, given no explanation, over the peculiar movements of iron before a loadstone.[3] Wonder, in Adam Smith, has clearly begun to be reflected upon naturalistically, but it is obviously taken as a central component in religion's sensibility, even when such a genius as he was ponders the emergent Newtonian paradigm of the Universe.[4]

For the putative founder of the discipline of comparative religion, "Anglo-German" Friedrich Max Müller (1823–1900), a century later, wonder was a very wellspring of religiosity, but in his envisaging of things, the Enlightenment tends to give way to the Romantic. What he described as the natural "appreciation of the infinite" was the naïve, childlike freshness with which the most ancient poets continually experienced their worlds:

> A new life flashed by every morning before their eyes, and the fresh breezes of dawn [that] reached them like greetings wafted across the golden threshold of the sky, from "the rainer, the thunderer, the measurer," or especially from those "bright beings, the Sun, the Sky, the Day, the Dawn...opposed to the powers of night and darkness" as a "contrast of very ancient date."[5]

On the other hand, Müller was inferring all this from what he took to be the earliest *textual* evidence of humanity's spiritual life; namely the signs of reverence behind the Rg Veda (and he trusted little else but texts for revealing the nature of religions in the distant past). Perhaps, in his earlier Enlightenment context, Smith seems only to make a little jump back from what he knew of the Graeco-Roman "polytheism" to the "primitive condition";[6] but by Müller's time, the corpus of ethnographic reports on indigenous peoples had expanded exponentially, and the new fashion of evolutionism tempted the mind to extrapolate from the "most apparently primitive" among contemporary "savages" back to the prehistoric origins of religion.[7] Müller, however, "historist" to the core, took a rather different tack by giving such priority to the Vedic hymns and what could be inferred behind them.[8] Yet for him, long *after* the more aware stage reflected in these hymns, many dispersed human groups lapsed into a confusion of thought – through a "disease of language" – that brought about the enormous "curious array of belief systems...too often called savage," found in the "anthropological religions" of tribal Africans, Australians, Pacific Islanders, and the like.[9] The true son of Romanticism, Müller placed the primordial impetus of an authentic wonder first, and the peoples his contemporaries were calling primitives and savages were, by the scientifically analyzable logic of language, more susceptible to errors of metonymy, anthropomorphism, and unintelligibility.[10] Herein lies the seedbed of the assumption that primitives, while they may be struggling with the connections of things, as Smith would say, may also be very curious – but only "to get it wrong."

It was on Christmas Eve, 1856, that an equally important figure in the proto-history of "religious studies," and as much an armchair theorist as Müller, was recuperating from an illness on a farm in Devon. Herbert Spencer (1820–1904), the great "social evolutionist," arguably the first sociologist of religion, found himself in simple, rustic, and (for a Londoner) not particularly stimulating company. To amuse himself one day, he followed his well-known inventive bent by making a holly berry with a pod thrust through it "dance about on a vertical jet of air," and demonstrated the experiment to the farmer and his small daughter. To Spencer's great interest, the farmer (whom most reading this chapter could presume might well have been very tired) showed not the slightest fascination over his antics. In the mind of the irrepressible evolutionist, though, when later reflecting on the incident, there could only be one obvious deduction:

> I was reminded of…accounts given of the comparative indifference which low savages display, when shown looking-glasses, watches, or other remarkable products of civilized life. Surprise or curiosity are not the traits of the utterly ignorant.[11]

By the act of imagination, or an extrapolation from an alleged relic in the English countryside both across to the inexperienced modern primitive and then back to the "original" one, we find here that "first peoples," or the members of most small-scale, traditional societies, are represented as "duller of wit," often lacking in curiosity and a sense of wonder – being the very logical opposite, in fact, to Spencer's ideal scientist as someone naturally prepared for surprise and educated by higher religion to marvel in a civilized way.[12]

Professor Kitson Clark once remarked that Spencer had as much influence on the West as Karl Marx on the East (though neither were that widely read).[13] Marx (1818–83) was as much an "evolutionist" (or, strictly speaking, a developmentalist), except that in the greater matter of political economy he shared with Müller a certain Romanticism, to the effect that the present order would have to throw off the chains of the new slave society of capitalism, and cure its disease through scientific socialism. Thus, to contemplate the famous paradigm in *The German Ideology*, history begins with a primal fear of overwhelming elements in the environment and ends with a complete mastery over both technology and sociality.[14] Although there may have been some reason to admire the earliest societies – especially because they had not dissolved "their relations to the earth"[15] – primitives are nonetheless in utter awe of external forces and inevitably create the gods out of them because they are at the mercy of the "not-yet-controllable." One might suspect again the shadow of Giambattista Vico here, and the famous exemplum of promiscuous couples startled into feelings of guilt and thus morality by claps of thunder, as the very voice of Jove.[16] But Marx is more patently neo-Epicurean in his envisagements; it is fear before the odds that counts, and humans are naturally driven through it to a mutual (Engels would add "classless") dependence on each other.[17]

By the turn into the last century, the European projection of the "wondering savage" had taken on newer and more various aspects. By then, Melanesia – the main subject of this chapter – had come into the picture. What R.H. Codrington told of Solomonese and eastern Melanesian notions of *mana* – that "power or influence, not physical," belonging "to the region of the unseen"[18] – had been construed as an apprehension of the "supernatural" that surprised "the natives" in their daily round. Thus, while F.B. Jevons (1858–1936) rejected on the basis of the flow of new ethnographic data the (Müllerian) thesis that "primitive man lived in a state of perpetual surprise," it was fair to assume that, "at any rate occasionally," any unexpected, "startling *frustration*" in *calculations* during the "natural" routine of life made primitives realize they were "in the hands of a mysterious and supernatural power."[19] The Scot James George Frazer (1854–1941) was having some effect here, because he had given back to the primitive (in spite of Spencer, and also Smith) a sense of "the experimental" – magic, for all the mistaken assumptions, being the predecessor to modern science (and also prior to religion).[20] For Jevons, though, it was implicitly the failure of expectations in a world of magic that induced wonder, and thus religiosity.

Another important English theorist of religion, R.R. Marett (1866–1943), paid homage to Jevons' approach when he argued, almost a decade before Rudolf Otto in Germany, that the word "awe" is "the one that expresses the fundamental religious feeling most nearly," that sense of "thrill" "whereof the component 'moments' are fear, admiration, wonder, and the like, whilst its object is, broadly speaking, the supernatural."[21] The Melanesians' *mana* was invoked, as was the comparably vague (and for Marett pre-animistic) conception of the supernatural among the African Masai, who, significantly enough for our present purposes, not only took mysterious steaming holes as *ngai*, but also the white man Joseph Thompson and his lamp.[22] Marett, however, was influenced enough by Scotsman Andrew Lang (1844–1912) and what he had written about primitive actions to the unexpected – and to the spooky[23] – to play down talk of magical experimentation and heighten the emphasis on feeling and states of uncertainty before the supernatural. The psychology of wonder became of greater importance.

The story of such European imaging has further chapters, both simultaneously on the Continent and further in time in the Anglophone world. A chapter by Austrian Sigmund Freud (1856–1939) in *Totem and Taboo* (1918) on the "omnipotence of thought" among infants and savages is essentially an argument for inferring "latent" psychological states that are generated from or coexist with the surprises of life "present to the senses and the consciousness."[24] When the would-be phenomenologist of religion Dutchman Gerardus van der Leeuw (1890–1950) once reflected on the greater suggestibility of primitives,[25] it was to make a pejorative-looking judgment, not too distant from Freud's, that "the natives" have a habit of making too much of things, of over-exaggerating and letting their thoughts run away, as little known expeditions to Melanesia – one by Anglo-American psychologist William McDougall to the Torres Strait in 1898, and another by psychological anthropologist Richard Thurnwald to German *Neuguinea* in 1906–09 – had already been designed to confirm.[26]

Less denigrating models were canvassed in part reaction by the German Rudolf Otto (1869–1937) and the Swiss Carl Jung (1875–1961). For Otto, "the feeling of something 'uncanny,' 'eerie' or 'weird' [i.e. basically *unheimlich*]...emerging in the mind of the primitive human being forms the starting point for the entirety of religious development in history."[27] Of this shuddering before the numinous, however, apprehension of "the 'supernatural' has nothing to do with the case." In qualifying Marett, he contended that this was "much too imposing an expression" for the primitive case. What he called "the vestibule of religion" was the product of "naive, rudimentary fancies" paying "homage to natural objects that were frightening or extraordinary."[28] Otto, however, wrote of this incipience of holy dread less out of empirical interests than a desire to solve a philosophical problem, that of giving the religious sense a status *sui generis*; and thus the primitive, embodied above all in the savage wonderer, was constituted as the "preface" to high theological insights.[29] As for Jung, that which

Otto conceives more in terms of outer relations, with primitives responding to shadows and lakes, and eventually theological minds to the "Wholly Other," comes to be transformed in analytical psychology into interior events. Primitives operate in a world affected by "unconscious regulators" – "dominants" that invade the inner *numinosum*, generating astonishment, awe, and fear.[30] This view, however, entailed Jung's problematic subscription to Frenchman Lévy-Bruhl's theory of the indigene's "mystical participation" with non-human agencies in this cosmos, or pre-logical mentalities that conditioned the fearful images and phantasms erupting as interior astonishments in dreams.[31]

The goalposts for the better understanding of *les sauvages*, in any case, tended to be shifted in accordance with specialist games played in European academic disciplines. That earthier English soul D.H. Lawrence (1885–1930), for one, who was a theorist of religion in his own right, and who knew some Jung but surprisingly never read Freud, was wondering where bodies had gone to in all this. He apparently wanted primal wonder to be re-located in the close encounter with or near touch of nakedness, when "blood," not just mind, was thinking.[32] When blood did come into it further down the track, the interest in awe and wonder assumed a sinister undertone, and the Dionysians' cultivation of fascination for the lost pagan *mysterium* led to the sacred Teutonic grottos of the Nazis, and the tragic misappropriations of Otto's *Das Heilige*.[33] Concern for wonder, on this account, began to lose what momentum it had left. If the *unheimlich* could metamorphose into the *grausig* politically, that had to be reckoned with experientially. Awe, dread, and curiosity became in psychological texts "mixed emotions" – of surprise and fear, fear and expectancy, and surprise and acceptance respectively – sometimes indistinguishable from other mixed emotions, and wonder hardly coming into view at all.[34] The American psychologist B.F. Skinner was quick to categorize wondering under "superstition," when, in consolidating earlier work by fellow countryman Thorndike and the Russian Pavlov, he found animals were "startled" to find reinforcement (food availability) by performing some action "totally irrelevant" to the norm (pressing a bar),[35] and so by experiencing what in the language of Jevons and Marett "defeats reasonable expectation."[36] The Western intellectual community was losing its own sense of wonder – symptomatically perhaps, given the "Era of Violence" – and from Durkheimian talk about collective excitations or effervescence to fancy new language about "cognitive engrossment" and "effortless dissociation," wonder was obscured behind other categories rather tangential to it.[37] That "naive and knowing" state, apparently being "dis-spelled" by a hundred-and-one photographic books, by the exponentially quickened appearance rate of new inventions, and by an ethos combining smart technology with the blasé, became steadily eviscerated. It has just managed to hold on with children (we are still delighted with the child's responsive explicatives of "Wow!" and "Cool!") and it is held in the back of the mind with the "politically correct" recognition that one should not play (too long) on the susceptibilities of others.[38] The perceptive, theologically educated Rollo May sensed the dilemma all too clearly. The culture of high technology has subtly and tragically so suppressed our sense of wonder that it has become central to *Man's Search for Himself* to recover it, if psychic health is to be maintained.[39] Concerning wonder, paradoxically, through which Western intellectuals created the culture of the primitive, the West requires recultivation – to forestall the pressures against utterly disenchanting the world.[40] For the decline of wonder seems symptomatic of the decay of religion itself.

II

The Melanesian region, the most complex ethnographic scene on earth, is a very obvious place from which to ponder further the wondering of once isolated indigenous peoples. It is the region made famous by the so-called "cargo cults," or collective activities arising from local expectations that "abundant Western-style cargo" will be sent to the living by the dead or by other spirit-powers.[41] Such phenomena have much to do with encounters between lithic (sometimes called "stone age") cultures[42] and modern humanity at the height of its technological prowess. Hence a common and strong association of Melanesia with a "primitivity of response" to outside contact, with an astonishment before the intrusive unknown, with black bodies falling fearful and worshipful under the roar of the noise of the "big birds," as Gasseau's Oscar-winning documentary film *The Sky Above the Mud Below* archetypally portrayed.[43] The story is an incredibly complex one, from earlier coastal contact situations, when the Russian explorer Baron Miklouho-Maclay landed by sailing ship at Astrolabe Bay in 1871, and was "moon man" to the local Madang Sek and Som groups,[44] up until the time when sophisticated Trobriander poet John Kasipwalova would look up at the Boeing 747s flying over the University of Papua New Guinea in the 1970s and declare: "Ah, whiteman!" The history of responses to intrusion in the southwest Pacific, however, does not lend itself to easy generalization. To the farthest west, on the *Vogelkop* of West Papua, contact with outside cultures was age-old, with Muslims who taught iron-smelting before serious white contact in the 1880s (see below, note 42); while to the far east in Fiji, encounters with whites since the late 1830s (ahead of the second Industrial Revolution), as well as a very significant involvement of Polynesians in the Christianization process, have meant that "neither cargo nor cult" has been characteristic of Fijian reactions to socio-technological change.[45] Towards the tail-end of the whole story of impact/response, however, completely landlocked, small-scale cultures were being "found" by outsiders right into the post-War period. One learns of white-besuited geologists landing in a helicopter on a mountainside in the remote Kopiago district of the Southern Highlands of Papua New Guinea in 1975, stopping briefly to chip at rocks like moonrakers while frightened and scattered locals watch them from behind trees, and then quickly flying off again, as if visitors from another planet.[46]

In this context, we can only set our agenda for reflective study; and it is one that I will set in reacting to those Western theoretical constituters of "the primitive," concentrated as it will remain on the intriguing question of wonder. An obvious starting point is with lexical issues, with the *vocabulary of wonder*. What is of interest here is the way in which the traditional language of the astounding, the unusual, and the numinous gets adjusted with the arrival of the "total outsiders" and their goods.

For a highly pertinent sample, take Papuan Motu, the language of the cultural complex in Papua New Guinea most affected by social change, for it is within Motuan (coastal) country that the capital Port Moresby has arisen. The expression *namehoa* was used for being startled, as in an ambush by another tribe, and this, interestingly, was the term applied to initial contact with whites or other connected newcomers. The LMS missionary Rarotongan Ruatoka, for example, evoked the response *namehoa*, presenting as he did in a white suit.[47] The whiteness of the suit, and of the Europeans' skins, as one would have expected, was also connected with the dread of spirits – or *lauma daure*, as the Motuan phrase had it – but the flesh-and-blood, mortal nature of the newcomers was soon established, and this expression came to be applied for a longer time and more specifically to the discharge of guns (until their common use by Motuan hunters). The word *ganora*, traditionally used of something astonishingly sharp (such as bone or bamboo points or weaponry), was taken to be still more appropriate in referring to the metal knives borne by the outsiders. *Kiama kiama*, a doublet denoting mysterious lights – luminescent fungus, for example, which one would avoid in the forest as attesting the presence of spirits, or lights flashing across the sea, taken as flying witches arriving from the east[48] – was naturally applied also to the unusual lights of European vessels out from the coastline.

Lexically speaking, Motuans reckon *lauma daure*, the dread of the spirits, to be more centrally important and, equivalently speaking, nearer the heart of their religion. Reactive *angst* over the sanction of the ancestral spirits, if one did not keep tabus, or did not behave correctly in a ritual context, was of greater consequence than confrontation with the unusual as such.[49] Western theorists may facilitate the asking of relevant questions, but we are left wondering whether they have been on the right "wave length." Marx, of all people, looks to have the most apt approach, with his focus on fear, yet we must be careful that we do not reduce fear to alarm over environmental eruptions, when in the main, as with most Melanesian traditions, it is a consensus-accepted anxiety about doing the right thing within the community of *both* the living and the dead.[50]

For another case, in an area barely affected by the outside world, because it is swamp-ridden, indeed flooded for half the year round, one can usefully ponder the hinterland Keraakie people, of the Trans-Fly region of the Western Province of Papua. For these people, some of the other Western theorists' views seem more pertinent. The Keraakie, for example, speak about the sun and the moon as if they come up afresh, as entirely new objects, every day and night – a notion to please Max Müller – yet on being pressed to consider whether this entails a renewed wonder for each morning or evening, they insist that the newness has no importance from any "practical" point of view. Of great daily consequence, however, yet bearing interesting connections with such Western theoreticians of wonder as Jevons, Marett, and Codrington, the Keraakie possess a general concept – articulated as *E'3rembah* – for anything unusual that occurs, or which calls for their attention. The term is used not just for events that genuinely startle, but also for a variety of "noticed happenings" – branches falling from trees, birds taking flight, dogs barking a little protractedly, etc. – that make up a "memorable" day. The arrival of the first white, the LMS missionary Samuel McFarlane in 1882, was predictably *E'3rembah*; in fact, it was such that the locals took flight.[51] As for goods, and then the cargo, it is of intriguing importance for Trans-Fly cultures that they lacked stones, which were traded in from Marind-Anim country (across the colonial border) from the west, and were considered to derive from the ancestors in the sky. In enough quantities, certainly, they were *E'3rembah*, and so, as one anticipates, were the belongings and items of cargo, many of them harder than stone, accompanying the whites.[52]

The traditional language of wonder was typically transferred to cover new experiences in Melanesia, yet, as the above cases indicate, each society has its own unique story of lexicon-semantic shift. Furthermore, the histories of adapted significations do not have to be overly cast as the reactions of primitivity towards the civilized. Marvel and alarm before the unknown there clearly was, yet the traditional conceptual frames themselves, examined as deeply as they have been for the Motu and Keraakie by my doctoral students Sibona Kopi and Graham Martin respectively,[53] are already very subtle, even – when their ramifications are the more fully explored – defensibly profound. If there is scope to document the naïvety of the initial impressions of the cargo of most Melanesian groups, however, one soon has to move "beyond primitivism" when discovering how very quickly and readily they sought to trade and negotiate for the new items and accommodate them within their own "reciprocal systems."[54]

Allusion to the absorption of the cargo into everyday worlds portends an obvious second fixture for our agenda, viz. reflection on *the actions, whether group or individual,* by which Melanesians responded to the new goods. Already we have noticed signs of initial *fright*, even *trauma*. The extraordinary character of new objects, considering first fears, evoked the need to settle that they were indeed present, as things, for further dealings, and thus for a *"reconciliation"* over their very existence; this was followed by a pronounced *curiosity* as to what they were, how they "worked," and from whence they came; and finally there emerged the *desire* to acquire them, if not take them from people who soon came, more than often, to be perceived as strangers (rather than retaining their earlier status of visiting or returning spirits). Actual possession of mysterious items, of course, entailed *experimentation*, usually by *imitation*; and imagined possession, fuelled by a belief that "magical manipulations" of "like objects" brought into being the desired ones, could issue in *mimicry*.

An act of "reconciliation" has been nicely documented by Ronald Berndt in connection with the landing of a "shining bird" on a strip between Kamano and Taiora territories in the eastern highlands of New Guinea in 1930. From the airplane were disgorged hundreds of shirts that were laid out on the grass as suitable acquisitions and tokens of self-improvement for "the natives." In their suspicion, local tribesmen "circumperambulated" the shirts, as if reconciling them to themselves before each took one.[55] Curiosity, however, got the better of the initially hesitant. Spencer, in fact, had to adjust his impressions of the Melanesians when reports about their genuine interest in the Europeans' possessions arrived on his London desk. Trying to be consistent with his preconceived methods, he remained satisfied in 1885 that "where curiosity exists we find it among races of not so low a grade," and so the known inquisitiveness of "the New Caledonians…and New Guinea people" forced him to notch them up a peg or two on his evolutionary scale, though their excitations towards enquiry were not so "decided" as the Polynesians' or as "insatiable" as the Dyaks'.[56] In fact, the adjustment was sheer rationalization, though at least indicative of what has steadily emerged as an impressive datum of Melanesian cultures nonetheless: the rapid passage from fear to fascination.

Ritual culture itself often played on the necessity of this passage. The primary impact of the spirits' arrival within ceremonial contexts was, most commonly, one of terror. The silence of the night was suddenly broken, as a famous passage from Francis Williams about the Papuan coastal Elema has it, and the villagers left stunned and riveted, when

> [s]uddenly far down the beach there is heard a noise – a faint one because of the distance, but so meaningful as to electrify every feminine soul in the village. It is weirdly distinctive, a conglomeration of voices, which defies all description…we hear…what seems like the shriek of some tremendous, superhuman voice. The shriek gives place to, and alternates with, a deep-toned roar; and the whole volume of mixed sounds swell terrifyingly, drawing momently nearer.[57]

Eventually the opening tensions give way to the consensus realization, sometimes an almost enforced change of tone, that the group is participating in its *cultus*, reconciled and captivated. The repertoires of rite and ceremonial exchange in Melanesia, however, were mainly expressed through corruptibles – the distributing of non-durable fruits and tubers, the killing of pigs, or even, as with the *Hevehe*, the burning of masks – though certain types of "valuables," such as shells or feathers, were more long-lasting.[58] The challenge, indeed wondrous quality, of the new goods was their very durability, symbolized especially by steel as against stone and wood,[59] yet also relatively by bottles and tins; and their presence for the Melanesians, just as Robert Beverley had seen it long before with the Iroquois in early colonial North America, was bound to multiply "their Wants, and put them upon desiring a thousand things, they never dreamt of before."[60]

I once illustrated the surge of desire, the urge of experimentation, and imitation, along with the alluring possibilities of mimicry, in a detailed study of contact among the central New Guinea highland Wahgi, from the 1930s into the 1950s. The "ethnohistory of acquisition" turned out to be a rich and important field. In the founding of the Mingende Catholic mission, for example, Divine Word Fathers had to cordon off their workplaces and building sites, resorting to physical discipline if overly eager Wahgi crossed the rope or attempted to steal any of their supplies. Occasionally the missionaries discarded objects. Used tins were appropriated as ornamental armbands, for example, a few young women dying through cuts from lead poisoning. As temporary laborers, Wahgi men could secure confidence by returning home with a steel hatchet. The news of their luck would long precede them; by the time they reached their hamlets, their wives' kitchen areas would be piled high with tubers, and a long queue of people would be stood waiting, anxious for their turn to use the coveted axes. When patrol officers passed through the Wahgi Valley, their carriers bore wooden cases of shell money for the purchase of local foodstuffs and services. There were enough shells to make elderly folk swoon, and tribesmen were prepared to offer anything to acquire as many shells as possible, in a market flood that turned out to be "inflationary." Guns in the hands of whites were crucial for keeping previously warring tribes at relative peace while all the new transactions were going on, but the time came, in 1949, when one local *illuminé* announced that he had the right method for turning sticks into guns, as well as fungi into axes or the precious gold-lipped *pinctades maximae*.[61] Clans and their members prided themselves on *mongi* ("the expression of wealth ready to be relinquished in exchange"), and the new goods were especially prized as the keys to opportunity and prestige in altered power relations. Not only were a limited number of objects acquired and then believed by some to be multipliable by imitation and experimentation, but this story of technological and cultural interface also includes independent attempts to set up *gavman* (government), with a king like that of the whites, and to mimic drilling in the hope that the dead would turn staves into superior weaponry.[62] The fervid engagement in "trying it" (in pidgin: *train tasol*) – such as coastal Papuan Toaripi sitting with imitation knives and forks at tables, or marching (ni-Vanuatu) Tannese emblazoning "GI" on their chests[63] – is patently attendant upon the fascinations and enticements of wonder(s). The responses never stopped at curiosity; they gave way to would-be active involvement with the "perceived worlds" in which the new goods moved, and sped on – well beyond "the mimetic propensity" (as Spencer dubbed it)[64] – into creativity.

The third and by far the most contentious item on the agenda concerns local and regionally disseminated *explanations of the cargo and its relative accessibility*, together with *individual and collective actions in the light of these explanations*. This topic is the one most connected with the so-called "cargo cultism" of learned literature,[65] but, as should be clear already, this chapter is hardly confined to reflection on "religious movements" of one kind or another; rather, it is meant to be more generally reflective about reactions to the cargo "across the board," and is thus as much about "cargo thinking," or "cargoism," as attitudes of excited interest towards material novelties and the remarkable innovations they brought.[66] The footprints of wonder that a "sociology of knowledge" in Melanesia soon reveal do not normally manifest in a fervent group belief that the imminent procurement of the new goods will come through preternatural agencies. "Cargo cultism" is not the Melanesian norm; it is an extreme among a majority of less dramatic reactions, and the glaring indication or prime symptom of crises that could and did erupt within a vast complex of acculturative adjustments.

Apropos less exceptional developments, one documentable tendency under pressure from post-contact colonization, missionization, or even invasion, is the indigenous depreciation of traditional, culture-specific sources of awe. From early mission preaching to expatriate business bosses' demands to "smarten up," there have been outside reasons enunciated as to why many "native notions and sentiments" were misguided or falling short of "white standards," and this has generated self- or group inferiorization of old marvels. Among the western Motu, for example, one of the longest-lasting ceremonial spectacles of traditional life was the harvest festival, when, to initiate the picking of the heavily laden fruit trees, dance leaders wore extraordinary ten-foot-high wicker-worked masks. Upon witnessing the bombing of Port Moresby in 1942 by the Japanese, however, this customary practice was spontaneously dropped forthwith (and without direct encouragement from the LMS missionaries, who had worked towards "baptizing" it as a Christian harvest festival).[67] The utterly uncanny simply rendered the conventionally weird irrelevant, at a certain point in a complicated process.

The Second World War to the north-west of the whole Melanesian region often had the effect of undermining prolonged commitments to the old ritual power, where these had managed to persist, and of unleashing the wildest dreams about ancestors (or Jesus) returning in cargo-laden vessels or wishing cities into existence. If Paliau Maloat, on Baluan Island in the Admiralties group, had already sensed as a youth a lack of efficacy in his people's initiation rites, so that he took off to begin his adventurous experiences of the wider world in a Chinese tradestore in circa 1924, by the time he returned to his home as a war hero in 1946 the phenomena of modern military power in his island region had been beyond even a white planter's imaginings.[68] During the preceding two years, American warships and transport planes had disgorged jeeps, tanks, DUKWs, and over a million Allied servicemen alone on Los Negros Island, a bitumened, double-laned highway soon traversing it from north to south. Against the background of this "transformation scene," Paliau was to found Melanesia's first independent church, yet in an atmosphere already tinder-dry for the fires of "cargo cultist" expectations. And certainly the "new fashion" (*nupela pasin*, as Paliau's pidgin phrase propounded it) was associated with wonders far outshining the "old."[69]

We should not exaggerate the problematic of acculturation, though, when it is the Melanesians' remarkable adaptability before and within the processes of rapid change – their ongoing "reconciliation" to what turned out to be the persistent presence of the "initially extraordinary" – that more accurately characterizes the broad-majority response to the cargo. Perhaps it will be of some use here to return to the history of Western theory to help pick up our bearings. After all, Europeans in the eighteenth century were reflecting on their own reactions to the surprises of industrial enterprise. Adam Ferguson, an early Scottish sociologist and a noted contemporary of Adam Smith, once astutely observed in that context how "Things new and strange bring people together from

Curiosity to know what they are; and when the passion of Curiosity is gratified there is pleasure which comes when Novelty no longer exists,"[70] and this has been as true of most Melanesians in practical terms as it has of most peoples before a technological revolution. On the other hand, the "eschatological" dimension of introduced cargo has been most striking in Melanesia, in drawing lithic techniques to a dramatic close, and in manifesting within the same plenum of "new time" when the Gospel was being proclaimed, with its hopes of divine consummation.[71] Moreover, the contrast between the lithic and the "hi-tech" put the greatest demands on human *explanatory* skill – to unlock the "secret" of the white man's possessions and power, to divine the "true origins" not only of the goods but also of possession itself. This thus reveals how the blacks, who had relied so faithfully on their ancestors for material blessings, had come to be without the totally new repertoire of artifacts before the possibilities of the eruptive Now.[72]

Of course, exceedingly high hopes in the face of very radical alterations to the technological and cognitive landscapes can be all too easily dashed by disillusionment. If traditional rituals of renewed fertility and social cohesion could "cultivate surprise and excess" on a periodic and therefore more relatively predictable basis,[73] the arrival of the cargo was as an intrusive flush that, for all its captivations, threatened to upset long-inured socio-economic stability. Here we are forced to address the prospect of a wonder turned "sour." This is a reality almost entirely neglected in the Western theory under our purview. Although a founder-figure of psychology, the Scot Alexander Bain was apparently the first to spot the relevant problematic. "Wonder, or the marvelous," he assessed,

> is felt on the view of what rises above, or what falls beneath, our expectations. In the one case, it is an elating emotion, of a kindred with the Sublime; on the other, it tends to depression, or else to contempt.

With wonder as "pure surprise," then, we must also counter-pose a kind of negative marvel in "the shock of contradiction."[74] The contrast is left undeveloped, and is poorly formulated in any case, yet it is not unhelpful as a clue to understanding the paradoxes of Melanesian "cargoism," or more particularly of active group preparations to receive cargo from a spiritual source.

The central paradox of "cargo cultism," as I have previously argued, is the continuing desire to possess attractive new goods contradicted by the souring realization that access to these goods is too limited. A kind of "cognitive dissonance" occurs even before the "failed prophecy" of someone whose portentous announcement of the arrival of much cargo is not borne out by harsh realities.[75] This is the earlier, nearer-to-contact disappointment: high anticipations attendant upon interchanges between indigenes and newcomers lead to much less than the local peoples have been hoping for. The concessive side to Melanesian (cultural-religious) life centered on successful reciprocity with material goods always being integrally involved. A breakdown of reciprocity usually betokened conflict and the possibility of inter-tribal war. The newcomers brought goods that they were expected to circulate as readily as traditional goods. What more than often happened was that they possessed too many accepted "currency" (or valuables-type) items (shell money, for example, or, at early stages, beads), and this caused inflation, or the raising of prices that destabilized traditional exchange practices.[76] On top of that, the newcomers could not afford to relinquish prized goods, or simply did not possess enough of them, to satisfy the local hopes that these items would be incorporated into their reciprocal arrangements.

Enough of a certain kind of object might enter a "local system" so that its use would become everyday, attitudes towards it blasé, and no "intensity of want" would be set upon it. We see this reflected in the observations of explorer-magistrate C.W.A. Monckton, when he climbed into the Owen Stanley Ranges (of the Papuan highlands) in 1906. In many Fuyughe hamlets he was surprised to find steel axes lying around, though the inhabitants themselves were absent, and he surmised that the high possession quantity had come as much through theft (in the lowland end of trade routes) as with actual trading or employer/employee relations between whites and blacks.[77]

The lack of access, however, tended to increase the desire, in time the sense of frustration and disappointment in the non-realization of portended reciprocities, and further in time the greater vulnerability of peoples to offered explanations as to why the problems and disappointments have occurred, and as to how they will be solved. In the so-called cargo cult, earlier wonder is played upon, or reconsidered by the propounders of new hope, who look to a supreme Wonder, the dramatic arrival of a great flush of goods so that the longed-for reciprocity, indeed even the "time of perfect reciprocal relations" or a kind of Eschaton, can be fulfilled.[78] This response is more likely than not to occur in locations where colonial or postcolonial infrastructural developments, by way of roads, tradestores, and government and mission stations, are lacking or at the edges of their existing limits.[79] Thus, where the same dilemma is perceived to present itself in "more developed" areas, other posed solutions – to start businesses, to try cash cropping, to lobby politicians, etc. – are more likely to be aired. But more often than not, the leaders and explainers will have to address the souring of wonder or the "culture of complaint" issuing from the failure of elevated expectations.

High hopes are usually imaged by scholarly interpreters as thoroughly dashed by the non-arrival of projected marvels. However, one of the various conundrums of "cargo cultism," or "cargoism," in general is that failure can be rationalized, often by blaming the enemies of the collective anticipators, sometimes through leaders accusing followers of faithlessness or, more rarely, through adherents rejecting prophets as in error. The objects of the hopes can still retain their "pull," and if the political administration reacts strongly against the altercation of cargo activity and "rumor mongering," then the agitators may be all the more convinced that they are "onto something" and closing in on a Grand Realization.[80] The temptations to follow Van der Leeuw, McDougall, and Thurnwald in claiming a greater credulity among primitives will tend to rise somewhat spectrally here, but we must think again about the premises of indigenous logic and explanations before rushing to confirm old theories of suggestibility.

We should also not forget, as is typically the case, that ostensible wonders may occur within the life of a cargo movement or during impulses in which "cargoist" beliefs are being diffused. Visions may be reported (lights out to sea among them), or leaders' dreams, and these have often constituted traditional consensus reasons for taking projections of change very seriously.[81] Occasionally, something even more dramatic takes place. During the time that some New Guinea highland cells of Yali's famous coastal (Madang) movement were being established among the Asaro in the 1970s,[82] for example, a meteorite fell from the sky. It is intriguing that this event among already disaffected villagers (who were turning to the cargo cult through disillusionment with other "avenues of improvement") made them all the more sullen and serious. It was as if the wonder gave them all the more reason to show their bitterness when the dropping of the meteorite was publicized and geologists showed their scientific interest by making a special visit to their "backwater."

What about those people who find themselves suddenly thrust into the arena of central economic importance because precious resources for wider humanity have been uncovered where over-development occurs? The objects of wonder are taken to portend great promise at an earlier stage. Enormous manifestations of high technology can be brought in, relatively quickly, to transform a given area. The first clear example of "heavy air traffic" anywhere in the world, if truth be told, was in New Guinea during the 1920s, with the air-freighting of large-scale mining equipment from Lae to the gold-bearing sites of Bulolo, Wau, and Eddie's Creek in the Morobe highlands.[83] Further on in time, during the 1970s and 1980s, some of the largest vehicles in the world were used to excavate and remove the mountain called Panguna in central Bougainville. There was astonishment enough among the villagers proximate to both these happenings, and such that cargo cult-type expectations arose.[84] Yet we must note that when wonder turns sour, other kinds of responses, if not wholly unrelated, occur. Papua New Guinea's labor movement, interestingly, and a sense of regional group identity, grew up in the Morobe highland goldfields during the 1930s and 1940s.[85] War, disastrously, erupted on Bougainville in 1991, because a mining bonanza was leaving the lands of neighboring people badly polluted, and there, as also has become obvious in other quarters, at Freeport in Irian Jaya included, those who have felt most dispossessed of "Wonder's boons" have sought to pay back the perceived enjoyers of these benefits most vehemently.[86] The Melanesian hatred of the non-reciprocal is, underneath it all, the hatred of a primal warrior.

In Melanesia, one can wonder about wonder endlessly. It is perhaps the last place in the world in which a few discrete cultures have remained uncontacted by the outside world; yet the flashiest emporia of Boroko and Port Moresby will be selling as high a quality range of furniture, electronics, and "white goods" as obtainable anywhere in the Western world, and to a multicultural mix of handsomely paid expatriates. I remember vividly, one hot afternoon in 1976, 80 miles from Moresby, being taken up a mountain to meet a Fuyughe who had never met a white, who had been instructed by a recently deceased prophet leader to avoid such contact if the local cosmos was to be kept intact, and who visibly struggled before me with the pressure to retreat on the one hand and the urge towards long-overdue reconciliation on the other. We quickly held hands, wondering at each other, and for me my watch and glasses seemed to impose themselves on his "natural space."

Thus it is that in the parallel processes of modernization and postcolonial postmodernity, assumed reasons for wonder are played off against each other. Newspapers, billboards, and televisual advertisements parade the magic of the cargo while neo-traditionalists, some with university degrees, try to reinvigorate the lost wonders of masked dances and initiation mysteries. The missionary arrives in a helicopter (in pidgin, a *mixmasta bilong Jesas*) while across the seas an airline company sells its product by photographing its in-flight magazine in the hands of an Irian Jayese Dani highland warrior, dressed only – as a "primitive wonder" – in his penis gourd. In this system, "the native" is in a better position than ever "to strike back,"[87] by displaying – very colorfully – before moderns the cultural wonders and senses of wondering that the modern world is, or would be, the worse for losing.

Notes

1 The book, subtitled *The Story of Great Britain's Industries and the Workers who Man the Machines*, was put together by W. Muckle and sixteen other authors (no editor cited), London, n.d. (my father's handwritten dedication was dated Christmas 1945).

2 Adam Smith, "The history of astronomy," in W.P.D. Wightman and J.C. Bryce (eds) *Essays on Philosophical Subjects*, The Glasgow Edition of the Works and Correspondence of Adam Smith, vol. 3, Indianapolis, 1982 (first published 1795), III(1–2), 48–9.

3 *Ibid.*, III(1–2), 48–9; cf. *ibid.*, II(5, 9), 40–2. See also G.B. Vico, *La scienza nuova* (1744 edn), in P. Rossi (ed.) *Opere*, Milan, 1959, and David Hume, *Treatise of Human Nature*, London, 1774 (especially on the invisibility of apparent causation).

4 Smith, "Astronomy," IV(76), 104–5.

5 Friedrich Max Müller, *The Science of Language*, London, 1899, vol. 2, 618 (longer quotation), *Anthropological Religion*, The Gifford Lectures, London, 1892, 61, and *Science*, vol. 2, 568–9 (two shorter quotations, respectively).

6 Smith, "Astronomy," III(2), 49; cf. David Hume, *Dialogues concerning Natural Religion*, London, 1779.

7 Cf. E.J. Sharpe, *Comparative Religion: A History*, London, 1986, Ch. 3.

8 For methodological background, see E. Troeltsch, *Historismus und seine Probleme, Gesammette Werke* 3, Aulen, 1977 (first published 1922). Events were to catch up with Müller, of course, because more ancient texts were being deciphered.

9 G.W. Trompf, *In Search of Origins*, Studies in World Religions, London and New Delhi, 1990, 42 (first quotation), and Müller, *Anthropological Religion* (second quotation).

10 Müller was in fact the son of the famous German Romantic poet Wilhelm Müller. For this mythopoetic stage and the mythological theory of religion, see G.W. Trompf, *Max Müller as a Theorist of Comparative Religion*, Bombay, 1978, Ch.3, Pt.2. However, for Müller at his most cautious and restrained about this side to his theorizing, see his "Preface" to W.W. Gill, *Myths and Songs from the South Pacific*, London, 1976, ix–xii, xvii–xviii.

11 H. Spencer, *An Autobiography*, London, 1904, vol. 1, 476–7; cf. also *The Principles of Sociology*, London and Edinburgh, 1885, vol. 1, 85–91, where Spencer postulates a scale of relative curiosity to deal with missionaries' and explorers' accounts apparently contradicting his generalizations.

12 See esp. H. Spencer, *First Principles*, London, 1890, Ch. 1.

13 G.K. Clark, "Nineteenth century social thought," seminar presented to the History Department, Monash University, Melbourne, 1964.

14 K. Marx (with F. Engels), *The German Ideology*, 1845–46, Ch.1, a convenient translation of which is provided in K. Marx/F. Engels, *On Religion*, trans. Progress Publishers, Moscow, 1975, 67–8.

15 K. Marx, *Grundrisse*, trans. M. Nicolaus, Harmondsworth, 1973, 497.

16 For alleged Vichian influences on Marx, see E. Kamenka, "Vico and Marxism," in G. Tagliacozzo and H. White (eds) *Giambattista Vico: An International Symposium*, Baltimore, 1969, 137–43.

17 On the limits of Vico's "Lucretianism," see G.W. Trompf, "Vico's universe," *British Journal for the History of Philosophy* 2(1), 1994, esp. 82–3. Marx, as is well known, wrote his Jena doctoral thesis on Epicurus; cf. T.I. Oizerman, *The Making of Marxist Philosophy*, trans. A. Khmelyakov, Moscow, 1977, Pt. 1, Ch. 4. For Engels' point, see, for example, K. Marx/F. Engels, *Selected Works*, trans. Foreign Languages Publications, Moscow, 1958, vol. 2, 134.

18 R.H. Codrington, *The Melanesians*, Oxford, 1891, 118–19; cf. *ibid.*, 51, 57, 103, 115, etc., the second quotation being from Max Müller and welcomed as doing Codrington an honor. For details of the Müller–Codrington connection, see N. Gunson, "Victorian Christianity in the South Seas," *Journal of Religious History* 8(2), 1974, 188–93.

19 F.B. Jevons, *An Introduction to the History of Religion*, London, 1927 (first published 1896), 18 (first quotation), 20 (others).

20 J.G. Frazer, *The Golden Bough*, London, 1911 (first published 1890), vol. 1.

21 R.R. Marett, *The Threshold of Religion*, London, 1914 (first published 1909), 13, cf. 8 (shorter quotations), 10 (longer quotation).

22 Marett, *Threshold*, 12 (quoting J. Thomson, *Through Masai Land*, London, 1887, 445); cf. Marett, *Threshold*, 14ff.

23 Cf. A. Lang, *The Making of Religion*, London, 1900.

24 S. Freud, *Totem and Taboo*, trans. A.A. Brill, New York, 1946, 122; cf. *ibid.*, Ch. 3, on the influences of Spencer, Marett, etc. Freud brings neurotics into a triangular paradigmatic parallelism with children and primitives, a relationship now little tolerated in child psychology; cf., for example, S.H. Fraiberg, *The Magic Years*, London and New York, 1968, 22–3.

25 G. van der Leeuw, published as "Gebeuren en willen bij natuurvolk en culturmensch," in W.J. Aalders, H.J.F.W. Brugmans, F.J.J. Buytendijk, I.H. Gosses, H. van Goudoever, G. van der Leeuw, L. Polak, E.D. Wiersma, and F. Zernike, *Causaliteit en Wilsvrijheid*, Groningen, 1936, 79ff.; cf. also Sharpe, *Comparative Religion*, 234–5.

26 See R.S. Woodworth, "Racial differences in mental traits," *Science* 31(788), 1910, esp. 176–85. Cf. W. McDougall (1871–1938), *An Outline of Psychology*, London, 1926, 373, and R. Thurnwald (1869–1954), *Ethno-psychologische Studien an südseevölken, Beihefte, Zeitschift für die angwandte Psychologie und psychologische Samelforschung* 6, Stuttgart, 1913 (cf. *Psychologie des primitiven Menschen, Handbuch der vergleichenden Psychologie* 1/2, Munich, n.d.).

27 R. Otto, trans. J.W. Harvey, Harmondsworth, 1959 (first published 1917), 29 (my amended translation).

28 Otto, *Idea*, 134–5 (my amended translation); cf., on Marett, *ibid.*, 29n, 34n, 89n.

29 For orientation, see J. Wach, "Rudolph Otto und der Begriff des Heiligen," in H.M. Garner *et al.*, *Deutsche Beiträge*, Chicago, 1953, 200ff. In Britain, W.L. Davidson, for one, was engaged in this same theological pursuit; see his "Awe," in J. Hastings (ed.) *Encyclopaedia of Religion and Ethics*, Edinburgh, 1909, vol. 2, 276–7.

30 See, for example, C. Jung, *The Structure and Dynamics of the Psyche*, Collected Works, trans. F.R.C. Hull, vol. 8, Bollingen Series 20, Princeton, 1969, 204ff.; cf. *ibid.*, 104, 131, 309, etc. Note, by comparison, R. Otto, *Religious Essays*, trans. B. Lunn, London, 1931, Chs 8–9.

31 See C. Jung, *Man and his Symbols*, London, 1964, esp. 93–9; cf., for example, L. Lévy-Bruhl (1857–1939), *La Mentalité Primitive*, Herbert Spencer Lecture, Oxford, 1937.

32 See T. Swain, "D.H. Lawrence as a theorist of religion" in C.M. Cusack and P. Oldmeadow (eds) *This Immense Panorama: Studies in Honour of Eric J. Sharpe* (Sydney Studies in Religion 2), Sydney 1999, pp. 291–301.

33 For background, see, for example, W.J. McGrath, *Dionysian Art and Populist Politics in Austria*, New Haven and London, 1974; G.L. Mosse, *The Nationalization of the Masses*, New York, 1875; and P.R. McKenzie, "Introduction to the man," in H.W. Turner and P.R. McKenzie, *Rudolph Otto: The Idea of the Holy*, Aberdeen, 1974, 6–7. Debate goes on as to whether Otto dispatched himself because of this ideological misappropriation.

34 See, for example, R. Plutchik, *The Emotions*, New York, 1962, 117–18.

35 B.F. Skinner, "Superstition," *Journal of Experimental Psychology* 38, 1948, 168–72. For background, see B.R. Bugelski, *The Psychology of Learning*, New York and London, 1956, 54–6.

36 Thus Marett, quoting Jevons, *Threshold*, 12.

37 I quote here from E. Goffman, *Encounters*, Harmondsworth, 1972, 35. Not only the French sociologist Durkheim (1858–1917), cf. *The Elementary Forms of Religious Life*, trans. J.W. Swain, London, 1976 (first published 1915), but also Frazer, *Golden Bough*, lacks interest in wonder, the latter through turning pre-religious magic into "early science" (see above).

38 I allude here to moral pressure against everything from prolonged hoodwinking (especially of children) to missionaries giving out to indigenous peoples trinkets and cargo items (that could be misunderstood as "bribes" or creators of dependence).

39 Alluding to his book of that title, New York, 1953, esp. 211–13.

40 See esp. W. Berman, *The Reenchantment of the World*, Ithaca, NY, 1981. But in these last assertions I fly somewhat blind, and offering these views here I seek insights from friends both old and new who may have something interesting to say on these matters.

41 On defining "cargo cultism" in this way, see G.W. Trompf (ed.) "Introduction," *Prophets of Melanesia*, Port Moresby and Suva, 1981, 8.

42 The small amount of iron-forging that occurred in the area took place on the region's extremities to the west, under the influence of trade relations with the Sultan of Tidor; cf. F.C. Kamma and S. Kooijman, *Romawa Forja: Child of Fire. Iron Working and the Role of Iron in West New Guinea (West Irian)*, Leiden, 1973 (booklet offprint). Melanesia usually features in histories of technology for its pottery; see, for example, C. Singer, E.J. Holmyard, A.R. Hall and T.I. Williams (eds) *A History of Technology*, Oxford, 1965, vol. 1, 406–7.

43 P.D. Gasseau, 1962.

44 Cf. E.M. Webster, *The Moon Man: A Biography of Nikolai Miklouho-Maclay*, Berkeley, 1984, Chs 4–5.

45 F. Kamma, *"Dit wonderlijk werk" – het probleem van de communicatie tussen oost en west gebasseerd op de ervaringen in het zendingswerk op Zieuw Guinea (Irian Jaya), 1855–1972*, West Papua, n.d., vol.1, *passim*; re Fiji and quotation, see M. Kaplan, *Neither Cargo Nor Cult: Ritual Politics and Colonial Imagination in Fiji*, Durham, NC, and London, 1995 (written to ensure that Fiji's highland Tuka movement of the 1870s to the 1880s should be dissociated from cargo movements on and around New Guinea). For Polynesian involvement in the Fijian conversion movement, see esp. D. Scarr, "Cakobau and Ma'afu: contenders for preeminence in Fiji," in J.W. Davidson and D. Scarr (eds) *Pacific Island Portraits*, Canberra, 1976, 95ff.; and note that the eastern Fijian, or Lau, group is culturally "Polynesian."

46 Sciences Department (Geology) report, Goroka Teachers College, University of Papua New Guinea, August 1975.

47 On Ruatoka, see esp. R. Lovett, *James Chalmers: His Autobiography and Letters*, London, 1902, 78, 132ff.

48 These two responses are better known as coming from the Papuan highland Fuyughe (cf. R.W. Williamson, *The Ways of the South Sea Savage*, London, 1914, 281), and from the Coastal Mailau to the east (W. Saville, *In Unknown New Guinea*, London, 1926, Ch. 5), respectively.

49 For most of the above, I am grateful for the field research conducted by my doctoral student Sibona Kopi, 1977–95.

50 See esp. W. Ferea, "The nature of fear in traditional Melanesian region," unpublished Honors sub-thesis, University of Papua New Guinea, Port Moresby, 1984.

51 Cf. S. McFarlane, *Among the Cannibals*, London, 1888, 380ff.

52 For background, see, for example, F.E. Williams, *Papuans of the Trans-Fly*, Oxford, 1936, 43ff., 201ff., 318ff.; cf. J. van Baal, *Dema*, Koninklijk Institut voor Taal-, Land- en Volkenkunde, Trans. Ser. 9, The Hague, 1966, 112ff.

53 S. Kopi, "Traditional medicine among the Motu," unpublished Ph.D. thesis, University of Sydney, Sydney, 1996; G. Martin, "A study of time as Being according to the Keraakie people of Papua New Guinea," unpublished Ph.D. thesis, University of Sydney, Sydney, 2001.

54 For a start, examine the case of the Bonarua Islanders discussed early in G.W. Trompf, *Melanesian Religion*, Cambridge, 1991, 7–9.

55 See R.M. Berndt, "A cargo movement in the Eastern Central Highlands of New Guinea," *Oceania* 23, 1952, 52ff.

56 Spencer, *Principles*, vol. 1, 86 (s. 46) (the sources cited being Cook, Earl, and Jukes); yet cf. earlier, for example, G. Duncan (ed.) *Descriptive Sociology*, London, 1874, Pt. 1, tables VI–VII.

57 F.E. Williams, *The Drama of Orokolo*, London, 1940, 210–11; also discussed in T. Swain and G.W. Trompf, *Religions of Oceania*, Library of Religious Beliefs and Practices, London, 1995, 149–50.

58 See G.W. Trompf, *Payback*, Cambridge, 1994, esp. 97–127; cf. C. Gregory, *Gifts and Commodities*, Studies in Political Economy 2, London, 1982.

59 Cf. R. Salisbury, *From Stone to Steel*, Melbourne, 1962.

60 R. Beverley, *The History and Present State of Virginia*, ed. L. Wright, Chapel Hill, 1947 (first published 1705), 233.

61 A form of frenetic activity, usually taken as "cargo cultist," resulted: G.W. Trompf, "Doesn't colonialism make you mad? To so-called 'Mur Madness' as an index to the study of new religious movements in Papua New Guinea," in S. Latukefu (ed.) *Papua New Guinea: A Century of Colonial Impact 1884–1984*, Port Moresby, 1989, 247ff.

62 Trompf, "Colonialism"; cf. M. Reay, *The Kuma*, Melbourne, 1959, 196–7.

63 See, as examples, H. Brown, "The eastern Elema," unpublished Postgraduate Diploma sub-thesis, University of London, London, 1956, 56–7; M. Lindstrom, "Cult and culture: American dreams in Vanuata," *Pacific Studies* 4, 1981, 101ff.

64 Spencer, *Principles*, vol. 1, 89 (s. 48).

65 As in, esp., P. Lawrence, *Road Belong Cargo*, Manchester, 1964; P. Christiansen, *The Melanesian Cargo Cult*, Copenhagen, 1969; K. Burridge, *New Heaven, New Earth*, Oxford, 1969, esp. Pt. 2; F. Steinbauer, "Die Cargo-Kulte als religionsgeschichtliches und missionstheologisches Problem," unpublished Ph.D. thesis, University of Erlangen-Nürnberg, Nürnberg, 1971; Trompf, *Payback*, Pt. 2, esp. Ch. 6.

66 On cargo thinking and cargoism, see Trompf, "Introduction," *Prophets*, and G.W. Trompf, *Cargo Cults and Millenarian Movements*, Religion and Society 29, Berlin, 1990, 1ff. and the literature cited therein.

67 G.W. Trompf, "Oral sources and the study of religious history in Papua New Guinea," in D. Denoon and R. Lacey (eds) *Oral Tradition in Melanesia*, Port Moresby, 1981, 62.

68 For background, see M. Mead, *New Lives for Old*, New York, 1981; T. Schwartz, *The Paliau Movement in the Admiralty Islands, 1946–1954*, Anthropological Papers of the American Museum of Natural History 49, New York, 1962, esp. 240–9.

69 G.W. Trompf, "Independent churches in Melanesia," *Oceania* 54(1), 1983, 59–60; on the language, cf. I. Hogbin, *Transformation Scene*, London, 1951.

70 A. Ferguson, "Essay 9," unpublished transcript by W. Philip, University of Edinburgh Special Collection, item DC.1.42, n.d., 5.

71 Trompf, *Payback*, 266–76.

72 For important reflections on such issues, begin with P. Gesch, *Initiative and Initiation*, Studia Instituti Anthropos 33, St. Augustin, 1985. For detailing indigenous explanations of the cargo in ways that space cannot allow here, see Lawrence, *Road Belong Cargo*, 71ff., 101ff.; J. Strelan, *Search for Salvation*, Adelaide, 1977, esp. Chs 3–4; Trompf, *Payback*, Ch. 6.

73 See P. Gesch, "The cultivation of surprise in excess," in Trompf, *Cargo*, 213ff.

74 A. Bain, *Mental and Moral Science*, London, 1875, 231.

75 For background, see L. Festinger, *The Theory of Cognitive Dissonance*, Stanford, 1957, and L. Festinger, H.W. Riecken and S. Schachterin, *When Prophecy Fails*, Chicago, 1964.

76 For guidance, see esp. R. Brunton, "Cargo cults and systems of exchange in Melanesia," *Mankind* 8, 1971, 115ff.

77 C.W.A. Monckton, personal communication, 2 June 1906, in Parliament of the Commonwealth of Australia, *British New Guinea: Annual Report*, Melbourne, 1906, 85ff.

78 See Trompf, *Payback*, Ch. 5.

79 See esp. L. Morauta, *Beyond the Village*, London School of Economics Monographs on Social Anthropology 49, London, 1974.

80 For the relevant theory, see H. Desroche, *The Sociology of Hope*, trans. C. Martin-Sperry, London, 1979, esp. Chs 3, 5.

81 See esp. W. Jojoga Opeba, "Melanesian cult movements as traditional religious and ritual responses to change," in G.W. Trompf (ed.) *The Gospel is Not Western*, Maryknoll, NY, 1987, 49ff.

82 For the background to these developments among the neighboring Bena Bena, see esp. G.W. Trompf, "The theology of Beig Wen, the would-be successor to Yali," *Catalyst* 6(3), 1976, 166–7.

83 W. Gammage, cited in Trompf, "Bilalaf," in Trompf (ed.) *Prophets*, 25.

84 Cf., for example, A.M. Maahs, "A sociological interpretation of the cargo cult of New Guinea and selected comparable phenomena in other areas of the world," unpublished Ph.D. thesis, University of Pittsburgh, Pittsburgh, 1936, 20; H. Sipari, "The Kopani 'cargo cult,' " in C.E. Loeliger and G.W. Trompf (eds) *New Religious Movements in Melanesia*, Port Moresby and Suva, 1985, 34ff.

85 Cf. esp. A. Kuluah, "Wokim Gol long Morobe – 1922–1942," unpublished typescript, University of Papua New Guinea, Port Moresby, 1993.

86 Begin with G. Lafitte, "Nations within nations: the obscure revolt of Bougainville against Papua New Guinea," in G.W. Trompf (ed.) *Islands and Enclaves*, New Delhi, 1993, 272ff.

87 Cf. J.E. Lips, *The Savage Hits Back*, London, 1937.

Chapter 21

Thinking and teaching with the indigenous traditions of Melanesia

Mary N. MacDonald

In 1973, as an Australian Catholic missionary, I first went to Papua New Guinea. My encounters there with indigenous religious traditions and with Melanesian styles of Christianity have influenced my subsequent thinking about religion and, indeed, my thinking about thinking.[1] Today, as a historian of religions, I spend most of my time teaching undergraduates at Le Moyne College in Syracuse, New York. Traditional Melanesia and an American college classroom provide the frameworks within which I think about indigenous traditions and modernity. I shall begin by explaining my current job, which, no doubt, bears similarities to the work of many who are concerned with the interaction of indigenous wisdom and modern knowledge. Then, I shall describe traditional ways of knowing among the Kewa and Huli of the Southern Highlands of Papua New Guinea, focusing in particular on Kewa sky people and ancestors, and on Huli sacred geography. From there I shall reflect on the colonial incursion, the coming of Christianity to Papua New Guinea, and the changes in consciousness that it has occasioned. Finally, I shall return to the American classroom where, I suggest, indigenous and modern approaches to knowledge can complement each other and where there is need to develop appropriate pedagogies for teaching about indigenous traditions.

In 1988, having recently completed a Ph.D. at the University of Chicago, I found a job at Le Moyne, a small college of liberal arts and sciences in the Jesuit tradition. I was hired as a generalist in the study of religion. In the interview process, I was told that the college desired to hire someone who could teach about "submerged cultures." I discovered that in the then recent revision of the core curriculum, there had been considerable debate about the teaching of non-Western philosophy, literature, history, and religion. A sense had developed of the need to acquaint students, most of them from the eastern United States, with cultures that had been disregarded or even disparaged, cultures that did not think in the modes of modernity.

The term "submerged cultures" suggests ways of understanding the world, ways of living, that we ("we" being the academy or, more specifically, the Le Moyne faculty), intent on inculcating modern ways of thinking, have buried or drowned, have suppressed or hidden from ourselves. There is a nostalgic tone to the term, a regret for what we have lost. Another way of stating the situation would be to speak of "oppressed cultures," those that modern cultures have tried to destroy. My colleagues-to-be engaged with the core curriculum revision. I recognized that there are ways of thinking that have not been part of modern literature, modern philosophy, modern history, modern religion, and that might confront and complement the Enlightenment theories on which the curriculum, not only at Le Moyne, but also in hundreds of similar colleges, is built.

My job, then, is that of a cultural and religious broker of sorts, co-opting Melanesia to serve as a stimulus to thought in Le Moyne classrooms. I ask myself whether I am genuinely expanding my students' horizons and giving them a deeper understanding of the human condition, or whether I am giving them a taste of the exotic without providing enough context for them to appreciate that Melanesian religious ways are, on the one hand, viable options for their practitioners and, on the other, human expressions and ways of thinking that are instructive for all of us. Many theorists in the study of religion have turned to Melanesian materials in trying to understand the human condition. Codrington, Leenhardt, Malinowski, Bateson, and Mead have developed theories as a result of field-work in Melanesia. Lévy-Bruhl, Marett, and Mauss have made use of Melanesian materials, encountered second-hand, in furthering their projects.

There is a difficulty for the cultural broker in handling the experiences of others. It is not easy to accurately situate the thinking of Melanesians and one's own thinking, let alone bring the differently situated perspectives into conversation. Situating ourselves is a complicated process because, for one thing, we all keep moving. And, for another thing, no one in the so-called West can speak to an agreed-upon "Enlightenment view" and no one in Papua New Guinea can speak to a "Melanesian ideal" that others would not, through their rituals and myths, contest. For example, most of the Melanesians I know, whether they be university graduates or rural horticulturists, have slipped or been dragged into the world of modernity; at the same time, many of the students I teach are strongly influenced by cultural currents of the pre-modern.

Indigenous religious traditions, it is often noted, are rooted in particular landscapes and particular histories. Their members think with these mountains and these ancestors, with these plants and these animals. The emphasis is on the local and particular experience, in contrast to the universal and general that scientific thought abstracts from many particulars. Papua New Guinea is home to an amazing diversity of natural environments and particular human cultures. It holds the largest rainforest area in the Asia-Pacific region,[2] and its myriad of microclimates supports a range of plants and animals that includes over 1,200 species of tree, half of them endemic to Papua New Guinea, and some 700 species of bird, 445 of which live in the rainforests. The first people to settle in what is now known as Papua New Guinea are believed to have come from South-East Asia some 50,000 years ago. Bands of migrants probably arrived over a period of hundreds of years. The major distinction between the Austronesian and non-Austronesian language families in the region is evidence of a long time period between earlier and later arrivals and probably also of different areas of origin.

Today, Papua New Guinea's human population numbers about 4 million, of whom 87 per cent live in rural areas. Only 3 per cent of the land has been permanently removed from customary tenure, but certain areas have been rented out to developers and others used for cash crops. The overall population density of 8.4 persons per square kilometer is relatively low by world standards. Subsistence agriculture remains, as it has done for more than 9,000 years, the basis of the total economy, and the principal means of livelihood for three-quarters of the population. Despite the serious economic and social problems that Papua New Guinea faces today, most of the people can feed themselves and shelter them-selves most of the time without reliance on the cash economy. However, Melanesians did not, like some other peoples, move from agriculture to the building of cities. Towns came only with the colonial intrusion of the late nineteenth century. Nor did Melanesians invent writing or make an industrial breakthrough. Their knowledge, their tools, their rituals, and their stories supported relatively small communities engaged in subsistence gardening, hunting, and fishing. Therefore, at the time of their encounter with Western technology, Melanesians were observed to be technologically "primitive" and, extrapolating from that observation, were characterized by colonial officials, traders, and missionaries as intellectually, socially, and religiously "primitive." For those pursuing an evolutionist hypothesis about religion and culture, their "primitivism" represented ways of thinking correlative with the early consciousness of humankind. For those engaged in industrial enterprises and, therefore, interested in the raw materials to be had in the Pacific, the Melanesians' lack of machinery relegated them to the "primitive" position of digging-stick cultivators. What a difference 9,000 years makes! Had the encounter occurred when the Melanesians were at the forefront of the agricultural breakthrough, they would clearly have had much to teach the outsiders. In fact, as the practice of cultivation has developed over the past century in Papua New Guinea, indigenous peoples and outside experts have come to appreciate each other's practical knowledge.

Some 840 distinct languages are spoken today in Papua New Guinea. The larger area of Melanesia, which includes Irian Jaya, the Solomon Islands, Vanuatu, New Caledonia, and Fiji as well as Papua New Guinea, has over 1,000, or more than one-quarter, of the world's languages. In speaking of "Melanesian religions," I am grouping together a wide range of understandings of the human condition and diverse systems for interaction with sacred powers that have developed over a long period of time in a variety of ecological and cultural-linguistic environments. The term "religion," which, in the spirit of postmodernity, we might agree, with Jonathan Z. Smith, is "a product of the scholar's study," can serve as a framework within which to explore ideas about making connections and sustaining meanings. I take it to be the field within which communities discern and divine and create worlds of significance.

Although ideas about the world and symbolic practices for participating in, and maximizing, cosmic life differ from group to group, there are commonalities that enable a term such as "Melanesian religion" to make some sense. For example, throughout Melanesia, ancestors are believed to have an ongoing relationship with the living community. Spirits are associated with particular features of the landscape. Rituals facilitate communication with spirits and sustain and renew cosmic life. Tradition is passed on and shaped to present needs in the telling of myths, and particular objects are repositories of cultural meanings and values. Practical work, such as hunting, fishing, and gardening, is accompanied by what an observer might call symbolic work. Symbolic work includes hunting magic, garden prayers, and the ritual feeding of spirits. Kewa discourse about sky people and ancestors and Huli mythic geography provide entrée into particular indigenous worlds of meaning. As we pursue these notions, we shall see that an idea of reciprocity informs understandings of social life and ritual work. There is an emphasis on the exchange of wealth in order to maintain social relationships, relationships that extend beyond death, and on the exchange of life power in order to heal persons and relationships that are in a weakened state.

The Kewa and Huli[3] are located on opposite sides of the Southern Highlands Province, the Kewa in the east and the Huli in the west. The languages of both are thought to derive from the same stock as Enga, the language that today has the largest number of speakers in Papua New Guinea. Kewa and Huli ancestors probably moved south from the Enga–Western Highlands region about 2,000 years ago. Throughout Melanesia, social relationships are typically initiated and sustained through the ritual exchange of goods.

Among the Kewa, the most spectacular of such exchanges is the pig kill that occurs in most communities at intervals of about seven years. It is possible to interpret the cargo cults of the colonial period as attempts to develop such exchange networks with Europeans.

The Kewa tell of a benevolent sky being, Yakili ("the man in the sky"), to whom appeal is made in times of hardship in the community. Pigs are killed for Yakili and he is asked to restore the fertility of the land, the prosperity of the pigs, and the well-being of the community. Myths relate that sky people came and settled the earth long ago and, for a time, maintained contact with their relatives in the sky. Then, as the result of a dispute between brothers, a connecting rope or tree – there are several versions of the tale – was severed, cutting off the earthly community from the more abundant life of the sky realm.

If the relationship with Yakili is important, then the relationship with the ancestors is just as significant. Kewa communities cluster around communal men's houses. Each woman has her own house where she lives with her children. In recent times, under Christian influence, some men have begun to live in their wives' houses, while retaining compartments in the men's house. Until the 1960s, and perhaps later, members of male cults periodically performed rituals, directed towards the ancestral spirits, the *remo*, to sustain and renew the fertility of the land, the pigs, and the community. On a day-to-day basis, Kewa women and men carry out rituals for gardening, for the health of pigs, for hunting, and for attracting members of the opposite sex. Some who have become Christian also pray to God for help and blessing in their daily endeavors. Individuals make use of words and potions for healing, and specialist healers are called upon to divine the causes of serious illness and to take corrective actions. Illness is thought to result from damaged relationships in the community, a community that includes the spirits of the dead and a variety of land spirits. The healer's task is first of all to identify the offence that has caused the tension or rupture in a relationship. Then he, or, less often, she, prescribes a remedy. It may be a meal of foods suggestive of strength and healing, which is shared by the sick person and the offending, because offended, spirit. The other side of the healer's power is sorcery. He may be engaged to redress social wrongs by directing symbolic words, substances, and actions against one who has offended those who commission the sorcery.

Like the Kewa, the Huli have an idea of a sky world. They say it is occupied by Datagaliwabe, the "one who sees everything," and other sky beings. The Huli maintain that at death, an ordinary person's spirit goes to a domain located somewhere inside the ground, but that the spirits of warriors killed in battle go to the sky world. The Kewa also think of the spirits of the dead residing in a "ghost settlement," passage to which may be found, they say, by entering a cave or sinkhole in the forest. With the coming of Christianity to the Kewa and the Huli in the 1950s, notions of Yakili and Datagaliwabe began to change and to become invested with Christian understandings of God. Similarly, the God preached by the missionaries has come to be invested with attributes of the all-seeing Yakili and Datagaliwabe. A major influence on the indigenous religions has been the fact that the Christian God is universal, watching everyone, not only, as Datagaliwabe does, those in Huli territory or, as Yakili does, those in Kewa territory.

The Huli are well known for the *haroli* bachelor cult in which male identity is cultivated by separation from women and through the observance of taboos and the performance of rituals. The cult teaches young men what their society considers to be appropriate male behavior and introduces them to their origin myths and the rituals that they need to perform to sustain their world, a world which is conceived of in an image that we might call "sacred geography." The Huli do not have villages or longhouses. Each man lives in a house in the midst of his gardens, and his wife and children live in another house some distance from him. Each family is part of a territorial grouping called *hameigini*. This group occupies land associated with an ancestor who, it is said, emerged in the origin time from underground.

Within *hameigini* territory is a shrine for the ancestor who, now in spirit form, is said to be willing to help the inhabitants of the territory, provided that they kill pigs for him and keep his house in good repair. Spirit houses for the *dama*, unpredictable non-human spirits whom the Huli seek to placate rather than to engage in relationships of positive reciprocity, are also located within the *hameigini* territory. Similarly, the Kewa practice avoidance rituals with regard to their forest spirits, the *raa ali*. The Huli conceive of a "root of the earth" extending from north to south and linking the Huli with communities on either side of them. The spirit houses are situated at places where the mythical root comes close to the surface. Thus, according to the Huli, the communities along the "root" all have their part to play in sustaining the world. Actually, the communities on either side do not know about this sacred geography and are unaware of the part the Huli expect them to play in sustaining it.

The Huli say that a python is entwined around the root of the earth and will keep the land fertile as long as it is fed with ritual offerings and does not become angry. Snakes, and pythons in particular, figure in many Huli and Kewa myths and, indeed, in myths and rituals throughout Melanesia. A snake shedding its skin suggests new life; its phallic form evokes fecundity. In 1987, when a vast amount of alluvial gold was discovered at Mt. Kare to the north of the Tari Basin in Enga Province, in a place regarded as a Huli sacred site, people speculated that the gold was flakes from the skin shed by the snake, or that it was specks from the snake's faeces. When many people became ill at the site, it was said that the snake was angry because its home had been disturbed and because women had been allowed at the site.[4] Thus, local discourse about environmental and social disturbance began not with scientific theories but with a traditional tale. How should such a discussion then proceed? Traditional tales can open up discussions on indigenous values related to land and community. However, the tales do not themselves contain answers. Rather, like biblical parables, they are a stimulus to thought. Most tales have to do with relationships between people, spirits, and land. As these relationships become strained and require restructuring, the telling of the tales permits a reflection on the situation and an implicit negotiation of change.

According to the Huli, the physical and social worlds go through cycles of decline and renewal. To restore their vitality it is necessary to carry out a ritual cycle called *dindi gamu* (earth ritual). Associated with the *dindi gamu* is the story of Pajapaja, a Duna youth whose name means "good, good." The Duna are neighbors of the Huli. It is told that in the past a small amount of blood from Pajapaja's finger would be shed to restore the fertility of gardens, pigs, and people. However, on one occasion, *dindi gamu* officiants decided to kill him, shedding all his blood at once, so that the land would be fertile forever. His mother, in utter distress at his death, returned to Duna country uttering a curse on the Huli, their pigs, their gardens, and their social relationships. In the wake of missionary teaching, which began in the mid-1950s, many Huli have come to identify Pajapaja with Jesus.

When I was in Tari in 1991, some Catholic women were discussing their experiences of Christianity. They asked me, "Do you think it is all right for our old people to address their prayers to Pajapaja?" Subsequent discussion revealed that while the younger women tended to address Jesus, but not Pajapaja, the older ones, who had become Christians as adults, would address Pajapaja. When questioned about this, they would say that Jesus was surely Pajapaja. Both Pajapaja and Jesus are represented as shedders of blood and restorers of life. Pajapaja is seen as being for the Huli in particular, while Jesus-Pajapaja is seen as being for everyone.

Some Huli worry today that their world is in decline, and that if it is not renewed through ritual – whether traditional ritual or Christian ritual is a matter of opinion – it will come to an end. Hence, the "end of the world" preaching by recently arrived Christian groups finds receptivity within traditional Huli modes of thought. A traditional ritual specialist, Yaluduma-Dai of Gelote, explaining the perceived situation of decline to Stephen Frankel, cited the behavior of young people as evidence of the end of the world. He observed:

> [Nowadays] young men mature too soon. They refuse to work the land, dig ditches, or look after pigs. They just roam around fighting, stealing, fornicating, and will not listen to their fathers. People take what is not theirs, they help themselves to others' belongings and wives. This is the time for us to die. It is now the afternoon. There is not much time left to us now. The world is dry...Before it was new ground, but now the earth is old and worn out.
>
> (Frankel 1986: 24)

The traditional Huli vision of the world, the sacred geography, which I have sketched out all too briefly, is being challenged by a larger world, a world that intrudes, for example, via national government and mining companies, via churches and schools. To be citizens of that larger world, the Huli need another geography. Whereas the traditional geography can say what it means to be Huli, an extended geography is necessary to say what it means to be a Papua New Guinean. For many Melanesians, Christianity, spread as it is throughout the nation, is that geography.

Even as the Kewa and Huli adopt Christianity, there are values in their traditional visions that are important for them and for us all. The sense of relationship to the land and of responsibility for its continued vitality, for example, speak to those who see care of the environment as a challenge for Papua New Guinea today, or even as the religious challenge of our time. Despite the Papua New Guinea Constitution's acknowledgment of both the "noble traditions" of the ancestors and "the Christian principles that are ours now,"[5] it has not been easy to incorporate local visions with national legislation.

Europeans became aware of the large island of New Guinea in the sixteenth century, but colonial control was not asserted until the nineteenth century. The Dutch took West Papua (Irian Jaya,[6] since 1963 a province of Indonesia), the Germans took the north-eastern section and outlying islands, while the British claimed the south-eastern section and outlying islands. In 1906, the British territory of Papua passed to Australia, and after the First World War the League of Nations placed the former German New Guinea under Australian administration. The two Australian-administered territories came to independence in 1975 as Papua New Guinea.

Missions followed the colonial powers into Papua and New Guinea, though not without resistance in some areas. But over time, the peoples of Melanesia came to embrace

Christianity. About 90 per cent of Melanesians acknowledge themselves to be Christian, and in a region of such cultural diversity, Christianity is clearly an important ingredient in the forging of a common identity. At the same time, however, the relationship to land and to ancestors has a complexion that is not that of Christianity in industrialized societies. In the earlier missionary work of the mainstream churches, conversion was presented in terms of a choice between the old and the new – the way of the ancestors and the way of God. With the churches came educational and health services and development projects predicated on the vision of industrial culture. Today, with indigenous ritual abandoned in many regions, the mainstream churches acknowledge that they have a responsibility to help in the quest for indigenous religious roots. On the other hand, many of the hundreds of fundamentalist missions that entered Papua New Guinea in the 1960s continue to condemn traditional religious practices. However, many Melanesian Christians desire to be reconciled with the indigenous religions. They turn to groups such as the Melanesian Institute, the Seminaries, the Teachers' Colleges, the University of Papua New Guinea, and the National Research Institute to provide courses and undertake research on indigenous religions. These groups record and reconstruct tradition. They instruct teachers and church workers about Melanesian traditions so that they may help young people and congregations to recognize the value and ongoing influence of such traditions.

Most young people in Melanesia have grown up in an environment in which Christianity is a significant presence. Indeed, to ask young people about religion is, in most cases, to ask about Christianity. Those who have little, or no, personal experience of Christianity are few. For many, the church has been an influential institution in their village or neighborhood – gathering people to express commitment to God and each other, providing educational and health services, promoting development works, addressing social concerns. Today among most Papua New Guineans, a notion of following Jesus' example, and of obeying God's law, is held as a moral norm.

For some Melanesian communities, a particular denominational affiliation is regarded as part of their common cultural identity. A few years ago, a Chambri man lamented to me that some young people from his area had joined a Pentecostal Church. "They shouldn't do it," he protested. "They are Chambri and to be Chambri is to be Catholic." Since the 1950s, many Chambri communities have associated themselves with the Catholic Church. The association of a whole village or cultural group with a particular denomination was part of the first experience of Christianity in Papua New Guinea. In both British Papua and German New Guinea, the colonial administrations encouraged a "spheres of influence" approach whereby different denominations worked in different areas. The man with whom I conversed had grown up Catholic and Chambri and experienced Catholicism and Chambriness as integral aspects of his identity. Since Catholicism had been integrated into his "tradition" and "culture," it was difficult for him to accept that his children might see Pentecostal versions of Christianity as compatible with authentic Chambri identity.

The Christianities that are pervasive in modern Melanesia are Christianities that have located themselves within indigenous world-views and which have modified these world-views in the process. Indigenous ideas about powers and spirits continue to influence people's behavior and to influence the styles of Christianity we encounter today. In all regions there are ideas about the relationship of living people to the dead and to spirits that dwell in various parts of the environment. In the past, each group had its own repertoire of ritual performances for communication with the spirits. Each group also had its own set of stories, some of which were related to the ritual cycle, and some of which discussed the roles and exploits of spirits. Regular communication with the spirits was considered to be necessary communal work to ensure the well-being of the living community. Food, wealth, health, fertility, individual partnerships, and groups were all supported by rituals. Certain aspects of ritual work were entrusted to ritual experts, while the entire community supported ritual performances by providing the necessary resources of food, decoration, and wealth.

In the process of appropriating Christian myth and ritual, Melanesian communities have either discontinued the practice of traditional rituals or have reinterpreted them. In the former instance, people may be able to tell how a particular ritual was practiced in the past but may not yet have any personal experience of that ritual. For example, in Kalauna village on Goodenough Island, in a community dependent largely on yams and taro, *manumanua*, an anti-hunger ritual, was, prior to mission and colonial contact, performed every year around December at the onset of the "hungry" time. With the introduction of sweet potatoes and other crops, and with the introduction of the rituals of the Methodist and Catholic missions, *manumanua* became, from the 1920s onwards, a contingency ritual. That is to say, it was no longer performed annually but only when famine threatened. Since 1958 it has not been performed at all, but accounts of its performance continue to be related, as do a number of stories associated with its institution.[7]

The pig killed in several highland communities has been reinterpreted and modified in the light of Christianity.[8] In Catholic communities in the Simbu, for example, Mass is celebrated at the beginning of the pig kill and a cross is erected in the middle of the pig-kill ground. Before a pig kill in a South Kewa community at Waro in the Southern Highlands in 1983, one of the sponsors, Ruri, who was associated with the Evangelical Church of Papua, told me, "We are brothers and sisters eating and sharing things among us as Jesus told us to do. That is why we have the men's house and why we kill pigs." The people of Waro had not significantly changed the form of the pig kill but they had recast its ideology in the light of Christianity. In both the Simbu and Waro cases, it may be presumed that in its new situation the pig kill expresses and furthers Melanesian Christian values that are rooted in land and community.

In June–July 1995, I worked at the Melanesian Institute in Goroka analyzing data on youth and religion, which had been collected in interviews with 1,630 young people in four regions of Papua New Guinea. Youth is a time of developing patterns of association and loyalty – to family, to clan, to region, to friends, to clubs, to jobs, to school, to religion. Responses to the Young Melanesians Project questionnaire suggest that some young people are successfully working out patterns for living that draw on both past and present and are finding appropriate support networks. However, the responses also suggest that some of them are alienated from "traditional" life, that they lack role models for pursuing a "modern" life, and that they are confused about where they belong. It is not surprising that young people in Papua New Guinea are confused and frustrated. Their school system, like that of the Australians who first developed it, is based on an industrial model. It assumes that young people will finish school and find factory and service jobs. In fact, paying jobs are not available for them all, but having studied in expectation of such jobs, students are reluctant to settle for a life of subsistence agriculture.

Stories such as that of Pajapaja, his mother, and the *dindi gamu* may be starting points for discussions about relationships and work today, just as the biblical texts with which Melanesian youth engage in an overwhelming number of Bible study groups are also starting points. When I talked with people in Tari in 1991, it seemed that in fact the story was a starting point of a Huli Christian theology. Pajapaja-Jesus was a paradigmatic figure, a model incorporating the hopes and disappointments of the human condition in the Huli context.

I began by asking what the study of indigenous traditions contributes to undergraduate education in the US. Where I teach at Le Moyne, a strong emphasis is placed on a liberal arts core curriculum and on values of education. All students in our undergraduate programs are required to take two courses in religious studies and three courses in philosophy. In addition, they must take a senior seminar in either religious studies or philosophy. In a recently introduced physician's assistant program, students are required to take a course in religious studies that focuses on religion and healing. In colleges such as Le Moyne, there is the opportunity in religious studies and in other "core" areas, such as history, literature, and philosophy, to bring the perspectives of modernity into a dialog with the insights of indigenous traditions. Yet there are issues of appropriate pedagogy that we need to address.

I teach a course entitled "Local Religions," in which about one-quarter of the ethnographic material is from Melanesia. The other three-quarters, when last I taught it, were divided among the Dogon, the Walbiri, and the Iroquois. The focus on "local" is meant to encourage students to look at religions – both the indigenous traditions that are the focus of the course and also the so-called world religions with which students have some familiarity from an introductory course – within geographic and ecological as well as cultural contexts. The course offers the opportunity to explore religion in its concreteness. The curriculum committee hopes, no doubt, that the course contributes to expanding our students' knowledge and modes of thinking. In the fall of 1995, I taught two sections of the local religions course – one in the afternoon to mostly traditional-age college students, and another in the evening to a group of continuous learning students. The afternoon group, like other daytime groups to which I have taught this course in the past, tended to have difficulties in getting a "big picture" of religions and cultures different from their own. They had problems in seeing a culture as a whole, and in seeing religion as enmeshed in the culture. At times, students would become fixated on a particular aspect of a myth or ritual (the infliction of pain in the Walbiri fire ceremony, for example) and then words such as "primitive," or phrases such as "don't know any better," would surface. One young man found the content of Walbiri dreams so strange that he was convinced that the Walbiri must be lying! This led to a helpful discussion on the ways we respond to friends and classmates who see things in ways that we cannot grasp, and to the expression of concerns about respect and truth.

At times, students in both classes would find indigenous ideas or practice immensely appealing. For example, a number became convinced that traditions which prescribe interaction with ancestral spirits afford their members a valuable way of connecting with those who have gone before them. Some then looked for parallels to this interaction in their own culture, but found them only in attenuated form – visits to graves, memorial services, celebrations of famous people, prayers to saints. The evening group, which included some teachers, showed greater sensitivity to "other" understandings of person and community. They built on their own experiences of encountering people whose religions and worldviews differed from their own. However, a couple of New Age devotees in the evening group had romantic and unrealistic notions about the capacity of indigenous traditions to save the world. In order to validate indigenous perspectives, they almost wanted to demonize Christianity and themselves.

In addition to the course on local religions, I teach a course on Native American religions, a course on oral tradition and religion, and a course on ritual performance. All of them make use of at least some materials from indigenous traditions in encouraging students to think about the ways in which human beings construct worlds of meaning. They all explore the role of religion in personal and communal life. One of the issues that frequently emerges in teaching undergraduate courses on indigenous religions is well presented in Charles Long's article, "Primitive/civilized: the locus of a problem" (Long 1980: 43–61). The article has helped many students think through the following question: "Do I need to put someone else down to claim my own identity?"

Even with the use of slides and film, it is not possible for me to provide students with direct Huli and Kewa experiences of their traditional and changing religious ways. I am limited to re-presenting Melanesian experiences, to reconstructing them in terms that I can understand and in terms that are accessible to students who may, as I said at the outset, be studying in an institution that prizes the modern but who may, nevertheless, sense an affinity with other ways of thinking and being. I can explicate Melanesian ideas about sky people and ancestors and sacred geography and invite students to consider the webs of relationships implicit in them. I can encourage them to become engaged, for example, with the image of communities aligned along a "root of the earth," with the image of a life-giving python wrapped around the root, with the ritual practices the Huli say sustain the earth. With faith in the power of images I can hope that they will think about the world and human responsibility for it, not only with the tools of modernity, but also with the rich images and insights of traditional Melanesia.

Notes

1   I lived for eight years (in 1973–77 and 1980–83) in Papua New Guinea and have since then spent shorter periods there (in 1988, 1989, 1991, and 1994). Given my missionary role, teaching first in a catechist training center and later working for an ecumenical research institute, it is not surprising that I have been interested in the interaction between indigenous Melanesian religions and Christianity. No doubt being a Catholic, a missionary, an Australian, and a woman influenced my first perceptions of Melanesian culture and religion, just as being a college teacher influences my current reflections. The population of Papua New Guinea in 1995 was just over 4 million (p. 315, l. 36). Today it is more like 5 million. In 1995 the western part of the large island of New Guinea was officially called Irian Jaya (p. 319, l. 38). Today it is officially called Papua.

2   With the depletion of forests in Sarawak, Sabah, and Borneo logging companies have moved into Papua New Guinea and the Solomons and pose a serious threat to a fundamental resource. It has been estimated that if current levels of logging are permitted to continue the forests will be lost within a generation (Duncan 1994).

3   On the indigenous religion of the Kewa, see Apea (1977) and MacDonald (1991). On the Huli, see Frankel (1986), Glasse (1968), and Goldman (1983).

4   On speculation about the illness at Mt. Kare, see Clark (1993: 742–57).

5   Preamble to the Constitution of Papua New Guinea, 1975.

6   At the time of writing (mid-January 1996), the Free Papua Movement has taken hostages in an attempt to draw the world's attention to the destruction of Melanesian ways of life. They are protesting the resettlement of people from other parts of Indonesia in Irian Jaya and the Indonesian Government's support of the ecologically disastrous Freeport Copper Mine. My

knowledge of the hostage-taking came first via Asaonet and later via Australian newspapers. I have yet to see anything about it in the US media.

7   For more information on *manumanua*, see Young (1983).

8   See Schaefer (1981). In the past several years there has been a decline in the practice of the pig kill in the Simbu.

References

Aerts, Theo (ed.), *The Martyrs of Papua New Guinea*, Port Moresby: University of Papua New Guinea Press, 1994.

Apea, Simon, "The problem of God in Ialibu," unpublished B.Th. thesis, Holy Spirit Seminary, Bomana, Papua New Guinea, 1977.

Beckford, James A. and Thomas Luckmann (eds), *The Changing Face of Religion*, London: Sage, 1989.

Clark, Jeffrey, "Gold, sex and pollution: male illness and myth at Mt. Kare, Papua New Guinea," *American Ethnologist* 20(4), 1993, 742–57.

Connell, John and Richard Howitt (eds), *Mining and Indigenous Peoples in Australasia*, Sydney: Sydney University Press, 1991.

Duncan, Ronald C., *Melanesian Forestry Sector Study*, Canberra: National Centre for Developmental Studies, The Australian National University, 1995.

Foster, Robert (ed.), *Nation Making: Emergent Identities in Postcolonial Melanesia*, Ann Arbor: University of Michigan Press, 1997.

Frankel, Stephen, *The Huli Response to Illness*, Cambridge: Cambridge University Press, 1986.

Glasse, Robert, *The Huli of Papua*, The Hague: Mouton, 1968.

Goldman, Laurence, *Talk Never Dies: The Language of Huli Disputes*, London: Tavistock, 1983.

Long, Charles, "Primitive/civilized: the locus of a problem," *History of Religions* 20, 1980, 43–61.

MacDonald, Mary N., *Mararoko: a study in Melanesian religion*, New York: Peter Lang, 1991.

Schaefer, Alfons, "Christianised ritual pig-killing," *Catalyst* 11, 1981, 213–23 (first published in German in 1959 in *Steyler Missionschronik*).

Swatridge, Colin, *Delivering the Goods: Education as Cargo in Papua New Guinea*, Melbourne: Melbourne University Press, 1976.

Trompf, Garry W., *Melanesian Religion*, Cambridge: Cambridge University Press, 1991.

Young, Michael W., *Magicians of Manumanu*, Berkeley: University of California Press, 1983.

Chapter 22

The Hawaiian lei on a voyage through modernities

A study in post-contact religion[1]

Steven J. Friesen

Introduction

The title of this volume highlights the problem of trying to move beyond a paradigm in religious studies (and in other disciplines) that requires the concept of the primitive. Charles Long has suggested that such a move would be profoundly disorienting because any attempt to transcend primitivism threatens to throw the meaning of modernity itself into disarray. According to Long, the idea of the primitive is inextricably enmeshed within the concept "civilization" (Long 1986: 79–96). "The problematical character of Western modernity created the language of the primitives and primitivism through their own explorations, exploitations, and disciplinary orientations" (*ibid.*: 93). Thus, the Western concept of the "primitive" has signified the inferior Other, the marker of alterity, against which "civilization" defines itself, its activities, and its knowledge.[2]

If the paradigm "modernity" collapses, through what lens shall we view the world? I am not ready to suggest some new general theory. Rather, my strategy is to excavate archives from a specific moment in the colonial history of the Hawaiian islands. In this way, I begin to construct new knowledge that is motivated by these concerns and that might play a part in the effort to generate a more equitable theory of the nature of the worlds in which we live. This chapter focuses on one object, the Hawaiian floral lei, and traces the transformations to which it was subjected in a colonial setting. I make use of the discussions unleashed in 1928 when Caucasians proposed a new holiday honoring the lei. In these discussions, we can discern both one chapter in a "biography" of the lei (Thomas 1991: 188), as well as one mechanism for the renegotiation of modernity in Hawai'i, as the lei was forcibly relocated from a Hawaiian socio-religious setting through a variety of post-contact situations.

This approach results in several conclusions. First, the concept of modernity needs to be fragmented to allow for its diverse manifestations in the world, as well as the transformations of modernity that occur in any given locale. Secondly, specific contact settings may be viewed as complex, negotiated, or imposed settlements between parties unequally yoked, through which all parties are changed. Thirdly, the transformations of meaning undergone by the Hawaiian lei as modernities were renegotiated highlights certain aspects of post-contact religion. In the first section of the chapter, I recount briefly some developments from the 150 years between contact and Lei Day in order to show the phase of post-contact interaction within which Lei Day was conceivable.

From contact to Lei Day

In the century and a half between contact and 1928, tremendous changes took place in Hawai`i. At the time of contact with Europeans in 1778, Hawaiian chiefs were vying for control of various portions of the islands. Kamehameha I was victorious and established a dynasty that ruled the main islands until the last decade of the nineteenth century. For much of that century, the islands were populated by native inhabitants and by a small minority of foreigners, most of whom were Caucasians.

One century after contact (1876), disease and disruption brought the population of the islands to its lowest point, at just under 54,000, nearly all of them Hawaiian.[3] The reason the population began to grow after 1876 was that plantation owners had begun importing foreign laborers. The number of Hawaiians continued to decline after 1876, but the total population grew with the importation of Chinese and Japanese workers. Later, Portuguese, Puerto Ricans, Koreans, Filipinos, and others were also brought in to work the fields (Armstrong 1983: 107).

The Kingdom of Hawaii came to an end in 1893, when a coalition of American businessmen protected by American Marines overthrew the native monarchy.[4] Annexation to the United States was delayed, and so the islands were declared a republic by the new rulers in 1894. In 1900, changes in American politics made annexation possible and the islands became known as the Territory of Hawaii, under the control of the United States of America.

The demographics of the territory continued to change rapidly during this period. By 1920, the population of the islands had grown nearly fivefold in less than fifty years – from 54,000 to over 255,000. Of the 255,000 residents in 1920, only 9 per cent were Hawaiian, and another 7 per cent were listed as mixed Hawaiian. Thus, in fifty years, Hawai`i had gone from having a predominantly Hawaiian population of 54,000 to a multiracial population of 255,000, where Hawaiians made up less than one-fifth of the population while Caucasians accounted for about 12 per cent (*Hawaiian Annual* 1928: 11).[5]

In 1928 – in the wake of these rapid political, economic, and demographic developments – a new holiday was initiated in the Territory of Hawaii in honor of the Hawaiian floral lei. They called it Lei Day, and it has been celebrated on an annual basis ever since.[6] The effort to drum up support for this new holiday provoked numerous discussions on the meaning of living on the islands and the place of native Hawaiians in territorial society. Some of the discussions can still be accessed in libraries and archives. These sources demonstrate that the holiday began in a situation characterized by "massively knotted and complex histories of special but nevertheless overlapping and interconnected experiences" (Said 1993: 32). Lei Day emerged from this tangle of relationships between Hawaiians, Caucasians, and Asians; between Hawaiian royalty and commoners; between high-, middle-, and lower-income settlers; and between populations of various cultural backgrounds.

Island modernities

Negotiations about the shaping of modernities are never discussions among equals. The process is always complicated by wealth, power, class, emotion, personality, personal history, and corporate history. These entanglements are not benign. They bind people in relationships that are fundamentally unequal and have consequences that are often destructive.[7] Because the interests of various peoples in the Hawaiian lei overlapped and conflicted, the discussions reveal some of the perceived modernities within which a religious object such as the lei was recontextualized.

The first view of modernity to surface came from Don Blanding. Blanding considered himself a vagabond poet. He was born in Oklahoma in 1894. At the age of 21, he saw a production of *The Bird of Paradise* in Kansas City, and within a week he was steaming out of San Francisco Bay, headed for the tropics. From that first visit in 1915 until his death in 1957, he made uncounted trips to Hawai`i for varying lengths of time. In between, he traveled the globe (Lovell 1992), publishing over fifteen books of poetry, travel reports, fiction, and drawings (Northe 1976). Blanding prided himself on never staying anywhere for more than two years at one time, but, he maintained: "I like other places. I love Hawaii" (Blanding 1959).

When he lived in Honolulu, Blanding often worked for a daily newspaper called the *Honolulu Star-Bulletin*. On 13 February 1928, Blanding published an article in the paper in which he proposed a distinctive day for the city of Honolulu that would focus on the lei. The intentions for the holiday are clear in the subheading of the article in the day's late edition: "Not a solemn anniversary; no propaganda, no commercial drive! Just a happy spontaneous expression of joy of being alive and living in the beauties of Hawaii" (Blanding 1928a). A careful reading of the proposal indicates that his own thoughts focused more on his lifestyle in Honolulu than on the flowers:

> Honolulu should have a day that is distinctively, particularly and individually its own. A Honolulu day in flavor and gayety [*sic*], in laughter and friendliness, in aloha and mirth. Not a solemn anniversary of some historical event. Not a serious minded "eat a peach a day" day. No propaganda or commercial drive. Just a bubbly, happy, spontaneous expression of the joy of living in Hawaii, which is the essence of Honolulu...
>
> It would be a day in which we stop and think how delightful it is to live in Honolulu, when we really rest our active lives a moment and inhale the perfumes of Hawaii and are fully conscious of the sunshine and the blueness of Hawaiian skies and the friendliness and aloha of this enchanted spot.
>
> We are too much inclined to take things for granted. With such lavish outpourings of nature's generous gifts we are inclined to be spoiled and petulant, demanding more and more instead of appreciating the gorgeousness of what we have...
>
> This is not Pollyanna-ism. We do live in one of the most contented, easy-happy places on the globe. Why not throw out our chests and declare to the universe that we know what a fortunate people we are.
>
> (*ibid.*)

Blanding solicited suggestions from readers about the date and design of a lei holiday, but in his articles there is a clear sense of the character of modernity in Hawai`i. It is a view that I characterize as the "Caucasian in Paradise." His Lei Day proposal exhibits the main features in broad, optimistic outline: Hawai`i is the happiest place on earth, mostly due to the favored climate. There are references to aspects of native culture such as "aloha" (normally translated as "love"), but there are no clear references to any possible grievances, nor is there any sense that some people might not consider Honolulu to be the happiest place on earth. It is an ethereal view, relatively disconnected from history.

Later statements from Blanding help fill out his view of Hawai'i. As a purveyor of trop-ical imagery for the American public, Blanding was accused at times of misrepresenting Hawai'i to the world. Late in his life he replied as follows:

I do not idealize my Hawaii. There are two perfectly good eyes in this head of mine. One sees the gracious beautiful surface. The other sees the corrosive lavas surging beneath the crust.

But BOTH eyes see that the red lava of destruction becomes the dark cements of construction, with time. One eye sees the little painted fishes among the corals. The other sees the lurking shark. One sees the outgiving of generous hearts. The other sees the powerful selfish forces surging, like turbulent lavas, below.

But BOTH see (since mine is a hopeful heart) that recorded history proves that the constructive forces have always won over the destructive...OR WE WOULDN'T BE HERE TODAY IN OUR CONTEMPORARY WORLD...

The Hand of Destiny is strongly over our Islands. If we successfully and peacefully succeed in blending and amalgamating the many varieties of humanity here in the near future as we have in the present day, we will be a splendid proof and challenge to the rest of the world, that true brotherhood comes through individuals working at it.

More than all else, my Hawaii means ALOHA to me, in the true sense, and not merely as a greeting card word or a label for canned tuna. It is the very genius of Hawaii. It is immaterial but more real than structural steel. It is the anti-toxin for the viruses of Mainland "go-get-'em-at-any-cost" crusades which have crept in like a mildew. We need our organization; we need our progress; we need intelligent commercialism...but, Oh, how we need our Aloha.

And how the world needs it.

(Blanding 1959: 5; emphasis in original)

Three important themes from the Caucasian in Paradise paradigm surface in this excerpt. First, there is a claim to objectivity that acknowledges both destructive and constructive forces at work in history, but understands the lesson of history to be that the constructive forces always win out. Second, Hawai'i is viewed as a great experiment, where the peoples of many nations come together peacefully. His rhetoric includes the images of "blending" and "amalgamation," and suggests that Hawai'i might teach the peoples of the world to live in harmony. The precise political and economic factors that brought people into contact on the islands – including European voyages of exploration and domination, Protestant missionary zeal, strategic military concerns, commercial opportunism, and contract labor for plantation work – are not mentioned. They are instead mystified by the vague reference to the "Hand of Destiny."

Third, Blanding evokes nostalgia for simpler days on the mainland and for the bygone days of Old Hawaii. Rosaldo has described this kind of sentiment as imperialist nostalgia: a tendency on the part of people in a colonial setting to long for things they themselves have helped to destroy (Rosaldo 1993: 68–87). Such nostalgia tends to disguise relation-ships that are fundamentally inequitable (*ibid.*: 87). Blanding's double nostalgia contributes to the mystification, and finds its resolution in the hope that Hawai'i's endan-gered aloha might be the solution to problems in the capitalist world. For the "Caucasian in Paradise," there is no sense that some people might not consider Honolulu to be the happiest place on earth.

Blanding's vision of Hawai`i and of Lei Day was ultimately overruled by other kinds of responses to his proposal. His Hawai`i was the view of a minority that vacillated between the experiences of a tourist and those of a settler. Other views would win the battle for the public display of Hawai`i's identity, though Blanding's views continued to serve him and others quite well.

After Blanding proposed Lei Day on 13 February 1928, the first response that the *Star-Bulletin* chose to print came from Grace Tower Warren. Warren was a 49-year-old former journalist (*Star-Bulletin* 1964). Her letter to the editor appeared two days after Blanding's proposal and manifests a second view of modernity, which I call the modernity of the Euro-American diaspora. Warren supported the idea of a lei holiday and is credited with connecting the idea of Lei Day with the traditions of May Day.[8] What were her reasons?

> It makes a good slogan for catchy advertising purposes; it would come in a month when there are still many tourists here, and at a time when every street is a lei itself with both sides glowing with flowering trees, and last but most important, it is sentimentally appropriate.
>
> (Warren 1928)

The arguments regarding advertising, the tourist season, and readily available flowers are clear enough, but why was May Day sentimentally appropriate? Warren explains this in the next paragraph:

> Those of us who were born in New England have never gotten over the thrill of the May baskets hung upon our door on the night of May first, and I for one, still cling to enough of my old Yankee traditions to miss the charming custom and to wish that it might be revived in Hawaii in the form of leis instead of baskets. It used to be such fun to wonder from whom our various baskets came and the expeditions to various parts of town with our fragrant burdens gave us an evening's pleasure.
>
> (*ibid.*)

This view differs from that of Blanding in the sense that it focuses on the absent homeland. Whereas Blanding was professionally infatuated with Honolulu life and even suggested that the ethos of urban Hawai`i might be exported to the mainland, Warren talks about importing memories of her childhood from New England and finding a suitable replacement for them in the tropics. The native craft would give local color to an essentially foreign ritual.

Warren's perspective was no more successful than that of Don Blanding, but for different reasons. Her view of the relationship between Hawaiian and Euro-American traditions was one that characterized public culture in Honolulu from around 1900 to about 1920. A standard feature of 1 May celebrations during those two decades was the importation of European-based May Day traditions. These rites of spring were carried out in a continental fashion, with no recourse to the symbolic potential of Hawai`i's tropical vegetation or climate. Such imported rituals coincided with efforts to consolidate American control over the islands during that same period. In the mid-1920s, American control was firmly established and more attention began to be paid to the flowers and weather of Hawai`i on 1 May. This transition, which was making Warren's perspective obsolete, eventually led to the establishment of Lei Day in 1928. Honolulu's public culture had moved beyond the Euro-American diasporic view of modernity (Friesen 1996). Warren's suggestion that Lei Day be held on 1 May was accepted, but her interpretation of the importance of the holiday was not. Her interpretation was not sufficiently Hawaiian.

Two days after Warren's response, an unsigned editorial in the *Star-Bulletin*, which was certainly written by Don Blanding, declared that there had been a widespread response to the proposal for some sort of Lei Day, and he reported that all were in favor of it. The editorial rephrased Blanding's earlier conceptualization of the holiday as a celebration of the joy of island living, but added an important note of overt nostalgia to the mix by describing it as "[a] day reminiscent of the charm of a passing age" (*Star-Bulletin* 1928b).

For the next month, the topic of Lei Day incubated out of public sight, reappearing in the paper only on 17 March.[9] Blanding reported that bushels of letters had poured in and that 80 per cent of them favored 1 May as the date for Lei Day. The public had spoken and it was time to make preparations. This article signaled the opening of a six-week campaign to define the holiday and build support for it. The slogan for the events – which has endured to the present day – was announced: "May Day is Lei Day in Hawaii." This slogan is worth considering closely. In seven words, it accomplishes several tasks. The sentence situates Hawai`i within an international setting; it posits May Day as normative; and it defines Lei Day as a local variation on the Euro-American theme. The slogan simultaneously signifies what makes Hawai`i distinct and what binds it to European and American culture.

In the same article, Blanding lists categories of people who had supported the idea, including school children, hostesses, clubs, and organizations. In this context, native Hawaiians for the first time became a topic in the public written discussion of Lei Day. Blanding implies that they were, or should be, in favor of the holiday:

> The Hawaiians are not going to let their most loved symbol of aloha be slighted on that day. I can see the exquisite flower arrangements which will come from hands that are born with the skill of flower arrangement in their finger tips.
>
> (Blanding 1928b)

Other articles from the middle of March contain an element that had been mostly latent a month earlier in the Lei Day proposal and responses. That element was uncertainty about the historical continuity of the unabashedly innovative lei holiday. The vagabond poet's idea of a day of spontaneous joy and friendship touched on an important aspect of some people's experience of Honolulu, but it could not provide a foundation upon which to build a festival for the community. Lei Day needed a history, and so in March, references to old-timers and forgotten styles of leis began to surface in the public discourse, fleshing out the brief reference in February to "the charm of a passing age."

On 20 March, the Bank of Hawaii announced in the *Star-Bulletin* that it would officially sponsor Lei Day to assist "in the preservation of a beautiful Hawaiian custom." The support of this financial institution proved to be crucial. The bank provided a central site for the main municipal rituals in Honolulu by offering its lobby for the display of leis (*Star-Bulletin* 1928c). The bank's branch offices on other islands also provided the catalyst for the holiday to spread beyond Honolulu. By late March, it was clear that Lei Day would not be confined to Honolulu. The Bank of Hawaii branch in Hilo was going to sponsor festivities on the Big Island. Maui and Kauai would follow suit (Blanding 1928d). This participation of the neighboring islands was an important contribution to the effort of developing a historical rationale for the festival. Ever since Honolulu became the urban center and the capital, it has also been the center of innovation for, and outside influence on, the islands. This image of progressive Honolulu has also led to the perception that the city is less attached to local traditions than elsewhere in Hawai`i. Honolulu normally needs to look to rural areas and to the other islands for the "authentic" bearers of tradition. If the kama`aina[10] of the neighbor islands were behind the festival, its historical legitimacy would be enhanced.

In early April, Blanding and the *Star-Bulletin* took further steps to build support for the holiday by actively soliciting support for Lei Day from prominent native Hawaiians and recognized kama`aina. His appeals resulted in articles that allow us to reconstruct some native Hawaiian views on modernities of the islands.

One native perspective was that of Princess Kawananakoa, recorded in an interview with Don Blanding. She was a member of the royal family that had been deposed in 1893. Blanding's report of the interview indicates that the princess approved of the festival and that she expected friends of the Hawaiian monarchy to take part in Lei Day. "There will be many people downtown on Lei Day to see the exhibitions…and if they are not wearing leis themselves they should be ashamed," she said. "You may depend on it that all of my friends will be decorated and they will see that their friends wear leis, too" (Blanding 1928e).

In the interview, the princess exhibits a view of modernity in Hawai`i that advocates a reintroduction of some aspects of Hawaiian culture into public culture. According to Princess Kawananakoa,

> The nicest part of [the] Lei Day idea is that it brings kamaainas together again. With so many malihinis and malihini customs in Honolulu, the old-timers have rather withdrawn from public events. But Lei Day is so much in the old-time manner that they are planning to revive many "good old days" courtesies.
>
> (*ibid.*)

The princess does not describe Lei Day as a memory of earlier days. Rather, she alludes to the difficulties of Hawaiians in the face of foreign dominance and the power of foreign customs. The people had not disappeared; they had withdrawn to the margins of public culture. Princess Kawananakoa did more than talk about bringing this aspect of Hawaiian culture back into the public eye. Later in the month, she agreed to lead the three-member committee that would judge the lei competition to be held in the lobby of the Bank of Hawaii.

Blanding's reading of the situation was quite different from that of the princess. In a book published in 1930 – two years after the initiation of Lei Day – he holds forth on the condition of Hawaiian culture:

> The old men and women of Hawaii are nearly all gone. The chanters, the hula masters and court retainers, who are the only sources of information for research into the life that was Hawaii, are dying or dead. Photographs and dry statistics can keep only the shadow. Now that it is almost too late, there are frantic efforts under way to retain some records of the passing culture which had beauty although it was savage.
>
> (Blanding 1930: 243)

Thus, Blanding preferred to think of Lei Day as a holiday that preserves and reinvigorates a momento from a dying culture. The princess referred to Lei Day as a chance to reincorporate the old-timers and to readmit some aspects of Hawaiian culture into mainstream culture. The journalist and the princess both supported Lei Day, but for their own particular reasons.

A more ambivalent native interpretation of Lei Day came from John C. Lane, the Alii Aimoku of the Order of Kamehameha. Blanding had solicited the opinion of the leader of this prominent Hawaiian organization on 11 April. On 25 April, he printed Lane's response. Lane begins by affirming his support for the idea and adds two paragraphs on the importance of the lei to Hawaiians. Then, with about a week to go before 1 May, Lane made a new suggestion:

> It is my humble opinion that there should be two Lei Days in the territory. One on May Day, as already adopted by general public approval and the other on the 11th of June, Kamehameha Day, a day which was observed and celebrated as far back during the days of the monarchy. This day, as far as my recollections bear me, was the real Lei Day in Hawaii of the past. It was celebrated with horse races at Kapiolani park and bringing together the young and the old – from the king down to the common people – all wore a lei.
>
> This suggestion is offered with no idea to minimize the coming celebration of Lei Day, which will fall on May Day, but rather to kokua [assist] the beautiful idea of Lei Day in Hawaii.
>
> (Blanding 1928g)

Lane's comment is important because it constitutes one of the only statements in the mainstream press suggesting that Lei Day is an appropriation of a Hawaiian tradition. By invoking the monarchial period and the birthday of Kamehameha, Lane reminds readers that the lei had been an integral part of a sovereign Hawaiian social system. He does not oppose the transformation that a territorial Lei Day implies; indeed, he took part in the ceremonies and his wife was a member of the Bank of Hawaii's Lei Day planning committee (*Pacific Commercial Advertiser* 1928a). Lane's suggestion implies, however, that the modern holiday should not supplant the memory of an earlier period. Lane's modernity allows for a multi-ethnic appropriation of the lei while institutionalizing a distinctive identity for Hawaiians. It is a call to cooperate with contemporary developments but to resist complete absorption into post-contact society.

In early April, Blanding also requested a statement from Emma Ahuena Taylor, a noted native scholar and member of the Daughters of Hawaii. What he received from her was not simply support for the reinvigoration of a custom, but also an effort to restore cultural memory. Blanding printed his version of her essay on 27 April, a mere four days before 1 May. Her writing goes much deeper into the place of the lei in Hawaiian life, presenting to the reader a range of topics that had been completely absent from the earlier official discourse on Lei Day. One of these topics was the relationship of leis to non-Christian Hawaiian religion. Taylor begins: "Leis, I have always known, were, and are, an expression of love. Leis were the garments of Hiku, the god of love." Further on she writes:

> Different goddesses, like Pele's sisters, have certain leis to represent them. Kapoulakinau, one of the goddesses that "dwelt in the eastern gateway of the sun," so tradition tells us, always wore the hala lei.

When the young girls and boys were to be trained to dance the hula, an altar was built, dedicated to the goddess of the dance, Laka. Each morning when they went to the altar they always placed a lei thereon. Laka had two forms. If it was the God Laka then he was presented with a hala lei. If it was the Goddess Laka then she was presented with a maile lei.

Different leis were used for different ceremonies, but to the Hawaiian, the choicest lei to give to their monarch was the lehua blossom, or red petals of the budding lehua...The ilima has been used for some ceremonies, but has always been considered the people's lei.

(Blanding 1928h)

Here, Taylor rhetorically removes leis from 1928 Honolulu and resituates them within a native Hawaiian social, political, and religious system. In that context, the lei was related to worship, education, family relations, feasting, fertility, and governance. Taylor then goes on to give a gendered interpretation of Hawaiian history as a struggle with "new thoughts" from outside sources:

From king to cowboy, no horseback rider was complete in his garb unless he wore a lei upon his hat and around his neck. It was a common thing to go to homes in the evenings and find every woman there wearing a lei. It just seemed a part of her adornment.

I recollect so well when the young men were forbidden to wear leis upon their hats when they went down town, as the parents of that period did not consider it manly for them to do so, but that was one of the many new thoughts in taking us away from our old Hawaii. Now, when those customs are all slowly dying out, I am happy to see that Don Blanding and *The Star-Bulletin* are endeavoring to restore the beautiful custom to which attaches so much sentiment, for now we see the lei principally on the days when steamers depart, or a luau is in sway.

Before the days of modern street transportation few women would be seen in the evening without wearing a lei, but the hat seems to have taken its place, and hats for women at night seem so out of place. Why not eliminate the hat for evening wear and substitute the lei as it used to be, if one really has to wear something upon the head after dusk.

(*ibid.*)

In this last extract, Taylor lays out a succession of three modernities. The first is a robust, functioning Hawaiian society in which the lei is implicated in all parts of life. A second phase involves the repression or replacement of traditional behavior and adornment due to foreign ideas. A third modernity is possible, though. A restoration of certain native customs might be effected, even in the very different setting of the Territory of Hawaii. As such, Taylor's modernity makes the strongest appeal to Hawaiian traditions, but her article closes with the hope that certain native customs might be restored, even in the Territory of Hawaii:

It seems to me that anything that tends to perpetuate the beautiful custom of the lei is worth while. What is more beautiful and fragrant than the green maile of different varieties, as one of the standard leis of Hawaii? "Lei Day" and "May Day" almost seem synonymous [*sic*].

(*ibid.*)

The views of these elite Hawaiians are important indicators of the kinds of discussions about Lei Day that could not be fully aired in the mainstream press and are no longer accessible. In the end, however, Lei Day's public culture was dominated by images of modernity supplied by settlers. On 23 April, Blanding published excerpts of letters written by Walter F. Dillingham and Conrad von Hamm, "two real kamaainas of the islands" from whom he had solicited support for Lei Day. Both respondents focus on traditional uses for the lei. One real kama`aina gives a hearty endorsement "for the revival of our long-established and beautiful custom." The other real kama`aina recalls how moved he was to receive a lei when he first arrived on the islands in 1890:

> The beautiful Hawaiian custom of presenting visitors with leis has possibly done more than anything else to add to the natural charm of our lovely islands by its token of welcome and aloha, thus creating the longing to return.
>
> I shall never forget the first impression I received when landing on the islands in 1890. The flower girls on the street corners selling flowers and leis, the men and women wearing leis around their necks and on their hats sometimes even at work and always when on horseback (then the general mode of transportation) presented a picture which one does not forget...
>
> I agree with you that we cannot do enough to endeavor to retain the old Hawaiian customs and a movement to develop "more Hawaii in Hawaii" is a very excellent plan.
>
> (Blanding 1928f)

The visions of modernity offered by settlers were the ones adopted for public display. These views were not so effervescent as the Caucasian in Paradise, nor did they manifest the Euro-American diaspora's preoccupation with life in other parts of the world. The support of Hawaiians was appreciated, but the separatist implications of Lane's letter and the cultural history of Taylor were not incorporated into the main events. Lei Day was not going to be tied so closely to political history or native practice. For the purposes of Lei Day, Hawai`i would be a place where foreigners were welcomed to share the natural charm of the islands, where the sentiments of the natives became those of the general populace.

With the visions of the settlers predominant in public and a variety of other visions operating in the shadows, Lei Day won widespread support. On the first of May, visitors to the Bank of Hawaii encountered an eclectic decor of May Day and Hawaiian themes (Bank of Hawaii 1972: 7–8). The fountain in the middle of the lobby had been turned into a dais for the floral throne of the first Lei Queen. Behind the throne rose a large lei pole. Maile streamers radiated out from the pole to various points on lei displays that filled the lobby.

> The queen and her court wore yellow silk blouses and skirts of ti leaves, into which were woven gold day lilies and purple bougainvillea. Leis of pansies and yellow mamo and sandals made of ti leaves completed the strikingly beautiful costumes of the princesses. A long train of purple bougainvillea lined with gold cloth hung from the queen's shoulders.
>
> (*Star-Bulletin* 1928e)

The Bank was open from 10 a.m. until 5 p.m. When it came time to crown the queen at 2 p.m., the crowd was estimated to be between 2,500 and 3,500 in number. Don Blanding was given the honor of crowning the queen and they both made short speeches. Hawaiian music played throughout the day. The Bank reopened between 7 and 9 p.m. for further viewing and for the announcement of awards.

In the end, the day was declared a success. On the afternoon of 1 May, two articles appeared on the front page of the *Star-Bulletin* under the common headline: "Spirit of Lei Day reigns in Honolulu; thousands of flowers worn, on exhibit":

> Crowning of regal Miss Bowman as Queen of the Lei took place this afternoon in the Bank of Hawaii before a crowd that taxed the capacity of the building. Every available space in the building was crowded with throngs who gathered to see the climax of the most spectacular celebration Honolulu has seen in many a long day.
>
> (*ibid.*)

> Leis recaptured the old spirit of the islands – a love of color and flowers, fragrance, laughter and aloha...Lei wearers smiled easily today...Life for the day, if only in simple gestures, seemed more spontaneous and therefore more charming.
>
> (*Star-Bulletin* 1928d)[11]

The *Hawaiian Annual* agreed:

> [T]he bank and its vicinity was thronged with interested humanity, among whom it may be said Hawaiians predominated and joined appreciatively in the happy spirit of the day...All the city was imbued with its spirit which so filled the air that its counterpart was observed on all the other islands. Our streets seemed more alive with joyous cheer in sharing these floral tokens of comradeship, for few were those who were not bedecked with one or more leis to brighten the corner of every heart.
>
> (*Hawaiian Annual* 1929: 104–5)

Religion moving through contact

The previous section of this chapter is based on the hypothesis that archival work on colonial entanglements can build more useful knowledge about the relations of natives and foreigners, which might lead in turn to a better paradigm for understanding what we call indigenous religion (Long 1986: 94). In this final section, I reflect on the archival materials and the newly created knowledge, giving special attention to the way a religious object such as the lei was changed as it moved through contact and the ensuing modernities. My starting point is a native Hawaiian critique of Lei Day.

Journalistic reporting on Lei Day is one place where a discouraging word is seldom heard. One extraordinary piece came to print in 1962 that manifests a native awareness of the transformations to which the lei has been subjected in the colonial encounter (Richeson 1962).[12] The article reports an interview with Alice K. Namakelua, one of the most respected elders of her day in Honolulu who was better known as "Tutu [Grandma] Alice." Tutu Alice had spent a lifetime participating in and teaching Hawaiian arts such as hula, ukulele, songwriting, and lei-making. Richeson begins the article as follows:

Last week in Hawaii, we celebrated Lei Day; and in the minds of almost everyone, this was a wonderful thing.

But in the minds of some, it was the symbol of a great tragedy. To them, Lei Day is something we could well do without.

The article then goes on to describe two criticisms of Lei Day from Tutu Alice (mediated, as is so often the case, by the journalist). The first problem was that Lei Day had made the wearing of leis into a special occasion rather than a part of everyday life:

When Tutu Alice was growing up into young womanhood on the Big Island, every day was literally Lei Day. Cowboys tending their cattle, wore leis on their hats. Women working in the home wore them as they went about their chores. The little girls, when they were old enough to handle the needle and thread, learned the gentle art and devoted long hours to keeping the family supplied. The work was considered almost as essential as preparing food...

It has been many years since this fine Hawaiian custom passed away; in Honolulu it has been even longer.

What caused its departure?

"Well, it was the haoles [Caucasians] and their rules and regulations," explained Tutu Alice.

"In their way of thinking, flowers were supposed to be worn on special occasions."

This first criticism from Tutu Alice echoes some of the opinions of Hawaiians recorded thirty-four years earlier in 1928. In an indigenous social system, leis had been woven into the fabric of life. Lei Day, on the other hand, was a day set aside for the giving and wearing of leis. From this perspective, Lei Day was not "Just a happy spontaneous expression of joy of being alive and living in the beauties of Hawaii" (Blanding 1928a). It was instead a reminder of the loss of sovereignty, with the lei as an icon of disenfranchisement. Princess Kawananakoa had been circumspect in identifying the problem as "so many malihinis and malihini customs in Honolulu" (Blanding 1928e). Tutu Alice was more frank in her diagnosis (though we might also allow for some elaboration of the systems of control in the decades between the two comments).

Tutu Alice's second criticism of the recontextualization of the lei had equally broad implications. The other problem with contemporary lei practice was commercialization:

When the commercial lei came on the market, much of the spirit of lei-giving disappeared, and also much of the beauty of the lei itself. In old Hawaii, when someone gave you a lei, you knew that it represented hours of work by the giver, who more often than not scavenged the hillsides to pick exactly the right flowers, than [sic] sat to weave or sew each into place. No two leis were alike. You picked the flowers and the arrangement to suit the personality of the person to whom you were giving it.

(Richeson 1962)

This second criticism, then, was that leis had become a commodity. In the process, people had been alienated from the world around them and from each other. Lei-giving no longer required the knowledge of nature necessary to recognize the correct plants, nor access to nature to choose and gather them. Furthermore, commercialization of the lei did not require anyone to infuse the labor with personal attention or skill. The creation of leis had been detached from the personal performances of giving and receiving. What had once been a labor of aloha was now available for purchase. Tutu Alice thus provided a grassroots critique of the alienation involved in the shift from an indigenous economy to a capitalist system. The vitality of community life no longer required the circulation of aloha, in this case through appropriate exchanges of crafted objects.

A careful examination of the 1928 texts reveals that the issue of community cohesion and material exchanges was at the heart of the discussions about the first Lei Day, with Hawaiians and long-term residents tending to understand the situation differently from the newcomers. All agree that the style of life on the islands is superior to other places and express strong emotional attachments to Hawai`i. For the Hawaiian writers surveyed here, however, Lei Day was a chance to recapture a sense of community that was retreating in the face of foreign ideas. A predominant theme in the writings of the Hawaiians is that the old style of community life was based on the act of giving. John C. Lane of the Order of Kamehameha writes: "The wearing of the lei and the giving of it to a friend, guest of honor, or to anyone – even though to a new acquaintance – carries the aloha, the friendship and the good thought one entertains towards another" (Blanding 1928g). Emma Taylor's historical treatment is also organized around leis as a gift of love, whether to family members, visitors, deities, or monarchs (Blanding 1928h). A letter from long-time resident James Wilder includes the importance of giving in the following lines, the first three of which were written as verse:

> One lei for each and all on May Day,
> But swap a lot! And with every swap Aloha kaua,
> "Fidelity and love between us two."
> That's what a lei means, not merely hello or goodbye.
>
> (Blanding 1928i)

Thus, the Hawaiian and kama`aina writers emphasized that the quality of life on the islands was founded upon the practice of giving. For them, the power of Lei Day was the power of sharing that produced community. Their sentiment was more than just nostalgia for a lost past, for the act of giving partially approximated an older practice and elicited some of the same reactions.

Writers who had arrived in Hawai`i more recently also manifested a strong sense of attachment to the islands, but usually for different reasons. A persistent theme in the non-Hawaiian discussions of Lei Day was not giving, but rather what the writers thought they had received from the islands and from Hawaiian culture, which enabled them to become natives to some extent:

> Wonderful indeed is the wooing spirit of Hawaii. The natives of the fiftieth generation feel it as deeply as their ancient ancestors. And we, all of us, if you have lived in Hawaii for any length of time have been won by its seductive influence.
> No matter where you were born, nor how loyal you may be to your native state Hawaii has a separate and distinct place in your inmost heart.
>
> (*Pacific Commercial Advertiser* 1928b)

Flowers have always been used as the language of affection. But nowhere else has one form of bouquet achieved the fame of symbolizing the spirit of an entire people. Not only are the Hawaiian people, as a race, symbolized in the word "Aloha" and the flower "Lei" but the sentiments they express have been adopted by all the people of the islands, irrespective of race or creed.

(*Pacific Commercial Advertiser* 1928a)

A similar text appeared in a periodical written especially for travelers:

Lei Day in Aloha Land, celebrated on this May Day, gives everybody a chance to emphasize the unique Hawaiian character of these islands of the Pacific. Everybody is interested...and the beautiful character of the old Hawaiian custom of giving and wearing leis just needed this one touch of universal cooperation to charm our tourist guests and draw out the sympathy and enthusiasm of old-timers and newcomers alike, to create a day of celebration when at least to a slight but distinctive degree everybody is Hawaiian.

(*Paradise of the Pacific* 1928: 3)

With the lei as an organizing principle, the flowers of 1 May were being transformed into an effective symbol for the indigenization of the peoples of Hawai`i on the basis of what they were all supposed to have learned from, or been given by, the natives. This interpretation of ethnic harmony and indigenization in Hawai`i was clearly the perspective of people who had moved to the islands. This settler perspective exhibited little or no awareness of the disastrous consequences of the Euro-American-sponsored invasion for Hawai`i's first inhabitants (Bushnell 1993). It did, however, occasionally shade into a mild criticism of the market-driven society of the capitalist mainland, suggesting in the process that Lei Day and aloha represented what was missing in American life:

[Lei Day] is a strong expression in favor of saving for all time those charming features of Hawaiian life that are the distinct contribution of the Hawaiian race. It is a challenge to the tendency of modern developments which bring in their wake standardization of cities. In other words, the vast majority of the people of Hawaii don't want the progress of the islands to destroy the character which the Hawaiians gave it.

(*Star-Bulletin* 1928a)

Lei Day should put big business in the background. It should banish caste and creed and doctrine. We should join with nature in one gesture to make the entire citizenry of the islands her children, renewing our faith in the Old Mother of us all. We should feel as if we were looking upon the gorgeous dawn of a new creation.

If Lei Day has this effect upon us it will live and grow to be an annual event which should find each year a fuller and freer expression of those feelings which we have in our hearts for Hawaii, but which have a subtle sacredness not to be shown in the market place.

(*Pacific Commercial Advertiser* 1928b)

For the people holding these views, the power of Lei Day was not so much in giving as in receiving. The new sense of community was based on superabundance. Out of the surplus came the goodwill and friendship that was lacking. According to this group, friendliness and acceptance characterized life on the islands, even after Western economic and social relations became dominant. This ambience came from the influence of Hawai`i's natural resources and from native Hawaiian culture. They concluded that anyone who stayed in Hawai`i long enough could assimilate the aloha spirit and become Hawaiian at heart.[13]

One conclusion from this study, then, is that post-contact Hawai`i was a place where everyone was changed in various ways to varying degrees (Long 1986: 6). The meeting of cultures involved a protracted process of exchange and transformation. In the case of Honolulu's Lei Day, the revival of lei-giving rituals represented a recognition of the importance of reciprocity in community life. The lei-giving rituals were not a return to earlier periods on the islands, though. This was hardly a restoration of a lifeway. It was only the recontextualization of a custom. The presuppositions of social organization were not changed; instead, an element of giving was simply grafted onto the existing system. The references in the Lei Day discussions to personal transformations should not be dismissed out of hand, however, nor should the sentiments be excised as unworthy of academic analysis. The reports of our informants' emotions must be taken seriously (Rosaldo 1993: 1–21). The mechanism of transformation was the act of giving that approximated the ethos of aloha. Newcomers, with their emphasis on receiving, were less familiar with the mechanism, and also more enchanted with the results. Those with more experience tended to be more realistic.

Conclusion

The voyage of the lei through several modernities raises some of the fundamental issues of our day. What will provide a foundation for community life in the early twenty-first century and beyond? Will social intercourse be based on some form of reciprocity, or on acquisition? What roles will natives and colonizers play in negotiating the shapes of those communities? What roles will there be for Asians, Hawaiians, Europeans, Caucasians, Aboriginals, Africans, Arabs, Native Americans, and others, not to mention admixtures of the above? Will the search for solutions always devolve to power and seduction? These are questions that should be a part of religious studies.

The voyage of the lei through various island modernities also asks other crucial questions of the discipline. The ambiguity of the colonial setting gave rise to many alternative modernities. The Lei Day texts manifest no monolithic response of Hawaiians to modernity, nor of the so-called moderns to Hawai`i. Rather, the colonial archives reveal tangled histories of transformation, of settlements negotiated within inequitable frameworks, of people and customs pushed to the center or to the margins, and of destruction. Any generalizations we might make about modernity in Hawai`i must recognize the many modernities that are attested, not to mention those that have vanished in the meantime. Further investigations into the mechanisms of modernity might help us see our way through some of the theoretical problems. Examinations into the ways in which rituals such as Lei Day have tried to define a normative modernity are productive enterprises, for such efforts to define society are bound to elicit resistances and alternative formulations (Said 1983: 10–14). In them we see the negotiations, standoffs, and power plays that make public culture possible. Lei Day has not eliminated contending definitions of the problems and possibilities of Honolulu life in the territorial period. It has restricted the options, has given one pre-eminence, and has allowed for the coexistence of a limited range of minority opinions (Friesen 1996).

Given the messiness of these relationships, is it any wonder that the concept "religion" has itself become ambiguous in post-contact societies? I do not intend to reopen, again, the question of the definition of religion. In the context of this study, I only note the difference between a lei in the Kingdom of Hawaii and a lei in the Territory of Hawaii. In the kingdom, the lei was clearly a religious object, though the term hardly does the object justice. The lei was a delicately crafted gift that functioned within a system of exchange that easily transcended foreign conceptual boundaries such as "sacred" or "secular." Leis were given to – and received by – family, friends, monarchs, deities, and nature, and in the process they helped give order to community life in a proper fashion. The act of giving and receiving was not simply an exchange of commodities but rather a commitment of selves, and thus it was profoundly religious. The floral garlands bound the people, plants, animals, land, and deities together. They were the physical poetics of community life.

In the Territory of Hawaii, the lei was a curiously isolated object. Most people did not know how to make them, what materials to use, or which stories to invoke as a rationale. But stripped bare, with only the act of giving, the natural beauty of flowers, and memories of an Old Hawaii at its disposal, the lei was still effective and affective. Was it still a religious object? Certainly, but it was not so powerful anymore. As a commodified native craft in a colonial setting, the lei's energy was drained. The problem was partially epistemic: restricted notions of the religious were at fault to some extent. But the problem was also economic: it has not yet been proven that the long-term health of any community can be founded on the principle of acquisition. If the lei helps us to understand these transformations better, then perhaps its arduous journey will not have been in vain.

Notes

1   I thank Puanani Burgess and Geoffrey White for helpful discussions of the issues raised in this study. The research was made possible by grants from Laurence and Mary Rockefeller, and from the Research Board of the University of Missouri. The assistance of the staff and fellows of the East–West Center in Honolulu proved invaluable at several points.

2   In this chapter, I use a definition of "modernity" that is based on this understanding regarding the place of the "primitive" in Euro-American self-understandings. I also take seriously the suggestion of Smith that modernity can mean any number of things, given its geographic spread and historical locations (Smith 1982: 77–95). Thus, I define modernities as modes of community existence characterized to varying degrees by: (1) a privileged position granted to Western rationality; (2) some form of a capitalist economy; and (3) the inequitable and symbiotic interdependence of primitives and civilizers. The contact has usually been initiated by the civilizers who have also retained the right to define the primitives.

3   Population figures for 1853 indicate a population that was 95.8 per cent Hawaiian and 1.3 per cent part Hawaiian (Armstrong 1983: 112).

4   On the overthrow, see Kuykendall (1967: 523–650), Daws (1968: 251–92), and Russ (1992).

5   The Japanese constituted by far the largest ethnic group in 1920, at 43 per cent of the population, but their presence in Hawaiian public and political life was far outweighed by that of Caucasians.

6   The only exception was in 1942, when Lei Day was not observed because of American involvement in the Second World War after the Japanese attack on Pearl Harbor (Chun 1953).

7   Thomas has argued that "entanglement" or "interpenetration" provide useful ways of describing relationships in colonized settings. Many treatments of colonial situations tend to treat indigenous peoples as reactive or even passive in the face of overwhelming violence. Thomas concluded that this does not do justice to the dynamics at work in the societies of the colonized. As a framework, entanglement encourages the analyst to look at the multifaceted interactions on all sides of asymmetrical colonial encounters (1991: 185–9, 204–6).

8   1 May also happened to be her birthday (Blanding 1928c).

9   In light of the competition between the *Pacific Commercial Advertiser* and the *Honolulu Star-Bulletin*, it is not surprising that the *Advertiser* remained almost completely silent about the Lei Day proposal until late April.

10 Normally translated as "child of the land" – in other words, someone who has lived long enough on the islands to become acculturated to the distinctive lifestyle. The correlative term is "malihini," indicating someone who is newly arrived or has not adjusted to local norms.

11 The style and vocabulary of this second article suggests that it was written by Don Blanding.

12 I thank Ms. Janet Zisk, archivist for the Kamehameha Schools in Honolulu, for this reference.

13 The appropriation of native culture remains a lively issue. For a rebuttal to the continuing presence of these sentiments, see Trask (1994: 64–5).

References

Armstrong, R. Warwick (ed.), *Atlas of Hawaii*, Honolulu: University of Hawaii Press, 1983.

Bank of Hawaii, *A Brief History of the Bank of Hawaii*, Honolulu: Bank of Hawaii, 1972.

Blanding, Don, "Why not a distinctive day for Honolulu? A Lei Day for us all," *Star-Bulletin*, 13 February, 1928a, 1 (the article appeared on the editorial page, 6, of the late edition).

——, "May Day seems to be the choice of Honolulu for its 'Lei Day,'" *Star-Bulletin*, 17 March, 1928b, 1, 3.

——, "Lei Day plans assuming more definite and promising form," *Star-Bulletin*, 24 March, 1928c, 1, 2.

——, "Whole territory getting behind plan to observe 'Lei Day' here," *Star-Bulletin*, 26 March, 1928d, 1, 3.

——, "Princess Kawananakoa gives generous kokua to 'Lei Day,'" *Star-Bulletin*, 7 April, 1928e, 1, 2.

——, "Lei Day kokua comes from two real kamaainas of the islands," *Star-Bulletin*, 23 April, 1928f, 1, 5.

——, "City already blossoming out in anticipation of Lei Day," *Star-Bulletin*, 25 April, 1928g, 1, 3.

——, "Leis, their meaning and their history told by Mrs. A.P. Taylor," *Star-Bulletin*, 27 April, 1928h, 1, 5.

——, "There's tomorrow and the next day, and then Lei Day arrives," *Star-Bulletin*, 28 April, 1928i, 5.

——, *Hula Moons*, New York: Dodd, Mead, & Co., 1930.

——, "My Hawaii," *Saturday Star-Bulletin*, 17 January, 1959, 4–5 (reprinted from *Star-Bulletin* "Hawaiian Life" magazine, 1954).

Bushnell, O.A., *The Gifts of Civilization: Germs and Genocide in Hawaii*, Honolulu: University of Hawaii Press, 1993.

Chun, Amos, Jr., "Lei Day 25 years old on Friday and thriving; founder is back," *Star-Bulletin*, 25 April, 1953, B 10.

Daws, Gavin, *Shoal of Time: A History of the Hawaiian Islands*, Honolulu: University of Hawaii Press, 1968.

Friesen, Steven J., "The origins of Lei Day: festivity and the construction of ethnicity in the Territory of Hawaii," *History and Anthropology* 10, 1996, 1–36.

Hawaiian Annual, "Comparative race population of Hawaii, 1920–1910," 1928, 11.

——, "Inaugurating Lei Day," 1929, 102–5.

Kuykendall, Ralph S., *1874–1893: The Kalakaua Dynasty*, vol. 3 of *The Hawaiian Kingdom*, Honolulu: University of Hawaii Press, 1967.

Long, Charles H., *Significations: Signs, Symbols, and Images in the Interpretation of Religion*, Philadelphia: Fortress, 1986.

Lovell, Charles, "The man who gave Hawai'i Lei Day," *Aloha* 15(3), 1992, 38–42, 52.

Northe, James Neill, "Don Blanding, 1894–1957: a bibliography," unpublished manuscript, 1976.

Pacific Commercial Advertiser (superseded by the *Honolulu Advertiser*), "Lei Day contest may be annual, Bank announces," 13 April, 1928a, 3.

——, "Lei Day, May Day, that will be a gay day," editorial, 27 April, 1928b.

Paradise of the Pacific, "Lei Day's message to aloha land," May, 1928, 3, 4.

Richeson, Dale, "Once-a-year Lei Day has its sad side," *Star-Bulletin*, "Hawaiian Life," 6 May, 1962, 19.

Rosaldo, Renato, *Culture and Truth: The Remaking of Social Analysis*, Boston: Beacon, 1993.

Russ, William Adam, *The Hawaiian Revolution (1893–94)*, Selinsgrove, PA: Susquehanna University Press, 1992 (first published 1959).

Said, Edward W., *The World, the Text, and the Critic*, Cambridge, MA: Harvard University Press, 1983.

——, *Culture and Imperialism*, New York: Vintage Books, 1993.

Smith, Wilfred Cantwell, *Religious Diversity*, New York: Crossroad, 1982.

Star-Bulletin, "A national celebration," editorial, 29 February, 1928a.

——, "We all welcome Lei Day," editorial, 17 February, 1928b.

——, "Speaking of Lei Day—," 20 March, 1928c, 3.

——, "All classes join in celebration of Old Hawaiian custom today," 1 May, 1928d, 1.

——, "Bank of Hawaii bower of magnificent flowers from all islands," 1 May, 1928e, 1, 6.

——, " 'Lei Day is May Day' : Kamaaina was part of its beginning," 25 April, 1964, 8.

Thomas, Nicholas, *Entangled Objects: Exchange, Material Culture, and Colonialism in the Pacific*, Cambridge, MA: Harvard University Press, 1991.

Trask, Haunani-Kay, *Light in the Crevice Never Seen*, Corvallis, OR: Calyx Books, 1994.

Warren, Grace Tower, "Likes proposal of Lei Day," *Star-Bulletin*, 15 February, 1928, 6.

Index

Printed in the USA/Agawam, MA
November 29, 2011